Dream Routes
of the World

Dream Routes
of the World

Contents

Pictures:

Page 2–3: The Lysefjord with its majestic promontory, the Prekestolen ('Preacher's Pulpit'), is one of the major natural attractions in southern Norway. The 40-km-long (25-mile) narrow sea channel stretches east of Stavanger.

Page 4–5: The Terracotta Army, 30 km (19 miles) east of Xi'an, is one of China's best-known historic attractions. The army of soldiers, officers, archers and horses contains some 7,000 figures.

Page 6–7: Marrakech's Djemma el Fna – the Square of the Hanged – comes to life as soon as the sun sets. Hundreds or even thousands of people congregate on the square in Morocco to form dense crowds around the cookshops, snake charmers, storytellers and acrobats.

Page 8–9: As if joined by giant hands – the mammoth stone cubes of the Inca fort Sacsayhuamán above Cuzco in Peru. It is still unclear how the nearly 200-tonne monoliths were brought here because the Inca were familiar with neither the wheel nor rollers.

Page 10–11: Marble Canyon in northern Arizona/USA. The Colorado River has cut into the earth here over millions of years to form a steep-walled canyon.

Page 12–13 top: One of Würzburg's icons in Germany is the Old Main Bridge with its imposing statues of holy personages.

Page 12–13 bottom: Morning fog in the hills of Tuscany in Italy.

Page 14: Potala Palace, the winter residence of the Dalai Lamas, rises majestically above Lhasa in Tibet.

Page 16–17: The famous Bay Bridge in San Francisco/USA.

About this book

Many of the routes featured in this book have become legendary over the centuries and still echo the footsteps of explorers, traders and pilgrims whilst offering excitement and promise to modern day travellers. You are about to experience the journey of a lifetime with every page you turn; touring the world from the comfort of your armchair. Who amongst you will be able to resist the temptation to travel the Dream Routes for real and the chance to create everlasting memories? Tread with caution, this book will cause 'itchy feet'!

How it works

These carefully researched road trips take you to the most fascinating travel destinations on the planet, with magnificent natural landscapes, unique cultural monuments, bustling cities and even peaceful, holy places. The spectrum ranges from the Camino de Santiago in northern Spain, the Romantic Road in Germany, the Friendship Highway in the Himalayas and the Garden Route in South Africa to the Stuart Highway in Australia, the Alaska Highway, Route 66 in the USA and the Inca Trail in Peru and Bolivia.

Route descriptions

An introduction to each chapter provides an outline of the route and introduces each of the countries and regions together with their scenic, historic and cultural features. The signifi-

cant locations and sightseeing attractions are then described according to the routes and accompanied by numerous high-quality colour images. The numbers corresponding to the locations and sightseeing attractions can be found on the map at the end of each chapter.

Important travel information on the time required and the length of the tour, national traffic regulations, weather and the best time to go, as well as useful addresses, is given in an information box for each route. Interesting natural and cultural aspects are also explained in the sidebars, and the shaded boxes in the sidebars indicate worthwhile side trips.

City maps

Cities on the route are described on separate pages with a city map and a detailed outline of the sightseeing attractions.

Touring maps

Special touring maps at the end of each chapter indicate the course of each route and the most important places and sightseeing attractions. The main route is clearly indicated and is supplemented with suggestions for interesting detours.

Specially designed icons (see adjoining list) indicate the location and type of significant sightseeing attractions along the route. Particularly outstanding destinations are also highlighted with colour images and brief descriptions next to the map.

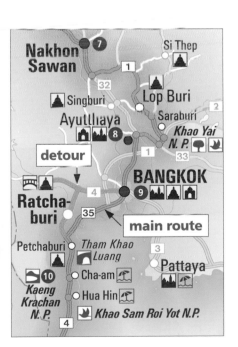

**Remarkable landscapes
and natural monuments**
- Mountain landscape
- Extinct volcano
- Active volcano
- Rock landscape
- Ravine/Canyon
- Cave
- Glacier
- Desert
- River landscape
- Waterfall/rapids
- Lake country
- Geyser
- Oasis
- National Park (fauna)
- National Park (flora)
- National Park (culture)
- National Park (landscape)
- Nature Park
- Cultural landscape
- Coastal landscape
- Island
- Beach
- Coral reef
- Underwater Reserve
- Zoo/safari park
- Fossil site
- Wildlife reserve
- Whale watching
- Protected area for
  sea-lions/seals
- Protected area for penguins
- Crocodile farm

**Remarkable cities
and cultural monuments**
- Pre- and early history
- The Ancient Orient
- Greek antiquity
- Roman antiquity
- Etruscan culture
- Indian reservation
- Indian Pueblo culture
- Places of Indian cultural interest
- Mayan culture
- Inca culture
- Other ancient American cultures
- Places of Islamic cultural interest
- Places of Buddhist cultural interest
- Places of Hindu cultural interest
- Places of Christian cultural interest
- Places of Jainist cultural interest
- Places of Abor. cultural interest
- Aborigine reservation
- Phoenician culture
- Prehistoric rockscape
- Early african cultures
- Cultural landscape
- Castle/fortress/fort
- Palace
- Technical/industrial monument
- Memorial
- Space telescope

- Historical city scape
- Impressive skyline
- Festivals
- Museum
- Theatre/theater
- World exhibition
- Olympics
- Monument
- Tomb/grave
- Market
- Caravanserai
- Theater of war/battlefield
- Dam
- Remarkable lighthouse
- Remarkable bridge

**Sport and
leisure destinations**
- Race track
- Skiing
- Sailing
- Diving
- Canoeing/rafting
- Mineral/thermal spa
- Beach resort
- Amusement/theme park
- Casino
- Horse racing
- Hill resort
- Deep-sea fishing
- Surfing
- Seaport

ICELAND

Norwegian
Sea

North Cape

SWEDEN

NORWAY

FINLAND

1

Oslo

ESTONIA

Baltic

Sea

LATVIA

2

North Sea

Glasgow   Edinburgh

DENMARK

LITHUANIA

IRELAND

UNITED
KINGDOM

NETHERLANDS

Berlin

BELARUS

3

London

BELGIUM

GERMANY

Würzburg

POLAND

5

6   Paris

CZECH REPUBLIC

UKRAINE

8

FRANCE

SWITZERLAND

Füssen

4

SLOVAKIA

AUSTRIA

Budapest

HUNGARY

MOLDOVA

San Sebastian

Bayonne

SLOVENIA

CROATIA

ROMANIA

PORTUGAL

Roncesvalles

7

Menton

10

Florence

BOSNIA AND
HERCEGOVINA

SERBIA

BULGARIA

MONTENEGRO

Barcelona

ITALY

Rome

ALBANIA

MACEDONIA

Sevilla

SPAIN

11

Brindisi

GREECE

9

Mediterranean Sea

Istanbul

GEORGIA

UZBEKI

Bucha

12

TURKEY

TURKMENIS

Arctic Ocean

Greenland
(Denmark)

Alaska
(USA)

Homer

21

Juneau

Prince Rupert

C A N A D A

Tangier

18

TUNISIA

MOROCCO

SYRIA

ISRAEL

IRAQ

I R A N

AFGHA

JORDAN

KUWAIT

Alexandria

23

Jackson

Chicago

U N I T E D

Portland

22

ALGERIA

LIBYA

19

EGYPT

SAUDI
ARABIA

QATAR

UAE

OM

24

S T A T E S

25

Washington

Abu Simbel

Los Angeles

Tucson

Amarillo

A T L A N T I C

BAHAMAS

CUBA

MAURITANIA

MALI

NIGER

CHAD

ERITREA

YEMEN

M E X I C O

26

Cancún

BELIZE

DOMINICAN
REPUBLIC

HAITI

CAPE VERDE

SENEGAL

GUINEA-BISSAU

BURKINA
FASO

BENIN

SUDAN

DJIBOUTI

GUATEMALA

HONDURAS

NIGERIA

CENTRAL
AFRICAN
REPUBLIC

ETHIOPIA

EL SALVADOR

NICARAGUA

GUINEA

SIERRA LEONE

GHANA

SOMALIA

COSTA RICA

LIBERIA

IVORY
COAST

CAMEROON

UGANDA

KENYA

P A C I F I C

VENEZUELA

GUYANA

PANAMA

SURINAME

GABON

CONGO

RWANDA

BURUNDI

COLOMBIA

D.R. CONGO

TANZANIA

ECUADOR

O C E A N

B R A Z I L

ANGOLA

ZAMBIA

MALAWI

Lima

PERU

27

BOLIVIA

ZIMBABWE

MOZAMBIQUE

MADAGAS

Sucre

NAMIBIA

BOTSWANA

MAUR

PARAGUAY

SWAZILAND

O C E A N

Córdoba

URUGUAY

LESOTHO

20

CHILE

SOUTH AFRICA

Cape Town

ARGENTINA

28

Ushuaia

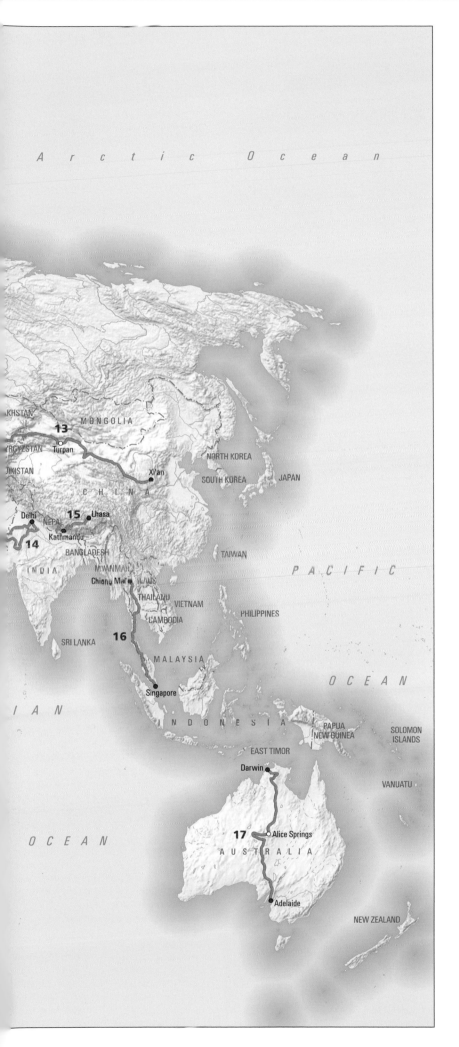

Route overview

Route 1

Norway

Autumn tundra in the Finnmark Province of Norway's far northern expanse.

Over fjord and fell: the spectacular natural world of northern Europe

Norway shares its borders with Russia, Finland and Sweden and is enveloped by the Norwegian Sea, the North Sea and the Skagerrak. It is a natural realm of truly unmatched beauty – alternately wild and delicate. One tip – make sure you allow plenty of time for the enormous distances.

As you might expect from industrious Scandinavians, the Norwegian mainland has an astonishingly well-maintained road infrastructure. In places where the rugged terrain would have you think the onward journey has come to an end, there appears a ferry, a tunnel or a bridge. Even the smallest hamlets and remote coastal villages are generally easy to reach. And yet progress in this expansive land inevitably takes longer than you've planned, mainly due to the unusual physical geography and strict speed limits. But you won't have to worry much about traffic jams and red lights.

The *Hurtigruten* is Norway's legendary passenger ship, which has been plying the 2,500 nautical miles between Bergen in the south and Kirkenes on the Russian border in the very north for well over a hundred years. It was originally used to transport post and supplies. Nowadays the permanent route, known as 'Imperial Road 1', has become famous as one of 'the world's most beautiful sea voyages'. From a geographical point of view, Norway is unlike any other European country. No other country in Europe is longer (1,752 km/1,089 miles), almost none is as narrow, and despite its odd

Mountain landscape in Kjerringøy in the north.

shape it is (without its polar provinces) three times the size of England.

Almost half of Norway is over 500 m (1,640 ft) above sea level. Its mountains are not particularly high – the highest does not even measure 2,500 m (8,200 ft) – yet nearly a quarter of the country is covered by alpine or high-alpine landscape, glaciers or wide, treeless plateaus at over 1,000 m (3,280 ft) altitude. The generally barren, high plateaus – known as fjells, or fells – are covered in snow for a large part of the year and consist mainly of moors, lakes and rivers.

Above the Arctic Circle and in the highland areas of the interior there is often no sign of human life at all. With the exception of Oslo, Bergen, Trondheim and Stavanger there is no town with more than 100,000 inhabitants in this relatively large country. Four out of five people live on

View from the mountain of Aksala over Ålesund past the town centre to the harbour.

Historic warehouses in Bergen, member of the Hanseatic League from the 14th to 16th century.

the coast or the banks of a fjord. Norway's very craggy coastline, including the fjords and bays, is over 28,000 km (17,398 miles) long – more than half the circumference of the earth.

The country is very sparsely populated and, thanks to the Gulf Stream, free of ice all year. Were it not for these warm ocean currents, the Norwegian mainland would be covered with a crust of ice, as is the case in large areas of the Norwegian polar provinces. On the other hand, the Gulf Stream is also to blame for the high level of summer rainfall, which is common.

Norway's fjords – the most famous of which are Geirangerfjord, Hardangerfjord and Sognefjord – are the number one tourist attraction here. These former valleys and canyons of various sizes and shapes were carved out by massive gla- ciers and ultimately flooded by rising sea levels following the last ice age.

The short summer months in Norway are quite mild. North of the Arctic Circle – in the 'Land of the Midnight Sun' – summer days actually don't end and the special atmosphere during this time of year often inspires wild parties. The opposite is the case during the cold period, which is snowy and dark in the very north – no sun for two months straight.

Norway is not in the EU and still uses the Norwegian Krone as its currency. After hundreds of years of occupation and invasion by the Danes, the Swedes and the Germans, they feel they have earned this 'exclusivity'. But things are going swimmingly here – fishing and tourism, as well as plentiful oil and natural gas reserves in the North Sea, have made the beautiful 'Land of Utgard' quite prosperous.

Fishing boats in the harbour of Hamnøy on the Lofoten island of Moskenesøya.

Oslo

At the end of the fjord of the same name, stretching nearly 100 km (60 miles) inland and surrounded by wooded hills, is Norway's capital Oslo, a city dating back to the 11th century. Oslo was called Kristiania until 1925 and had varying political and industrial significance. Although the city is home to a mere half-million inhabitants, it is one of Europe's largest cities in surface area. It is the largest port in Norway and the country's trading and industrial centre.

Worth seeing in the centre of town: the new town hall (1931-50), the city's trademark with a sumptuous interior and Europe's highest clock tower; Akershus Fort (from 1300), one of the country's most important

Top: Oslo town hall.
Bottom: Akershus Castle.

medieval buildings; Nasjonalgalleriet, the largest collection of paintings and sculptures in Norway; the royal castle (changing of the guard at 1:30 pm). Highlights outside the city centre include Holmenkollen, a winter-sport resort with skiing museum; Munch-Museet; Vigelandpark (Frognerpark) with 200 monumental works in bronze and stone by Gustav Vigeland; Bygdöy peninsular museum with the Vikingskipshuset (three ships from the 9th century); Kon-Tiki Museet with the Thor Heyerdahls Raft (Kon-Tiki, RA I, RA II); Fram-Museet.

North Cape Route: On the 4,000-km (2,484-mile) trip to the North Cape you get to experience just about everything Norway's fascinating natural landscape has to offer: glaciers, waterfalls, mountains, high plateaus, rugged coastline and endless fjords. The cultural highlights include old harbour and mining towns, interesting stone carvings and charming old churches.

❶ Oslo (see sidebar left). From Oslo follow the coast to Kongsberg.

❷ Kongsberg The Mining Museum here casts you back to the times of silver mining, which ceased in 1957 after more than 330 years. In the Saggrenda pit you can see what is probably the world's first ever elevator – it consists of ladders that go up and down.

❸ Heddal and Eidsborg Norway's first stave church (1147) is in Telemark and has an outer gallery that was used to protect people from the weather and to store weapons.
Road 45 (direction Dalen) splits off towards the Eidsborg stave church at Ofte. The walls of the

church are covered with shingles, which is unusual. About 4 km (2.4 miles) beyond Rødal, Road 13 turns off towards Stavanger.
The E134 also passes through Hardangervidda further on.

❹ Hardangervidda Europe's largest plateau is a fascinating area for hiking and is home to rare wildlife. From Skarsmo our route leads north on Road 13. Alongside the road are the wild frothing waters of the Låtefossen. It is definitely worth a short detour (50 km/31 miles) from Kinsarvik, along the Eidfjord to Fossli, to the edge of the Vidda where the Vøringfossen Falls drop 170 m (557 ft) into the depths of Måbø Canyon.
From Kinsarvik, ferries cross the Utne to Kvanndal on the Hardangerfjord. The 'King of the Fjords' reaches far inland at a length of 179 km (111 miles) and a depth of 830 m (2,723 ft). The

Travel information

Route profile
Length: approx. 4,000 km (2,484 miles), excluding detours
Time required: at least 4 weeks, ideally 6–8 weeks.
Start: Oslo
End: The North Cape
Route (main locations): Oslo, Kongsberg, Bergen, Jotunheimen, Trondheim, Fauske, Narvik, Tromsø, Alta, North Cape

Traffic information:
This route requires some driving skill and good planning as the ferries are often fully booked. Drive on the right in Norway. Customs laws are strictly enforced. Headlights are obligatory even during the day. Bridges, tunnels and

mountain pass roads mostly charge tolls. Mountain roads are often only opened in June/July.

When to go:
The best time to go is from June to August. Even in these months, snowfall is common in the north and on the plateaus.

Accommodation:
Mountain inns, known as fjellstue or fjellstove, and chalets are attractive.

General information:
www.visitnorway.com
www.norway.org
www.norway.com
Customs:
www.toll.no

Detour

Stavanger and Lysefjord

Instead of the E134 south, you can take a spectacular mountain road (13) from Røldal to Stavanger. You will have to cross a good many fjords on this route.

Stavanger, founded in 1125, was still the centre of the herring and fish-canning industry in Norway until just three decades ago. In 1970, plentiful oil reserves were discovered in the Ekofisk Field, instantly making Norway's third-largest town the oil capital of the country.

Top: A colourful harbour town.
Bottom: Stavanger Oil Museum.

As a result, some flamboyant buildings were erected, but much of the architecture still recalls the more tranquil times prior to the oil bonanza – the Canning History Museum, for example.

The old town is called Gamle Stavanger and has 173 listed wooden houses in cobblestone lanes. The Gothic cathedral (1125–1300) is noteworthy for being the purest example of medieval church building in Norway. The Kongsgaard, where the Danish kings stayed on their travels between the 14th and 19th centuries, appears spartan in contrast. The Valbergturm, an old fire watchtower and local icon, offers a good view of the town.

The long, narrow Lysefjord is among the prettiest in the country, plunging to a depth of 400 m (1,311 ft) and stretching 40 km (25 miles). Its stone walls rise as high as 1,000 m (3,300 ft).

An impressive suspension bridge spans the fjord at its western end. A boat trip to Lysefjord and the Prekestolen promontory – the Preacher's Pulpit – is a must.

route then leads over the plateau of Kvamskogen on to Bergen.

5 Bergen The most famous street in this old Hanseatic League town is Bryggen, a UNESCO World Heritage Site with picturesque warehouses right on the waterfront. The fishing harbour, the cathedral, the 12th-century church and the Gamle Bergen open-air museum are also worth visiting.

6 Viksøyri The E16 passes many lakes on the way to Voss, home of the oldest wooden house in Norway – 'Finneloftet' from the 13th century. Further along the route you should take a detour to Viksøyri (with a charming stave church) where you can see the Sognefjord about 40 km (25 miles) away. It is Norway's greatest fjord – 180 km (112 miles) long, in some places only 5 km (3 miles) wide, and up to 1,200 m (3,937 ft) deep.

7 Stalheimskleiva and Nærøyfjord About 13 km (8 miles) past Oppheim, a road leads to the Hotel Stalheim, which has wonderful views. Norway's steepest road leads round thirteen hairpin bends down to the Nærøyfjord. It is the narrowest one in the country with walls up to 1,200 m (3,937 ft) high.

Two impressive waterfalls are also on the route – the Stahlheimfoss (126 m/413 ft) and the Sivlefoss (240 m/787 ft). The main road goes from Gudvangen to Kaupanger and on to Songdal. The fjord route leads past Nærøyfjord, Aurlandsfjord and Sognefjord, among the most beautiful in Norway.

1 UNESCO World Heritage Site: the picturesque wooden houses of Bryggen in Bergen, once a member of the Hanseatic League.

2 An isolated farmstead in the bare fell landscape – Telemark in southern Norway.

3 The Vøringfossen falls cascade from the Hardanger Plateau into the deep and narrow Måbø Canyon.

4 The 800-year-old stave church of Borgund near Borlaug, deep in the Lærdal Valley.

Detour

Ålesund and the bird island of Runde

This little detour first takes you about 120 km (75 miles) out to Ålesund, an island town with stone buildings (unusual for Norway) that were built by art nouveau architects from all over Europe after a fire destroyed the place in 1904. It is this uniform view of the harbour town that makes a visit so worthwhile.

The main attractions of the town include a visit to the 189-m-high (621-ft) Aksla Mountain – from its terrace you can enjoy a great panoramic view over the town, the skerry (rock) belt and the Sunnmøre Mountains in the west. From the town park it's about 400 m (1,312 ft) to the viewpoint.

Top: Sheep on the cliffs.
Bottom: A farmstead on the Kløfjellet.

The Atlanterhavsparken Aquarium displays marine flora and fauna local to this Norwegian coastal area. To the east of town is the Sunnmøren open-air museum with more than forty old houses and farms.

The island of Runde, which is only 6.4 sq km (2.5 sq mi), is a must for anyone who loves nature. Although only 150 people live there, up to 700,000 sea birds also call it home. You can get the best view of 'Bird Island', which hosts puffins, uria, razorbills and several varieties of gulls, by booking a boat trip around the island.

Even divers value the area as much as ornithologists – in 1725 a Dutch ship carrying nineteen cases of gold and silver coins sank off the island, as did a Spanish treasure ship in 1588!

1

2

Trollstigen

Surrounded by waterfalls, deep valleys and mountains as high as 1,760 m (6,316 ft), Norway's most photographed mountain pass, the Trollstigen, snakes its way from Langdal to Åndalsnes at elevations of up to 850 m (2,789 ft). Eleven hairpin bends with a gradient of ten per cent take some skill to master. The road was built in 1936 and winds along almost vertical rock faces. As a result, it is unfortunately closed to camper vans.

8 Borgund The best-preserved stave church in the country can be viewed by taking a short diversion inland after driving through the new 20-km (13-mile) Lærdals Tunnel on the E16. The church was erected around 1150 and is known for its ornate carvings. The pagoda-shaped bell tower is next to the church.

9 Jotunheimen and Sognefjell road Norway's highest and most spectacular mountain pass runs from Sogndal to Lom. It climbs a steep, winding trail into the Jotunheimen Mountains where over two hundred peaks of at least 2,000 m (6,561 ft) form a bizarre ring. The two highest among them are Galdahøppigen

at 2,469 m (8,100 ft) and Glittertind at 2,452 m (8,045 ft). The Sognefjell is a plateau littered with lakes of all sizes. To the west of the road is Europe's largest mainland glacier, the Jostedalsbree, which is about 100 km (62 miles) long.

10 Urnes A small single-lane road now leads from Skjolden on the east bank of the Lustrafjord to the town of Urnes and an 11th-century stave church, the oldest of twenty-nine listed Norwegian stave churches and a UNESCO World Heritage Site. The robust design of the exterior is fascinating and the carvings of fable characters in the interior are lovely.

11 Geirangerfjord The route continues through some pretty landscape on its way to the Geirangerfjord, a 15-km (9-mile) arm of the Sunnylvsfjord. Its walls are up to 800 m (2,625 ft) high and many waterfalls feed into the fjord. The panorama from the viewpoint at Dalsnibba before Geiranger is fabulous. The winding road 'Ornevein' (Eagle Route) leads up into the mountains offering frequent

views over the fjord. After crossing the Nordalsfjord you get your first chance to turn off to Ålesund Island (80 km/50 miles). The main route then continues through the Gudbrands Gorge to the Trollstigen mountain road and on to Åndalsnes. Here you have a second possibility to head towards Ålesund about 120 km (74 miles) down the E136.

The E136 continues east in Romsdalen to Dombås, and from here

Røros

A number of buildings, hangars, pits and slag heaps recall an era when Røros was a great mining centre. The oldest copper mine in

The church of Bergstaden Zir, built between 1780–1884.

through the hilly mountainous countryside to the Dovrefjell.

⑫ Dovrefjell Norway's tallest mountain, Snøhetta, at 2,286 m (7,500 ft) dominates the plateau and you can get a great view from the road's highest point (1,026 m/3,366 ft). The national park is classified as the only remaining intact high-altitude ecosystem in Europe.
The road passes through Drivdalen to Oppdal with its modest open-air museum. On the way to Trondheim (E06) you will be presented with a diversion to the old mining town of Røros (120 km/74.5 miles), with a massive stone cathedral and some charming historic buildings.

⑬ Trondheim Trondheim was Norway's capital for quite some time. To this day, royal coronations still take place in the mighty Nidaros Cathedral, built in 1070 over the grave of Olav the Holy. The western facade has some particularly interesting sculptures. The Tyholt Television Tower, Fort Kristiansen and the cathedral tower all offer wonderful views over the rooftops of Trondheim.
The scenic E16 leads from Trondheim to Grong, following the banks of numerous fjords along the way. In Grong, Road 760 links up with the R17, the Kystriksveien. The E06 goes north towards Fauske, rolling through the charming Namdalen.

⑭ Kystriksveien The 560-km (348-mile) Kystriksveien is in effect the mainland counterpart to the legendary Hurtigruten coastal journey – one of Europe's dream routes. Many ferries ply the fjords and lakes in this region and the landscape is varied. But the coastal road requires a lot of time and money, and waiting times are to be expected for the various ferries. The crossing fees can indeed add up to a considerable sum.
A few kilometres beyond Sonja there is a small road to Mo I Rana where you can get back on the E06 to the Saltfjellet-Svartisen National Park.
The section of the coastal road north of the turnoff to Mo I

1 The Jostedalsbreen National Park, the 'Land of the Giants', in southern Norway protects the largest land glacier in Europe, which has four glacial tongues.

2 Picturesque fishing boats reflected in the Lusterfjord, a northern arm of the Sognefjord.

3 South of Oppdal lies the Dovrefjell National Park with Snøhetta (snow cap) in the background (2,286 m/7,500 ft), Norway's highest mountain just outside Jotunheimen.

4 Typical mountainous and fjord landscape in Nordland, the Norwegian province that straddles the Arctic Circle.

town is a UNESCO World Heritage Site dating back to 1644.
The stone baroque church of Bergstaden Zir (1784) in the town centre is surrounded by wooden buildings and is worth visiting. With a capacity of 2,000, it is the third-largest church in the country. It was reserved for miners who lived alongside the slag heaps or in the side streets in shacks. Rich citizens, civil servants and mine managers lived in the avenues and pleasant areas of town, as usual.

1

Lofoten and Vesterålen Islands

Lofoten and Vesterålen, its northern extension, have been popular holiday destinations for Norwegians since the 19th century. The grandiose scenery of mountains and sea, the colourful villages and the surprisingly mild climate make them exceptional even amid the already spectacular Norwegian landscape. Infrastructure here is excellent, with all the main islands connected to one another as well to the mainland by tunnels or bridges. Ferries take you to the smaller islands.

Both groups of islands reach 250 km (155 miles) out into the Norwegian Sea like a wildly shattered wall of stone, with snow-capped mountains and deep, verdant valleys. Because of the steep cliffs, often only the narrow coastlines are inhabited.

Colourful wooden houses – called Rorbuer – are built on stilts over the water. At places like Austvågøys, wonderful white sandy beaches are hidden in the fjords and bays – not what one would expect this far north. The bird life on the islands is also impressive. In addition to the typical sea and migratory birds, majestic sea eagles are also at home here. The plant life on these once wooded islands is stunted but varied. Mountain, beach and meadow plants grow side by side.

Despite the fact that the Lofoten and Vesterålen are between 150 and 300 km (93–86 miles) inside the Arctic Circle, the air temperature, even in winter, rarely drops below freezing thanks to the warming effects of the Gulf Stream. Due to the constantly warm currents, the Vestfjord has become a preferred spawning-ground for herring and cod, which in turn benefits salmon and trout breeding in the fjords and bays.

Dried and cured cod are considered delicacies. From March to June they are to be found in their masses drying on wooden racks. Dried fish chips, which like the vitamin C-rich cloudberries are easy to store for long periods, are beloved souvenirs for the 200,000 tourists who visit Lofoten every year.

The detour to Lofoten is a long 587-km (365-mile) drive, but the effort is definitely worth it. The best time of year to visit this stunning archipelago is from the end of May to the middle of July, when the interplay of midnight sun and mountains will dazzle the uninitiated. Remember to bring your eye masks if you are sensitive to light when you sleep!

Another one of Lofoten's attractions that is worth visiting is Hinnøya, the northernmost medieval church in the world located in Harstad on Norway's largest island. Orcas and porpoises are a very common sight in the Vest-

fjord, but a whale safari is still an unforgettable experience. They are offered from Andenes on the northern point of the northernmost Vesterålen island, Andøya, from June to September and you are likely to see sperm whales in the waters off the shore of the whaling station.

The museum in Stokmarknes on the Vesterålen island of Hadseløya tells of the legendary Hurtigruten liner, which

3

4

5

1 A scene typical for the archipelago – small fishing villages in front of impressive cliffs on the rare flat areas along the coast.

2 Hamnøy, sheltered at the entrance to the Reinefjord, is one of the oldest fishing villages on the Lofoten island of Moskenesøya.

3 Midsummer's night: from 2 May to 17 July the sun never sets on the north and west side of the Lofoten Archipelago.

4 The fishing village of Reine is surrounded by steep mountain scenery and considered to be one of the prettiest Lofoten villages. The red-painted Rorbuer houses that line the banks have been used by fishermen since the 12th century.

5 The *hjeller*, wooden racks used to dry fish (especially cod), are common sights on the Lofoten Islands.

was 'founded' here in 1881. Hadseløya has no fjords or bays, but is remarkable from a sporting point of view – its circumference Is 42.195 km (26 miles 385 yards), precisely the length of a traditional marathon. Naturally, every year in August there is a race around the island.

Svolvær, the capital of the Lofoten on Austvågøya, is overshadowed by a craggy rock that is shaped like a goat,

the Svolværgeita. Don't pass up trips to: the highest peak of the Lofoten islands, the Higravstindan at 1,146 m (3,758 ft); to Raftsund with the second-longest cantilever bridge in the world; and the boat trip to Raftsund in the Trollfjord, which has walls as high as 1,146 m (3,759 ft) in some places and narrow passages that are definitely among the best that the Norwegian landscape has to offer.

From February to April Kabelvåg is northern Norway's cod fishing centre. During this time, thousands of fishing boats cast their nets into the waters of the Vestfjord. Around AD 600 there were Vikings living on Vestvågøya. Make sure to pay a visit to the 86-m-long (270-ft) Norman meeting hall in the reconstructed settlement at the Lofotr Museum in the town of Borg.

The 19th-century church in nearby Flakstad on the island of Flakstadøya is considered the prettiest church in the Lofoten Archipelago. Hamnøy, on the beautiful neighbouring island of Moskenesøya, is a particularly rustic fishing village.
From Moskenes there is a regular ferry crossing to Bodø on the mainland, and from there you get back on the E06 to Fauske.

Flora and fauna in the Finnmark

Long, cold winters with astounding temperatures of -40°C (-40°F) and short but pleasant summers are characteristic of the tundra of northern

Top: Musk oxen.
Bottom: Reindeer run wild here.

Norway. During the few snow-free weeks the small flora in this area seem to explode into berries and blossom, offering direct or indirect nourishment to animals like reindeer, Arctic hares, Arctic foxes, lemmings, snow owls, wolves, bears and lynxes.
In addition, a variety of whale species live in the coastal waters. But the most common encounters are with reindeer and mosquitoes!

Rana is called Helgeland-Salten, the 'Green Road'. A natural tidal spectacle is visible near Løding – every six hours the water trapped behind the 'Eye of the Needle' forces its way through the strait.
From Løding it is a 43-km (27-mile) drive back to the E06 at Fauske. An interesting alternative is the road through the Saltfjellet-Svaryisen National Park. Norway's second largest glacier is high in the Arctic Circle here. The tremendous glacier is hard to reach, however – gravel track turns off at Skonseng towards Svartisdalhytta. Inside the Arctic Circle and above the tree line, only moss and shrubs grow here. The road to Rognan on Saltdalsfjord leads through the high valley of Saltfjells, and then follows the eastern bank to Fauske. The E06 then goes north to Ulsvåg,

where you can turn off to Skutvik, the most important Lofoten harbour.

15 Narvik Swedish iron ore from Kiruna is shipped around the world from the permanently ice-free harbour of Ofotenfjord here. The warehouses and transport systems are best viewed from the panorama point up on Fagernessfjell (656 m/2,151 ft). Ferries also travel to Lofoten from Narvik. The E08 turns to Tromsø at Nordkjosbotn.

16 Tromsø Northern Norway's largest town ironically benefits from a mild climate. The Polarmuseet has interesting exhibits covering various international polar expeditions. The Tromsøbrua connects the island town to the mainland. Next to it is the town's icon – the pointed Arctic Cathedral (1965). Back on

the E06 you drive through some spectacular fjords.

17 Alta This town on the fjord of the same name is a centre of Sami culture. The stone carvings of Hjemmeluft, which date back between 2,000 and 6,000 years, are definitely worth a visit. They depict animals, hunting and everyday scenes and are listed as a World Heritage Site. The Alta Canyon is also a must-see, with impressive depths of 500 m (1,634 ft) and a length of 15 km (9 miles).
The route then crosses the tundra landscape of Finnmarksvidda to the harbour town of Hammerfest. After that, the E06 crosses a plateau before the E69 turns off at Olderford towards the North Cape.

18 North Cape The road then heads past Porsangerfjord to the

ferry port of Kåfjord, where ferries travel to Honningsvag on the North Cape island of Magerøya. There is now a tunnel to the island. Across the harsh landscape we reach the North Cape, the end of our trip.

1 The Lyngenfjord is over 10 km (6 miles) wide and one of the prettiest in northern Norway.

2 The Finnmark is characterized by wild, harsh landscape, deep fjords, craggy coastal cliffs and expansive plateaus.

3 The midnight sun shines on the North Cape from 14 May to 30 July, yet the Cape is often immersed in thick fog, rain or snow. A globe marks Europe's northernmost point.

Lofoten Typical for the Lofoten are the craggy mountain tops with steep faces, deep green meadows and colourful wooden houses on stilts. Here we see winter, but the climate of the islands is actually quite mild due to the warm Gulf Stream.

Lyngenfjord This mountain panorama is one of the most beautiful in Norway. It feels a lot like the Alps.

North Cape Usually foggy and mainly promoted to tourists as the northernmost point in Europe, Magerøya is still worth seeing despite neighbour Knivskjellodden actually being further north.

Ålesund This island, which was rebuilt by Art Nouveau architects from all over Europe following a devastating fire in 1904, is characterized by stone houses, which are unusual for Norway. An aquarium displays Norway's sea life and the view from Aksla Mountain above town is a treat.

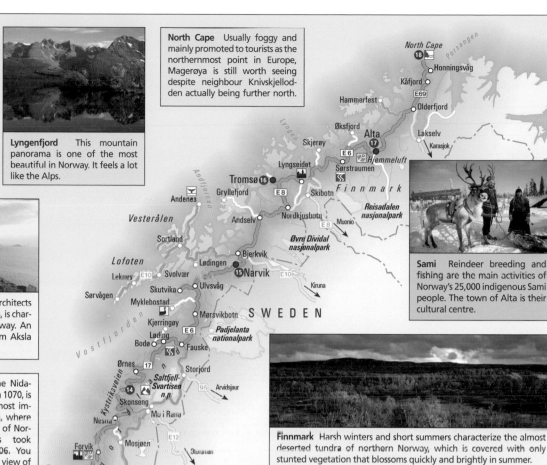

Sami Reindeer breeding and fishing are the main activities of Norway's 25,000 indigenous Sami people. The town of Alta is their cultural centre.

Geirangerfjord About 15 km (9 miles) long and flanked by cliff walls of up to 800 m (2,625 ft), this is truly one of Norway's natural wonders.

Trondheim The Nidarosdom, built in 1070, is Scandinavia's most impressive church, where the coronation of Norwegian kings took place until 1906. You can get a great view of Trondheim from the Nidarosdom tower.

Finnmark Harsh winters and short summers characterize the almost deserted tundra of northern Norway, which is covered with only stunted vegetation that blossoms quickly and brightly in summer.

Trollstigen Norway's most famous mountain pass takes some handy driving – eleven hairpin bends await you at a gradient of ten per cent over an altitude change of 850 m (2,789 ft).

Sognefjord Norway's largest fjord is 180 km (112 miles) long, up to 5 km (3 miles) wide and 1,200 m (3,937 ft) deep. Nearby is the longest car tunnel in the world.

Røros The wooden buildings in the centre of town recall a more prosperous era when Røros was a wealthy copper-mining town. The stone church, built in 1784, was reserved for miners.

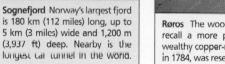

Bergen The Bryggen road, with numerous historic warehouses nestled together at the fishing harbour, a charming cathedral, a 12th-century church, the Gamle Bergen open-air museum and one of Europe's largest ocean aquariums all make the old Hanseatic League town of Bergen well worth visiting.

Urnes The oldest Norwegian stave church has ornate wood-carvings and a unique wooden construction. It is located near the Lustrafjord.

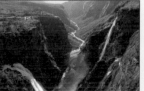

Vöringfossen Europe's largest plateau, the Hardangervidda, is the starting point for the 170-m-high (557-ft) Vöringfossen, a spectacular waterfall that plummets into the Måbø Canyon.

Prekestolen This 600-m-high (1,969-ft) promontory, 'Preacher's Pulpit', is one of the must-see attractions in southern Norway.

Oslo World-famous museums, plenty of greenery and water make this sprawling metropolis a fascinating experience. The new town hall on the harbour is the icon of the Norwegian capital.

Map labels:

North Cape · Porsangen · Honningsvåg · Kåfjord · E69 · Olderfjord · Hammerfest · Øksfjord · Alta · Lakselv · Skjerøy · E6 · Hjemmeluft · Karasjok · Lyngseidet · Sørstraumen · Finnmark · Tromsø · Gryllefjord · E8 · Skibotn · Andenes · Andselv · Nordkjosbotn · E8 · Muonio · Vesterålen · Reisadalen nasjonalpark · Sortland · Øvre Dividal nasjonalpark · Bjerkvik · Lofoten · Lødingen · Narvik · E10 · Leknes · Svolvær · Kiruna · Sørvågen · Skutvika · Ulvsvåg · Myklebostad · Mørsvikbotn · S W E D E N · Kjerringøy · E6 · Padjelanta nationalpark · Løding · Bodø · Fauske · Ørnes · Storjord · Saltfjell-Svartisen n.p. · Arvidsjaur · Skonseng · 95 · Nesna · Mu i Rana · Forvik · Mosjøen · E12 · Storuman · Brønnøysund · Rørvik · Norge · Holm · Børgefjell nasjonalpark · Namsos · Grong · Gressåmoen nasjonalpark · Bølareinen · Steinkjer · Trondheimsfjorden · Østersund · Trondheim · Orkanger · Stjørdal · Kristiansund · E39 · Støren · E14 · Molde · Ålesund · Åndalsnes · Røros · Trollstigen · Oppdal · Sveg · 63 · E136 · Dovrefjell nasjonalpark · Femundsmarka nasjonalpark · Måløy · Geirangerfjorden · Lom · Stryn · Dombås · Rondane nasjonalpark · Jostedalsbreen nasjonalpark · Otta · Nordfjord · Skei · Jotunheimen nasjonalpark · Førde · Urnes · Sogndal · Lillehammer · Viksøyri · Borgund · Hamar · Nærøyfjord · E16 · Aurlandsvangen · E16 · Sognefjorden · Dale · Voss · Bergen · Kvanndal · Eidfjord · Geilo · Mjøsa · Utne · Voringfoss · Steindalsfossen · Kinsarvik · Hardangervidda nasjonalpark · Folgefonna · Hønefoss · Hardangerfjorden · Røldal · OSLO · Haukeligrend · Heddal · Haugesund · E134 · Drammen · Hjelmeland · Sand · Eidsborg · Kongsberg · Karlstad · Boknafjorden · Stavanger · Prekestolen · Seljord · E18 · Lysefjord · Telemark · Valle · Ulefoss · Larvik · Sandnes · Göteborg · E18 · E39 · Kristiansand

The summit of Buchaille Etive Mor is a challenge for mountain climbers.

Route 2

Scotland

Clansmen, whisky and the solitude of the Highlands

Whether you're a romantic, a lover of the outdoors or a culture con-noisseur, Scotland's raw beauty rarely fails to move the souls of people who make the journey there. Those who choose to experience the rugged, often solitary landscape of the Highlands and the rich history and tradition of this country will be rewarded with unforgettable memories.

Jagged escarpments covered in a lush carpet of green grass, deep lakes in misty moorlands, and torrential rivers tumbling down craggy valleys often typify our image of the Highlands and Scotland in general. But there is more to Scotland than the Highlands in the north, notably the interesting groups of islands to the west and a couple of lovely cities. Glasgow and the capital, Edinburgh, offer modern city living, with cultural events, attractive shopping possibilities and re-nowned festivals, while idyllic sandy

'Clansmen' in Scottish national costume.

beaches await discovery, for example on the Western Isles. On the mainland, Scotland's first national parks were recently opened around the Cairngorm Mountains and Loch Lomond.

Poets such as Sir Walter Scott and the 'national poet of Scotland', Robert Burns, have written of this country's unique beauty. The modern revival of Gaelic music and language has long since spread beyond Scotland's borders, and Scottish customs like caber tossing and wearing kilts may seem peculiar to outsiders, but to the Scots they are part of their identity. If you take one insider tip, make it this one: Scottish cooking. Once you have tried Angus steak, grouse or Highland lamb, you will no longer limit your praise of the country to single malt whisky. Hav-ing said that, there are about 110 whisky distilleries in Scotland, mainly spread

around the Highlands and on the West-ern Isles. These world-famous single malt elixirs age for up to thirty years in old whisky and sherry barrels.

Scotland's territory covers a total of 78,000 sq km (30,014 sq mi), roughly the top third of the island of Great Britain. Most of its many islands are part of either the Hebrides (Inner and Outer), the Orkneys or the Shetlands. During the last ice age, glaciers formed deep valleys throughout the region. When they melt-ed, they left behind lochs (lakes) and firths (fjords) along the country's 3,700 km (2,300 miles) of coastline.

Among the characteristics of the Highlands, the most sparsely populated area of Scotland, are steep rock faces, heath-covered moors, deep lochs and rushing mountain streams. The Great Glen (valley divides the Highlands into

Kilchurn Castle on the northern edge of Loch Awe dates from the 15th century.

Eilean Donan Castle lies on Loch Duich in Glen Shiel and is linked to the mainland by a small dam and a bridge. The castle was rebuilt last century from its former ruins.

two parts. South of the Highlands are the Lowlands, a fertile and densely populated area containing both Glasgow and Edinburgh. The Southern Uplands make up the border with England.

Despite what one might think, Scotland's oceanic climate rarely produces extreme weather conditions – but the weather really can change from sun to rain in a hurry. Wide areas of Scotland are renowned for their characteristic flora (heather, pine trees, ferns) and a wide variety of wildlife.

The Scots are the descendants of a mix of different peoples including the Picts, the Scots, who gave their name to the country, as well as the Scandinavians and the Anglo-Saxons. It was in the 9th century, under Kenneth MacAlpine, that Alba was founded, the first Celtic Scottish kingdom. From then on Scotland's history

was plagued with struggles for independence and resistance against the evermightier forces of England. In 1707, the 'Acts of Union' created the Kingdom of Great Britain and with that came the end of Scotland's independence.

Things unfortunately went from bad to worse after that. The characteristic solitude of the Scottish landscape was a direct result of the Highland Clearances, a move by their own clan chiefs and aristocratic land owners in the 18th century to run small Highland and island farmers off their plots to make room for more lucrative sheep breeding.

After 300 years, Scotland now has its own parliament again, in Edinburgh, and about 5.1 million people. Although the official language is English, many Scots in the Highlands and on the Hebrides speak Scottish Gaelic, a Celtic language.

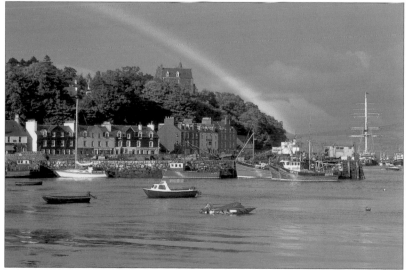

Tobemory with its colourful houses lies on the northern end of the Isle of Mull.

Detour

Blair Castle

At Arbroath the A933 makes its way west before you get to Forfar, where the pink-grey walls of Glamis Castle appear through the trees. It is a place steeped in history, from the murder of Duncan by Macbeth to numerous ghost apparitions and the childhood tales of the late Queen Mother, who grew up here.

The trip then continues north-west to Blair Atholl via the Killiecrankie Pass, scene in 1689 of a bloody battle between the English and the Scots.

The origins of Blair Castle date back to the 13th century.

From there an alley lined with lime trees leads to Blair Castle, the residence of the Duke of Atholl. This fabulously equipped, brilliant white castle is among the most beautiful buildings in Scotland.

The Atholl Highlanders, as the Duke of Atholl's private army is called, are a curious band. Every year at the beginning of June an impressive parade is staged in front of the castle with a backing of bagpipe music.

A journey through Scotland: time-honoured buildings, mysterious stone circles and the occasional whisky distillery line your route, which begins in Edinburgh, takes you through the Highlands and ends in Glasgow. Detours to the Orkneys and Hebrides are highly recommended and can be easily organized from the various harbour towns.

❶ **Edinburgh** (see p. 33). Your route begins in the cultural metropolis of Edinburgh, travelling initially north westward towards Stirling.

❷ **Stirling** The charming city of Stirling, roughly 58 km (36 miles) west of Edinburgh, is built on the banks of the Forth at the point where it first becomes part of the tidal firth (fjord). It is often called the 'Gateway to the Highlands' and is dominated by a large castle. The oldest part of Stirling Castle dates back to the 14th century. The Church of the Holy Rood (cross), which was in the 13th century, is historically significant in that it is one of the very few churches from the Middle Ages to have survived the Reformation in Scotland.

❸ **Fife Peninsula** The Fife Peninsula juts out between the Firth of Forth and the Firth of Tay. In the 4th century the region here made up one of the seven Scottish kingdoms.

The northern coast of the Firth of Forth leads initially to Culross, a small town that blossomed as a trading centre in the 16th cen-

tury. Wealthy trade houses have remained intact and make for an enchanting atmosphere here.

About 11 km (7 miles) to the east of Culross you'll come to Dunfermline, once a long-standing residence or 'burgh' of the Scottish kings. The ruins of the old castle, abbey and monastery can still be seen atop a hill to the south-west of the town.

A little further east, behind the Chapel Ness headland and between the coastal towns of

1 View from the Nelson Monument of the Old Town and castle in Edinburgh.

2 The Scottish national sport of golf was already being played in the 15th century on the sandy beaches of St Andrews.

3 Glamis Castle was the childhood home of the late Queen Mother.

Travel information

Route profile
Length: approx. 1,200 km (745 miles), excluding detours
Time required: 2–3 weeks
Start: Edinburgh
End: Glasgow
Route (main locations): Edinburgh, Stirling, Dundee, Dunottar Castle, Ballater, Inverness, John o'Groats, Durness, Fort William, Inveraray, Glasgow

Traffic information:
Drive on the left in Scotland. Ferries connect the mainland with the various islands:
www.northlink-ferries.co.uk
www.scottish-islands.com

Weather:
The weather in Scotland is generally 'unsettled':

summers are relatively cool, winters on the coast are mild, but in the Highlands bitterly cold, and it can rain at any given moment.

When to go:
Between April and October is the best time. You can check weather forecasts at:
www.onlineweather.com

Accommodation:
An interesting option is a private bed & breakfast:
www.bedandbreakfast scotland.co.uk
www.aboutscotland.com

Information:
wikitravel.org/en/ Scotland
www.visitscotland.com
www.scotland.org.uk

Edinburgh

Both the Old Town and New Town of Scotland's capital have been listed as UNESCO World Heritage Sites, and both are a fascinating display of architectural unity and its exceptional cultural activity. Summer is especially lively during the renowned Edinburgh Festival weeks. The city has been the cultural centre of the north since the 18th and 19th centuries, with famous authors such as Robert Burns and Sir Walter Scott making it their home.

The oldest core of the city, inhabited since the Bronze Age, is Castle Rock, a volcanic outcrop upon which King Edwin built the first castle in the 7th century – hence the name Edinburgh. The castle is still the city's eye-catcher but other higher buildings from the 17th century rise up around it like battlements.

The attractions most worthy of a visit in the Old Town include Edinburgh Castle, a large edifice with buildings from numerous eras, of which St Margaret's Chapel (11th century) is the oldest; the Scottish royal insignia in the castle's Crown Room; the Palace

Edinburgh Castle has served as a fort, a royal residence and a prison.

of Holyroodhouse, the Queen's official residence in Scotland; and the Royal Mile between her residence and the castle with its many side streets.

The New Town, built at the end of the 18th century, is home to the National Gallery of Scotland with one of Europe's most important collections of paintings, the Museum of Antiques for early and art history, and the Scottish National Gallery of Modern Art (20th-century art), all of which are worth a visit.

Detour

Balmoral Castle

This royal castle on the River Dee is in the Grampian Mountains, and thus within the limits of the Cairngorms National Park in Aberdeenshire. Prince Albert, Queen Victoria's consort, bought Balmoral Castle in 1846 and later had it replaced with a magnificent granite building in grand Scottish style.

He personally oversaw the interior decoration, which was inspired by Scottish hunting lodges, with large check patterns and floral designs on upholstery that bear witness to the country style. The royal family came here to get away from court ceremonies in London.

Cairngorms National Park, established in 2003, is Great Britain's largest national park and stretches from Grantown on the Spey to Angus Glens near Glamis. Twenty five per cent of Great Britain's endangered species live in the reserve and numerous rare plants

Top: Iconic Highland cattle graze in front of Balmoral Castle.
Bottom: A royal garden party.

grow only at the foot of the central Cairngorms range (Scottish Gaelic for 'Blue Mountain'). The various moorlands, heath and forests are typical of the area. Fields and pasture typify the lovely Spey and Dee valleys.

Stone-Age monuments, medieval castles and towns steeped in tradition are testimony to the historical importance of the region.

Elie and Crail, is a series of picturesque fishing villages, castle ruins and old churches.

❹ St Andrews Continuing on around the north-east side of the peninsula you will come to the proverbial golfing mecca of the world, St Andrews, about 10 km (6 miles) north of Crail. This, the first ever golf club, was founded here in 1754, and it is still possible to play on the famous Old Course.

The 16th-century ruins of Blackfriars Chapel, at one time Scotland's largest church, are also worth a visit if golf isn't your cup of tea. There is a fabulous view of the grounds from the top of St Rule's Tower.

The route then follows the coast through Dundee to Montrose, about 12 km (8 miles) north of Arbroath. A worthy detour here takes you to Blair Castle, roughly 65 km (40 miles) inland from Arbroath.

❺ Montrose This harbour town and 'burgh' is built like a defensive wall on the peninsula of a natural bay. The House of Dun Mansion, built in 1730, stands on the bank of the Montrose Basin. The coastline north and south of Montrose impresses with long sandy beaches and steep cliffs.

❻ Dunnottar Castle Following the A92 to the north you'll reach one of Scotland's most

fascinating ruins just a few kilometres before Stonehaven – Dunnottar Castle. Built on a rock more than 50 m (60 yds) out to sea, the fortress is connected to the mainland only by a narrow spit of land.

In the 17th century, the Scottish imperial insignia were stored here. Nowadays, only the ruins of the turret, a barrack and the chapel remain of the once formidable construction.

❼ Aberdeen This town is the capital of Europe's oil industry and one of the largest European ports. Despite its industrial leanings, however, there are a number of historic highlights to visit, including Kings College, St Andrew's Cathedral, St Machar's Cathedral and the Maritime Museum.

From Aberdeen the route leads inland to Ballater. (Here we recommend taking a detour to

Balmoral Castle about 50 km (31 miles) away. The mountain road (A939) then goes from Ballater through Colnabaichin to Tomintoul, the starting point of the whisky trail, before heading to Dufftown and Keith.

You then go west through the Spey Valley to Aviemore where the A9 takes you to Inverness.

❽ Inverness This modern-day industrial centre at the northern

Detour

The Orkney Islands

The Orkney Islands, of which only eighteen are inhabited, are around 30 km (19 miles) off the north-eastern coast of Scotland. They are best reached from the ferry ports of John o'Groats and Thurso.
Mainland, Hoy and South Ronaldsay are the larger of the islands in the archipelago, with rolling hills formed by glaciers from the last ice age. Despite their northerly location, the islands benefit from a comparatively mild climate caused by the warm Gulf Stream.

Top: An historic lighthouse.
Middle: The 'Standing Stones of Stennes', a prehistoric stone circle.
Bottom: Impressive rocky coast.

The inhabitants of the Orkneys, descendants of Scots and Scandinavians, live mostly from farming, fishing and tourism these days. Rock climbers and ornithologists are also fascinated by Britain's highest coastal cliffs (347 m/1,138 ft) on the island of Hoy, while the spectacular landscape and monuments, like the Stone-Age village of Skara Brae or the stone circle of Brodgar on Mainland, are popular with everyone who visits.

along the north coast towards Bettyhill past deserted beaches that are often only accessible by short footpaths. Dunnet Head is the most northern point of the Scottish mainland. The popular holiday destination of Thurso, which is also the ferry port for travel to the Orkney Islands, was the scene of a memorable battle between the Scots and the Vikings in 1040.
To the west of the village of Bettyhill, in the county of Sutherland, the A836 leads over the impressive Kyle of Tongue Fjord and on to Durness. Shortly before Durness is the Cave of Smoo, which was used as shelter by the Picts, then the Vikings, and later still by Scottish smugglers. Organized trips to Cape Wrath, the rocky outcrop on the north-westernmost point of Scotland, are offered from Durness.

1 The once strategic position of Dunnottar Castle is unmistakable: built on a solid rock promontory, a deep ravine separates the castle from the mainland.

2 Inverness is the 'capital' of the Highlands, and its business and administrative centre.

3 View from the harbour over Aberdeen.

4 Mighty waves from the Atlantic crash against the cliffs of Cape Wrath on the north coast of Scotland. The lighthouse was built in 1828.

The Whisky Trail

The famous 110-km-long (68-mile) Speyside Malt Whisky Trail, which sets off from Tomintoul, is a well-signposted route leading past seven whisky distilleries. Among them are some well-known names such as Glenlivet, Glenfiddich and Glenfarclas.

tip of Loch Ness is the ideal starting point for trips to the home of 'Nessie', Urquhart Castle and into the wild and romantic Highland landscape.
Due to its exposed location, Inverness was regularly involved in military disputes, to the extent that few of its old buildings remain. Most of today's structures were erected in the 19th century.

9 East Coast of the North-west Highlands From Inverness the A9 (and the A99) snake northwards along the striking east coast. Various sites like Dunrobin Castle, Helmsdale Castle or the mysterious Bronze-Age rock lines near Greg Cairns are worth short visits on your way. One option is to take a long walk from the former fishing village of Wick out to the picturesque cliffs of Noss Head. Nearby are the ruins of Sinclair and Girnigoe Castles.

10 John o'Groats The village of John o'Groats is about 17 km (11 miles) north of Wick on the north-eastern tip of Caithness. Just before you get there, Warth Hill will offer an exceptional view of the area.
Ferries travel between John o'Groats, the Orkneys and the coastal seal colonies.

11 North Coast The A836 then takes you from John o'Groats

Detour

The Outer Hebrides

The Atlantic islands to the west of Scotland are made up of the southern Inner Hebrides, near the Scottish mainland, and the Outer Hebrides (Western Isles) farther out towards the northwest. The main islands of the Outer Hebrides are, from north to south, the double islands of Lewis and Harris, North Uist and South Uist, joined by a dam, and Barra. You can reach the Western Isles by ferry from Ullapool or from Skye, the largest of the Inner Hebrides islands, which include Rum, Coll, Tiree, Mull, Jura and Islay.

The Hebrides have a long and chequered past. In 563 the Irish minister Columban the Elder (who later became St Columba) established a Celtic monastery on the small island of Iona and began the process of Christianizing Scotland. In the 8th century the islands were invaded by the Norwegian Vikings, who kept their rule over much of the region for many hundreds of years. It was only in 1266, after the signing of the Treaty of Perth, that the Scots regained the upper hand and the islands were henceforth run by the clans MacDougall and MacDonald. Their rulers were thereafter called 'Lord of the Isles'.

Today's visitors are met by a world in which life is still greatly influenced by natural forces and the isolation of the Atlantic. History and time have left some clear traces in the partly undulating moor and heath landscape. In geological terms the islands consist of the oldest rocks in the entire British Isles. Stone-Age graves, Celtic Christian ruins, Viking settlements and Scottish forts can all be found around the various Hebrides islands.

In addition to the historical attractions, the magnificent natural environment includes lakes and valleys, pristine white sand beaches, and rich animal and plant life that all help to attract a good number of adventurous tourists each year.

The Isle of Lewis and Harris

The two halves of the island of Lewis and Harris are connected by an isthmus and are not just the largest of the Western Isles, but the largest island around Great Britain after Ireland. Lewis and Harris have very differing landscapes: Lewis is littered with rocky hill ranges, fjords and bays, while Harris is covered with moors and heath. The A859 leads from the main town of Stornoway to south Harris, which is noteworthy for its fabulous sandy beaches. Don't miss the mysterious stone circles of Callanish on Lewis, which, like Stonehenge, were built thousands of years ago, presumably for cult rituals.

North Uist und South Uist

North and South Uist, and the island of Benbecula between them, are covered with countless lakes. Deep ocean bays line the east coast to such an extent that it resembles a series of islands that have grown together.

The Stone-Age burial chambers on North Uist and the low, reed-covered crofter houses, some of which have survived hundreds of years of wind and weather, are worth visiting.

The A865 leads all the way around North Uist and down to the southern tip of South Uist, passing the prettiest areas of the island on the way. The east coast of South Uist has two 600-m (2,000-ft) peaks – Beinn Mhór and Hecla.

Barra

Ferries from Ludag on South Uist to the small island of Barra, the southernmost island of the Outer Hebrides, only take about 40 minutes. Barra's small neighbouring islands include Berneray with it tall lighthouse.

The island, named after St Finbarr, is regarded as one of the prettiest islands of the Outer Hebrides due to the thousands of colourful flowers that grow

there. Kisimuil Castle, the old residence of the MacNeils, dominates the harbour of the main town, Castlebay.

The ring road, the A888, goes as far as Cille Barra in the north, with its ruins of a monastery built in the 12th century. A 12th-century chapel has been restored and houses some sacred objects. A cemetery lies on the hill.

1 Isle of Lewis: the monumental 'Standing Stones of Callanish' form a 13 m by 11 m (40 ft by 35 ft) circle and were erected around 1800 BC.

2 The Taransay Sound separates the island of Taransay from the south-west coast of Harris. This island of beautiful beaches is uninhabited.

3 Lovers of treeless, wild landscapes will be contented on the Isle of Lewis in the north of the Outer Hebrides.

4 This is the inlet of Loch Sealg on the east coast of Lewis at dusk. The natural life of this stretch of land has inspired many an artist.

1

2

3

Isle of Skye

Skye, the largest island of the Inner Hebrides, is known for being one of the wildest, roughest and yet most beautiful islands in Scotland. Mountains like the 1,009-m-high (3,310-ft) Cuillin Hills, or the Quiraing Hills and bizarre geological formations like the Old Man of Storr give the island its unique character.

Fog, brief showers and plentiful rainbows make a trip around this island an unforgettable adventure. Dunvegan Castle, lounging seal herds, the Talisker whisky distillery, otter colonies and other fun sights invite the traveller to make pleasant stops along the way.

Next to an open fire in a little restaurant offering local specialities like venison and raspberry dessert, you can imagine what may have come to pass on these remote islands while enjoying a glass of whisky and a Gaelic tune.

14 Eilean Donan Castle A bit further along the A87 is Eilean Donan Castle, a picturesque natural stone castle rising up from St Donan Island in Loch Duich. This edifice, which was badly damaged by the Jacobite Wars, was only rebuilt at the start of the 19th century.

Around 5 km (3 miles) from the castle, the A890 feeds into the A87, which leads to Kyle of Lochalsh. A toll bridge from there takes you over to the Isle of Skye. From Ardvasar in the south-west of Skye there is a ferry back to Mallaig on the mainland. Take the 'Road to the Isles' (A830) 40 km (25 miles) to the east to reach Fort William.

If you are short on time, travel directly from Eilean Donan Castle eastwards on the A87 and then turn south onto the A82 at Invergarry to reach Fort William.

15 Ben Nevis The highest mountain on the British Isles, at 1,344 m (4,409 ft), rises magnificently from the Grampian Mountains above Fort William. While the north-western face of the mountain is relatively easy to hike, the 460-m (1,509-ft) north-eastern rock face is reserved for experienced climbers.

Before travelling on to Glencoe, take the A828 15 km (9 miles) to Castle Stalker near Portnacroish.

16 Loch Rannoch Fort William is the starting point for a small detour by train into the other-

12 North-west Coast up to Ullapool The wild north-west portion of Sutherland is not your typical holiday destination. Its steep mountains and fjords, deep blue lakes and glistening waterfalls are too secluded for the average traveller. The impassable valleys and deserted coastlines have thus become a paradise for hikers, hunters and fishermen. Naturalists can observe seabirds, seals and dolphins and sometimes even whales from these remote environs. Innumerable small alcoves are perfect for a relaxing break.

A narrow road, the A838, then leads from Durness towards the south-west. Just before Scourie you can take the A894, which branches off towards Handa

Island, a seabird sanctuary with imposing cliffs where puffins and guillemots nest.

From Kylesku, which is further south, you can take boat trips to seal colonies and to Great Britain's highest waterfall along Loch Glencoul (200 m/656 ft).

If you want to follow the tiny roads along the coast, turn off after Kylesku on to the B869. Otherwise follow the wider roads, A837 and A835, south to Ullapool. This beautiful stretch passes Loch Assynt and the ruins of Ardvreck Castle.

If you are interested, you can take the ferries that travel from Ullapool on Loch Broom to Lewis in the Outer Hebrides, and the steamers that travel to the nearby Summer Isles.

After Ullapool, stay on the A835 until shortly after Corrieshalloch Gorge (61 m/200 ft), a ravine with waterfall, where you will turn onto the A832.

13 Inverewe Gardens After Little Loch Broom and Gruinard Bay you come to Loch Ewe and the Inverewe Gardens. These gardens were planted in 1862 and exhibit a wonderful collection of rhododendron and hibiscus bushes. Next you will come to Kinlochewe, in the Torridon Mountains, where the road to Shieldaig on the coast follows the Liathach Ridge out to a seabird sanctuary. Thrill seekers can then follow the tiny coastal road south from Shieldaig.

1 Eilean Donan Castle was destroyed in 1719 by the English because it was a Jacobite stronghold.

2 View from Loch Eil to the east with Ben Nevis.

3 Mountain stream in the snow-covered Highlands near Glencoe.

Top: Beinn Edra (611 m/2,005 ft) on the Trotternish Peninsula. Middle: Dunvegan Castle in the north-west of Skye has been the official residence of the MacLeod Clan since the 11th century. Bottom: The green cattle and sheep pastures are mainly down in the southern part of the Isle of Skye.

Detour

Isle of Mull

Mull, one of the islands of the Inner Hebrides at the entrance to Loch Linnhe, has an unusual effect on visitors with its craggy, hilly landscape and castles. It is also one of the easier islands to reach by taking the quick ferry from Oban.

The west coast of Mull is particularly pretty. This is where you'll find The Burg nature reserve, among other things, and picturesque bays lining the northern side of the Ross of Mull Peninsula.

Just off the peninsula is the legendary Isle of Iona, the cradle of Christianity in Scotland, where the Celtic monk Columban the Elder

Abandoned boats on the coast of the Isle of Mull.

founded the first monastery here in 563. For a long time Iona was even the final resting place of Scottish, Norwegian and Irish kings. The island has been inhabited since the Stone Age, as archaeological digs have proven.

Also off the west coast of Mull is the Isle of Ulva, which was inhabited until the Highland Clearances in the middle of the 19th century before farmers were driven from their land in order to make way for more lucrative sheep farming.

wise intractable Rannoch Moor. Rannoch Station, a tiny house in the wide landscape of the moor, is one of the most isolated stations in Great Britain. Small ponds and trout-rich streams cross the boulder-scattered moor and marshland. To the east of the moor lies the impressively calm Loch Rannoch.

17 Glencoe The Glencoe Valley begins roughly 16 km (10 miles) to the south of Fort William and is one of Scotland's must-see destinations. After the Jacobite Risings of the 17th century, the English attempted to take control over Scotland by exploiting clan rivalries and disputes. So it was that in 1692, soldiers led by the Clan Campbell of Glencoe and loyal to the new king, William of Orange, massacred the opposing Clan MacDonald almost in its entirety. Women and children were apparently left to perish in the elements. An impressive monument marks this gruesome event.

Following the A82 you will soon cross the A85 at Tyndrum. If you are planning a trip to the Isle of Mull, follow the A85 west to Oban, a harbour on the Firth of Lorne. Ferries sail from here to Mull and the other islands of the Inner Hebrides.

18 Kilchurn Castle If you turn east from the A82 onto the A85, you will reach the northern tip of Loch Awe where you will find the ruins of the 15th-century Kilchurn Castle. The ruins were hit by lightning in the 18th century and completely abandoned. One of the turrets still lies upside down in the courtyard. Restored steamboats navigate Loch Awe, the longest freshwater loch in Scotland.

19 Inveraray The town of Inveraray, 15 km (9 miles) south of Loch Awe, was constructed alongside Loch Fyne according to plans drawn up in the 18th century by the Duke of Argyll. He had his castle built in artistically arranged gardens. A prison museum in the old Inveraray Jail is also worth a visit. You can appear in court there, and even be locked up.

20 Loch Lomond The A83 leads further east to the holiday destination of Loch Lomond, Scotland's largest loch in surface area. The area is loved by hikers, water-sports enthusiasts and families looking to take a steamboat trip to the islands.

In 2002, Loch Lomond and the Trossachs National Park was opened to the east of the lake.

21 Glasgow For culture fans this city is one of Europe's hot destinations. Renowned museums and galleries as well as countless cultural programmes vie for your attention. The millionstrong city on the Clyde River is also an important industrial centre. To get an overview of Glasgow's various highlights and attractions, take a double-decker bus tour.

Only a few of the buildings in Scotland's largest city date back to before the 18th century. Among them are the Gothic St Mungo's Cathedral and the classical Pollok House. The Hunterian Museum (with works by Charles Rennie Mackintosh, for example), the Burrell Collection (art and craftwork) and the Gallery of Modern Art are worth a visit.

A little way out of town is the New Lanark textile mill from the 18th century, which was recently listed as a UNESCO World Heritage Site – one of four in Scotland. This interesting museum town provides insight into factory life at the start of the 19th century.

1 Kilchurn Castle in the shadow of the 1,125-m-high (3,691-ft) Ben Cruachan.

2 The inaccessible Rannoch Moor is Britain's largest uninterrupted moor. The landscape is made up of wild streams, crippled trees and thousands of boulders carried here by a glacier.

3 View over the industrial city and port of Glasgow.

The Isle of Skye The largest of the Inner Hebrides islands is a craggy refuge for all kinds of animals: sheep, cattle, otters and seals all find their home here.

The Hebrides Islands Most of the islands off the west coast of Scotland in the Atlantic are raw, isolated and covered with ancient flora and fauna. Because of the great distances between them, the Outer Hebrides are vastly different from the Inner Hebrides in this respect. The Hebrides are also the home to most of Scotland's native Gaelic-speaking population.

The Orkney Islands Only eighteen of the seventy islands off Scotland's north-eastern coast are actually inhabited, despite the fact that the Gulf Stream blesses them with an exceptionally mild climate, which helps farming, fishing and tourism. The island of Mainland is interesting due to its many prehistoric finds, including the Stone-Age grave Maes Howe.

Eilean Donan Castle This formidable castle sits on the island of St Donan in Loch Duich. It was destroyed in 1719 and reopened in 1932.

Fort William With all the necessary tourist amenities, this town at the south end of the Great Glen on the shore of Loch Linnhe is an ideal starting point for trips to the Isle of Skye or Ben Nevis.

Stalker Castle This 15th-century castle stands alone on a small island in Loch Laich. Due to its situation, it was well-protected from attacks.

Glencoe An important event in Scottish history took place here in the Glencoe Valley: in 1692 faithfuls to the new king, William of Orange, massacred the Clan MacDonald. The North Lorn Folk Museum provides more information.

Dunrobin Castle The earls and dukes of Sutherland were among the most powerful landowners in Europe when they built 'Scotland's Neuschwanstein' in the middle of the 19th century. Many of the 150 rooms can be visited.

Inverness This industrial city on Loch Ness is an ideal jumping-off point for trips to the watery home of the famous monster, 'Nessie', or into the wildly romantic Highlands.

Dufftown This town, referred to historically as early as AD 566, is home to several well known whisky makers including the Glenfiddich Distillery.

Dunottar Castle This castle from the 14th century was home of the Scottish insignia in the 17th century. Although thought of as impenetrable due to its prime location, today it lies in ruins.

Rannoch The large (130 sq km/50 sq mi) and nearly impassable Rannoch Moor is home to Rannoch Station, one of Britain's most isolated train stations. East of the moors is the tranquil Loch Rannoch.

Glasgow Museums like the Hunterian Art Gallery, the Burrell Collection and the Gallery of Modern Art have put Glasgow back on the map. Only very few buildings date back to before the 18th century.

Edinburgh Scotland's capital captivates visitors with its architectural consistency and cultural diversity. Edinburgh Castle (11th century), the royal residence of Holyrood Palace and the lanes around the Royal Mile are but three of the highlights of this incredible city.

St Andrews This town in the region of Fife is the home of golf, and it was here that the first golf club was founded in 1754. Its course is still playable. The view here is from St Rule's Tower in the church ruins of Blackfriars Chapel, once Scotland's largest religious building. St Andrews on the North Sea is also home to Scotland's oldest university, founded in 1410.

The most famous prehistoric construction in Europe – Stonehenge, erected around 3000 BC.

England

Magical locations in southern Britain

Ancient trading routes crisscross the south of England, and monumental stone circles bear witness to prehistoric settlements in the region. The Celts, the Romans, the Anglo-Saxons and the Normans came after the original inhabitants of the island and eventually transformed the magnificent natural environment here into a diverse cultural macrocosm with monuments, cathedrals, quaint fishing villages, parks and country houses.

Generally, the 'South of England' refers to the region along the south coast, extending northwards to Bristol in the west and London in the east. For some, however, the south only includes the coastal counties south of London like East and West Sussex, Hampshire and Dorset. Others think of just the southeast including London, while others of the south-west with Cornwall and Devon. In some references, the south even reaches up to the middle of England. Some areas, like Greater London (with around

Bodiam Castle near Hastings.

eight million inhabitants) are densely populated, whereas others like Dartmoor in Devon appear at first glance to be deserted. In the end, the South of England is unspecific, but Britons look at it as an area 'steeped in history' and known for its contrasts: picturesque cliffs and small sailing villages, busy seaside resorts and modern port towns, green pastures and barren moorland.

Indeed, the bustling metropolis of London dominates the south-east, while the more relaxed south-west has a real holiday feel to it. The area has always attracted writers and artists: Shakespeare, Jane Austen, Turner and Constable all lived here, or at least gave the south a recognizable face in their various works. Numerous nature reserves and magical, manicured gardens invite you to take peaceful walks.

Geologically speaking, the British Isles 'separated' from the continent roughly 700,000 years ago. At the time, there had been a land bridge connecting what is now England to the mainland, with a river running through (now the English Channel). The water trapped in the ice at the end of the ice age about 10,000 years ago was then released, causing sea levels to rise and gradually wash away the land bridge. The characteristic white limestone cliffs that we now see in places along the south coast like Dover and Eastbourne are the result of this 'river' flooding through the weakest point between the now divided land masses. The West Country consists mostly of granite, whereas the limestone is typical of the south-east. At the narrowest point in the channel, the Dover Strait, the distance between the United Kingdom and

The western facade of Wells Cathedral is decorated with countless sculptures from the medieval period.

The natural arch of Durdle Door on the Jurassic Coast of Dorset is the result of erosion by the pounding sea.

the European continent is only around 32 km (20 miles).

Demographically, countless generations have created a rich landscape in Britain. Due to the geographical proximity to the continent, the south was always the arrival point for immigrants, invaders and traders. In about 3500 BC, farmers and livestock breeders migrated to the island. The fortuitously warm Gulf Stream provided them and their modern-day ancestors with a relatively mild climate and even some subtropical vegetation. Natural resources like tin and copper also attracted invaders over the centuries.

England has not been successfully subdued by an enemy power since 1066, when the Normans under William the Conqueror emerged victorious at the legendary Battle of Hastings. The vulnerability of the south coast is revealed by countless castles and fortresses, and also by installations from World War II.

The varied history of settlements also features in the endless stories and myths that originate here. King Arthur and his Knights of the Round Table are among the prominent characters in these tales. Castles, cathedrals and grand old universities testify to the historical importance of the south while small fishing villages on the coast have developed into significant harbour towns that enabled the British Empire's rise to naval dominance. In return came exotic goods and peoples, changing yet again the cultural fabric of the traditional island inhabitants.

'High society' discovered the coast in the 19th century, and from then on vacationed in resort towns like Brighton and Eastbourne. Today the coastal economy relies primarily on services and tourism.

Tower Bridge is a masterpiece of Victorian engineering completed in 1894.

1

Brighton

The well-known seaside resort of Brighton, which once attracted London's high society and even became a royal city of sorts, is still a wildly popular getaway for city dwellers and

Top: The Mughal-style Royal Pavilion is one of Brighton's main attractions.
Bottom: Chandeliers in the banquet room of the Royal Pavilion.

beach lovers. One of the attractions is the Royal Pavilion from the 19th century, a palace built in Indian Mughal style with minarets, columns and an ostentatious interior. It is still used for exhibitions and concerts. Before the advent of cheap package holidays, Brighton was famous for its West Pier, which was unfortunately destroyed by fire and storms in 2003.

This dream route through the South of England begins in London and heads down to the coast, which it then follows west until bending northwards at Land's End back towards Oxford and eventually back to the capital, London. Along the way you will experience everything from fashionable seaside resorts and Roman ruins to awe-inspiring cathedrals, desolate moors and craggy cliffs.

1 London (see pp. 44–47 for a detailed description of the sights and sounds that await you in England's capital).

2 Hastings Around 40 km (25 miles) south of London (A21) is possibly one of the most important battlefields in the long and distinguished history of the British Isles: Hastings, scene of the legendary battle in 1066 between Duke William of Normandy and the Saxon army under King Harold of England. The outcome of the Battle of Hastings was the coronation of the Duke of Normandy as the third king of England in Westminster following his victory. The first building he commissioned was the Battle Abbey on the site of the struggle.
Nearby Bodiam Castle is also worthy of a visit. Purportedly intended as a fortress to protect against French attacks during the Hundred Years War, it has come to light that it was actually more for show, a purpose it fits well: the castle is guarded by eight mighty towers and is artistically placed in the middle spring-fed moat.

3 Eastbourne and the Seven Sisters The traditional sea resort

of Eastbourne, about 17 km (11 miles) west of Hastings, is noteworthy for its wonderful sandy beaches and noble Victorian architecture. Just beyond Eastbourne is the fascinating Seven Sisters Country Park, named after seven bright limestone cliffs on the coast. A short walk leads to the South Downs Way, which meanders along the shore and over the remarkable limestone landscape.
From Beachy Head, the highest limestone cliff in Britain at 163 m (535 ft), you get a breathtaking view over the English Channel and the 100-year-old lighthouse out in the sea. The postcard panorama of the Seven Sisters, however, is only visible from the next cliff, South Hill.

4 Portsmouth and the Isle of Wight The narrow coastal road now travels past the elegant seaside resort of Brighton towards Portsmouth, an old harbour and trading port that is home to the Royal Navy. Some of the attractions here include Lord Nelson's flagship from the Battle of Trafalgar (the most significant naval victory of the Napoleonic Wars), the Sea Life Centre and the house where Charles Dickens was born.

2

Travel information

Route profile
Length: approx. 1,200 km (746 miles), excluding detours
Time required: 2–3 weeks
Start and end: London
Route (main locations): London, Hastings, Brighton, Portsmouth, Salisbury, Weymouth, Exeter, Torquay, St Austell, Land's End, Barnstaple, Bridgwater, Bath, Stratford-upon-Avon, Oxford, Windsor, London

Traffic information:
Drive on the left in Great Britain. The green insurance card is necessary.
Info: www.theaa.com

When to go:
Thanks to the Gulf Stream, the weather in southern

Britain is better than reputed with warm summers and mild winters. Recommended travel season: April to October. Further information available at:
www.onlineweather.com

Accommodation:
As well as hotels and guesthouses, bed-and-breakfast accommodation (B&B) is in private houses recommended. Useful information:
www.bedandbreakfast nationwide.com
www.accommodation britain.co.uk

Information:
British Tourist Office
www.visitbritain.com
London sights and travel
www. visitlondon.com

Salisbury Cathedral was built between 1220 and 1258 in what is known as 'Early English' style to the Britons, an English Gothic form that identifies with the early-Gothic architectural style. The cathedral has the tallest spine in England.

The silhouette of the diocesan city of Exeter is dominated by the Cathedral Church of St Peter, built between the 11th and 14th centuries in 'Decorated' style. England's largest surviving collection of 14th-century sculptures cover

Top: Exeter Cathedral in Devon. Bottom: The impressive quire of Salisbury Cathedral.

the western facade and include angels, kings and apostles. The lusciously decorated interior contains an impressive carved arch.

The city of Winchester was England's capital until 1066, a pivotal year in the island's history when the Normans invaded and conquered it. The transepts and tower survive from the Norman cathedral (1079) while the Perpendicular nave and choir loft (with vertical framework on the windows) are from the 14th century. At 170 m (560 ft), the cathedral is Europe's tallest medieval church.

Ferries sail from Portsmouth to the Isle of Wight, the smallest county in England at 381 sq km (146 sq mi), once inhabited by the Romans. The island benefits from a varied landscape thanks to the warm Gulf Stream, which gives it a mild climate and allows colourful subtropical plants to blossom here between palm trees.

Off the west coast are three limestone formations – The Needles. At the base of the last rock outcrop, a lighthouse defies the constant pounding of the waves. Back on the mainland, we continue inland to Winchester, which was the capital of England until 1066, and then on to Salisbury. About 16 km (10 miles) to the north of the town lies Stonehenge.

5 Stonehenge It should come as no surprise that the most famous prehistoric site on the British Isles has been listed as a UNESCO World Heritage Site. Stonehenge is believed to have been erected in four stages between 3100 BC and 1500 BC by successors of the Bell-Beaker culture. The unbelievable 'engineering' and building capacity of these Stone-Age peoples inspires awe to this day: they transported eighty-two gigantic building blocks from the Welsh mountains, nearly 160 km (100 miles) away, presumably using rivers and rollers of some sort all the way to Stonehenge. Later, at the start of the Bronze Age, these blue stones were replaced by even larger sandstone blocks measuring 7-m (23-ft) high.

Indeed, the site was modified a number of times. Today two concentric stone circles make up the middle section. The outer circle, with a diameter of 30 m (98 ft), is made up of seventeen trilithons and two vertical monoliths with a horizontal stone. The inner circle is made up exclusively of monoliths. It is a source of discussion as to whether the site was used as a place of worship, an observatory or for monitoring the sun's behaviour. On the day of the summer solstice, the sun rises exactly over the Heel Stone, following the axis of the entrance, and throws its light through a stone window. Stonehenge has been a magical place for thousands of years. Celtic druids also used the site for their rites.

6 Shaftesbury About 20 km (12.5 miles) to the west of Salisbury, one of Britain's rare medieval hill towns continues to enchant visitors. Time seems to have stood still in Shaftesbury: ancient town walls and Gold Hill are reminiscent of a long forgotten time. The steep, cobbled lanes are lined with small, sometimes thatched houses and were at one time part of the pilgrimage route to the grave of Edward the Martyr, whose bones are now kept in Westminster Abbey. In the Middle Ages there was a prosperous Benedictine monastary here, but it was disbanded in 1539 and for the most part demolished.

The oft-photographed Gold Hill is classified today as Britain's prettiest street. From the top of

it you get a view over green, hilly pastureland that is interrupted only by lush, dark-green hedges.

The A350 then leads south, back to the coast, past Blandford and on to the coastal town of Swanage on the lovely Purbeck Peninsula.

7 Corfe Castle and Swanage On your way to Swanage it is worth stopping at Corfe Castle, a wild and romantic set of ruins out on a high promontory. In 1646 the fort fell through a betrayal on the part of Oliver Cromwell's soldiers and was almost totally destroyed.

Swanage is a charming seaside town at the end of the narrow Purbeck Peninsula. The Old Harry Rocks are just a walk away from here. Like the Needles on the Isle of Wight, the limestone rocks in this formation were formed by the emergence of the Alps over thirty million years ago.

8 The Jurassic Coast The coast between Swanage and Weymouth is not called the Jurassic Coast for nothing. The cliff formations here date from the period and because of their location are only partially accessible by car. In 2001 this stretch of coastline was classified a Natural World Heritage Site by UNESCO – the first site to be listed as such in the UK – because it documents nearly 185 million years of the earth's history.

The beaches and the cliffs here bear witness to periods within the Mesozoic Era, effectively the geological 'middle ages'. Ever

since the spectacular find of an Ichthyosaurus, an enormous fish dinosaur, in the 19th century, this area has also become world-famous among hobby fossil hunters.

Yet the region is also perfect for walks with breathtaking views. Shortly before Weymouth is the enchanting Lulworth Cove, a natural harbour with steep cliffs and golden sands. A footpath then leads you along the cliff edge to the impressive Durdle Door, a natural bridge that extends out into the ocean. St Oswalds Bay, with its fine sand beach, can also be reached from here by a steep path.

Between Weymouth and Exeter there are many small coastal villages that invite you for a break. In the dreamy village of Abbotsbury, the Swannery swan colony is home to about 1,000 swans, a sight to behold.

Chesil Bank is a gravel bank that is over 80,000 years old and stretches more than 29 km (18 miles). It resembles a pebble dune. Beyond the dune is a bird sanctuary in the brackish water of the lagoon.

9 Torquay Torquay is around 40 km (25 miles) south of Exeter on what is commonly known as the English Riviera. This 30-km-long (19-mile) stretch of coast

1 The white lighthouse of Godrevy, which sits atop an isolated rock, is not far from Gwithian in Cornwall. The lighthouse inspired Virginia Woolf's famous novel To the Lighthouse.

2 One of England's most recognizable medieval streets: Gold Hill in Shaftesbury.

3 The limestone cliffs of the Seven Sisters between Seaford and Eastbourne are visible from far away.

4 The Needles and lighthouse west of the Isle of Wight.

5 The yacht harbour of Torquay on the 'English Riviera' in Devon.

London

England's capital, London, is the seat of British government and an international financial centre of massive proportions, but above all it is a cosmopolitan city in the truest sense of the word. For a few centuries, London was the heart of the British Empire, and this is still very much perceptible in its dynamic atmosphere. Due to numerous restrictions for cars in the city centre, use of the excellent public transport network or a tour on a red sightseeing double-decker bus is highly recommended.

The western part of central London is typified by diversity – the administrative centre of Whitehall in the historic district of Westminster; posh residential and business districts like Knightsbridge and Belgravia; busy squares like Piccadilly Circus and Trafalgar Square; and the fabulous parks like St James's and the Kensington Gardens.

Starting with the district of Westminster, here is a handful of things to

18th century), the city residence of the Queen, Green Park and St James's Park, and the Tate Gallery with a first-class selection of English art.

In Whitehall you'll find 10 Downing Street, residence of the Prime Minister; the Palladian-style Banqueting House, opposite Horse Guards Parade for the Changing of the Guard; Trafalgar Square with Nelson's Column; the National Gallery with works from the

Top: Buckingham Palace – London residence of the Queen.
Middle: Bustling Trafalgar Square with Nelson's Column.
Bottom: Houses of Parliament with Big Ben.

see, the first two being UNESCO World Heritage Sites: Westminster Abbey, the mighty Gothic church where English kings are crowned and buried (not to be confused with nearby Westminster Cathedral, a Catholic church from the 19th century), and the neo-Gothic Houses of Parliament on the Thames. Then we have the only remaining part of the original medieval building, Westminster Hall, and next to that the clock tower housing Big Ben (1858). Westminster Bridge crosses the Thames. After that we have Buckingham Palace (early

16th to 20th centuries, the National Portrait Gallery; Hyde Park, a public park from the 17th century with the famous Speaker's Corner; Madame Tussaud's Wax Museum.

In Knightsbridge are the Victoria and Albert Museum, the largest arts and crafts museum in the world; the Natural History Museum, with a famous dinosaur section; the Science and Technology Museum; the legendary Harrods department store with something for everyone; and the younger and less conventional Harvey Nichols department store.

London

In 1851, when Great Britain was at the height of its imperial power and had just celebrated itself in a World Fair, London had around one million inhabitants. Today there are over twelve million people in Greater London and around eight within city limits – the latter makes it the largest city in Europe.

It began modestly almost 2,000 years ago, when the Romans conquered the island that is now England and founded Londinium on the Thames. Many peoples have come to the British Isles, but since William the Conqueror made London his capital in 1066, the city has remained the administrative centre of Britain, not least due to its strategic position – near the continent, yet protected in an estuary. The first block of the Tower of London, the city's most venerated building, was in fact laid by William the Conqueror in 1078.

A large fortress and medieval royal residence, the Tower of London complex is centred around the White Tower (11th century) and it is here that the Crown Jewels are on display. Another one of the most recognizable icons of London's cityscape is the Tower Bridge

centre – and the famous London Stock Exchange from 1773.

In the West End you'll find countless theatres, cinemas, pubs and restaurants around Piccadilly Circus, London's most colourful square. Covent Garden, once a market, is now a pedestrian zone in the West End. The Royal Opera House and the British Museum, with a number of world-famous collections, are also here.

Interesting places in the Southwark area include the cathedral of the same name, which is the oldest Gothic church in London. It has a memorial for Shakespeare, whose Globe Theatre was rebuilt nearby almost in its original form. The Tate Modern is a striking art museum in a disused power station across the Thames on the Millennium Footbridge. The Docklands and Canary Wharf both feature

Top: St Paul's Cathedral stands in the centre of London.
Bottom: Walls from the 13th century protect the Tower of London.

(1894) with its double towers and distinctive bascule bridge.

In the City district of London you should take time to go to St Paul's Cathedral (1674–1710), a Renaissance masterpiece with a walkway that goes all the way around its dome. North of St Paul's Cathedral are the futuristic Barbican towers – a culture and arts

modern architecture – Canada Tower and Canary Wharf Tower, respectively. The latter is the tallest building in the UK at 244 m (800 ft).

In Greenwich is the Royal Maritime Museum with sailing history, the historic Cutty Sark clipper ship, and the observatory, which crosses the prime meridian.

Through Dartmoor National Park

From Torquay, a route leads through Dartmoor National Park, a largely untouched area of moorland and forest on the south-west coast of England that covers approximately 945 sq km (363 sq mi) at an elevation of roughly 500 m (1,640 ft) above sea level. It is one of Europe's largest nature reserves.

Dartmoor is not a primeval landscape, but rather an area that has been cultivated for thousands of years. Numerous archaeological sites – remains of Stone Age villages, stone paths and circles, monuments such as burial sites, and more – testify to the extensive human presence here.

Heather-covered moor landscape in Dartmoor National Park.

An 800-km-long (500-mile) network of footpaths crisscrosses the countryside, and in some places the granite rises out of the earth in formations called tors, or craggy hills. Reddish-brown ferns, heather, windswept trees and shaggy Dartmoor ponies are among the park's simple selection of things to see, especially in the sparse western reaches. Tidy lanes and little villages are common on the more inhabited east side.

From Ashburton, a pretty town near idyllic Widecombe-in-the-Moor, your drive goes through the hilly landscape to Two Bridges, past Princetown with the infamous Dartmoor Prison. Tavistock, an earlier centre for tin and copper mining, was famous for hundreds of years because of its rich Benedictine monastery.

has been given this name because of its numerous idyllic bays, palm-littered beaches, mild climate and its urbane atmosphere. Three towns – Torquay, Paignton and Brixham – have become known as Torbay, though they have kept their own individual styles. Elegant hotels, Victorian villas and countless bars and restaurants around the little harbour give the area a holiday feel.

After the impressive mountain road through Dartmoor National Park (with grades of up to twenty-five per cent), the A390 leads from Liskeard back down towards the coast and St Austell.

10 St Austell and the Eden Project Since the discovery of kaolin in the 18th century, the economic welfare of the town has been closely linked to the mining of this important base product used in the manufacture of porcelain. The story of china clay or 'white gold' is retold in St Austell's museum. The Eden Project was constructed over 14 ha (35 acres) on a disused kaolin quarry near Bodelva. In two gigantic greenhouses, gardeners have reproduced two climatic zones – tropical rainforest and Mediterranean. The greenhouses are densely populated with plants from these respective regions in order to allow a natural ecosystem to develop. In another area, a cool zone was set up, in which indigenous plants from Britain and exotic plants from temperate Cornwall flourish. The larger of the greenhouses, the Humid Tropics Biome, is the largest greenhouse in the world covering an area of 1,559 ha (4 acres) at a height of 55 m (180 ft).

11 Mevagissey The Lost Gardens of Heligan north of Mevagissy are every bit as fascinating as the Eden Project – strange, prehistoric fallen tree trunks lie amid a subtropical landscape with giant bamboo, ancient tree ferns and mysterious ponds. The gardens were initially planted in the 18th and 19th centuries, but then fell into a long dormant phase.

In 1990, the developer Tim Smit cut through the 5-m-thick (16-ft) thorn bushes and discovered a site that had been forgotten for nearly a hundred years. After a painstaking reconstruction of the original gardens, the microenvironment was saved. The 32-ha (80-acre) site includes a ravine, an enchanting Italian garden, a grotto and ancient

rhododendron bushes. Lost Valley, a jungle environment with a view over Mevagissey, is another highlight of the gardens.

12 Penzance The largest town in Cornwall lies 50 km (31 miles) to the west of here. A drive over the Penwith Peninsula to Land's End is definitely recommended. Due to its temperate climate, this striking region is also called the 'Cornish Riviera'.

Penzance was an important tin trading point for the Roman Empire and medieval Europe. The centre of town, between Chapel Street and Market Jew Street, is the oldest part of Pen-

zance, where the long since vanished times of the seafarers can still be felt. The Barbican, which is an old storage house, and the Egyptian House (1830) are both worth visiting.

Opposite the town stands the old castle of St Michael's Mount on top of a granite island in the bay of the same name. This former Benedictine monastery came into the Crown's possession in 1535 and was then converted into a fortress. Historians date the founding of the monastery back to the 8th century. At that time Celtic monks had built a monastery on Mont St-Michel in Normandy, which is remarkably,

but not coincidentally, similar to its Cornish counterpart.

At low tide you can cross the bay on foot. At high tide there is a boat service. If you climb to the top of the 70-m-high (230-ft) outcrop, you'll get a fabulous view over Penwith Peninsula.

From Penzance, there is a 35-km (22-mile) road that leads round the peninsula to Land's End and on to St Ives.

13 Land's End The westernmost point of England is covered with an open moor and heath, and is absolutely riddled with archaeological treasures. Headstones from the ice age and

5

6

Bronze Age, Celtic crosses and entire villages that date back to times before the birth of Christ all bear witness to thousands of years of settlement in the area. The continual breaking of the waves from the Atlantic over the mighty rocks led the Romans to christen the place Belerion – Home of the Storms.

14 Scilly Isles About 40 km (25 miles) off the coast to the south-west lie the 140 Scilly Isles, which are reachable by ferry from Penzance. The 2,000 inhabitants, who live mostly from tourism and flower exports, are spread over only seven inhabited islands. With their rough granite rocks, white sandy beaches and turquoise bays, the Scilly Isles are best discovered on foot or by bicycle. A collection of the exotic palms and plants that traditionally flourish in this mild climate can be seen in the Abbey Garden at Tresco.

Back on the mainland, the often steep coastal road then follows the Atlantic coast around to St Ives. Ornithologists come here to find rare visitors like thrushes, New World warblers and vireos that have come over from America accidental on the omnipresent Westerlies. Some of the best observation points are the lighthouses.

15 St Ives Grey granite houses populate this former fishing village, which also happens to have one of Cornwall's most beautiful beaches. Numerous artists and sculptors have been coming here since the last century, fascinated by the light and landscape. The Tate Gallery has even opened

a 'branch' high above Porthmoor Beach where works by artists from St Ives are on display including paintings by Patrick Heron and Ben Nicholson, who lived here with his artist wife Barbara Hepworth. The village of Gwithian just up the road is also worth a stop.

The tiny fishing village of Port Isaac is near by, just off the A30. It has been spared a lot of the mass tourism that has become rampant in these parts, which makes it a refreshing alternative. The extremely steep streets probably put off a lot of visitors, so the best bet is to park the car above the village, and walk to Kellan Head on the coast.

16 Tintagel The legendary ruins on Tintagel Head are said to be the birthplace of King Arthur. Beyond the village of Tintagel a path leads over the cliffs to a green outcrop on the Atlantic that is crowned with crumbling ruin walls and can be reached via the steep staircase. As digs have proven, a Celtic monastery from the 5th century once stood here with a library, chapel, guest house, refectory and even a bath house.

The castle, however, whose ruins are also still visible, only dates back to the 13th century, a fact that would cast a doubt over the speculation of it being the birthplace of the legendary king of England.

And yet he who stands in the fog on the cliffs looking down on waves crashing by the dark entrance to Merlin's Cave can easily feel himself transported back to the times of King Arthur. The Norman church graveyard

has a number of half-buried tombstones telling tales of dead seamen and grieving widows.

The A39 leads further north from Tintagel along the coast, passing between Blackmoor Gate and Dunster across Exmoor National Park. In order to fully appreciate the coast and the moorland here, you should walk a section of the Somerset and Devon Coastal Path, from Bossington for example.

17 Glastonbury and Wells At Bridgwater, the coastal road A39 finally turns inland and leads to Glastonbury, a mythical place that attracts countless esoteric types. There are many reasons for the concentration of mystical and supernatural activity here: the remains of King Arthur are thought to be buried under the ruins of Glastonbury Abbey, and Glastonbury is often thought to be the legendary Avalon – a paradise to which Arthur was carried after his death.

Historical facts date the foundation of the first monastery back to the 7th century while the construction of England's largest abbey came around the year 1000 and the dissolution of the monastery in 1539.

The small city of Wells, on the other hand, is known for its glorious cathedral, the first Gothic building in all of England. The main section was completed in 1240, but the western tower and chapel came much later. The western facade was at one time covered with 400 figures, testimony to the skill of the medieval masons here – one picture book carved into the stone relates biblical and world history. Adjacent

to the cathedral is the Bishop's Palace, which is still used by the Bishop of Bath and Wells.

Bath, your next stop, is the cultural centre of the county of Somerset and is around 30 km (19 miles) north of Wells on the A367.

18 Bath The Romans knew this hot-springs town as Aquae Sulis. They built magnificent swimming pools, Turkish baths and saunas, and turned the town into a meeting place for the Roman elite. Oddly, the unique baths were only discovered in the 18th century.

Bath's rebirth as a health resort began in earnest in the 19th century when the city's grandiose Georgian architecture, concerts and balls enticed London's upper class to enjoy the recuperative benefits of its historic facilities. Visitors could also admire the dignified limestone buildings such as Queen Square, Royal Crescent and Pulteney Bridge.

1 Kellan Head on the striking north-west coast of Cornwall.

2 Street in the picturesque town of St Ives.

3 The West of England begins in the Wiltshire countryside.

4 A great boulder near Lower Slaughter in the Cotswolds.

5 The harbour of Port Issac on the west coast of Cornwall.

6 Land's End – in Cornish, Penn an Wlas – the steep, Atlantic-battered cliffs on the westernmost point of Great Britain.

The Romans in England

It's true, the Romans even ruled England, as Britannia, from around 55 BC to AD 410. After Julius Caesar's failed attempt, Emperor Claudius was the first to conquer the island all the way up to what is now Scotland, then called Caledonia, or 'Wooded Land'. Emperor Hadrian had built a wall there in around 122 BC to keep the fearsome Picts (Scottish predecessors) out of the Roman territories in Eng-

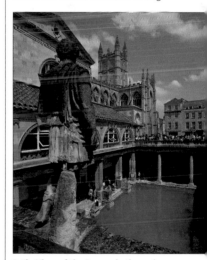

Bath: View of the Roman baths and the abbey.

land. The Romans remained on the island for a good 400 years.

The Romans selected Londinium as their capital and founded numerous other cities, with common suffixes like 'caster' or 'chester' being a throwback to the Roman word for fort. Some of their roads are still in use as well, for example the Fosse Way through the Cotswolds. When the Pict resistance grew too strong, the Romans retreated. Their ruins are now monuments.

Today, you can taste the healing waters and take in the atmosphere in the Pump Room.

A short detour of about 12 km (7.5 miles) via Chippenham leads you to the archaeological site at Avebury in Wiltshire. Avebury is home to the remains of England's largest and most impressive stone circle, made up of over 100 stones erected around 3,500 years ago. Nearby, the 40-m-high (130-ft) Silbury Hill looks like a pyramid, but it was not used as a burial site.

19 The Cotswolds The A429 takes you through the deep, wooded valleys and gentle hills of the Cotswolds, an area that has been populated since prehistoric times. After the Romans, the Cotswolds bloomed through the Middle Ages thanks to wool production. The region then sank into a long period of dormancy before being reawakened by tourism.

The typical Cotswolds architectural style and fairy-tale charm can be best seen in places such as Bouton-on-the-Water where golden stone buildings stand side-by-side with little bridges crossing streams in quaint and colourful meadows.

The town of Stow-on-the-Wold with its stone market hall sits atop a hill and was once a thriving sheep market. On the other side of the hill are the tiny villages of Upper Slaughter and Lower Slaughter, whose miniature appearance have made them into much-loved postcard images.

20 Stratford-upon-Avon The birthplace of William Shake-speare (1564) is the northernmost point of your route. In 1594, the famous playwright left for London, where he was able to establish his legendary reputation as actor and writer in one of the leading theatre companies of the time. In 1610 he returned to his home town of Stratford, where he died in 1616. Despite thousands of tourists walking in the footsteps of the poet every year, Stratford has been able to retain some of its Shakespearian atmosphere.

Visitors can tour the house where the playwright was born, learn about his life and work in the Shakespeare Centre, or watch one of his plays performed by the Royal Shakespeare Company in the Swan Theatre. A boat trip on the Avon rounds off the visit.

The A44 towards Oxford passes the impressive Blenheim Palace at Moreton-in-Marsh.

21 Blenheim Palace This impressive palace near Oxford was finished in 1722 and is Britain's largest private home. It was originally a gift from Queen

Wells This town was originally founded by the Romans. Its cathedral was begun in AD 700, and the Bishop's Palace is over 800 years old.

Bath 2,000 years ago the Romans established a bath complex that was later rediscovered in 1870. In the 18th century, Bath became a fashionable health resort.

Stonehenge This world-famous prehistoric site was erected between 3100 and 1500 BC by a late Stone-Age people and given some detailed inscriptions in the Bronze Age. Some of the artistically sculpted stones originate from mountains in 'nearby' Wales.

Blenheim Palace This controversial baroque palace completed in 1722 was a gift from Queen Anne to the Duke of Marlborough for winning the Battle of Blenheim (1704). Another famous personage was born here in 1874 – Winston Churchill, a descendant of the Duke.

Scilly Isles Fabulous bays and an exceptionally mild climate make the Scilly Isles a popular holiday destination. Roughly 45 km (28 miles) south-west of Land's End, only seven of the 140 islands are inhabited.

The Cotswolds Typical of this wooded, hilly area are the constructions of Cotswold stone used in bridges, cottages, churches, country houses and walls. Fine examples can be found in Bourton-on-the-Water, Upper Slaughter or Stow-on-the-Wold.

Land's End The stunning scenery from here, the westernmost point of England, has made it into a popular destination for visitors and artists alike.

St Ives Two museums in St Ives show works by a group of landscape-inspired artists who 'discovered' the fishing village at the end of the 1920s.

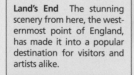

St Michael's Mount Its resemblance to Mont St-Michel in Normandy was the inspiration for this isle's name.

East Devon Coast The lovely coastline of Devon is seemingly endless, quite diverse and littered with holiday resorts.

Shaftesbury Ruins of a cloister and Gold Hill, the most picturesque street in England, make this a charming town.

Anne to John Churchill, the 1st Duke of Marlborough, after his defeat of Ludwig XIV in Blenheim, Bavaria (actually Blindheim near Höchstädt on the Danube). Blenheim Palace is recommended for a relaxing afternoon walk followed by tea. Many garden-lovers come here to visit the palace park, created by landscape gardener Capability Brown in typical English style.

22 Oxford The many spires of Oxford, especially Tom Tower of Christ Church and Magdalen Tower, are visible from the approach road. Oxford is known throughout the world as England's most prestigious university town. Its cathedral and the Picture Gallery, containing masterpieces from the Renaissance and baroque era, are worth a visit. Don't miss the Radcliffe Camera, Sheldonian Theatre and the Bodleian Library with its five million books. A coffee break with a book can be taken in the Blackwell Bookshop with a view over Radcliffe Camera.
The college tour is a classic, and leads around the buildings of

Merton College, Corpus Christi and New College, among others. Take a relaxing walk through the botanical gardens and its old greenhouses as well.

23 Windsor and Ascot Windsor Castle is in the Thames Valley west of London, and has been the primary residence of the English royal family since the Middle Ages. The fort, built in the 12th and 13th centuries, has been frequently remodelled over the years.
Many sections of Windsor Castle, one of the largest inhabited castles in the world, are open to

1 Stratford-upon-Avon: the tower of the legendary Holy Trinity Church, site of William Shakespeare's grave.

2 Winston Churchill was born in 1874 in Blenheim Palace (UNESCO World Heritage Site), a baroque masterpiece.

3 The countless spires and towers of colleges and churches give the skyline of Oxford a dignified and unmistakable appearance.

the public. A trip to St George's Chapel and the Albert Memorial Chapel to view the burial sites of the monarchs is recommended. The Round Tower offers a wonderful view of the castle and the Great Park.
Opposite Windsor Castle is Eton College, founded in 1440–41.

This exclusive private school favours a traditional English education with emphasis on the Classics and sport.
Windsor and Ascot, the famous racetrack, are separated only by a few kilometres. The Hippodrome, built in 1711 by Queen Anne, is among the most famous

tracks in the world. From 1825 until 1945, the four-day Royal Meeting race was the only event staged there. Today twenty-five races take place each year.
The last stop now is London, with its historical monuments, impressive museums and world-famous churches.

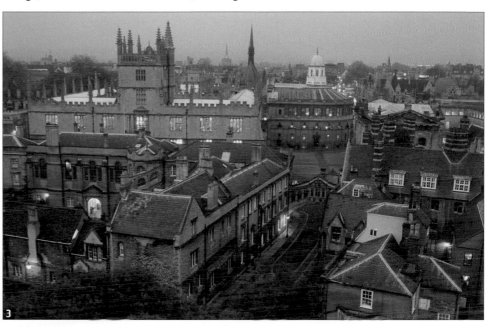

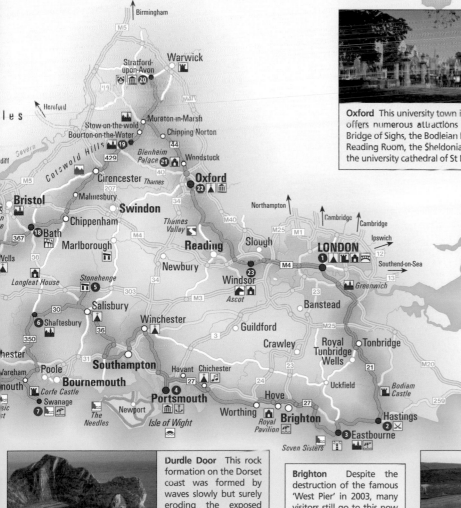

Oxford This university town is England's education mecca and offers numerous attractions – the Ashmolean Museum, the Bridge of Sighs, the Bodleian Library with the Radcliffe Camera Reading Room, the Sheldonian Theatre, thirty-six colleges and the university cathedral of St Mary the Virgin.

Windsor This castle in the Thames Valley was begun in 1070 and regularly extended over the centuries. It has been the principal residence of the royal family since the Middle Ages. Many parts of the castle are open.

London England's capital is at once old-fashioned and modern. A few of the must-sees in London are Westminster Abbey, the Houses of Parliament, Westminster Hall with Big Ben, Buckingham Palace, the Tower of London, St Paul's Cathedral and the British Museum.

Bodiam Castle This moated castle from the 14th century is like a picture from a fairy tale in the heart of south-east England. The castle, though quite large, was built under the guise of protecting the area from French attacks.

Durdle Door This rock formation on the Dorset coast was formed by waves slowly but surely eroding the exposed limestone.

Brighton Despite the destruction of the famous 'West Pier' in 2003, many visitors still go to this now hip seaside resort.

The Seven Sisters At 163 m (535 ft), Beachy Head is Britain's highest limestone cliff. It is to be found in Seven Sisters Country Park, named after the seven distinctive limestone monoliths.

Four city gates and fourteen towers surround the medieval fortress town of Dinkelsbühl.

Germany

A fairy-tale journey – the Romantic Road

From the vineyards of Mainfranken through the charming Tauber Valley, to the geologically unique meteor-crater landscape of Ries and along the Danube, into the foothills of the Alps and the limestone mountains of Bavaria, the Romantic Road leads past myriad cultural sites from different centuries while giving you a glimpse of Germany's diverse natural landscape.

For the millions of visitors who travel the Romantic Road each year, it is a route that makes the cliché of charming and sociable Germany a reality. The stress of modern living seems to have had no effect in towns like Rothenburg ob der Tauber, Dinkelsbühl or Nördlingen, where the Middle Ages are still very much a part of the atmosphere. Yet they are dynamic towns that have understood the value of preserving the relics of their great past and carefully rebuilding those that were destroyed in World War II.

Plenty of culture awaits the traveller along this route. Alongside the well-known highlights there are numerous architectural gems that are also worth viewing if time permits. Some examples of these are Weikersheim Castle, the small church in Detwang with its Riemenschneider altar, Schillingsfürst Castle, the old town and castle at Oettingen, Harburg high above the Wörnitz Valley, the convent in Mönchsdeggingen, the churches in Steingaden and Ilgen, the little church of St Koloman near Füssen and other

King Ludwig II by Ferdinand von Piloty.

treasures along the way that have – per-haps luckily – not yet been discovered by the tourist hordes.

And yet the natural highlights should not be forgotten either as you cruise the Romantic Road to places like Würzburg, Rothenburg, Dinkelsbühl, Nördlingen, Donauwörth, Augsburg, Landsberg, the Wieskirche or Füssen, whose unique beauty is underscored by their rustic set-tings in romantic valleys, enchanting forests or impressive mountains.

Two of the most visited buildings on the route have been classified as UNESCO World Heritage Sites: the Würzburger Residenz and the Wieskirche, important baroque and rococo works. A trip to Munich, the charming and cosmopolitan capital of Bavaria, or to the Werdenfels region with its famous sights such as Oberammergau, Linderhof Castle, Ettal

Donauwörth with its Gothic parish church and 15th-century Tanzhaus from the. The once 'free city' has an incredible medieval old town.

The St Koloman Pilgrimage Church stands in a field against the backdrop of the Schwangauer Mountains.

Monastery and the twin villages of Garmisch-Partenkirchen enhances this aspect of your German experience.

For those who have the time, a visit to one of the numerous festivals that take place along the Romantic Road is highly recommended. Some are based around regional history like the Meistertrunk in Rothenburg ob der Tauber, a re-enactment of a drinking contest from the 17th century, or the Kinderzeche in Dinkelsbühl, a children's festival originating in the 17th-century Thirty Years War.

Classical music lovers should try to obtain tickets for the Mozart Festival in Würzburg, the Jeunesses Musicales concerts in Weikersheim, the Mozart Summer in Augsburg or the Richard Strauss Days in Garmisch. The Cloister Theatre performances in Feuchtwangen are staged before a magnificent backdrop.

In addition to all this, there are festivals where anybody can participate, like the Free Town Festival in Rothenburg ob der Tauber or the Peace Festival in Augsburg. All these events take place in summer. Then of course there is the world-famous Oktoberfest in Munich, unmatched on the entire planet in its degree of debauchery and its sheer size. In winter the Christmas markets set up stalls that invite you to stroll, shop and drink a mulled wine with gingerbread cookies and other delicacies.

To sum it up, the Romantic Road has myriad attractions throughout the entire year, and takes you through the prettiest regions of Bavaria and Baden-Württemburg. Like no other road in Germany, it connects regional history with broad cultural landscapes, and brings the country's rich past to life.

The majestic throne room in Neuschwanstein Castle.

Johann Balthasar Neumann and Giambattista Tiepolo

Johann Balthasar Neumann was born in 1687 in Eger. Following an apprenticeship as a cannon fouder, he went to Würzburg in 1711 to work in this trade. But his passion lay in architecture and he took every possible opportunity to learn more, supported by Prince-Bishop Johann Philipp Franz of Schönborn.

In 1720 he began his greatest work as royal architect of the Würzburger Residenz. Other important works by Neumann include the Würzburg Chapel, the pilgrimage churches in Vierzehnheiligen and Gößweinstein, Weißenstein Castle in Pommersfelden, Augustusburg Castle in Brühl and the Bruchsal Castle. When the master builder died in 1753 in Würzburg he was buried with military honours.

Top: Staircase in the Würzburger Residenz.
Bottom: Self-portrait of Tiepolo in the ceiling fresco over the staircase.

Most of the works of the Venice-born painter and etcher Giambattista Tiepolo can be found in Italy and in the royal castle in Madrid. Yet his principal works were the ceiling frescoes in the staircase and emperor's rooms of the Würzburger Residenz.
Tiepolo died in 1770 in Madrid. In the ceiling fresco of the staircase in Würzburg the painter immortalized himself and Neumann. Neumann is sitting upon a cannon.

The Romantic Road – The fascinating route between Würzburg and Füssen is lined with picturesque towns, forts, castles and priceless works of art. The road starts in the Main River Valley on its way through the charming Tauber Valley into the Wörnitz Valley and then crosses the Danube to follow the Lech towards the impressive Alps.

① Würzburg The Romantic Road begins with a sensation: the majestic Würzburger Residenz (1720), a baroque masterpiece. Despite the devastating bombings of 16 March 1945, which left even the most optimistic people with little to be optimistic about, this city on the Main offers many sights: the late-Gothic chapel of Mary and the rococo Haus zum Falken blend nicely on the market square.
The cathedral, which was consecrated doors in 1188, has unfortunately lost some of its character due to war damage. Near the baroque Neumünster lies the tranquil Lusamgärtlein, where the minstrel Walther von der Vogelweide lies buried. And all of this is dominated by the mighty fortress (13–18th centuries) on the Marienberg with its Main-Franconia Museum containing many works by Tilman Riemenschneider.

② Tauberbischofsheim This town in the Tauber Valley is famous for its history in the sport of fencing. It is distinguished by the Kurmainzisch Castle, whose storm tower is a masterpiece from the turn of the 16th century. The Riemenschneider School altar in St Martin's Parish Church is also worth seeing.

③ Bad Mergentheim The Old Town in this health resort is dominated by the Castle of the German Knights (16th century). Don't miss the baroque castle church designed by B. Neumann and François Cuvilliés. A small detour to see 'The Madonna' by Matthias Grünewald in Stuppach Parish Church is worth it.

④ Weikersheim Continuing through the Tauber Valley, Weikersheim invites you to visit its Ren-aissance castle and baroque gardens, which are among Germany's prettiest. The small former royal capital is surrounded by numerous vineyards.

⑤ Creglingen The Tauber Valley houses many of the works of

Travel information

Route profile
Length: approx. 350 km (217 miles), excluding detours
Time required: 7–10 days
Start: Würzburg
End: Füssen
Route (main locations): Würzburg, Tauberbischofsheim, Bad Mergentheim, Rothenburg ob der Tauber, Dinkelsbühl, Nördlingen, Donauwörth, Augsburg, Landsberg, Schongau, Füssen

Traffic information: Drive on the right in Germany. There is a 420-km (261-mile) cycle path that runs parallel to the Romantic Road. More information about this route can be found on the

Internet at:
www.bayerninfo.de.

Information:
There is a lot of information available on the Romantic Road but no definitive site for the entire route. The following sites might help you get an idea of how to organize your trip.

General:
www.romantischestrasse.de
en.wikipedia.org/wiki/Romantic_Road

Town sites:
www.rothenburg.de
www.dinkelsbuehl.de
www2.augsburg.de
www.fuessen.de

Jakob Fugger, known in his day as simply 'the Rich', lived from 1459 to 1525. As financier and creditor to Habsburg emperors Maximilian I and Charles V, he almost had more power than the rulers themselves since they were dependent on him for capital. But as a man of faith Jakob Fugger also wanted to do something for his salvation, so with his brothers he founded the Fuggerei in 1516, the world's first social housing project.

People who found themselves in need through no fault of their own were provided with accommodation in one of the 67 buildings containing 147 apartments. The 'town within the

Top: The apartment blocks of the Fuggerei, the oldest low-income housing estate in the world.
Bottom: The Fuggerei Museum, showing an original sleeping area.

town' even had its own church and a well. Indeed, the flats in the Fuggerei are still available to Augsburgers in need. And the rent is still one Rhine Taler as it was when it was built – the equivalent of 0.88 euros.

House rules still oblige the daily recital of the Lord's Prayer, Hail Mary and 'believe in God for the founder'. The site is run by the Royal Fugger Foundation. It is impressive that people in the 21st century profit from Fugger's prosperity in the 16th century.

Riemenschneider here. In fact, the triple-nave St Jakob Basilka houses his Holy Blood Altar. Further along the route heading south you'll cross the Frankenhöhe, the European watershed between the Rhine and Danube.

7 Feuchtwangen This one-time collegiate church, part Romantic, part Gothic, is worth a visit any time of the year. The marketplace has an attractive mix of bourgeois town houses.

8 Dinkelsbühl The main attraction of this town in the idyllic Wörnitz Valley is the perfect medieval town centre with its town walls. Other highlights include the Deutsches Haus, a fabulous half-timbered house, and the St Georg Parish Church (second half of the 15th century). The town is more than 1,000-years-old.

9 Nördlingen Ideally you would approach fabulous Nördlingen from above in order to fully appreciate the nearly perfectly circular city centre. Its original town walls have been masterfully preserved and its five town gates are still in use today.

St Georg is one of the largest late-Gothic German hall churches, its icon being 'Daniel', the 90-m (295-ft) bell tower. On a clear day from the tower you can make out the rim of the Ries crater, especially towards the south-west, the south and the east.

10 Donauworth This 'free town' developed from a fishing village on the Wörnitz island of 'Ried' at the confluence of the Wörnitz and the Danube. Most of its attractions are located along the main road, the Reichsstrasse: the Fuggerhaus from 1536, the late-Gothic Maria Himmelfahrt Parish Church, the Tanzhaus from around 1400, the town hall and the baroque Deutschordenshaus. The baroque church of the old Benedictine monastery Heiligkreuz is also worth visiting.

11 Augsburg 'Augusta Vindelicorum' was the original name given to Augsburg by its Roman founders. By the 16th century the 'free town' was one of the most important cultural

1 View of the Würzburger Residenz from Residenzplatz with the Franconia Fountain (1894).

2 The town hall in Augsburg with its remarkably symmetrical facade and 78-m (256-ft) Perlach Tower.

3 View from 'Daniel' over the Nördlingen market square.

---

the wood sculptor Tilman Riemenschneider. The altar in the Creglingen Herrgottskirche is among the most beautiful. The Old Town here is a lovely mix of half-timbered houses and medieval fortresses.

6 Rothenburg ob der Tauber This small town is synonymous

around the world with German medieval Romanticism. A walk along the well-preserved town walls offers an overview of the place and great views across the Tauber Valley. The market square is dominated by the town hall, which has Gothic and Renaissance wings. You can also view more works of Tilman

Beer gardens

The Munich beer gardens were born from the need to store the beer in a cool place. To do this the brewers built large cellars, usually right next to their breweries. In order to protect them from the heat, they planted the area with chestnut trees. And because a rest in the shade of the

Beer garden at the Chinese Tower in the Englischer Garten.

trees became popular, they set up tables and benches.

King Ludwig I allowed them to serve beer there but the breweries were forbidden to sell food. And so it came about that the citizens brought their own snacks with them – often meatloaf, cheese, radishes and pretzels. This custom has survived to this day, although now many beer gardens serve snacks or even full meals alongside their beer.

So, Cheers!

Detour

Munich

There are many ways to discover Munich – by bike through the differrent neighbourhoods, a museum tour or shopping in Old Town. Or you can do it by theme.

The Munich of artists

Important paintings and sculptures are on display in the large and impressive Munich museums: the Alte and Neue Pinakothek, Pinakothek der Moderne and Haus der Kunst. The Lenbachhaus and the Villa Stuck show how successful artists lived in Munich at the end of the 19th century. The Lenbachhaus was designed by the architect Gabriel von Seidl in 1887 for the painter Franz von Lenbach and is a fantastic little museum with a wonderful variety of art and photography.

Today it is home to a municipal gallery and contains major works by the Blaue Reiter group. The Villa Stuck was designed by the aristocratic painter Franz von Stuck in 1897–98 and hosts a variety of exhibits. A wander into the heart of Schwabing is also part of any trip on the trail of artists – at the beginning of the 20th century, 'bohemian Munich' used to gather near Nikolaiplatz. Schwabing has been able to preserve some of its old flair.

Green Munich

For those who have had enough of the city it is also easy to find a bit of nature in this wonderful city. The first and foremost of the green oases is of course the Englischer Garten. At 4 sq km (1.5 sq mi) it is the world's largest city park – even larger than Central Park in New York. Beyond the vast lawns and brooks that flow through this wonderful park there are a few architectural highlights as well: the Chinese Tower, the Monopteros and the Japanese teahouse. The best way to explore the Englischer Garten – and Munich in general – is by bike. Take a break along the way at one of the beer gardens.

The Isar River runs straight through Munich and on a summer day can be a nice way to cool down. To get there just walk to the Deutsches Museum. There are stony riverbanks to stroll and dip your feet in the water, and even a few places to jump right in!

In the centre of town, just a few steps from Karlsplatz (also known as Stachus), is the old botanical gardens park. The of Nymphenburg porcelain statues spread around the park are beautiful. Take a tram to Nymphenburger Park, another oasis of relaxation where you'll find landscaped gardens and a baroque castle.

Munich theatre town

For theatre lovers, Munich offers interesting shows and fantastic theatre architecture. The majestic Cuvilliés Theatre is part of the former royal Residenz. François Cuvilliés designed the fabulously ornate rococo structure. A second building that attracts theatre lovers and architecture enthusiasts is the Kammerspiele in the Maximilianstrasse. Architects Richard Riemerschmid and Max Littmann allowed their art-nouveau

fantasies free rein here in 1900–01. A lengthy restoration was finished recently.

Another building with a bit of history is the Prinzregenten Theatre, which was badly damaged during World War II and not reopened until the renovation was completed in 1996. It was built in 1901 to celebrate the works of Richard Wagner. You can see international operas in the Prinzregenten Theatre and in the classical National Theatre. Munich also has a lively free theatre scene, some of which moves around regularly.

1 Munich by night: View over the Frauenkirche with its imposing spires and the neo-Gothic town hall tower. To the far right is the Olympia Tower.

2 The Siegestor gate in Schwabing separates the two great avenues of Leopoldstrasse and Ludwigstrasse.

3 The Cuvilliés Theatre is the city's oldest surviving opera house. Only the interior remains of the original building.

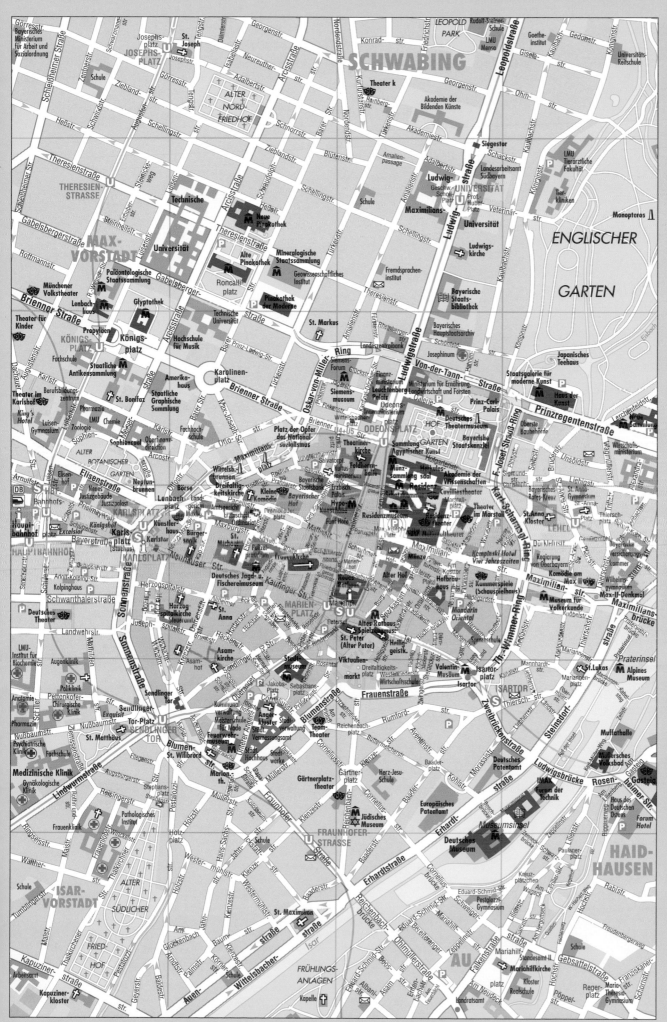

Munich

Munich exudes the magic of an old city that still manages to remain youthful, multicultural and very much itself.

Munich was originally founded by Guelph Heinrich the Lion, but the royal Wittelsbacher family controlled the city until 1918 and played a much greater role in its history. They are to be thanked for most of the city's monuments and works of art and the prettiest stretches of road. Ludwig I was particularly energetic, claiming that he wanted to build 'Athens on the Isar'. The Old Town lies between the Isartor, Sendlinger Tor, Karlstor and the Feldherrnhalle. Schwabing, the university and museum district, gives Munich its reputation for being a fun-loving and cultured city of the arts.

Attractions in the historic city centre include Marienplatz with the new town hall from the 19th century, the old town hall from the 15th century and the baroque Mariensäule; the late-Gothic Frauenkirche with its two iconic spires; Asamkirche, a rococo masterpiece; the Residenz with the treasure chamber, Residenz theatre (rococo) and court garden, which was expanded during the Renaissance; the National Theatre; the baroque Theatinerkirche; the Renaissance church of St Michael's; the

Top: National Museum, on Max-Joseph-Platz.
Bottom: Nymphenburg Castle.

Hofbräuhaus and Viktualienmarkt and the bronze Bavaria on the Theresienwiese.

There is also the Nymphenburg Castle and Park and the Olympic Park from 1972. Don't miss the museums: Deutsches Museum, the Alte Pinakothek, the Neue Pinakothek, the Pinakothek der Moderne, Lenbachhaus, Glyptothek, Bayerisches Nationalmuseum; Stadtmuseum in the old Zeughaus and the Villa Stuck.

King Ludwig II

In 1864 Ludwig II ascended to the Bavarian throne. He soon withdrew into a dream world, where fantasies of Louis XIV's palace took over and Richard Wagner's operas influenced the architecture of the Linderhof, Neuschwanstein and Herrenchiemsee

King Ludwig II's *Night time Sled Ride*, by Rudolf Wenig.

castles. Wagner would not have been able to create the Bayreuther Festival had it not been for financial support from Ludwig. Yet the king's passions tore great holes in the state's finances and so he was certified insane in 1886. A few days later he drowned in mysterious circumstances in Lake Starnberg and thus became a popular myth.

and financial metropolises north of the Alps. The town hall was built between 1615 and 1620 and was designed by Elias Holl, as was the Zeughaus of 1607. Stained-glass windows depicting the five prophets in St Maria Cathedral are among the oldest in the world. The streets are lined with many patrician houses like the Schaezler and Gignoux palaces. A few towers and gates (such asthe Red Gate) are left over from the old town defences.

From Augsburg it is a quick half-hour drive to Munich (see pp. 56–57). From there you can take the Lindau motorway straight to Landsberg.

⑫ Klosterlechfeld This monastery was built on the site of an historic battlefield from the year 955. Elias Holl was the architect of this pilgrimage church, which was erected in 1603. It was based on the Pantheon in Rome.

⑬ Landsberg am Lech The first wall surrounding the Old Town between the Lech River and the Lech bluff was built in the 13th century. It included the Schmalzturm at the top end of the triangular main plaza, which

is dominated by the town hall. The stucco facade of the town hall was designed by Dominikus Zimmermann in 1719.

The Bayer Gate, built in 1425, is part of the third wall and is one of the most beautiful of its kind in southern Germany. The four churches in Landsberg am Lech are especially noteworthy: the Gothic, late-baroque Maria Himmelfahrt; the Johanniskirche by Dominikus Zimmermann; the Ursuline Convent Church by J.B. Gunetzrhainer (begun in 1740) and the Heiligkreuz Monastery church. Portions of the 15th-century

Landsberg town wall are also quite well-preserved.

⑭ Altenstadt St Michael's is one of Upper Bavaria's most significant Romantic churches. It was built in the early part of the 13th century and is surrounded by a mighty protective wall. It houses frescoes from the 14th and 15th centuries as well as the 'Grosser Gott von Altenstadt', a Romanesque crucifix from around 1200. Because of its enormous size, it is one of the most important works of art of its type, radiating an expressive calm in the church.

⑮ Schongau The drive to Schongau follows the Lech River through Claudia Augusta. The Gothic Ballenhaus of 1515 bears witness to its previous importance as a trading town.

The town walls with their battlements are still conserved in part, as are five towers and the Frauen Gate to the west (14th century). The Maria Himmelfahrt Parish Church, which was remodelled by Dominikus Zimmermann in 1748, has frescoes by Matthäus Günter and is well worth a visit.

If time permits, you can continue from here into the Werdenfels

area to enjoy some wonderful mountain scenery (see Detour, p. 60).

16 Rottenbuch The old Augustine canonical church in Rottenbuch was remodelled

charming baroque church after another. Add the natural environment of the area and you've got a delightfully attractive combination for walks such as the one leading through the Ammerschlucht to Wieskirche.

17 Wieskirche One of this route's best highlights is the Wieskirche, built by Dominikus Zimmermann in 1745. Against the backdrop of the Trauchberge Mountains, the ceiling frescoes and a large part of the stucco here were done by Johann Baptist Zimmermann.
The white and gold interior appears light and cheerful, as if music had been turned to stone. The Wieskirche near Steingaden is visited by hundreds of thousands of tourists every year. It is considered to be a complete work of art.

18 Hohenschwangau and Neuschwanstein These two royal castles are picturesquely set in a striking mountain scene. Crown Prince Maximilian gave Castle Hohenschwangau (12th century) a neo-Gothic facelift in 1833 – Ludwig II, the man behind nearby Castle Neuschwanstein, had spent part

between 1737 and 1742 and now shines with baroque cheerfulness. Stucco artist Joseph Schmuzer and painter Matthäus Günter were responsible for the wonderful interior. In this area it isn't hard to stumble over one

of his youth here in Hohenschwangau. Neuschwanstein is the idealized image of a medieval castle with towers, battlements and majestic rooms.

19 Füssen The Romantic Road comes to an end in this small town on the Lech River. Don't miss the St Mang Monastery or the baroque St Magnus Parish Church. The medieval edifice here was also given a generous baroque remodel. The trompe l'oeil on the facade of the Hohen Schloss castle courtyard is particularly noteworthy. The facade of the Heilig-Geist-Spital Church (1748–49) is sumptuously painted. To finish off the trip, how about a wild nature experience: take a gander at the nearby Lechfall.

1 Neuschwanstein Castle with the Allgäuer Alps as a backdrop.

2 The pilgrimage church of the Gegeißelter Heiland auf der Wies lies in the Pfaffenwinkel and is a UNESCO World Heritage Site.

3 The two-storey choir in the Wieskirche with the painting of Christ in the centre.

Dominikus Zimmermann

Born in 1685 in Wessobrun, this trained carpenter actually reached his masterful heights as a builder and stucco artist. He became rich and famous thanks to his trade and even became mayor of Landsberg am Lech

View from the ornate pulpit above the choir stalls in the Wieskirche.

from 1749 to 1754. In 1756 he moved into the house he had built next to his masterpiece, the Wieskirche near Steingaden, and lived there until his death in 1766. His other works include the Steinhausen Pilgrimage Church and the Frauenkirche in Günzburg.

The Oberammergau Passion Play

In 1633 a plague epidemic occurred during the Thirty Years War that inspired the people of Oberammergau to inaugurate this 'play of suffering, death and the resurrection of our Lord Jesus Christ', which they would perform every ten years.

The play was enacted for the first time in 1634 at the cemetery where the victims of the plague had been buried. This location was then used until 1820. In 1830 it was moved to its current venue where, in the year 2000, the play was performed for the 40th time.

Over 2,000 people from Oberammergau – all amateurs – took part in the most recent Passion Play, as actors, musicians, singers or stagehands. The story lasts around six hours and the text has been modified numerous times over the years. It is a regular source of dispute.

The people of Oberammergau are not always in agreement when it comes to the Passion Play. For example, the decision as to whether or not to allow married or older women to participate had

Top: Backdrop of the Passion Play in 2000.
Bottom: Crucifixion scene in Oberammergau.

to be decided by the Upper Regional Court. The result was that they are allowed to participate.

The current open-air stage was originally built in 1930 but was fully renovated between 1997 and 1999. As the theatre was brought up to date with technology, the town can now host other events, such as operas, in the years between the Passion Plays.

Detour

Werdenfelser Land

A small detour from the Romantic Road takes you into the Werdenfelser Land, a magnificent mountain landscape with numerous romantic towns and villages. To take this detour, do not continue on to Füssen from the Wieskirche. Instead turn east towards Unterammergau and Oberammergau.

Oberammergau

The prettiest house in this picture-book village is the so-called Pilatushaus, which is richly decorated with paintings by Franz Seraph Zwink. The outside wall on the garden side of the house depicts the Judgement of Jesus by Pilate, hence the name of the house. Today Pilatushaus is home to a gallery and 'live-work studio' where you can watch local wood-carvers ply their trade. Oberammergau has been renowned for its wood-carving tradition since the Middle Ages and there are around 120 of them here. When the Passion Play is not scheduled you can take a tour of the theatre.

Linderhof

After a short drive through the romantic Graswang Valley you reach Linderhof Castle, the only castle built by Ludwig II that was actually finished during his lifetime. The baroque construction is surrounded by large grounds containing other odd and interesting buildings, for example the Venus grotto, which was built to resemble the Hörselberg grotto in Wagner's *Tannhäuser*. Other sites include a Moorish Kiosk, a Prussian pavilion from the 1867 World Exhibition, which Ludwig II had majestically redecorated to his tastes, and the Hundinghütte, a perfect Germanic log cabin based on Wagner's Valkyrie.

Ettal Monastery

Standing in front of the majestic church of Ettal Monastery, you have the feeling of having stumbled across a little piece of Italy in the middle of the Bavarian Werdenfelser Land. The painting of Christ, the centrepiece of

the church, was donated in 1330 by Emperor Ludwig of Bavaria. There was initially a Gothic abbey here that was remodelled in 1710 in a majestic baroque style. The building, erected by the Italian Enrico Zucalli, was decorated with stucco by artists J.B. Zimmermann and J.G. Ueblherr, and a magnificent ceiling painting by J.J. Zeiller and M. Knoller. The layout, a twelve-sided central construction is unique in Germany and was actually necessary for the facade. The Benedictine monks had not only God in mind when they built their monastery, but also the awe it would inspire in its visitors.

Garmisch-Partenkirchen

In 1935 the two villages of Garmisch and Partenkirchen were joined into a market town. Many houses here are decorated with frescoes. Haus zum Husaren is a particularly well-known example. In Garmisch the old Gothic parish church of St Martin, with its

well-preserved frescoes, and the new baroque parish church of St Martin are worth visiting. In Partenkirchen the pilgrimage church St Anton, built on the Wank, the local mountain, dates back to the middle of the 18th century. Music lovers should head for the Richard Strauss Institute and the Strauss Villa, where the composer spent a large part of his life.

You shouldn't miss taking the gondola up to the Zugspitze (2,962 m/9,718 ft), Germany's highest mountain.

1 The golden cross marks the eastern peak of the Zugspitze, which offers a great panoramic view.

2 The north facade of Linderhof Castle reflected in the lake.

3 The town of Garmisch-Partenkirchen, one of the most renowned health resorts at the base of the Wetterstein Mountains.

Bad Mergentheim The Old Town here is dominated by the Castle of the German Knights (16th century). Its church was designed by B. Neumann and F. Cuvilliés.

Weikersheim This precious royal town in the Tauber River Valley has a Renaissance castle and a baroque garden, one of Germany's prettiest.

Dinkelsbühl More than 1,000 years of history bless this town in the Wörnitz Valley, perhaps the best example of medieval architecture. Surrounded by formidable walls, its main attractions are the Deutsches Haus and St Georg Cathedral.

Augsburg The Renaissance town hall and Perlach Tower are highlights in this 2,000-year-old city.

Wieskirche This pilgrimage church is considered in its entirety to be one of the major works of Bavarian rococo art.

Linderhof Castle The only one of Ludwig II's three castles to be finished during his lifetime is surrounded by a park with unusual buildings, some of which are derived from Wagner's operatic fantasy world.

Füssen/Neuschwanstein The old city between the Ammergau and Allgäu Alps awaits you with two royal castles: Hohenschwangau (12th century, transformed to neo-Gothic in 1837) and the world-famous fairy-tale castle of Disney fame, Neuschwanstein (1869–86).

Würzburg Despite the bombings of 1945, this wine city on the Main offers a number of attractions. The most important of these are St Kilian Cathedral (opened in 1188), the old Main bridge and Fort Marienberg (13th–18th centuries).

Feuchtwangen This former 'free town' with rows of pretty houses has a collegiate church that is part Romantic and part Gothic. There is also a handful of museum collections worth seeing.

Nördlingen St Georg is one of Germany's largest late-Gothic hall churches. From the bell tower 'Daniel' you can get a good view of this almost perfectly circular town.

Würzburger Residenz The majestic construction, started in 1720, was supposed to replace Fort Marienberg. Its scale is amazing, both inside and out.

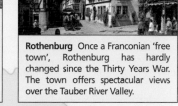

Rothenburg Once a Franconian 'free town', Rothenburg has hardly changed since the Thirty Years War. The town offers spectacular views over the Tauber River Valley.

Nymphenburg This baroque castle in Munich is a majestic site indeed. The expansive grounds make for a lovely walk or picnic. The state porcelain factory is next door.

München A detour into the Bavarian capital should be part of any trip along the Romantic Road. With the Old Town and the Schwabing district, the Viktualienmarkt, the Englischer Garten, the impressive Olympic Park as well as churches from almost 850 years ago and world-famous museums, this 'international village' has much more to offer than just the 'Oktoberfest'.

Route 5

In the heart of Europe

The Route of the Emperors: Berlin – Prague – Vienna – Budapest

Schönbrunn Palace in Vienna – a former Habsburg summer palace with

On this journey along the ancient European transport and trade arteries of the Elbe, Vltava and Danube rivers, Europe presents itself in all its historical and cultural diversity. On the various riverbanks, cities like Dresden, Prague, Vienna and Budapest show off their abundant monuments of art, and everywhere along the route are palaces, castles and urban gems surrounded by unique natural scenery.

No emperor could ever have imagined that at the beginning of the 21st century you would be able to travel all the way from the Spree River (Berlin) to the Danube without any complicated border checks, particularly after the centuries of mini-states in the region and the tragic rift of the 20th century. What happened to the days when autocratic despots jealously erected border checkpoints and threw up 'iron curtains' to protect their territories? When the Viennese knew nothing of Budweis or Bratislava, and to the people of West Berlin, Dresden might as well have been further away than the Dominican Republic? Gone indeed are those days. These days, the road is free to explore what is so close and yet still quite unfamiliar, and there really is a lot to discover.

Berlin, Germany's old and new capital, is its very own unique tourist cosmos. It would take weeks to see even a fraction of its museum treasures, its continuously

The landmark of Vienna: St Stephen's Cathedral.

changing skyline with so much contemporary architecture, an art and restaurant scene that is just as dynamic as that of any other cosmopolitan city, and its large green parks. On this route, however, Berlin is but the starting point of a fascinating journey across Europe.

In Brandenburg and Saxony, both core regions of German intellectual history, one highlight seems to follow the next. Potsdam, the royal residence of the Prussian kings, provides a magnificent overture to the Lutheran town of Wittenberg, to Weimar, the focal point of German classicism, and to the porcelain metropolis of Meissen, your next stops.

Dresden is simply irresistible as a tourist destination. The capital of Saxony, which rose like the proverbial phoenix from the ashes (and from the floodwaters in 2002), enchants with its baroque and rococo

extensive gardens.

Charlottenburg Palace in Berlin, the summer residence of Sophie Charlotte, wife of Frederick I.

Hradčany Castle above the Charles Bridge, Prague's most famous bridge, on the Vltava River.

buildings and its art galleries. Music lovers flock to highlights like the Semper Opera, the Staatskapelle orchestra and the famous Kreuzchor choir.

Attempting to describe in words the exquisite beauty of Prague is often an exercise in futility. The views across the Vltava River towards Hradčany Castle are some of the most unforgettable city sights anywhere on earth. And just like one of Mozart's melodies, the magic hovering above the picturesque alleyways in the Small Quarter and around the Old Town Square will leave no soul untouched.

From the splendidly restored spa towns of Karlovy Vary and Mariánské Láznů, to Litoměřice, Hrad Karlštejn, České Budějovice and Český Krumlov – the number of five-star attractions in Bohemia is just incredible.

There are just as many amazing sights on the journey through Upper and Lower Austria – Freistadt, Linz, Enns, Grein and Krems, not to mention the Melk and Klosterneuburg monasteries.

Away from urban attractions, nature will also spoil you along the route – the heathlands of lower Fläming and Lower Lausitz, the sandstone mountains on the River Elbe, the Vltava Valley, the Bohemian Forest, the Mühl Quarter, Wachau and the Viennese Forest. Between city tours and museums you can tank up on oxygen everywhere on this trip. On top of that, you can always sample the tasty delicacies that local cuisine has to offer.

An almost exotic piece of scenery awaits you at the end of your tour, east of Budapest across the River Tisza – the Hortobágy National Park, a real piece of the idyllic Hungarian Puszta.

East of Budapest's Matthias Church is the Halászbástya, the Fisherman's Bastion.

Wittenberg, the town of Luther and one of the focal points of German intellectual history, is located 30 km (18 miles) west of the impressive medieval town of Jüterbog. To get there, take the B187.

As a university town, the cradle of the Reformation and the 'workshop' of seminal humanists, Wittenberg was one of the intellectual centres not only of Germany in the 16th century, but of Central Europe. It was here that the influential scholar Martin Luther came in 1508 to hang his famous ninety-five Theses fulminating against the clerics on the Castle Church door, thereby kicking off the Reformation.

Memories of him and of the theologian Philipp Melanchthon are still very much alive. In the house where

Wartburg Castle near Eisenach.

Martin Luther lived from 1508 to 1546, there is a museum on the history of the Reformation. The house where Melanchthon lived, studied and died is also open to the public, and is also the only private home remaining from the 16th century. The town church of St Mary where Luther used to give his sermons is also worth seeing.

Despite it being off your route, a visit to Wartburg castle is highly recommended. About 250 km (160 miles) from Dresden you'll find Eisenach, where Luther went to school. Southwest of Eisenach, atop the Wart Mountain, in the middle of the Thuringian Forest, is the medieval Wartburg Castle, built in 1150. It was in this castle that Luther translated the New Testament from Greek into what was then the first-ever German version of the bible in 1521–22. The rest, as they say, is history.

From the Spree in Berlin to the Danube in Budapest – a journey through the European heartland of old empires is now possible without border checks, through five countries from the German capital to the Hungarian capital. It will give you a comprehensive overview of its cultural depth and scenic beauty.

❶ Berlin (see pp. 66–67).

❷ Potsdam Our first stop outside the city limits of Berlin is Potsdam, the state capital of Brandenburg. It is famous mainly for the beautiful baroque and neoclassical buildings and its magnificent parks dating from the era of the Prussian kings. The best-known attraction of this town, which is 1,000 years old and has been partially declared a UNESCO World Heritage Site, is Frederick III's pompously decorated summer palace. Its park covers 300 ha (740 acres) and was designed by Lenné. It is an architectural gem in itself, full of statues and monuments such as the neighbouring park of Charlottenhof.

In Potsdam's Old Town, the Old Market with the St Nicholas Church and the former town hall, the Marstall stables, the Dutch Quarter and the old Russian colony of Alexandrowka are all worth a visit. Another must-see is the New Garden with its Marble Palace and Cecilienhof Castle.

From Potsdam, drive to the old town of Beelitz, and from there east to the B101 south towards Luckenwalde.

❸ Luckenwalde At first glance, this medieval market town may seem dull and industrial, but its interesting historical centre has been well preserved. Its landmark is the steeple of St Johannskirche with its Gothic frescoes and important altar statues. A former hat factory, built at the beginning of the 1920s by Erich Mendelsohn, is also remarkable.

❹ Jüterbog This town, located 15 km (9 miles) further south at the edge of the lower Fläming heathlands, still has most of its original fortifications, including three beautiful gates. Sites here include the Liebfrauenkirche, the Nikolaikirche and the town hall, but the main attraction is really 5 km (3 miles) to the north: the ruins of the Cistercian monastery of Zinna, with important Gothic wall paintings.

Driving along the edge of the Lower Lausitz heathlands for

Travel information

Route profile
Length: approx. 1,100 km (700 miles), excluding detours
Time required: at least 2 weeks
Start: Berlin, Germany
End: Budapest, Hungary
Route (main locations): Berlin, Potsdam, Dresden, Prague, České Budějovice, Linz, Krems, Vienna, Bratislava, Komárno (Komárom), Budapest

Traffic information:
Drive on the right in all the countries on this trip. Speed limits are signposted. If not, 50 km/h (35 mph) in built-up areas, 90–100 km/h (55–60 mph) outside of towns. Autobahns in Germany have no speed limit

unless otherwise indicated. In the other countries, 130 km/h (80 mph) is usually the limit. Roads are typically good in all five countries.

When to go:
Central Europe is typically quite warm in summer, cold in winter, and inconsistent in spring and autumn. Always have a rain jacket, regardless of season.

General travel information:
Here are some sites that may help get you started with planning:
wikitravel.org/en/Berlin
www.saxonytourism.com
www.czech.cz
www.aboutaustria.org
www.oberoesterreich.at
www.hungary.com

Detour

Weimar

This Thuringian city with wonderful museums and monuments attracts visitors from far and wide. You reach Weimar from Dresden via the A4 Autobahn. In 1990 it was the European Capital of Culture and it certainly dressed itself for the occasion. Luther, Bach and Cranach all worked here; Goethe, Schiller, Wieland and Herder took German classicism to its peak; and Walter

Gropius started Bauhaus architecture here. Attractions are the Goethe House and Schiller House, the Bauhaus Museum, the Duchess Anna Amalia Library, the historic cemetery and the castle with its collection of art.

Top: Goethe and Schiller in front of the National Theatre in Weimar.
Middle: Weimar Castle, home to the state art collection.
Bottom: Lucas Cranach House on Weimar Market.

about 100 km (62 miles) on the B101, you will pass Elsterwerda and Großenhain before you reach the Elbe River and the porcelain centre of Meissen.

5 Meissen In the 12th century, this 'Cradle of Saxony', where the German emperors founded the first settlement on Slavic soil, was a royal residence of the House of Wettin. Until the devastations of World War II it was able to preserve its medieval imprint, with the Gothic cathedral and Albrecht Castle representing both religious and worldly power. These are still visible from the historic Old Town with its market square and half-timbered buildings.
Today the town is more famous for its 'white gold' than for its 1,000 years of history. Home of Europe's first hard porcelain, Meissen has produced this valuable product since Augustus the

Strong founded the factory in 1710. It continues to be exported all over the world.
Past Radebeul, the route along the B26 takes us to Dresden, the Saxon state capital 25 km (16 miles) away.

6 Dresden This former elector's residence, which has also been praised as the 'Florence of Germany' or the 'Baroque Pearl', is doubtless one of Europe's major cultural centres. In 1485 it became the seat of the Albertinian government, and during the 17th and 18th centuries, Augustus the Strong and his successors turned it into one of the most magnificent baroque residence cities in all of Germany.
The devastating bomb raids in February 1945 were unfortunately fatal for the city, destroying the Old Town almost beyond recognition. However, many of the famous buildings have either

already been restored or are still works in progress, chief among them being the Zwinger, housing the 'Old Masters' art gallery; the Semper Opera; the castle; the Frauenkirche; the Japanese Palace; the Albertinum, housing the 'New Masters' art gallery; the Green Vault; and the Brühl Terraces high above the riverbank. You should definitely visit the important attractions in the surrounding area, above all Pillnitz Castle, Moritzburg Castle and the so-called Elbe Castles.
If you are not intending to do the detour to Weimar and Wartburg Castle, you now follow the B172 upriver from Dresden. You'll pass Pirna, with its picturesque centre and the interesting Großsedlitz baroque gardens, and enter the spectacular Elbe Sandstone Mountains.

7 Elbe Sandstone Mountains In order to get the best possible

views of these bizarre sandstone rock formations, you would really have to do a boat trip on the meandering river. Barring that, you can get some magnificent views from the road. Most of the area is now included in the 'Saxon Switzerland' National Park, with its monumental plateaus. Königstein Castle and the bastion in the spa town of Rathen are quite popular. Bad Schandau is the starting point for hiking and climbing tours to

1 Dresden owes its nickname, the 'Florence of Germany', to its baroque cityscape, which includes the Semper Opera and the Frauenkirche Church.

2 View of Sanssouci Palace, Friedrich II's summer residence, considered a rival to Versailles.

3 Moritzburg Castle was used by the Elector Friedrich August II of Saxony as a hunting lodge.

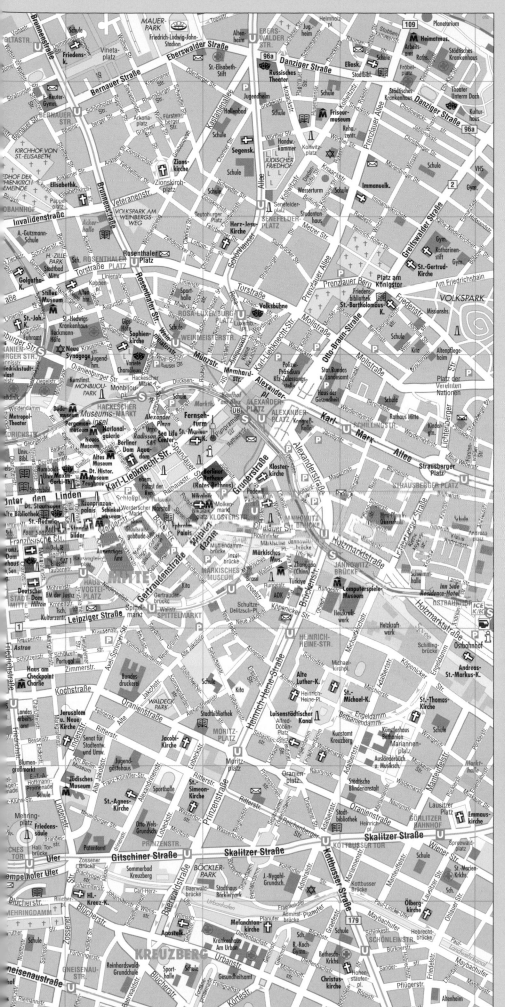

Berlin

Things have been changing incredibly rapidly in Berlin since the Berlin Wall came down in 1989. Now it seems the whole world knows that the lively German capital on the rivers Spree and Havel is a cosmopolitan city on a par with the likes of New York, Tokyo and London.

Berlin, whose history began in the 13th century, is not one of Germany's older cities. It was Prussia's rise to a great European power in the 18th century that made the capital significant. Berlin then became larger and more beautiful, finally being named the capital of the German Empire in 1871. Under the National Socialists, terror and annihilation spread from the capital, but in 1945 it was reduced to rubble. After being divided in 1961, it went on to inspire the reunification of East and West Germany in 1989 with the opening of the Berlin Wall. Since then it has changed dramatically. Today, Berlin is still not one entity but rather a grouping of districts. In a way, however, this is a blessing – for it is the city's variety and its contrasts that define this metropolis.

In the Charlottenburg district visit: Kurfürstendamm, the city's principal shopping boulevard, the ruins of the Emperor William Memorial Church and the Zoological Gardens.

Outside the city centre visit the Charlottenburg Castle and Park, the 'German Versailles', palace of the Prussian kings (built 1695–1746); the Egyptian Museum with Nefertiti; and the Museum Berggruen with great modern art.

In the Tiergarten district check out Berlin's largest city park with Bellevue Castle and Park, the residence of the German president; the Cultural Forum with the Philharmonic, the Museum of Musical Instruments, the Arts and Crafts Museum, a gallery with European paintings to the 19th century, the New National Gallery with 20th century art, the memorial to the German Resistance in the former Wehrmacht headquarters; the Road of 17 June with Victory Column (67 m/220 ft)

between Brandenburg Gate and Ernst-Reuter-Square.

West of city centre go to Grunewald, Berlin's forest, the Wannsee, and the Dahlem Museum with an outstanding collection of ethnological exhibits.

In Kreuzberg see the ruins of Anhalt Station, the Martin Gropius Building, the Jewish Museum by Daniel Liebeskind, the German Technology Museum, and Victoria Park with Kreuzberg Memorial.

Berlin 'Mitte' (centre): the Brandenburg Gate (1791); 'Unter den Linden' historic boulevard with a memorial of Frederick the Great; the New Guard by Schinkel; St Hedwig's Cathedral from the 18th century; the neoclassical public opera house, the baroque Zeughaus with the German Historical Museum; the Crown Prince's Palace (18th century); Humboldt University; the Gendarmes Market; the French and German Cathedral (18th century); the Schinkel Theatre (1821); the Reichstag (Parliament) with glass dome by Sir Norman Foster; Potsdam Square's modern architecture, Museum Island with Pergamon Museum, the Old Museum (antiquities), the New Museum, the Old National Gallery, the Bode Museum and Lustgarten. Beyond that is the Berlin Cathedral (late 19th century), 'Alex' TV tower (365 m/1,198 ft), old Checkpoint Charlie with the Berlin

Brandenburg Gate, built in the late 18th century, is considered the most important landmark of Berlin and of the German Reunification.

German president; the Cultural Forum with the Philharmonic, the Museum of Musical Instruments, the Arts and Crafts Museum, a gallery with European paintings to the 19th century, the New National Gallery with 20th century art, the memorial to the German Resistance in the former Wehrmacht headquarters; the Road of 17 June with Victory Column (67 m/220 ft)

Wall museum; St Mary's Church (13th century); historic Nikolai Quarter; Märkisches Museum of the city.

In the Scheunenviertel go to the Hamburger Bahnhof Gallery (modern art), the New Synagogue with its centre on the history of Berlin's Jewish community, and the Hackesche Höfe from 1906, once the largest working and living compound in Europe.

Karlovy Vary and Mariánské Lázně

Just over 40 km (25 miles) south of the German-Czech border, near Ústí nad Labem, follow the N13 west via Most and Chomutov to the Karlovy Vary, formerly the German Karlsbad ('Charles Bath'). Legend has it that it was actually Emperor Charles IV himself who found the hot salty springs in the area when he was out hunting deer in the 14th century.

Top: Town centre of Karlovy Vary.
Bottom: Health spa facilities at Mariánské Lázně.

Over the next 500 years, Bohemia's most famous and most glamorous spa town developed around these springs, with European elites from politics, art and society all making their way here to see and be seen. After fifty years of drabness during the Communist era, a glittering rebirth followed in 1989. Most of the Wilhelminian buildings, including the Mühlbrunn Colonnades, the town theatre and the Grandhotel Pupp, now radiate again with all their former glory.
From the densely settled banks of the Tepla River, take the turnoff onto the N21 just outside Cheb and drive just 60 km (37 miles) to the second legendary spa town of Mariánské Lázně ('Mary's Bath'), where Goethe wrote his 'Marienbad Elegies' in 1823. Its stucco facades were completely restored in the original Schönbrunn imperial yellow. Especially magnificent are the 120 m (131 yds) of cast-iron colonnades.

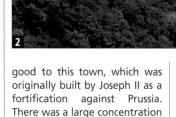

the Schrammsteine rocks and through Kirnitz Valley up to the Lichtenhain waterfalls.

8 Děčín The rocky sandstone scenery continues in all its grandeur here on the Czech side of the border. From the town of Hřensko, for example, there is a beautiful 4-km (2.5-mile) walk to the spectacular Pravčická Gate stone formation. An ideal starting point for trips into the park area is Děčín, where the famous 'Shepherd's Wall' towers 150 m (492 ft) over the river.
On the way to the Ústí nad Labem region you'll find another magnificent rock formation, crowned by the ruins of Strekov castle. From here you can take a detour heading west on the N13 via Most and Chomutov to the renowned spa towns of Karlovy Vary and Mariánské Lázně.

9 Litoměřice At the confluence of the Eger and the Elbe (Labe), where the Bohemian hills flatten out towards the plains, is the ancient town of Litomŭfiice surrounded by vineyards and orchards. Its Old Town is among the most beautiful in Bohemia. At its centre is the market square, which is around 2 ha (5 acres) in size. Don't miss the 'Kelchhaus', the town hall and St Stephen's Cathedral on Cathedral Hill.
About 4 km (2.5 miles) to the south, Terezín invokes memories of darker times. In World War II, the German occupation was not good to this town, which was originally built by Joseph II as a fortification against Prussia. There was a large concentration camp here.

10 Mělník High above the junction of the Vltava and Elbe Rivers is the much-visited town of Mělník, with its market square surrounded by beautiful stately houses. The town's most eye-catching sight, however, is its castle, a cherished possession of the local nobility for more than 1,100 years. The terrace of the castle restaurant has some fantastic views over the idyllic river valley.
From Mělník it is 40 km (25 miles) to Prague, the fairy-tale city on the Vltava River, and only 30 km (18 miles) to what is considered Bohemia's most famous castle.

11 Prague For detailed information see p. 69.

12 Karlštejn After 16 km (10 miles) on the R4, you head westbound at Dobřichovice for around 40 km (25 miles) until you get to this monumental castle perched majestically on a limestone rock 72 m (236 ft) above the Berounka Valley. It was built in the mid 14th century by Emperor Charles IV as his royal residence and a depository for the treasures. Its highlight in terms of art history is the Chapel of the Cross in the Great Tower with its gold-plated arches.
Back on the R4, you go to Příbram, which is located 50 km (31 miles) south-west of Prague, just off the main road.

13 Příbram This industrial and mining town, where silver has been mined since the 14th century and uranium since 1945, would not be worth mentioning if it were not for one of the Czech Republic's most visited pilgrimage destinations at its south-eastern edge – the Church of Our Lady of Svatá Hora with its baroque additions.
South-east of Příbram, not far from the B4, are two imposing castles on the bank of the Vltava River, which actually forms a reservoir more than 100 km (62 miles) long in this area. One of them is Zvíkov Castle, built in the 13th century on a towering rock outcrop; this former royal residence is worth a visit for its Chapel of St Wenceslas and the late-Gothic frescoes in its Great Hall. Orlík Castle, owned by the Schwarzenberg family for more than 700 years

1 View over Prague's Charles Bridge with the Old Town bridge tower and the church of St Franciscus in the background.

2 Hrad Karlštejn was used as a summer residence by Charles IV.

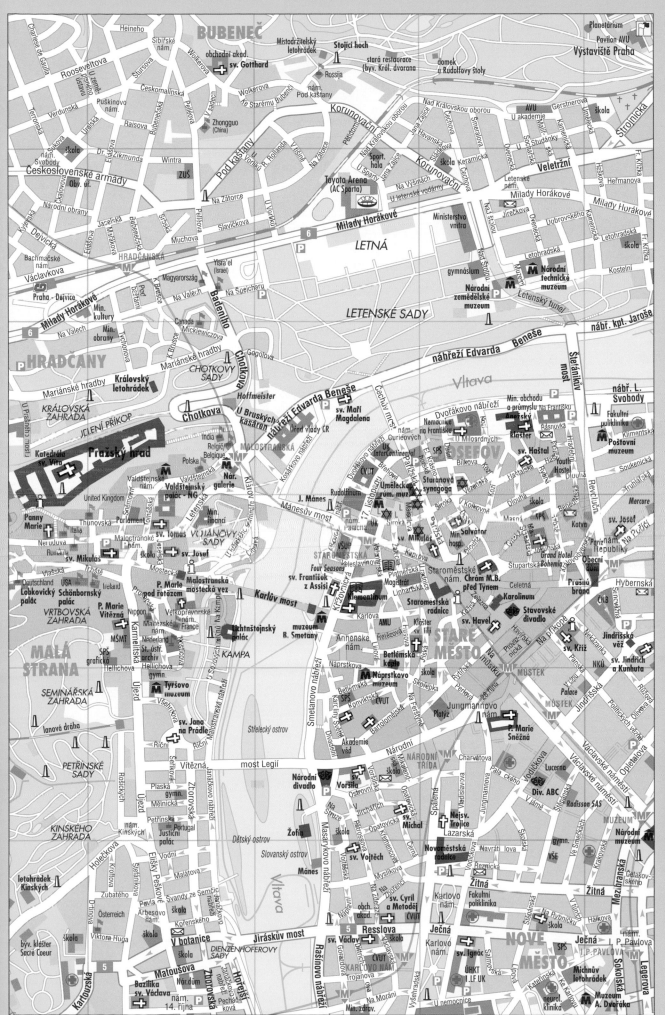

Prague

For centuries, the 'Golden City' has been an important intellectual and cultural centre, characterized by unique and beautiful architecture throughout the entire city.

Although Prague escaped destruction in World War II, time has still taken its toll on the city's buildings over the centuries. Thanks to an expertly managed restoration, however, Prague can once again show off the magnificence of more than 1,000 years of history.
The Czech people can be proud of their capital, which is the former residence of Bohemian kings and Habsburg Emperors. Hradčany Castle, where they used to reside, provides you with the best views of this masterpiece of historical urban architecture – the entire city is designated a UNESCO World Heritage Site.
In the Old Town go see the Altstädter Ring with rows of historic houses; the baroque Týn Church and Jan Hus Memorial; the art-nouveau Representation House; St Wenceslas Square with buildings from the 19th and 20th centuries; the Gothic town hall with its astronomical clock; and the late-Gothic gunpowder tower.
In the Castle Quarter on the Hradčany visit the castle (royal residence since the 10th century); the Golden Alleyway; the King's Palace with Renaissance Hall; the St Veit's Cathedral, with relics from

Town hall and Týn Church, Prague.

St Wenceslas, the national saint; St George's Basilica (12th century).
In the Josefov district see the Old Jewish cemetery, the Old New Synagogue, and the Pinkas Synagogue.
In the Lesser Quarter visit the Charles Bridge (14th century); St Nicholas Church, Prague's most important baroque church and the Waldstein Palace of the commander Wallenstein.

The castle of Český Krumlov

There are many good reasons why the castle of Český Krumlov, located high above the Vltava River, is a UNESCO World Heritage Site – it comprises forty buildings and palaces with a total of 320 rooms and halls, as well as five courtyards and castle gardens measuring 7 ha (17 acres), with some very interesting detailing.

The castle buildings, erected on different rock formations, are connected by a three-storey viaduct with a canopied three-level walkway. The entrance is dominated by the tower, painted in 1590. The rococo castle theatre dating from 1767 still has its original, and still functional, stage engineering. This open-air stage in the castle park is unique because it is the audience – not the stage – that turns when there is a change of scene.

The gigantic castle of Český Krumlov rises up high above the city.

The Masque Hall is also worth seeing. It is painted with figures from polite society and the *Commedia dell'Arte* (completed by J. Lederer in 1748). Also worth mentioning are the four bears guarding the entrance to the compound.

and reconstructed in neo-Gothic style in the 19th century, captivates with its richly decorated interior.

14 Písek On your way south on Road 20 you'll cross the Otava River after 50 km (31 miles). The well-manicured centre of this little town used to be an important stopping point on the so-called Golden Path, the trade route between Prague and Passau. Deer Bridge recalls the town's importance as an ancient traffic hub. The bridge, which was built in the second half of the 13th century, is Bohemia's oldest stone bridge.

15 České Budějovice Another 50 km (31 miles) on, you come to České Budějovice, which is world-famous for its breweries. Since Ottokar II founded the town in 1265, its centre has been the market square. The most dramatic sight on this huge square, which covers an area of 133 by 133 m (145 by 145 yds) and is surrounded by arcades on all sides, is the Samson Fountain. From the viewing platform of the steeple (72 m/236 ft), you can easily spot the other sights of the town – the baroque cathedral

of St Nicholas, the town hall, the Dominican Monastery and the Church of Our Lady, as well as the Salt House.

Around 10 km (6 miles) to the north, the battlements of Hluboká Castle appear on the horizon. Considered 'Bohemia's Neuschwanstein', this lavishly furnished castle was also owned by the Schwarzenberg family until 1939.

16 Český Krumlov Upriver from České Budějovice, it is another fifteen minutes by car along the Vltava River to the famous town of Český Krumlov. UNESCO certainly had its reasons for declaring this gem of more than 700 years as a World Heritage Site. Its location on both sides of a narrow hook in the river is incredibly scenic, and the labyrinthine alleyways of the Old Town and the Latrán with its shingled roofs are almost unsurpassably quaint. Highlights of every city tour are the Gothic St Vitus Church and the Schiele Centre. The painter Egon Schiele worked and lived in Český Krumlov in 1911.

The defining attraction of the town, however, is its castle. It is Bohemia's second-largest,

and is surpassed only by the Hradčany in Prague. It was originally owned by the Rosenberg family for 300 years, then by Emperor Rudolph II before landing in the hands of the counts of Schwarzenberg in the early 18th

century. A guided tour of the castle shows you the living quarters, gallery, chapel, the Masque Hall with frescoes and a fine rococo open-air theatre. It has been a designated UNESCO World Heritage Site since 1992.

Your next stop is Linz, the capital of Upper Austria, and from there our route follows the northern banks of the Danube (B3) towards Vienna.

18 Linz (see sidebar on the right).

19 Enns This attractive town near the Danube dates back to a Roman fort called Lauriacum and is one of the most ancient towns in Austria. Its landmark is the city's free-standing tower, which measures 60 m (197 ft). Antiquity is brought to life in the Museum Lauriacum, which is located on the town square. On the left bank of the Danube, some miles north of Enns, lies the market town of Mauthausen. A monument in the local granite quarries commemorates the fact that the Germans ran a concentration camp here, where

1 View of Český Krumlov castle and the Old Town.

2 Samson Fountain on the square in České Budějovice, also known as Budweis of Budweiser fame.

3 The old cathedral on Linz's central square.

Linz

In the last couple of decades, Linz, which had long endured a bad reputation as an unattractive industrial town, has radically polished up its image. Contemporary art, using the most modern media and technology available, now defines Linz's cultural identity.

The Lentos Museum of Modern Art, the Ars Electronica Festival and the Design Centre all pay their tribute to modern times. Every year, the bigwigs of computer art turn up for the Ars Electronica Festival, and a multimedia wave of sound and light descends on the city.

Beyond all this modernism is also the neatly restored historic centre around the town square, which includes the Renaissance Landhaus (house of the provincial government), the castle, the Church of St Martin, the parish church and the old and new cathedrals, as well as a number of interesting galleries and museums.

An integral part of any sightseeing trip should also be a boat ride on the Danube with the Linz City Express, or a journey up the Pöstlingberg mountain on the ancient mountain railway.

17 Freistadt Right across the border in Austria you'll come to the next delightful example of medieval town planning. The centre of the northern Mühl District, developed under the Babenberg Dynasty, quickly became the most important trading post between Bohemia and the Danube. To this day it has kept its 14th-century fortifications. Take a stroll through the narrow alleyways between the Linz Gate and the Bohemia Gate, past the town's handsome mansions and the huge town square to the church. Make sure not to miss the Mühl District House in the castle, which has a superb collection of reverse glass painting.

The Melk Abbey – a spiritual centre on the Danube

As far back as AD 976, Margrave Leopold I had established Melk Castle as his residence. Over the years, his successors equipped it with valuable treasures and relics. Then, in 1089, Margrave Leopold II handed the castle over to the Benedictine monks of the nearby Lambach Abbey. To this day, the monks continue to live at

The monastery library, decorated in shades of brown and gold, houses roughly 100,000 books.

the abbey according to the Rule of St Benedict.

Over the course of centuries, the monks not only collected but also produced valuable manuscripts for the abbey's vast library. In many areas of the natural and social sciences, as well as in music, the members of the Melk Abbey have chalked up some outstanding achievements during the establishment's illustrious history.

To this day, the monks continue to be active in the areas of counselling, economy, culture and tourism. Ever since it was founded, Melk Abbey has been an important spiritual and religious centre in Austria.

around 100,000 people lost their lives.

Around 30 km (18 miles) downriver, at the start of the 'Strudengau', a stretch of river that is feared for its strong currents and dangerous sandbanks, is the little town of Grein. It originally became wealthy because local mariners would guide travellers through the dangerous waters. It also has a very delightful rococo theatre. Close by, the castle ruins of Klam are also worth seeing.

20 Ybbs This traditional market and toll location marks the beginning of the next section of the valley, the so-called 'Nibelungengau'. North of the power station (1958), the historic castle of Persenbeug keeps vigil over the valley. The castle remains the property of the Habsburg family and can only be viewed from outside.

A little further east, there are two reasons for a short excursion up to Maria Taferl, a Lower Austrian market town with no more than a thousand inhabitants. In addition to the baroque pilgrimage church, whose exuberant colours and shapes are truly beguiling, it is mainly the view from the terrace that is so captivating – the entire Nibelungengau of Burgundian legend sprawled out at your feet. In

good weather, you can even see large parts of the Eastern Alps.

21 Melk A real baroque icon salutes us from a rock outcrop 60 m (197 ft) above the south bank across the river, around 10 km (6 miles) east of the pilgrimage church. It's the Benedictine abbey of Melk with a church, two steeples and a facade of more than 360 m (393 yds) – undoubtedly one of the most magnificent of its kind in the world. This religious fortification, which was built in the

early 18th century, impressively symbolizes the euphoria among the clerics and the nobility after their dual triumph – over the Reformation and over the Turks. There is exuberant splendour everywhere in the edifice: in the Emperor's Wing with the Emperor's Gallery, which is nearly 200 m (219 yds) long; in the marble hall with its frescoes by Paul Troger; in the vast library with approximately 100,000 volumes; and also in the church, with ceiling frescoes by Johann Michael Rottmayr.

Back on the northern riverbank, the B3 takes us past the Jauerling Nature Park via Aggsbach, Spitz, Weißenkirchen and Dürnstein to the spectacular transverse valley of the Wachau River. Many of these places have an interesting history, like the Aggstein Castle on a rock outcrop high above the Danube. It is said that a series of unscrupulous men abused the castle's position on the river to rob passing Danube boats and charge exorbitant tolls. The ruin of Dürnstein tells the tale of the capture

Wachau

The transverse valley of the Danube, between Melk and Mautern and Emmersdorf and Krems, is the very image of a central European cultural landscape. No surprise, then, that it has been listed as a UNESCO World Heritage Site.

Blessed with a sunny climate and surrounded by picturesque, painstakingly terraced vineyards, it is just as famous for its good wines and fruit, especially its apricots, as for its history and stone memorials.

Top: Aggstein Castle ruins, Aggsbach. Bottom: A lovely vineyard near Weißenkirchen.

Danube, it takes just under thirty minutes to get to Tulln.

㉔ Tulln This town on the Danube, which started out as a Roman fort called Comagenis, has an impressive architectural ensemble of parish churches and a former charnel house. A visit to the mighty salt tower with its Roman core is also worth doing, and can easily be combined with a stroll along the riverside promenade. A museum with around ninety original paintings commemorates Egon Schiele, the town's favourite son and groundbreaking expressionist.

1 The Melk Abbey, founded c. 1000 AD, received its distinguished baroque makeover between 1702–39.

2 The icon of Wachau – the baroque monastery at Dürnstein contains a Renaissance castle, a former Augustinian monastery and a former Clarissan nunnery, all forming a unique ensemble on the bank of the Danube.

3 High above the Danube, not far from Aggsbach, is the Schönbühel Castle dating from the 12th century.

4 Impressions of Wachau – Weißenkirchen, the local wine-growing centre, with its mighty Gothic parish church.

In addition to the historic treasures of Krems, Stein, the old Kuenringer town of Dürnstein and the monasteries at Göttweig and Melk, the many small towns with their Gothic churches, covered arcades on the vineyards and medieval castles are among the highlights of a drive through this region 'wrapped in the silver band of the Danube'.

Must-sees along the northern river bank are Spitz with the Museum of Navigation, St Michael with its bizarrely decorated filial church, Aggsbach, the wine-growing towns of Weißenkirchen, Joching and Wösendorf, and last but not least, Dürnstein with its monastery and legendary castle.

of Richard the Lionheart and Blondel, the singer, who recognized him.

㉒ Wachau (see sidebar right).

㉓ Krems This town is located on the exact spot where the Danube trade route meets one of the main routes between the Alpine foothills and the Bohemian Forest, and where traders and mariners as far back as the early Middle Ages came to exchange their goods. This mercantile centre at the eastern entrance to

the Wachau is not only one of the oldest, but also one of the most beautiful towns in the whole area. As a way into its restored alleyways, take the Steiner Tor ('Stone Gate'). From here, there is a circular walk across Corn Market to the Dominican Church, which houses the wine museum, and on to Gozzoburg on the High Market. From the gunpowder tower you have a beautiful view onto the more modern districts, the harbour and the Danube over to Göttweig Monastery. On the

way back you go along the road, past such architectural gems as the Bürgerspitalkirche, Gögl House and the town hall.

At the western end of Krems is the town of Stein. Must-sees here are the Minorite and St Nicholas Churches and a number of magnificent buildings as well as a former monastery which now houses the 'House of Lower Austrian Wines'.

Driving along the Wagram, a steep slope where lovely vineyards drop colourfully and abruptly down towards the

1

Lake Neusiedl

This steppe lake in the northern Burgenland region, which is 30 km (18 miles) long and a maximum of 2 m (6.5 ft) deep, is not called the 'Sea of the Viennese' for nothing. In summer, it is a paradise for water sports. For the rest of the year. It is a Mecca for amateur ornithologists who can observe a large number of rare birds in the reed belt around the lake that is 1–3-km wide (0.6–2-miles). From Illmitz, you can take regular guided tours through the national park by bike, horse-drawn carriage or on horseback.
The areas in the west, north and south of Lake Neusiedl (its south-eastern corner is part of Hungary)

Top: Rust, a famous wine-growing town on Lake Neusiedl.
Bottom: Burgenland farmhouse.

are among Austria's most famous wine-growing regions. Villages in the area like Rust, Mörbisch, Donnerskirchen, Breitenbrunn or Podersdorf are worth seeing because of their picturesque town centres and neat farmhouses with stork's nests crowning their chimneys. From mid July to late August, operettas are regularly performed on the open-air stage in Mörbisch as part of the Lake Festival.
You definitely should not miss the 'excursion within the excursion' here to Eisenstadt, where you can visit the palace of the Esterházy princes and the mausoleum of Joseph Haydn in the Bergkirche church.

25 Klosterneuburg This small town right outside Vienna on the southern bank of the Danube is world-famous thanks to its Augustinian monastery. The monumental building was built in the early 12th century by the Babenberg Duke Leopold III and soon after donated to the order. For centuries, it was the scientific centre of the country. The dazzling emperor's rooms, the emperor's staircase and the marble hall are the primary attractions. Don't miss the enamel Verdun Altar by Nicholas of Verdun in Leopold's Chapel. The monastery also houses the largest religious library in the country, a museum and a treasury.

26 Vienna (see p. 75). After ample time in Vienna, the capital of Austria, you can take an interesting excursion to Lake Neusiedl. Your best option is the A4 to Neusiedl on the lake's northern shore. Alternatively, carry on along the Danube.

27 Carnuntum Around 35 km (22 miles) east of Vienna, where the 'Amber Road' (between the Baltic Sea and the Mediterranean) and the East-West Route along the Danube meet, are the Roman remains of Carnuntum, south of the river. Nowhere else in Austria have archaeologists found such rich ancient heritage. The excavation site, officially made into an 'archaeological park' in 1996, comprises the whole of the civilian town with its network of ancient walls and streets, a reconstructed Diana Temple and a long piece of the original Roman Limes Road (Border Road). A little further away

are the ruins of a palace, baths, an amphitheatre and the Heathen's Gate. Many of the rich findings are on display in the Museum Carnuntinum in Bad Deutsch-Altenburg.

28 Bratislava When the Turks conquered Budapest in the middle of the 16th century and kept it for nearly 150 years, Bratislava, now the capital of Slovakia, was called Pozsony and was the capital of free Hungary until 1848. In modern times it was behind the Iron Curtain until 1989. Since then, it has not only forged closer ties to the Western world, but also undergone a radical beautification and rejuvenation.
The sins of socialist town planning cannot be undone, and the prefabricated tower blocks in Petržalka on the southern bank of the Danube, for example, will continue to be an eyesore for quite some time. Staré Mesto, by contrast, the largely car-free Old Town, has done itself up rather nicely. Its most important sights are St Martin's Cathedral, the archbishop's palace, the Slovak National Gallery, the National Theatre and Museum and the castle residing above the river. East of Bratislava, Road 63 (E575) takes you down into the Danube Plains (Podunajsko), which are completely flat and extremely fertile. During the summer months fresh fruit and vegetable stands are everywhere.
During World War II, this region was particularly hard hit. Reconstruction led to local towns looking very much alike. This route, however, now takes us away from the Danube to the south – back through Austria to Fertőd in Hungary.

2

3

29 Fertőd/Esterházy Palace Around 5 km (3 miles) east of Fertő-tó (the Hungarian name of Lake Neusiedl), we come to Fertőd and Esterházy Palace. The Esterházys are an old Hungarian dynasty from which many politicians and military men have come.

30 Győr This large city has an important harbour on the Danube and is worth seeing for its 12th-century cathedral which was given a baroque makeover in the 17th century.

31 Komárno/Komárom Located where the River Váh meets the Danube, the town has

always been of the utmost strategic importance. The Romans even had a fort here called Brigetio. In the course of the 19th century, the Habsburg Dynasty turned the town into

1 The classical Austrian Parliament Building in Vienna (1874–84) with the Pallas-Athene Fountain.

2 The ceremonial hall, the main hall of Vienna's National Library, was begun by Johann Bernhard Fischer von Erlach in 1719; his son finished it.

3 Esterházy Castle in Fertőd was the royal residence of the Esterházy princes and the workplace of the composer Joseph Haydn.

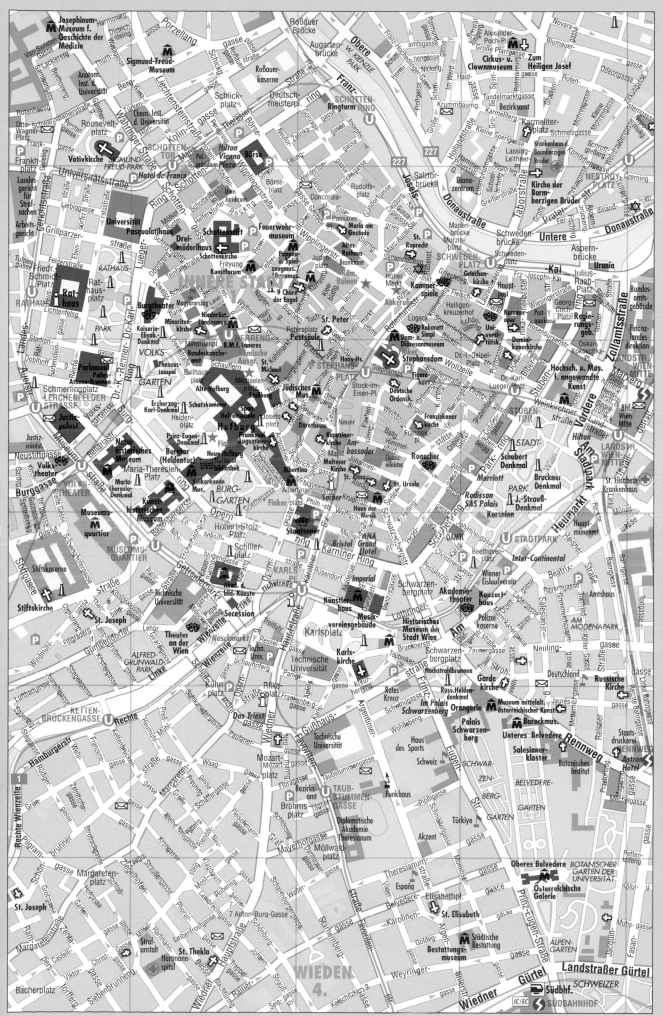

Vienna

Located on the 'beautiful blue Danube', the Austrian capital has a uniquely charming atmosphere and seems still to radiate the Old World feel of the Dual Monarchy.

Vienna, the old royal city and former centre of the 'multicultural' Habsburg Empire, has architecture and art treasures from all eras of its long history. As a result, you will need some time to explore this city, especially if you want to catch a bit of its famous atmosphere, which is largely communicated through the pleasures of food and drink. Your best bet is in the 'Heurigen' wine taverns, in the coffee houses or on the traditional 'Naschmarkt' (literally 'Nibbles Market').

Definitely visit the Stephansdom with Romanesque, Gothic and late-Gothic sections, richly ornate facade and precious interior; the Hofburg, until 1918 the imperial residence with treasure chamber, emperor's rooms and palace chapel; the Art History Museum with its collection of European paintings; and the baroque Josefsplatz with National Library; the Gothic Augustinerkirche with its baroque Capuchin crypt of the Habsburg emperors; the Spanish Riding School; the Karlskirche, the most beautiful baroque building in Vienna; the Museum of Applied Art; Belvedere

Top: View over Vienna's sea of houses and the Stephansdom cathedral (right).
Bottom: Karlskirche by Fischer von Erlach.

Castle with Lower Belvedere (baroque museum) and Upper Belvedere (19th- and 20th-century paintings); Schönbrunn, a baroque Versailles imitation with park, Gloriette classical arcades with a beautiful view of the castle and town. The historic centre and Schönbrunn Palace are UNESCO World Heritage Sites.

Detour

Puszta – the central European steppe

Driving east from Budapest on the M3 motorway and then from Füzesabony on the N33, you reach Hortobágy, Hungary's oldest national park. Here, ancient prairie lands stretch out between the Tisza and Debrecen Rivers, the last vestige of the puszta landscape that once covered the entire steppe.
Crossing this grassland by car (it was designated a UNESCO World Heritage Site in 1999), you can hardly see anything but flat, monotonous

Top: The Puszta's landmarks are draw wells and herdsmen's huts. Bottom: Field of sunflowers in the Puszta.

countryside. Therefore, in order to see it in all its beauty you need to go exploring on foot, by bike, by boat or by horse-drawn carriage.
Right next to the famous Bridge of Nine Arches in Hortobágy Village, a museum takes you back to the everyday life of the Puszta herdsmen, a lifestyle that has all but disappeared. You can encounter old animal breeds in this area such as grey cattle, woolly boars and Raczka sheep.
Riding performances and bird watching or a visit to a pottery and a meal of the local savoury pancakes round off your visit.

a 'city of fortifications' like no other in the monarchy. After Ferenc I, King of Hungary, had found shelter from Napoleon's army in Komárno in 1809, it was made the central defence post of the Habsburg Empire.
Ever since the Treaty of Trianon (1920) marking the Danube as the border of the realm, the city has been divided into two parts. The former Old Town on the northern shore is now part of the Slovakian town of Komárno. On the Hungarian side, three fortifications are an interesting attraction for military history enthusiasts.
Monostor, the largest of the forts with 640 rooms and 4 km (2.5 miles) of underground shelters, is sometimes nicknamed 'Gibraltar of the Danube' and there are guided tours around it. The Igmánd fort, which is significantly smaller, houses a museum with findings from Roman times.

32 **Tata** This spa town at the bottom of Gerecse Hill gives off an atmosphere of cosiness and charm with its lakes and complex labyrinth of rivers and canals. But its location and its history have not been kind to the 'City of Water' – for 150 years it was situated on the border between the territories of the Habsburgs and the Ottoman Empire, which resulted in consistent large-scale devastation of its buildings
But every cloud has a silver lining. In around 1730, the Esterházy princes, then rulers of the town, initiated the reconstruc-

tion of the Tata, whose myriad baroque architectural ensembles shape the town to this day. Be sure to visit the ruins of the castle, built in the 14th century and later expanded into a magnificent Renaissance Palace by Matthias Corvinus. Don't miss Esterházy Castle and the former synagogue, which houses about 100 plaster-of-Paris copies of famous antique sculptures.
Halfway between Tata and Budapest – you can see it from the M1 motorway – is an apogee of Hungary's Romance architecture reaching high up into the sky. The Zsámbék Church itself actually collapsed in the middle of the 18th century, along with the adjacent Premonstratensian priory. Even as ruins, though, the colossal dimensions of the building are truly spectacular.

33 **Budapest** The Magyar metropolis has around two million inhabitants on a location where the Romans had already founded a town called Aquincum. Like many others, the two medieval communities of Ofen and Pest were devastated by the Mongols in 1241.
After the reconstruction, Ofen became Hungary's most important city, but was overtaken in the early 19th century by its sister town of Pest. The two cities were finally united in 1872. In the early 20th century, Budapest was considered the 'Paris of the East', a reputation it is still hoping to regain despite the devastation of World War II and more than four decades of Soviet rule.

The first thing on a long list of things to do just has to be the castle mountain. It is here on this limestone rock, nearly 1.5 km (0.9 miles) long, above the right bank of the Danube that the country's historical heart has been beating ever since the first king's castle was constructed upon it by Béla IV. Combining the Matthias Church, the Fisherman's Bastion and the castle, which houses several first-rate museums, this quarter has some of the most important sights in the city. And there are also some unforgettable panoramic views down to the city and to the river. The view from the neighbouring Gellért Mountain is just as scenic. The majority of the city's sights are located on the left bank of the Danube, in the Pest district. Once you leave behind the narrow Old Town centre, the cityscape is typified by extensive Wilhelminian ring and radial roads.

You can visit St Stephen's Basilica, the National Opera, the National Museum, the Grand Synagogue and, directly by the river, the large market hall and the even larger houses of parliament. Out in the city forest are Vajdahunyad Castle, the Széchenyi Baths and the Museum of Fine Arts.
A must-see is, of course, the baroque palace in Gödöllő 30 km (18 miles) north-east of the city centre, where Emperor Franz Joseph I and his wife Elizabeth ('Sisi') lived.

1 Budapest – the Houses of Parliament on the banks of the mighty Danube. In the foreground is the city's suspension bridge.

2 Hungarian grey cattle in Hortobágy National Park.

Sanssouci The rococo ensemble, whose name means 'Carefree', is the most visited attraction in Potsdam, capital of Brandenburg, where you can take a carefree stroll through the summer residence of Friedrich II.

Berlin The old and new German capital has become even more attractive since the Berlin Wall came down. Located on the Spree and Havel rivers, it has a lot of greenery, vibrant nightlife and myriad cultural highlights both in the former east and in the west. Pictured is the Charlottenburg Palace.

Meißen The centre of this porcelain town and 'Cradle of Saxony' has a medieval atmosphere. Above it is the towering cathedral and the Albrecht Castle.

Wartburg Legend has it that the castle was founded in 1067. Located at the edge of the Thuringian Forest it was probably the site of the German minstrels' contest. Luther translated the bible into German here.

Dresden Buildings like the Zwinger and the Semper Opera House, as well as precious collections like the Old Masters Gallery, have made Dresden a leading European cultural metropolis.

Saxon Switzerland Whether you prefer hiking or a boat trip on the Elbe River, the bizarre plateaus, rock outcrops and gorges of the Elbe Sandstone Mountains near Dresden are fascinating. Most of the area has been made into a national park.

Prague The Czech capital is located on the Vltava River and has an unusual skyline. Hradčany Castle, Charles Bridge and the art-nouveau buildings of this 'Golden City' are unique. This photograph is of Týn Church.

České Budějovice The centre of this world-famous city of breweries and beer is the market square with Samson Fountain.

Karlovy Vary This spa town on the Eger River has some healing springs as well as historical and modern spa facilities.

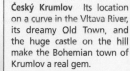

Český Krumlov Its location on a curve in the Vltava River, its dreamy Old Town, and the huge castle on the hill make the Bohemian town of Krumlov a real gem.

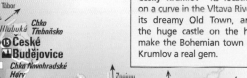

Wachau The forest and wine-growing area of Wachau extends from Melk to Krems – a transverse valley of the Danube that is 30 km (18 miles) long.

Melk The Benedictine abbey high above the Danube is baroque architecture in all its perfection.

Vienna The Austrian capital is always worth a visit. The number and quality of the sights in this metropolis on the Danube is simply overwhelming. Pictured here is the Austrian Parliament Building.

Fertöd, Esterházy Palace The 'Hungarian Versailles' in Fertöd used to belong to a family of princes. There is even an opera house and a puppet theatre inside.

Budapest One of the landmarks of the Hungarian capital is the mighty suspension bridge (1839–49). The list of further sights in the metropolis on the Danube is a long one – from Fisherman's Bastion and the crown of St Stephen in the National Museum to the neo-Gothic Houses of Parliament and the terrific art-nouveau bath houses.

The old harbour of La Rochelle and the watchtowers of St-Nicolas and Tour de la Chaîne.

France

Via Turonensis – on the old pilgrimage route from Paris to Biarritz

The Via Turonensis was mainly travelled by pilgrims from the Netherlands and northern France on their way to Santiago de Compostela in Galicia, the far north-west corner of Spain. They mostly went on foot to their imminent salvation. Today, there are still pilgrims who follow the Camino de Santiago (St James' Way) and its various 'side streets' for religious purposes, but most people these days are simply interested in seeing the wonderful sights along the way.

Four different trails originally led pilgrims through France to the tomb of St James in Santiago de Compostela – the Via Tolosana from Arles through Montpellier and Toulouse to Spain; the Via Podensis from Le Puy through Conques, Cahors and Moissac to the border; the Via Lemovicensis from Vézelay through Avallon, Nevers and Limoges; and finally, the fourth route, the Via Turonensis, known as the 'magnum iter Sancti Jacobi' (the Great Route of St James).

The route's name comes from the city of Tours, through which it passed. The pilgrims started at the tomb of St Dionysius in St-Denis before heading through Paris, down the Rue St-Jacques to the church of the same name, where only the tower still stands on the right bank of the Seine. The tomb of St Evurtius was the destination in Orléans, while the tomb of St Martin, who was often compared to St James, awaited pilgrims in Tours. In Poitiers, there were three churches on the

Jeanne d'Arc Arriving at Orléans, a painting by Jean Jacques Scherrer.

intinerary: St-Hilaire, Notre Dame la Grande and Ste-Radegonde. The head of John the Baptist was the object of worship in St-Jean-d'Angély, and pilgrims would pray at the tomb of St Eutropius in Saintes. Bordeaux was also the custodian of important relics like the bones of St Severin and the Horn of Roland.

The pilgrims of the Middle Ages would most certainly have been amazed and would have shaken their heads at the buildings that the modern pilgrims along the Via Turonensis today find so fascinating. While the largest and most beautiful buildings in the Middle Ages were erected to honour and praise God, modern man seems obsessed with himself and his comforts. 'Pilgrims' nowadays are most interested in visiting the castles along the Via Turonensis, drawn to the extravagance as if by magic.

Château de Chambord, in the middle of a large forest, is a structure of fairy-tale proportions.

The modern glass pyramid by I.M. Pei in front of the magnificent Louvre building has been the museum's main entrance since 1989.

Perfect examples of this absolutism are just outside Paris in the Île-de-France – the enormous palace complex of Versailles and the castle of Rambouillet which, as the summer residence of French presidents, continues to be a centre of power. Many other magnificent buildings are scattered along the Loire River and its tributaries, the Indre, Cher and Vienne, including the colossal Château de Chambord, a dream realized by King Francis I, the Château de Chenonceaux, and others like Beauregard, Chaumont, Valençay, Loches, Le Lude and Langeais.

The area around Bordeaux is home to a completely different kind of château. Médoc, Bordeaux and Entre-Deux-Mers are names that make the wine-lover's heart skip a beat. This region is the home of myriad great wines, in particular red wine. The wineries around Bordeaux, most of which look like real castles in the middle of vast vineyards, are referred to as châteaus and include internationally renowned names such as Mouton-Roth-schild, Lafitte-Rothschild and Latour.

Last but not least, today's 'car pilgrims' are attracted to destinations that are far off the beaten track and would have seemed rather absurd as a detour to the pilgrims of the Middle Ages – namely, those on the Atlantic coast. The sandy beaches and coves of the Arcachon Basin and the sections of coast further south on the Bay of Biscay provide wind and waves for windsurfers and surfers. The elegant life of the 19th century is celebrated in the charming seaside resort of Biarritz and, from here, it's not much further to the Aragonian section of the Camino de Santiago, which stretches along the northern coast of Spain.

The Médoc on the left bank of the Gironde is one of the best red wine regions in the world.

Chartres

Even from a great distance, Chartres Cathedral is an impressive edifice, soaring like a mirage above the vast expanse of cornfields in the Beauce region. Up close, any doubts of its stature vanish immediately. This masterpiece of Gothic architecture, a large portion of which was built in the second half of the 12th century, simply overwhelms with its dimensions and design.

Chartres Cathedral

The facade and, in particular, the entrance area are a dazzling sight full of lavish ornamentation, but the cathedral's greatest treasure is inside: glass paintings unsurpassed in their number and beauty anywhere else in the world. The colourful stained-glass windows depict both biblical and historical scenes, and thus provided literate and illiterate believers alike with their wealth of information.

The rose windows are also stunning, and their engraved tracery contains an extensive range of images. The southern and western rose windows illustrate the Last Judgement, while the eastern rose window is dedicated to the Virgin Mary.

Chartres Cathedral, a UNESCO World Heritage Site since 1979, should definitely not be missed.

The Via Turonensis follows one of the four major French routes of the St James' pilgrimage trail. Starting in the Île-de-France, you'll head to Orléans on the Loire, continue downstream past some of the most beautiful and famous Loire châteaus and then, from Saumur onwards, make your way south into the Gironde to Bordeaux. Prior to arriving in Biarritz, you stop in St-Jean-Pied-de-Port, the former last stop for pilgrims before crossing the Pyrenees.

❶ St-Denis The actual pilgrim route begins in St-Denis, north of Paris. During the heyday of the Camino de Santiago (St James' Way) pilgrimages, this town was located north of the former city border and was the meeting place for the pilgrims coming from Paris. The French national saint, Dionysius, is buried in the city's cathedral. The basilica, where almost all of France's kings are entombed, is considered the first masterpiece of Gothic architecture.

❷ Paris (see pp. 82–85). South-west of Paris is Versailles. The name of the palace is intrinsically tied to the Sun King, Louis XIV, and is a symbol of his display of absolutist power.

❸ The Palace of Versailles Louis XIII first had a small hunting lodge built on the site where this magnificent building now stands. Under Louis XIV, the lodge was gradually expanded to the immense dimensions we know today, followed by some 'insignificant' extensions like the opera, built under Louis XV.

During the reign of the Sun King, Versailles was the place where anyone who wanted to have any sort of influence in the State had to stay. Apart from the large, opulent reception rooms such as the Hall of Mirrors, the Venus Room, the Hercules Room or the Abundance Salon, there were also the king and queen's lavishly furnished private chambers. The opera is a real gem, completed in 1770.

Beyond the water features of the Bassin d'Apollon is the vast park complex, which is home to the Grand Trianon, Petit Trianon and Le Hameau. The Grand Trianon was built under the orders of Louis XIV – one wing for him and the other for his beloved, Madame de Maintenon. The Petit Trianon was built for

Louis XV's mistresses. Le Hameau is almost an absurdity – a small village with a homestead, dairy farm, mill and pigeon loft, where Marie Antoinette played 'peasant', a game that did not win her any fans among supporters of the revolution – she wound up under the guillotine on the Place de la Concorde.

❹ Rambouillet Although the palace is the summer residence of the French president, it can be visited most of the time. The building consists of wings designed in different architectural styles including Gothic, Renaissance and baroque.

This castle only became royal property in 1783, when Louis XVI

Travel information

Route profile
Length: approx. 1,100 km (684 miles), excluding detours
Time required: 10–14 days
Start: Paris
End: Bayonne
Route (main locations): Paris, Versailles, Orléans, Blois, Tours, Saumur, Poitiers, Saintes, Cognac, St-Émilion, Bordeaux, St-Jean-Pied-de-Port, Bayonne

Traffic information:
Drive on the right in France. The speed limit in built-up areas is 50 km/h (31 mph), 90 km/h (56 mph) on rural roads, 110 km/h (68 mph) on expressways and 130 km/h (81 mph) on highways. Headlights are required when driving in foggy, rainy or snowy conditions.

Weather:
The best seasons to visit the Île-de-France and the Loire Valley are spring and autumn, when the Loire Valley shows off its most beautiful side and is ablaze with all shades of yellow and red. For more information go to:
www.meteofrance.com

Information:
General
www.francetourism.com
www.franceguide.com
www.theviaturonensis.com
Paris
en.parisinfo.com
Loire Valley
www.westernfrancetourist board.com
Bordeaux
www.bordeaux-tourisme. com

acquired it as a hunting lodge. The park and the adjacent Rambouillet forest are ideal places to take a relaxing stroll. On the way to Orléans to the south of Paris, it's worth making a detour to Chartres, whose name is automatically associated with its Gothic cathedral, the largest in Europe.

5 Orléans This city's cathedral, Ste-Croix, is built in Gothic style, though only very small parts of it date back to the Gothic period. The original building, destroyed during the French Wars of Religion, was rebuilt under Henry VI, and the architects of the 18th and 19th centuries continued to use the Gothic style.

The city's liberator lived in the house named after her – the Maison de Jeanne d'Arc. The half-timbered house, which was destroyed in World War II, was reconstructed identically to the original. Only very few of the beautiful old houses and noble palaces were spared from the severe attacks of the war, but the Hôtel Toutin, with its gorgeous Renaissance interior courtyard, is one that was. Of course, Orléans wouldn't be complete without the statue of Jeanne d'Arc, erected on the Place du Martroi in 1855.

Before heading on to Blois, it's well worth making a detour to the beautiful moated castle of Sully-sur-Loire, some 40 km (25 miles) south-east of Orléans. From Orléans, you have two options for reaching Chambord, which is somewhat outside of the Loire Valley – either along the right bank of the Loire to Merand and across a bridge, or along the left bank of the Loire on small rural roads.

6 Chambord King Francis I had this château built on the site of an older hunting lodge. Lost among the vast forests, the result was a vast dream castle with an incredible 440 rooms, seventy staircases, corner towers, a parapet and a moat. Leonardo da Vinci was apparently involved in its construction as well, designing the elaborate double-helix staircase whose two spirals are so intertwined that the people going up cannot see the people going down, and vice versa.

One of the château's real charms is its unique roof silhouette with its numerous turrets and chimneys. Francis I did not live to see the completion of his château, and work was not continued on it until the reign of Louis XIV. Louis XV gave it as a gift to the Elector of Saxony, who had it gloriously renovated. The château fell into temporary neglect after his death.

7 Blois In the first half of the 17th century, Blois was the centre of France's political world. The town revolves around its castle, where the individual building phases are very easily recognized. The oldest section is Louis XII's wing, constructed in red brick with white limestone decorations. The Francis I wing is far more lavish, built in Renaissance style with traces of French Gothic in parts. The king would often have his heraldic animal, the salamander, displayed in certain areas. What really catches your eye is the Renaissance-style staircase tower in the interior courtyard, where the royal family could attend events.

Noble palaces such as the Hôtel Sardini, the Hôtel d'Alluye and the Hôtel de Guise are proof that, apart from royalty, numerous other aristocrats also had their residences along the Loire. The St-Louis Cathedral is not Gothic and only dates back to the 17th century, the previous building having been extensively destroyed by a hurricane. An

1 View of the Eiffel Tower lit up at night from one of the many bridges along the Seine.

2 The Palace of Versailles – the Cour de Marbre courtyard is paved with marble slabs.

3 The oldest bridge in Paris, the Pont Neuf, spans the Seine on the north and south sides of the Île de la Cité. Despite its name 'New Bridge', the Pont Neuf was opened in 1607 and connected the city to the island in the river, its medieval centre.

Ludwig XIV and Absolutism

L'état c'est moi – I am the State. This statement by Louis XIV aptly characterizes his understanding of power. The 'Sun King' was born in 1638 and, following the death of his father in 1643,

Louis XIV – a painting by H. Rigaud, 1701, Louvre, Paris.

proclaimed king at the tender age of five. His reign was subsequently defined by his love of all things opulent and gaudy, and the Palace of Versailles is the most impressive and repeatedly copied example of this.

After the death of Cardinal Mazarin, Louis XIV limited the rights of parliament and the aristocracy and strengthened the army. He ruled with absolute power until his death in 1715.

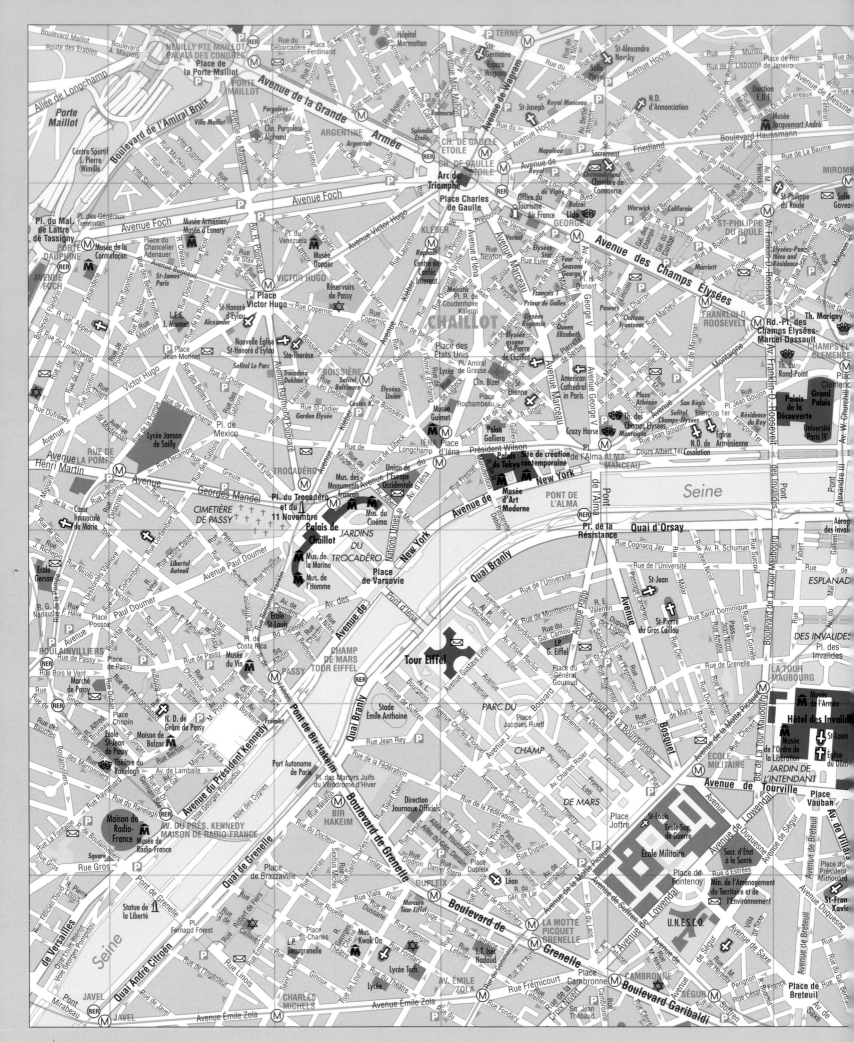

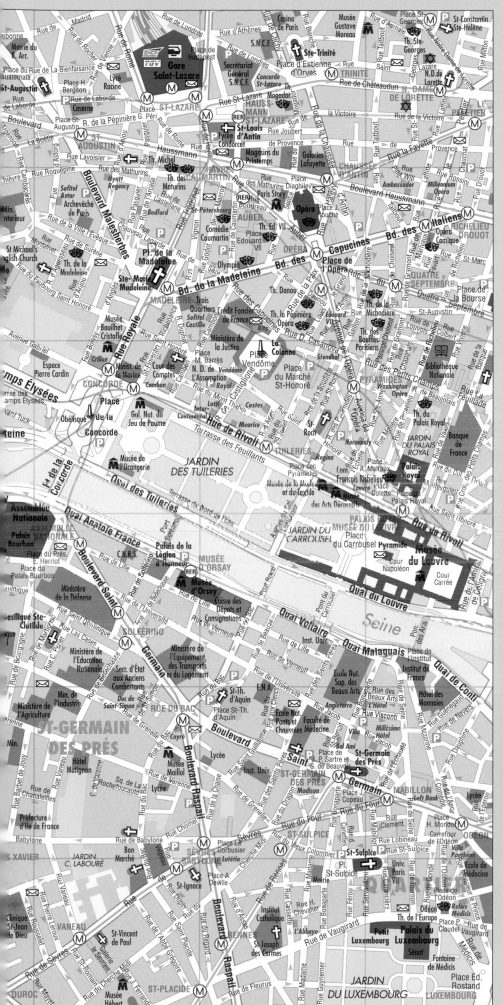

Paris

The French capital is a city of thrilling contrasts – rich in tradition and at the same time avant-garde, enormous in size and yet captivatingly charming. Paris is also a university city and the place of government, a global centre for fashion and art, incredibly multicultural and yet still very much the epitome of all things French.

Throughout its long history, Paris has continually been in a state of expansion. The city always appeared to be bursting at the seams. Today, greater Paris covers an area of about 105 sq km (40 sq miles) and is home to some twelve million people – more than twenty per cent of the entire population of France. This city's non-stop growth is not least due to the fact that Paris does not accept any rivals. The nation's capital has always been unchallenged in its political, economic and cultural significance.

On the south side of the Seine you won't be able to miss the Eiffel Tower, the symbol of Paris built for the World Fair in 1889. The iron construction, towering 300 m (984 ft) over the city, took engineer Gustav Eiffel just sixteen months to completed. The viewing platform, accessed by

Be sure to see the Place de la Concorde, an excellent example of wide boulevards and geometric plazas that gave the French capital its 'big city' look during its renovation in the 18th century. Also visit the park complex Jardin des Tuileries, which leads up to the Louvre; the Place Vendôme with its upmarket shopping; the Palais Garnier, an opulent 19th-century opera house; and the 17th-century Palais Royal.

Montmartre, on the north side of town, is great for exploring both day and night. Things to see include the historic Moulin de la Galette with its outdoor garden restaurant; the Sacre Coeur basilica up on the hill, with fantastic views of the city; the Père Lachaise Cemetery (east, outside city centre), one of three large cemeteries built around 1800 with the graves of numerous celebrities (Oscar Wilde, Jim

Top: Place de la Concorde, one of the most magnificent plazas in Europe.
Middle: The striking Arc de Triomphe on the Champs-Elysées by night.
Bottom: The Eiffel Tower was erected in 1889 for the World Fair.

elevator, is one of the city's major attractions. The Hôtel des Invalides, a complex crowned by the Dôme des Invalides, was built by Louis XIV for the victims of his numerous wars.

North of the Seine is probably the most magnificent boulevard in the world, the Champs-Elysées, with the Arc de Triomphe providing a great view of the streets emanating from its centre.

Morrison, Edith Piaf, Eugène Delacroix and Frédéric Chopin, for example). All the cemeteries have detailed maps available at the main entrance.

In the northern suburb of St-Denis you will find the early-Gothic church of St-Denis, the burial place of the French kings, and the Stade de France, a massive football stadium with capacity for 80,000, built for the 1998 World Cup.

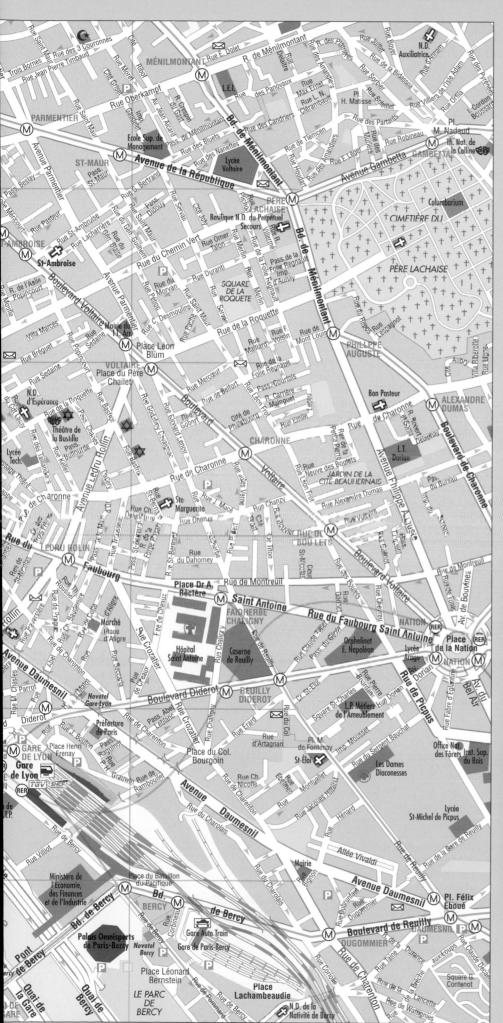

Paris

The historic centre of the 'City of Light' is relatively easy to navigate, and many sights can be reached on foot. However, you should allow yourself copious amounts of time – after all, if you fancied it, you could spend days just wandering around the Louvre.

During the Middle Ages, when Paris was arguably the most important city in Europe, three factors determined the city's development and status – the church, its royalty and the university, all of which have left their mark on the historic city centre. Out on the Île de la Cité – the city's oldest core settlement where the Romans, Merovingians and Carolingians based their dominions – stands one of France's most splendid cathedrals: Notre Dame.

As of 1400, medieval royalty focused their power on the northern banks of the Seine at the Louvre, which was begun in 1200 as part of a first ring of fortifications and developed into a magnificent residence over the centuries. On the other side of the river, in the Latin Quarter, professors and students united to establish the Sorbonne at the end of the 12th century. The riverbank, with its grand buildings, is a UNESCO World Heritage Site.

the former palace chapel of Ste-Chapelle, a high-Gothic masterpiece; the Conciergerie, part of the medieval royal palace; Pont Neuf, one of the most beautiful bridges on the Seine; and the idyllic Île St-Louis, south-east of the Île de la Cité, with its Renaissance buildings.

North of the Seine visit the Louvre, first a medieval castle, then the royal residence until the 17th century, then rebuilt and made into one of the largest art museums in the world; the Centre Pompidou, a cultural centre with exemplary modern architecture; the Hôtel de Ville, the 19th-century town hall at the Place de Grève; the Marais quarter with the romantic Place des Vosges, the avant-garde Opéra National de Paris, the Gothic church of St-Gervais-et-St-Protais, the Picasso museum, and the Hôtel Carnavalet's museum on the city's history.

Top: The illuminated Louvre pyramid was built at the end of the 20th century as part of the costly modernization of the largest art museum in the world.
Below: From the 12th to 14th centuries, the Gothic Notre Dame Cathedral was built on the Île de la Cité in the medieval city centre.

On the Île de la Cité, don't miss the early-Gothic Cathédrale Notre Dame (12th/13th centuries), where you can climb both 68-m-high (223-ft) towers;

South of the Seine go to the famous Latin Quarter; the St-Germain-des-Prés and Montparnasse Quarters and the Jardin du Luxembourg park.

Jeanne d'Arc (Joan of Arc)

Jeanne d'Arc was born in 1412, the daughter of a rich farmer in Domrémy in the Lorraine region. At the time, France had been heavily involved in the Hundred Years War with England since 1337, and the English had advanced as far as the Loire.

At the age of thirteen, Jeanne began hearing voices in her head telling her to join forces with the French heir apparent, Charles VII, and expel the English from France. After she recognized him in Chinon, despite his disguise, people started believing in her divine mission. She was then given his support and went with the French army to Orléans, which was occupied by the English. With

A golden statue of Jeanne d'Arc on the Place des Pyramids in Paris.

her help, the city was liberated on 8 May 1429.

Jeanne was also able to persuade Charles VII to follow the dangerous road to Reims to be crowned. The ceremony took place in July 1420 in the Reims cathedral. However, the farmer's daughter from Lorraine, who was now France's heroine, had enemies too. In 1430, the Burgundians, who were allied with England, succeeded in imprisoning and handing Jeanne over to the English. She was accused of heresy and witchery in Rouen in 1431 and, as Charles VII thought it to be politically incorrect to help her, condemned to be burned at the stake on 30 May 1431. The conviction was overturned in 1456 and in 1920 Jeanne d'Arc was granted sainthood.

especially lovely half-timbered house, the Maison des Acrobates, is located on the cathedral square. If you are interested in Gothic churches, pay a visit to the 12th-century St-Nicolas.

8 Cheverny This castle, built between 1620 and 1634, is still owned by the family of the builder, Henri Hurault. It is also probably thanks to this fact that the castle still contains a large part of the original, opulent interior decor. The ceiling frescoes in the dining hall and bedroom are particularly worth inspecting.

9 Chenonceaux Powerful women played a large role in the history of this romantic pleasure palace. For example, Cathérine Briçonnet supervised its construction in the early 16th century while her husband was in Italy. After Thomas Bohier's death, the building fell into the hands of the king and Henry II gave it as a gift to his beloved, Diane de Poitiers, who extended it to include a bridge over the Cher. Following Henry's death, his wife, Catherine de Medici, kept the castle for herself, and it is thanks to her idea that the Florentine-style bridge was built, including its own gallery.

After Catherine de Medici, the widow of the assasinated Henry III, Louise de Lorraine, proceeded to live a life of mourning in what was actually a very

bright and cheerful-looking castle. This spirit returned in the 18th century with the arrival of middle-class Louise Dupin, who saved the castle from the destruction of the revolution. Only very little remains of the original decor, but Renaissance furnishings have been used to give an impression of what the interior may have been like.

Located on the bridge pier is the gorgeous kitchen, where copper pots and pans still hang in an orderly fashion.

10 Amboise Perched on a hill sloping steeply into the Loire is France's first major Renaissance château. Although only parts of the construction have been preserved, they are still very impressive in their size and grandeur.

Following an expedition to Italy in 1496, Charles VIII brought back with him Italian artists, craftsmen and works of art to decorate the palace. The interiors of the mighty towers were constructed in such a way that a rider on a horse could reach up into the storey above. The Chapelle-St-Hubert is a good example of Gothic architecture. Not far from the château is the Le Clos-Lucé mansion, where Leonardo da Vinci spent the final years of his life. Francis I had originally arranged for the Italian universal genius to come to France, and a small museum displaying models of Leonardo's inventions pays homage to this influential man.

The small town located below the château, a row of houses,

and the clock tower all date back to the time of this region's heyday. From Amboise, a small road leads through the middle of the Loire Valley to Tours.

11 Tours This is the town that gave the Via Turonensis its name, and the tomb of St Martin here was an extremely important stop for St James pilgrims. Revolutionaries demolished the old St-Martin Basilica at the end of the 18th century. The new St-Martin Basilica, in neo-Byzantine style, contains the tomb of the saint, consecrated in 1890. It is an example of the monumental church architecture of the time, one that made use of many different styles.

The St-Gatien Cathedral is the city's most important historic

Romanesque church art in Poitiers and Parthenay-le-vieux

The Romanesque style of the Poitou region is typified, for the most part, by rich sculptural decorations. The facade of the former collegiate church

Top: The western facade of the Notre Dame Cathedral in Poitiers.
Bottom: A look inside the church.

of Notre Dame la Grande in Poitiers, completed in the mid 12th century, is a particularly good example of this. Above the three portals, as well as to the left and right of the large second-storey window, is an ornately sculptured series of images depicting themes from the Old and New Testament such as Adam and Eve, the prophet Moses, Jeremiah, Josiah and Daniel, the Tree of Jesse, the Annunciation, the birth of Christ, the twelve apostles and, in the gables, Christ in the Mandorla with two angels.
The church of St-Pierre in nearby Parthenay-le-Vieux was built in the late 11th century. The most striking part of this building is the eight-cornered transept tower, but the most beautiful features are the decorative figures on the facade. Samson's battle with the lion is depicted here, as well as the horseman, which is typical for the Romanesque style in Poitiers. The image of the Melusine fairy, which appears more than thirty times, is an original element.

3

4

church. The two-storey cloister provides a great view of the towers' tracery and the finely carved flying buttresses.
In some parts of the Old Town, like the Place Plumereau, you could be forgiven for thinking you were back in the Middle Ages. Charming half-timbered houses with pointed gables and often ornately carved balconies are proof of the wealth of the traders at the time. A waxworks cabinet is located in the historic rooms of the Château Royal (13th century).

12 Villandry The last of the great castles to be built in the Loire during the Renaissance (1536) fell into ruin in the 19th century and its Renaissance gardens were then made into an English-style park. The Spanish Carvallo family eventually bought it in 1906 and it is thanks to them that the castle has been renovated. More importantly, the gardens were remodelled in

the original Renaissance style. This explains why a lot of the people who visit the castle today are lovers of historic landscaping. Whether it be beds of flowers or vegetables, everything is laid out artistically and trees and hedges are perfectly trimmed into geometric shapes.

13 Azay-le-Rideau This castle on the Indre, built between 1519 and 1524, captivates visitors with the harmony of its proportions and its romantic location on an island in the river. However, it did not bring its builder, the mayor of Tours, Gilles Berthelot, much luck. Like other French kings, Francis I could not tolerate his subjects openly displaying their wealth. Without further ado, he accused the mayor of infidelity and embezzlement, and seized the castle.

14 Ussé The Château d'Ussé was built on the walls of a fortified castle in the second half of

the 15th century. With its turrets and merlons, as well as its location at the edge of the forest, it's easy to see how it was the inspiration for authors of fairy tales. The Gothic chapel houses an important work of art from the Italian Renaissance, a terracotta Madonna by the Florentine sculptor Luca della Robbia.

15 Saumur Horse lovers around the world should be very familiar with the name Saumur. The cavalry school, founded in 1763, is still France's national riding school. The castle was built in the second half of the 14th century and is located on a hillside above the city.
Today, it houses two museums, an art museum and the Musée du Cheval. In the Old Town, half-timbered houses like the town hall on the Place St-Pierre, which was created in 1508 as a patrician palace, and the numerous 17th-century villas are all worth a look. In the Gothic church of

Notre Dame de Nantilly, the side aisle, which Louis XI had built in a flamboyant style, is home to a prayer chapel that an inscription identifies as being the royal oratorio. On rainy days there are two interesting museums worth visiting: a mask museum (Saumur produces a large quantity of carnival masks) and a mushroom museum. These

1 After Versailles, the fantastic 16th-century water palace in Chenonceaux is the most visited château in France.

2 A stone bridge crosses the Loire in Amboise, home to the grand château of the same name.

3 Located on the left bank of the Indre, the 15th-century Château d'Ussé is like a fairy-tale castle made into reality.

4 Saumur – a view over the Loire to the Château de Saumur and the church tower of St-Pierre.

La Rochelle and Île de Ré

A detour to Île de Ré first takes you to La Rochelle, an important harbour town since the 11th century and considered one of France's most beautiful cities. In 1628, Cardinal Richelieu seized the town, which had for too long taken the wrong side in the political debate of the day – over 23,000 people died during the brutal occupation.

Today, its main attraction is the Atlantic harbour, where yachts bob up and down in a picture-perfect

Top: An aerial photo of Île de Ré.
Bottom: A view of the harbour at St-Martin-de-Ré.

scene. The city's best-known tourist sites are down by the Old Harbour – the Tour St-Nicolas and the Tour de la Chaîne. In times of war, an iron chain was stretched between the two towers to protect the harbour from enemy ships. The town hall (1595–1606) is built in Renaissance style with a gorgeous arcaded interior courtyard.

The Île de Ré – also known as the 'White Island' – is connected to the mainland by a 4-km-long (2.5-mile) bridge. Vineyards and salt marshes dominate the scene and are surrounded by pretty villages whose houses are decorated with lush flowers. The main town on the island is St-Martin-de-Ré, with a citadel that was constructed in the 17th century by the famous fort builder, Vauban.

St-Clément-des-Baleines near the north-western tip of the island is also interesting – it has two lighthouses worth seeing.

precious fungi are grown in the surrounding area in numerous limestone caves.

From Saumur, the westernmost point of the journey through the Loire, the road heads 11 km (7 miles) back towards Fontevraud-l'Abbey.

16 Fontevraud-l'Abbaye This abbey was founded in 1101 and existed as such until the 19th century. In the tall, bright church (consecrated in 1119) is the tomb of Eleonore of Aquitania. Southwest France 'wedded' England when she married Henry Plantagenet, later Henry II of England. Eleonore's husband and their son, Richard the Lionheart, are also buried in Fontevraud.

The 16th-century cloister is the largest in all of France. However, the abbey's most original building is the monastery kitchen, which almost looks like a chapel with six arches.

17 Chinon This castle-like château high above the banks of the Vienne played an important role in French history. This is where Jeanne d'Arc first met Charles VII and recognized him despite his costume, his courtiers, who were hiding him, and the fact that she had never seen him before. It is for this reason that the large tower, the Tour de l'Horloge, houses a small museum dedicated to her. Other

parts of the castle, originating from the 10th to 15th centuries, are only ruins now. A highlight of any visit to the castle is the view over the Vienne valley.

18 Châtellerault This town, no longer of much significance, was once an important stop for pilgrims on the Camino de Santiago. Pilgrims would enter the town, as did Jeanne d'Arc, through Porte Ste-Cathérine.

The church of St-Jacques, the destination of all pilgrims on the Camino de Santiago, was furnished with an ornate set of chimes. Some of the houses, such as the Logis Cognet, enable you to imagine what life was like in the 15th century.

19 Poitiers This old city, which was an important stop for pilgrims on the Camino de Santiago, found an important patron in Duke Jean de Berry. In the second half of the 16th century, it became a centre of spiritualism and science and its churches still show evidence of this today.

20 Marais Poitevin The marshland located west of Poitiers and stretching all the way to the coast seems to have remained stuck in time. The most important and often the only means of transport in the 'Venise Verte' (Green Venice) is one of the flat-bottomed boats.

The Romanesque churches of Parthenay-le-Vieux, some 50 km (31 miles) west of Poitiers, are well worth a visit. You have to return to Poitiers before continuing on to St-Jean-d'Angély.

21 St-Jean-d'Angély Although it has now paled into insignificance, this town was once an important destination for St James pilgrims as it was here that they had the opportunity to pay their respects to John the Baptist. Only ruins remain of the Gothic church, but a row of beautiful half-timbered houses, the Tour de la Grosse Horloge (clock tower) dating from 1406, an artistic fountain (1546), and the 17th-century abbey enable modern visitors to take a trip back in time.

From here, it's worth making a detour to the harbour town of La Rochelle on the Atlantic, where you can make an excursion out to the Île de Ré.

22 Saintes The capital of the Saintonge looks back on a long history, traces of which can still be seen today. The Arc de Germanicus, which was originally the gateway to a bridge, dates back to Roman times. When the bridge eroded, it was saved and rebuilt on the right bank. The ruins of the amphitheatre, dating back to the 1st century and today overgrown with grass,

once seated 20,000 people. There are also some impressive remains from the Middle Ages. The Abbaye aux Dames, for example, was founded in 1047, and the Romanesque church was built in the 11th and 12th centuries. The Gothic St-Pierre Cathedral was constructed in the 13th and 14th centuries and the tower was added in the 17th century. The church of St-Eutrope, dating from the late 11th century, was one of the destinations of the St James

Château Mouton-Rothschild

In the Bordelais wine region, château does not mean castle, but rather a large vineyard. One of this region's world-famous vineyard abodes is the Château Mouton-Rothschild in Pauillac on the Gironde. Predominantly upmarket Cabernet-Sauvignon grapes are grown here, on a piece of land covering about 80 ha (198 acres). Baron Philippe de Rothschild came up with the idea to make his wine bottles into small works of art. As a result, for over half a century artists have been creating labels for the property's top red wines. The list of contributing painters reads like a 'Who's Who' of modern art – Jean Cocteau (1947), Georges

to the St-Émilion appellation, which produce very high-quality wines, is the small town whose beginnings trace back to a monastery. The sizeable rock-hewn church here (9th–12th centuries), whose understated facade faces towards the pretty market place, is a special attraction. The collegiate church was built in the 12th century and its main aisle is Romanesque. By no means should you miss having a look at the very well-preserved cloister. The donjon, a relic from the royal fort, towers high above St-Émilion where the 'Jurade' wine confrérie meets to test the new wines. Every year, from the tower platform, the members ceremoniously declare the grape harvest open.

26 Bordeaux This old city on the Garonne has long been dominated by trade – predominantly the wine trade. An historic event had a profound effect on the city – in 1154, Bordeaux fell under English rule

Top: Vineyards as far as the eye can see.
Bottom: The château's wine cellar.

Braque (1955), Salvador Dalí (1958), Juan Miro (1969), Marc Chagall (1970), Pablo Picasso (1973), Andy Warhol (1975), Keith Haring (1988). You can admire these artworks, as well as many other exhibits, in the château's wine museum.

pilgrims. They prayed here in the spacious crypt at the tomb of the city's saint, Eutropius.
From Saintes you head southeast towards Cognac.

23 Cognac This town, on the banks of the Charente, today very much revolves around the drink of the same name, which expert noses will be able to catch whiffs of as they stroll through the town. The Valois Castle, from the 15th and 16th centuries, has a cognac distillery.

An exhibition at the town hall allows you to get a better understanding of the history and production of the precious brandy, which takes between five and forty years to mature. Some of the distilleries offer interesting tours of their facilities.
You head south-west from here to Pons before continuing on to Libourne.

24 Libourne This small town is a typical bastide, a fortified town, built at the time when

South-West France was an apple of discord between England and France (1150–1450). Every bastide is surrounded by a wall and has a grid-like layout and a large market square. Libourne was founded in 1270 and was for a long time a very important harbour for shipping wine out of the region. Today, it's worth taking a stroll around the Place Abel Surchamp.

25 St-Émilion Soaring out of the sea of vineyards that belong

1 Storm clouds over the harbour of La Rochelle with its 15th-century Tour de la Lanterne.

2 With its medieval houses, squares and streets, St-Émilion is a charming little town in the middle of the lovely wine region of the same name.

Côte d'Argent and Côte des Basques

The Côte d'Argent refers to the stretch of coast between the Bassin d'Arcachon and Biarritz, where it turns into the Côte Basque, straddling the French-Spanish border. Apart from excellent swimming, the Côte d'Argent also hosts a unique natural landscape.

The Dune de Pilat is Europe's highest dune, fluctuating between 105 m and 120 m (345 ft and 394 ft), with a width of 500 m (1,640 ft), and a length of 2.7 km (2 miles). The

The romantic coast of Biarritz.

Parc Ornithologique du Teich is also worth a visit.

The Côte Basque is home to one of few swanky seaside resorts in the region – Biarritz. It experienced its heyday during the Belle Époque, when Napoleon III and his wife, Eugénie, spent their holidays here. The Rocher de la Vierge (Rock of the Virgin) and its statue of the Madonna have a charming location out in the sea. A footbridge leads you out to the isolated formation. The casino and many of the hotel palaces are evidence of the glitz and glamour of Biarritz' golden age. St-Jean-de-Luz is a picturesque old town and several of its houses display the typically Basque half-timber style.

The Sun King met his bride, the Spanish Infanta Maria Theresa, for the first time here in the Maison Louis XIV. Her house, the Maison de l'Infante, is located just a little further on.

and, thanks to their huge interest in the region's wines, trade boomed. Even when Bordeaux was again part of France, it still maintained a close relationship with the British Isles.

The Place de la Comédie, with the classical columned facade of the Grand Théâtre, is an ideal place to start a stroll through the city. The Esplanade des Quinconces here is considered the largest square in Europe. You shouldn't miss seeing the city's churches. The St-André Cathedral was built between the 13th and 15th centuries and fascinates visitors with its Porte Royale, a magnificent door lavishly decorated with sculptures. Apart from the church, there is the Tour Pey-Berland, a freestanding tower. St-Michel was constructed somewhat later, in the 14th/16th centuries, and is furnished in 17th-century baroque style.

Those following in the footsteps of Camino de Santiago pilgrims should pay a visit to St-Seurin. Worshipping St-Severin (St-Seurin) was an important part of the route. The early-Romanesque crypt dates back to this time.

Bordeaux has a lot more to offer than just St James relics – the city gates of Porte de Cailhau, Porte d'Aquitaine, Porte de la Monnaie and Porte Dijeaux, for example. The Pont de Pierre (a stone bridge) and the tall, modern bridge, Pont d'Aquitaine, datingfrom 1967, are also worth a look.

Those interested in seeing the region's world-famous vineyards should make the 50-km (31-mile) journey along the Gironde to the Château Mouton-Rothschild in Pauillac.

② Les Landes This is the name given to the landscape typical of the area south of Bordeaux – flat, sandy earth with sparse pine forests. The forests are planted by hand and are still used for their lumber by-products, predominantly for the extraction of resin.

Pont-Vieux

The small town of Orthez was already of strategic importance during the Middle Ages because of its Gothic bridge over the Gave du Pau. The medieval pilgrim bridge dates back to the 13th and 14th centuries and is home to a striking bridge tower.

The region's capital is Mont-de-Marsan, located somewhat off the beaten track in the southeast and home to some interesting Romanesque houses, the 15th-century Lacataye donjon and some very pretty parks.

② Dax This small town on the Adour is one of France's most frequently visited thermal baths. Water at a temperature of 64°C (147°F) bubbles out of the Fontaine de la Néhé.

The 17th-century cathedral here is also worth seeing. The apostle gate from the earlier Gothic building is significant in an art-history context.

A visit to the Musée Borda in a beautiful city palace and a stroll along the banks of the Adour round off the visit.

If you want to go to the seaside, you can can drive 40 km (25 miles) from Dax to the southern end of the Côte d'Argent and then further on to the Côte des Basques around Biarritz.

On the other hand, those wanting to get a whiff of the mountain air in the Pyrenees should continue south-east along the spectacular route to Orthez.

② St-Jean-Pied-de-Port In the Middle Ages, this mountain

town was already an important stop for pilgrims – and the last before the strenuous crossing of the Pyrenees over the Roncesvalles Pass and across the Spanish border. 'Saint John at the Foot of the Pass' manages to preserve its medieval character even today. The banks of the Nive River are lined with houses from the 16th and 17th centuries and the Gothic church of Notre Dame du Bout du Pont.

③ Bayonne The capital of the Pays Basque is a densely settled area but it has managed to retain much of its charm in its centre with bridges on two rivers, large squares and rows of houses packed closely together around the Gothic cathedral of Ste Marie. Its city festival is famous, held every year on the second weekend in August.

1 The Bay of Biarritz with its tiny harbour and the main beach.

2 The Pont du Pierre crosses the Garonne in Bordeaux, with the striking tower of the Cathédrale St-André in the background.

Paris France's capital is, and remains, the City of Love: zest for life, art, fashion, 100 museums and exquisite cuisine all inspire romance. You definitely need more time than you think to see everything, from the Eiffel Tower, Montmartre, and the Louvre to the Champs-Elysées and Arc de Triomphe.

Versailles The 580-m-long (1,903-ft) building and the park in front of the Paris gates are some of France's most visited attractions. Versailles was the centre of power under Louis XIV's rule. Anyone looking to influence politics had to be present here.

Amboise Ruins of what was once the most important château in France lie on the banks of the Loire. Italian artists – including Leonardo da Vinci – played an important role in its construction.

Orléans This town, which was liberated in 1429 by Jeanne d'Arc, is graced by the Gothic Ste-Croix Cathedral, and has a statue of the heroine in the Place du Martroi.

La Rochelle This old harbour city is both a fishing town and a seaside resort. Arcades and quaint houses characterize the 'St-Tropez on the Atlantic'.

Blois The cathedral and the castle where Catherine de Medici spent much of her life are the focal point of this Loire town, which was once a political powerhouse.

Arcachon The great pride of the Belle-Epoque seaside resort is the Dune du Pilat, Europe's highest dune – up to 120 m (394 ft) high, 3 km (2 miles) in length and 500 m (1,640 ft) wide, it's like a small desert. The Cap Ferret headland and the fishing towns of the Arcachon Bay are also worth seeing.

Château de Chenonceaux It was mainly women who influenced the tone of this Renaissance building on the banks of the Cher in the Loire Valley.

Château de Chambord With 440 rooms, a wide moat, and scores of towers, chimneys and gables, this dream castle is truly one of a kind. Leonardo da Vinci created one of the château's seventy staircases, an intricate double-helix spiral.

Poitiers Numerous churches and the cathedral are evidence of this town's location on the Camino de Santiago.

Bordeaux This wine, trade and harbour city on the Garonne is home to a multitude of tourist attractions including the Place de la Comédie with the Grand Théâtre; Europe's largest square, the Esplanade des Quinconces; the ornate St-André Cathedral (13th–15th centuries).

The vineyards of the Médoc This region north of Bordeaux is dominated by vineyards. More than 130 wineries, often called châteaus, produce red wine.

Biarritz Winter guests made this former whaling town on the Basque coast popular in the 19th century. Its beaches and promenades still enjoy huge popularity.

Bayonne This town is the heart and soul of the French Basque region. Its Gothic cathedral, famous for its folk festival in August, is definitely worth a visit.

St-Émilion Amid the vineyards are the fortress complexes of St-Émilion, with its famous cathedral and rock-hewn church.

Lavender fields – a symbol of Provence. The plants are cultivated for their scented oil.

France and Spain

The 'Land of Light' – from Côte d'Azur to Costa Brava

The coastline along the Côte d'Azur, the Golfe du Lion and the Costa Brava could hardly be more diverse or enticing. At the southern edge of the Alps, the Côte d'Azur showcases a landscape of breathtakingly unique beauty. Provence is a paradise for nature lovers and culture enthusiasts, while the Camargue is a near pristine delta landscape. The Costa Brava gets its name from the mountains which drop away steeply into the sea.

An incredibly varied stretch of coast between Menton on the Côte d'Azur and Barcelona on the Costa Brava greets visitors with all the beauty the French Midi and the north-eastern Spanish coast have to offer.

Directly behind Monte Carlo's sea of houses and apartments are the captivating mountains of the Alpes-Maritimes, which only begin to flatten out near Nice, allowing trendier cities like Cannes and Antibes to sprawl a bit. The foothills of the Massif des Maures once again

straddle the coast beyond St-Tropez where there is really only enough room for small, picturesque villages – your search for sandy beaches will be in vain. But not to worry, you'll find them again around Hyères and the offshore islands in the area.

Wine-lovers will get their money's worth between Toulon and Cassis – the wines grown between Bandol and Le Castellet are some of the best in the Midi. Marseille then presents itself as the harbour city with two faces. Founded by the Greeks,

The Calanques cliffs near Cassis.

and later a stronghold of the Romans, its cultural history dates back 2,500 years. At the same time, it was long the gateway to the cultures on other Mediterranean shores – Europe, North Africa and the Near East are all represented in Marseille's multicultural population.

West of Marseille, in the delta between the two mouths of the Rhône, sprawls a breathtakingly beautiful wetland of ponds, marshes, meadows and plains abundant with springs, grass, and salt fields – the Camargue. North of here is where you'll discover the heart of Provence. Cities such as Arles, Avignon and Nîmes are strongholds of European cultural history with their unique examples of Roman architecture.

The Languedoc-Roussillon region begins west of the Rhône delta and stretches to the Spanish border with a mix of long

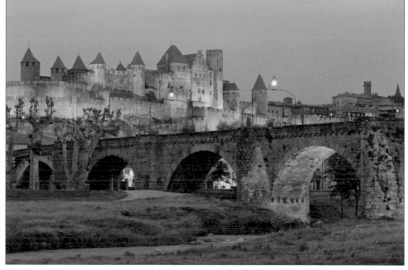

St-Tropez: The international jet set discovered this idyllic fishing town in the 1950s and since then there have been more yachts than fishing boats anchored in the harbour.

Isolated bays along the rocky coast of the Costa Brava near Cadaqués.

beaches and mountainous hinterland. The Languedoc is home to the troubadours, and the Roussillon was part of Spain until the 1659 Treaty of the Pyrenees. The Catalán legacy in this region can still be seen at every turn. Even bullfights are still held here. The Languedoc was also home to the Cathars, who broke away from the Catholic Church in the 13th century.

Between Narbonne and Carcassone in the hills of Corbières, where an invitation to taste wine should never be refused, are numerous ruins of the proud castles that once stood here. With its fortress complexes, Carcassonne takes you back in time to the Middle Ages. South of Narbonne, near Leucate, marks the start of long, brilliantly white sandy beaches stretching to the Franco-Spanish border and the eastern foothills of the Pyrenees.

The last of the French villages before reaching Spain are self-assured fishing villages virtually embedded into the mountains. The Costa Brava, as this coastline is called, owes its name to the steep seaside cliffs at the eastern end of the Pyrenees. Bravo also means 'brave' or 'outstanding' in Spanish, so travellers should expect much more than just a wild coast.

The further south you go, the bigger the beaches become and the more towns and villages appear. The Catalán capital, Barcelona, is Spain's second-largest city. Carthaginians, Romans, Visigoths and Moors have all left their legacy here, making the city into a European metropolis with a special Catalán charm. The numerous art-nouveau buildings by Gaudí and Domènech i Montaner are quite spectacular. Life pulses day and night on the Ramblas, Barcelona's pedestrian zone.

The Old Town of Carcassonne enclosed by a double wall.

The Principality of Monaco

The area where the skyscrapers of 'Manhattan on the Côte d'Azur' soar above Monaco's modest 190 ha (222 acres) was first settled by the Greeks, followed by the Romans, and then later ruled by the powerful maritime city-state of Genoa.

In 1297, the coastal strip came under the rule of the mighty Grimaldi family, aristocrats from Genoa who later created the principality in 1612. The Grimaldis built their residence on a rock south of the harbour and have been able to retain their mini principality to this day.

Monaco owes its wealth to Prince Charles III, who built a casino on the headland north of the harbour in 1865. The revenues were so great that five years later the prince was able to abolish all taxes and thus lay

The Monaco casino.

the second foundation for the small state's successful history, a tax haven. In his honour, the rock on which the casino was built was given the name of Monte Carlo in 1878, a name that now applies to the entire region north of the harbour.

The casinos and the tax privileges guarantee Monaco's incessant growth. Nowhere else in Europe do so many Rolls Royces cruise the streets, nowhere else in the world are there so many millionaires living in such a small area, and nowhere else in the world will you find so many tax evaders. Tennis players and film stars alike ensure that the fairy tale of perpetual wealth never ends, and that the yachts in the harbour never get smaller.

The most important sights are the Palais de Monaco (16th–17th centuries), the houses of government; the casino, built by Charles Garnier in 1878; the Musée Océanographique, one of Europe's best aquariums; and the Jardin Exotique with a unique cactus collection.

Along the north-western Mediterranean coast – our dream route from Menton to Barcelona takes you on forays into the hinterland of Provence, leads you along impressive rocky coasts, white beaches, the Rhône delta and the foothills of the Pyrenees, and passes through famous seaside resorts on a journey that includes 2,000-year-old towns in a region with unmatched cultural history.

❶ Menton Rich Englishmen discovered the pleasant climate of the Côte d'Azur quite late – around 1870. But they didn't waste any time. Villas and magnificent hotels from this Belle Époque recall the glory days of their 'winter residences' between the Alps and the sea. The most beautiful view over Menton and the bay here can be seen from the cemetery above the city. Its attractions include the baroque Church of St-Michel, the Register Office in the town hall with frescoes by Jean Cocteau, and the Musée Cocteau in a 17th-century fort. Just a few kilometres beyond Menton is the Principality of Monaco, where a steep street heads into the mountainous interior towards Èze.

❷ Èze This tiny village sits on the top of a 427-m-high (1,401-ft) rock formation overlooking the Mediterranean Sea as if from a throne. It is one of Provence's most beautiful medieval fortified villages, the so-called 'villages perchés'.

A thick stone wall surrounds the houses, which are clustered around a castle donjon high in the mountains. An exotic garden was created around the former fort, and the view from here reaches as far as Corsica on a clear day.

Following the N7 towards Nice, the route heads back along the sea to Villefranche-sur-Mer.

❸ Cap Ferrat In the shadows of mighty pines and hidden behind high walls, the magnificent villas of millionaires cling to the coastline of Cap Ferrat, which drops steeply into the sea. The Fondation Ephrussi de Rothschild, probably the most beautiful villa on the Cap Ferrat peninsula, is even open to the public. The stately building, in gorgeous gardens, displays the furnishings bequethed by Baroness Rothschild.

Travel information

Route profile
Length: approx. 1,300 km (808 miles), excluding detours
Time required: 2–3 weeks
Start: Menton, France
End: Barcelona, Spain
Route (main locations): Menton, Monaco, Nice, Toulon, Marseille, Aix-en-Provence, Arles, Avignon, Orange, Nîmes, Camargue, Narbonne, Carcassonne, Perpignan, Barcelona

Traffic information:
Drive on the right in both countries. The speed limit for urban areas is 60 km/h (37 mph), 90 km/h (56 mph) on rural roads, and 130 km/h (80 mph) on highways (120 km/h/75 mph in Spain). In rainy conditions, the speed

limit for rural roads is 80 km/h (50 mph) and 100 km/h (62 mph) for highways. The 'right before left' rule almost always applies in built-up areas in both France and Spain!

When to go:
Spring and autumn are the best seasons for the Mediterranean coast. Summer is often very hot, while winter can be quite cold, rainy and even snowy, particularly higher up.

Information:
France
General: *www.france.com*
Provence: *www.beyond.fr*
Spain
General: *www.spain.info*
Costa Brava:
www.costabrava.org

red rocks, cliffs, many gorges and secluded bays.

7 **Fréjus** The Roman legacy of this settlement, founded by Julius Caesar in 46 BC, is still clearly visible in the cityscape. Parts of the Roman city wall, the aqueduct and, most importantly, the amphitheatre have all been very well-preserved. The area around the Cathédrale St Léone is also worth seeing.

The fortified church and the monastery were founded in the

1 The marina in Menton on the eastern Côte d'Azur.

2 The famous Promenade des Anglais in Nice is 8 km (5 miles) long and separates the beach from the Old Town.

3 This view of the village of Èze shows its exposed location.

4 The château in Mandelieu-la-Napoule, a spa resort west of Cannes, dates back to the 14th century.

5 Red cliffs dominate the Corniche de l'Esterel between St-Raphaël and Agay.

6 The view of the Old Town in Cannes on the slope of Mont Chevalier.

Antibes and Picasso

Antibes dates back to the ancient Greeks, who originally founded it as Antipolis. It has been a fortress town throughout its history, the harbour and Fort Carrée being creations of French architect Vauban.

Medieval towers and the beautiful Grimaldi Castle dominate the Antibes cityscape, and the old watchtower is now used as the bell tower for the Eglise de l'Immaculée Conception.

The Old Town of Antibes.

The Château Grimaldi (12th century) was the residence of the Grimaldis of Monaco between 1385 and 1609, and the city allowed Pablo Picasso to use some rooms as his studio in the autumn of 1946, after the war, to 'free himself from the evils of civilization'. He produced 150 works in a very short time, which he then gave to what is now the Musée Picasso in return for the hospitality.

4 **Nice** The 'unofficial' capital of the Côte d'Azur is a city of contrasts – the grand boulevards try to rekindle the memories of the Belle Époque while parts of the Old Town are still like an Italian village. The Greeks founded Nikaia here, the 'Victorious City', in the 5th century BC, but the Romans preferred the hills further up for their township of Cemenelum, today Cimiez.

The most powerful icon of Nice is the Promenade des Anglais, which is directly on the sea. Wealthy British made Nice their retirement home in the mid 19th century and the most impressive mansions from that era are the famous Hotel Négresco and the Palais Masséna.

The main square in the Old Town, with its maze of small alleyways and Italian-style houses, is the Cour Saleya, with a remarkable flower and vegetable market. The castle hill provides a great view over the Old Town and the sea.

The city's most interesting museums are the Musée d'Art Contemporain, the Musée Chagall and the Musée Matisse in Cimiez, which displays works by the artist, who moved to Nice in 1916. Some of the most impressive Roman ruins in Nice make up the 67-m-long (220-ft), 56-m-wide (184-ft) arena, which used to hold some 5,000 Romans. The city's most exotic landmark is the Cathédrale Orthodoxe Russe St-Nicolas (1912).

After passing the airport, the route now leaves the coastal road for a trip into Provence's hilly interior. For art lovers, it is worth taking the 10-km (6-mile) detour into St-Paul-de-Vence, a medieval town where the Fondation Maeght displays modern artwork. From the coast, the D2085 heads to Grasse, a perfume manufacturing centre.

5 **Grasse** Perfume brought this town its early prosperity, traces of which can still be seen in the medieval alleys and streets of the Old Town. The International Perfume Museum will tell you everything you wanted to know about the manufacture of these valuable essences, and the large factories hold daily tours. From Grasse, the N85 heads back to the sea towards Cannes, one of the swankier places on the already swanky Côte d'Azur.

6 **Cannes** This city is of course known for its annual film festival, where the world's rich and famous gather on the Boulevarde la Croisette. Cap d'Antibes, with the holiday resorts of Juan-les-Pins and Antibes, is just 11 km (7 miles) from here.

The N98 heads from Cannes to Fréjus along the Corniche d'Esterel, which is one of the highlights of the journey with its

The Romans in southern France

When the Romans elected to overrun southern France, the decision was strategic in nature – after the victory over Carthage in the 2nd century BC they needed a safe land route to Spain. The hammer fell in 102 BC when Marius crushed the Teutons at the foot of the St-Victoire Massif. The resulting region was called Aquae Sextiae Saluvorium – Aix-en-Provence.

Soon after, the Greek settlements throughout the entire region were remodelled to reflect the design of Rome. The streets were built according to an ordered grid pattern using blocks approximately 100 m (328 ft) in length. This layout can most clearly be seen in Orange and Arles.

A city's centre point was its forum, a square lined with colonnades around which temples and other public buildings were grouped. Extravagant stages and large amphitheatres satis-

The Pont du Gard was built around 19 BC and towers 48 m (157 ft) over the Gard. Once part of the aqueduct between Uzès and Nîmes, today it is a UNESCO World Heritage Site.

fied the Romans' need for cultural entertainment.

The triumphal arches, public baths and aqueducts continue to provide testimony to the architectural and engineering mastery of the Roman occupation army.

12th century, and the older baptistry dates back as far as the 5th century.

❽ St-Tropez Between Fréjus and Hyères, thick pine, oak and chestnut forests line the coast, and the hills drop away steeply into the sea, leaving no room for townships of any size on the Corniche des Maures. The coastal road is nothing less than spectacular here, and although it winds partly into the hills it continually provides stunning views of the sea. Small villages that were once dedicated to fishing are nestled tidily into the small bays, many of them retaining most of their original charm.

St-Tropez is no exception. In this town – which first became famous after the film *And God Created Woman* (1956) with Brigitte Bardot – it's all about seeing and being seen. The image of the extravagant life in the film captivated the youth of the world and ultimately drew mass tourism to the sleepy coastal town.

❾ Hyères This small town east of Toulon is the oldest seaside resort on the coast. The medieval Vieille Ville, with its

Place Massillon, is delightful. The old castle ruins provide an amazing panoramic view of the coast. Offshore from Hyères are the Iles d'Hyères, a group of islands that President Pompidou ordered the French state to make into a nature preserve in 1971. A visit to Porquerolles allows you to imagine how the entire Côte d'Azur must have looked before tourism began.

❿ Toulon The capital of the Département Var owes its importance to the large natural harbour here, which continues to be an important marine base. Architect Vauban built Toulon into a war harbour in the 17th century under King Louis XIV.

⓫ Route de Crêtes La Ciotat is the starting point for a trip over the Route des Crêtes to Cassis. The 'Mountain Ridge Road' leads over the steep slopes of the Montagne de la Canaille and provides magnificent views of both the sea and the country. The small harbour town of Cassis has been able to retain much of its early charm, particularly in the old alleys directly behind the harbour. The shops and businesses give an insight

into the original Midi way of life. West of Cassis, white limestone walls rise straight out of the crystal blue waters. You can take a boat ride to the cliffs from Cassis. If you take the rural road N 559 direct towards Marseille and turn left, you'll see narrow access roads leading to three bays that are worth seeing – Port Miou, Port Pin and En-Vau.

To drive into the heart of Provence, take the highway or the N559 to Aubagne and then the N96 to Aix-en-Provence.

⓬ Marseille (see p. 97).

⓭ Aix-en-Provence The Romans originally founded the colony of Aquae Sextiae Saluvorium on the former Celtic-Ligurian township of Entremont in 122 BC – what is now Aix-en-Provence. This spa and university town eventually became the capital of Provence at the end of the 12th century and remained so for hundreds of years. It also developed into a city of artists and academics.

The Old Town is tucked between the Cours Mirabeau, an avenue of sycamores with a gorgeous 18th-century city palace, and the Cathedral of St-Sauveur with

a baptistry from the Merovingian era.

Other attractions include the town hall (17th-century), the Musée des Tapisseries and the Atelier de Paul Cézanne. A favourite source of inspiration of the city's most famous son is the Mont St-Victoire in the eastern section of the town, which is also worth a detour to see for yourself.

The shortest connection to Arles heads along the A8 and A7 to Salon-de-Provence and from there crosses the eastern part of the Rhône delta.

⓮ Arles The gateway to the Camargue was an area settled by the Celts, the Greeks and the Romans. Emperor Constantine had a splendid residence here, where he once summoned a council in AD 314.

Today, Arles is still home to impressive and important buildings from Roman times – the amphitheatre, a grandiose oval

1 Les Arènes, a former Roman amphitheatre in Arles.

2 The view of St-Tropez from the walls of the citadel.

Marseille

The second-largest city in France and the country's most important harbour town boasts a long history of 2,500 years. Its significance as an important gateway to North Africa is reflected in its multi-cultural population.

Marseille was originally founded as Massalia by Greeks from Asia Minor who built the city on the hill where Notre Dame de la Garde now stands. It then came under the yoke of the Romans, with Caesar eventually conquering the Greek republic in 49 BC. The harbour city experienced its first big boom in the 12th century when legions of crusaders embarked from here on their journeys to Jerusalem and the Holy Land. For the next few centuries, Marseille was the most important harbour in the entire Mediterranean.

The heart of Marseille continues to beat in the old harbour quarter. It marks the beginning of the city's main road, the Canebière, which connects the harbour with the rest of the city and was once the icon of a lively town. The entrance to the old harbour is flanked on the north side by the Fort St-Jean and on the south side by the Fort St-Nicolas.

The best view over the harbour and the city is from the Plateau de la Croix in front of the Basilica of Notre Dame de la Garde, Marseille's most visible landmark. Another good vista point is the rock peak of Château d'If, which

Notre Dame de la Garde watches over the harbour city of Marseille.

looks out over Marseille from across the harbour.

Other attractions include the Basilique St-Victor, a 5th-century church with early-Christian sarcophagi and sculptural fragments in its crypt; Basilique de Notre Dame de la Garde (19th century), a neo-Byzantine church with a gold-plated figure of Mary on the bell tower and mosaics inside and the Chateau d'If (1516–28) on the rock in front of the harbour, accessed from the Quai des Belges. The citadel was the state jail from 1580.

Museums include Vieille Charité, Musée des Docks Romains, Musée du Vieux Marseille, and Musée Grobet-Labadié with relics of the 19th century.

Roussillon in the Luberon range was the centre for ochre mining at the end of the 19th century. Over fifteen different shades were obtained from the rock quarries near the town. Some of these old quarries can be explored on hiking trails.

1

2

3

4

Detour

Luberon and Haute Provence

East of Avignon, halfway between the Alps and the Mediterranean, is the sprawling limestone Luberon massif. The rocky region is home to lonely oak forests, small mountain villages and ancient stone huts, which all add to its natural beauty. The mountains, which reach 1,125 m (3,691 ft) in places, still contain wide swathes of uninhabited land where over 1,000 different types of plants thrive. The Parc Naturel Régional du Luberon was established in 1977 to protect the vegetation.

However, the seclusion of many parts of the Luberon today belies the fact that this tertiary limestone range has been settled by humans for thousands of years. In the Middle Ages, this place was home to villages nestled in vales and hollows, with thick-walled houses and churches that also doubled as refuges. Inhabitants of the region lived on meagre agricultural cultivation. When incomes were no longer sufficient, the villages in the northern sections were abandoned.

One of the symbols of the Luberon are some 3,000 'bories', unique one- or two-storey stone huts located seemingly randomly in the fields either on their own or in picturesque groups. The bories were made using lime slabs without mortar and were used by farmers as stalls and sheds.

During construction, each row of stones was staggered a little towards the middle so that when a height of about 3–4 m (10–13 ft) was reached, the final opening on top could be closed with a single slab. The most beautiful bories are found around Gordes, at the edge of the Plateau de Vaucluse on the north side of the Luberon.

Nestled into a hilly knoll like a picture postcard, Gordes welcomes visitors with arcaded lanes and a 16th-century castle. In the south is the Village des Bories with about twenty restored bories.

Another of the Luberon's landmarks are its ochre quarries, which are grouped around the picturesque tourist area of Roussillon. One of the most impressive is the now closed quarry at Sentier des Ochres.

One understands the partially dry climate of the Luberon after a visit to Fontaine de Vaucluse. Here, in a grotto at the foot of a massive rock formation is the source of the Sorgue River, the largest spring in France and one of the largest karst springs in the world with up to 90,000 litres (409,090 gal) of water bubbling up from the mountains of the Luberon and the Vaucluse per second.

Hidden in a small gorge on the Plateau de Vaucluse is a very different sort of attraction – the Abbey de Sénanque. Founded in 1148 by Cistercians, the abbey had its heyday in the early 13th century and was destroyed in 1544. It wasn't until 1854 that seventy-two monks took the risk of rebuilding it. Lavender fields surround the monastery with its church and cloister.

To observe the Luberon from above, hike up the 1,125-m (3,691-ft) Mourre Nègre, east of Apt. The 1,909-m (6,263-ft) Mont Ventoux is the highest point in Provence and also provides great views. You can get there on foot or by car. The diverse vegetation here is impressive, from lavender fields and vineyards to oak, beech and pine forests and bare rock mounds with cushion plants.

1 Lavender fields surround the 12th-century Abbaye de Sénanque.

2 An isolated homestead in Haute Provence at the foot of the Vaucluse Mountains.

3 A symbol of Provence – endless rows of blossoming lavender fields.

4 Fields of sunflowers dominate the Luberon along with vineyards and wheat fields.

The horses of the Camargue

Covering a marsh, meadow and grasslands area of roughly 140,000 ha (345,940 acres), the delta between the two main forks of the mouth of the Rhône is one of the largest wetlands in Europe. Agriculture – predominantly rice cultivation – is concentrated on the northern part of the Camargue, while salt is extracted in the flat lagoons of the south-eastern section.

The southern part, on the other hand, is a nature paradise not found anywhere else in Europe. The delta's grassy meadows are home to not only the well-known Camargue horses and Camargue bulls, but also to numerous water and marsh birds – around 10,000 pairs of flamingos breed in the marshes, the largest of which is the Etang de Vaccarés. Twice a year, more than 350 species of

Wild Camargue horses.

birds stop at the Parc Ornithologique du Pont de Grau in the Camargue's south-west.

The black Camargue bulls are distinguished by their lyre-shaped horns. The white Camargue horses, semi-white thoroughbreds found in the Solutré cave paintings, often frolic among the bulls. Their physical characteristics include a compact body, angular head and thick mane, and they are born black or dark brown in color only growing their white coat after the age of five. If the wild horses are broken in to saddles and bridles at a young age, they can be perserving riding animals and very useful to herdsmen for controlling herds of cattle. A number of guided tours offer even amateur riders the chance to go for a gallop into the marshes, to the beaches or to see the bull herds, allowing people to experience many parts of the Camargue that would be otherwise inaccessible.

structure about 137 m (446 ft) by 107 m (351 ft) wide with a capacity of 20,000; and the theatre, which could fit an impressive 12,000 people into its semicircle. The tidy Romanesque Church of St-Trophime is a masterpiece of Provencal stonemasonry, with a portal that dates back to 1190. The Romanesque-Gothic cloister adjacent to the church is considered the most beautiful in all of Provence.

From Arles, a rural road heads north-east to one of Provence's best-known villages, Les Baux.

⑮ Les Baux-de-Provence This stone village is perched on a 900-m-long (2,953-ft) by 200-m-wide (656-ft) rocky ridge that rises dramatically out of the modest Alpilles range. In the Middle Ages, troubadours performed their courtly love songs in the once proud fort of Les Baux. The fort's unique location on a rock combined with the gorgeous view over the expanses of the Camargue and

the Rhône delta draw countless visitors to this car-free town every year.

From Les Baux, the road crosses the Alpilles to St-Rémy, a 24-km-long (15-mile) mountain range between Rhône and Durance.

⑯ St-Rémy-de-Provence Nostradamus was born in this quintessential Provencal town in 1503, and van Gogh painted his picture of the cornfield and cypresses here in 1889. St-Rémy's predecessor was the old city of Glanum, about 1 km (0.6 miles) south of the present-day centre. An 18-m-high (59-ft) mausoleum dates back to this time and the Arc Municipal traces back to the time of Emperor Augustus.

⑰ Avignon This former papal city dominates the left bank of the Rhône and is still surrounded by a 4.5-km-long (3-mile) city wall. The Rocher des Doms and the enormous Palais des Papes (Papal Palace) are an impressive sight even from a distance.

Seven French popes resided here between 1309 and 1377, the time of the Papal Schism. The last 'antipope' did not flee his palace until 1403. The mighty fort-like Palais des Papes was built during this century-long schism, but next to nothing remains of the once ostentatious interior decor.

The famous bridge, Pont St-Bénézet (also known as Pont d'Avignon), was built in 1177, and four of its original twenty-two arches still stand today. From Aix, the journey heads north to two more of Europe's most beautiful Roman constructions. Near Sorgues, the D17 turns off towards Châteauneuf-du-Pape. The popes of Avignon built yet another castle here in the 14th century. Today, the wine from this region is one of the best in the Côtes du Rhône region. If you have enough time, you should make a detour into the Luberon or Villeneuve-les-Avignon on the way to Orange (see p. 99).

⑱ Orange Emperor Augustus founded this location as Arausio in 35 BC. The theatre was built soon after, and today it is one of the most beautiful Roman works in Provence. The large stage wall is 103 m (338 ft) wide and 38 m (125 ft) high.

On the north side of the city is the third-largest triumphal arch of its kind, with a height of 22 m (72 ft), a width of 21 m (69 ft) and a thickness of 8 m (26 ft). Travelling south-west along the A9 you reach the Pont du Gard, a famous Roman aqueduct.

⑲ Nîmes This city of temples, public baths and theatres was founded in AD 16, also by Emperor Augustus. The Romans' most impressive building is the amphitheatre, with an oval arena and tiered stone benches that seated 25,000 guests. The Maison Carrée, from the second and third centuries AD, is one of Europe's best-preserved Roman temples, with columns and decorative friezes. Many public baths,

Canal du Midi

The dream of connecting the Mediterranean to the Atlantic existed for many years but wasn't made a reality until Paul Riquet, an engineer from Béziers, took on the task between 1666 and 1681. With the 240-km-long (149-mile) Canal du Midi he connected the Mediterranean harbour town of Sète to the industrial city of Toulouse, which he in turn connected to the Atlantic via the Garonne River, navigable from Toulouse onwards.

The canal, with its countless dams, aqueducts, bridges and locks, was an engineering masterpiece for the 17th century and, with regard to trade, became the backbone of goods transport in the Languedoc region. Today, the canal is a romantic waterway for leisure skippers for whom the French way of life is more important than a quick journey.

The Canal du Midi is a UNESCO World Heritage Site.

Houseboats can be rented in Sète, Béziers, Narbonne, Castelnaudary, Carcassonne and Toulouse, and they indeed make for some interesting excursions. The journey is done at a leisurely pace and in some parts passes beneath long avenues of sycamores, through impressive landscapes and grand vineyards, and near cultural attractions.

Along the way, there is still time for fishing, swimming or simply relaxing. A boat licence is not required to charter a boat, as all important instructions are given at the start.

24 Narbonne This town was once the most significant Roman harbour in the area. The Horreum, an underground granary built in the first century BC, is visible evidence of this time. The Cathédrale St-Just, with its beautiful sculptures and colourful stained glass windows, dates back to the 13th century. The Palais des Archevêques is a fort-like complex with massive towers (14th century). Some 60 km (37 miles) west of Narbonne is Carcassonne, a prime example of medieval fortress architecture.

25 Carcassonne This city on the steep bank of the Aude is visible from quite a distance. Its double walls with distinctive merlons and towers date back to King Louis IX, who began construction in the 13th century. Porte Narbonnaise takes you to the Old Town, where the most

Pont du Gard

This 2,000-year-old bridge at 49 m (161 ft) in height is the highest bridge ever built by the Romans and probably the best example of Roman bridge construction. The 'bridge' was actually also an aqueduct carrying water from Uzès to Nîmes. It was in operation for about 500 years.

temples and a theatre (today a park) are concentrated around the Jardin de la Fontaine. About 20 km (12 miles) north-east of Nîmes is the Pont du Gard. From Nîmes, the route heads along the north-western edge of the Camargue to Aigues-Mortes.

20 Aigues-Mortes This town impresses visitors with the mighty walls of its fort, which are still completely intact. Aigues-Mortes, or 'Place of Dead Water', was constructed by Louis XI in the 13th century to consolidate his power on the Mediterranean coast. One part of the city wall can still be accessed. The Tour de Constance provides the best view over the city and the Camargue.

21 Saintes-Maries-de-la-Mer A 30-km-long (19-mile) road heads through the Camargue to the département capital, Les Saintes-Maries-de-la-Mer, well-known for the gypsy pilgrimage held every year in May. The Roman church here looks like

a medieval castle with its battlements and crenellated platform.

22 Montpellier The capital of the Département Hérault is home to France's oldest Botanic Garden, among other things. The focal point of the city is the Place de la Comédie, with a 19th-century opera house. Its most important attractions include the 17th-century patrician houses.

23 Béziers The route now heads through Montepellier to this lovely city on the Canal du Midi. The town's most recognizable landmark is the massive Cathédrale St-Nazaire (14th century), which is perched like a fort on a mountain above the city.

1 Along with the Cathédrale St-Nazaire, the historic fort town of Carcassonne has been listed as a UNESCO World Heritage Site.

2 Some of France's best wines are grown in the mountainous hinterland of the Languedoc.

3 Visible from a distance – the Cathédrale St-Nazaire, the landmark of Béziers on the Canal du Midi. This Romanesque-Gothic church was built between the 12th and 14th centuries. In the foreground is the Pont Vieux (13th century) over the River Orb.

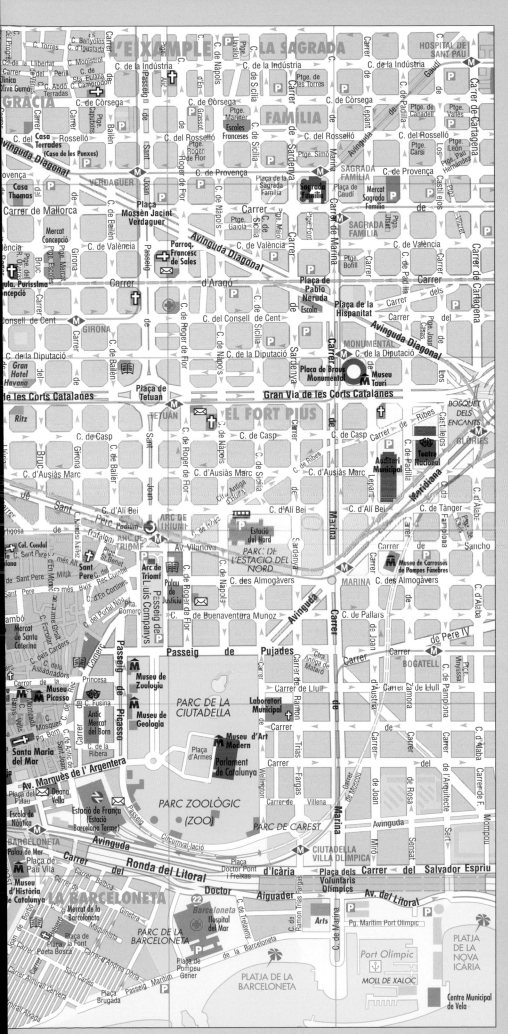

Barcelona

The capital of Catalonia, with its striking monuments, exciting nightlife and beautiful walks along the harbour and the sea, combines cosmopolitan flair with independent local tradition. Of course, it is also the city where Antoní Gaudí erected his largest and most compelling architectural feats.

Madrid's eternal competitor has a history that spans more than 2,000 years. Founded by the Romans, it was later conquered in 236 BC by the Carthaginian Hamilka Barcas, who named it Barcino. Control over this Mediterranean city changed hands between the Visigoths in 415, the Arabs in 713 and the Franks in 803.

When the kingdoms of Catalonia and Aragon were united (1137), it rose to become an important Spanish harbour and trading city. It unsuccessfully tried to become independent from Spain in the 17th century, and during the Spanish Civil War in the 20th century, Barcelona sided with the Republicans – against the eventual victor, Franco.

Towards the end of the 19th century, a completely new style of art and architecture developed in Barcelona – Modernism, the Catalán version of art nouveau, which has shaped the city's contemporary image like no other. Apart from Antoní Gaudí, the most important figures in this movement were architects Josep Puig i Cadalfalch and Lluís Domènech i Montaner. Many of their buildings are found in the Eixample neighbourhood.

The best views of the city are seen from Montjuic in the south, or the 532-m-high (1745-ft) Tibidabo in the west, both of which are accessed by cable car. Particularly worth seeing are the Barri Gòtic, the oldest, elevated part of the city; the medieval square; Plaça del Rei with the palace of the Catalán and Castilian kings; Palau Real Major; the mighty Gothic cathedral; La Seu with its crypt and cloister where geese traditionally guard the tombs; Plaça del Pi, a square full of atmosphere; Las Ramblas, Catalonia's most famous pedestrian and shopping strip; the nostalgic market hall of La Boqueria (the 'gorge') with a wide range of products; Museu Nacional d'Art de Catalunya, whose collection of Romanesque frescoes and altar paintings is internationally reputed; Museu Picasso, with 3,600 works by the artist, who studied in Barcelona; and the Museu Maritim, a maritime museum in old shipbuilding halls.

The city's most magnificent building, and Antoní Gaudí's (1852–1926) masterpiece is the huge, still-incomplete church of La Sagrada Familia with its flamboyant, deeply symbolic design. Gaudí's other works include the counts' private residence of Palau Güell in the Barri Xines; the apartment blocks of Casa Milà, with bizarre sculptural decorations and a magical roof landscape; Casa Calvet and Casa Batlló in the modernist Eixample; and the Avinguda de

Gaudí, with its wide avenues very much in keeping with the great architect's style. Palau Güell and Casa Milà are UNESCO World Heritage Sites.

Domènech i Montaner has various works throughout the city, including:

Top: La Sagrada Familia by Gaudí.
Middle: Palau de la Música Catalana.
Bottom: Las Ramblas, Barcelona's 'pedestrian mall'.

Casa de l'Ardiaca, Casa Lleó Morera, Palau de la Música Catalana, Fundació Antoni Tàpies, Illa de la Discòrdia, Hospital de la Santa Creu i de Sant Pa and Museo de Zoologia.

Dalí Museum

Salvador Dalí (1904–89) is without question the favourite son of the city of Figueres. The artist, a prominent ambassador of surrealism, built his own museum here in the old glass-domed city theatre, which he bought

Inside the Dalí Museum in Figueres.

himself. You'll not only find numerous works from all of his different periods, but there are also portraits and busts of Dalí himself – without any false sense of modesty.

important buildings are the Château Comtal and the Basilique St-Nazaire, home to France's most beautiful stained-glass windows. The castle, a mighty fort inside a fort, was constructed in the 12th century and has five defence towers.
The next part of the journey heads towards Perpignan along the D118 as far as Quillan, and it's worth making a detour on the D117 to the Château de Peyrepertuse, probably the most impressive Cathar castle ruins in the Corbières hills.

26 Perpignan The capital of Roussillon had its heyday under the kings of Mallorca in the 13th and 14th centuries. The fortified Palais des Rois de Majorque, picturesquely built around an arcaded courtyard, is evidence of this time. The two-storey chapel, a Gothic masterpiece with Moor-

ish elements, is also a real dazzler. The Cathédrale de St-Jean was begun in 1324 and completed in 1509 and the houses on the palm-lined River Têt promenade are painted in colourful hues. Catalán influence is particularly noticeable in summer in Perpignan. The Place de la Loge becomes a stage for Sardana, a Catalán dance in which both young and old participate. You'll also find the most beautiful building in the city here, the Loge de Mer, built in 1397.
At the point where the Pyrenees meet the Mediterranean, the coastal road snakes along the red (vermillion) rocks of the Côte Vermeille, where ancient fishing villages are tucked into picturesque bays. The most significant of these old towns are Argelès-Plages, Cerbère and Banyuls on the French side and Portbou on the Spanish side.

27 Cadaqués One of the most beautiful fishing villages on the Costa Brava, which stretches from Empordà to Blanes, is behind the Coll de Perafita and can only be reached on a narrow side road. Cadaqués is home to tidy white houses and a stunning 16th-century baroque church. The Museu Perrot Moore has a collection of European art from the 15th to 20th centuries.
North of Cadaqués, the cape of Creus is the last of the Pyrenees foothills and also the eastern-most point of the Iberian Peninsula. The Parc Natural del Cap de Creus combines nature and sea and is a vast uninhabited region. The Greeks were some of the first to recognize the beauty of the Badia de Roses with its long beaches. From here it's worth making a detour to the Dalí museum in Figueres. Continuing south, you cross a plain where

1

Béziers This city, dominated by the Cathédrale St-Nazaire (14th century), has an interesting regional museum.

Pont du Gard The 49-m-high (161-ft) bridge was built by the Romans over 2,000 years ago and also served as a water channel. For 500 years it supplied the citizens of Nîmes with cool mountain water.

Arles This city, located at the gateway to the Camargue, was Vincent van Gogh's temporary place of residence and has many Roman buildings. The amphitheatre has a capacity for 20,000 people.

Carcassonne This city is encircled by two protective walls dating back to the 13th century. It is also home to the 12th-century Château Comtal Castle.

Nîmes The most impressive buildings in this city, which was founded in the 16th century, are the amphitheatre with a former seating capacity of 25,000, and the Maison Carrée, one of Europe's best-preserved Roman temples. Other sites include the Romanesque Cathédrale Notre Dame et St-Castor and the 18th-century Jardin de la Fontaine.

Tossa de Mar This former Roman city is located in one of the most beautiful areas on the Costa Brava. Below the town is a lovely bay and beach.

Cadaqués This fishing village on the Costa Brava captivates visitors with its white houses and a mighty baroque church.

Avignon A mile-long wall encircles this city on the Rhône River – the city of the Papal Schism (13th–14th centuries). Behind it tower the Rocher des Doms and the enormous Palais des Papes.

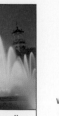

Barcelona Catalonia's proud capital has a Gothic old town as well as numerous quarters in the characteristic Modernism style – art nouveau. Here we see the Museu Nacional d'Art de Catalunya (1929).

Camargue Black bulls, semi-wild white horses, huge mountains of salt and flocks of flamingos and other unique birds are typical of the vast Rhône delta.

there is an amazing view of the eastern Pyrenees.

28 Costa Brava Pals, the most beautiful village on the entire Costa Brava, is located just north and inland of Palafrugell. It enchants visitors with its quaint back alleys. Back on the coast is one holiday resort after another. Around Palamós are some isolated bays and beaches, but Platja d'Aro is lined with high-rise hotels. The medieval old town of Tossa de Mar is a great place for a stroll while the famous Botanical Gardens of Mar i Murtra rise high above the town of Blanes.

29 Barcelona (see pp. 102–103). Our journey ends here, in Spain's second-largest city.

1 Cadaqués on the Costa Brava. Dalí spent many years of his life in the Port Lligat area.

Luberon The limestone massif, up to 1,125 m (3,691 ft) high, is known for its flora and fauna. Typical of the region are bories, huts and stalls built without mortar at the edge of the vineyards and lavender fields. Other sights include the ochre quarries of Roussillon and the Vaucluse spring

Menton Grand villas and hotels in Belle Époque style define the 'winter residence' once so prized by the English. Its attractions are the baroque Church of St-Michel, the Register Office in the town hall with frescoes by Jean Cocteau, and the Musée Cocteau in a 17th-century fort.

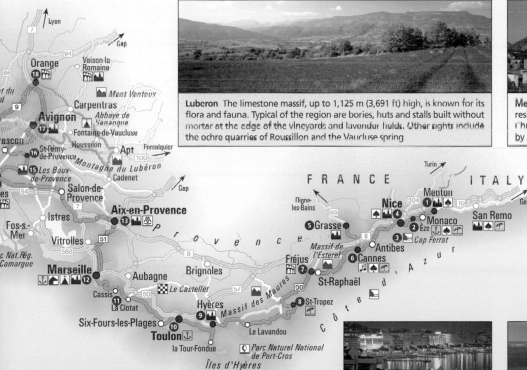

Monaco The principality is a mix of high-rise and grand buildings including the famous casino, the cathedral and the Grimaldi palace. 'Monte Carlo' is actually a rock formation that juts out into the Mediterranean on a headland below a rock that is almost 800 m (2,625 ft) high.

Antibes Pablo Picasso used the 12th-century Château Grimaldi as his studio in 1946. Many of his works can be seen here.

Cannes The trendiest place on the Côte d'Azur has a city wall around the Old Town. The Boulevard de la Croisette is world renowned.

Nice The Promenade des Anglais, the Hotel Négresco and the Palais Masséna are symbols of the 'unofficial' capital of the Côte d'Azur. Also worth seeing are the maze-like old town, the flower and vegetable market, the Musée d'Art Contemporain and the Musée Chagall.

Marseille France's largest harbour city has many tourist attractions. High above the city is the Basilique of Notre Dame de la Garde. Small, stepped streets, idyllic squares and the lively harbour and fish market lend the city its charm. The Château d'If is located on an island offshore from the city and offers great views.

St-Tropez This fishing village, located on a little peninsula, has been a popular Côte d'Azur seaside resort since the 1950s. The former citadel dates back to the 16th/17th centuries.

Esterel Red rock, steep cliffs and gorges, and very remote bays distinguish this coastal area between Cannes and St-Raphaël: an off-the-beaten-track location on the southern French coast.

A picturesque village crowned with a pilgrimage church along the Camino de Santiago in Galicia.

Spain

Camino de Santiago and Costa Verde – a journey through verdant Spain

Since the Middle Ages, pilgrims from all over the world have been drawn to the shrine of the apostle St James in Santiago de Compostela. Picturesque villages and towns, monasteries and castles, and the mighty cathedrals of Burgos and León line the 'Camino', which stretches from the Pyrenees on the border with France to Galicia in the north-western corner of Spain. The return journey skirts the rugged northern Spanish coast.

Legend has it that the apostle St James was beheaded in Palestine in the year AD 44 and his remains were sent by boat to the extreme north-west of Spain, where he had previously taught the gospel. It was not until much later, after the apostle's grave was discovered in the early 9th century, that the first St James' Basilica was built.

Subsequently, in 950, Gotescalco, the Bishop of Le Puy, became one of the first to make the pilgrimage to Compostela with a large entourage. Cesareo, the

Abbot of Montserrat, followed suit in 959. The stream of pilgrims grew so much that in 1072 Alfonso VI suspended the toll for the Galician Trail. Just one century later, Aymeric Picaud, a priest from Poitou, wrote the first guidebook for the pilgrimage to Compostela, which was published throughout all Europe's monasteries as *Codex Calixtinus*.

Paris, Vezelay, Le Puy and Arles became the main meeting points from which the groups of pious travellers would continue on their way. Before starting their jour-

The bulls entering the arena of Pamplona.

ney, the pilgrims and their equipment – a hat and coat to protect against the weather, a gourd for water and a staff for defence – were ceremoniously blessed. The seashells that the first pilgrims brought back from Galicia quickly became the symbol for future pilgrims. Those who arrived in Santiago and could prove the pilgrimage by showing their pilgrim book to the cathedral's secretary received the 'compostela', an official pilgrim certificate. To this day, every pilgrim who travels along the Camino de Santiago for at least 100 km (62 miles) either by walking or riding a bicycle or a horse also receives such a certificate.

Picaud described the meeting points in France: the two trails over the Pyrenees and the main trail from the Puente la Reina. Pilgrims coming from Paris, Vezelay and Le Puy would go over the Puerto

Every pilgrim's goal – the Cathedral of Santiago de Compostela. According to legend, the remains of the apostle St James were brought to Galicia from Jerusalem and were later found in the city on this site.

The Cuevas del Marbei Llanes beach lies on the Costa Verde at the foot of the Sierra de Cuera.

de Ibaneta (1,057 m/3,468 ft), and those coming from Arles would go over the Puerto de Somport (1,650 m/5,414 ft). In his trail guide, Picaud even describes the townships, hospitals and accommodation options along the way in great detail – the classic pilgrim trail still follows these today.

Nowadays, the thousand-year-old trail is signposted with blue signs depicting hikers or yellow St James shells. You can also experience the beauty along the way as an 'independent pilgrim', perhaps learning even more about the country, the people, the art and the culture of this stunning area. The rugged mountains stretch from the western Pyrenees to the Cantabrian Mountains, over the plateaus of the northern Meseta, mostly moorland, to the semi-desert area of the Navarran Bardenas Reales.

While the pilgrims' destination is Santiago, you have the option of heading back along the northern Spanish coast, which partly corresponds to the Aragonian pilgrim route, and experiencing the charming interplay of mountains and sea on the rugged, craggy Atlantic coast between Galicia and the Basque country (País Vasco).

On the way to the Basque country, the tour passes through the historic province of Asturias, with its mountain pastures, and Cantabria, with its impressive Atlantic coniferous forests. The mountains then go east into the Pyrenees. Both routes also offer a multitude of art and culture, with historical relics dating back 1,500 years. From the treasures hidden in the tiniest of village churches to the lavishly filled chambers of major cathedrals, St James' Way will not disappoint.

Chaparral scenery along the Camino de Santiago, from the Pyrenees to Galicia.

Fiesta San Fermin in Pamplona

Ernest Hemingway called the Feria del Toro (Festival of the Bull) a 'damn good party' and eternalized it as 'The Running of the Bulls' in his novel Fiesta. The festival is held in honour of St Fermin and the days of the event, held every year in Pamplona from 6 to 14 July, are also known as San Fermines, when the town is reduced to a chaotic state of emergency for a long 204 hours.

People begin celebrations early in the morning and party all night until

Top: Bulls run through the old town alleys of Pamplona.
Bottom: The evening bullfight.

exactly 8 am, when the encierro begins – the 900-m (2,952-ft) chase through the city with the bulls hots on the tails of people. The run starts at the stalls of the Cuesta de Santo Domingo, goes through the town hall square, and ends at the entrance to the arena.

In front of, next to and behind the six bulls, thousands of people follow the same route and try not to end up on the bulls' horns. After the race comes all kinds of merrymaking, and in the evening the bulls are finally able to demonstrate their fighting strength in the arena.

Everywhere you look, peñas (circles of friends) trundle through the streets and alleys playing loud music, spurred on by free-flowing sangria and endless cerveza. The inspiration for the festival was to honour Bishop Fermin, who died as a martyr in Amiens in AD 287. In 1186, his remains were brought back to Pamplona.

The Camino de Santiago and the northern Spanish coast are home to several pilgrim trails that lead from the Pyrenees to the shrine of St James in Galicia. This particular route starts in Roncesvalles and heads through Burgos and León to Santiago de Compostela. The return trip along the Atlantic coast unleashes the beauty of the Galician, Asturian, Cantabrian and Basque coastline.

❶ Roncesvalles In the year AD 778, this small village below the Ibañeta Pass decided the fate of one Marquis Roland, who in the wake of Charles the Great had tried to expel the Moors from Zaragoza. When the armies retreated, Roland led the rearguard but got caught in an ambush and was killed. The heroic sagas surrounding his death became the 'Song of Roland' in 1080.

The historic Augustine Hostel in Roncesvalles is one of the oldest along the pilgrimage route and the collegiate church dates back to 1127. The Gothic Church of Santa Maria was built in the 13th century and is home to the Madonna of Roncevalles, a silver-plated statue with a core of cedar wood.

❷ Pamplona The city of the San Fermines, with the famous 'Running of the Bulls', was founded by the Roman General Pompeius in 75 BC. The Moors ruled here in the 8th century, but starting in 905 it became the capital of the Kingdom of Navarra, which transformed into the Castillian Empire in 1512. Today, the Plaza del Castillo, with its

rows of houses from the 18th and 19th centuries, is the lively centre of the city. The facade of the town hall at the Plaza Consistorial is really quite impressive with its interesting Doric, Ionic and Corinthian features. Opposite the plaza is the Church of San Saturnino, once a military church, and next door is the hostel for pilgrims travelling the Camino de Santiago.

The symbol of Pamplona is, however, the Santa Maria Cathedral, with its 50-m-high (164-ft) towers. Behind its classical facade is a French-style Gothic interior. The dominating feature of the cathedral is the Virgen del Sagrario, who looks over the main altar. In the Middle Ages, the kings of Navarra were crowned here under the Romanesque statue of Mary. Make sure not to miss the Gothic cloister, built in 1472, with its numerous tomb slabs.

❸ Puente la Reina This town's name traces its origins to the Puente Regina, the five-arched pedestrian bridge built in the 11th century that was a donation from Doña Mayor, the wife of the Navarran King Sancho el

Travel information

Route profile
Length: approx. 1,800 km (1,119 miles), excluding detours
Time required: at least 2 weeks
Start: Roncesvalles
End: San Sebastián
Route (main locations):
The main Camino de Santiago including Roncesvalles, Pamplona, Logroño, Burgos, León, Astorga, Ponferrada, Santiago de Compostela, then back through La Coruña, Gijón, Santander, Bilbao, San Sebastián.

Traffic information: Drive on the right in Spain. The speed limit in urban areas is 50 km/h (31 mph), 90 km/h (56 miles) on rural roads, 100–120 km/h (62–75 mph) on expressways and 120 km/h (75 mph) on freeways. Important: you must carry two

warning triangles and a set of spare bulbs for the vehicle lights in the car at all times.

Accommodation:
The pilgrim hostels along the Camino de Santiago are reserved for hiking pilgrims with an official pilgrim book. Pilgrims are only accepted on bicycles if they have vacancies. Drivers are not normally accepted. You may only stay once in each hostel, except in Santiago itself, where three nights are allowed.

Information
www.aragonguide.com
www.euskadi.net (Basque)
www.galiciaguide.com
www.turismodecantabria.com
www.visitasturias.co.uk
St James' Way:
www.caminodesantiago.me.uk

Romanesque churches on the Camino de Santiago

From approximately the 10th century onwards, church builders all over Europe began erecting structures with classic Roman features like rounded arches, columns, pillars and vaults, and uniting them in the standard Basilica shape. Originally they had flat roofs – only the crypts had arches, and in the 11th century this was also introduced over the aisle.

Not much later, however, the Mediterranean countries in particular began adopting dome vaults as well as barrel vaults. The round shape, dictated by

Mayor The Romanesque pilgrim bridge over the Río Arga is the most beautiful on the entire pilgrimage route.

Right at the entrance to the town, next to the old pilgrim hospital, is the Iglesia del Crucifijo, built in the 12th century by the Knights Templar and housing a crucifix from the 14th century. This parish church has a Romanesque facade with a baroque interior and contains the interesting little carving Santiago Beltza, the 'Black James'.

4 Estella In its heyday, this old royal residence included no less than twenty churches, monasteries and chapels, the most beautiful of which is San Pedro de la Rúa (12th century). Its three Gothic naves each have Romanesque arches, and the main arch was completed in the 17th century. The most precious pieces are the figure of Mary dating from the 12th century and one of Christ from the 14th century. The finely crafted column capi-

tals in the ruins of the cloister are also interesting.

5 Logroño The most beautiful part of La Rioja's capital is its old city centre around the Plaza del Mercado, where you will find the Cathedral of Santa Maria la Redonda. Its baroque towers are visible from quite a distance. The building dates back to the 15th century, and its most precious piece is an image of the crucifixion by Michelangelo.

6 Nájera This small town, which was the capital of La Rioja and Navarra until 1076, experienced its heyday under King Sancho el Mayor until 1035. The monastery of Santa María la Real also dates back to this time. The Knights Cloister in the monastery was built in the 16th century and the church of Santa Maria in the 15th century.

At the centre of the golden baroque altar is a wonderful image of Mary. However, the most beautiful feature is the

magnificently decorated late 15th-century choir stalls.

7 Santo Domingo de la Calzada The main attraction of the local cathedral is an ornate chicken coop where a white hen and a white rooster have been kept for centuries. According to legend, the two birds are said to have saved the life of an innocent boy who was condemned to the gallows.

The church itself was founded by St Domingo, who rendered outstanding services to the pilgrims along the Camino de Compostela in the 11th century. An impressively high altar dating back to 1540 fills the Romanesque choir of the church.

8 Burgos Over the centuries, this city was one of the most important stops on the Camino de Santiago. At the end of the 15th century it had no less than thirty-two hostels for those making their way to or from Galicia. Its importance was also

due to the cathedral, the construction of which began in 1221 under the auspices of Bishop Mauricio. Work continued on this, the third-largest cathedral in Spain, for more than three centuries – 108 m (354 ft) long and 61 m (200 ft) wide with a central arch measuring 20 m (66 ft) in height. Its Gothic towers, completed in the 15th century, soar to 80 m (262 ft) while its main, lavishly decorated facade displays eight statues of kings. All four entrances are sculptural

1 The Puente la Reina over the Río Agra was built as a pedestrian bridge in the 11th century.

2 The cloister in the Gothic cathedral of Pamplona.

3 The Gothic cathedral of Burgos was inaugurated in 1221.

4 San Pedro de la Rua in Estella, an important stop on the Camino de Santiago.

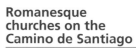

Top: San Martín in Frómista.
Bottom: San Pedro de Tejada in Puente Arenas in the Valle de Valdivielso.

the simple structural calculations involved in these buildings, was softened with pedestals, pilaster strips, pilasters and half columns while the cornices and mini galleries gave the plain walls a sense of elegance. Romanesque artists displayed their work on decorative friezes, portal and window soffits and, last but not least, the column capitals.

Las Médulas

This small town near Carucedo, some 25 km (16 miles) south-west of Ponferrada, sits on a throne of gold – at least this was the case during Roman times. The Romans systematically dug up so many square kilometres of land in the search for this precious metal that the bizarre land formations can still be seen today.

Cave and shaft entrances are interspersed with tombs, ancient washing systems and hills in a unique eroded landscape of gorges and rock. Everything points to the fact that this place was the site of an extremely well-organized search for gold, despite having only the most basic of means.

Contemporary sources provide evidence of the hard labour carried out by entire legions of slaves, who had to dig like moles for the prized metal while being whipped by their masters. The Lago de Carucedo, south-west of Ponferrade, is also a by-product of the search for gold. This is where the slaves

The scenery around Las Médulas.

were forced to dig an artificial lake which, along with the network of canals and channels, was used to wash the millions of tonnes of rock from the surrounding hills.

The Romans eventually mined around 500 tonnes (550 tons) of the precious metal from the area. Today, the ancient gold-mine site is a UNESCO World Heritage Site accessible by a 2-km-long (1-mile) track.

The Mirador de Orellán provides the most beautiful view of the rugged, orange-red rock landscape and can be reached by car. Las Médulas itself, after which the gold-mine was named, also offers good views over the region.

masterpieces and the interior is similarly awe-inspiring.

Art lovers will be blown away by the nineteen chapels, thirty-eight altars and numerous sculptures, reliefs and paintings. The chapels, in particular, house many centuries' worth of individual works of art. In the centre of the opulent high altar stands the silver statue of Santa Maria la Mayor, patron saint of Burgos. A visit to the 13th-century cloister and the adjacent chapels is also not to be missed.

The city's most famous son, El Cid (1043–99), who retook Valencia from the Moors in 1094 and was immortalized through the poem *El Cantar del mio Cid*, is buried in the cathedral.

Those who are short of time to see all the many interesting churches the city has to offer should at least visit the old Carthusian monastery of Cartuja de Santa María de Miraflores in the east of the city.

The Gothic minster, which was completed in 1499, contains a masterful Renaissance choir stall, a high altar decorated in gold, and the alabaster tomb of Juan II and Isabel of Portugal.

9 Frómista This tiny town is home to what is probably the most beautiful, stylistically sound Romanesque church on the entire Camino de Santiago. Begun in 1066, both the eight-cornered intersecting tower and the two round towers in the west look almost like defence fortifications. The eaves extending out over the walls were decorated with more than three hundred mythical creatures, animals, plants and designs.

Inside the sacred building is a 14th-century portrait of St Martin, and another of St James from the 16th century. The column capitals are also unique, ornately decorated with animal motifs and biblical scenes.

10 León The old royal city of León on the Río Bernesga was founded in the 1st century. It quickly became an important stop along the Camino de Santiago, and its grand churches were built accordingly. The best of these is the Gothic Cathedral of Santa María de la Regla, begun in the 13th century, with its two 65- and 68-m-high (213- and 223-ft) towers.

The lavishly decorated western facade is impressive with its rose window and three entrances adorned with exquisite relief work. The southern facade also has a large rose window and the ruins of Roman baths under glass casing.

The cathedral's main treasure, however, is its more than a hundred stained-glass windows covering an area of about 1,800 sq m (19,368 sq ft). The oldest of these dates back to the 13th century, with the most recent dating back to the 20th

century, and all of them cover a variety of themes from mythical creatures to plant motifs.

Similarly significant is the royal collegiate church of San Isidoro, tracing back to the 11th century. It is an example of Spanish Romanesque architecture and has housed the relics of St Isidor of Seville since 1063.

Next to the church is the Panteón Real (Royal Pantheon), which can be visited as a museum and is the final resting place of no fewer than twenty-three kings and queens. The ceiling was painted with unique Romanesque frescoes as early as 1160, which gave the Pantheon its nickname, the 'Sistine Chapel of Spain's Romanesque Art.' Go through the cloister to get to the actual museum with its countless artistic treasures.

Catholic kings were responsible for the Monastery of San Marcos, which was founded at the start of the 16th century.

St James

The apostle St James was active on the Iberian Peninsula for seven years before being beheaded in Jerusalem in the year AD 44. His disciples allegedly transported his remains to Galicia thereafter.

The altar in the Cathedral of Santiago de Compostela.

Behind the monastery's ornate facade – considered one of the most impressive examples of the Spanish Renaissance style – is a hotel. If you are are interested in seeing the beautiful cloister of the old monastery you can go into the hotel hall and take the second door on the right.

⑪ **Astorga** This city's finest treasures can all be seen from the Avenida de las Murallas – the impressive city wall dating back to Roman times, the Episcopal Palace built by Antoni Gaudí, and the Santa María Cathedral. Gaudí's palace, completed in 1913, was never actually used by the bishops and today serves as an interesting Camino de Santiago museum (Museo de los Caminos).
Construction on the late-Gothic Santa María Cathedral began in 1471 but wasn't completed until the 18th century. Its main altar dates back to the mid 16th cen-

tury, as does the richly decorated choir stall.

⑫ **Ponferrada** The Knights Templar built this enormous castle with a surface area of 160 m by 90 m (525 ft by 295 ft) on the 'Pons Ferrata', an 11th-century iron bridge, to protect pilgrims travelling on the Camino de Santiago. The attractions of the old town include the Mozarabic Iglesia de Santo Tomás de las Ollas, with its horseshoe arches. It's worth taking a trip out of Ponferrada to the ancient gold-mine of Las Médulas (see sidebar left).

⑬ **Cebreiro** This tiny village is home to the oldest little church on the Camino de Santiago. It was built in the 9th century and its well-fortified walls house a painting of the Madonna from the 12th century.

⑭ **Santiago de Compostela** In the Middle Ages, the tomb of

St James was the most important Christian pilgrimage site outside of Rome and Jerusalem. In 1075, after the Moors were expelled, Bishop Diego Pelaez began building a cathedral to reflect the importance of this pilgrimage destination, although it was not completed until the mid 18th century. In fact, the two solid exterior towers were only finished in 1750.
The long construction time meant that simple Romanesque styles and opulent baroque touches existed side by side. This fusion also dominates the facade. The Pórtico de la Gloria, with its ornate sculpture work, is now within a late-baroque building placed in front of it, and the mix of styles continues inside as well. The impressive Romanesque design of the building is partially covered in the most lavish of baroque decor, and the entire structure is crowned with a golden high

altar with a 13th-century silver-plated figure of St James in the centre. Under the high altar is the mausoleum of the saint, whose remains rest in a silver shrine.

1 The Cathedral at León illuminated at night.

2 San Martin de Frómista – the most beautiful Romanesque church on the Camino de Santiago.

3 A typical mountain landscape north of León.

4 The core of the Cathedral Santiago de Compostela is unchanged since the 11th century.

5 The Palace of Astorga was designed by Antoni Gaudí.

6 The Knights Templar built the Castle of Ponferrada between the 12th and 14th centuries to ensure the safety of pilgrims on the 'Camino'.

The holy cult around James began in earnest after a monk was repeatedly guided by a group of stars back in 813 (Lat. Campus stellae = Compostela = field of stars) to the location of the present-day church, and the king saw an apparition of St James during his victorious battle against the Arabs.

Detour

Picos de Europa

The 'Peaks of Europe' form the centre of the national park of the same name, dominated in particular by forested mountains that range between 800 and 1,500 m in height (2,625–4,922 ft). The thick-trunked, ancient chestnut trees, oaks and yews all provide an ideal habitat for a wide range of wildlife.

Top: The Picos de Europa.
Middle: Stone bridges over the Duje River.
Bottom: San Salvador de Cantamuda near Potes.

The national park can be accessed from the towns of Unquera in the east and Cangas de Onis in the west. The most famous gorges include the Desfiladera de los Beyos and the Desfiladero del Río Cares.
A cable car from Fuente Dé takes visitors up to a 900-m-high (2,953-ft) rock plateau. On the west side are Covadonga and the grotto of the same name where Don Pelayo is buried. Just 15 km (9 miles) further up, at about 1,150 m (3,773 ft), are the glacial lakes of Enol and Ercina, which mark the start of numerous hikes in the national park.

The cathedral museum includes the treasure chamber, the chapter house and the cloister from the 16th century. The city itself practically grew around the cathedral and is today similar to an historic open-air museum. Countless churches, particularly ones built in baroque style, await the eyes of connoisseurs, while picturesque old town alleys offer recreation of all kinds to both tourists and religious pilgrims.
In addition to the journey along the historic Camino de Santiago, it is worth heading further out to the Galician coast. The road then heads back along the shores of northern Spain to the Basque town of San Sebastián back near the French border.

⑮ Carnota The 7-km-long (4-mile) sandy beach on Spain's north-west coast is a surfer's par-

adise. The small village itself is home to the longest (over 30 m/98 ft) and probably also the most beautiful granary in Galicia, built out of granite at the end of the 18th century. To protect the grain from mice, the granary stands on two rows of pillars, secured with a corbel.

⑯ Cabo Finisterre The *finis terrae*, the end of the world, is a peninsula that towers above the Costa da Morte. Even today, the Atlantic tides and the dangerous cliffs mean numerous ships are wrecked on this 'Coast of Death'. The westernmost point of continental Europe is further north at Cape Touriñana. Both places are hauntingly beautiful and were important cult sites for the Celts.

⑰ La Coruña The Romans built this, the second-largest city in Galicia, into an important har-

bour city. The Torre de Hércules on the western side of the peninsula dates back to those Roman times. Begun in AD 100, it is said to be the oldest lighthouse in the world. Today, the tower is 60 m (197 ft) tall and can be climbed in summer.
The Old Town of La Coruña grew out of the former pescaderia, the fishmongers' quarter. Apart from Romanesque and baroque churches, two museums are of particular interest – the Museum of Archaeological History in the San Antón Castle displays findings from Celtic and Roman times as well as medieval sculptures; and the Fine Arts Museum at the Plaza de Zalaeta exhibits works from Rubens to Picasso.

⑱ Rías Altas Those following the coastal road between La Coruña and Ribadeo will see picturesque estuaries, small holiday

and fishing towns, ancient farmhouses and even older granaries. Flat coastal plains are interspersed with steep coastal mountains and striking promontories and headlands. The interior is dominated by pine and eucalypt forests and the weather is dictated by the windy and wet Atlantic.

⑲ Ribadeo This is the easternmost town in Galicia. It is situated on the Ría, the Atlantic mouth of the Río Eo, which cuts deep into the interior like a Scandinavian fjord. Old manors surround the Plaza de España, and the Convento de Santa Clara dates back to the 14th century.

⑳ Luarca This harbour town on the Costa Verde is undoubtedly one of the most beautiful parts of the Asturias region. The fishing harbour is so tightly

Altamira

The world-famous Altamira Cave is located in the hills above Santillana del Mar and was discovered in 1879. The ceiling paintings were first thought to be fakes, as no one could believe that the early civilizations were capable of such artistic talent. Only after the discovery of similiar Stone-Age caves in the area were the paintings in Altamira further researched, proved to be authentic and given more specific dates.

The Stone-Age drawing of a European bison.

The 270-m-long (886-ft) cave opens up from an anteroom into a large, natural hall whose walls and ceiling are covered with depictions of buffalo, deer, horses and all sorts of other game animals either lying on the ground or running.
The individual drawings can measure up to 2.2 m (7 ft) tall, are in colour and are even partially carved into the rock. Brown, yellowish and red ochre colours, black manganese soil and coal were all used in the depictions. The bison, in particular, are painted in so many different shades that the animals look plastic and realistic. The overall effect of the hall also resulted in the cave being nicknamed the 'Stone-Age Sistine Chapel'.
Using the most modern of tests, researchers have proved that the drawings dated back to the Old Stone Age (Palaeolithic times) and were thus around sixteen thousand years old, making them the most important example of pre-historic art in the world.
At some point, the cave purveyors realized that visitors' breath and perspiration was starting to damage the drawings, so the original cave was closed to the general public and an authentic replica was created in the museum. Those who wish to see the original cave, in which only 25 people a day are admitted, must ask to do so at the Museo y Centro de Investigación de Altamira (39330 Santillana del Mar) – the waiting time is three years.

today. The town's main points of interest are, however, its picturesque alleys, the variety of lovingly tended flowerpots, and the old walls, romantically overgrown with ivy.
Hidden about 2 km (1 mile) up from the village is the world-famous Altamira Cave.

26 Santander Cantabria's capital, jutting out on a long peninsula, is a harbour city, seaside resort and secret 'Capital of Promenades'. The city grew from a small fishing harbour into a relatively large trading port. In 1941, however, many of its buildings went up in flames during a devastating city fire. That's why walkers are again in demand in Santander, and their main destination should be the La Magdalena Peninsula. King Alfonso XIII chose the Palacio de la Magdalena, built in English style at the start of the 20th century, to be his summer residence.
Sprawling north-west of the peninsula are the beautiful

jammed in between the rock faces and the rows of houses that there is only a tiny bit of room for the fishing boats to come in and out. The fish market quarter is especially picturesque, and you'll get the best view from the city hill of Atalaya.

21 Costa Verde The coast between Ribadeo and Santander showcases a series of spectacular, as well as very isolated, sandy bays and impressive cliffs that are only interrupted once by the long Rías. The town of Cudillero has a gorgeous fishing harbour, cosy pubs and, more importantly, a number of isolated and often empty beaches.Turning off from the coastal highway, there are plenty of peaceful spots for everyone. It's worth taking a detour inland at Avilés to visit Oviedo, the beautiful capital of Asturias.

22 Luanco North-west of the industrial city of Gijón, this beach town has its own oceanography museum. A vast beach sprawls from Banugues to the windy and exposed Cabo de Peñas. Swimming can be dangerous along some sections of this coast.

23 Ribadesella The Old Town at the mouth of the Río Sella and the long promenade around the fine sandy beach are what make this town so attractive. It also has a point of interest worth seeing – the cave of Tito Bustillo, which was discovered in 1968. This dripstone cave contains Stone Age rock paintings that are around twenty thousand years old depicting red and black deer and horses. For preservation purposes, the number of visitors allowed in per day has had to be limited, similar to the caves in Altamira.

24 Cueva del Pindal Beneath the small farming village of Pimiango, the Pindal cave also contains prehistoric rock paintings. It is best to come in the early morning, as only 200 people are admitted each day.
In Unquera it's worth taking a detour away from the coastal road to head south into the Picos de Europa. The Desfiladero de la Hermida Gorge starts after Panes, with some nearly vertical rock faces that reach 600 m (1,969 ft) in height. Potes is the main town in the eastern Picos de Europa.

25 Santillana del Mar This small town, located slightly away from the sea, owes its existence to the remains of St Juliana. Monks built a monastery around her remains and its Romanesque collegiate church is the area's most important building even

1 The view of the harbour of Castro Urdiales between Santander and Bilbao.

2 Cabo Finisterre above the vast Atlantic.

3 Closely-packed fishing boats at the harbour of La Coruña.

4 A view of the harbour in Ribadesella on the Costa Verde.

Bilbao: architecture old and new

To improve the image of the city, which does not have much to offer in the way of tourism, Bilbao's city planners asked a series of famous architects

Siete Calles in Bilbao.

to contribute to the city's lacklustre facade. Apart from Gehry's Museo Guggenheim, the pedestrian bridge Puente del Campo Volantin and the futuristic airport, both by Santiago Calatrava, as well as the metro stations by Norman Foster, are some of the most important additions. The most beautiful old buildings are found in the Siete Calles in the old town – seven streets of neoclassical buildings from the 19th century with lovely gazebos and wrought-iron balconies.

beaches of Primera Playa and Segunda Playa. Following the coastal road further east you will eventually come to Castro Urdiales, an attractive harbour town dominated by a Knights Templar castle.

27 Bilbao Now an industrial town, Bilbao originally grew out of a fishing village started back in the 11th century. Steelworks were eventually established here in the second half of the 19th century, which brought considerable wealth to the city. Only the Old Town is really worth seeing, in particular its Siete Calles, the 'Seven Streets', between the cathedral and the river. The 14th-century cathedral was completely burnt down in 1571 so its current form and its cloister date back to the 16th century. A more elegant life is reflected in the 19th-century neoclassical Plaza Nueva. North of the square you should visit the 15th-century church of San Nicolas. It has a gorgeous Gothic carved altar, as well as some interesting sculptures.
Always worth a visit is the Museum of Fine Arts with important works by El Greco, Goya and Gaugin. The gigantic Guggenheim Museum, designed by

Frank O. Gehry, is an absolute must. It alone attracts over one million people a year to the city.

28 Costa Vasca The 176-km-long (109-mile) Basque coast is defined by bays and estuaries lined by numerous cliffs. The landscape of the hinterland is one of wooded hills. Travellers stumble across heavenly beaches near Algorta on the eastern coast of the Ría of Bilbao.
Far more interesting, however, is the chapel of San Juan de Gaztelugatxe, west of Cape Machichaco, perched on a protruding rock in the middle of wildly romantic, windswept cliffs. It is only accessible on foot up a uniquely beautiful set of steps formed out of the rock. The 11th-century sailors' chapel on the rock is also of interest.
Whalers set off from Bermeo towards Iceland and Labrador. The Museo del Pescador in the 16th-century Ercilla military tower has all the answers on the topic of fish.

29 Guernica This city is evidence of one of the darkest chapters in Spanish-German history. During the Spanish Civil War, an air raid by the German Condor Legion on 26 April 1937

destroyed virtually the entire city. Some two thousand people died in the inferno, but the world did not see it as a precursor to the disaster that was World War II. Only Pablo Picasso captured the horror in his world-famous *Guernica* painting, which now hangs in Madrid's Museo Nacional Centro de Arte Reina Sofía. Guernica is considered the 'holy city of the Basques' because the Basques held their regional meetings here in the Middle Ages. When the Basque region became part of Castile, the Spanish kings had to swear that they would forever respect the rights of the Basques.
Everything worth knowing about the Basques can be found in the Museo Euskal Herria.

30 San Sebastián The journey across northern Spain ends in this beautiful seaside town from the Belle Époque, which was for a long time the summer resort of the Spanish kings. Aristocracy from all over Europe would stay in the mansions from this era that still dominate the cityscape. The Monte Urgull and the Castillo de la Mota tower above the Old Town, at the centre of which is the Plaza de la Constitución. Bullfights used to be

held in this square – the large number of balconies is evidence of this.
The other attractions of the Basque city include the aquarium, the Museo de San Telmo in a 16th-century monastery, and the Palacio del Mar – and of course the best tapas in Spain. On the west side is an enormous bay with two popular beaches. The view from the Monte Igueldo is by far the most beautiful.

Cabo Finisterre This cape is feared by sailors because of its cliffs, but it is a popular viewpoint for the mighty Atlantic.

La Coruña This Galician harbour city is home to the only Roman lighthouse left in the world. It also has astonishing rows of houses enclosed in glass to withstand the harsh elements.

Picos de Europa Homecoming sailors gave this massif its name, which appears to soar out of the sea. Part of the mountains form Europe's largest national park. The highest peak is the Torre Cerredo (2,648 m/8,688 ft).

Santiago de Compostela The capital of Galicia is one of the world's most important Christian pilgrim destinations. The entire old town and the cathedral are works of art built of stone.

Las Médulas The Romans made their slaves dig for gold here, creating a bizarre landscape left over from excavations.

Ponferrada The 11th-century Templar castle was built to protect the pilgrims. Worth seeing are the baroque town hall and the Iglesia de Santo Tomás de las Ollas.

Astorga This city's main attraction is the Episcopal Palace and the Santa María Cathedral built by Antoni Gaudí.

León Churches like the Santa María de la Regla show León's importance along St James' Way.

Frómista This small town has one of the most beautiful and stylistically sound Romanesque churches along the Camino de Santiago, the Iglesia de San Martín. It is lavishly adorned with mythical creatures, animals, plants and biblical scenes.

Guggenheim Museum in Bilbao

The museum, which was designed by star architect Frank O. Gehry, opened in Bilbao in 1997 and is located on the banks of the Rio Nervion. It is a prime example of modern architecture. The structure, made of limestone, titanium and glass, cost around 100 million dollars and took four years to build. Its fusion of flat surfaces and shapes, as well as its silver exterior, are an impressive sight even from afar. The locals refer to the mighty metal roof as a 'metallic flower'. The uniquely designed parts of the building are loosely grouped around a central, glazed atrium 50 m (164 ft) high from which all parts of the building can be accessed. The entrance hall alone is 130 m (427 ft) long and 30 m (98 ft) wide and contains no obstructive pillars. Nineteen exhibition halls with a total surface area of 24,290 sq m (261,360 sq ft) provide enough space for gigantic displays.

1 The glittering facade of Gehry's Museo Guggenheim was covered in 60 tonnes (66 tons) of titanium. Its exterior shell is just 3 mm (0.1 in) thick.

2 San Sebastián is located on La Concha (shell) Bay. The sides of the semicircular bay mark the border of the rock massif of Monte Igueldo and Monte Urgull. In the entrance to the bay is the small rock island of Santa Clara.

Altamira When the cave was discovered, the images of hunting and animals on the walls were first thought to be fakes. A replica of the cave now means that everyone can experience artwork from the Old Stone Age.

San Sebastián 'Donostia' in Basque, this centre of Basque culture is dominated by lovely buildings, beautiful beaches and exquisite tapas restaurants.

Castro Urdiales This lively fishing town is a good starting point for visiting Cantabria's beaches and historical sites. It is home to a natural harbour with elegant riverside walks while above it all are the Gothic Iglesia de Santa Maria and a castle built by the Knights Templar.

Bilbao The old town of this industrial Basque city has mostly understated buildings. But the Museum of Fine Arts with major works by El Greco, Goya and Gaugin, as well as the glinting silver Guggenheim Museum (1997) by Frank O. Gehry, are definitely worth a look.

Burgos Construction started on Spain's third-largest cathedral in 1221 and took three centuries to complete. The Carthusian monastery is another attraction here.

Estella Many of its attractions lie on the other side of the Ega Bridge. The most beautiful church in Estella is the lavishly decorated San Pedro de la Rúa (12th century).

Puente la Reina This stone bridge was built in the 11th century as a donation from the wife of the king of Navarra.

Pamplona This city was made famous by Hemingway's novel *Fiesta*, in which he called this the 'Running of the Bulls'.

Puerto Banus near Marbella, one of the best-known yacht harbours on the Costa del Sol.

Spain

Andalusia – a Moorish legacy in southern Europe

Andalusia is a region filled with passion and culture. The fertile agricultural land here is blessed with plentiful sun where olives trees grow against a backdrop of snow-covered mountains and the tidy whitewashed houses recall Moorish architectural styles. This natural setting coupled with the local aromas of leather and sherry and the rhythms of the castanets and flamenco all combine to create a truly unforgettable experience.

'Al Andaluz' – the 'Land of Light' – is what the Arabs called this sunny southern part of Spain. Interestingly, it was not meant as a metaphor. This region, where two continents and two seas meet, actually possesses a unique light that seems not to exist anywhere else in the world, and whose clarity never ceases to amaze its inspired visitors.

Andalusia covers an area of more than 87,000 sq km (33,582 sq mi). Its landscape is defined by the Sierra Morena Mountains and the Betic Cordillera Range,

whose 3,481-m-high (11,421-ft) Sierra Nevada Mountains are covered in snow almost all year long.

The area is home to ancient settlements that pre-date the Romans, including Cadiz, which was first settled by the Phoenicians in around 1100 BC. Since then, Greeks, Romans, Vandals and Visigoths have taken turns settling and farming the sun-drenched land in the south of Iberia. It wasn't until the 8th century that the Arabs ended the reign of the Visigoths and took control of the area.

Flamenco – a dance and a way of life.

It turns out to have been an easy campaign for the Arabs to gain their foothold in Andalusia. When they secretly crossed the Strait of Gibraltar under Tariq ibn Ziyad, and later Musa ibn Nusair in 711, they only needed gradually to seize the already deteriorating kingdom of Roderic, the Visigoth ruler. After that, virtually no one else stood in their way and their expansion reached as far as Galicia and the Pyrenees. They were only halted by Charles Martell in 732 at the Battle of Tours in France.

In Spain, however, the Arabs reigned supreme for over half a century. Abd ar-Rahman I made Córdoba the capital of his Caliphate and adorned the city with an exquisite mosque. In Granada, Islamic culture developed with consummate splendour. Over the centuries, the Moors erected some truly magnificent buildings

The 'White Village' ('Pueblo Blanco') of Zahara de la Sierra is a national monument.

The Puente Nuevo across the rock gorge in Ronda, which is more than 100 m (328 ft) deep, is a technical masterpiece dating from the 18th century.

all throughout this region, in architectural styles that remain the defining element of Andalusia even to this day.

In the 13th century, the Christian 'Reconquista' of the Iberian Peninsula began in earnest and a huge victory was won for the Catholic monarchs Ferdinand and Isabella when Seville fell in 1248. When Granada was taken as well in 1492, the last Muslim minorities were expelled, marking the start of a new Andalusia that would not just ride the tide of good fortune that came with the discovery and conquest of the 'New World', but even dictate its development. Following the conquests of Mexico and Peru, the city of Seville became the most important trading centre in all of Spain.

Today, the autonomous region of Andalusia, which enjoys 3,000 hours of sun a year and where oranges, olives, wine and almonds all flourish, is home to some seven million people and has around 760 towns and communities. Traditional festivals and religious life are of extreme importance to Andalusians, and these are celebrated with full fervour and devotion especially during the Semana Santa, or Holy Week, when numerous pilgrimages and processions take place.

Community culture is reflected in the local festival weeks, the ferias, as well as in the bullfights and diverse flamenco styles. These events show the true Andalusia, the land of bold caballeros, beautiful señoritas, formidable black bulls – the land that gets your blood pumping like no other place. And the natural landscape is breathtaking and diverse, from the glorious beaches of the Costa del Sol to the magnificent snow-covered peaks of the Sierra Nevada.

The famous stone pillars in the lion courtyard of the Alhambra in Granada.

Flamenco

Flamenco is 'the' dance of Spain, but it was actually a mix of non-spanish minorities who were responsible for its survival. The gitanos (gypsies) who travelled the area around Cádiz and Seville in the 15th century are said to have invented the 'cante andaluz' (Andalusian canto) or 'cante jondo' (deep canto). Flamenco was later used as background music in brothels until it became acceptable in the 1920s.
The musical form has been internationally renowned since Carlos Sauras'

A flamenco festival in Andalusia.

sensational film *Carmen*. Flamenco is not just a dance to an exciting rhythm or a simple form of entertainment with catchy tunes, it is also a way of opening up the soul. For many, it is also the impressive reflection of a way of life – pride and passion under the torrid Andalusian sun.

Your Andalusian excursion takes you 1,600 km (994 miles) through the mountains of the Sierra Nevada Range, across the fertile plains of the Guadalquivir River and on down towards the Costa del Sol and the Costa del Luz. You'll visit the charming 'white villages' and the magnificent cities that are home to Moorish architectural masterpieces.

1 **Seville** For detailed information see p. 119.

2 **Vega del Guadalquivir** After leaving Seville on the C431 towards Córdoba you will emerge onto the flat, green and fertile plains known as the Vega del Guadalquivir. It is one of Andalusia's primary agricultural regions, with orange plantations, cornfields and sunflower fields sprawling across a wide valley formed by the river that made Seville a world power in the days of the explorers.
Small villages pop up along the route, with tidy white houses perched on top of lush hills. Most of the people in the area live off the rich agricultural bounty.

3 **Palma del Río** Its prime location at the confluence of the Guadalquivir and Genil is romantic enough. Add to that the verdant green surroundings and you've got two good reasons why this area is called 'Andalusia's Garden'.

The impressive 12th-century city walls have been well preserved in parts and recall the town's rich history, which goes back to the Romans who founded it. Palma del Río then played a special role in Spain's history from the 16th to 18th centuries when the Convento de San Francisco regularly sent missionaries to the New World. One of them was Brother Junípero Serra, who was responsible in large for the fabulous mission churches that can still be seen in California. But those times have long passed and the monastery has been given a new purpose now – beautifully renovated, today it is used as a hotel.

1 The mighty Moorish bell tower of La Giralda overlooks the Gothic cathedral and the Archivo General de Indias in Seville.

2 The Santa Maria Cathedral in Seville was built on the foundation walls of the Almohada Mosque.

Travel information

Route profile
Length: approx. 1,600 km (994 miles), excluding detours
Time required: at least 8–10 days
Start and end: Seville
Route (main locations): Seville, Córdoba, Granada, Almería, Málaga, Ronda, Olvera, Arcos de la Frontera, Cádiz, Sanlúcar, Jerez, Seville

Traffic information:
Drive on the right in Spain. The speed limit in built-up areas is 50 km/h (31 mph), 90 or 100 km/h (56 or 62 mph) outside built-up areas, and 120 km/h (75 mph) on high-

ways (generally tolls are required).

When to go:
The recommended times to travel are spring (around 26°C/79°F) and autumn (up to 32°C/90°C in September). Summer can be brutally hot.

Accommodation:
Paradores are state-run hotels in historic buildings. Bookings and reservations are made through Ibero Hotel (*www.iberotours.de*).

Information:
www.tourspain.es
Info on Andalusia:
www.andalusien-web.com

Seville

To experience Spain you simply have to visit Seville, the capital of Andalusia.

Seville is one of the country's most charming cities, competing directly with Granada, Andalusia's second Moorish treasure, for the position. After America was discovered, Seville had its heyday as a river port on the Guadalquivir and as an important trading centre where goods from Spanish colonies overseas were unloaded and transported to the interior. This brought extreme wealth and a breath of fresh air from the New World to this old city!

Particularly worth seeing here are the 15th-century Santa María Cathedral, a complex with lavishly designed porticos, the Patio de los Naranjos, the former mosque courtyard with early medieval marble bowls, and the Giralda bell tower, built as a minaret in the 12th century; the Reales Alcázares, built in the 12th century by the Almohadas, used as a Christian royal palace from 1248 and continually expanded until the 16th century.

Highlights of any visit also include the exquisitely decorated interior courtyards around which the palace buildings are grouped, as well as the gardens there (the cathedral and the Alcázares are UNESCO World Heritage Sites), the Barrio de Santa Cruz, the Jewish quarter with its narrow alleys, tiled inner courtyards and wrought-iron balconies; the Casa de Pilatos,

Ceramic works on the Plaza de España.

a rambling private palace combining a fascinating mix of styles; the Hospital de la Caridad (17th century), the most important piece of Sevillian baroque architecture; the Museo de Bellas Artes with collections focusing on Spanish baroque art; the Plaza de España, a dazzling structure with ceramic paintings in the city park, Parque de María Luisa. Outside the city are the ruins of the Roman Itálica.

Moorish art

Andalusia owes its most magnificent buildings to the Arabs who once ruled the area – the Mezquita in Córdoba, the Alhambra in Granada, and the Alcázar and the Giralda in Seville. One of the outstanding features of Moorish style is its ornate attention to detail. Because Islam prohibits the depiction of any of Allah's creatures, exquisite wall patterns were created in inscriptions and by combining geometric, floral and calligraphy motifs. The grandiose ornamentation often incorporated mosaics, ceramics, Koranic proverbs sculptured in marble and glass compounds adorned with Byzantine patterns imported from the eastern end of the Mediterranean. Mosques usually contained extravagant domes and entire halls of columns.

Top: The Myrtle Courtyard.
Middle: Lion courtyard with fountain.
Bottom: Courtyard of the Alcazar.

The style of arch most frequently used are the rounded, spiked or the Moorish horseshoe arch. The most popular building material during the time of the caliphs was ashlar rock. The Almohadas used natural stone for foundations and pedestals, and fired bricks and stamped clay for other parts of the structures.
Apart from the religious buildings and the palaces, Moorish architecture is still visible in the maze of streets in many of the Old City quarters in Andalusia.

4 Medina Azahara Just before reaching Córdoba, a road turns off towards the ruins of Medina Azahara, the old palace city built on three terraces where the caliphs lived together with their royal suite between the mid 10th and early 11th centuries. Parts of the complex have been renovated and give you a pretty good idea of the former beauty of the 'Flower City', a masterpiece of Islamic architecture.

5 Córdoba This city was an important political and cultural centre as early as Roman times – one of its most famous sons is the philosopher, Seneca, from the 3rd century BC. By AD 929, Córdoba had risen to become one of the Caliphate's most resplendent metropolises on Spanish soil, competing even with the likes of the former cosmopolitan city of Baghdad. Jews, Arabs and Christians lived in harmony with each other. Science and philosophy flourished like never before.
In the old city centre, traces remain of this heyday when the mighty Caliphate city had over a million inhabitants. It has now become a provincial capital with a population of just 300,000, but Córdoba remains a gem indeed: the Old City's narrow little alley-

ways, whitewashed houses and inner courtyards decorated with flowers all create an idyllic scene. At the centre of it all is the Mezquita – previously a mosque and now a cathedral – standing strong like an old fortification. The enormous building, with the magnificent prayer hall supported by 856 ornate columns, was declared a UNESCO 'Legacy of Mankind'. Nineteen naves and thirty-eight transepts, exquisite Oriental decorations and light casting mysterious shadows on the pillars make the Mezquita a truly unforgettable sight.
Just next to the Mezquita is the Judería, the former Jewish quarter with narrow streets adorned with flowers. One of the most beautiful of these is the aptly named Calleja de las Flores. The former synagogue and the bullfighting museum, which inci-

dentally is one of the most interesting in all of Spain, are also worth a visit.
The Alcázar de los Reyes Cristianos, a royal residence built as a fort in the 14th century, has really lovely gardens. The Museo Arqueológico Provincial, located in a Renaissance palace, has a number of Roman, Visigoth and Arabic exhibits. In the quarter around the Christian churches, Córdoba has another tourist attraction in store – the Palacio de Viana, a mansion with twelve inner courtyards and spectacular gardens.
The two most important centres during Spain's Moorish period, Córdoba and Granada, are connected by the Caliphate Route. Today it is known as the N432, a slightly less romantic name, but it still passes through a hilly region with relatively little

settlement, some small homesteads and a handful of well-fortified castles and towers.
At the town of Alcalá la Real, nestled in the shadow of the Moorish Castillo de la Mota, you leave the N432 for a leisurely drive through the villages of the fertile highlands of the Vega.

6 Montefrio This town lies in a unique mountain landscape and is known for its castle, Castillo de la Villa, which was built around 1500 on the walls of an old Moorish fort.
After some 20 km (12 miles) you come to the A9 heading towards Granada.

7 Granada The geographic location of this city is fascinating in itself – bordered in the west by a high plateau, in the south by the northern bank of the

river Genil, and with the snow-capped peaks of the Sierra Nevada as a background setting. However, what really gives Granada its 'One-Thousand-and-One-Nights' feel is the extensive Moorish legacy that has defined this city for more than seven hundred years now.

Granada experienced its heyday between the 13th and 15th centuries, before the Moors were pushed south by the gathering armies of the Christian 'Reconquista'. At that point the city had been the capital of the independent Kingdom of the Nasrids for 250 years, and it was during this time that its most magnificent edifice was built – the Alhambra.

A total of twenty-three sultans from the Nasrid Dynasty contributed to this tour de force of Spanish-Arabic constructions. Now the castle, at once fortress-like and elegant, is the pearl of the city of Granada.

The Alhambra, whose name 'The Red One' derives from the reddish ochre of its walls, is an enormous complex of fortifications, towers, royal residential palaces, mosques and gardens. It comprises four main sections – the defences, or Alcazaba, on the western tip of the hill; the Palacio Árabe (Alhambra Palace); the Palacio de Carlos V, a Renaissance palace with the Museum of Fine Arts in the centre of the hill; and the gardens of the Generalife in the east. Apart from the gardens, which were part of a summer residence, all other buildings are surrounded by fortified walls with towers.

The Palacio de los Leones, with its arcade passage adorned with filigree work, and the lion fountain are two of the most impressive parts of the Alhambra, along with the water features in the gardens, which have a real oasis feel. But the Alhambra is not all that this splendid city has to offer.

The Albaicin is also something to behold – the whitewashed Moorish quarter is an architectural gem in its own right, with tiny alleyways and the mirador, the San Nicolás lookout. In addition, there is the area around the 16th/17th-century cathedral, the Capilla Real, the late-Gothic royal chapel and the Carthusian monastery, founded in the early 16th century – each and every one of them worth a visit.

A must for poetry-lovers after all this is the small detour from Granada to Fuente Vaqueros,

1 To get the most beautiful view of the Alhambra in Granada and the Sierra Nevada Mountains, go to the Mirador de San Nicolás in Albaicín.

2 The prayer room of the former Umayyad Mosque in Córdoba has 856 columns.

3 The churches of Iglesia de la Villa (16th century) and Iglesia de la Encarnación (18th century) tower over Montefrío.

Carretera Granada–Veleta

Europe's highest mountain road runs for 46 km (29 miles) from Granada to Pico Veleta, the second-highest peak in the Sierra Nevada at 3,392 m (2,108 ft). The mountain is normally only free of snow from August to September, meaning snow fields are quite common along the road, which has an average incline of 5.1 per cent from Granada and 6.5 per cent from the actual start of the slope. The view from the top is sensational, spanning from the mountains of the Sierra Nevada over Granada, the Mediterranean 30 km (19 miles) away and all the way to the North African coast.

Detour

Sierra Nevada

The Sierra Nevada, whose name literally means 'Snowy Range', is Spain's highest mountain range. Its name obviously says a lot about these mountains – they are often

Fields in front of the snow-covered peaks of the Sierra Nevada

snow-capped, even in summer. There are fourteen peaks here over 3,000 m (9,843 ft), in front of which are mountain ranges also reaching up to 2,000 m (6,562 ft) in height. The highest point is the Cerro de Mulhacén at 3,481 m (11,421 ft). Between the second-highest peak, the Pico Veleta, and the town of Pradollano, located at an elevation of 1,300 m (4,265 ft), is an excellent region for skiing with nineteen lifts and a total of 61 km (38 miles) of trails.

Costa del Sol

'Costa del Sol' – the Sunshine Coast – refers to a roughly 150-km-long (93-mile) stretch of the south-eastern coast of Spain. And rightly so, because this lovely area of Andalusia enjoys a pleasant, sunny climate, with mild temperatures even in winter.

Marbella's yacht harbour.

It is certainly one of the reasons that the Costa del Sol has become one of the most popular holiday destinations in the world. Many of the small, once poor, fishing towns like Fuengirola and Torremolinos have now become tourist hot spots with enormous hotel and apartment complexes, holiday villas, golf courses and yacht harbours. Some of the former villages have kept their Andalusian charm, including Estepona.

Even Marbella, the luxurious and glamorous city favoured by the international jetset, has preserved traditional houses, lanes, squares and gardens in its historic centre.

the birthplace of García Lorca, 17 km (11 miles) away on the plains. From there it is up into the mountains for a detour into the Sierra Nevada over Europe's highest pass.

As you leave Granada heading east on a small road parallel to the A92, the landscape becomes sparser and wilder. This effect is enhanced when you see the first cave dwellings dug into the rocky hillsides.

8 Guadix This truly ancient city with grand Moorish ruins and a history that dates back to Roman times also has a section with cave dwellings – some five thousand gitanos (gypsies) live here underground in the Barrio de Santiago. Their homes, painstakingly carved into the steep loess slopes and actually comprising multiple rooms, are even connected to the city water supply and electricity network. The landscape remains sparse for a while now. After Guadix, the castle of La Calahorra is worth a detour. The Gulf of Almería soon comes into view.

9 Almería This fine city has always benefited from its special geographic location. Protected from the mainland by mountain ranges, the vast Gulf of Almería fulfills all the right conditions for a nice harbour and a good centre for trade. The Phoenicians even recognized this and built a harbour that became the foundation for the Roman Portus Magnus. Pirates later found it to be an ideal hideout, too.

During the time of the caliphs, Almería experienced yet another rise as an important trading centre, becoming the capital of a kingdom to which the likes of Córdoba, Murcia, Jaén and even parts of Granada temporarily paid allegiance. In 1489, the city was reconquered by the Christians and from then on only played a secondary role.

Today, Almería is very much an agricultural town. The surrounding area is home to rows of enormous greenhouses where fruit and vegetables are grown for export. The nearby Andarax Valley is home to the region's orchards and vineyards.

Almería is a predominantly modern town with wide, palm-lined streets dominated by the massive alcazaba (fort), which sits on top of a hill as if on its own throne. Construction began on the alcazaba in the 10th century and it is one of the most powerful and best-preserved fort complexes in all of Andalusia.

The Old Town, with its picturesque fishing and gitano quarter on the castle hill, La Chanca, still has an undeniable Moorish feel to it. The colourful cubic houses and the cave dwellings look like relics from distant times.

For the next part of the journey there is an alternative route to the highway – the very picturesque 332/348, which take you inland through the mountains of the Sierra Nevada and then back down the coast.

Passing through Motril, the road continues towards the Costa del Sol through the fertile plains where tropical fruits are a speciality. Along the way, a good place to stop is Nerja, about 50 km (31 miles) before reaching Málaga. Perched on a ridge, this

town is home to the amazing Cueva de Nerja dripstone cave.

10 Málaga Málaga is a very important economic centre, Andalusia's second-largest city with over half a million inhabitants, and the second-largest Spanish port on the Mediterranean after that of Barcelona. It is the main trading centre for the agricultural products from the nearby plains, in particular wine and raisins.

In terms of tourist attractions, Málaga does not have a lot to offer. However, it is well worth climbing up to the Gibralfaro, the Moorish citadel and lighthouse that gives you a beautiful view of the semicircular expanse of land.

Today, next to nothing remains of the splendour of the alcazaba – often compared to the Alhambra in Granada – and the cathedral, whose construction started in the 16th century but was not completed: the middle section of the tower, 'La Manquita', (the missing one) is still open for all to see.

Detour

Gibraltar

The first impression is imposing: the 425-m-high (1,394-ft) limestone rock of Gibraltar suddenly soars out of the sea, connected to the mainland only by a flat alluvial plain. This is where the airfield was built, and where every visitor must pass upon presenting their passport or personal ID.

The British enclave, just 6 sq km (2.3 sq mi) in size and with a population of 30,000, controls the strait between Europe and Africa. Its name derives from Djebal al-Tarik, – Tarik's Mountain – the name of its Arab conqueror from 711.

The British originally seized the strategically important southern tip of Spain in 1713 during the War of the Spanish Succession, and at the start of the 19th century they built the Anglican Church here. Today, the British governor resides in a former Franciscan monastery dating back to the 16th century.

The official language on the island is English and the most interesting

The rock of Gibraltar towers over the strait of the same name.

From Málaga, the Costa del Sol continues along coastal road 340 with its large holiday resorts. After Marbella, the main road turns off into San Pedro de Alcántara. For those who want to enjoy some beautiful scenery, however, drive another 30 km (19 miles) west and take the route at Manilva that heads up into the Serranía de Ronda. If you wish to to visit Gibraltar you can do so by continuing another 40 km (25 miles) from Manilva along the coastal road.

⑪ **Ronda** If for nothing else, this town is worth seeing for its adventuresome location. It lies at the edge of a high plateau divided by the Río Guadalevín, which flows by in a gorge that is up to 200 m (656 ft) deep. Its houses and numerous mansions are built right up to the edge of the cliff.

The 98-m-high (322-ft) Puente Nuevo, built in the 18th century, spans the gorge. Ernest Hemingway was as fascinated with the city, the deep gorge, the houses and the cliffs as was the poet

Rainer Maria Rilke, who once wrote: 'I have searched everywhere for my dream city and I have found it in Ronda.'

Ronda is divided into three sections. The oldest, La Ciudad, lies in the middle of the limestone plateau and is bordered on one side by a Moorish wall and on the other by steep terrain; sprawled at its feet is the San Francisco Quarter, with a street network lined with farms; and on the other side of the 'Tajo' gorge is the modern area El Mercadillo, where most of Ronda's 35,000 inhabitants live.

One of the most important attractions here is the Casa del Rey Moro in the La Ciudad. Inside the rock, a staircase with 365 steps leads down from this Moorish palace into the gorge. The cathedral, the Palacio de Mondragón and the Casa del Gigante with their Arabic ornamentation and decorative elements are worth seeing.

Then there is the bullfighting arena. Built in 1785, it is one of the oldest in Spain. Ronda was also the place where bullfights

were given a sort of 'constitution' in the 18th century.

It is absolutely essential to do day trips around Ronda where the 'white villages' are charmingly tucked into the rugged mountains and valleys – Prado del Rey, with its neatly planned streets; Ubrique, capital of the Sierra de Cádiz, known for its leather products; Zahara or Setenil, which look like large eyries with their houses clinging to the rock; and of course Olvera, a town whose architecture is still entirely Moorish and whose walled upper city is dominated by a 12th-century castle.

⑫ **Arcos de la Frontera** The route now continues towards the Atlantic coast, passing by Embalse de Zahara. This town has a population of 30,000 and sits on a rocky ridge basically in the middle of the Guadelete River. Its whitewashed houses still create a Moorish atmosphere, while the church of San Pedro is most definitely worth a look, perched directly on a cliff with an impressive view of the

gorge and the plains with their seemingly endless olive groves. The route now follows Highway 328 towards the Atlantic coast, although it is worth making a detour to Cádiz beforehand.

⑬ **Cádiz** This city is considered the oldest in Spain; the Phoenicians were already making good use of its narrow, 10-km-long (6-mile) peninsula as a storage

1 The view over the harbour city of Málaga on the Costa del Sol.

2 White houses in Ronda look out over the abyss on the high plateau.

3 Setenil, one of the 'white villages' around Ronda.

4 Casares, west of Marbella, was founded by Julius Caesar.

5 The mountain town of Arcos de la Frontera captivates visitors with its Moorish quarter.

6 An olive grove in the Sierra de Grazalema.

tourist attraction is the cable car to the top of the rock. From the top there is an amazing view of the Bay of Algeciras, the Gibraltar harbour and the North African coast.

The darlings of all visitors to Gibraltar, however, are the frisky Barbary apes, which can be fed without any problem. Legend has it that Britain's rule of Gibraltar will be protected as long as the apes continue to inhabit the rock.

1

Detour

Coto de Doñana

This region covering 757 sq km (292 sq mi) of the Guadalquivir delta

Top: Swamps in the national park.
Bottom: An indigenous pearl lizard.

area has been a national park since 1969. Formerly a royal hunting ground, a sand dune separates the marsh from the sea. This allowed numerous biotopes to develop where rare and endangered animal species live and migratory birds make temporary stops.

yard. Much later, after America was discovered, the city became extremely wealthy. Cádiz is still the second most important shipyard in Spain after El Ferrol. Fish is also an important source of revenue, as is salt, which is obtained from enormous salt refineries in the south-east of the city.

The best way to discover Cádiz is to take a taxi ride around the Old Town, which is especially picturesque with the golden cupola of the Catedral Nueva towering over the tiny square houses. The treasures of its church include the largest and most precious processional monstrance in the world. The Church of San Felipe Neri downtown is also worth a visit as the location where the Cádiz Cortes government in exile declared Spain's liberal Constitution in 1812. The Museo de Bellas Artes has some beautiful works by Spanish masters such as Francisco de Zurbarán and Murillo.

North of Cádiz on the Atlantic coast is a series of lovely resort towns – Puerto Real, Puerto de Santa Maria, Rota and Chipiona all have long, wide, fine sandy beaches.

⑭ **Sanlúcar de Barrameda** This dignified city, located at the

2

mouth of the Guadalquivir, is the export hub for the famous Manzanilla sherry. The Fino variety is only produced here in Sanlúcar.

The city is divided into two sections, the upper and lower city. Be sure to pay a visit to the palace of the once influential dukes of Medina-Sidonia and the superb Mudejar portico of the Church of Santa Maria. Another attraction is the royal equestrian school, the Real Escuela Andaluza de Arte Ecuestre, where you can witness Spanish dressage riding styles. This famous port saw Columbus begin his third voyage to America, and Magellan also set off from here on the trip on which his ship became the first to circumnavigate the globe.

Long before that, the Holy Virgin is said to have appeared here, hence the name Coto de Doñana (Coast of the Mistress). Today, you can take a boat to the Parque Nacional de Coto de Doñana from the quay.

From Sanlúcar the C440 'Ruta del Vino', or Wine Road, leads into the home of jerez (sherry).

⑮ **Jerez de la Frontera** A visit to one of the most wonderful bodegas – wine cellars – is a must in this charming city so rich in tradition. Many of these bodegas also have something special to offer apart from sherry. The Bodega Domecq in Calle Ildefonso, for example, enchants visitors with its Moorish interior, while the ironwork in the Bodega González Byass was done by

none other than Gustave Eiffel. Those still keen on seeing more sights after the enticing bodegas should head to the Old Town and have a look at the 17th/18th-century Church of San Salvador, the 11th-century Alcázar and the 'Cartuja', somewhat outside the city, whose Gothic church is particularly ornate.

From Jerez, highway E05 then heads back to your starting point, Seville.

1 Jerez de la Frontera: in the vaults of the Bodega Pedro Domecq, sherry matures painstakingly in hundreds of barrels until it can be bottled and drunk.

2 The Catedral Nueva offers a magnificent view of the Cádiz headlands.

Seville The capital of Andalusia and host of the 1992 EXPO lies on the banks of the Guadalquivir. It was an important trading centre after the discovery of the Americas. The 15th-century cathedral, with Moorish elements from the 12th century, the former royal palaces, the museums, the Plaza de España and the former Jewish quarter all make this city an absolute must.

Córdoba The hometown of the philosopher, Seneca, was already of importance during Roman times and in 929 became the centre point of the Spanish Caliphate. There are still traces of this around the great Mezquita – once a mosque, now a cathedral.

Granada Surrounded by the Sierra Nevada and the Río Genil, Granada's greatest treasure is the Alhambra, a sultan's residence with fortress walls, towers, residential palaces, mosques and gardens, inhabited by twenty-three Nasrid rulers over the centuries.

Palma del Río The Romans first founded this city at the confluence of the Guadalquivir and the Genil. It is also known as 'Andalusia's Garden'. The ruins of the city wall and the Monasterio de San Francisco are worth a visit.

Montefrío A lovely view of Montefrío from the south with its white houses, quaint churches and Moorish ruins all clinging to the jagged slopes.

The Sierra Nevada National Park The country's highest mountain range is home to excellent ski slopes and is often covered in snow until well into summer.

Guadix Some 1,300 of this village's dwellings are caves, the first of which were created in pre-Roman times. Today they are equipped with modern comforts.

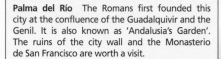

Jerez de la Frontera Upon arriving in the 'Sherry City', the first things to see are the Church of San Salvador (17th/18th century) and the 11th-century Alcázar – before you pay an inevitable visit to the bodega.

Casares A 13th-century Moorish fort towers over this village, originally founded by Julius Caesar in the Sierra Bermeja.

Ronda Hemingway was one of many famous artists and writers to have spent long periods of time in this fascinating town.

La Calahorra The protective walls and towers of the Renaissance castle south of Guadix surround a two-storey interior courtyard made of the finest marble.

Arcos de la Frontera White-washed houses give the town a slightly Arabic feel. The views from the village over the area and the gorge are fantastic.

Zahara 'White villages' like Zahara are scattered throughout the area between Ronda and Arcos de la Frontera.

Gibraltar A trip up the 425-m-high (1,394-ft) rock inhabited by the famous Barbary apes is worth it: the view of the British outpost and North Africa is spectacular.

Costa del Sol The 150-km-long (93-mile) 'Sunshine Coast' is a charming part of Andalusia with loads of long sandy beaches.

Almería This coastal city has a picturesque Old Town and a mighty cathedral, towered over by the Alcazaba (10th century), the largest Moorish fort in Spain.

The area north of Siena is the traditional wine growing region for Chianti Classico.

Italy

From Riviera di Levante fishing villages to famous Renaissance cities

From golden rolling hills, aromatic pine forests and stylish cypress boulevards to extraordinary art treasures and mouth-watering cuisine – Tuscany is a perfect holiday destination for nature lovers, art connoisseurs and gourmets. With rustic villages, a rich history and unique landscapes, this attractive region presents itself as one of Europe's 'complete artworks'.

Travelling in Tuscany is simply an intoxicating experience for the senses. Your eyes feast on the magnificently cultivated landscape, the delicate hints of rosemary and lavender please the nose, and your palate is spoilt for choice with world-famous Chianti wines and a cuisine that, with great help from the Medici family, had already begun conquering the world during the Renaissance. If that were not enough, nearly all Tuscany's charming ancient towns offer abundant art treasures as well.

Historically, central Italy is a region that has been inhabited for thousands of years, and proof of that fact is not hard to find. The ubiquitous remains of Etruscan necropolises, ruins from Roman settlements or the medieval town of San Gimignano make the point clear enough. Tuscany reached its zenith primarily during the medieval and Renaissance periods, and rightly regards itself as the 'Cradle of European culture'. Modern art, including painting, sculpture and architecture, can be traced back to this region.

Michelangelo's *David* in Florence.

The most important role in the region's rise to glory was played by the Medici, a Florentine family of vast wealth and influence that decisively dictated politics and the arts in that city for almost three hundred years, between 1434 and 1743. The pronounced cultural interest of the Medici drew the renowned artists of the time into their fold and, as patron of the arts, the family commissioned some of the most important works of the Renaissance period.

The cultural bounty of Tuscany attracts a great number of tourists every year. But a visit to Tuscany should include not only the well-known towns but also the countryside, as Tuscany is as famous for its ancient rural aesthetic as it is for its urban culture. This extraordinary countryside was planned in incredible detail and cultivated for centuries, with the landed

Cypresses, wine, an isolated farmhouse in the rolling hills – Tuscany presents a unique cultural landscape.

View from Pienza across the Tuscan plain with the cathedral tower in the background.

gentry as well as the farmers playing a part in the development. The farms, with a geometrical layout unchanged over the years, were placed on hilltops and all boasted a cypress-lined drive to their entrances. These splendid, centuries-old cypress lanes indicate their penchant for precise planning here.

Geographically, Tuscany stretches from the Apennine Mountains in the north to the Monte Amiata in the south, offering a varied landscape with rugged mountains, gentle rolling hills, the fertile coastal area of the Maremma and the green valleys of the Arno river. Southern Tuscany differs considerably from other Tuscan regions, being much hotter and having a less lush vegetation, dominated by maquis – dense, evergreen shrubs.

Industry and tourism are the economic backbones of Tuscany. Agriculture's main product is olive oil, but agriculture nowadays only supports a small part of the population. As a holiday destination, Tuscany is almost perfect all year round – between May and June an abundance of plants blossom in an extraordinary range of colours, while summer is dominated by the radiant red of the poppies and the glowing yellow of sunflower fields. Autumn is the time of the grape harvest, when the chestnut trees and the beeches change colour in late October and transform the landscape into a sea of mellow golden and red.

Your tour also enters the Emilia, a region between the river Po and the Apennine Mountains where Bologna is the city of note. On the west coast you reach Liguria with the Riviera di Levante and the tourist mecca, La Spezia. And from the hills of eastern Tuscany you finally reach Umbria.

Built on cliffs, the coastal village of Rio Maggiore in Cinque Terre.

The Medici

Almost no other Italian family managed to attain as much power and influence in politics and the arts as the Medici. A Florentine family of wealthy bankers, the Medici began their rise under Cosimo 'the Elder' (1389–1464) and reached their peak under the tutelage of Lorenzo 'the Magnificent' (1449–92).

Cosimo was basically able to rule his home town without ever holding any political office. He and his grandson Lorenzo were generous patrons of the arts and sciences and, under their auspices, geniuses such as Brunelleschi and Donatello eventually made Florence their home.

Equestrian statue of Cosimo I at Piazza della Signoria, Florence.

In the 16th century the family rose to princely status, but its decline began soon thereafter, continuing until the Medici line died out in 1737. The Grand Duchy of Tuscany then fell to the Habsburgs.

Tuscany – your tour through this magnificent region is also a journey through the Middle Ages and the Renaissance, starting in the lovely city of Florence. A highly recommended day trip leads to three towns on to the Ligurian coast, and the romantic country roads offer you a unique chance to get to know the varied Tuscan landscape in all its glory.

❶ Florence (see p. 129). Your circular tour through Tuscany begins in beautiful Florence. Only 8 km (5 miles) north of there is the village of Fiésole.

❷ Fiésole Founded in the 6th century BC by the Etruscans, this hilltop village is a far cry from the hustle and bustle of the big city and offers a fantastic panoramic view of Florence. In centuries past it was an ideal summer retreat for Florence's aristocracy, who were looking for respite from the city's heat and dust.

The wide Piazza Mino da Fiesole with the San Romolo Cathedral (begun in 1028) is the centre of the village. North-east of the cathedral, remains of some partially well-preserved Roman settlements were discovered, including the ruins of a theatre that seated up to three thousand people. Continuing via Florence you come to lively Prato, Tuscany's third-largest town.

❸ Prato With its daring mixture of medieval buildings and modern architecture, Prato is a city of stark contrasts. As it was the metropolis of textile manufacture, wool-weavers began

settling here in the Middle Ages. Medieval ramparts enclose the historic town centre, which has a cathedral modelled on the cathedrals of Pisa and Lucca. The imposing Castello dell' Imperatore, built by Emperor Frederick II between 1237 and 1248, is a remarkable sight.

❹ Pistóia Following the SS64, an often very winding road that negotiates considerable differences in altitude, you reach Pistóia, a lively town steeped in tradition that is surrounded by nurseries and colourful flora. The picturesque markets and the beautiful 9th-century church of Sant'Andrea is worth a visit with its legendary pulpit by Pisano (1298).

❺ Bologna Tuscany is not alone in the area as a custodian of Italy's art treasures. The SS64 leads you to the neighbouring province of Emilia-Romagna and three cities that are as richly steeped in history as any Tuscan locations.

Like so many of the cities in this area, Bologna, the capital of

1 The Ponte Vecchio was built in 1345 and is the oldest bridge in Florence. Since 1593, goldsmiths and jewellers have been working in the bridge's workshops.

2 The Romanesque church of San Sepolcro houses the tomb of Saint Petronius and is one of Bologna's many artistically and historically significant ecclesiastical buildings.

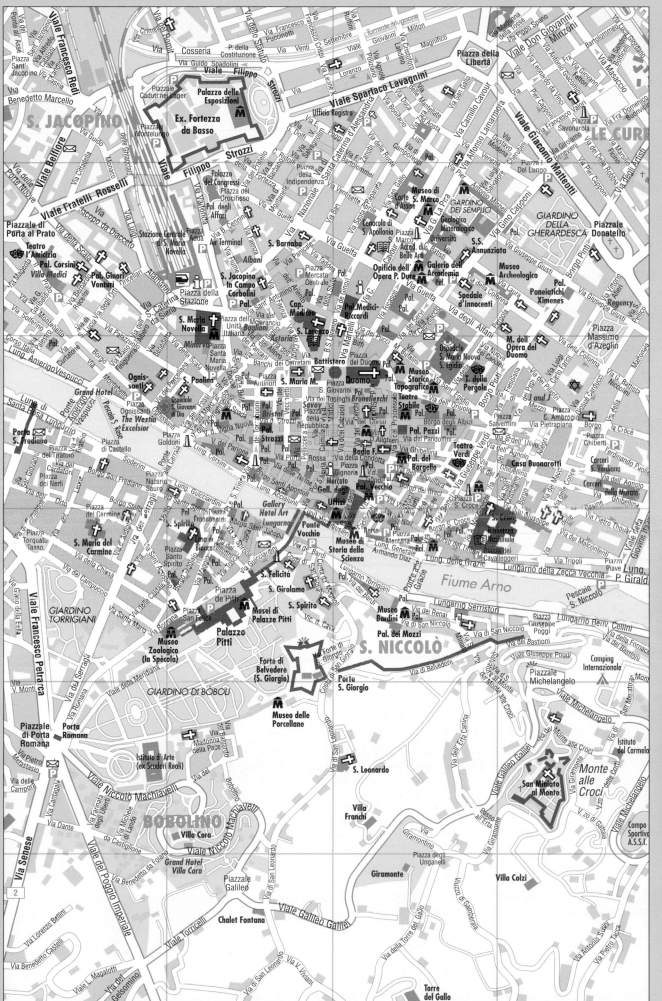

Florence

Florence's influence on the history of Western civilization is unequalled – it is considered the birthplace of the Renaissance. The city boasts a long list of famous sights, and attracts a phenomenal number of tourists each year. If you want to see the city from above, go to the Piazzale Michelangelo, situated 104 m (341 ft) above the historic town centre – the view of Florence stretching picturesquely over both sides of the Arno river is breathtaking.

Almost all the sights in the old part of town are within walking distance of one another. Florence's architectural jewel, the 'Duomo' (Santa Maria del Fiore, built 1296–1436), dominates the Old Town with its magnificent octagonal dome by Brunelleschi. Opposite that is the Baptistry of San Giovanni (11th–13th centuries) with its three sets of bronze doors by Pisano and Ghiberti, and the famous 'Gates of Paradise' doors.
The Uffizi Gallery houses one of the oldest and most important art collections in the world, including masterpieces by Giotto and Botticelli. Nearby, the Ponte Vecchio, Florence's oldest bridge, is famous for the goldsmiths' and jewellers' shops built on it in the 16th century.

Top: Duomo Santa Maria del Fiore.
Bottom: The Fountain of Neptune.

Back on the Piazza del Duomo, be sure to take a stroll along the Via Calzaiuoli to the Piazza della Signoria, Florence's most beautiful square and home to the 14th-century Palazzo Vecchio, the city's massive town hall with a slim, crenellated tower. A visit to the Giardino di Boboli is then a lovely finish to your leisurely stroll through town.

Portofino

An excursion to the picturesque village of Portofino is highly recommended – but leave your car behind! This swanky seaside resort is among the most beautiful on the Italian Riviera coast, and as such

Luxury yachts anchored in Portofino's harbour.

the traffic on the one small road to get there is generally horrendous. It's better to take the ferry over from Santa Margherita Ligure. The charming fishing village of Portofino and its cute little harbour is surrounded by olive groves, vineyards and cypresses. In the 19th century, rich industrialists started to come to the village with its tidy red- and ochre-coloured houses and left their imprint by constructing luxurious villas.

After strolling through the narrow alleys and hilly streets, you come to the medieval church of San Giorgio on the esplanade. The location offers a spectacular panoramic view. The Castello di San Giorgio (16th century) is your next stop. Towards the end of the 19th century, Baron von Mumm converted this former military hospital into a luxury villa.

If you follow the picturesque path up to its southern peak, you reach the lighthouse of Punto Capo, which affords magnificent views across the Tigullian Gulf.

Emilia-Romagna, was founded by the Etruscans. It lies in a fertile plain in the foothills of the Apennines and is home to one of Europe's oldest universities, dating back to 1119.

Important churches, arcaded lanes, towers and palaces bear witness to Bologna's period of prominence back in the Middle Ages. Among other sights, the Church of San Petronio is worth visiting. Its interior ranks up there with the most exemplary of Gothic architectural works. The two 'leaning towers', built in brick for defence purposes, are the hallmark of the city.

The SS9 now leads you on to Módena, about 40 km (25 miles) to the north-west.

6 Módena Located in the Po river valley, Módena is worth a visit for its magnificent cathedral and celebrated art treasures. The centre of town boasts extensive squares and leafy arcades. The Cathedral San Geminiano (1184), with its impressive 88-m (288-ft) bell tower, and the Piazza Grande have been given joint status as a UNESCO World Heritage Site.

7 Réggio nell'Emília Like Módena, Reggio nell'Emília was founded by the Romans and mainly belonged to the House of Este. The town is situated on the edge of Italy's northern plain, a fertile area with great agricultural yields.

The cathedral, whose construction began in the 9th century, the 16th-century San Próspero Church and the Church of the Madonna della Ghiaira, a baroque edifice featuring stucco and frescoes (1597–1619), are all well worth visiting.

8 Parma The city of Parma, near the Apennine Mountains, was founded by the Etruscans, but now has a modern layout due to reconstruction after devastating bombings in World War II. The Piazza Garibaldi, with the Palazzo del Governatore, marks the centre of town.

On the Piazza del Duomo stands the 12th-century Romanesque cathedral with its famous fres-

Detour

Lucca

Lucca, situated in a fertile plain near the Appuan Mountains, is rightly regarded as the archetypal Tuscan city. It boasts a number of palaces and towers and fully intact Old Town walls. This erstwhile Roman settlement retained its independence for a very long time and only fell under the rule of nearby Pisa for a brief period.

The traditional trading city today has an important silk, paper and

Medieval edifices surround the Piazza del Mercato.

textile industry. You enter the historic centre through one of the seven old gates and are immediately enthralled by the ambience of its tiny streets and alleyways.

The Duomo San Martino (c. 11th century), with its magnificent arcaded façade, is Lucca's most prominent religious structure. Its nave and transepts were rebuilt in the Gothic style in the 13th and 15th centuries. The Church of San Michele in Foro has a spectacular Romanesque arcaded facade and is named after the Roman forum that once stood here. For centuries the Piazza San Michele was regarded as the centre of town, with its exquisite medieval houses built by the wealthy merchant classes of old. Nearby is the villa of the Guinigi family, with an unusual tower that has trees sprouting from it. After a climb to the top, you are rewarded with a wonderful view across the red roofs of the Old Town. Afterwards you should consider taking a walk on the 4-km (2.5-mile) wall around the Old Town, which offers magnificent views of the surrounding countryside.

On the way out of town to the resort of Bagni di Lucca you come to the famous Ponte del Diavolo – the 'Devil's Bridge' – from the 11th century, which dramatically spans the River Serchio.

coes, while further west you'll find the Palazzo della Pilotta. Inside this unfinished brick edifice is a beautiful inner courtyard and some museums, such as the Galeria Nazionale.

The journey continues now across the 1,055-m (3,460-ft) Cento Croci Pass (SS62 and SS523), a very curvy road with breathtaking scenery that runs from Varese Ligure via Rapallo along the Riviera di Levante.

9 Cinque Terre These five legendary coastal villages built on the cliffs of the Riviera di Levante have become one of the most popular tourist areas in all of Italy. Ever since the steeply terraced landscape in the area was made accessible to automobiles, the villages – Monterosso, Vernazza, Corniglia, Manarola and Riomaggiore – are practically household names.

However, visitors are strongly recommended to leave their cars in Levanto and take the train instead. The roads leading to the villages are very steep and winding – and often full of traffic.

To be able to enjoy the natural beauty of this place to the full, you need to take the five-hour walk on the footpath that links the five villages. Italy's most beautiful walking trail offers absolutely awe-inspiring views of the Mediterranean and the magnificent cliffs.

After a short excursion to Portofino, another elegant former fishing village, the journey continues south to La Spézia.

10 La Spézia One of Italy's most beautiful bays is located at the

southernmost point on the Gulf of Genoa, with the spectacular Apennine Mountains as a backdrop. La Spézia, Liguria's second-largest town, is one of Italy's most important military and commercial ports, a fact that has rendered the town less attractive over the years.

However, its charming shopping streets date back to the 19th century and the museum of archaeology and the shipping museum make a visit worthwhile. A short trip south leads to Lerici.

11 Carrara Here in the northwest of Tuscany, Carrara marks

1 Baptistry on the Piazza del Duomo in Parma.

2 Módena's Romanesque cathedral also has a leaning tower – the Torre Ghirlandina.

3 Vernazza on the Italian Riviera, one of the five villages of beautiful Cinque Terre.

4 A medieval castle rises above Lerici's marina.

Detour

Elba

Even the ancient Etruscans and Romans recognized the unique beauty of this mountainous island. Its iron resources were already wellknown in Roman times when mines were established. Due to its mild climate, Italy's third-largest island offers a diverse natural landscape that includes not only chestnut trees, vineyards and olive groves, but also Mediterranean scrub brush. Hills, mountains and low plains are all wonderfully mixed together.

Taking the ferry from Piombino, you reach the island's capital of Portoferraio on the north coast in one

Porto Ferraio on the island of Elba.

hour. Napoleon's former summer residence, with the somewhat uninspired name of Villa Napoleonica, is in San Martino just 6 km (3.7 miles) from the dock.

On a round trip of the island, you first arrive in Procchio, with a beautiful bay that is ideal for swimming. Continuing along the picturesque winding road, you come to the island's favourite seaside resort, Marciana Marina, where the Pisan Tower offered shelter from the Saracens. Shady pine forests stretch from here to the sea.

Marina di Campo on the south coast has a broad sandy beach and is the island's main tourist resort. Porto Azurro is popular because it is sheltered from the constant wind. Above the town rises the star-shaped Fort Longone, which has served as a prison for the last 150 years.

the beginning of the Versilia Coast, a beautiful stretch scattered with white sandy beaches and the Apuan Alps providing the film-set backdrop.

The road takes you through a unique marble region where exhausted marble quarries have left rather bizarre formations that now seem to dominate the landscape. Even in Roman times, Carrara was famous for its fine-grained white and grey marble. Today, Carrara is home to an academy for sculptors, where artists have the luxury of learning to work with the rock directly at its source.

In the workshops of the Old Town of Pietrasanta, you can see stonemasons at work, happy to let tourists watch while they create. It is also well worth taking a stroll through the historic town centre to admire the 13th-century Cathedral San Martino with its charming brick campanile.

12 Viaréggio Even in the coastal resort town of Viaréggio, people's livelihood depends to an extent on the marble industry. Other options, however, include shipbuilding and, of course, tourism. Europe's high

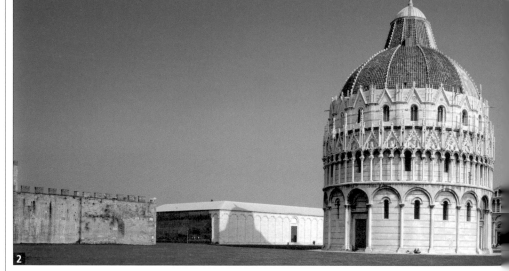

society discovered this picturesque fishing village in the 19th century, as the art deco villas and audacious rococo-style cafés will illustrate.

From Viaréggio it is only 25 km (15 miles) to Lucca, which is not to be missed on your trip. The road now leaves the coast and runs parallel to the regional nature reserve, Parco Naturale Migliarino-Massaciúccoli, which stretches all the way down to Livorno.

13 Pisa About 21 km (13 miles) south of Viaréggio is Pisa, well-known for its unique buildings around the Campo dei Miracoli, the 'Field of Miracles'. Among the masterpieces here are the Duomo (the cathedral) and the Baptistry – and most important of all, the Leaning Tower of Pisa, which began leaning to the south-east almost immediately after construction began in 1775. Although these structures were built at different times,

they were all erected with white Carrara marble and therefore have the effect of being one harmonious entity.

Pisa's role as an important commercial and naval port earned the city the epithet of 'Queen of the Sea', and its influence was considerable. Its decline came when Pisa was defeated by powerful rivals from Genoa and Venice, and the port silted up. The only leading institution remaining in Pisa is its university,

proof of a deep-rooted educational tradition. If you wish to relax, visit the romantic botanic gardens, established in 1543.

⑭ Livorno One can hardly believe that Livorno is part of Tuscany, its ambience is so different. But this is probably due to the late construction of the town. It was not until 1571 that this small fishing village was expanded into a port by Cosimo I (see the Medici sidebar p. 128)

because Pisa's port was in danger of silting up. The dyke protecting the port here was built between 1607 and 1621.
Today, Livorno is Tuscany's most important port. At the seaside visitors can admire the 'Old Fortress' (1521–23) and the 'New Fortress' (1590) and enjoy a visit to the aquarium.
South of Livorno the route continues along the cliffs to San Pietro in Palazzi, past some sandy bays. From here you take the exit onto the SS68 heading east and continue for another 33 km (20 miles) inland until you get to Volterra, high above the road on a hillside.

⑮ Volterra Medieval ramparts surround Volterra's historic town centre with its narrow and dark little alleyways and tall rows of houses. The town's livelihood comes mainly from the alabaster industry. The Etruscan Museum, containing thousands of funerary urns and sarcophagi, is a must for anyone interested in this ancient culture.
The view from the top of the city hall's tower is breathtaking – on clear days you can even see the sea. The old town has been left

intact for a rather dramatic reason – Volterra is in danger of subsiding because the steep hill it is built on frequently suffers landslides, making the town unattractive to developers.
A turn-off from the SS68 leads onto a small road of outstanding natural beauty – this is the heart of Tuscany, with its typical landscape of vineyards and olive groves.

⑯ San Gimignano For a time, the merchant families of San Gimignano built tall towers to display their wealth – the taller the tower, the richer the family. Seventy-two of them guarded the dreamy Piazza della Cisterna in the historic centre of town. Only fifteen are standing now, but these perfectly preserved 14th-century towers, the iconic skyline of San Gimignano, make you feel as if transported back to the Middle Ages.
Returning along the same route, you reach the coast again about 72 km (45 miles) further along. Follow the old Via Aurelia south to San Vincenzo, and continue on a small coastal road until you get to a series of beaches that look inviting for a dip.

⑰ Piombino The ferries for Elba leave from Piombino, a port town with an interesting harbour promenade and charming views of the old anchorage and the island of Elba. Populonia, an ancient Etruscan port town with the impressive necropolis of San Cerbone, is nearby and worth a visit
Getting back on the S1 at San Vincenzo, continue to Follónica, where the SS439 turns inland.

⑱ Massa Marittima Roughly 26 km (16 miles) from the sea, the small town of Massa Marittima lies on the edge of the Maremma, a former marshland that was drained in the 19th century. From the upper part of town – in particular the Torre del Candeliere – you can get a magnificent view of the Old Town's red roofs and the surrounding

1 View across the plains of the Maremma, from Massa Marittima on the hills of the Colline Metallifere. The Romanesque-Gothic cathedral is the town's icon.

2 Pisa's famous symbols – the Baptistry, Duomo and 'Leaning Tower' in the Field of Miracles.

Dynastic towers

In the medieval towns of yore, noble families who had made it rich in the wool, wine or spice trade competed with one another by erecting fortified towers that also served as dwellings. These rivalries between families were focused mainly on the height of the towers – the height being an indication of power. But apart from being symbols of power, the towers actually

The medieval 'skyline' of San Gimignano.

served the very real purpose of providing shelter from enemies. They were also the sites of family feuds.
The 'skyline' of San Gimignano is unique – fifteen towers of varying height are still intact and have earned the city the rather fanciful name of the 'Manhattan of the Middle Ages'.

Assisi

A short trip to Assisi in nearby Umbria is highly recommended. The famous basilica in Assisi is entirely dedicated to St Francis (1182–1226), who was born here. Everywhere you will find churches and memorials

Frescoes in the Basilica di San Francesco.

erected in honour of this worldly saint, also known as the 'Patron Saint of Animals and Ecology'.

Since the time of Francis, the impressive layout of the small village on the flank of Mount Subasio has hardly changed. One event, however, was far-reaching – the construction of the basilica, three years after the saint's death. The upper church houses works by many of Italy's renowned late-Romansque and early-Gothic artists. Nowhere else in Italy can you find a collection of this calibre. The lower church, where the saint is buried, is the pilgrimage site. Damage from the earthquake in 1997 has been almost completely repaired.

Tuscan countryside. A diocesan town in the 12th and 13th centuries, Massa Marittima boasts magnificent medieval buildings such as the Duomo San Cerbone (1228–1304).

Stay on the SS441 and SS73 for 75 km (46 miles) to Siena.

19 Siena Siena's red-brick palaces and extraordinary flair often give this town a more authentic ambience than its great rival Florence. The 'Gothic City' stretches over three hillsides in the heart of the rolling Tuscan countryside. Its historic centre has long been designated a UNESCO World Heritage Site. Siena is also home to what is arguably Italy's most beautiful square, the shell-shaped Piazza del Campo, surrounded by Gothic palaces. Twice a year it hosts the legendary Palio horse race, which attracts up to fifty thousand spectators and causes total chaos throughout the city.

The Duomo (12th century) is Siena's cathedral and one of the jewels of the Gothic period. It should not be missed. Other architectural treasures include the Palazzo Pubblico (1288–1309) and the slim 102-m (334-ft) Torre del Mangia, one of the most daring medieval towers.

The centre of the Chianti area is north of Siena. From here, small roads lead to the domain of Chianti Classico, carrying the emblem 'Gallo Nero' (black cockerel) as proof of its outstanding quality. The vineyards advertise 'Vendita diretta' for wine tasting and direct sales.

Follow the S222, S249 and S408 in a clockwise direction to visit a number of quaint villages – Castellina in Chianti, Radda in Chianti, Badia a Coltibuono, Moleto and Brolio with its castle Castello di Brolio.

20 Montepulciano About 70 km (43 miles) south-east of Siena is Montepulciano, a Renaissance town of outstanding beauty on top of a limestone hill. The small town, with its lovely brick buildings, is a Mecca for wine and art connoisseurs. Just outside Montepulciano you'll find San Biagio, an architectural treasure dating back to the 16th century. The pilgrimage church is laid out in the form of a Greek cross and is surrounded by cypresses – in perfect harmony with the landscape.

From Montepulciano the S146 leads to Chiusi and south-east to the junction of the S71, which runs along the west side of the Lago Trasimeno before bringing you to Cortona 40 km (25 miles) away. From the lake we recommend a detour of about 75 km (46 miles) to visit Assisi on the S75 – birthplace of the legendary St Francis of Assisi.

21 Cortona Cortona, one of the oldest Etruscan settlements, is another Tuscan hill town situated above the plains of Chiana. We recommend a stroll through the maze of the Old Town, full of alleyways and steps. The Piazza Garibaldi offers a spectacular view of the Lago Trasimeno.

22 Arezzo Arezzo, 80 km (50 miles) south-east of Florence, is the last port of call on your journey. The palaces of rich merchants and influential families dominate the scene, along with the ubiquitous religious buildings. The town is wealthy, partly due to its worldwide gold jewellery export industry.

The Gothic Basilica of San Francesco has become a Mecca for art lovers. The main attraction is the *History of the True Cross*, a series of frescoes by Piero della Francesca. *La Leggenda della Vera Croce*

(The Legend of the True Cross) is also one of Italy's most beautiful frescoes. Its theme is the wood from the tree of knowledge in the Garden of Eden that became the cross on which Christ was crucified. The colour and the perspective are extraordinary.

1 The pilgrimage church of Tempio di San Biagio (1518–34) is a masterpiece by architect Antonio da Sangallo just outside Montepulciano.

2 The Duomo and the 102-m (334-ft) bell tower of the Palazzo Pubblico dominate the modest skyline of Siena.

3 Because they grow so straight and tall, cypresses are the local favourite for delineating recreation areas or a landmark.

Parma This town is famous for its food – the delicious prosciutto di Parma and of course Parmesan cheese. After being destroyed during World War II, the Old Town was not restored. The Lombardian-Romanesque Duomo (12th century) and the Palazzo della Pilotta are the only remains.

Módena A Duomo (1184) with an 88-m-high (29-ft) bell tower and leafy arcades are the prominent features of this town.

Bologna This university town in the province of Emilia-Romagna is steeped in history and well worth a visit. The Church of San Petronio, with its two famous leaning towers, and the interesting alleys and palaces keep you wandering.

Portofino This seaside town in the Gulf of Rapallo is surrounded by olive and cypress groves. The quaint fishing village has long attracted the rich and famous, who have built luxury villas here.

Prato The historic part of this textile industry hub is surrounded by medieval fortifications. Prato is home to its own Duomo and the Castello dell'Imperatore, built by Emperor Frederick II from 1237 to 1248. The rest of the Old Town is an interesting mix of ancient and modern buildings.

Florence A trip to Florence should start at the Piazzale Michelangelo, to get a perfect view of the 'Birthplace of the Renaissance', before visiting the other main attractions – the Duomo Santa Maria del Fiore (1296–1436), the Uffizi, the Ponte Vecchio and the Palazzo Vecchio.

Assisi This town on the western flank of Monte Subasio is the birthplace of the famous St Francis (1182–1226).

Cinque Terre The villages of Monterosso, Vernazza, Corniglia, Manarola and Riomaggiore on the Riviera di Levante are among Italy's most photographed.

Lucca Seven arches open onto the historic centre of this walled town, to the Duomo San Martino (11th century) and to many merchants' houses, towers and villas.

Volterra This ancient city is still very well preserved and surrounded by medieval ramparts. Volterra is famous for its alabaster products, and its History and Etruscan Museum ranks among Italy's best.

Elba Italy's third-largest island offers an amazingly varied landscape with mountains, lowland plains, olive groves, pine forests and bays for swimming. In the northern part of the island is Napoleon's summer residence, the Villa Napoleonica – a must-see.

Massa Marittima The upper part of town offers a breathtaking view over the historic centre's red roofs, with the Duomo San Cerbone (1228–1304), and the surrounding Tuscan countryside.

San Gimignano Many of the medieval buildings here have been expertly preserved, among them fifteen of the original seventy-two medieval towers, which offered shelter against enemy attack.

Pisa Not only the Leaning Tower, but all the buildings on the Campo dei Miracoli (the Field of Miracles), including the Duomo and Baptistry, are worth visiting. Although these edifices in elegant Carrara marble were constructed at different times, they convey perfect architectural harmony.

Siena Florence's eternal rival is defined by the Gothic period. The Piazza del Campo, one of Italy's most beautiful squares, is a perfect example. Also visit the Duomo and the bold Torre del Mangia.

The Temple of Hera in Paestum, also known as the 'Basilica', was built around 530 BC.

Route 11

Italy

On the Via Appia from Rome to Brindisi

In the time of the Imperium Romanum, the motto of the day was 'All roads lead to Rome', when Romans saw their capital as the cradle of not only their own empire but of the civilized world. Large parts of Europe and the entire Mediterranean were ruled from here, and military roads ensured the necessary logistical infrastructure. Probably the best known of these ancient roads is the Via Appia Antica, the basis for your journey.

Relatively little remains of the brilliant splendour of ancient Rome, but what is left is indeed impressive enough – the Colosseum, the Baths of Caracalla, the Pantheon, Domus Aurea, the Arch of Titus, Forum Romanum, the emperors' forums and the Capitol. Contemporary Rome, on the other hand, is defined more dramatically by the unremitting desire of the popes to build magnificent churches, palaces, squares and fountains using the best architects of their times. The popes

were particularly active during the Renaissance and baroque periods. To this day, St Peter's Square and St Peter's Cathedral remain the heart of the city and of the Catholic Christian world.

The ancient Via Appia began at what is today Porta Sebastiano, and originally only went as far as Capua. It was then extended past Benevento and Taranto to Brindisi in 190 BC. Around AD 113, Emperor Trajan added yet another ancillary road that led through Bari.

Statue of Emperor Marcus Aurelius in Rome.

The 540-km-long (336-mile) basalt route, lined as it is by countless ancient tombs, temples, villas, ruins and even early Christian catacombs, can still be driven today and is considered 'the longest museum in the world'.

The road initially takes you out of Rome and into the hills of the Colli Albani where, in the Middle Ages, popes and Roman nobles had numerous villas and castles built – collectively known as the Castelli Romani. From Velletri, the Via Appia continues in almost a dead straight line to what is today Terracina on the Tyrrhenian Sea, then through Gaeta and inland towards Cápua.

From here, there is still an access road to the former Greek city of Neapolis, known today as Naples. This is home to the infamous Mount Vesuvius, a still-active volcano that once destroyed Pompeii and

The Ponte Sant'Angelo bridge in Rome leads over the Tiber to the Castel Sant'Angelo, built in AD 139 as a citadel, prison and papal residence.

The 13th-century Cathedral of Matera (Apulia) is maintained in the late Romanesque style.

Herculaneum, and whose next eruption remains a concern for some geologists. For the time being, the view from the crater's rim provides a wonderful view of the bustling city of Naples and the Island of Ischia in the Gulf of Naples.

From Naples, the journey continues along the sea around the Gulf to Sorrento. Since the time of the Roman emperors this picturesque area has been a meeting place for aristocracy. The southern side of the Sorrento Peninsula is where the steep cliffs of the Amalfi Coast begin, with its quaint, pastel-coloured villages nestled between the azure sea and the brilliant yellow lemon trees. At the end of the famous Amalfitana coastal road lies Salerno, where the actual Mezzogiorno begins. The stunning coastal road then continues on to Paestum, with ancient golden-yellow Greek temples that are some of the most beautiful examples of their kind in Europe. Indeed, the Greeks settled in southern Italy long before the Romans and left some magnificent relics of a blossoming civilization.

After Sapri the route leaves the coast and heads east through the inland province of Basilicata towards the Gulf of Taranto. At Metaponto on the gulf, the route again swings inland towards Matera, whose 'sassi' – former ancient cave dwellings – are a UNESCO World Heritage Site. Taranto marks the starting point for the journey through the 'Land of the Trulli', whose capital is Alberobello.

After passing through Ostuni you finally arrive in Brindisi, where one of the two ancient harbour columns is a reminder of how important this city at the end of the Via Appia once was for the mighty Imperium Romanum.

Remains of a colossal statue of Constantine the Great in the Palazzo dei Conservatori in Rome.

The Imperium Romanum

History teachers of every generation will tell their students that 'Rome was born in 753'. However, the creation of Rome more likely took place around the turn of the 6th century BC. It began with the merging of several towns into a municipality (still) under Etruscan rule.

In 510 BC the citizens chased away Tarquinius Superbus, their Etruscan king, and created an aristocracy from which the Roman republic eventually emerged. This officially lasted until 31 BC when Emperor Augustus came to power.

The expansion of Rome initially proceeded very slowly and was hardly noticed by the Greek colonists in southern Italy or the Carthaginians in North Africa (present-day Tunisia). However, after the three Punic Wars

Stairway to the Palazzo Senatorio.

(264–241 BC, 218–201 BC, 149–146 BC), almost all of Italy, including the surrounding islands, was under Roman rule. Victories over the Etruscans, Greeks and Carthaginians further guaranteed Roman dominance in the western Mediterranean and the Imperium Romanum was born.

The advances of Roman legionnaires were highly visible throughout almost all of Europe, sections of North Africa and in the Near East. At its largest, under Emperor Trajan (AD 98–117), the Imperium Romanum stretched all the way from the British Isles to the Persian Gulf. It had reached its zenith, which in turn marked the beginning of the end.

By AD 395 the no-longer governable western Imperium and the East Roman Empire were divided, with Byzantium as the capital of the eastern part. Germanic tribes then invaded the West Roman Empire and in AD 476 the Germanic ruler Odoaker dethroned the last West Roman emperor, Romulus Augustulus.

On the trail of the ancient Via Appia: this route begins in Rome and follows the famous highway of classic antiquity to Cápua, where it was later extended to Benevento, Taranto and then Brundisium (Bríndisi). The stations recall the country's important historic periods.

1 **Rome** For a detailed description of the myriad attractions here, see pp. 284–285.

Porta Sebastiano used to be known as Porta Appia because this ancient city gate marked the start of the Via Appia. The area around the porta includes the burial site of the Scipios, the famous Temple of Mars and the tomb of Cecilia Metella on the cypress-lined road to Frascati.

2 **Frascati** This is the most famous town of the Castelli Romani. Its glorious location, numerous patrician villas (e.g. the 17th-century Villa Aldobrandini), its exceptional white wine and 'porchetta', crispy grilled suckling pig, all contribute to this renown. And the popes enjoyed it all, which is why Frascati was their long-time summer residence before they moved to Castel Gandolfo. Roughly 5 km (3 miles) east of the city are the ruins of the ancient Tusculum, the favourite abode of Cicero, one of Rome's greatest orators and philosophers.

A few smaller places around Frascati are also worth a visit. The main attraction of the Grottaferrata, 3 km (2 miles) south of Frascati, is the castle-like monastery of San Nilo, founded in 1004, with frescoes from Domenichio (17th century).

Travel information

Route profile
Length: approx. 650 km (404 miles), excluding detours
Time required: 10–12 days
Start: Rome
End: Bríndisi
Route (main locations): Rome, Frascati, Velletri, Latina, Terracina, Gaeta, Cápua, Naples, Sorrento, Salerno, Paestum, Rotondella, Metaponto, Matera, Taranto, Martina Franca, Bríndisi

Traffic information:
Drive on the right in Italy. Speed limit in built-up areas is 50 km/h (31 mph), on highways 130 km/h (81 mph). International licences are required unless you have a new photocard licence from a European nation. Spare bulbs and warning triangle required.

When to go:
The best times to travel are spring and autumn, as temperatures are pleasant. In summer, temperatures can rise to over 40°C (105°F), though by the sea it is often cooler with the breezes. For current weather conditions at many holiday destinations visit:
www.italy-weather-and-maps.com

Information:
www.italiantourism.com
www.justitaly.org
For accommodation and events:
www.slowtrav.com/italy

Until a larger replica was built on the Ivory Coast in the 1990s, San Pietro in Vaticano was the world's largest Christian church. San Pietro was built under the auspices of master architect Giovanni Bernini between 1656 and 1667, and towers above St Peter's Square (Piazza San Pietro). This absolutely massive plaza is in turn lined with four semicircular colonnades containing a total of 284 columns and 88 pillars. In the middle of the square is the 25.5-m-high (84-ft) Egyptian obelisk, to which two fountains were added, one in 1613 and the next in 1675.

St Peter's Basilica was originally built in 1506, on the site where Constantine the Great had previously placed a basilica over the tomb of Petrus in 320. The most reputable Renaissance builders and artists helped construct the church, including Bramante, Raffael, Michelangelo and Bernini.

The enormous double partition cupola, started by Bramante and finished

The light-filled altar area with Bernini's altar canopy.

It's worth taking a small detour into the Alban Hills (Colli Albani – 740 m/2,427 ft) to see the township of Rocca di Papa, some 8 km (5 miles) south-east of Frascati. Monte Cavo at 949 m (3,114 ft) provides a wonderful view out over the province of Lazio.

The town of Marino is also located roughly 8 km (5 miles) away to the south of Frascati. During the wine festival on the first weekend of October, wine flows from the Fontana dei Mori instead of water!

❸ Castel Gandolfo This small town, idyllically located on Lake Albano (Lago Albano), has been the summer residence of the popes since 1604. The Papal Palace (1629–69) and other impressive homesteads like Villa Barberini and Villa Cyco, are the defining buildings in the area. The Piazza, with the Church of

San Tommaso and a stunning fountain by Bernini, is also worth seeing.

❹ Albano Laziale High above Lake Albano, the legendary Latin Alba Longa is said to have once been located here before the rise of Rome even began. The remains of a villa belonging to the famous general Pompeius is still open to the public. In Arrica, the neighbouring town designed by Bernini, it's worth visiting the Palazzo Chigi and the church of Santa Maria dell' Assunzione (1665) at the Piazza della Republica.

❺ Genzano This small town between the Via Appia Antica and Lago di Nemi is famous for its annual 'Infiorata' – on the Sunday after Corpus Christi a carpet of flowers adorns the Via Italo Belardi all the way up to the church of Maria della Cima.

The flowers come from the neighbouring town of Nemi, which is also a local strawberry-growing centre.

❻ Velletri The southernmost of the Castelli Romani communes is Velletri, located at the edge of the Via Appia Antica. Like Frascati, it is known for its excellent wines, but apart from this there are architectural attractions including the Piazza Cairoli with its 50-m-high (164-ft) Torre del Trivio from 1353, the Palazzo Communale from 1590, and the cathedral, which was completed in 1662.

The Via Appia then continues from Velletri to Latina.

❼ Latina This township is a good starting point for a day trip to the lovely forests and lakes of the Circeo Nature Park, which stretches over the mountainous promontory of Monte Circeo. At

the tip of the peninsula is the alleged grotto of the sorceress, Circe, from Homer's *Odyssey*.

From Latina, the route leads into the coastal town of Terracina.

❽ Terracina This town, which is today a famous spa resort,

1 The impressive complex of St Peter's Square, Rome, a masterpiece created by Bernini between 1656 and 1667. The obelisk in the middle of the square was erected in 1586 with the help of horses and winches.

2 The Arch of Constantine in Rome, constructed in AD 315, is next to the Colosseum, the largest amphitheatre of ancient times and the scene of countless gladiator battles.

3 An icon of Rome and a popular meeting place – the Spanish Steps. They get their name from the Piazza di Spagna.

by Michelangelo, is 132 m (433 ft) high. Michelangelo also created the famous Pietá statue in the aisle.

St Peter's itself is 186 m (610 ft) long and 136 m (446 ft) wide, with a height in the main aisle of 45 m (148 ft). It has capacity for up to 60,000 people. The papal altar stands over the tomb of Petrus and beneath the Confessio, which is vaulted by Bernini's 29-m-high (95-ft) bronze canopy.

Over the centuries, the faithful have kissed the right foot of the bronze statue of Petrus at the Longinus pillar so often that it is now shiny. Bernini's Cathedra Petri lies in the Apsis while left of the main altar is the papal treasury and the Vatican grotto, a crypt with the tombs of many popes.

Rome

The 'Eternal City', with its unparalleled artistic treasures and architectural monuments from basically every period of Western culture, is the centre of the Catholic world and at the same time the lively and vibrant capital of Italy - you just have to see Rome at least once in your life!

Rome, built on seven hills around the Tiber River, obviously has a long and eventful history that has left endless marks on the city. Its neighbourhoods, squares, monuments, buildings and architectural treasures have been built in every style imaginable.

Today, not all seven of the ancient hills are recognizable in the sea of houses, but from the Piazza del Quirinale on the Quirinal, the highest of these hills, you can get a fantastic view over the entire city. It is said that Rome was founded in 753, but the first traces of

the city eventually regained political importance in the 19th century when Italy was reunited and Rome was made the capital of the Kingdom of Italy.

Ancient Rome includes the Forum Romanum, the main square of the Old City; the Colosseum with its four-storey arena; and the Pantheon, the domed masterpiece of ancient architecture. In the Vatican City is St Peter's Basilica, the domed, Renaissance-style monument; the Vatican museums and galleries, probably the largest collection of art in the world; the Sistine Chapel;

Top: Nicola Salvis' masterpiece, the Trevi Fountain, was completed in 1762.
Bottom: The view of Ponte Sant'Angelo and the Castel Sant'Angelo.

settlement are clearly older. In fact for centuries before that there was significant activity here. The year 509 BC, for example, was a dramatic one in which the Roman Republic was established – and one oriented towards expansion. Rome soon became the mistress of the Mediterranean and ultimately, during the time of the emperors, the ruler of the known world. The Age of the Popes began after the fall of the Roman Empire. Rome then became primarily a religious centre. However,

and the Santa Maria Maggiore with original mosaics from the 5th century (exclave of the Vatican). Be sure to visit the Villa Giulia, once a papal summer residence with the national Etruscan museum.

The baroque square of Piazza Navona, the baroque fountain Fontana di Trevi, and the Spanish Steps are great meeting places.

For day trips, take the Via Appia to the catacombs of San Callisto and San Sebastiano, or go to Tivoli.

The frescoes of Pompeii

On 24 August in AD 79, the enormous plug that had sealed the cap of Mount Vesuvius for centuries exploded out of the mountain into the sky above the volcano. A huge cloud of cinders, stone and ash obscured the sun and glowing red magma spilled over the edge of the crater into the valley, burying the Roman cities of Pompeii and Herculaneum.

It all happened so quickly that some people could not get away. Like their cities, they were buried under 6 m (20 ft) of ash, lava and cinders – virtually mummified. Due to the sudden nature of the event and the quickness with which it engulfed these towns, it actually preserved homes and people in precisely the positions they were in when the eruption happened. As a result, much of what we know today

The portrait of Terentius Nero and his wife (1st century BC).

about ancient Roman life was discovered in the ruins of the towns.

Following the disaster, Pompeii was subsequently forgotten until the 16th century. Excavations only began in 1748 and gradually uncovered an almost completely preserved ancient city – not only temples, theatres and forums, but also houses and many other aspects of everyday Roman life – shops, kitchens, hostels, latrines, tools, public baths and, of course, the famous Pompeii Red Frescoes.

The most beautiful and best-preserved of these are in the Casa del Menandro, the Casa dei Vettii and the Villa dei Misteri, including a 17-m-wide (56-ft) series of images depicting the mysteries of the cult of Dionysus.

It is no wonder that Pompeii has long been designated a UNESCO World Heritage Site. However, the hordes of visitors and vandalism mean the excavation site is unfortunately in disastrous condition.

was once an important Roman trading town. Evidence of this can still be seen here.

The devastating bomb attacks during World War II actually had one fortuitous result – they uncovered a number of ancient sites, including a section of the Via Appia and the original foundation of the Roman Forum.

The cathedral is from the Middle Ages and is located on a former temple site. It contains some artistic treasures such as a mosaic floor dating back to the 13th century. The spectacular coastal road leads from here to your next coastal town.

9 Gaeta The Old Town, whose silhouette is dominated by the Aragonian fort and the Church of San Francesco, has a picturesque location on a small peninsula. However, the town is particularly worth visiting for the unique bell tower in the 12th-century cathedral – its bricks are fired in bright colours. The small Church of San Giovanni a Mare, dating from the 10th century, also contains a small oddity – the builders wisely designed the floor on a slope so that the sea water could run off again at high tide. For a long time Gaeta was a fortress for the kingdom of Naples.

After a few kilometres, the road leaves the coast and heads inland towards Cápua.

The ancient Via Appia

The most famous of ancient Rome's legendary roads was named after its builder, Appius Claudius Caecus, and was designed using large hexagonal blocks laid on an extremely solid foundation. First constructed as a military transport route, it was later used more heavily for trade. It originally led from the Porta Sebastiano in Rome to Cápua, but was extended through Benevento and Taranto to Brindisi in 190 BC. As Roman road architects mainly preferred straight lines, the road actually runs 'perfectly straight', despite steep rises in the Alban Hills and the Pontine Marshes. The Via Appia is 4.1 m (13 ft) wide, enough for two large transport wagons to pass each other at the time. You can still drive its complete length of 540 km (336 miles).

10 Cápua When it was initially built, the first 'section' of the Via Appia ended here in Cápua. This former Etruscan centre, with its enormous amphitheatre from the 1st century AD, was destroyed after the collapse of the West Roman Empire and rebuilt by the Lombards in the 9th century. The cathedral's bell tower dates back to this time. The Museo Campagna on the nearby Palazzo Antignano houses numerous discoveries from the city's ancient burial sites.

The tour now leaves the Lazio landscape and continues on towards Campania.

11 Caserta Just a stone's throw away from Cápua is the town of Caserta, sometimes boastfully called the 'Versailles of the South' – Bourbon King Karl III built the monumental French-style Palazzo Reale here. The palace is grouped around four large interior courtyards and is

Vesuvius

Mount Vesuvius is the youngest and only remaining active volcano in mainland Europe – it's 12,000 years old and last erupted in 1944. It is unknown how long its current dormant phase will last, but one thing is for certain – the pressure is rising inside. At present, a 3-km-deep (2-mile) plug is blocking the crater hole, and the magma continues to bubble up from a depth of 5–7 km (3–4 miles).

In the event of another eruption, more than 600,000 people living around Mount Vesuvius are potentially in harm's way. Since the last eruption, the volcano now has two peaks – Vesuvius itself at 1,281 m (4,203 ft) and Monte Somma at 1,132 m (3,714 ft). The main crater has a depth of up to 300 m (984 ft) and a diameter of about 600 m (1,969 ft).

The crater of Mount Vesuvius.

For those adventurous enough to climb the mountain, the view over the Gulf of Naples from the edge of the crater is gorgeous. These cinder cones and their most recent lava layers have virtually no vegetation, but halfway up are some sturdy oaks and chestnut trees making a go of it. Below 500 m (1,640 ft) there are even oleander, gorse, silver lichen, olive and fruit trees as well as the vines of the 'Lacrimae Christi' wine region. Despite its deadly outbursts over the millennia, the fertile soil on the slopes of Vesuvius continues to draw people back after every eruption.

There are a number of options for getting right up close to Vesuvius. The simplest is taking a ride on the Circumvesuviana, a train ride around the volcano that takes about two hours. Alternatively, there is a bus ride from Ercolano that takes you to the former chairlift station. From there, it takes about half an hour to climb to the top.

church of Gesù Nuovo, dating from the 16th century. The Old Town of Naples, with its 300 churches, castles and town houses, was declared a UNESCO World Heritage Site in 1995.

In addition, there are three castles in the centre of the city: Castel dell'Ovo from 1154, the residence of the Normans and Hohenstaufen of Swabia; Castel Nuovo (1279 82) in the harbour area; and the star-shaped Castel Sant'Elmo (14th–16th century) on Vomero Hill, just opposite the former Carthusian monastery of Certosa di San Martino. The Palazzo Reale and the Teatro San Carlo (1737) are also worth visiting.

Next to the Gothic Duomo San Gennaro (13th century) is the Gothic church of Santa Chiara (14th century), burial place of the Anjou kings with an interest-

1 The view over the Bay of Naples with the yacht harbour and Vesuvius in the background.

2 One of the important country villas of the ancient city of Pompeii – the Villa dei Misteri. Its wonderfully colourful paintings (80–30 BC) depict occult celebrations.

3 The church of San Francesco di Paola in Naples was modelled after the Roman Pantheon. Its cupola is 53 m (174 ft) high.

an impressive five storeys high. The whole complex – declared a UNESCO World Heritage Site – is 247 m (810 ft) long, 184 m (604 ft) wide and has 1,200 rooms with 1,800 windows.

No less extraordinary are the 120-ha (297-acre) baroque gardens with statuaries and water features including the Great Waterfall, which are a mighty 78 m (256 ft) high!

Somewhat in contrast to this extravagance here is the modest medieval mountain town of Caserta Vecchia 10 km (6 miles) to the north-east. There is a Norman cathedral here that was consecrated in 1153.

From Caserta, it's roughly 40 km (25 miles) to Naples, originally founded as Neapolis by the Greeks in the 7th century BC.

12 Naples Italy's third-largest city is often considered the 'most Italian' in the country. It is probably the noisiest and most hectic, but also the most likeable of Italy's big cities, where washing

lines still hang over the narrow alleys and the gap between rich and poor provides a somehow fascinating cultural mix.

The Spaccianapoli (literally 'split Naples'), a boulevard that cuts right through the city, widens at the turn-off to the north-south axis, Via Toledo, and leads you into the Piazza del Gesù Nuovo. At the centre of the square is a 34-m-high (112-ft) baroque column dedicated to the memory of plague victims from the 17th century. Opposite this is the

Detour

Capri

Emperor Augustus and his successor, Tiberius, had already discovered the beauty of Capri's legendary sunsets before the birth of Christ – ruins still remain from Tiberius' Villa Iovis on the island.

With a length of just 6.25 km (4 miles) and a width of just 2.5 km (1.5 miles), Capri is relatively small, but the jagged and, in parts, bizarre

Top: The 'Faraglioni' rocks off the south-east coast of Capri.
Bottom: Marina Grande, Capri.

limestone cliffs soar to heights of 589 m (1,932 ft) out of the Gulf of Naples. Along the coast is a series of caves and grottoes formed over the last 2,000 years because the island has sunk some 15 m (49 ft). The entrance of the Blue Grotto, for example, is only 1 m (3 ft) above the waterline. The grotto itself, however, is quite big at 54 m (177 ft) long, 15 m (49 ft) wide and up to 30 m (98 ft) high. The Grotta Azzurra gets its name from the mystical blue light that glows inside it from the early morning sun.

Ferries from the mainland dock at Marina Grande. A trip to the island would be incomplete without seeing the towns of Capri and Anacapri on the slopes of Monte Solaro, the rock cliffs of the Arco Naturale in the east and the three 'Faraglioni', rock formations in the south-east.

ing cloister. Behind the church Della Madre de Buon Consiglio is the entrance to the catacombs from early Christian times with frescoes dating back to the 2nd century. After the caves take a ride on the Funicolari, cable cars that bring you to the higher parts of the city.

The Museo Archeologico Nazionale has some priceless discoveries including the 'Farnese Bull' from the Baths of Caracalla in Rome and the mosaics from Pompeii depicting Alexander the Great's battle. A must on the way to Sorrento is Pompeii, which documents the devastating powers of Mount Vesuvius like no other place on earth.

13 Sorrento A beautiful coastal road leads you around the Gulf of Naples to Sorrento, with gorgeous views over the sea on the opposite side of the peninsula from Capri. The Roman emperors had villas and temples built in this small town upon high, steep rock faces as if on their own natural throne.

Sorrento experienced a Renaissance in the 18th century, when it was inundated by artists. Today, the birthplace of the poet Torquato Tasso in 1544 is one of Italy's most popular health resorts and artist colonies. A marble statue in the Piazza Torquato Tasso pays homage to the poet.

The iconic 14th-century cathedral is worth seeing for its inlay

work alone, and the Villa Communale provides wonderful views out over the Gulf of Naples. Another popular holiday destination in the area is the medieval town of Massa Lubrense, south of Sorrento.

14 Positano One of the most beautiful spots on the Amalfi Coast is at the beginning of the Amalfitana. Famous for its picturesque location on two slopes of the Monte Angelo a Tre Pizzi (1,443 m/4,738 ft), Positano has been transformed from a once quaint fishing village into a sophisticated spa resort. Dominating the scene over Spaggia

Grande Beach is the glazed cupola of the Church of Santa Maria Assunta.

15 Amalfi The cultivated fields dotting the Amalfi Coast, itself a UNESCO World Heritage Site, stretch out along the southern side of the Sorrento peninsula. Amalfi, today a lovely resort with a population of 6,000, was an important maritime republic between the 9th and 11th centuries that competed with the likes of Genoa, Pisa and Venice – it was home to 50,000 people back then. The rowing regatta held every four years between these former rivals is now the

only legacy of those times. In the 14th century, Amalfi was extensively destroyed by a heavy storm tide. Little of its history has been preserved.

In the middle of the maze of alleys is the monumental cathedral dating back to the 9th century. It was built in 1203 in an Arab-Norman-Sicilian style. Two former monasteries have been converted to luxury hotels where the likes of Henrik Ibsen and Ingrid Bergmann have stayed.

A worthwhile day trip from Amalfi takes you into the Valley of the Mills where some of Europe's oldest paper mills were

constructed. Make sure you see the wild Castania forests on Monte Lattari, which form the impressive hinterland of the Amalfi Coast.

16 Salerno The capital of the province and gulf of the same name had its heyday under Norman rule in the 11th/12th centuries when it was home to the Scuola Medica, Europe's first medical school. The Duomo San Matteo, with its 56-m-high (184-ft) campanile, was also built during this time. After passing between the Roman lions you enter a large forecourt with arcades of twenty-eight ancient columns brought from Paestum. The crypt is a gem of baroque marble inlay work. The Castello di Arechi towers over the city.

17 Paestum In 1752, road workers on the southern bend of the Gulf of Salerno came across the ruins of the ancient city of Poseidonia, which was founded by the Greeks in 600 BC and later called Paestum by the Romans. After being extensively destroyed by the Saracens in the 9th century, it was forgotten until the road came. The imposing temple complexes (the Temple of Neptune, Temple of Ceres, Temple of Hera) have now been excavated and preserved.
Other attractions include the 4.7-km-long (3-mile) city wall, a forum, the Via Sacra and a Roman amphitheatre. Herds of

placid buffalo now graze between the monuments and supply milk for the reputedly best mozzarella in the world.

18 Agrópoli South of Paestum is Agrópoli, a fishing town that clings to a rock cape. It has picturesque alleyways, ancient steps, a Saracen castle and more wonderful views of the gulf. East of Agrópoli, the hilly Parco Nazionale Del Cilento surrounds Monte Cervati (1,898 m/6,227 ft). You can go hiking, enjoy the serenity of the idyllic mountain village of Castellabate, or bathe in the turquoise-blue bays at Capo Palinuro.
Circling the promontory separating the Gulf of Salerno and the

Amalfitana

The coast road running along the Sorrento Peninsula is considered by many to be the most beautiful in Italy. Hewn mercilessly from the steep cliff walls, the 45-km-long (28-mile) route makes its way along the sea through narrow serpentines and hairpins providing you with non-stop panoramic views over the azure blue sea and the Costiera Amalfitana. Villages dot the coastline like pearls amid lemon groves and vineyards, while the sturdy houses cling to the cliffs and cover the dramatic slopes. The road serves as a connection for the villages between Nerano and Salerno.

Gulf of Policastro, you finally arrive in Sapri. From here, the route leaves the southbound coastal road and heads east overland to Brindisi, the historic end terminus of the Via Appia. Just under half way to Metaponto, about 30 km (19 miles) out of Sapri, you should take a detour south at Lauría into the Parco Nazionale del Pollina. The rugged landscape of the Basilicata is home to some lovely verdant forests, and peaks like Monte Pollina (2,248 m/7,376 ft). Two of this region's specialities are the rare stone pines and the Apennine wolf.

19 Metaponto Founded by the Greeks, this ancient city on the

Gulf of Taranto used to be called Metapontion before it fell to the Romans. It was also where the philosopher Pythagoras died in 497 BC. Numerous artefacts from excavations in the surrounding area are exhibited in the Museo Nazionale. The ruins of four temple complexes, the agora and amphitheatres are located in the Parco Archeologico. Drive to the Lido di Metaponto for a swim.

20 Matera Matera owes its fame to its 'sassi' – medieval cave dwellings dug into the steep tuff walls of the Gravina (gorge). Inextricably nestled into one another, houses later built in front of them stretch up the western slope. The caves were originally inhabited by Benedictine and Greek monks who built chapels, halls and altars and

1 The Duomo di Sant'Andrea in Amalfi was rebuilt in Romanesque style in the 11th century. An impressive perron leads from the Piazza Duomo up to the church.

2 The Costiera Amalfitana near Positano – pastel-coloured houses cling to the steep slope in terraces.

3 The Temple of Neptune in Paestum was built in 450 BC and is one of the best-preserved Greek temples in all of Europe.

The Greeks in southern Italy

Greek sailors had settled in southern Italy and Sicily back in the middle of the 8th century BC, long before the Romans arrived. On Sicily they found-

The Temple of Hera in Metaponto dates from the 6th century BC.

ed the city of Siracusa which, in its heyday in the 4th century BC, was the most important Greek city outside Greece and a metropolis of the ancient world. There were early Greek colonies on Ischia as well, just as the later Roman city of Cumae was also a Greek colony. These settlements were all grouped under the term 'Magna Graecia'.
Some of Europe's most beautiful Greek ruins can still be found in southern Italy – on the mainland are the Temple of Paestum and the ancient sites in Metaponto, while on Sicily there are the amphitheatre and the Temple of Segesta, the Valley of Temples near Agrigent, the Temple of Tyndaris and the Taormina Theatre.

The trulli of Alberobello

These traditional stone dwellings (trulli) are only found in the Apulia region, more precisely in the hilly Murge dei Trulli, a high karst plateau where the sparse landscape is defined by olive groves, vineyards and some fruit orchards. The word 'murge' itself comes from the Latin meaning 'sharp stone'.

It is here in the Itria Valley that you will find thousands of these small, round, stone houses with cone-shaped roofs topped with capstones called 'cippos' or 'pinnacolos.' Some of the houses have even been connected.

Until the 1930s, no one was really interested in the cute whitewashed houses of the poor farmers of the Apulia hinterland. Today, they are a national legacy and a UNESCO World Heritage Site.

Farmers used to store their crops in the high cone-shaped roofs. Many of the trulli were extended with another trullo by breaking through a wall each time a new child was born. Unique and bizarre structures were

The classic cone-shaped roofs of trulli in Alberobello.

thus created, the sizes of which were an indication of the owner's wealth. The clever Count Gian Girolamo II originally designed these strange little houses back in 1635 to save taxes. At the time, brick houses were subject to tax so he got his starving farmhands to pile rubble slabs on top of each other, without any mortar, to form round constructions with cone-shaped roofs. Using mud for grouting he developed the trullo – a non-brick building that helped him avoid further taxes.

The trulli were originally located on fields before entire trulli settlements were later formed. Alberobello, with around a thousand trulli, is the capital of the Murge dei Trulli and is located just a few kilometres northeast of Martina Franca.

painted priceless historic frescoes. Farmers later followed their example. Almost 20,000 people lived here in incredibly tiny spaces and in very primitive conditions until the start of the 1950s – sometimes even with their animals.

To eradicate them as a source of 'national shame', the sassi inhabitants were eventually relocated. Since the 1970s the structures were restored and made into a very popular tourist attraction. The town's other sights include the Norman-Roman cathedral (13th century), the Castello Tramontano (1515) and the Chiesa del Purgatorio (1770) with macabre depictions of purgatory. In 1993, UNESCO declared the city with its two sassi areas a World Heritage Site.

The route heads through Castellanetta towards the coast near Chiatona. The next stop on your trip is Taranto.

㉑ Taranto Also originally a Greek settlement (Taras), Taranto became one of the richest and most powerful cities in Magna Graecia in the 4th century because of its colour production using the spiny dye-murex snail. Most of its inhabitants were still Greek at the time of Emperor Augustus.

Taranto is divided into three sections connected by two bridges. The Old City is perched on a small rock island and is still quite charming despite a long decline. It is dominated by the towers of the Castello Aragonese (15th century). The Museo Archeologico Nazionale is really worth

seeing, with its precious gold and silver treasures. The cathedral in the Città Vecchia (Old City) was built in the 12th century but later remodelled. Its cave-like crypt and ancient marble columns are worth a look.

㉒ Martina Franca Further down the road you cross the Zona dei Trulli and reach the town of Martina Franca. In contrast to the nearby trulli style, this town is defined by baroque and rococo buildings like the Palazzo Ducale (1668–1742). The Church of San Martino, built from 1747–75, has a beautiful altar and is located at the gorgeous Corso Vittorio Emanuele. A detour to the trulli after Alberobello is a must (see sidebar left).

㉓ Ostuni The 'white' town lies at the eastern edge of the Zona dei Trulli, just 6 km (4 miles) from the sea. The picturesque village

is full of tiny alleyways and terraced white houses sprawl over its three hills. The late Gothic cathedral (15th century) and the town hall at the Piazza della Liberta (14th century) are also worth visiting.

㉔ Bríndisi The ancient city, Brundisium, has been the terminus of the Via Appia since 190 BC. Its original icons were two 19-m-high (62-ft) marble columns down on the waterfront. As back then, Bríndisi continues to be a gateway to the eastern Mediterranean – it isn't much further to Greece and 'Asia Minor' from here.

A plaque on the Colonna Romana pays homage to the poet Vergil who died here in 19 BC. Not far from the Colonna Romana is the cathedral square complex, a 12th-century work that was later given a baroque look in 1743.

Other churches include the Temple Church of San Giovanni al Sepolcro (12th century) and, further west, the church of the same name with a Norman cloister. The Church of Santa Maria del Casale has striking frescoes and the castle on the Seno di Ponte was built under Friedrich II from 1227.

1 The cave dwellings in Matera are divided into an upper and lower district, which are in turn made up of Sasso Barisano and Sasso Cavoso. Over thousands of years, new caves and houses were continually dug into the tuff in the two horn-shaped rock gorges. A total of 150 rock churches have been preserved here.

2 Trulli are the round white houses made of stone with a cone-shaped roof that is really a false dome. The architecture is unique to Apulia.

Rome The city gate of Porta Sebastiano, constructed around 312 BC, marks the start of the Via Appia and was once known as the Porta Appia. The area surrounding the ancient city gate is home to burial sites of the Scipios, the famous Temple of Mars and the tomb of Cecilia Metella, among other worthy sights. You'll find them on the cypress-lined road to Frascati.

Vatican City This 'city within a city' covers an area of 44 ha (108 acres) and has 400 permanent residents whose leader is the Pope. The Vatican's 'territory' spans the Vatican itself, the Papal Gardens, St Peter's Basilica and St Peter's Square, as well as some basilicas outside the Vatican and the summer residence of Castel Gandolfo.

Frascati Fabulous villas and the white wine of the same name have made the former papal summer residence famous. It also has some historic buildings to see.

Castel Gandolfo This small town on Lago Albano has been the papal summer residence for 300 years. The Papal Palace (1629–69) and some grand estates such as the Villa Barberini and the Villa Cyco define the town. The Piazza del Plebiscito, with Bernini's San Tommaso Church, is also worth seeing.

Genzano This small town on Lago di Nemi is famous for its 'Infiorata' – every year on the Sunday after Corpus Christi, the Via Italo Belardi turns into a carpet of flowers.

Gaeta Visit the colourful cathedral tower (12th C.) and the Church of San Giovanni a Mare (10th C.) in this ancient town neatly perched on a promontory.

Cápua The city, destroyed after the fall of the West Roman Empire, is home to an enormous amphitheatre (1st century AD) and an interesting museum.

Caserta The Palazzo Reale (1752–74) has 1,200 rooms with 1,800 windows. It is sometimes rightly called the 'Versailles of the South.' No less impressive is the 78-m-high (256-ft) waterfall in the palace garden.

Naples 'Italy's most Italian city' is noisy and hectic but its location on the coast, the narrow alleyways and small steps of the Old Town, and its wealth of artistic treasures easily compensate for that.

Pompeii This former provincial capital was buried under a metre of pumice and ash following the eruption of Mount Vesuvius in AD 79. Around three-fifths of the ruins have been unearthed since the 18th century. Nowhere else can Roman domestic culture be so vividly experienced.

Matera Cave dwellings called 'sassi', numerous chapels and buildings from the early Middle Ages buried into the tuff slope have made this picturesque area famous. Old caves were later 'modernized' with facades.

Alberobello Thousands of trulli – including a church and a two-storey stone house built in the typically Apulian style – define the look of this unique area.

Capri This oft-praised isle in the Gulf of Naples is only very small, but thanks to its location and the 'Blue Grotto' it has a mighty reputation on the Mediterranean.

The Amalfi Coast The 45-km-long (28-mile) road on the southern coast of Sorrento is considered Italy's most beautiful coastal stretch. The serpentine route itself is as spectacular as the views it affords.

Amalfi The 9th-century cathedral dominates the Old Town here. A regatta held every four years commemorates Amalfi's past as an important maritime republic (9th–11th century).

Paestum This city was founded by the Greeks in the 7th century BC and later destroyed by the Saracens. Its ruins from the 5th century BC are the most important Hellenistic sights on the Italian mainland.

The tombs of Hasan Pasa Kümbet at Ahlat, on the northern shore of Lake Van.

Turkey

Temples, mosques and gorgeous coves

Olive orchards, beaches and the snow-capped peak of Mount Ararat – Turkey welcomes visitors with an enormous wealth of scenery and landscapes. Beyond that, cultural landmarks and monuments of numerous empires spanning more than nine thousand years play a huge role in making your trip to Turkey an unforgettable experience.

Your journey through the Republic of Turkey begins in a surprisingly rural setting. Istanbul's lively arterial roads are full of all sorts of businesses, but they soon give way to the green fields of East Thrace, a totally different landscape where traditional tearooms, bazaars and caravanserais coexist with modern highways, cargo vessels, Roman ruins and monuments like those in Gelibolu (Gallipoli) National Park.

It was here that Turkish troops managed to defeat the British and Australian Armies after months of fighting in 1915 –

all under the command of Mustafa Kemal Pasha, later to become known as Atatürk, 'Father of the Turks', founder of modern Turkey.

All along the Mediterranean shores of western Anatolia, the 'Coasts of Light', there are historical sites of ancient Greek and Roman culture in all their breathtaking beauty. Among them are Pergamon, Ephesus and Milet, some of the most incredible examples of art and architecture from those times. The Hellenic mathematicians and philosophers living in Ionia, on Asia Minor's western

Head of Medusa in the ancient city of Didyma.

frontier, transformed that city into one of the cradles of European civilization.

On the south coast between Marmaris and Alanya you will be delighted by the plentiful beaches where water sports and relaxation are high on the agenda. For more adventurous travellers, there is also rafting, paragliding, cave excursions and mountain climbing. With a bit of searching you can find secluded coves and pristine natural settings.

Between the Olympus Mountains and the coast, a region of fishing villages, farms and winding pathways has been converted into a holiday destination where sensitive infrastructure and environmental considerations were taken into account right from the beginning. The project, known as the 'South Antalya Project' or 'Kemer project', has been called a 'total success'. The motto was 'Less is More', and

A strange sight – wind and rain have exposed these tuff pillars near Göreme in Cappadocia.

The Hagia Sophia in Istanbul is a masterpiece of Byzantine architecture. The building is no longer used for religious purposes, but as a museum.

it seems to have worked with the upmarket boutiques and hotels.

East of Anamur Castle, built on a magnificent location above the sea, your 'Turkey adventure' can really finally begin. Very few people come this far to see the wide horizons of eastern Anatolia. For hours, and over considerable distances, the land appears completely empty, with low-lying, dust-coloured villages barely standing out from the surrounding countryside. Yet this easternmost region of Turkey is where you find the country's largest lake, Lake Van, and its highest peak, Mount Ararat. Due to Ararat's remote location, however, we recommend you visit Nemrut Dagi in the Taurus Mountains, a man-made mountain with a 2,000-year-old king's tomb.

Lake Van and the town of Van, on the other hand, are worth a longer visit.

In central Anatolia you can experience Muslim culture at its most intense, especially in the highlands between the Taurus Mountains to the south and the Pontic Mountains at the Black Sea. Towns like Sivas or Konya are centres of Islamic mysticism.

Cappadocia, a must-see, is home to the bizarre erosion landscape around Nevsehir and Göreme. The tuff formations are a truly fantastic experience, both in terms of nature and culture. Byzantine monks once sought shelter here from Muslim Arab attacks. Today the cave dwellings and churches form a giant open-air museum.

An even older culture exists near Ankara, Turkey's modern capital. The Hattusas ruins are now a UNESCO World Heritage Site – one of a total of nine UNESCO Cultural and Natural Sites in Turkey.

The Celsus Library in Ephesus with its restored facade.

The Byzantine Empire

When the Western Roman Empire was shattered by the invasions of various central European hordes, the rulers of the 'Eastern Roman Empire' carried on. Constantine the Great turned the old Greek colonial town of Byzantion into the empire's new capital in AD 330 and renamed it Constantinople.

The Byzantine Empire, as the 'Eastern Roman Empire' came to be known, was at its largest geographically under Emperor Justinian (482–565), who ruled from 527 until his death. At that time, it encompassed all of Anatolia, the Balkans, Italy and Andalusia as well as the North African coasts of the Mediterranean.

Byzantium initially played the role of a protective buffer in defending ancient Europe from the Persian Sassanids, but the reward for this position was centuries of confrontation with the fighters of Islam. Seljuk and Ottoman armies continued gradually to reduce the scope of the empire until it ultimately encompassed nothing but its capital. On 29 May 1453, the Ottomans finally stormed Constantinople, killing Constantine XI, the last Byzantine emperor, and the empire was left to its own fate by the rest of Christian Europe.

Christ as Pantocrator: A magnificent mosaic in the Hagia Sophia shows Jesus as the 'Almighty'.

Ever since the Great Schism of 1054, Roman Catholicism had seen the Byzantine Eastern Orthodox Church as more of an undesirable competitor than as a Christian brother.

How much worse off would the European world be without East Rome? Well, the Codex Justinianus formed the historical foundation of the Roman legal system, which improved the rights of women, for example. Byzantine scholars also passed on antique texts from Greek philosophers and scientists. Furthermore, Byzantine art and architecture have been very influential in southern and central Europe, as evidenced by the mosaics in Ravenna. From St John's Basilica in Ephesus to the cave churches of Cappadocia and the Ani churches on the Armenian border, traces of Byzantium are simply everywhere in Turkey.

Turkey – a travel adventure even today? Beach-hopping along the west and south coasts is no problem at all – it's pure enjoyment. But what a bold contrast to the dust clouds on some of the dirt roads in eastern Anatolia! This journey takes you from touristy coastal towns to the central Anatolian hinterland, a fascinating excursion through the cultural and natural landscape of this diverse nation.

❶ **Istanbul** (see pp. 152–153). This city, where Black Sea currents flow through the Bosporus Strait, the Marmara Sea and the Dardanelles into the Aegean Sea, seems more closely linked to the sea than most other cities on earth. The coastal roads are generally wide and modern, with marvellous panoramic views of the Bosporus and the Golden Horn. Following Highway 03, this dream route first takes you across the Bosporus through the gentle, fertile hills of Thrace. There is peace and quiet in the fields and villages of this ancient agricultural region.

❷ **Lüleburgaz** The Romans knew it as Arkadiopolis but modern Lüleburgaz is a modest town on National Road 100. It does have a place of interest, however – in the 16th century, the architectural genius Sinan (1490–1578) built a mosque here for a pasha.

❸ **Edirne** From 1365 until the conquest of Constantinople in 1453, the former Adrianople (Turkish: Edirne) was the capital of the Ottoman Empire. Buildings dating back to the sultanate and an historical town centre with picturesque wooden houses have been well preserved throughout the ages.

The Selimiye Camii Mosque, built by Selim II, was called Sinan's masterpiece by none other than the great architect himself. This terrific building has a giant dome that possesses enchanting harmony and grace. Back on the coast, Sarköy is the centre of the wine-growing area on the northern shore of the Marmara Sea. Leave the E90 at Bolayir towards the east to get there.

Towards the south, the E90/550 ends in Eceabat, where you can catch one of the several ferries that cross the narrow Dardanelles each day to Çanakkale. The straits are only 1,200 m (1,300 yds) wide.

❹ **Çanakkale** Burly 15th century fortifications, a marine museum and a reconstruction of a World War I minelayer leave no doubt about the military importance of the Dardanelles. Along

Travel information

Route profile
Length: approx. 6,000 km (3,730 miles), excluding detours
Time required: 8–12 weeks
Start and end: Istanbul
Route (main locations): Istanbul, Edirne, Çanakkale, Troy, Pergamon, Izmir, Ephesus, Bodrum, Fethiye, Antalya, Alanya, Silifke, Şanliurfa, Diyarbakir, Van, Göreme, Konya, Ankara, Safranbulo, Bursa

Traffic information:
Beware of the three-lane system where the middle lane is used for overtaking in both directions! The middle lane is not always empty! Speed limit outside towns is 90 km/h (56 mph), inside towns it is 50 m/h (31 mph).

When to go:
Spring and autumn in general; due to relatively long winters in Eastern and central Anatolia, however, not before April/May and not after September. On the coasts, you can travel as early as March and as late as September.

Information:
www.turkeytravelplanner.com
www.travelturkey.com
www.turizm.net
www.exclusivetravelturkey.com

Around ninety-eight per cent of Turkish citizens are officially Muslim, but there is also a tiny minority of Greek Orthodox, Armenian Christians and Jews. As a strictly monotheistic epiphany, Islam considers itself the consummation of the two 'book religions', Judaism and Christianity.

However, since its foundation by Atatürk in 1923, the Republic of Turkey has had a secular constitution that separates church and state – and in 1928, Islam also ceased to be the country's official religion.

Sinan's Sellmlye Mosque in Edirne is an architectural masterpiece.

At the crossroads between being a democratic state and a Muslim theocracy, Turkey has definitely made a lot of progress towards 'Western' values – even if the theory of gender equality, so self-evident in western Turkey, is nothing but a theory in remote villages.

In some cases, physical violence by a man against his wife is considered a justified. A rigid code of honour sometimes even demands a vendetta by fathers or brothers if patriarchal sexual morals are overstepped.

the quays there is a row of cafés, shops and restaurants to explore. Away from the bustle of the harbour, the constant currents ensure that the waters are clean enough for swimming. We recommend Güzelyali on the southern shore of the Dardanelles.

⑤ Troy (Truva) This is where Heinrich Schliemann celebrated the discovery of the 'Priamos Treasure' and Homeric Troy in 1871. Archaeologists are still at work today but, due to a lack of written records, there is still no absolute certainty that this actually is the Troy of Homer's epics. An interesting and attractive exhibition presents the excavation findings.

⑥ Assos The Bagi Peninsula, an alternatingly flat and moun-

tainous strip of land with plentiful forests, separates the Marmara Sea from the Gulf of Edremit. More densely populated in the past than it is today, the coastal road (not the E87!) takes you past the overgrown remains of a few ancient sites – Alexandreia Troas, a port town near Gülpinar; the temple walls of the Apollon Sminteion sanctuary; and, at dizzying heights with fantastic views above the southern seashore, the ruins of old Assos (around three thousand years old). At the foot of the mountain is the tiny picturesque harbour of Behramkale.

⑦ Ayvalik After passing through Edremit on Highway 550, the main town on the 'Olive Riviera', you come to the tourist destination of Ayvalik with its seaside promenade, Old Town

alleyways, diving resorts and twenty-three islands just off the coast. Further inland are some wine-growing villages tucked in among the hills. Farmers, vintners and innkeepers have recently joined forces here to prevent the opening of a gold mine because of the environmental damage that it would most likely cause.

After turning off the E87 further inland, follow the signs for Pergamon (50 km/31 miles).

⑧ Pergamon The rulers of Pergamon used the steep slopes of the local rock plateaus, some up to 300 m (1,000 ft) high, to build the 'acropolis' of their capital city. Today, the acropolis' altar to Zeus can only be admired in Berlin's Pergamon Museum, but there are still abundant ruins in this ancient

town of kings. Bergama, the modern city at the foot of the castle mountain, also contains some historical ruins.

⑨ Izmir Cosmopolitan and full of energy, Izmir's two million people make it the only big city on Turkey's west coast and the country's most important port. Its bazaar is still as lively as ever.

1 The Temple of Hadrian in Ephesus is decorated in lavish relief.

2 Ortaköy Mosque, one of Istanbul's grand religious buildings.

3 The 'Blue Mosque' (Sultan Ahmed Camii Mosque) is so-named because of its 21,000 mostly blue tiles.

4 The ruins of Hercules Gate in Ephesus, vestiges of a former imperial power.

Istanbul

Its fairy-tale location on the Bosporus Strait and the Golden Horn makes Istanbul worth a visit. There is a lot to see and do in this historically charged city so perfectly placed between East and West, and its friendly people will not disappoint.

This city of three names – Byzantium, Constantinople, Istanbul – was the mistress of two empires that both decisively shaped the history of the Mediterranean for almost two thousand years – the East Roman or Byzantine Empire and its direct successor, the Ottoman Empire. Art treasures from every era of its history as well as the variety and vitality of modern Istanbul make the city an ideal destination for lovers of art and culture.

In the Old Town between the Golden Horn, Bosporus and the Marmara Sea there are a few things you shouldn't miss – Hagia Sophia, the religious centre of ancient Byzantium built by the emperor Justinian I from 532 to 537. It has a magnificent dome and some beautifully preserved mosaics. Hagia Eirene goes back to pre-Constantine times, the current building having

the 'Blue Mosque' (17th century); the Hippodrome, an antique carriage race track; the Museum of Turkish and Islamic Art; the Sokollu Mehmet Pasa Mosque (16th century); the Mosaic Museum; the beautiful ancient steam baths of Haseki Hürrem Hamam (1557) and Cagaloglu Hamam (18th century); Sogukcese Sokagi, a road lined with restored timber buildings from the Ottomans; and the High Gate, a rococo gate.

In the Old City check out: the Grand Bazaar, the world's largest indoor market; the Egyptian Bazaar, a book bazaar; the New Mosque (17th century); the Rüstem Pasa Mosque dating from the 16th century with its colourful tiles; the Beyazit Tower, a fire tower from 1828; the Beyazit Mosque (16th century); Nuruosmaniye Mosque (18th century); the Constantine Col-

Top: Hagia Sophia was originally used as a Byzantine coronation church.
Bottom: The Grand Bazaar is the world's largest indoor bazaar.

been erected in the 8th century. The Archaeological Museum has an interesting collection of antique exhibits. In the Ottoman city centre be sure to visit – Topkapi Sultan's Palace, a spacious compound with magnificent buildings structured by courtyards and gates; the well of Sultan Ahmed III (1728); the Sultan Ahmed Mosque –

umn from AD 330; and the Sultan Süleyman Mosque.

At the edge of the Old City visit the Hagios Georgios (1720), the cast-iron Church of St Stephen (1871), Tefur Palace (11th century), some ruins of the Theodosian wall (5th century), the Mihrimah Mosque (16th century), the Chora Church and the Victory Mosque.

Detour

Hierapolis and Pamukkale

The gleaming white sinter terraces above the valley are something right out of a fairy tale – albeit a recent one. Concerns for both tourism and the environment were fortunately taken into account when the greying terraces were restored over the past few years. The reason for this bizarre landscape is the high concentration of lime in the steaming hot water (36°C/96°F) that cascades down from mountain springs. As it cools, layer upon layer of lime is deposited onto the terraces.

Top: Monument of the apostle Philippus in Hierapolis.
Middle: View of Hierapolis above Pamukkale.
Bottom: Ancient ruins of Hierapolis.

The extensive ruins of the ancient town of Hierapolis are also part of this UNESCO World Heritage Site. In around 190 BC, these hot springs were probably an important reason that Eumenes II of Pergamon founded this town here, which was later to become an important Roman spa complex.
Besides the Roman baths and Nymphaeum (a huge fountain), the theatre is particularly impressive with its 15,000 seats and a stage house. South-west of Pamukkale are the ruins of Aphrodisias.

The parks, promenades and baths of Balcova provide a charming Mediterranean atmosphere, along with the lovely beaches of the Çesme Peninsula. From Izmir, there are two ways to reach the sinter terraces at Pamukkale – through the mountains via Sardes and Salihli (210 km/130 miles) or more quickly via Aydin on Road 320 (270 km/168 miles).

10 Ephesus This city of ruins near the town of Selçuk really defines the concept of ancient – the Lydians and Carians worshipped the mother goddess of Kybele here long before Greek traders and settlers arrived on the Ionian coast and built their own temple to Artemis in the tradition of the mother goddess. In approximately AD 129, Ephesus became the capital of the Roman province of Asia. At the time it had about 200,000 inhabitants. Archaeologists have been able to reconstruct more of Ephesus' temples, streets, baths and living quarters than any other site in Turkey. The city harbour, however, has silted up over the centuries and the sea is now several miles away.
Not far from Kusadasi is the important Ionian town of Milet.

11 Milet Like Ephesus and Priene, the trading town of Milet had to be relocated several times because its harbour was threatened by silt buildup. Today the former harbour is hardly visible among the ruins, which nearly disappear into the flood plains of the Meander River (Büyük Menderes). Only one field with a mighty theatre, an agora (square) and the walls of the baths have survived.
The area that was once the largest town in ancient Greece is now home to frogs and storks. Historically, however, the cities of Thales, Anaximander and Anaximenes formed the centre of philosophy and mathematics in the empire.
Road 525 first takes you to the forested region around Lake Bafa before reaching the well-preserved temple of Euromos. South of Milas you take National Road 330 to Bodrum, a pleasant drive with plenty of opportunities for excursions and breaks.

12 Bodrum This former fishing village is now a tidy white-washed town on a striking blue bay. Its centre is the Castle of the Knights of St John (1413). If you want, you can hire a gulet, one of the traditional sailing vessels from these parts, to take you out to a secluded bay for a picnic.

13 Knidos/Datça The road now takes a sweeping curve along Gökova Bay, which is almost 80 km (50 miles) long, through Milas, Yatagan, Mugla and Marmaris, and out onto the 'panhandle' of the Datça Peninsula.

The Turkish Riviera

Only late in the 20th century did tourism strategists set their sights on the Turkish south coast, a coastline once visited only by traders, crusaders and pirates. In the early 1980s they worked out how many holidaymakers would be enticed by a trip to sunny Turkey given available flight capacity. The target area was 'within six hours' by plane to the holiday destination. This radius made Turkey available to people from Oslo, London or Kuwait. At the edge of Antalya, planners brooded over road maps near Konyaalti Beach, nowadays home to one luxury hotel after another. The final hour had struck for the small orange groves along the coast.

But with the establishment of the Olimpos and Termessos National Parks and other national parks further upcountry, some grand scenery was saved from the scramble to develop

Top: The lagoon near Ölü Deniz is now a protected area.
Bottom: The castle of the Knights of St John is the icon of Bodrum.

A national park here covers an area of roughly 1,500 sq km (580 sq mi) and protects the local forests and bays from the sadly unbridled development taking place in the area.

From the fishing and holiday village of Datça you can take a boat across to Knidos, a town founded in 400 BC at the end of the peninsula. Among the sights of this important antique trading and military post are an acropolis and the temples of Aphrodite and Demeter.

Leaving Marmaris behind we now drive through forested landscapes, over mountains and rivers, back along the coast, and then past Lake Köycegiz and some antique sites (Kaunos Rock Tombs) to the small town of Fethiye. National Road 400 starts here and follows Turkey's south coast. The rock tombs at Fethiye are well worth a climb at sunset. Ölü Deniz has attractive clear waters and an 'almost' white sand beach. It is the most famous bay south of Fethiye.

houses make this town, situated at the foot of an impressive mountain range, a worthy stop.

15 Antalya This town has been called 'Smiling Beauty of South Turkey'. In only two decades, this lovely place has become the undisputed tourist destination of southern Turkey. From the terrific mountain backdrops, city beaches and bustling nightlife to lively bazaars and outstanding museums, Antalya has everything the tourist's heart desires. In springtime you can go skiing in the mountains and take a plunge in the sea later all in one day, or you can take trips to Termessos National Park or the ancient town of Termessos. Golfers are drawn to nearby Belek, Turkey's upmarket golf centre.

14 Phaselis On your way to Olimpos National Park you will be amazed by the antique Lycian town of Xanthos, miles of hotel-free beaches around Patara, the ancient towns of Kalkan and Kas, and the island world of Kekova with its submerged city. All of these are worth a visit.

A short detour from National Road 400 then takes you to Phaselis, an ancient port with a unique atmosphere. The ruins of three harbours, an amphitheatre, an agora and bath

16 Manavgat/Side Just one hour east of Antalya is the ancient harbour of Side, now home to idyllic sandy beaches. In Side and the provincial town of

1 Sunset over the sinter terraces of Pamukkale.

2 Kaunos: Lycian rock tombs near the holiday destination of Dalyan.

3 Beautiful beaches for bathing and snorkelling near Fethiye.

the land. Care was also taken to provide adequate water and electricity, install a waste disposal system and effectively combat forest fires. It didn't take long for investors to start arriving in droves, followed by guests – initially in their tens of thousands, and soon after in their millions.

The South-East Anatolian Project

Ever since the giant reservoirs of the 'South-East Anatolian Project' began helping to irrigate large stretches of land and providing hydroelectric power, the Euphrates River has turned the steppes of Turkey's far east into fertile agricultural lands. The 'world's largest water pipes' – as Sanliurfa locals proudly boast – are part of one of the most extensive irrigation projects on the planet.

From Atatürk Dam, water flows through 26 km (16 miles) of pipes measuring almost 8 m (26 ft) in diameter onto the Harran Plains. Some farmers in the area continue to live in

The Euphrates south of the Keban Dam near Elazig.

old-fashioned beehive-like houses. Behind the dam is the Atatürk Reservoir, the world's sixth largest and only one in a series of massive reservoirs that have submerged several rocky gorges on this formerly wild river. Places like Kahta on the way to Nemrut Dag, which used to be in the middle of a dry plain, are now located right on the lake shore.

Turkey's reserves of hydroelectric power are enormous, and the conditions for its exploitation are very favourable. There are many large rivers that flow from the mountains and highlands, cutting through the coastal mountain ranges in narrow valleys.

When it comes to the Tigris and Euphrates, however, Turkey's Arab neighbours are suspicious of the country's intentions. How much water will be left downstream if the Anatolian cotton fields are harvested three times per year? Indeed, the battle for water in this region is far from over.

Manavgat a little further inland you have a vast range of accommodation to choose from.

Using this area as a base, there are interesting trips to Köprülü Canyon National Park and the Manavgat waterfalls. Thrill-seekers can take organized rafting tours on the Köpru River.

17 Alanya This is the third holiday destination on the south coast after Side and Antalya. The impressive red Seljuk castle on a steep rock outcrop above the town has 146 towers, stunning views and offers romantic sunsets. It's definitely Alanya's biggest attraction.

The town's palm-lined alleyways and subtropical flora are wonderful for relaxing strolls, and Alanya's extensive beaches are well-suited to all kinds of sports and activities. Not long ago, one of Turkey's most beautiful stalactite caves – Dim Magarsi – was made accessible to the public.

18 Anamur From here, the distances between towns will start getting longer. Blasted out of coastal cliffs, National Road 400 is made up of a never-ending series of breathtaking sea views. Spiny, fragrant scrubland dominates the landscape while trees are rare in the area. The town and castle of Anamur, however, are strikingly different – on the

flood plain of the Dragon River you'll find lush green fields.

Greek settlers established the port of Anamurium as far back as 400 BC at this southernmost point in Asia Minor, and for a long time their trade with Cyprus flourished. The remains of a palestra (sports stadium), an odeon (theatre) and baths several floors high still bear witness to these times.

The inhabitants of Anamurium were eventually driven out by Arab invasions in the 7th century. In the 12th and 13th centuries the town was resettled. Soon thereafter, Anamur Castle was built by a ruler of the Karaman principality. With its battlements and gallery, thirty-six towers and three courtyards, this is one of the most impressive medieval fortifications in all of Anatolia. Its location also makes it unforgettable – right above the coastal rocks, the waves crash against the castle walls. Later Ottoman rulers added a mosque, a bath and a well to the courtyards.

19 Silifke In 1190, Frederick I Barbarossa ('Red Beard') wanted to take this town during the third crusade, but one day in June a few miles outside of it he drowned in the Göksu River. Silifke, which was founded around 300 BC by Seleukos I Nikator, is the most unchanged of any

town on Turkey's south coast. It is set against the majestic backdrop of the Cilikian Mountains close to the sea and makes a good base for a handful of day trips and excursions to islands, caves and ancient sanctuaries. Among the town's sights are the Roman ruins of Olba and Diocaesarea (Ura/Uzuncaburç) set in some terrific scenery; the Byzantine monastery of Alahan; and also Cennet ve Cehennem ('Heaven and Hell'), two deep, round rock valleys.

20 Adana This area is dominated by the nearby Taurus Mountains, which rise to an impressive 4,000 m (13,000 ft). Between Adana and the sea are the

Çukurova Plains with their endless fields of cotton. Turkey's largest mosque was recently constructed on Adana's Seydan River. In recent decades, 3,500-year-old Adana has grown to become Turkey's fourth-largest city. Its thousands of shops, bazaars and minarets are typical of the historical Old Town while the new city is home to tree-lined boulevards, modern banks and high-rise buildings.

After passing Kahramanmaras, Adiyaman and Kahta, your route ascends the desolate mountain regions of the Taurus Range.

21 Nemrut Dağı The monumental eagles and statues sitting curiously at 2,150 m (7,050 ft)

The translation of Göreme means 'thou shalt not see'. This landscape of volcanic tuff extends from Kizilirmak ('Red River') in the north to the underground cities of Kaymakli and Derinkuyu in the south. It is hardly imaginable these days that more than a thousand years ago local people carved extensive tunnels and living quarters several storeys high into the crumbling rock, often as a refuge from repeated attacks by Muslim fighters. The systems often went to depths of over 85 m (273 ft) and giant millstones were used to seal off the entrances on each individual level. The designers integrated narrow shafts to circulate air, and water was taken from large cisterns.

Top: Rock Church near Göreme.
Bottom: Tokali Kilise, 'Buckle Church'.

above sea level have become the leading icon of adventurous, exotic Turkey. The tomb monuments, which continue to baffle scientists to this day, were erected by King Antiochos I of Commagena (an Anatolian state around the birth of Christ). Today there are only ruins where cities once thrived. Two of the tomb's three original terraces have been well preserved, with fragments of statues seemingly randomly placed around the site. Their heads gaze out over the land towards the rising sun. Greek as well as Oriental gods were worshipped here.
Road 875 now takes us via Adiyaman west of the Atatürk Reservoir to Şanliurfa.

22 Şanliurfa On the vast plains of Upper Mesopotamia, a rock promontory bears the ruins of an ancient fortification. Soldiers serving under Alexander the Great founded this city and gave it the Macedonian name Edessa. Şanliurfa was an important place for early Christianity as well as for Arab scholars. Its spring was already sacred to the Greeks and to this day there are sacred Muslim carp swimming in it ('Abraham's Pond').
From Şanliurfa, National Road 360 takes us to Diyarbakir, the largest town in eastern Anatolia.

23 Diyarbakir To this day, the Old Town here is surrounded almost completely by the origi-

nal Roman-Byzantine walls of basalt rock. East of these walls is the legendary Tigris River. Palaces, mosques and madrasahs (Koranic schools), caravanserais, churches, lively bazaars and modern boulevards all give this city its many faces. You reach Lake Van in the east by taking a winding mountain road for about 250 km (160 miles).

24 Van Lake Van covers an area of 3,750 sq km (3,225 sq mi), is located at an altitude of 1,600 m (5,250 ft) and is surrounded by mountain ranges more than 4,000 m (13,000 ft) high. Roughly 3,000 years ago, the town of Van on the south-eastern shore was called Tuspa. It was the capital of the Urartu Kingdom, famed for its highly skilled metalworkers and grand fortifications. The Armenian church (915–921) on Ahtamar Island sits amid quaint olive groves and is definitely worth a visit for its stucco work and frescoes.
Your route to Sivas circles Lake Van and goes through some wonderful mountain scenery past Elazig, the Keban Reservoir to the north and Divrigi, whose large mosque is a UNESCO World Heritage Site.

25 Sivas This town's architecture is impressive, above all the intricately decorated gates of

the Gök Madrasah. The 'Mukarnas', little niches in the building, are decorated to look like stalactites. Depictions of plants and animals cover the walls of these niches, giving them a labyrinth feel. The financial means for such intricate ornamentation were provided by Sivas' fortuitous location – the main trade routes to and from Russia, Egypt, Iran and south-eastern Europe all pass through here.

26 Kayseri In ancient Rome, Kayseri was called Caesarea. At the time it was the capital of Cappadocia. The modern town sprawls out onto the plains at the foot of the Erciyes Dagi Mountain, whose mighty summit reaches 3,916 m (12,848 ft) and is always covered in snow. The Old Town of this industrial city has a lot to offer to lovers of art and architecture. The buildings from the heyday of the Seljuk Empire (11th–12th centuries) are worth seeing, along with those from later centuries. The mosque of Huand Hatun, a Seljuk princess, is well worth a

1 Panorama of Cappadocia with bizarre tuff towers near Göreme.

2 The impressive, 1,000-year-old Armenian church on Ahtamar Island in Lake Van.

Visitors to Cappadocia can explore not only the narrow tunnels of this fascinating underworld, but also the bizarre canyons, semi-arid lunar landscapes and wide, green valleys above the surface. The now abandoned rock churches of Christian hermits and monks are well worth seeing too. Imitating church buildings, the monks carved vaults and cupolas, arches and pillars out of the tuff rocks. There are around 150 of these churches, many of them with beautiful frescoes.
After severe and long-term depredation, UNESCO finally got involved. Since the 1970s it has been aiming to secure and restore what has not yet been completely lost. Among the most beautiful churches are Elmali Kilise ('Apple Church'), Carikli Kilise ('Sandal Church'), Tokali Kilise ('Buckle Church') and Yilanli Kilise ('Snake Church').

Whirling Dervishes

If you want to see whirling dervishes dancing in their bell-shaped white gowns, go to Konya in Central Anatolia or, during the summer, to the ancient theatre of Aspendos on the south coast. In 1925, the order of the dancing dervishes or 'Mevlevî' was forbidden in Atatürk's secular republic.

Whirling dance of Mevlevî dervishes.

In 1990, however, the 'Mevlana Culture and Art Foundation' was founded. Known as 'Mevlana' among his followers, hence the name of the order, the mystic and meditative teachings and ecstatic poetry of its founder, Celâleddin, may be alien to most Westerners. Yet it is hard to resist the magic of the whirling dances: '... they were spinning with such surprising speed that I could do nothing but admire them', wrote the Briton Samuel Purch in 1613.

visit with its madrasah, large baths and the mausoleum of the benefactress.

㉗ Nevsehir/Göreme The former is a predominantly modern town, but its Seljuk castle on the local mountain and its mosque and madrasah (Koranic school) are worth seeing. These were donated by a Grand Vizier of the Ottoman Empire in the 18th century, who was initially lauded but later decapitated.
For many visitors, however, the town is simply a good starting point for excursions to the picturesque lunar landscape of Cappadocia. The cones, obelisks and tuff pillars here are the result of erosion over millions of years as well as extensive use by local people as cave dwellings, monks' habitations and lookout posts. Cappadocia is basically one big open-air museum with a terrific setting for this unique 'natural architecture' and some good hiking.

㉘ Konya The crusaders marvelled when they arrived in Konya in the Middle Ages, and modern Konya keeps up the tradition of beauty with wide boulevards and more parks than any other town in central Anatolia. Lovers of historic architecture and sculpture will find many precious stone carvings on

the mosques and madrasahs of this former Seljuk capital.
The monastery of the Mevlevî dervish order (Mevlânâ Tekkesi) has been a museum since the order was outlawed by Atatürk back in 1925. For centuries this was a centre of the Mevlânâ sect. The Huzuri Pir Hall ('Presence of the Saint') is always filled with crowds of visitors wanting to touch their hands and lips to the sarcophagi of Celâleddin and his closest followers. The founder of the order came from Persia, lived in Konya for almost half a century and died in 1273. There are several museums in Konya with outstanding collections. Don't miss them if you have enough time.
The road across the Anatolian highlands to Ankara 300 km (185 miles) away is well developed and easy to drive. You cross a deserted, dry plain with some impressive mountain scenery. From March to May the plains are in full bloom and the colourful carpets of wild tulips are one of the most popular themes of Turkish art.
Between Cihanbeyli and Kulu, you drive along the Tuz Gölü salt lake (1,500 sq km/580 sq mi). In the summer it shrinks to a bog with salty white edges.

㉙ Ankara This town was crucial in the Turkish National War

of Liberation, which saved the country from being divided up among the victorious powers of World War I. At the time, around 1920, this small town only had about 30,000 inhabitants. By 1980, there were two million and today there may be as many as four million. Only a fraction of this city actually dates back more than eighty years.
Atatürk's decision to move the capital into the Anatolian plains 600 km (375 miles) away from the Aegean coast at first seemed absurd to many people, but it was a way to make Ankara (the Roman Ankyra) the instrument and symbol of a new orientation for the country. The move was designed to bring not only the Aegean Coast but the whole of Turkey closer to Europe. The ploy seems to have worked, at least in this young metropolis. The German architect Hermann Jansen was responsible for much of the town planning in modern Ankara. For an encounter with the 9,000 years of Anatolian history, be sure to visit the Museum of Anatolian Civilization.
Allow at least two days for an excursion to Hattusas (Turkish: Bogazkale), the almost 4,000-year-old capital of the Hethitan kingdom, which has a number of palaces and temples.
Heading north, a winding road takes us into the Köroglu Daglari

and Ilgaz Daglari forests. The route to the Black Sea coast then ends among some gentle, hilly scenery in Kastamonu on the northern slopes of the Pontic Mountains.

㉚ Kastamonu Numerous terraces and the well-proportioned Ottoman mosques dating from the 15th and 16th centuries are among the town's noteworthy sights. Sultan Suleyman the Magnificent's chef and storehouse overseer was the architect of Yakub Aga Külliyesi, a stately mosque with a central dome and neighbouring madrasah.
Even more impressive than its mosques, however, are Kastamonu's two-and three-storey timber-framed houses, or 'Konaks'. The ground floors were made of stone, with bays and mostly flat roofs and they give the city an attractive provincial feel. The small river in the valley terminates in the Kizilirmak River a little to the east, which in turn flows into the Black Sea.

㉛ Safranbolu Since its Old Town was designated a UNESCO World Heritage Site in 1994, this town has been more famous than Kastamonu, its neighbour to the east. The 'Saffron City' had its heyday in the 18th century, at a time when it was the trade hub for this much sought-

Atatürk

After the disaster of World War I, Mustafa Kemal Pasha became the saviour of Turkey. His people called him Atatürk, 'Father of the Turks'. In other parts of the world very little is known about this man, who instilled new confidence into a downtrodden, under-developed country and also opened the door for Turkey's social and political shift towards the 'West'.

He introduced Western legal principles and constitutional systems, separated church and state, created new schools, supported women's rights and gave up the previously used Arabic letters in favour of Latin script.

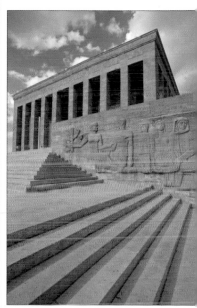

An eternal remembrance of modern Turkey's founding father: the Atatürk Mausoleum.

Born in 1881 in Saloniki, Mustafa Kemal Pasha eventually decided to pursue a career in the military. In 1915, when the Ottoman Empire was pushed into World War I by Germany, the Allies under British command landed at the Dardanelles in an attempt to take Istanbul. With large numbers of casualties on both sides, Mustafa Kemal Pasha forced the attackers to retreat.

Four years later, when the victorious powers divided the Ottoman Empire among themselves, Kemal Pasha founded a government in Ankara and organized the resistance. Skilful in military and diplomatic matters, he abolished both the Sultanate and the Caliphate. The modern Republic of Turkey was established in 1923.

monuments have been well preserved in park-like settings amid the urban surroundings. The former inhabitants of Prusa ad Olympum, its ancient predecessor, had long ago learned to appreciate the local hot springs. The town received its nickname from Mount Uludag, the 'Mystical Olympus'. In 1326, Bursa became the capital of the Ottoman Empire.

Bursa is now a large city, but in winter Mount Uludag provides respite with ski resorts and a gondola that takes you to the top. Some pastel-coloured houses adorn the Old Town, and there are some babbling fountains beneath green cypresses. Due to its elevation the climate is pleasant even in summer, making Bursa a nice final stop on your way back to Istanbul.

Taking National Roads 575 and 130 you will pass through Gemlk. From Kocaeli (Highway 04), it is only 240 km (150 miles) back to Istanbul.

1 The Mevlânâ Monastery in Konya has been the destination of pious pilgrims for centuries.

2 Traditional houses on the slopes of Safranbolu.

3 The Kocatepe Mosque in Ankara was consecrated in 1987.

after yellow plant dye that was used as a spice, medicine and, above all, dye for various foodstuffs. The 'Konak' houses here have been lovingly maintained and restored; most of them are built with two storeys around a central courtyard and brick roofs. The Old Town (Carsi) is easy to explore on foot, and a little further out on a hill in Baglar are the summer residences of some wealthier families. In the Carsi there are a few worthwhile museums as well as crafts workshops, a lively bazaar, typical tearooms and hotels – almost all of them located in historic buildings.

Taking National Road 755 south from Safranbolu you'll arrive at National Road 100 (E80) at Eskipazar after about 60 km (37 miles). When you get to Gerede, the road becomes Highway 04. At Sakarya, take National Road 650 south towards Bözüyük. After roughly 120 km (75 miles) you follow National Road 200 (E90) north-west, which takes you to Bursa (another 120 km/75 miles), your last stop on the tour before we head back to Istanbul.

32 Bursa Its location on the slopes of Mount Uludag combined with the magnificent architecture of its palaces, mosques and mausoleums all make Bursa one of the most beautiful towns of the former sultanate. The city's

Pergamon This temple was begun by Emperor Trajan and completed by his successor, Hadrian, on the highest point of the ancient city of kings on the castle hill of modern Bergama. The Pergamon Empire reached its peak after the death of Alexander the Great and later fell to Rome without a fight.

Assos There is a terrific view across to the island of Lesbos from the ruins of the Temple of Athena, which is on the town hill of Assos where Aristotle used to teach. It is worth driving down the steep hill to the stone houses, tea terraces and harbour of Behramkale.

Ephesus Few modern libraries can compete with the glorious columns of the Celsus Library. Built to commemorate the Roman Proconsul in the 2nd century AD, it is probably the most beautiful ancient library still standing.

Pamukkale The limestone terraces of Pamukkale ('Cotton Castle') are now gleaming white again. They were recently renovated after years of neglect. The cascading formations are formed by hot spring water with a high lime content.

Kaunos The unique rock tombs in south-west Turkey go back to the Lycians who presumably came from Crete even before the Greeks did. The picture shows tombs in a steep rock face near the fishing village of Dalyan, not far from Bodrum.

Turkish wine-growing around the Marmara Sea Wine has been grown around Sarköy and Mürefte since time immemorial. Annual harvests reach 70,000 tonnes (77,000 tons). Recently, local vintners started to offer professional wine tastings and local wines are improving in terms of both variety and quality. The stiffest competition for Turkish vineyards comes from Raki, a traditional anise-based liqueur from nearby Tekirdag.

Istanbul The Blue Mosque, with its six minarets (a very unusual number) was named after a Turkish speciality – the roughly 21,000 mostly blue tiles, which are indeed very intricately made. The 'Blue Miracle', right next to the Hagia Sophia in Turkey's capital, took five years to build between 1609 an 1616.

Bodrum This town has a modern-Mediterranean feel, but the castle of the Order of the Knights of St John was built here in 1413.

Aphrodisias This remote area has a number of ancient ruins, was once a centre for stone carving, and is a Mecca for archaeologists.

Fethiye Famous mainly because of the nearby dream bay of Ölü Deniz as well as numerous islands and beaches, Fethiye itself is a charming place with lively bazaars and picturesque mosques.

Antalya This city of half a million people has its share of parks, long beaches, ancient architecture and old-town romance, all of which contribute to its well-deserved nickname – the 'Smiling Beauty of South Turkey'.

Safranbolu Near the Black Sea and the coal mines of Zonguldak, the old quarters of Safranbolu have been preserved, with 'Hanes' (traditional trading houses with a central courtyard), restored wooden and stone houses and narrow alleyways on the cosy slopes that shape the town.

Ankara This former one-horse town is now one of the country's most modern cities. Kocatepe Camii Mosque (above), was built between 1976 an 1987 and is one of the country's largest. Many public buildings were inspired by Bauhaus architectural styles in the 1930s at a time when the budding Turkish state sheltered a number of architects persecuted in Nazi Germany.

Konya Mevlânâ Mosque recalls the preacher Mevlânâ Celâleddin Mehmed Rumi (1207–73), in whose name the Mevlevî order of dervishes was founded when he passed away. Konya, the capital of Islamic mysticism in Turkey, was also the capital of Seljuk knights and is now a modern metropolis.

Nevsehir/Göreme Many of the rock towers in the volcanic tuff landscapes of Cappadocia look like massive pieces of Swiss cheese. Above and below ground, both natural erosion and the human desire for shelter have been responsible for the carved-out sections in the rock. Innumerable caves, tunnels and even entire church halls such as Uçhisar (above) were constructed.

Divriği This town's most famous building is Ulu Camii, the Great Mosque, a UNESCO World Heritage Site built in 1240–41. It has portals designed in different styles. The north gate is adorned with large-scale depictions of plant themes.

Elazığ Tucked in among the rocks and rivers around this town is the Byzantine castle of Harput, which is over 1,000 years old. The Keban Baraji reservoirs, part of the East Anatolian Project on the Tigris and Euphrates rivers, are very close by.

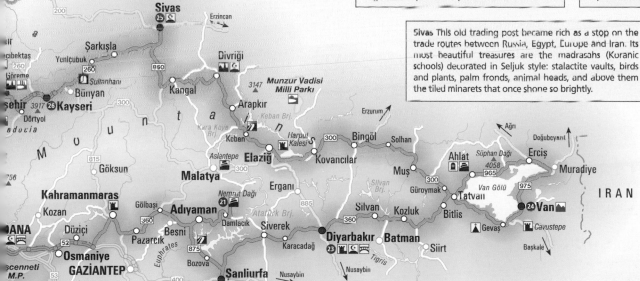

Sivas This old trading post became rich as a stop on the trade routes between Russia, Egypt, Europe and Iran. Its most beautiful treasures are the madrasahs (Koranic schools) decorated in Seljuk style: stalactite vaults, birds and plants, palm fronds, animal heads, and above them the tiled minarets that once shone so brightly.

Şanliurfa In the Old City of Urfa (its older name; before that it was called Edessa), the Halilür Rahman Mosque is worth a visit for its decorative stone carvings. The picture shows the pond that backs up to the little mosque.

Uzuncaburç Less than an hour from Silifke are the remains of the ancient twin cities of Olba and Diocaesarea. Their city gates, aqueducts and ruins are a magnificent sight against the backdrop of an untouched mountain landscape.

Nemrut Dağı The large heads and other stone monuments on the eastern terraces of Antiochos I of Commagena's monumental king's tomb date back to the 1st century BC. This place in the lonely, bare highlands is one of the most spectacular tombs in the world.

Lake Van The Armenian church on the island of Ahtamar in Lake Van is over a thousand years old. Its partially well-preserved reliefs and frescoes of biblical tales make it one of the most fascinating buildings in East Anatolia. The lake is surrounded by mountains more than 4,000 m (13,000 ft) high.

Route 13

Central Asia and China

On the Silk Road from Bukhara to Xi'an

For more than a thousand years, Europe and Asia were connected primarily through the ancient 'Silk Road' trade route. The importance of this caravan route was not, however, only restricted to the trade of goods. It also provided the backdrop for a lively exchange of culture and ideas between the Mediterranean, Central Asian and Chinese realms.

When silk products originating from the Han and Tang dynasties of China (200 BC and 7th century, respectively) were discovered in Iran, Syria and Italy, the significance of this sought-after commodity immediately became clear. 2,000 years ago, silk was as expensive as gold in Rome. Julius Caesar drew extra attention to himself when he attended theatre performances wearing silken robes. At the time, the Romans believed that silk grew on trees and was combed from the leaves as a fine fluff.

The Chinese, on the other hand, did not want to reveal the secrets of silk production, for it ensured their powerful monopoly in the trade. They were able to maintain this upper hand for centuries until, as legend has it, monks smuggled silkworm eggs and mulberry seeds out of China in hollow bamboo canes and brought them to the Eastern Roman Empire in the 6th century.

Western products that the Chinese had never heard of were, in turn, taken back to China – perfumes, pearls, grapes,

A Kyrgyz family in their yurt, the round tents lined with carpets used as dwellings by the nomads.

Fort Jiayuguan in Gansu was built at the eastern end of the Great Wall and fitted with gates adorned with towers. It has a wall over 10 m (33 ft) high and 733 m (2,356 ft) long.

The Lamaistic monastery of Ta'er Si is 26 km (16 miles) south of Xining in the Qinghai province.

pomegranates, walnuts, sesame, coriander and incense. Another incentive for the Chinese to keep the trade route alive was the acquisition of the highly regarded Fergana horses. The Romans paid for the silk not only with jingling coins, but also with gold, glass, wool and African slaves, who were very desirable in China at the time. The high price for silk is understandable if you take into account that, at the time, the Silk Road passed through thirty-six dominions, each demanding their own customs duties.

During the Tang Dynasty (618–907), the Chinese were particularly open to foreigners. At that time, the Chinese upper class was interested in music and instruments from Central and West Asia, as well as the handicrafts from the West. Clothing, metal and glass products, and even sculpture were all influenced by the West.

The cultural exchange between East and West also helped develop astronomy, calendars, mathematics and medicine. Mediterranean acrobatics and circuses, the game of polo from Persia, as well as exotic songs and dances were all extremely popular. Chinese poetry and painting also incorporated influences from the West and thus developed new styles during the period.

The Silk Road was also a place where new and old religions were evangelized. In the first century AD, Buddha's teachings spread from the kingdom of Gandhara in north-west Pakistan through the Central Asian khanates to the Middle Kingdom. The teachings of Zarathustra, as well as Manichaeism, Nestorianism and Islam, were later transported on this road through Central Asia to China, where they all found followers.

The wooden figure in the Haizang Temple in Wuwei, an oasis town in the Gansu province.

Faiences

South-west of Ravenna is the Italian town of Faenza, the old Faventia, after which faiences were named. As early as AD 1400, a factory here manufactured and sold plates, tiles and stove tiles, often with blue and yellow Moorish patterns.

However, the art of pottery goes back much further. Faiences were already being produced in Egypt and northern Syria in the 4th century BC and, shortly after, throughout all of Mesopotamia. In the middle of the 2nd century BC, faience production in Asia Minor experienced new prosperity when palace walls, city walls and gates were clad in varnished

Samarkand: Mausoleum in the necropolis of Shohizinda.

bricks – a prime example being the Ishtar Gate of Babylon.

From the 9th century, faiences played an increasingly important role in the creation of Islamic art. The architecture and building ceramics eventually spread throughout the Islamic world and continue to adorn countless mosques and madrassahs in Central Asia. Some of the better-known examples of this are the madrassahs at the Registan in Samarkand and those in Bukhara.

After firing, soft-fired clay becomes red or ochre and very porous. The clay fragments are coated in a tin or lead glaze, painted and then fired again. At the start, only underglaze firing colours (blue, manganese, yellow, green, red, brown and black) were produced. Later, the manufacture of so-called 'muffle' colours at lower firing temperatures enabled all hues to be used.

In addition to the spectacular desert landscapes of the Kysylkum and Takla Makan, high mountain regions such as the Tian Shan between Tashkent and Ürümqi or the Qilian Shan south of the Hexi Corridor await you along the eastern Silk Road.

❶ Bukhara During the European Middle Ages, this oasis city at the edge of the Kysylkum was one of the most significant religious and economic centres of the Islamic world, boasting 350 mosques and more than 100 madrasahs. The old city's most important sights include the Ulughbek madrasah (the oldest mosque in Central Asia), the Khalif-Niazkul Mosque (Chor Minor) with four 17-m-high (56-ft) towers, and the Ismail-Samani mausoleum (9th/10th century). The Kaljan Mosque (1127) minaret is also an impressive sight at 47 m (154 ft). A navigational light used to guide approaching caravans a thousand years ago, and the tower provides you with a striking view of the old town. A museum of local history and popular art is today located in the citadel Ark

(7th–8th century), once the castle of the Emir of Bukhara.

Bukhara owes its existence to the Zarafshan river, whose waters feed the irrigation canals of oasis gardens; the main city canal, the Shachrud; and the Labihauz (1620), a large basin in the centre of the city. The latter used to provide the city's inhabitants with water, as no irrigation system could be implemented owing to the narrow streets and alleys. In the old days, water bearers brought water to the courts and bazaars in leather buckets. Nowadays, after a long day exploring the old city, you can sit and relax on a bench outside the tearooms, eat excellent food and soak up the atmosphere.

Out on the old Silk Road you enter the desert steppe and the shifting sand dunes of the

Travel information

Route profile
Length: approx. 4,800 km (2,983 miles), excluding detours
Time required: about 6 weeks
Start: Bukhara, Uzbekistan
Finish: Xi'an, China
Route (main locations): Bukhara, Samarkand, Tashkent, Kokand, Bishkek, Issyk Kul, Almaty, Ürümqi, Turpan, Astana, Minghoshan, Jiayuguan, Zhangye, Wuwei, Lanzhou, Xi'an

Traffic information: Drive on the right on this trip. It is not always possible to drive from Tashkent into the Fergana Valley. Those using a diesel-powered vehicle must pay a weight tax upon entry.

Information:
www.centralasiatravel.com
www.dostuck.com
www.eurasianet.org
www.fantasticasia.net
www.marcopolo.uz/en/

Kysylkum. As was the case west of Bukhara, the sun beats down relentlessly on the vast cotton fields along the road here. Summer temperatures can reach 45°C (113°F), while in winter they fall to -25°C (-13°F) – these variations are typical of this landlocked area.

❷ Samarkand At an altitude of 725 m (2,379 ft), Samarkand is

situated in the foothills of the Pamiro-Altai. Upon entering the city, the apartment blocks and factories do not initially reflect the glorious past of one of Central Asia's most important cultural and trading cities, and one of the oldest inhabited cities in the world. Having survived the imperial conquest of Alexander the Great and the destruction inflicted by Genghis Khan's

2

3

tion systems and thus called it Shakhrisyabz, or 'green city'. It is also where Timur built his summer residence, Aq-Saray, the 'White Palace'. As a result of his great successes (often looked upon with derision in the Persian and Arab regions that he conquered), an imposing monument was dedicated to the city's great son in the main square in front of the ruins of Aq-Saray.

❹ **Tashkent** Highway 39 takes you to the Uzbek capital of Tashkent, located in the foothills of the Tian Shan. This is a place

troops, Samarkand has continually been rebuilt.
Today, its architectural monuments (15th–17th centuries) give it an almost fairy-tale feel and in 2001 it was selected as a UNESCO World Heritage Site. Attractions include the Registan, or main square of Old Samarkand; the famous Gur-e Amir, cemetery and family mausoleum of the notorious conqueror Timur Lang; Shah-i-Zinda, or 'Tomb of the Living King'; the glorious Bibi-Khanym Mosque; and the Ulughbek observatory, dating back to the early 15th century. Some 90 km (56 miles) south of Samarkand is Shakhrisyabz.

❸ **Shakhrisyabz** The now exalted Timur Lang, known as Tamerlane in Europe, was born around 1330 in the immediate vicinity of Shakhrisyabz. He established a kingdom which, at his death in 1405, stretched from northern India to Damascus, and from the Chinese border to Hungary. Samarkand lay at the heart of his dominion. He provided his place of birth, Kesh, with irriga-

1 A glimpse of the artistic dome in the Tilla-Kari (the 'one decorated in gold') madrasah in Samarkand, Uzbekistan.

2 Three madrasahs from the 15th–17th centuries line the Registan, the main square of Samarkand – Ulugh Bek, Tilla-Kari and Sherdar.

3 Muslim arts have been taught in the Mir Arab madrasah in Bukhara (1530–36) for over 400 years.

The Kyrgyz

There is a variety of theories about the origin of the Kyrgyz 'nation'. The most plausible seems to be the unification

Kyrgyz woman with traditional headdress.

of forty Turkic-speaking tribes living as nomads in the high mountains of Central Asia (their flag has forty rays of the sun at its centre). Regardless, by the mid 19th century, after periods of regional dominance and even longer periods as vassals of the Mongols, the Kyrgyz came under the influence of the expanding Russian kingdom and in 1876 were controlled by the general governorate of 'Turkestan'. Attempted revolts against the Tsarist politics were unsuccessful, whereupon thousands migrated to western China with their herds.

Today, from a total 2.7 million Kyrgyz, some 2.2 million live in Kyrgyzstan, 140,000 in the autonomous region of Xin Jiang, China, and others in Uzbekistan, Tajikistan, Kazakhstan, Afghanistan and Pakistan. Kyrgyzstan became independent in 1991.

where two worlds collide: where traditional Asia meets the modern world, mud houses meet towering glass palaces, veiled women meet children in fashionable designer clothing, the colourful bazaars meet the supermarket, narrow alleyways meet vast leisure parks, and Islamic domes with decorative patterns meet colourful neon signs.

The city acquired its modern-day image in the 1970s. An earthquake in 1966 nearly destroyed the entire city, leaving around 300,000 people homeless and only very few historic buildings still intact. Soviet architects took advantage of this and built a city with surprisingly numerous green areas in its place.

Since the country's independence in 1991, Tashkent's planners have been trying to give the modern buildings more of an Uzbek look. There are also several new monuments in memory of important persons in Uzbek history. At Amir Timur Square, you immediately notice the imposing monument of the kingdom's founder, Timur, on horseback. Increasing tourism means Tashkent is today a popular starting place for trekking tours in the Tian Shan mountains or the Pamir range.

Tashkent used to be a junction in the old Silk Road – the northern branch led through Bishkek, while the older, southern route first takes you into the Fergana

Valley before travelling east through some difficult, dangerous mountain passes. Nowadays, the road into the Fergana basin is occasionally closed owing to fear of terrorist attacks.

5 Kokand Green mountainsides, clear blue lakes and fertile plantations all await travellers in the Fergana Valley, whose diverse interior even includes deserty sections. Sheltered from cold, northerly winds by high mountain ranges, the valley provides optimal climatic conditions for agriculture. Minimal rainfall (25–30 cm/10–12 in per year) means the fertile oases are watered by a complex network of canals, and modern industry was really first introduced when the region was taken over by the Russians. Today, visitors see a Fergana basin that is well-settled and intensely cultivated. Kokand is located directly on the old caravan route. An earlier colony was destroyed by the Mongolians in the 13th century.

The city today, which was the religious centre of the valley until the 19th century, offers sights such as the 19th-century Khan's palace, the Jummi Mosque and the mausoleums at the cemetery, all well worth seeing. One of the small silk factories at the edge of the city or in the surrounding area also make for an interesting visit.

The route leads through Andijan to the Kyrgyz border. Osh, an

ancient city said to be 3,000 years old, has now become the second-largest city in Kyrgyzstan and is a well-known pilgrimage site. Passing through Uzgen, with three mausoleums from the 11th and 12th centuries and a tall minaret that stands 27 m (89 ft) high, you will then come to Kara Kul before reaching Bishkek. Several 3,000-m-high (9,843-ft) pass-

es must be overcome on the way to the Kyrgyz capital.

If the road through the Fergana Valley is blocked off, or for those who do not want to travel through the mountains, there is an alternative route along the northern edge of the mountain range. This well-built road leads for 450 km (280 miles) through Kazakhstan. In the footsteps of

Kazakhs

Kazakh territory stretches from the Caspian Sea to the Gobi Desert, and from the mountains of Central Asia to the steppes of the west Siberian lowlands. Like the Kyrgyz, they are a Turkic-speaking people whose independent development began in the 15th century with the separation from the Uzbeks.

A clear social structure of aristocrats and commoners was characteristic of this society. As nomads, the Kazakhs were involved in livestock farming

Hunting with golden eagles is an old Kazakh tradition.

based on horse, cattle, sheep and camel breeding. Their early dwellings were the easily disassembled yurts, which enabled them to migrate between summer and winter pastures. In terms of religion, they practised a form of Islam adapted to their essentially nature-oriented Shamanist beliefs.

Around the middle of the 19th century, the Kazakhs' territory was integrated into the Russian kingdom. Russian farmers settled and Kazakh revolts were brutally defeated. During the Stalin era, collectivization, settling of nomads, arrests and relocation forced many Kazakhs to flee. Their numbers decreased by one-fifth between 1926 and 1939 alone.

There is currently a total of approximately 9.3 million Kazakhs, out of which 8.1 million still reside in Kazakhstan. The rest live as minorities in the neighbouring Central Asian republics. Although many Kazakhs migrated from Mongolia, Iran and other states, and Russians fled the country after Kazakhstan's independence in 1991, the titular nation continues to be in the minority.

diverse scenery. Oddly enough, winds coming from the north- and south-west bring plenty of rainfall to the windward side of the mountains, yet basins and valleys remain dry and have to be irrigated.

About 30 km (19 miles) from Bishkek you will come to another border crossing, this time into Kazakhstan. The numerous border checks on the northern route of the historic Silk Road are a tedious legacy from the collapse of the Soviet Union.

The next destination is the former capital of this vast country, Almaty (formerly Alma-Ata).

1 The Tian Shan mountains stretch for 2,500 km (1,554 miles) through Central Asia. The highest peak is Pik Pobeda at 7,439 m (24,407 ft), on the Kyrgyz-Chinese border.

2 The 16th-century Kukeldash Madrasah in Tashkent is decorated with brightly coloured faiences.

3 A regional museum now stands at the site of the former palace of Khudoyar Khan of Kokand.

4 The beautifully decorated yurts of a Kazakh family.

5 Nestled in the impressive mountain landscape of the Tian Shan is Issyk Kul, the highest lake in Kyrgyzstan at 1,608 m (5,276 ft).

the old Silk Road, the route first heads north towards Shymkent, crossing a recreation area in the foothills of the Tian Shan before heading west. East of Shymkent, the Khrebet Karatau, or 'Black Mountains', which reach elevations of 1,000–1,500 m (3,281–4,922 ft), must be traversed. These foothills of the mighty Tian Shan are sparsely covered in grassy vegetation.

The southern outskirts then follow the 'Starving Steppe' through the Muyunkum Desert. Here, the terrain rises from some 300 m (984 ft) in the north to around 700 m (2,297 ft) in the south-east. Occasionally you will witness barchans (shifting sand dunes). The arid land is used as a winter pasture, and groundwater close to the surface enables farming in some areas.

After crossing the border into Kyrgyzstan at the town of Merke, the Kyrgyz capital of

Bishkek is another 100 km (62 miles). This country's impressive mountains, idyllic lakes, deep valleys and fertile basins have earned it the nickname 'Switzerland of Central Asia'.

6 Bishkek This city lies in the fertile yet earthquake-prone Chu Valley at the foot of the Kyrgyz Alatau (Ala-Toosu in Kyrgyz), at altitudes ranging from 750 to 900 m (2,461–2,953 ft). From 1929 to 1990, the city was known as Frunse in honour of a Russian general. The Russians had conquered a fortress founded here in the early 19th century and set up a military settlement in the typical grid layout of Russian 'colonial' cities. Today, over 600,000 people live in this city, Kyrgyzstan's political, economic and cultural centre. Bishkek is home to universities, museums, theatres and industrial plants. South-east of the capi-

tal is one of the country's main attractions, the Issyk Kul.

7 Issyk Kul This high mountain lake at 1,608 m (5,276 ft) is lined with sandy beaches and encircled by snow-capped mountains. Despite the snowy mountains, however, the lake never freezes, hence its name, meaning 'warm lake' in Kyrgyz.

From Balykchy on the western shore, the southern frontage road leads to Karakol at the eastern end of the lake. Its main attraction is the Buddhist-style Dungan Mosque, built in 1910 completely out of wood, with no metal nails used at all. On the way back to Bishkek is another captivating mountain lake south-west of Issyk Kul, the Song Köl, over 3,000 m (9,843 ft) above sea level.

Heading east now from Bishkek towards Almaty you will be confronted with some extremely

Ürümqi

As the centre of the petrochemical industry, Ürümqi is also an important economic and transport hub where the rich natural resources and agricultural products of the hinterland are processed.

From time to time, tensions between the Turkic Uygurs and the Han Chinese, mostly as a result of 'encour-

The modern skyline of Ürümqi.

aged settlement' of Han Chinese by the government in Beijing, result in violent unrest. The unrest also explains the large number of Chinese officers in the capital and surrounding areas, as well as the tangible military presence in the city.

The capital of the Uygur Autonomous Region offers a wide range of culture. Ürümqi's opera complex hosts operas of various national minorities in their original language, while folklore events provide an insight into the traditions of the indigenous Uygur people.

⑧ Almaty Caravans have been making stops here since ancient times, though there are no traces of this history in this modern administrative and industrial city. In 1854, the Russians constructed a fort where several mountain streams from the Tian Shan converge. The city, at 700–900 m (2,297–2,953 ft) has the typical grid layout of Russian cities. Its few tourist sights include the 19th-century cathedral in Panfilov Park, one of the largest and tallest wooden buildings on earth. The high mountain ice stadium, Medeo, is located at 1,680 m (5,512 ft) in the mountain's foothills.

The long road to Ürümqi is marked by desert-like river valleys and steep passes over high mountains. Taking a well-built mountain road through the Korgas Pass you cross the Chinese border, which has only been re-opened since the 1980s. The journey through the Borohoro Shan mountains, with valley glaciers up to 20 km (12 miles) long, is a diverse one. Glacial mountains 5,000 m (16,405 ft) high never cease to captivate travellers.

After a few monotonous stretches over wide, desolate plateaus at the edge of the Dzungaria, you reach Ürümqi at the northern side of the Tian Shan. Vehicular travel on the road through to the 5,000-m (16,405-ft) Chinese

section of the Tian Shan has only been possible since 1955. From Tashkent on, the mountain chains and foothills of the Tian Shan accompany travellers along the Silk Road.

There is no rainfall in the basins between these imposing, land-locked mountains, but coniferous forests still exist at altitudes of over 1,600 m (5,250 ft). The mountains form the border between the extremely arid Tarim Valley to the south and the more humid Dzungaria north of Ürümqi.

⑨ Ürümqi This industrial city located at 870 m (2,854 ft) above sea level is the capital of the Xin Jiang Autonomous Region and home to 1.2 million people. Ürümqi is surrounded by a fertile oasis landscape and was an

extremely important trading centre on the Silk Road. This is reflected in the exhibits at the Qu Bowuguan Regional Museum and in the lively bazaars. The symbol of Ürümqi is the 900-m-high (2,953-ft) Red Mountain (Tiger Head Mountain).

⑩ Tian Chi A day trip out of Ürümqi into the Bogda Shan mountains 50 km (31 miles) to

Turpan Hollow

Between the main northern and southern ranges of the Tian Shan there are a number of expansive and very deep valleys. The Turpan Valley, for example, at the eastern end of the range, sits at 154 m (505 ft) below sea level. It is not only the deepest point in China but the second deepest

The Turpan Hollow lies in the rainy shadows of the Tian Shan foothills.

the east is well worth doing. Tian Chi, or Heaven Lake, has motorboats ready to take you around. The lake is at a height of 1,900 m (6,234 ft) and located at the base of the always snow-capped Bogda Feng, a peak 5,445 m (17,865 ft) high. When the snow melts in springtime, the depth of this relatively shallow lake suddenly reaches 90 m (295 ft). Dome-shaped yurts on the

shore can provide overnight accommodation.

⓫ **Turpan** Through desert valleys, the route heads 100 km (62 miles) down into the Turpan Valley, which the Chinese controlled over 2,000 years ago for the purposes of preserving safety on the Silk Road. Approximately 150 sq km (58 sq mi) in size, Aydingkol Hu (Moonlight

Lake) lies at the deepest point of the valley (154 m/505 ft below sea level). During the hot summer months, temperatures here rise to 47°C (117°F). Even when it rains, the rainfall very rarely reaches the ground – most of it evaporates on the way down. For this reason, no more than 16 mm (0.63 in) of rainfall is recorded each year. In addition to its fame as the source of the

1 The slopes of the Tian Shan mountains around Ürümqi.

2 The 'Precious Pagoda of the Red Mountains' in Ürümqi.

3 Bogda Shan peaks reflected like a painting in the Tian Chi.

4 The minaret of the Emin Mosque in Turpan.

depression on earth. The hot summers here are only bearable because of low air humidity.

The ancient, loess-covered lake bed has now been transformed into a productive oasis landscape. How? Once again, a carefully installed irrigation system based on groundwater transported through canals. The region is known for its exquisite wines and grapes, as well as the quality of its cotton. Turpan means 'Land of Abundance' in Uygur language.

Jiaohe Gucheng

About 10 km (6 miles) west of Turpan is the 'Old City on Two Rivers', Jiaohe Gucheng. The ruined city is located on a high plateau formed by two rivers. The walls, which drop away steeply on all sides, provided natural protection and saved the inhabitants from having to build their own city wall.

Around 200 BC, the city was founded as part of the Han emperors' troop stations. At the time, the city was known as Yarkhoto and was the centre of the kingdom until the 5th century. Between 745 and 842 it was the prosperous capital of the Uygur kingdom of Cheshi.

The ruins of Jiaohe Gucheng.

One Tang dynasty story read: 'The king resided in the city of Jiaohe, which was nothing more than the former royal court of Jushi at the time of the Han. The kingdom has over 2,000 elite soldiers. The ground there is fertile. Wheat and corn provide two harvests a year. There is a plant there called 'baidie' (presumably cotton); its blossoms are collected and canvas weaved out of it. Inhabitants need to tie back their long flowing hair.'

As the citizens feuded and drought led to material hardship, the Mongols finally attacked the territory and the city was eventually abandoned, falling slowly into ruin.

The centre of the settlement is marked by a precisely 350-m-long (1,125-ft) main road stretching from north to south with predominantly perpendicular side roads leading from it. The central sacral area, with well-preserved ruins of Buddhist monasteries and stupas, was unearthed in the north-west.

A handicrafts quarter and bazaar were once located at the eastern gate, and both differ greatly to the residential areas. The remains of underground dwellings protecting against the summer heat and winter cold are also something of note.

famous Hami melons, the oasis city of Turpan is also known for the grapes grown here for raisins. It is a good starting point for a series of interesting day trips: about 10 m (6 miles) west are the ruins of Jiaohe Gucheng, and east of Turpan is the Bezeklik Qianfo Dong (Caves of the Thousand Buddhas) in the Murtuq Gorge.

12 Flaming Mountains (Huoyan Shan) This mountain range owes its name to the steep mounds of red sandstone rock, which look like they are on fire in the gleaming sun. Here in the Xin Jiang Autonomous Region, the climate is extremely continental, with ice-cold winters and hot, dry summers.

On the way to the Flaming Mountains, the road passes homesteads made of yellow clay bricks and enclosing large interior courtyards. During the hot summer, these courtyards, which are mostly overgrown with creepers, are the scene of everyday family life.

13 Gaochang Gucheng About 47 km (29 miles) south-east of Turpan at the foot of the Flaming Mountains are the ruins of a city dating back to Tang times (618–908). The outline of the entire complex is still very recognizable even today. Sections of the once 5-km-long (3-mile) wall

made from stamped mud also still exist and are up to 8 m (26 ft) high in some parts, despite the relatively extreme conditions in these parts. It once surrounded a settlement 1.5 sq km (0.5 sq mi) in size that was divided into an external, internal and palace city. An entrance gate, the foundations of a pagoda and a temple hall are all well-preserved, and some brick buildings were rebuilt in parts.

14 Astana In the immediate vicinity of Gaochang Gucheng are the tombs of Astana (Uygur for capital). Even though the ancient tomb complex, containing some 400 tombs, was built between the 3rd and 8th centuries AD, the mummies are still very well preserved because of the hot, dry climate. 2,000 books and documents were also discovered in the tombs. Along with the coin, ceramic and silk findings, they are further proof of the enormous wealth this region possessed in the Silk Road's heyday.

The road follows the old trade routes along the northern edge of the eastern Tarim Basin through the oasis town of Hami to Minghoshan in what is today the Gansu Province.

15 Minghoshan (Dunhuang) It is in this famous oasis city, where fruit and cotton are culti-

vated in abundance thanks to clever irrigation, that the northern and southern forks of the Silk Road leading around the Taklimakan Desert converge.

In the past, if travellers heading east on the Silk Road had reached Mingoshan, it meant they had survived virtually every kind of danger, be it nature,

thieves or highway robbers. This meant the opposite was true for travellers heading west with their caravans. Minghoshan was the last safe haven in Chinese-protected territory. It is thus no surprise that wealthy travellers between the 4th and 14th centuries were told of supernatural powers here,

The Caves of the Thousand Buddhas

The old cave monastery of Bezeklik was built north of Gaochang in the Flaming Mountains, and is today one of the main attractions at the Turpan oasis. The vast monastery complex is reached via the gorge of the Murtuq River, where the ruins of a watchtower take you back to the 1770s. Opposite the large complex is another cave monastery, Sämgin, which was inhabited from 450 BC until the 13th century, but is not accessible to the public. The Caves of the Thousand Buddhas at Bezeklik were dug into the steep face of the western bank some 80 m

Buddha in Bezeklik.

(262 ft) above the river. Work began on the caves around 430 BC and continued until the 13th century. After the monks had left the monastery, it was forgotten about for several centuries.

The cave murals were damaged several times from the mid 19th century onwards. Initially, sometime after 1860, Islamic bigots destroyed most of the Buddhas' faces in their fanaticism. German and British archaeologists (Albert von Le Coq, Albert Grünwedel, Aurel Stein) later cut out the most important and most valuable murals and transported them back to Europe in boxes. Many of these were irrecoverably lost in World War II during the bombing attacks on Berlin.

The images of Buddhas and Bodhisattvas in particular fell victim to this type of 'scientific' meddling.

Among the still-preserved paintings of interest are those depicting emissaries from distant lands, for example one of a condolence ceremony.

The illustrations of people of different races and clothing are a clear indication of the lively cultural and economic exchange along the Silk Road.

and their donations helped to equip the Magao cave monastery in opulent style.

16 Mogao Ku This monastery complex is located in a river valley between the San Wei and Ming Sha mountains about 25 km (15 miles) from Minghoshan. Nearly 500 caves were unearthed here, with walls covering a total surface area of 45,000 sq m (484,200 sq ft). The illustrations are not just evidence of their creators' religious beliefs, but also depict a multitude of themes from everyday life.

The entire complex, including murals, reliefs and sculptures from the 8th century, is considered one of the most important examples of Buddhist art in China and was declared a UNESCO World Heritage Site in 1987.

17 Yueya Quan and Mingshashan The Minghoshan area's second-largest tourist sight are the dunes around Crescent Lake (Yueya Quan), which is fed by an underground reservoir. These flawlessly formed crescent dunes extend to the oasis gardens on the outskirts of town and are proof that the desert is near. You also get an amazing view of the eastern foothills of the Taklimakan Desert from the 200-m-high (656-ft) dunes of the Mingshashan, the 'Singing Sands'.

The next stretch of the journey via Anxi leads partly through semi-desert and partly through the steppe. Your next destination is Jiayuguan in the southeastern foothills of the Jiayu mountains. This is where you meet up with the western end of the Great Wall of China.

18 Jiayuguan This impressive fortress was built in 1372 and was the most remote western fort of the Ming Dynasty along the Great Wall. Over the centuries, it protected the strategically important Jiayu Pass between Qilian Shan and Bei Shan.

The fortress itself comprised a double wall with watchtowers in each corner and two double gates with 17-m (46-ft) watchtowers in the east and west. The wall in the inner city is 733 m (2,356 ft) long and 10 m (33 ft) high. In 1507, another 40 km

1 The Murtuq Gorge east of Turpan with the Caves of the Thousand Buddhas in Bezeklik.

2 The Mogao Grottoes with wooden porches near Minghoshan (Dunhuang) contain paintings, scripts and cult objects.

3 The western end of the Great Wall at the Jiayu Pass near Jiayuguan.

Detour

Ta'er Si

Near Xining, the capital of the Qinghai province, is the Kumbum monastery, called Ta'er Si by the Chinese, a very important site in Tibetan culture. The founder of the yellow-capped sect, Tsong Kapa (1357–1419) was born here. Con-

Lamaistic monks in a procession.

struction on this Tibetan-style monastery began in 1560 under the Ming emperors. The walls are whitewashed, the roof friezes red-brown and the ceilings gold-plated. A 14-m-high (46-ft) Chorten (stupa) stands at the entrance. The golden roof hall is the main building and houses a 1.3-m (4-ft) golden statue of the founder.

(25 miles) was added to the wall, which was especially well forti-fied on the west side where the enemy was expected to attack. Archers shot the attackers from the small towers. The entire 24,000-sq-m (258,240-sq-ft) struc-ture was built out of stamped mud and clad with bricks.

The Silk Road then continues towards Lanzhou through the Hexi Corridor along the Great Wall, surrounded by deserts and semi-deserts in the north and lined by the steep Qilian Shan mountains in the south. 'Hexi' means 'west of the Huanghe.' This natural transportation link is 1,000 km (621 miles) long and 100 km (62 miles) wide. The con-nection only became a safe transport route after the Han emperor Wudi fortified the pass-es, built the Great Wall on the north side and put a function-ing administration in place, all more than 2,000 years ago. The corridor was located in a crucial position for relations and trade between Central Asia and China, and the cultural, linguistic and religious influences flowed from both sides.

⑲ Zhangye The first stop is Zhangye, a place Marco Polo described as a metropolis on his one-year sojourn here. Great

Buddha Monastery, built in 1098 in the centre of the city, was one of the places he visited. With its 34-m-long (109-ft) reclining Bud-dha, the monastery continues to be Zhangye's main attraction. The next section of the journey towards the south-east through the loess landscape is a diverse one, and must have been even more so in earlier times. Mulber-ry trees, the basis for silk produc-tion, once flourished here where today there is only wasteland.

⑳ Wuwei Wuwei was, and still is, a strategically important set-tlement in the Hexi Corridor, and was established as the regional capital as early as 115 BC. To defend against attacking Huns, Han Emperor Wudi devel-oped a plan to breed govern-ment studs here, but the farmers did not know anything about horse breeding. Wudi brought horses from areas such as the Fergana Valley and mixed them with local breeds. A galloping bronze horse from the time of the Han Dynasty was discovered in a tomb near Wuwei. This mas-terpiece is the main attraction of the Wuwei Museum.

㉑ Lanzhou Lanzhou, the capi-tal of the Gansu province, is located where the Hexi Corridor

leaves the road and continues over the Huang He. It stretches from west to east along both banks of the Huang He. The

best view of the 'Orchid City' is from the hills of the White Pagoda (Baita Shan) on the northern riverbank. When in

4

Lanzhou, it's worth visiting the Park of the Five Wells (Wuquan Gongyuan) on the southern side of a hill with its 600-year-old temple complex. In summer and autumn, you can take a boat ride on Lake Liujiaxia to Binglingsi Shiku, the cave temple of the Thousand Buddhas. It is one of the most impressive Buddhist cave temples in China. Here, a 60-m (197-ft) rock face soars out of the reservoir, from which a 27-m (89-ft) figure of the Buddha and numerous grottoes and alcoves were fashioned. Craftsmen worked on the complex between AD 513 and the mid 19th century, when it was suddenly forgotten. Wooden galleries and steps connect the grottoes in the rock face, and their forms are shown in frescoes and murals.

From Lanzhou, it is also worth allowing a couple of hours for a detour 300 km (186 miles) west to the Lamaistic monastery Ta'er Si. It is located 26 km (16 miles) south of Xining and is one of the six monasteries of the yellow-capped sect.

㉒ **Tianshui** This route initially heads through well-maintained mountain roads to Tianshui, where a mountain towers up on the slopes of the Qinling Shan south of the city. The mountain resembles a haystack and is for this reason called Maiji (wheat storer). It is famous for the sculptures in its grottoes (Maijishan Shiku) which are some of the most significant Buddhist grottoes in China.

The road runs parallel to Wei Hei towards Baoji in the Shaanxi province, an early centre for breeding silkworms. It continues downhill through a rolling, fertile loess landscape, terraced in some parts and badly eroded in others, into the densely settled Wei Valley. Finally, you reach Xi'an, the starting or ending point of our section of the historic Silk Road.

㉓ **Xi'an** Today's provincial capital was also China's capital, known then as Chang'an, for over 1,000 years under a series of eleven dynasties. A visit to the colourful Neolithic settlement of Banpo Bowuguan illustrates how the region has been continually inhabited since ancient times. The historic city's mighty wall has been preserved from the 14th century and still surrounds the historic old city today. The bell and drum tower, pagodas and temples, as well as the Great Mosque, have all been very well preserved.

However, only very few of the old living quarters survived the frenzy to modernize, which sacrificed large parts of the historic old city to create an autonomous inner city.

Roughly 85 km (53 miles) northwest of Xi'an near Qian Xian is an important necropolis from the Tang Dynasty (618–906). It contains the tombs of the third Tang Emperor Kao-tsung (649–683), who was buried here in the Liang mountains.

Xi'an's biggest attraction is, however, the grave mound of the Emperor Qin Shi Huangdi, which towers 47 m (154 ft) above the plains not far from the city in the Lintong district. The tomb itself has still not been opened.

Just 1.5 km (0.9 miles) west of this is one of the main tourist sites of the route, where the 7,000-strong army of terracotta warriors, which was meant to protect the tomb, was uncovered in 1974.

1 Scenery near Lanzhou with 4,000-m (13,124-ft) peaks of the Qinling Shan range.

2 The Temple of the Great Buddha near Zhangye, an early garrison city on the old Silk Road.

3 The Great Wild Goose Pagoda in Xi'an is 73 m (240 ft) high.

4 Terracotta Army warriors, which the first emperor of China had erected not far from his tomb.

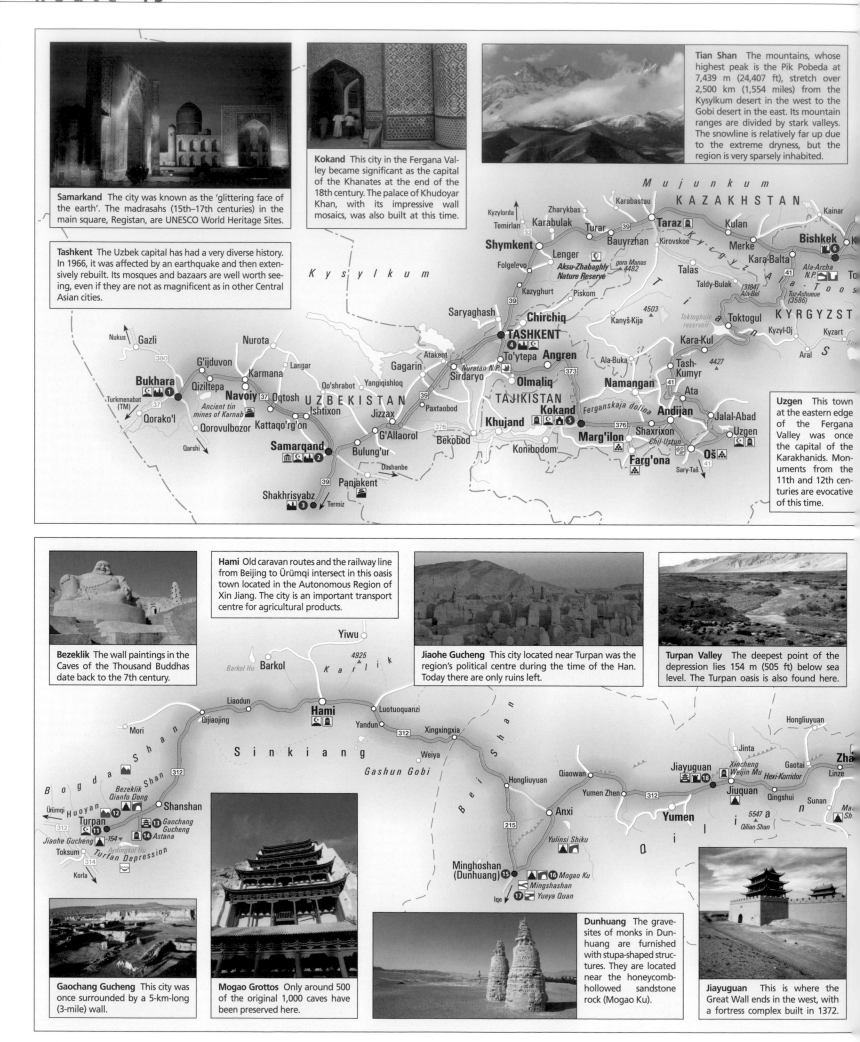

Samarkand The city was known as the 'glittering face of the earth'. The madrasahs (15th–17th centuries) in the main square, Registan, are UNESCO World Heritage Sites.

Kokand This city in the Fergana Valley became significant as the capital of the Khanates at the end of the 18th century. The palace of Khudoyar Khan, with its impressive wall mosaics, was also built at this time.

Tian Shan The mountains, whose highest peak is the Pik Pobeda at 7,439 m (24,407 ft), stretch over 2,500 km (1,554 miles) from the Kysylkum desert in the west to the Gobi desert in the east. Its mountain ranges are divided by stark valleys. The snowline is relatively far up due to the extreme dryness, but the region is very sparsely inhabited.

Tashkent The Uzbek capital has had a very diverse history. In 1966, it was affected by an earthquake and then extensively rebuilt. Its mosques and bazaars are well worth seeing, even if they are not as magnificent as in other Central Asian cities.

Uzgen This town at the eastern edge of the Fergana Valley was once the capital of the Karakhanids. Monuments from the 11th and 12th centuries are evocative of this time.

Hami Old caravan routes and the railway line from Beijing to Ürümqi intersect in this oasis town located in the Autonomous Region of Xin Jiang. The city is an important transport centre for agricultural products.

Bezeklik The wall paintings in the Caves of the Thousand Buddhas date back to the 7th century.

Jiaohe Gucheng This city located near Turpan was the region's political centre during the time of the Han. Today there are only ruins left.

Turpan Valley The deepest point of the depression lies 154 m (505 ft) below sea level. The Turpan oasis is also found here.

Gaochang Gucheng This city was once surrounded by a 5-km-long (3-mile) wall.

Mogao Grottos Only around 500 of the original 1,000 caves have been preserved here.

Dunhuang The grave-sites of monks in Dunhuang are furnished with stupa-shaped structures. They are located near the honeycomb-hollowed sandstone rock (Mogao Ku).

Jiayuguan This is where the Great Wall ends in the west, with a fortress complex built in 1372.

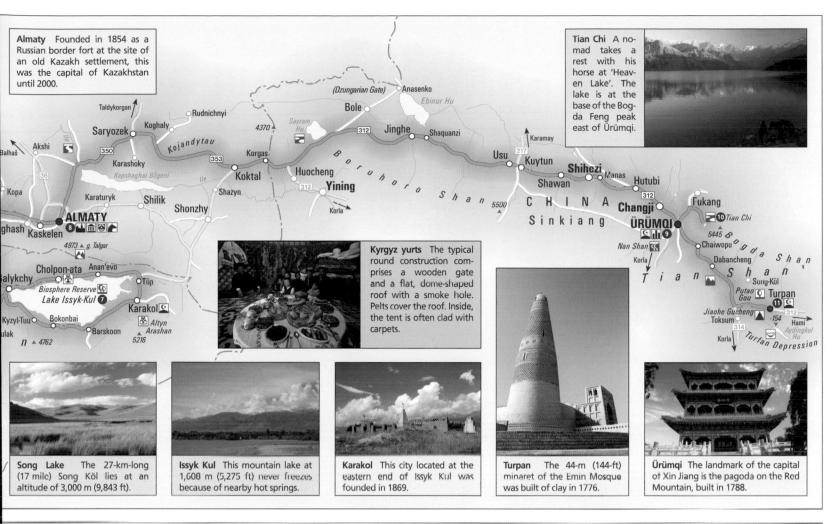

Almaty Founded in 1854 as a Russian border fort at the site of an old Kazakh settlement, this was the capital of Kazakhstan until 2000.

Tian Chi A nomad takes a rest with his horse at 'Heaven Lake'. The lake is at the base of the Bogda Feng peak east of Ürümqi.

Kyrgyz yurts The typical round construction comprises a wooden gate and a flat, dome-shaped roof with a smoke hole. Pelts cover the roof. Inside, the tent is often clad with carpets.

Song Lake The 27-km-long (17 mile) Song Köl lies at an altitude of 3,000 m (9,843 ft).

Issyk Kul This mountain lake at 1,608 m (5,275 ft) never freezes because of nearby hot springs.

Karakol This city located at the eastern end of Issyk Kul was founded in 1869.

Turpan The 44-m (144-ft) minaret of the Emin Mosque was built of clay in 1776.

Ürümqi The landmark of the capital of Xin Jiang is the pagoda on the Red Mountain, built in 1788.

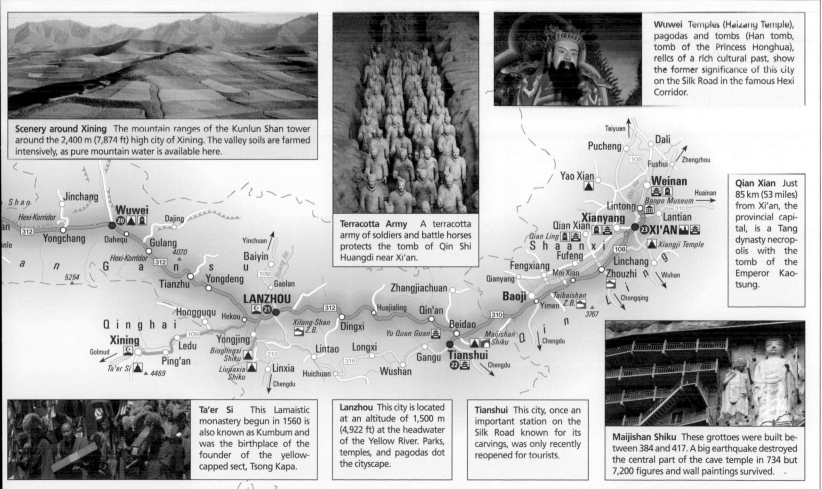

Wuwei Temples (Haizang Temple), pagodas and tombs (Han tomb, tomb of the Princess Honghua), relics of a rich cultural past, show the former significance of this city on the Silk Road in the famous Hexi Corridor.

Scenery around Xining The mountain ranges of the Kunlun Shan tower around the 2,400 m (7,874 ft) high city of Xining. The valley soils are farmed intensively, as pure mountain water is available here.

Terracotta Army A terracotta army of soldiers and battle horses protects the tomb of Qin Shi Huangdi near Xi'an.

Qian Xian Just 85 km (53 miles) from Xi'an, the provincial capital, is a Tang dynasty necropolis with the tomb of the Emperor Kaotsung.

Ta'er Si This Lamaistic monastery begun in 1560 is also known as Kumbum and was the birthplace of the founder of the yellow-capped sect, Tsong Kapa.

Lanzhou This city is located at an altitude of 1,500 m (4,922 ft) at the headwater of the Yellow River. Parks, temples, and pagodas dot the cityscape.

Tianshui This city, once an important station on the Silk Road known for its carvings, was only recently reopened for tourists.

Maijishan Shiku These grottoes were built between 384 and 417. A big earthquake destroyed the central part of the cave temple in 734 but 7,200 figures and wall paintings survived.

An impregnable rock face – Fort Meherangarh in Jodhpur on the edge of

Route 14

India

Rajasthan and the 'Golden Triangle'

Rajasthan means 'Land of the Kings', yet many villages in this region of India live in extreme poverty. Exploring the land of the Rajputs, you very quickly realize one irony about this 'desert state' – there is a lot more green than you might think. And where else does India dazzle with such vivid colours and magnificent palaces as in Rajasthan?

Due to Rajasthan's size and diversity, it can be difficult to decide what to do first after arriving in Delhi. Despite being the capital of the state, the glorious Maharaja city of Jaipur is not always the first stop. Instead, many visitors are initially, and naturally, drawn to the Mughal city of Agra in the state of Uttar Pradesh, which makes up the other corner of India's 'Golden Triangle' (Delhi-Agra-Jaipur). After all, it is the home of the immediately recognizable Taj Mahal, the white marble mausoleum built by Mughal Emperor Shah Jahan for his

favourite wife Mumtaz Mahal. The Islamic building has ironically become the most visible icon of India despite Hinduism being the dominant religious and ethnic identity factor in this culturally multifarious country. About eighty-two per cent of the people living in India are Hindus – the rest are a mix of Muslims, Christians, Sikhs, Buddhists and Jains.

Continuing westwards to Jaipur, now the capital of the whole of Rajasthan and barely four hours away from Delhi on the new motorway, you pass through

Vivid colours and ornaments – that's Rajasthan!

Mathura, the legendary birthplace of the god Krishna and a holy pilgrimage destination for Hindus. Again, though, one is struck by the number of large mosques here. You will see this type of religious coexistence almost everywhere in Rajasthan, not just in the so-called 'Golden Triangle'. The mighty walls of the Maharaja's fort bear witness to the centuries of power struggles between the Rajput dynasties and the Mughal emperors.

Part of the legacy of the Rajputs are their former hunting grounds, which are now some of India's most beautiful national parks and reserves. East of the long Aravalli Range near Bharatpur, for example, are three fabulous ones – Keoladeo Ghana, Sariska and Ranthambore. In the latter two it is possible to witness tigers in the wild, especially in the 400-sq-km (154-sq-mi) Ranthambore National Park.

The Taj Mahal: a monumental marble grave built by Shah Jahan on the Yamuna River in Agra not far from the 'Red Fort'. The mausoleum took twenty-two years to complete and houses the sarcophagus of the Mughal emperor's favourite wife, Mumtaz Mahal, who died giving birth to their fourteenth child in 1631. His own sarcophagus followed in 1666.

the Thar Desert, residence of the Maharajas of Marwar.

West of the Aravalli is the semi-arid Thar Desert, which extends far into Pakistan. Former caravan routes through the Thar have become tourist tracks in recent decades. The camel safaris to the sand dunes around Jaisalmer and Bikaner are a whole new riding experience and visits to desert villages, carpet weavers and potters are interesting. The indigenous population of this region, the Bishnoi, have been carefully cultivating native flora and fauna for 600 years.

Rajasthan is not all rustic – the engineering feat of the century, the Indira Ghandi Canal, brings water from the Himalayas and the Punjab into the Thar. Stony desert soil becomes farmland and the desert shrinks. Modernity has also changed transportation – instead of running on a narrow gauge, trains are now rolling into the desert on standard Indian gauge.

Looking for remnants of the magic of 'a thousand and one nights'? You'll find it in more than a few places – Rajasthan tempts visitors with bazaars, temples and palaces from Alwar to Jaipur, from Udaipur to Jodhpur, from Bikaner into the Shekhawati land of 'painted cities'.

Rajasthan also provided the model for Heritage Hotels, which are now all over India but nowhere as prevalent as in Rajasthan. Heritage Hotels are opulent palaces, glamorous merchants' houses (havelis) or relaxing country houses that have been turned into hotels by their owners. In some of them, royal personages stay under the same roof as normal hotel guests. From a comfortable bed to extreme luxury, every taste is catered for at Heritage Hotels – again a piece of 'a thousand and one nights' in Rajasthan.

A camel safari is almost a must – campfires under the starry sky included.

Opulent columned halls, defiant fortifications, tombs of Muslim saints and Indian Maharajas – the first stops on your journey to India offer some of the greatest architectural sights this ancient land has to offer. The state of Rajasthan, which is roughly the size of Germany, awaits you with magnificent fortresses, decadent palaces and the unique landscape of the Thar Desert.

1 **Delhi** (see pp. 180–181). From Delhi our journey leads us in two or three hours on mainly good roads to Agra, the former capital of the Mughal emperors. Roughly 150 km (93 miles) south of Agra, a town called Mathura is a worthy stop on our route.

2 **Mathura** East of Mathura's town centre you'll see the broad Yamuna River lined with ghats (steps) and cobblestone streets. It is a pilgrimage destination for hundreds of thousands of Hindus. The reason for this ist that Mathura is the birthplace of Krishna, and therefore one of the holiest cities in India.
Apart from Ganesha, the son of Shiva who provides success and wealth, Hindus worship virtually no other god more than the flute-playing Krishna. Mathura's many temples were destroyed by Muslim conquerors, in particular Mahmud of Ghazni in 1018. Sculptures from the school of Mathura dating back to around 100 AD are of remarkable quality and depict gods and 'Yakshis' – semi-divine beings. They are on display in the Archaeological Museum of Mathura.

3 **Agra** For quite a long time this city was chosen by the Mughal emperors as their capital, which makes the number of extravagant buildings hardly surprising. The Taj Mahal, which Shah Jahan built as a tomb for his favourite wife, Mumtaz Mahal, is known as one of the most beautiful buildings on earth.
Also well worth a visit here is of course the Red Fort, the two tombs Chinika Rauza and the slightly older Itmad-du-Daulah (a finance minister had them erected during his lifetime). The miniature example of the latter may have inspired the architect of the Taj Mahal.
Only 37 km (23 miles) to the south-west of Agra we find the ruins of another Mughal capital, albeit a shorter-lived one.

4 **Fatehpur Sikri** Akbar the Great was one of the most successful among a succession of very successful Mughal rulers. His reign lasted from 1556–1605 and his influence helped extend the empire throughout most of India.
For years Akbar waited in vain for the birth of an heir, and it was only after a pilgrimage to the Muslim saint Shaik Salim Chisti that his wife bore him a son. Out of gratitude for this gift and due to his victories over the Rajputs, Akbar had a new residence built on the spot where Shaik Salim Chisti had prophesied him a son – Fatehpur Sikri, the 'City of Victory'.
Built on a waterless plateau above the plains west of Agra, this city was abandoned soon after it was built. It remains nearly fully intact and is a place of particular fascination to this day. An hour from Agra you suddenly find yourself behind an enormous gate in the halls of an abandoned palace and in courts surrounded by columns. Individual marble structures are embedded like jewels into the sumptuous red sandstone architecture.
Pilgrims stream to the domed tomb of Shaik Salim Chisti, decorated with exquisite stone carvings. Children squat in the shadow of the mosque with their books and their teachers. Tourists admire the reception hall where Akbar discussed the possibility of a common religion ('Din-I-Ilahi') with the representatives of different faiths within his empire.
A trip to the Keoladeo Ghana National Park is well worth it for nature lovers and it is not too far from Bharatpur. In Bharatpur a street turns off in the direction of Dig to the north and from there it is 80km (50 miles) to Alwar via the town of Nagar.

1 The triple-nave reception hall in the Red Fort in Agra, built by Akbar in 1565–73, represents glamorous 16th-century architecture.

Detour

Gwalior

Gwalior is situated on the northern edge of the Vindhya Mountains in the state of Madhya Pradesh. Its fame comes mostly from two things – the truly enormous fort that dominates the city from a high plateau and the colossal Jain sculptures that reach 17 m (56 ft) and are hewn into the fortified mountain. Embattled for centuries, this city with over a million inhabitants is

The mighty walls of Man Singh's Gwalior Fort, built around 1500.

proud of its heroes, singers and poets. Hunting trophies and curiosities are shown in the Jaivilas Palace of the Scindia Maharajas, but parks and temples are also worth a visit. During the uprising against colonial rule in 1857 the Maharaja sided with the British, but his troops rebelled and fought against them, led by the much admired Rani (princess) Lakshmi Bai of Jhansi, who died weapon in hand.

Travel information

Route profile
Length: approx. 3,200 km (1,988 miles), excluding detours
Time required: 4–6 weeks
Start and end: Delhi
Route (main locations): Delhi, Mathura, Agra, Fatehpur Sikri, Bharatpur, Alwar, Sariska, Jaipur, Ajmer, Pushkar, Ranakpur, Udaipur, Chittaurgarh, Mount Abu, Jodhpur, Jaisalmer, Bikaner, Mandawa, Neemrana

Traffic information:
Drive on the left in India. Because of the chaotic traffic, rental cars are always rented with a driver. Reliable agencies offer qualified drivers and top-notch vehicles.

When to go:
The best time to visit Rajasthan is from October to March when the weather is milder and many of the important festivals take place.

General information:
www.rajasthantourism.gov.in
www.rajasthantourismindia.com
www.rajasthaninfo.org
Visa information:
www.india.gov.in

The precious little marble structure in front of this mighty mosque, Fatehpur Sikri, contains the sarcophagus of Sufi saint Shaik Salim Chisti. Like the Mughal emperor Akbar before them, Muslim and Hindu women come here to ask to be blessed with children and leave coloured cotton threads at the tomb.

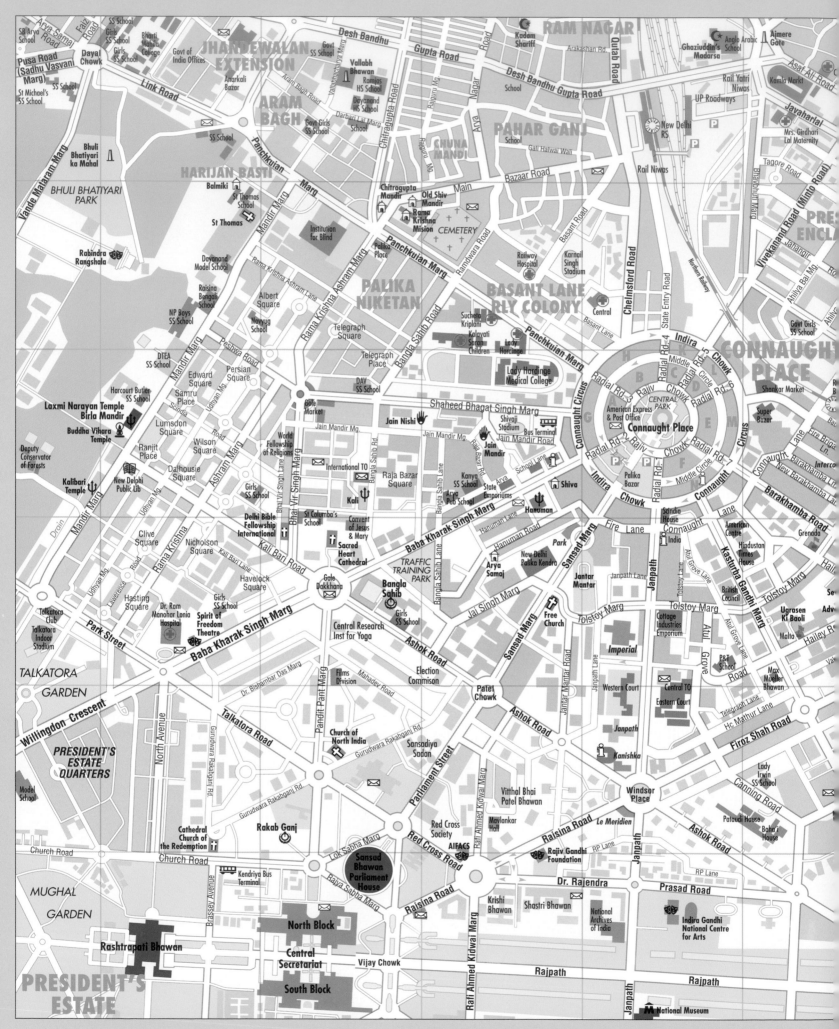

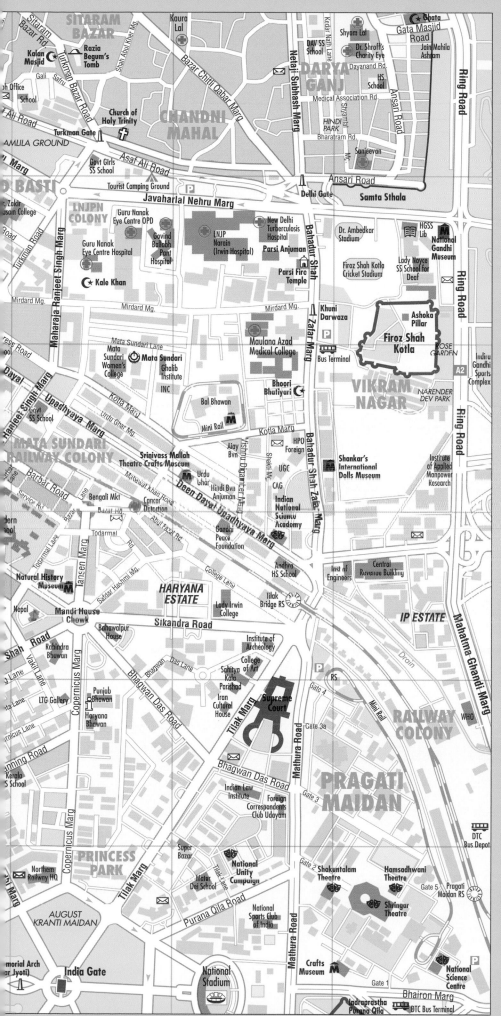

Delhi

Delhi has always been an important strategic town on the north Indian plain. Approximately as old as Rome, over the centuries this city was made the capital of many an empire. Since the end of British colonial rule in 1947, Delhi is the political centre of the Republic of India and a billion people are governed from here.

With its crowded bazaars, countless rickshaws and rumbling overcrowded buses, no traveller to Delhi would ever doubt that the population here has increased dramatically over the last century to its present 14 million. Indeed, Delhi has many faces.

One leftover from colonial rule is the expansive capital of India, New Delhi. Its broad avenues are home to ministries, the parliament, the presidential palace and magnificent museums, all of which form the centre of power for the apparatus of government.

Edwin Lutyens and Herbert Baker designed the circle of arcades that is Connaught Place in the heart of New Delhi in the first part of the 20th century. The circles and 'spokes' around it form Connaught Circus.

High-rise buildings from the last two decades tower over this attractive shopping and commercial area. Lutyens and Baker created New Delhi in a style that mixed neo classicism with Indian Palatial

Old Delhi, the old town, with its bazaars, temples and many mosques, is focused between the Yamuna River

Shah Jahan, grandson of the great Akbar. By no coincidence, he was also responsible for Old Delhi's other feature attraction, a fortification and palace for the great Mughal rulers, the Red Fort. The Persians stole the legendary 'Peacock Throne' from its imperial halls and other conquerors removed the inlaid jewels from the columns and walls.

Despite these thefts, a wide variety of art works from all the great epochs of Indian art can be found in Delhi. The National Museum displays great sculptures and miniatures, and nowhere else can you find as much contemporary Indian art and traditional arts and crafts as in Delhi. The Craft Museum is a good example, located in a village complex near the ruins of Purana Quila – said to be the location of Delhi's oldest city, Indraprashta. Basically, it's all here – numerous museums and parks, fine dining, luxurious shopping, theatres and cinemas.

Almost three million people a year also visit another temple, this one designed in the shape of a lotus flower with twenty-seven marble leaves: the Bahai

Top: The gate of the Red Fort. The fortification is surrounded by a sandstone wall and is almost a kilometre long and over 500 m (1,640 ft) wide. Right: A UNESCO World Heritage Site – Mughal Emperor Humayun's tomb from around 1570.

and the rail lines and has grown massively over centuries. Even if you have little time to spend in Delhi, we highly recommend a wander through the street bazaars of Chandni Chowk to experience the hustle and bustle of sellers, carts, cows and children – it certainly eclipses any department store adventure.

The two main monuments of Old Delhi are quite close to one another. The first is the Jama Masjid (Friday Mosque), India's largest, with a minaret that you can climb. The 'Mosque with a View of the World' – its original name – was commissioned by

House of Worship. The Bahai believe in uniting the faithful of all religions.

Everyday life in Delhi is dominated by contrasts – cosmopolitan and traditional, dire poverty and fairy-tale riches, bizarre and comfortable. Indeed, what most urban dwellers around the world take for granted has only just become reality in Delhi – a metro – and new satellite cities are springing up regularly in the surrounding countryside.

1

Keoladeo Ghana National Park

About 100 years ago, Maharajas irrigated the bushland south of Bharatpur using dams and canals in order to attract birds, which were subsequently shot in their thousands by Anglo-Indian hunting parties.

A family of storks in the Keoladeo Ghana National Park.

In 1983 the area was declared a national park covering 29 sq km (18 sq mi). It is home to more than 370 bird species, among them the Siberian Crane. The best time to visit the park is during the months of October to March.

5 Alwar Set into the rocky Aravalli Mountains, Alwar is an old trading centre with a royal palace and relatively few foreign visitors. Agra, Jaipur and the nearby national parks provide more of a draw for tourists than the ancient royal residence of Alwar, a town that received mention in India's great Mahabharata Epic from the 2nd century BC. All of this makes the city and the Rajput palace and gardens even more authentic.

Oddly, many of the palace's rooms serve the banal purpose of storing government files, which are stacked to the ceiling in places. Only the fifth floor has a museum with some of the hunting trophies, silver tables, metre-long scrolls and works of the Bundi school of painting.

6 Sariska National Park This reserve covers an area of about 800 sq km (308 sq mi) roughly 37 km (23 miles) south of Alwar, and was made a national park in 1979 with a focus on conserving the tiger. There is plenty of space for the tigers to live peacefully in the jungle here – they are actually rather afraid of people.

Failing a tiger sighting, you may catch a glimpse of beautifully spotted Chital deer, Chowsingha antelope, hyenas, a pack of wild boar or very likely a pack of rhesus monkeys.

2

There are also Mughal forts and temples both within and around the park. Take Highway 8 via Shahpura 100 km (62 miles) to Jaipur where you will be greeted first by magnificent Fort Amber.

7 Jaipur This old town, also known as the 'Pink City' for the colour of its facades, was planned on a nine-part rectangular grid in 1727 – very rational and geometric town planning. At the same time, the nine old-town quarters of Jaipur symbolize the Brahmin Hindu cosmos. The open-air observatory Jantar Mantar at the palace also fits in

well with this cosmic association and is one of the main attractions here. You can even walk on some of its 'instruments', which are made of brick.

Jaipur, which is the western point of the 'Golden Triangle' (Delhi-Agra-Jaipur), is home to over two million people and is thus the only town with over a million inhabitants in Rajasthan. To this day the city is full of palaces.

The first Maharaja of Rajasthan to convert Rambagh, his summer palace, into a hotel was Sawai Man Singh II in 1957. Since then his aristocratic brethren all over

India seem to have adopted the 'Palace and Heritage Tourism' concept.

Jaipur is also a centre for jewellery, jewels, precious inlaid marble and all sorts of other arts and crafts.

1 A symbol of India – tigers in the Sariska National Park.

2 The magic of an old town on the edge of the mountains – the 19th-century city palace of Alwar sits above the temple pond.

In Jaipur's mountainous surroundings there are numerous palaces, temples, gardens and forts to entice visitors, like here in the Galta valley. Hundreds of pilgrims worship the Sun god in the Surya Temple above a natural swimming pool in the rock (top) and below is the recently renovated Gaitor Palace

The Jains

Much like the Hindus, the faith of the Jains theoretically leads them through a series of reincarnations to 'Moksha', a sort of liberation from earthly existence. The Jains worship the 'Tirthankaras', the twenty-four

Head of Buddha in the Jain temple in Ranakpur.

forerunners, as their teachers, the last of which was Mahavira who lived in the 6th century BC.
Apart from 'Ahimsa' (peacefulness), Jains also preach 'Asteya' (not taking from others), 'Brahmacharya' (moderation as far as food, drink and sexuality are concerned) and 'Aparigraha' (inner distance from worldly possessions).

❽ Ajmer A defiant fortress built upon a stark rocky plateau overlooking a walled city, the model for many cities in this area where for centuries it was necessary to defend against the repeated attacks of ambitious conquerors. At Fort Taragarh in Ajmer, there is not much left of the often 4-m-thick (13-ft) walls built by a Hindu ruler some 900 years ago.
But Ajmer presents itself as a lively, pulsating city in many respects. It is home to many schools and universities and a pilgrimage destination for pious Muslims and Jains. In fact, about a quarter of the more than 400,000 inhabitants are Jains. Following the example of British public schools, the still highly regarded Mayo College in Ajmer was founded in 1873 for the sons of the Rajputs.
The Dargah Sharif Mosque Centre is even older and was developed around the tomb of Khwaja Moinuddin Chisti, who was a friend of the poor. In memory of his works, two enormous iron vats of food are still provided for the needy at the entrance to the holy district.

Even Emperor Akbar made a pilgrimage to Ajmer.
A more recent building that is worth a visit is the Nasiyan Temple from 1864, built by the Jains. A two-storey hall fantastically depicts the heavenly cosmos of the Jains, including golden temples and the airships of the gods. About 11 km (7 miles) from Ajmer you'll come to Pushkar.

❾ Pushkar The name Pushkar means 'lotus blossom'. But in this case we are not talking about just any lotus blossom. It is the one that Brahma allegedly dropped to the floor to create Pushkar Lake. That is why the little town of Pushkar with its 15,000 inhabitants is one of the holiest sites in India.
Half surrounded by mountains, this little town with tidy white houses and the fresh green fauna of a nearby oasis possesses a majestic beauty. Unfortunately, it has been so overrun by tourism in the last few years that Pushkar's priests, beggars and numerous self-appointed Sadhus ('holy men') have developed a business sense to accompany their piety.

They constantly invite travellers to the 'Puja', the washing ceremony, which takes place at the fifty-two ghats, the steps down to the lake. Then without delay they demand payment with rupees or, even better, dollars. The 'Little Varansi' at Pushkar Lake is therefore best visited in the morning – the temples open early. The view from the hill with the Savitri Temple, dedicated to Brahma's wife, is especially beautiful. It can be reached after a good half-hour hike.
From Pushkar you'll need a day of driving through winding mountain landscapes to get to

Ranakpur. On the way, you'll be tempted to take a detour to one of the biggest forts in Rajasthan – the 15th-century Fort Kumbhalgarh. The 36-km (22-mile) wall around the perimeter of this fort is said to be second only to the Great Wall of China in length and protects a total of 360 temples – 300 Jains and the rest Buddhist. You get a splendid view of the Aravalli Mountains from atop the wall.

⑩ Ranakpur Completely different from Pushkar, this holy temple town of the Jains typically allows you to enjoy its treasures in peace and quiet. It is set back from any larger neighbours in a forested valley with family farms, two reservoirs and a handful of hotels.
One of these is the Maharani Bagh Orchard Retreat, a former fruit garden and picknicking spot of the Maharaja of Jodhpur. It is just an hour's walk from the Jain temples and the pilgrim hostels. Before climbing the steps to the temples you will be required to remove anything you have that is made of leather or other animal products. The four temples here date from the 15th and 16th centuries. Three of them are dedicated to the 'forerunners' Adinath, Parsvanatha and Neminath, and the fourth is dedicated to the Sun god Surya. Take a look at the unique stonework on the hundreds of columns and domed prayer halls. Flowers are placed before the pictures of Jain saints and music echoes through the rooms.
It is now a good 80 km (50 miles) to Udaipur, the biggest city in the south of Rajasthan.

⑪ Udaipur Also known as the 'Queen of the Lakes', Udaipur is considered by many to be the most beautiful city in Rajasthan. Today it has 400,000 inhabitants, and from its founding in the year 1568 it was constantly under the rule of the Sisodia Maharanas until Indian independence in 1947.
The title Maharana ('Great King') is equivalent to Maharajah. In the old realm of Mewar, the Sisodias took the top position in the royal hierarchy of India, and their influence is still felt today. Nearly 500 years ago they were responsible for many of the reservoirs and artificial lakes that were built in the area. In the midst of the most beautiful of these, Lake Pichola, summer palaces were built on two islands opposite the mighty towering complex of the city palace. The bigger of the two island palaces became world famous as the Lake Palace Hotel. The list of celebrated guests is endless. The nightly spectacle of the lake bathed in lights is best enjoyed from one of the roof terrace restaurants in the old town.
Parks like the 'Garden of the Ladies of Honour' (Saheliyon ki Bari) contribute not only to the charm of Udaipur when the lotus ponds and roses are in bloom, but also reveal the artistic sense and craftsmanship present here. Behind the city palace and in the small side streets are countless studios and shops where you can witness hundreds of indigenous artists and craftsmen that still specialize in the miniature paintings of the old academies and the skilled carpet weaving of the region.

⑫ Chittaurgarh Seven mighty gates once secured the ascent to the plateau over the Berach River 100 km (60 miles) to the east of Udaipur. On the plain below is a city of 75,000 inhabitants founded in the 8th century and once the capital of Mewar.

1 In 1567 Maharana Udai Singh ordered the creation of Lake Pichola when he declared Udaipur the capital of Merwar. The Lake Palace Hotel is on an island in the lake.

2 Pushkar: India's holiest of lakes is supposed to have developed from Brahma's lotus blossom.

The Thar Desert

The only great desert on the subcontinent stretches from the foothills of the Aravalli Mountains to the Indian-Pakistani border to the Indu Valley, and occupies nearly half of Rajasthan, an area of 250,000 sq km (155,000 sq mi). But the Thar Desert is not like the Sahara desert. Sand dunes without vegetation are only found in small areas to the west and south of Jaisalmer. Geologists consider it a semi-arid region.

The journey from Jodhpur to Jaisalmer and from Jaisalmer to Bikaner takes hours. You'll see sand swirling in the hot wind, green, withered, thorny acacia bushes on the horizon, and maybe a tree, but only few villages.

But the Thar is not devoid of human life. Women by the side of the road balance all manner of supplies on their heads as they walk along the road – water jugs, or sand and stones for a building site. And they wear brightly coloured dresses threaded with silver.

Camel caravan in the Thar Desert.

Adolescents herd their goats and men drive colourfully painted trucks over the sandy road or journey on camels with turbans of yellow or red.

If you take the time for a detour from Highway 15, ideally with a guide, you'll come to a few farms and villages in the middle of the stony landscape where the stone or mud buildings are surrounded by thorny bushes to protect the sheep and goats from dogs and hyenas.

West of the Thar the landscape of the desert changes to green fields thanks to the Indira Ghandi Canal. Though it is not without its environmentally damaging effects, this 'engineering feat of the century' in India pumps water from the Punjab into Rajasthan and gives many farmers a chance to cultivate crops in an otherwise wasteland area.

The steep walls of the rocky plateau rise to 150 m (492 ft), but despite its formidable gates and walls it was still conquered three times by Mughal armies. Each of these invasions culminated in a 'Jauhar' by the women and children – the heroic ritual of collective suicide by throwing themselves onto burning pyres. The men then committed 'Saka': battling to their last breath.

Dozens of sprawling palace and temple ruins, a narrow 15th-century 'victory' tower, which you can climb, and some pavilions and ponds are all that is left of the glory and decline of this medieval residence.

Back in Udaipur the journey continues via Som straight through the Aravalli Mountains to the north-west in the direction of Abu Road. When the heat begins to hit the plains in April, the hotels in Rajasthan's 'hill station' Mount Abu begin to fill up. Close to the border to Gujarat, Abu Road winds its way to 1,200 m (3,937 ft) where you can live comfortably in this mountain village (20,000 inhabitants) even in the summer.

⑬ Mount Abu The hilly forest and hiking areas, Nakki Lake, the splendid view from 'Sunset Point' and a protected wildlife area for leopards, bears and red deer, all quite close to the centre of town, make Mount Abu an enjoyable diversion for tourists, particularly if you've come in hotter months. The Dilwara temples outside of Mount Abu are well-known among art lovers.

On a par with the Jain temples of Ranakpur, the skilful stone carvings and sculpture in the five main temples here (11th–18th centuries) are even considered by some to be the best Jain work ever done.

To the left and right of Abu Road heading towards Jodhpur there are a number of Rajput residences, small country palaces with gardens usually near a village, and some former 'havelis' in their modern guise as 'Heritage Hotels'. Among the 'havelis' are the Ghanerao Royal Castle, Karni Kot Sodawas, Bera, Bhenswara, Sardasamand, Fort Chanwar Luni and Rohet Garh.

⑭ Jodhpur In stark contrast to the rural landscape along the road, Jodhpur is Rajasthan's second-largest city and has more than 800,000 inhabitants. It is also the south-eastern point in the great 'Desert Triangle'.

Once you are in town, the streets of Jodhpur are dominated by hectic traffic and lively trade in the bazaar. But high above it all stands the mighty Meherangarh Fort, built by the Rathore rulers, more than 120 m (393 ft) above the Old Town alleys in the north-west of the city. The fort's palaces are known for their superb filigree stone patterns and spacious courtyards.

Across the city on Chittar Hill is the magnificent Umaid Bhawan Palace, the last of the monumental residences built by the Rajput (1929–43). Museums, markets, arts and crafts and antiques await you here.

⑮ Jaisalmer For many people, the most lasting impression of their desert travels in Rajasthan is the moment the honey-gold walls of Jaisalmer appear above the sandy plains. Since the 12th century the ninety-nine bastions of these fortifications have dominated the hills of the city of Jaisalmer.

Even until far into the 19th century, the caravans of the spice

and silk traders travelled in and out of the city. Ironically, it was the faraway Suez Canal that made the difference. By boosting sea trade with Europe it more or less put an end to the overland business. As a result, Jaisalmer's wealthy traders and their fairy-tale mansions with opulent facades, bay windows and balconies became a thing of the past virtually overnight.

After the tumultuous division of India and Pakistan in 1947, Jaisalmer's strategic location on the western border gave it renewed significance and India soon invested in streets and railways. Yet the conversion from the narrow-gauge railways to the Indian wide-gauge system is actually a recent development, and one that greatly benefited tourism. Since the 1990s the

industry has grown dramatically, and the population of Jaisalmer has doubled to 40,000 in the last decade. Jaisalmer is now the centre of desert tourism in India and a main gathering point for camel drivers and thousands of souvenir sellers.

The adventure is not all lost, however, on a trip to Desert National Park west of the city, which includes oases and deserted medieval cities like Kuldhara and Kabha. The Akal Wood Fossil Park, located 17 km (11 miles) south of Jaisalmer on the road to Barmer, has fascinating fossilized tree trunks 180 million years old.

In just two hours from here you can also reach Pokaran, a small desert town with only 20,000 inhabitants.

16 Pokaran The name of Pokaran went through the international press in 1998 when the Indian government demonstrated its status as a nuclear power by carrying out several test detonations near the neighbouring town of Khetolai. But what is also worth seeing in Pokaran is the fort built in the 14th century, whose imposing walls are an example of a private restoration initiative.

The family of the Thakur Rajputs has been living in this fort for thirteen generations and has

installed not only a Heritage Hotel but also a small museum, which specializes in archaeology and folklore. When the owner can spare the time, he willingly explains to his guests how the neglected rooms of the palace are being restored to former glory.

17 Gajner Wildlife Sanctuary This well-preserved old palace on the lake is surrounded by old trees and almost seems haunted. The grounds, which are only 30 km (18 miles) west of the large city of Bikaner, were once used by their owner as hunting territory until India's conservationists and biologists pressed for the creation of a nature reserve under the auspices of 'Project Tiger'.

The primary objective of the reserve was obviously to protect and increase the number of species living here. The secondary objective was to increase tourism in the area. The Gajner Wildlife Sanctuary is now a paradise for birds and wild animals, and the Gajner Palace itself was turned into a Heritage Hotel.

1 The Meherangarh Fort towers high above Jodhpur.

2 The Indira Ghandi Canal flows into the Gadi Sagar, the temple lake of Jaisalmer.

Desert fortresses

There is hardly a city in the Thar Desert that doesn't have an accompanying fort. Peaceful times were rare in this wild region all the way up until the 19th century, and protective walls were a necessity. Some fans of Rajasthan travel exclusively from fort to

Jaisalmer's upper city has ninety-nine mighty bastions.

fort, inspecting the wooden gates crowned by iron spikes and reinforced with iron bands, climbing steep steps and marvelling at the collections of weapons and opulent chambers.

Khimsar, one of the most romantic forts, lies by the side of a small road between Jodhpur and Nagaur south of Bikaner. It was restored by its owners and not only has an attractive dining room and a refreshing pool, but also a cosy private cinema.

Shekhawati

As long as their caravans crossed the country, the merchants in Shekhawati in the north-east of Rajasthan were rich. Well, they are still wealthy but have long since moved their houses

Typically painted facade in the Shekhawati region.

and businesses to Kolkata or Mumbai. The 'havelis', their opulently decorated town houses, are mostly deserted now. But it is with amazement that you behold the colourful facades of these mansions, which depict stories of gods, dancers, railways and first motor cars, all with a seemingly naive delight.

The rooms are decorated with antiques and enjoy a view of the bird-lake activities including boating, golf, cycling and hiking. However, during longer stretches of drought or a non-existent monsoon, there is nothing to be done – the lake dries out and the birds move on.

18 Bikaner The main roads to Bikaner, an old city of the Maharajas with a current population of about 500,000, have improved over the years as more and more palaces have recently converted to hotels. But the contrast between the present and the past, between bazaar alleys and shanty towns is more stark than in Jaipur or Udaipur.
The forward-planning Maharaja Dungar Singh had an electricity network installed comparatively early, in 1886. His successor then had schools, hospitals and canals built. A mighty ring of walls surrounds Junagarh Fort, which was built towards the end of the 16th century. Its mirrored cabinets, delicately decorated chambers and its opulent coronation hall make it one of the high-

lights of Indian palatial architecture in the region.
Away from the city on a visit to India's only state camel-breeding farm you get to see first-hand why 750,000 of the five million camels worldwide live right here in Rajasthan.
A slightly unusual facet of Hindu culture presents itself to visitors about 30 km (18 miles) south in Deshnok at the Karni Mata Mandir, a temple with silver doors and marble reliefs. Rats are worshipped here as holy animals and run around uninhibited. According to legend, they are the souls of dead poets and singers.

19 Mandawa There are no big cities in the Shekhawati region east of Bikaner and north of Jaipur. Mandawa, founded in 1790 and now the tourist centre of the area, is accordingly modest in size. Comfortable accommodation is limited here. The best option is the former Rajput palaces where the owner often lives in a separate wing. The Roop Niwa Palace in Nawalgarh is an option, or try the 18th-century Castle Mandawa.

Desert sands blow around the walls of the former fort of Mandawa (begun in 1760), behind which the Rajput Rangir Singh continues to restore the decaying splendour of palace halls and boudoirs to provide space for more visitors. No room here is the same as another. Exploring Mandawa you can find several large 'havelis' (Gulab Rai and Saraf, for example), a deep well with steps leading down to it, or a few antiques and arts and craft shops.
Mandawa is a convenient starting point for excursions into the partly green, partly desert landscape around the city and to a dozen other typical Shekhawati villages. The neighbouring village of Nawalgarh about 25 km (15 miles) away has more 'havelis' than any other town in the Shekhawati region. Several open their doors to visitors. The Poddar Haveli Museum from the 1920s has around 750 images on its facade, not counting the painted passages in the inner courtyard, as well as collections of musical instruments and historical photographs.

The drive to our last destination, Neemrana, takes around six hours (225 km/140 miles). Take the turn-off about 15 km (9 miles) north of Behror on Highway 8 between Jaipur and Delhi.

20 Neemrana For those who enjoy castles and exotic living, Neemrana is a very desirable destination. Some years ago a Frenchman and an Indian turned medieval Fort Neemrana above the village into a Heritage Hotel. With a sure sense of style and every detail of attention to the needs of their guests, they created an array of terraces, balconies, rooms and suites that spoil you without overdoing the decadence.
From the city of Neemrana it is another 120 km (74 miles) via the Delhi-Jaipur Highway back to the starting point, Delhi.

1 The 'Pushkar Mela' is not the only big camel market in Rajasthan. Nagaur, north of Jodhpur, is also famed for its own gathering, which takes place once a year in January or February.

Jaisalmer With ninety-nine bastions, Jaisalmer towers 80 m (263 ft) above the Thar Desert. It was the residence of the Bhati Rajputs, a contested headquarters for caravan trade.

Jodhpur In front of the steep rock of Meherangarh Fort sits the 'Jhaswant Thada', a white marble palace built in memory of Maharaja Jhaswant Singh II to honour his progressive policies.

Desert National Park This national park in the Thar Desert is a superb example of the ecosystems here and the rich variety of species (Dorkas gazelles, desert lynx, giant Indian bustards).

Fort Amber One of India's most beautiful, the Amber Palace (17th/18th century) in the fort of the same name is adorned with mirrors, marble halls, imposing gates and grand views of the stark mountains outside. The Mata Temple has a black marble depiction of Kali.

Delhi Mughal Emperor Shah Jahan had the Red Fort (Lal Quila) built between 1639 and 1648. The most beautiful of its buildings is the reception hall Diwan-I-Khas. Also worth seeing in Delhi are the Jama Masjid Mosque, the tomb of Mughal Emperor Humayun, the Lodi graves and the Qutb Minar minaret.

Fatehpur Sikri This city was founded by Akbar the Great in 1569 at the zenith of Mughal power in India. The Jama Masjid (Friday Mosque) is the centre of the city's holy district.

Sariska National Park Formerly the hunting ground of the Maharaja of Alwar, this region is alive with tigers and dense forest. Located in the Aravalli Range, it became a national park in 1979. The Maharaja's summer palace near the grounds is now an hotel.

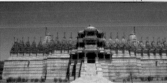

Ranakpur The 15th/16th-century temples built by the Jains contain unique halls with superb stone-carvings and domes considered among the most important masterpieces in all of India. They belong to a well-educated subculture in India.

Agra The Red Fort (1565–73), built as a fortification with deep and broad trenches, soon became an example of imperial luxury and prestigious architecture. It is accentuated with large courtyards, palaces, and opulent columned halls like the triple-nave marble hall of Diwan-I-Am shown here.

Udaipur The city palace of the Maharanas of Mewar, the oldest dynasty in Rajasthan, has been continuously expanded since it was built in the 16th century. It is still inhabited by the family.

Jaipur The 'Palace of the Winds' was built with stone lattice windows to allow the ladies of the court to see without being seen.

Gwalior Fort The enormous walls of this mighty fortress rise high above the town. It contains the Man Singh Palace, built around 1500, and four other palaces.

Taj Mahal Tomb and monument of a great love: the great Mughal Emperor Shah Jahan had this mausoleum built in Agra for his wife Mumtaz Mahal, who died giving birth to their 14th child.

The stupa in Boudhanath is 40 m (131 ft) high, the tallest in all of Nepal.

Nepal and Tibet

On the Road of Friendship across the Roof of the World

The path over the main crescent of the Himalayas easily makes it into our list of dream routes. After all, you cross part of the highest mountain range in the world, passing turquoise-coloured lakes and endless high steppe regions that are still traversed by nomads with yak, goat and sheep herds. Add monasteries perched on impossible bluffs and you've got an unforgettable journey. Our route begins in Kathmandu, meanders through central Nepal and ends in Lhasa on the Kodari Highway.

Foreigners have only been allowed to visit the previously sealed-off country of Nepal since 1950. Much has changed culturally since then, but fortunately the fascination that the country inspires has not. About a third of the country is taken up by the Himalayas, the highest point of which lies on the border to Tibet – Mount Everest, at 8,850 m (29,037 ft).
Between the protective Mahabharat Range in the south and the mighty main crest of the Himalayas in the north lies the valley of Kathmandu, which contains the three ancient and royal cities of Kathmandu, Patan and Bhaktapur.
Even in the age of the automobile the spirit of times past is palpable in the capital, and Kathmandu continues to impress visitors with its royal palace and the hundreds of temples, statues and beautiful wood-carvings on the facades and monuments. The second of the ancient royal cities, Patan, lies on the opposite shore of the Bagmati. Once again, a former royal

Buddha statue Amithaba/Tashilhunpo Monastery.

palace and over fifty temples remind us of Nepal's glorious past. South-east of Kathmandu lies Bhaktapur, where the alleys and streets are dominated by Newari wood-carvings.
Before you start off from Bhaktapur towards Lhasa, it is worth undertaking a journey to Pokhara in the north-west, on the shore of the Phewasees at the bottom of the Annapurna Massif. Via Lumbini, the birthplace of Buddha, and Butwal the round trip leads you to Bharatpur, the gate to the Royal Chitwan National Park, and eventually back to Bhaktapur.
The Kodari Highway then brings you over the main ridge of the Himalayas into Tibet. Along this panoramic route you are constantly under the spell of 7,000 to 8,000-m-high (22,967 to 26,248-ft) mountains. In Tingri, for example, you finally experience Everest as an impressive single

Sagarmatha National Park with its grandiose mountain landscape is listed in the UNESCO World Heritage register.

'Om mani padme hum' – Tibetan monks gather for communal prayer in the Sakya monastery near Lhaze.

entity. The journey here can become arduous at times, as the highway leads over passes where the air is rather thin – over 5,000 m (16,405 ft) above sealevel on the Lalung-La Pass, for instance.

Tibet, 'The Land of Snow', has been closely linked to China since the 13th century. The current Tibet Autonomous Region (TAR) of China has an extremely low population density – roughly 2.5 million Tibetans, and 350,000 Chinese live on 1.2 million sq km (463,000 sq mil) of land. The Chinese dominate the economy, politics and government. Since the 9th century, Tibetans have followed Lamaism, a Tibetan variant of Buddhism whose religious and political head is the Dalai Lama.

The route through Gutsuo, Tingri, Lhaze, Yigaze, Gyangze and Nagarze into the city of Lhasa, which was once forbidden to foreigners, is lined by Lamaist monasteries –

at least, the ones that weren't destroyed by the Chinese cultural revolution. Sakya is one of the oldest monasteries in Tibet and the 15th-century Buddhist monastery of Tashilhunpo has also been preserved – the latter contains a 26-m-high (85-ft) bronze Buddha. It is unlikely that anybody wouldn't be fascinated by the Kubum monastery in Gyangze, a monumental complex of temples with pagodas, stupas and palaces.

Lhasa, the 'Place of the Gods', lies at an elevation of 3,700 m (12,140 ft) and was chosen by Songsten Ganpo (620–49), the first Tibetan king, as his royal residence. Where today the famous red and white Potala Palace looks down on the city, Ganpo had built a fortification that later became Tibet's theocratic centre of power, including all pictorial works and national treasures – the icon of Tibetan religiosity.

Prayer flags on the Road of Friendship near Xigaze.

1

The royal cities of Nepal

In the 3rd century, Indian Emperor Ashoka brought Buddhism to the Kathmandu Valley and had five stupas erected in what today is Patan. From about 300 to 879 Lichchavi rulers from India dominated the Kathmandu Valley and for their part furthered the proliferation of Hinduism. The

Above: The royal palace in Patan.
Below: Durbar Square in Bhaktapur.

small principalities that developed between 879 and 1200, including Kathmandu, became centres of Buddhism.
The year 1220 marked the beginning of the Malla Dynasty, which reigned until 1768. Yaksha Malla (1428–82) bequeathed his kingdom to his three children who ended up falling out and founding their own royal cities: Kathmandu, Patan und Bhaktapur. For three hundred years they competed with each other by erecting increasingly elaborate buildings.

The Road of Friendship was built only twenty years ago, stretches 950 km (590 miles) and connects Nepal and Tibet. Apart from beautiful villages and monasteries that represent hundreds of years of history, it is the grandiose mountain scenery that so impresses travellers.

1 Kathmandu (see sidebar right).

2 Patan Over the years Patan (or Lalitpur), which has been famous for its metalworks for centuries, has almost completely melded with Kathmandu and is only separated from it by the Bagmati River. The Old Town here is particular worth visiting due to its royal palace. The more than fifty temples in Patan that are at least three storeys high were erected using either traditional wood or stone. The most important Shiva shrine is the five-storey Kumbeshvra Temple, not far from the 'Golden Temple'.

3 Bhaktapur Situated about 15 km (9.3 miles) from Kathmandu, Bhaktapur was founded in the 12th century and life here still seems to flow at a mostly rural pace. The potters' market is full of locally produced goods and there are wood-carvers all around town.
The main sights are at Durbar Square around the royal palace. The magnificently gilded Sundhoka Gate connects the two

2

wings of the palace and simultaneously marks the entrance to the Taleju Temple, the main shrine within the palace.

4 Langtang National Park North of Kathmandu and Patan is Langtang National Park. The southern entrance near Dhunche is about six or seven hours away. The park, which covers an area of 1,710 sq km (660 sq mi), gets its name from the 7,245-m-high (23,771-ft) Langtang Lirung peak and runs from Dhunche to the Tibetan border.
Luxurious pine, birch and rhododendron forests are home to musk deer, collar bears, small pandas, snow leopards, tahrs, and rhesus and langur monkeys. Starting from Kathmandu, a four-day trek leads you to the sacred lakes of Gosainkund via the monastery of Sing Gompa, which lies at an elevation of more than 4,400 m (14,436 ft). Back in Kathmandu the serpentine drive takes you through mountain landscapes on a road of varying quality into Pokhara.

5 Gorkha On your way back, you can make detour to the

Travel information

Route profile
Length: approx. 900 km (559 miles), excluding detours
Time required: 2–3 weeks
Start: Kathmandu, Nepal
End: Lhasa, Tibet
Route (main locations): Kathmandu, Patan, Bhaktapur, Pokhara, Lumbini, Bharatpur, Dolalghat, Nyalam, Gutsuo, Lhaze, Xigaze, Nagarze, Lhasa

Traffic information:
Drive on the left in Nepal, on the right in Tibet. The condition of the roads is generally very bad. So-called 'highways' are often full of potholes and asphalt is often missing. Landslides are common during monsoon season and after heavy rains.

Trekking:
The best time for trekking is after the monsoons. Any other time is too cold.
A trekking permit is required separately for each region (except the Langtang, Annapurna, Everest region). They can be acquired from the immigration offices in Kathmandu or Pokhara. From about 3,000 m (10,000 ft) altitude sickness may be a factor.

General information:
Nepal general info:
www.visitnepal.com
www.nepal.com
Tibet general info:
www.tibet.com
www.tibet-tour.com
Buddhism/Hinduism:
www.thamel.com

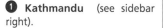
1 The fertile Kathmandu valley is the economic and population centre of Nepal.

2 Temple figures made of stone stand guard before the entrance to a temple in Bhaktapur, a UNESCO World Heritage Site.

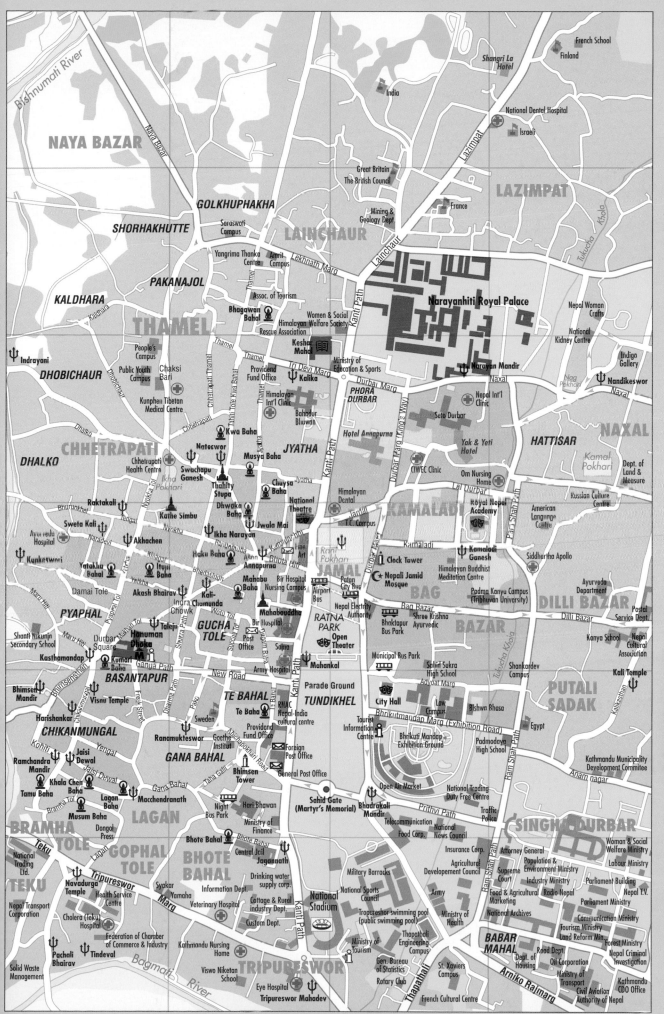

Kathmandu

This ancient royal city at an elevation of 1,300 m (4,265 ft) is the centrepiece of the Kathmandu Valley. Its many palaces, temples and monasteries mirror the centuries-old traditions and history of the Nepalese kingdom.

Even back in the 10th century this city, which is located at the confluence of the Bagmati and Vishnumati rivers, was an important marketplace that eventually developed into a religious, cultural and political centre competing with Patan and Bhaktapur ultimately to become the sole royal city. The Old Town presents the visitor with a plethora of streets and alleys where people, carts, bicycles, rickshaws and cars struggle to negotiate their way through the honking and screaming of the traffic.

In the centre of the city is Durbar Square, which the Nepali call Hanuman Dhoka. Here there are Buddhist and Hindu temples and shrines as well as the old royal palace where for centuries Malla and Shah kings resided. The oldest parts developed in the 16th century include the great inner courtyard Nasal Chowk, or coronation court.

In the centre of the Hanuman Dhoka is the Jagannath Temple, one of the most beautiful examples of Nepalese temple architecture. The Shiva Temple was built in 1690 and is flanked by two Vishnu temples and the Vishnu Parvati Temple with its two enormous drums. After the Hanuman Dhoka is the Basantapur, which has been taken over by countless souvenir sellers.

Some of the most startling buildings on the square are the nine-storey

The Swayambunath Stupa with its 'all-seeing eyes of Buddha'.

Basanthapur Pagoda, with beautiful wood-carvings, and the richly decorated palace of Kumari, a living goddess. Surrounding the old town are more UNESCO World Heritage Sites – about 5 km (3 miles) from the centre is the Boudhanath Stupa, the largest shrine of Tibetan Nepalese people; west of Kathmandu is the Swayambunath Stupa, dating from the 14th century; and on the eastern edge of the city is the temple of Pashupatinath with the sacred Lingam.

Veils of mist often cloak Lake Phewa near Pokhara in the morning. During a boat journey on the 5-sq-km (3-sq-mi) lake, the dreamy backdrop of the Himalayas can be a real vision of glory. Here the summit of Machhapuchare (left) and the Annapurna Massif (right), with its total of sixteen peaks, dominate the scene.

leopards, gaurs, sloth bears, gavial crocodiles, freshwater dolphins and more than 400 types of birds. A variety of options for enjoying the park are available to visitors here – elephant safaris, rafting boat rides or guided tours.

The road back to Kathmandu leads through Bharatpur and Hetauda to Kathmandu.

9 Dolalghat The Chinese gave the beautiful Kodari Highway its nickname – 'The Friendship Road' – when they built it in 1967. The route connects Nepal with Tibet and travels 114 km (71 miles) from Bhaktapur via Dolalghat to the border town of Kodari.

After a three-hour drive from Bhaktapur you arrive at the village of Dolalghat by the Sun Kosi at a modest elevation of 643 m (2,110 ft). The village is situated at the junction where the Bhote Kosi and the Indrawati rivers form the Sun Kosi (Golden River), which flows to the west along the Mahabharat. Dolalghat is primarily known as a jumping-off point for white-water rafting trips on the Sun Kosi.

Near Dolalghat a road leads to the Sagarmatha Nature Reserve. Once you have arrived in Kodari at 1,660 m (5,446 ft), the 'Friendship Bridge' takes you over the Bhote Kosi to Zhangmu. The route now follows Highway 318 all the way to Lhasa.

1 Trekkers ascend to the Thorung-La Pass when traversing the Annapurna.

2 The Deorali Pass cuts through the Annapurna Himal.

Annapurna Massif

The mountain massif north of Pokhara is one of the most popular walking and trekking areas of Nepal. The surrounding countryside is full of glorious variety and is easily accessible. In just three weeks you can circle the entire massif and get impressively near to most of the sixteen peaks of the range.

The Annapurna stretches over 50 km (31 miles) between the rivers Kali Gandak and Marsyandi. Its main peaks include Annapurna I at 8,091 m (26,547 ft), Annapurna II at 7,937 m (26,041 ft), Annapurna III at 7,555 m (24,788 ft) and Annapurna IV at

A marvellous view of the sacred mountain Machapuchare from the Annapurna Base Camp.

7,525 m (24,690 ft). The first ascent of Annapurna I was made in 1950 by a French expedition – three years before the first climbing of Everest.

Three well-signposted routes make their way through the Annapurna region, partly overlapping as they go: the Muktinath Trail, the Mustang Trail (a continuation of the Muktinath) and the Annapurna Circle Trail.

A shorter trail leads you to the Annapurna Shrine of the Gurung people who also live in these parts. It's an enormous moraine surrounded by peaks between 6,000 and 8,000 m (19,686 and 26,248 ft) where the Annapurna Base Camp is located.

Gorkha valley just before you reach the town of Mugling. The drive passes through green rice plantations set in a fascinating mountain landscape on its way to the village of Gorkha at 1,000 m (3,300 ft), which is overlooked by a fortification from the 17th century. The giant mountains Dhaulagiri, Ganesh Himal and Manaslu present an overwhelming panorama.

Ghorka has an important place in Nepalese history. In 1768, King Prithvi Narayan Shah conquered Kathmandu from Gorkha, then proceeded to Patan and Bhaktapur, thereby laying the foundations for his royal dynasty.

6 Pokhara Only on the last few kilometres to Pokhara does the road flatten out into a broad valley. Nepal's third-largest city lies at an elevation of 800 m (3,150 ft) on the shores of Lake Phewa. In stark contrast to the surrounding mountainscape, the

subtropical climate here has produced ample vegetation. For many trekkers the city is the 'Gateway to the Himalaya'. From Pokhara you get a magnificent view of the central Himalayas, which are now only 30 km (18 miles) away. Peaks that you can see from here include Dhaulagiri at 8,167 m (26,796 ft), the Annapurna Massif and the sacred mountain of Machapuchare at 6,977 m (22,892 ft). The sights nearby include the dripstone cave at Batulechaur, the ravine of Seti and Devin's fall. The seven-storey fortification of Nuwakot arguably offers the most beautiful view of Dhaulagiri, Annapurna and Manaslu.

The winding road to Lumbini leads down through a richly forested mountain landscape. After Butwal the scenery flattens out, giving way to rice fields and willows that come right up to the street.

7 Lumbini The birthplace of Siddharta Gautama, Buddha's birthname, is surprisingly off the beaten track. Excavations have been taking place in this previously forgotten place since the 1970s. Finds include Emperor Ashoka's column from the 3rd century, which was only discovered in the jungle in 1896, and the Maya Devi Temple, both grouped around a sacred pool of water in which Buddha's mother (Maya Devi) allegedly bathed shortly before his birth.

To head for the Royal Chitwan National Park from here, drive back to Butwal and from there to Bharatpur.

8 Royal Chitwan National Park This large national park covers 932 sq km (360 sq mi) and is bordered by the Rapti, Reu and Narayanif rivers. The park is dominated by jungle and grasslands that are home to elephants, rhinos, Bengal tigers,

Detour

Sagarmatha National Park

Chomolungma, the 'Goddess Mother of the Earth', is what the Tibetans respectfully call the highest mountain on earth. Mount Everest, as the rest of the world knows it, peaks at 8,850 m (29,037 ft) above sea level on the border between Nepal and Tibet. The Nepalese refer to the mountain as Sagarmatha, 'King of the Heavens', and in 1976 a national park of the same name was established in the Khumbu Himal region.

From the northern edge of the national park, Sagarmatha leisurely watches over the neighbouring monoliths of Lhotse I (8,516 m/27,941 ft), Makalu I (8,463 m/27,767 ft), Cho Oyu (8,201 m/ 26,907 ft) and Nuptse (7,879 m/ 25,851 ft), all surrounded by the 'Royal Court' of six-thousanders. This royal court is worshipped by locals as the residence of the gods.

Enormous glaciers flow into deep valleys, the largest of which reside on the Lhotse, Khumbu, Imja, Ngozumba and Nangpa mountains. The entire national park covers an area of 1,243 sq km (770 sq mi) and the entrance is between the villages of Monjo at 2,845 m (9,334 ft) and Jorsale. From bottom to top the park spans an elevation difference of 6,000 m (19,680 ft).

In October and November the park can get bitterly cold at night. Between December and February the temperatures reach a maximum of 5°C (41°F). From June to September you can expect daily monsoon rains and correspondingly bad views of the central ridge of the Himalaya.

Flora and fauna are extremely diverse due to the differences in altitude – below 3,500 m (11,484 ft) there are still pines or blue spruce trees, but above that, to the tree line at 4,500 m (14,765 ft), you find silver spruce, birch, junipers and rhododendron (in flower in April and May).

With a bit of luck you will run across not only the omnipresent yaks in the

(16,864 ft). Then comes Everest Base Camp at an elevation of 5,364 m (17,599 ft) after crossing the bizarre Khumbu Glacier.

1 Prayer flags all around Mount Everest.

2 Above 3,000 m (9,843 ft) the yaks are indispensable – they provide milk, meat and wool in addition to carrying loads and pulling ploughs.

lower zones of the national park but also Himalaya black bears, Himalaya tahrs, musk ox and the yellow-tailed pheasant, which is the Nepalese national bird. Further up are the very rare snow leopards.

The easiest way to reach the national park is by plane. Flights from Kathmandu to Lukla at 2,840 m (9,318 ft) last just 40 minutes and the two-day trek to Namche Bazar, the park offices, starts in Lukla and leads through the Dudh Kosi Valley, famous for its forests and rhododendrons.

On the way you pass Nepalese villages like Phadking, inhabited by the indigenous Sherpas who originally immigrated in the 16th century from Eastern Tibet and have been cultivating barley, potatoes, spinach, radishes and onions ever since, in addition to working as porters for climbers. Since the first ascent of Everest by Edmund Hillary and legendary Sherpa Tenzing Norgay in 1953, trekking has almost become a national sport in the park.

On the way into the Mount Everest Base Camp, Namche Bazar, at 3,446 m (11,306 ft) you'll notice that the air is already getting thinner. But it is from here that visitors can gaze upon Everest and Lhotse for the first time. The busy village is the starting point for all trekkers on their way to the Mount Everest Base Camp, and provides everything needed for the trip.

An hour north of Namche Bazar the famous Mount Everest View Hotel boasts the highest landing strip in the world. The journey then continues through the Sherpa villages of Khumjung and Kunde. Definitely worth seeing on the way is the Tengpoche Monastery at 3,867 m (12,688 ft), where the famous Mani Rimdu dances take place every year in autumn.

North of the Pangpoche Monastery trekkers cross the vegetation limit and the air gets unpleasantly thin. Many take an extended break in Periche (4,270 m/14,010 ft) to acclimatize before the trail continues with yak caravans up to Dhuka at 4,620 m (15,158 ft). The last stop before Base Camp is Gorakshep at 5,140 m

3 View of the south-west wall of Mount Everest (8,850 m/29,037 ft), Lhotse (8,516 m/27,941 ft) and Nuptse (7,861 m/25,792 ft).

4 View from the Khumbu Valley of Mount Everest and Lhotse.

5 The Tengpoche Monastery in the Khumbu Valley.

6 Yaks relaxing in the mountains around Everest.

Rongbuk Monastery

Shortly before Shergar a road leads over the Pang-La Pass at 5,150 m (16,897 ft) toward the main ridge of the Himalaya. It is a good 65 km (40 miles) from Tingri to the monastery, which is at the end of some pretty adventurous roads. At 5,151 m (16,900 ft) it is reputed to be the highest monastery in the world.

Above: Ruins of the Rongbuk Monastery.
Below: Prayer flags on the Chörten of the Rongbuk Monastery.

After more than 400 years of meditating in makeshift shelters, a proper monastery was finally built here in 1899. Rongbuk Lama, its founder, looked at the first climbers as heretics, but provided them with food and drink. During the Chinese Cultural Revolution the monastery was largely destroyed, but starting in the 1990s it has been partly rebuilt and reinhabited by monks. Whoever starts out for the Mount Everest Base Camp about 10 km (6 miles) away will be irresistably drawn to the magnificent view of the bizarre Rombuk Glacier and the north wall of Everest. Due to the 'passing trade' to the base camp, the monastery now offers a hostelry and a shop.

⑩ Nyalam On a clear day you get a magnificent view from Nyalam (4,100 m/13,452 ft) of the Xixabangma Feng at 8,012 m (26,287 ft) rising up to the west. All around the old town are typical flat-roof clay houses, makeshift shacks of the Chinese inhabitants.

The drive continues past snow-capped mountains 6,000–8,000 m (19,686–26,248 ft) high until you finally reach the Lalung-La Pass at 5,200 m (17,061 ft), which leads to the Tibetan plateau. Here you'll find the village of Gutsuo, which has accommodation and provisions as well as a small hospital.

Tingri is known for its fantastic view of Cho Oyu at 8,153 m (26,750 ft), Mount Everest at 8,850 m (29,037 ft), Lhotse I at 8,516 m (27,941 ft) and Makalu I at 8,463 m (27,767 ft). We recommend you head south from here towards Rongbuk Monastery.

⑪ Lhaze Beyond Tingri the road winds down to Lhaze at 4,030 m (13,222 ft), which has a hotel, restaurants, a gas station and a monastery. This village is

right on the road that leads west of the sacred mountain of Kailash and is located in a fertile valley whose green fields provide colourful contrast to the arid Tibetan plateau.

⑫ Sa'gya The fortified monastery of Sakya was founded in 1073 and was the original monastery of the Sakya Order. Of the original 108 chapels in the north wing, only one is left today. A white stupa stands nearby on the mountain's edge. The southern monastery is enclosed by mighty walls with four watchtowers, as the Sakya dynasty had to defend itself against many enemies.

Heading to Xigaze you cross the Tso-La Pass at 4,500 m (14,765 ft) where you have a good view of Everest on a clear day.

⑬ Xigaze After the devastation of the Cultural Revolution,

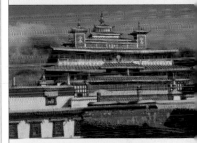

Detour

The Gonggar and Samye monasteries

About 70 km (43.5 miles) south of Lhasa is the Gonggar Monastery, which was founded in 1464 and was one of the centres of the Sakyapa school. There used to be about 160 monks living here. Today there are about thirty. During the Chinese Cultural Revolution large parts of the monastery were destroyed. Only the main temple remained untouched.

Especially worth seeing are the murals of Khyentse Chenmo, which depict scenes from the life of

Above: The monastery of Samye
Below: The main temple of Samye

Buddha, tantric deities and personalities from the Sakyapa School.

The Samye Monastery is 30 km (20 miles) north-west of Zetang on the northern shore of Yarlung Zangbo Jiang and is reachable by ferry and bus from Zetang. Situated on a steppe landscape, it is the oldest monastery in the whole of Tibet (c. 770) and an architectural symbol for the victory march of Buddhism in Tibet that began in the 8th century. The architect's concept of the monastery was an image of the universe – the three-storey gilded main temple was a symbol of the cosmic world mountain, Meru; around it are twelve temples that picture four continents with their subcontinents; and two smaller shrines to the north and south of it represent the sun and the moon. The geometrically symmetrical conception of the monastery makes it look like a 3-dimensional mantra image. Parts of the monastery fell victim to fire, earthquakes and the Cultural Revolution.

only the foundations of the once impressive fortifications of the Tsang Dynasty kings (16th/17th century) are left. Today the main sight in Xigaze, former capital of Tibet, is the Tashilhunpo Monastery, home of the Panchen Lama that once housed 6,000 monks. Founded by the first Dalai Lama in 1447, the complex at the bottom of the Drölma consists of red and ochre-coloured buildings whose gilded roofs glimmer from afar.

14 Gyangze This small town at 4,070 m (13,354 ft) on the north shore of Nyangchu still gives a traditional Tibet impression with its white facades and colourful eaves, windows and door frames. Towering over the city is an impressive Dzhong (fortification) from 1268, which offers a splendid view of the walled monastery city of Pälkhor Chode (15th century). The extensive grounds are dominated by octagonal Kumbum Chorten and the Nepalese-influenced stupa is a magnificent example of Tibetan architecture.

From Gyangzee to Lhasa the road leads past little villages through fertile valleys where yaks graze at leisure. Then you must traverse the Karo-La Pass at 5,045 m (29,906 ft). The landscape is of overwhelming beauty here. On the way you'll see the Karo-La glacier, stunning waterfalls and mountain streams. You then descend the serpentine pass via Lungmar to Ralung with its monastery dating from 1180 and continue on to Nagarze.

15 Nagarze The village of Nagarze at 4,200 m (13,780 ft) sits between the snow-covered Noijin Kangsang at 7,100 m (23,295 ft) and the sacred lake of Yandrok Tso, one of the biggest and most beautiful lakes in central Tibet. The street runs along the shore for several kilometres

1 View of the Tashilhunpo monastery near Xigaze.

2 The Kumbum Chorten in Pälkhor Chode Monastery near Gyangze is Nepalese in design.

3 Yandrok Tso is one of the largest lakes in Tibet.

1

Sera and Ganden

The Sera Monastery is situated in a rocky environment about 4 km (2.5 miles) north of Lhasa. As early as around 1770 there were roughly 2,850 monks living here and at the beginning of the 20th century there were 6,600. Today, after the trials of the Chinese Cultural Revolution, about 300 have returned – a success in itself.

Sera Monastery was founded north of Lhasa in around 1419.

Sera has always been a centre of monastic education in Tibet along with Drepung and Ganden. The Ganden Monastery is about 45 km (28 miles) east of Lhasa on the road to Sichuan. It was founded three years before Sera by Tsonkhapa and later became the centre of the Galupa School, which asserted itself in the whole of Tibet from the 17th century. Of the original 200 buildings, only fifty have been restored. In the centre of the monastery is the tomb of the founder and his relics are kept in a chorten.

2

passing grazing horses, yaks and goats. A visit to castle ruins and the 13th-century Samding Monastery is worthwhile. The way to Quxu leads over the Kampa-La Pass at 4,898 m (16,070 ft), then it is just 20 km (12 miles) into the valley.

16 Quxu The bridge over the Yarlung was opened in the mid 1970s and provides a connection between western and eastern Tibet. The place itself is a good starting point for trips to the monasteries of Gonggar and Samye to the east. North of Quxu is the region of Nethang, which houses the monastery of the same name founded by Atisha (982–1054), an Indian Buddhist. Now we head back to the Tibetan capital through the Lhasa Valley.

17 Drepung About 10 km (6 miles) north of Lhasa is a monastery dating from 1416 that used to be the biggest in

Tibet with 10,000 monks. As the religious and political centre of the Gelugpa School (yellow-cap sect) its abbots were decision-makers in religious as well as political matters. Before the Potala became their residence it even housed the first five Dalai Lamas. Despite the destruction by the Chinese Red Guards, the main buildings of the monastery have remained unharmed, including Ganden Palace, the four theological faculties and the great congregation hall. Today some 600 monks are living here again.

18 Lhasa The capital of the Tibet Autonomous Region lies on the Lhasa River (Kyichu) at an elevation of 3,658 m (12,002 ft) and was founded in the 7th century. Originally the residence of the Tibetan kings (7th–9th centuries) it became the seat of government of Lamaistic theocracy under Dalai Lama rule. For centuries Lhasa was a 'forbidden

city' to foreigners. It even closed its doors to Sven Hedin, the famous explorer of Asia.
In the heart of the old town you'll find the two-storey Jokhang Temple from the 7th century, the oldest Buddhist monastery in Tibet and akin to a national shrine. All roads in Lhasa therefore lead to the Jokhang temple, which is also once again home to monks.
Nearly as old as the Jokhang is the Ramoche Temple with fortified walls, which goes back to the times of the Chinese princess Wencheng. Unfortunately, the Red Guards destroyed or stole many of the statues here during the Cultural Revolution.
Many associate Lhasa with the Potala Palace towering impressively over the city with its thirteen storeys (110 m/361 ft). Its facade alone is 360 m (1,181 ft) long and it reputedly houses 999 rooms with 130,000 sq m (1,399,308 sq ft) of living quarters. The part of the palace

painted white houses administration and storage space while the red part was the residence of the Dalai Lama up to his flight in 1959. Since then the palace is only has been used as a museum. Opposite the Potala is the cave temple Drolha Lubuk with depictions of Buddhist deities that reputedly created themselves. The summer palace of the Dalai Lama, Norbulingka, is also in the west of the city and was built on an even larger scale. On the northern edge of the city is the monastery of Sera, and on the road to Sichuan (a good 45 km/30 miles east of Lhasa) is the monastery of Ganden.

1 View from the Jokhang Temple, the heart of Tibetan culture in Lhasa.

2 Monks during communal prayer in the Ramoche Monastery in Lhasa.

3 Colourful wall hangings in the Jokhang Monastery.

3

Lake Phewa Fishing, rowing, and swimming – this lake leaves no wishes unfulfilled, and you have a view of Annapurna.

Kathmandu In the 'City of the Gods' it is mainly Durbar Square, a colorful bazaar surrounded by wood and brick buildings, that is well worth a visit.

Patan The Bagmati River separates this mainly Buddhist-inhabited city from its neighbour, Kathmandu. Patan's old town has countless workshops to visit, as well as the Mahabuddha Bahal temple and Jawalakhel, a part of town that is inhabited by Tibetan refugees.

Lhasa The 'Red Palace' of the Potala was commissioned by the fifth Dalai Lama in the 17th century. The white buildings were added in the 19th century. The palace has some 999 rooms and thirteen storeys. Since the occupation of Tibet by China and the flight of the Dalai Lama, the palace is used only as a museum.

Annapurna Massif The tenth highest peak in the world was first ascended in 1950. It is surrounded by mountains that often seem higher than the peak that gives the region its name. Especially outstanding is the sacred, and thus unconquered, Machapuchare.

Royal Chitwan National Park This park can be explored on the back of an elephant or in a rafting boat. It is known for its 400 rhinoceroses as well as tigers, gavial crocodiles, leopards and buffalo.

Bhaktapur Time seems to have stood still in this beautifully restored town situated at the east end of the Kathmandu Valley. Highlights include the Dattatraya Square and the temple pagodas on Taumadhi Square.

Sera Elaborate religious ceremonies are still held in this former monastery and university village on the edge of Lhasa.

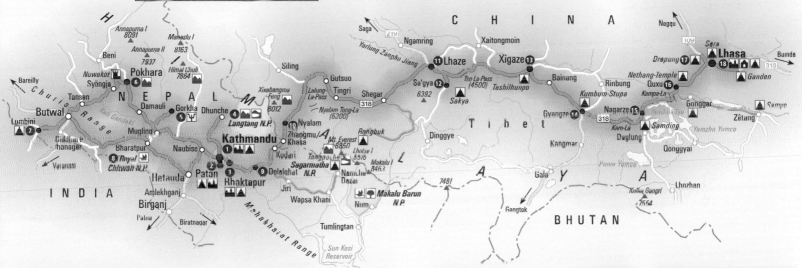

Mount Everest At 8,850 m (29,037 ft) this is the highest mountain in the world, and is locally known as Chomolungma or Sagarmatha. The first successful ascent was in 1953 by Edmund Hillary and Sherpa Tenzing Norgay.

Sakya Monastery 'Grey Earth' – such is the name of a monastery near Xigaze in South Tibet of the red-cap sect, a branch of Tibetan Buddhism founded in 1073. Until 1354 its leaders were the landlords of Tibet.

Xigaze Tibet's second-largest city is home to a the 15th-century monastery. The Panchen Lama residence survived the Cultural Revolution.

Gyangze This village south-west of Lhasa has a monastery worth visiting (Pälkhör Chode). The Kumbum Stupa is considered Tibet's most beautiful sanctum.

Lumbini Siddharta Gautama – aka Buddha – was born here in southern Nepal in the 6th century BC. Visit the sacred garden and the Maya Devi Temple.

Sagarmatha National Park This park, located in the Khumbu region at the base of Mount Everest, is home to a variety of rare animals like the black bear, snow leopard and musk deer.

Tengpoche Until a fire in 1989 this monastery at 4,000 m (13,124 ft) in the Khumbu Valley was the largest in the region. It is still well worth seeing.

Samye This rebuilt temple is part of the oldest Tibetan monastery. It was built around 770 and is situated in the mountains on the north shore of Yarlung Zangbo Jiang.

Penang Island is 285 sq km (110 sq mi) in size and located just off Malaysia's west coast.

Route 16

Thailand and Malaysia
Pulsing cities and tropical natural paradises

South-East Asia – teeming urban centres and quiet villages, tropical rain-forests and idyllic white sand beaches, historic sites and modern daily life. A trip along the region's North-South Highway will show you the many diverse faces of the region and immerse you in local life with all of glorious scenery and culture.

Starting in Thailand's mountainous north, this route first takes us down to the fertile plain of the Mae Nam Chao Phraya River and its many tributaries in Central Thailand. The Menam Basin, also nicknamed Thailand's 'rice bowl', has been the country's most densely settled economic region since the time of the first Thai kingdoms.

South of the Thai capital of Bangkok, the highway then takes us onto the Malay Peninsula, which stretches 1,500 km (930 miles) between the Indian Ocean

(Andaman Sea) and the Pacific Ocean (Gulf of Thailand and South China Sea). At its narrowest point, the Isthmus of Kra, the peninsula is a mere 50 km (31 miles) wide. Its backbone is formed by a mountain range that reaches its highest elevations in Malaysia at more than 2,000 m (6,500 ft).

The tropical plants and animals of Thailand and Malaysia are almost unbeatably varied and abundant. Nevertheless, in recent years the once so prevalent tropical rainforests have had to give way to

Sculpture at the entrance to Batu Caves.

large-scale plantations, rice paddies and urban sprawl. Only in mountainous regions and individual national parks can you still find real virgin rainforests with their wealth of plants and animals. You'll find giant trees, wild orchids and epi-phytes, and these South-East Asian rain-forests are also home to several species of apes as well as snakes and tigers.

As the climate of the area is very favourable, large areas of both countries have been devoted to agriculture. In some places in Thailand there are rice paddies as far as the eye can see, and in Malaysia there are massive oil palm and rubber tree plantations.

Being one of South-East Asia's most ancient kingdoms, Thailand has a large number of historic sites dating from different periods in its history. Many of these monumental buildings, such as

Petchaburi: In 1860, Rama IV had his summer palace of Phra Nakhon Khiri ('Heavenly Mountain City') constructed in this magnificent location. The palace is on a hill 92 m (302 ft) high.

The courtyard at the Ayutthaya temple is lined with innumerable statues of the sitting Buddha.

those of Sukhothai and Ayutthaya, are very well-maintained. Their size and the skill employed in their construction are truly impressive.

Malaysia and Singapore, by contrast, claim much shorter histories. Their oldest historic sites date from the colonial period. These days places like Georgetown, Melaka and Singapore have numerous preserved and restored colonial buildings that provide visitors with a lively impression of this bygone era.

All three states have ethnically diverse populations, and this variety makes the region all the more attractive. In Thailand a majority of around 80 per cent of the population is Thai, in Malaysia 50 per cent are Malay, and in Singapore 70 per cent are Chinese. The remainder of the Thai population is made up of mountain tribes and Chinese descendants.

Malaysia and Singapore also have large Indian populations. The Chinese, who account for a very small percentage of the population of Thailand, for example, exercise significant influence on the regional economy and local trade. In fact, they make up the vast majority of South-East Asia's economically powerful. Yet despite the region's ethnic diversity and the corresponding cultural and traditional differences, people mostly live together in harmony and welcome foreign visitors with all the legendary Asian friendliness.

A journey from northern Thailand to Singapore via Malaysia thus becomes a journey through a very diverse region in terms of scenery, ethnicity and culture. You will be both surprised and enchanted by the ever-changing human and natural landscape.

The temple of Wat Mahathat was once the spiritual centre of the Sukhothai kingdom.

Rice cultivation

In Thailand and Malaysia rice is the basis of most meals. Singapore, on the other hand, has a broader mix of Asian and Western culinary styles.

A large number of rice varieties are cultivated in the world. Distinctions are made between mountain rice – cultivated without irrigation in higher regions up to 2,000 m (6,500 ft) – and water rice, which is typical in Thailand and Malaysia.

During the dry season, rice seedlings are raised in small beds and the fields are ploughed using ploughs drawn by water buffalo. When the seedlings have been planted in the fields, the fields are irrigated until the rice plants flower. Then they are left dry until they ripen and fall.

Flooded rice paddy near Chiang Rai.

During the summer, the rice paddies that were once bright green turn more and more yellow. Rice grows up to 40 cm (15 in) tall and is finally harvested in November.

Because of the high levels of water in the area, the flood plains and large river mouths are the main rice-growing regions of Thailand. In contrast to oil palms, coffee and tea, which are all grown on large plantations, rice is mostly cultivated on small farms with low yields. These often do little more than provide for the farming families' most basic needs.

While modern irrigation techniques, fertilizers and the use of higher-yield varieties have managed to increase harvests, the total agricultural area continues to diminish. More and more agricultural land is needed for export-oriented plantation agriculture and the countries' urban centres.

The North-South Highway of the Thai-Malay corridor – if you want to get to know this exciting region, we recommend the long and winding road from Chiang Mai in northern Thailand to Singapore at the southern tip of the Malay peninsula. The road leads through tropical landscapes and urban centres for more than 3,250 km (2,020 miles).

① Chiang Mai The Thais call Chiang Mai the 'Rose of the North'. Thailand's second city is the tourist centre of northern Thailand. Using Chiang Mai as a base, you can take trekking tours into the mountains and visit the hill tribes who live in them. Under King Mengrai this settlement, founded in 1292, became the capital of the Lanna Kingdom and an important centre for Theravada Buddhism. The king and his successors built the majority of the numerous temples (wats) in the so-called Lanna style. The most important among them are Wat Phra Sing (1345), Wat Chedi Luang (c. 15th century) and Wat Chiang Man.

The quadratic centre of the Old Town, with its picturesque alleyways and traditional houses, is

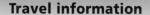

surrounded by well-preserved trenches that today separate the historic city centre from modern Chiang Mai.

Outside the Old Town you'll find the National Museum with its large and beautiful terracotta collection, a small ethnological museum and numerous other temples.

Nature and art lovers should make sure to pay a visit to the densely forested national park Doi Suthep Doi Pui, 16 km (10 miles) north-west of Chiang Mai. The park is the home of Doi Suthep, the most important Buddhist temple in northern Thailand, situated at an elevation of 1,600 m (5,250 ft) above sea level. Precisely 304 steep steps lead up to it.

Taking Highway 11 south you now drive through some lush green hills and mountains and pass some steep valleys with carefully maintained fields and rice paddies.

Travel information

Route profile
Length: approx. 3,250 km (2,020 miles), excluding detours
Time required: at least 3 weeks
Start: Chiang Mai
End: Singapore
Route (main locations): Chiang Mai, Bangkok, Ratchaburi, Hat Yai, Georgetown, Kuala Lumpur, Singapore

Traffic information:
Drive on the left throughout South-East Asia. Roads are generally in decent condition. Tolls are often charged on highways.
Singapore: Tolls are charged via an electronic device obtainable from car rental companies.
All three countries require international driving licences.

When to go:
North: November to February
East coast: Avoid the rainy season from October to February
West coast: April to October

Information:
Thailand:
www.thaiwave.com
www.gothailand.com
Malaysia:
www.allmalaysia.info
www.tourism.gov.my
Singapore:
www.visitingsingapore.com
www.stb.com/sg/

To find reasonable prices check the various national airline home pages at:
www.thaiair.com
www.malaysiaairlines.com
www.singaporeair.com

Padaung neck rings

From Chiang Mai you can take an interesting excursion 100 km (62 miles) along Highway 108 to the west into the scenic region of Mae Hong Son. Here at the border to Myanmar you will find a few villages of the Padaung people, whose women are probably among the most photographed in all of Thailand.

From early childhood, girls wear heavy bronze rings around their necks. Each year one more is added. Long necks are a thing of beauty to the Padaung and the rings also represent status and

Padaung girl with an artificially 'elongated' neck.

② Chae Son National Park This is a mountainous national park around 50 km (31 miles) further south-east. Its forests are home to black bears, wild boar and monkeys as well as some rarely seen tigers.

The main trail through the national park starts in Khuntan and after an 8-km (5-mile) hike it takes you up to the summit of Yot Se (1,373 m/4,505 ft). From there you have some wonderful views of the surrounding mountain scenery.

③ Mae Ping National Park Rafting tours and boat trips are the main reason that so many people come to visit Mae Ping National Park, located west of Highway 1. By car you get to it via Lamphum (30 km/19 miles south of Chiang Mai) on Highways 106 and 1087. The park is roughly 100 km (62 miles) away. Most visitors take a two-hour boat ride on the Ping River from

Doi Tao Lake, which takes them into the park. From there they carry on to the village of Ko. In addition to a white-water ride and some impressive limestone cliffs and caves, this national park offers a good insight into the different plants and animals living in the rainforests.

④ Lampang What is fascinating about this 7th-century town are its temples, traditional houses and an old market with a variety of different architectural styles represented in the surrounding buildings. In the 19th century Lampang became a centre for teak production. The town's brightly painted horse-drawn carriages date from this era and they are still Lampang's standard form of public transport.

The town's most important temple is Wat Phra Kaew Don Tao. In the south-west you'll find one of northern Thailand's most beauti-

ful temples – Wat Phra That Lampang Luang, dating from the 15th century.

Leaving Lampang, you take Highway 1 to the south. The mountains soon give way to more gentle hills that eventually flatten out towards the plains of the upper Menam Basin. Rice is cultivated in expansive paddies here for as far as the eye can see. From Tak you can take a worthwhile excursion on Highway 12 to Sukhothai, the former capital of Thailand, which is 80 km (49 miles) away.

⑤ Sukhothai UNESCO declared the ruined city of Old Sukhothai a World Heritage Site in 1991. With more than forty temples, this city recalls the heydey of the Sukhothai kingdom, the most powerful in the Menam Basin between 1240 and 1320. Founded in 1238, the city was the capital of the first Thai nation for more than 120 years. The

large compound stretches over 70 sq km (27 sq mi) and includes an historic park and so many other attractions that you can easily spend several days here. At the heart of the historic park is the Old Town, which is surrounded by a wall 1.6 km (1 mile) by 2 km (1.3 miles) long. The royal palace and the Wat Mahathat (13th century) temple alone encompass an area of more than 16 ha (40 acres). The complex is completely surrounded by a trench.

⑥ Kamphaeng Phet Founded in 1347, Kamphaeng Phet used to be a royal garrison town. In the north are the town's historic quarters, and in the south you will find the modern town. Surrounded as they are by a moat, the historic quarters give you an idea of what Old Sukhothai

1 Buddha statues several metres high at the Ayutthaya temple compound north of Bangkok.

2 The temples at Chiang Mai in north-eastern Thailand were constructed between the 13th and 16th centuries.

3 Ruins of a Bot (ceremonial hall) north of the main chedi in the Wat Mahathat temple compound in Sukhothai.

wealth. X-ray photographs have shown that the weight of these docs not stretch the neck but that, instead, the women's collarbones and shoulders are pushed down. The muscles normally supporting the head lose their function and with time, they wither. These women have problems drinking – they have to bend over forwards and use straws to drink.

In recent years, this idiosyncratic attire has come back into fashion after almost disappearing from Padaung culture.

Nakhon Pathom

Around 70 km (45 miles) west of Bangkok on Highway 4 is the little town of Nakhon Pathom, which was the capital of the Dvaravati kingdom from the 6th to the 11th centuries. Buddhist monks who had come from India founded this kingdom in the early 6th century directly in the heart of modern Thailand. Nowadays the town is a much-visited pilgrimage destination with two absolute highlights of Buddhist culture – Phra Pathom Chedi at 127 m (417 ft) is the highest Buddhist monument anywhere and the Buddha inside is the world's largest at 40 m (131 ft) high.

At the heart of this giant, bell-shaped chedi covered in orange bricks are the remains of another chedi, which was built during the Mon Period (6th century) in the same place. This means that it was probably the first Buddhist building ever erected on Thai soil. It was repeatedly destroyed and expanded and only achieved its current height

The chedi of Nakhom Pathom, the world's highest Buddhist monument (120 m/394 ft).

in 1860. In the middle of the 19th century King Mongut had tried in vain to restore the old chedi and finally ordered a new one to be built on top of the old.

The National Museum at Phra Pathom chedi houses some precious findings from the heyday of this early kingdom, among them some impressive wheels of law and beautifully made stone carvings. The gardens around the Sanam-Chan palace to the west of the temple compound are an oasis of peace and quiet.

might have been like. The National Museum and the temple compound with Wat Phra Kaeo and Wat Phra That are also worth seeing.

7 Nakhon Sawan The most interesting thing here is not the provincial capital itself but the confluence of the Mae Nam Ping and Mae Nam Yom rivers. They come together in this region to form the Menam Chao Phraya, whose flood plains are the most fertile and densely populated region in Thailand.

All you can see for miles are the thousands of rice paddies, dotted here and there with hills and mountains. From Nakhon Sawan take Highway 32 through the fields and hills towards Ayutthaya.

8 Ayutthaya From 1350 to 1767 Ayutthaya was the capital of Siam (Thailand). Historical sources claim that it was Asia's most impressive city at the time. Visitors from Europe back then were overwhelmed by its splendour and many said that they had never seen anything to equal it. The kings of thirty-three different dynasties ruled the country from here until the city was razed to the ground by the Burmese in 1767.

The historic Old Town is located at the confluence of three rivers and completely surrounded by water. The most impressive sights are located on the island in the middle of these three rivers. Among them are the temples of Wat Na Phra Men, which was not destroyed in 1767, and

Wat Phra Si Sanphet with its three chedis.

From Ayutthaya, it is only around 40 km (25 miles) to Bangkok.

9 Bangkok (see pp. 208–209). From Taksin Bridge the highway sweeps west along the bay onto the Malay Peninsula. West of Bangkok you can visit Nakhon Prathom with its giant temple compound and Kanchanaburi with the famous 'Bridge Over the River Kwai'. Both sights are relatively close to Highway 4.

Carry on southbound along the east coast (west side of the bay). Around 20 km (13 miles) after Ratchaburi, a road turns off to Thailand's largest national park, Kaeng Krachan National Park, which is well worth visiting.

The 'Bridge Over the River Kwai'

Not far from Kanchanaburi is the 'Bridge Over the River Kwai', which was made famous by the novel by Pierre Boulle. During World War II the Japanese constructed a railway line here. Its construction cost the lives of 16,000 allied prisoners of war and around 100,000 local labourers, most of whom died of starvation, malaria and cholera. The current bridge is a reconstruction.

Detour

Similan Islands

The Similan Islands are located around 100 km (62 miles) north-west of Phuket and it takes three hours to get there by boat from Thap Lamu. The archipelago with its nine islands really is a diving paradise.

In 1984 the islands were declared a marine national park because of their unique sea life. They have been attracting divers from all around the world for years. The

Top: Kuak-Ma-Bay
Middle: Hawksbill turtle
Bottom: A school of doctor fish.

⑩ Kaeng Krachan National Park Thailand's largest park is surprisingly unknown among travellers despite the fact that its dense, evergreen tropical rain-forests cover mountains that rise to 1,200 m (4,000 ft). The park is home to tigers, Malaysian bears, leopards, tapirs and elephants as well as gibbons and langurs. The next 370 km (230 miles) south of Ratchaburi run along the east coast before you get to Chumphon where Highway 4 changes to two lanes and you switch to the west coast for another 350 km (217 miles).

At Kra, the Malay Peninsula narrows to only 50 km (31 miles) wide. Soon after that you will arrive in Khuraburi and the next national park in the midst of a tropical mountain landscape.

⑪ Khao Sok National Park This hilly national park with luscious rainforests is regarded as Thailand's most beautiful forest. It has some very good hiking among the impressive limestone cliffs and the numerous waterfalls, which are the park's principal attractions.

Among them are Nam Tok Sip Et Chan, where the water cascades down eleven glorious levels. With a bit of luck you might even find a specimen of the world's largest flower, a species of Rafflesia with a diameter of around 1 m (3.5 ft).

After Thap Lamu (see sidebar right for a worthwhile excursion to the diving paradise of the Similan Islands) the road runs along the Khao Lak coast riddled with lonely beaches against the

backdrop of the extensive tropical monsoon forests of Khao Lak National Park.

Past the turn-off for the incredibly touristy island of Phuket you can carry on to Phang Nga, the starting point for trips into the Phang Nga Bay.

⑫ Phang Nga Bay This bay's dense mangrove forests make it one of Thailand's most impressive regions. It is protected as a national park and has some bizarre, partly overgrown limestone rocks that rise up to 350 m (1,150 ft) out of the clear azure waters. Many of the rock faces have karst caves and tunnels.

The most important stations on a boat trip in this bay are Panyi, a village on stilts, the Suwan-Kuha caves with a reclining Bud-

dha, and some other stalactite caves. To the east, the karst landscape continues on the mainland and into the Khao Phanom Bencha National Park north of Krabi.

1 Wat Arun on the shores of Chao Phraya in Bangkok.

2 Phuket, Thailand's largest and most popular island, is 48 km (30 miles) long.

3 Ko Phi Phi comprises the islands of Phi Phi Don and Phi Phi Ley. They are popular because of good diving and the film *The Beach* (Ley).

4 Phang Nga Bay is famous for its karst rocks rising out of the sea.

species-rich underwater landscape is probably unbeatable in Thailand. Just off the islands there are some granite rocks with many grottoes and tunnels. From turtles to doctor fish to whale sharks, many different marine animals call this home.

But even swimming or snorkelling will be a thrill. The most beautiful island is called Ko Miang. The months with the best underwater views are from December to April, just before the rainy season. The islands, which are not well developed for tourism, are partly covered in tropical rainforests.

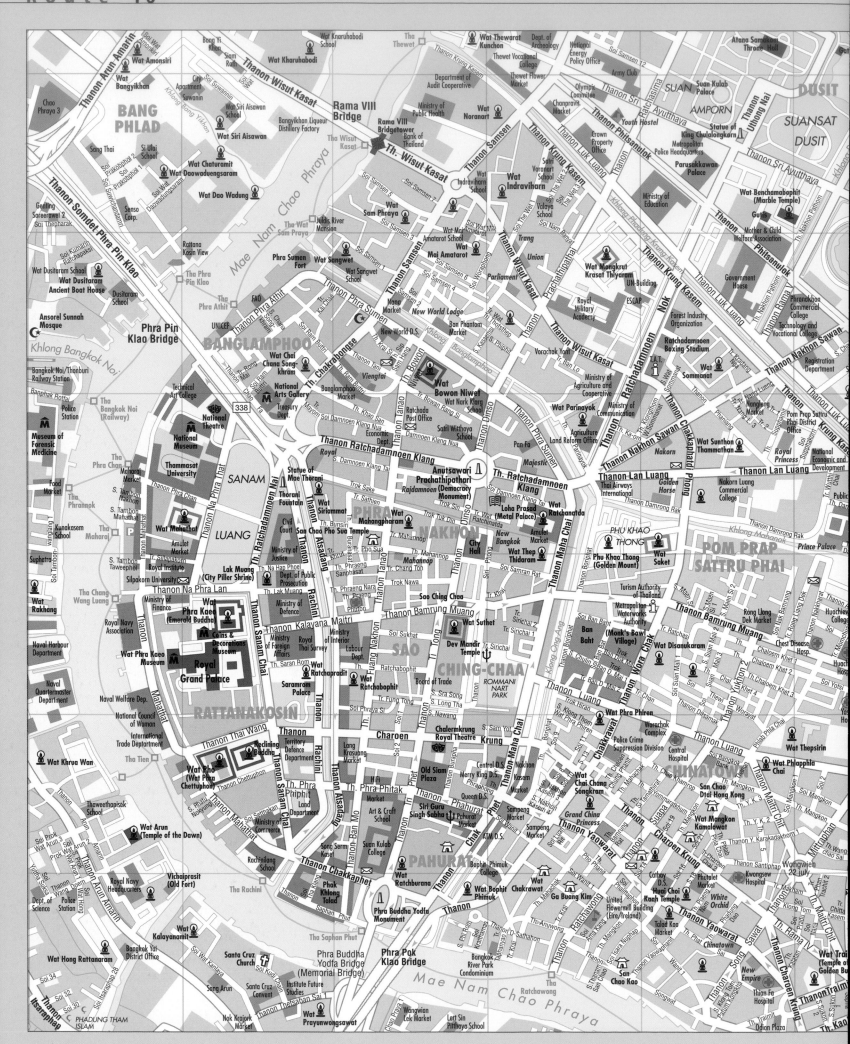

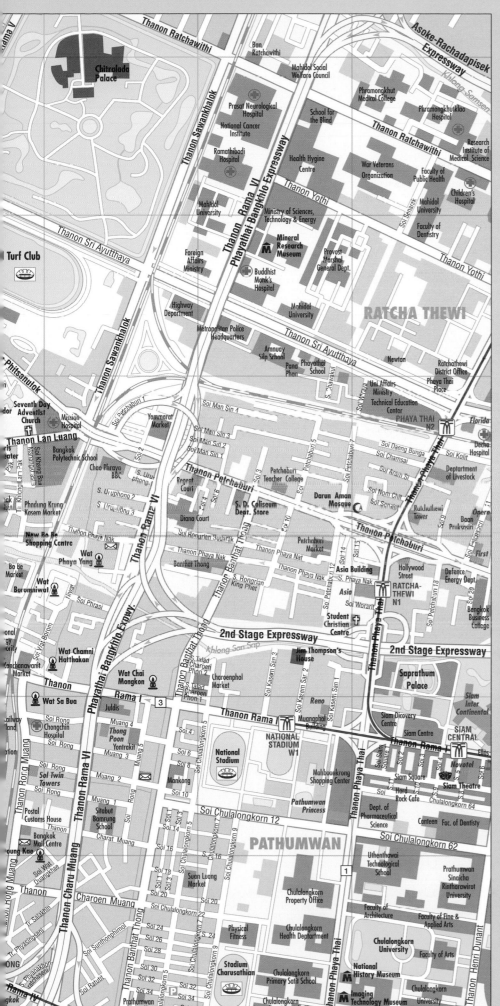

Bangkok

With its roughly twelve million inhabitants, Bangkok is Thailand's largest city and its cultural, political and social centre. The city's most important sight, the Grand Palace with the temple of Wat Phra Kaeo, is located on the eastern shore of the Chao Phraya River. These two form the centre of spiritual and worldly power in the kingdom.

As many as ten per cent of the Thai population lives in and around the capital, which as a result suffers from high levels of pollution, heavy traffic and incessant noise.

These days Bangkok is certainly one of the most lively and exciting metropolises in South-East Asia, but with its unspeakably chaotic traffic it can be quite stressful as well. Every day three million cars, trucks, motorcycles and bicycles fight their way through a city whose road network is simply not up to the task. In order to forestall a total collapse, some through roads have been constructed on stilts, but expensive road tolls are charged for their use and they do nothing to enhance the city's beauty.

The numerous palm lined Khlongs that once gave Bangkok the nickname 'Venice of the East' are only visible in some of the outer districts like Thon Buri or around Wat Arun. Most of

with its golden chedi and Emerald Buddha; Wat Po with its reclining golden Buddha, Bangkok's oldest temple and a centre for traditional medicine; and Wat Saket on the Golden Hill with a good view over the city.

The most important museums are the National Museum with exhibits on the history, arts and crafts of Thailand and the National Gallery, the largest gallery for contemporary Asian art.

Worth seeing in Chinatown, the 200-year-old Chinese trade centre of Bangkok, are Songwat Road, which still exudes a 19th-century atmosphere; the Buddhist shrine of Leng Noi Yee; different markets (Kao-Market, Pak-Khlong-Market, Phahurat-Market); Yaowarat Road, the main traffic artery of Chinatown and Wat Traimit with a golden image of Buddha.

Sights in the Dusit governmental centre are Dusit Park with its several museums; Wat Banchamabophit temple;

Top: King's Palace and Wat Phra Kaeo in Bangkok.
Bottom: View of the city centre and Chao Phraya.

them have been paved over in recent years. To visitors the city can seem extremely confusing. Many of the principal sights are far away from each other and it can be quite an adventure to get from one to the next.

The Old City's main sights include the King's Palace (construction started in 1782) with the Dusit Throne Hall, Amarinn Winichai Hall, Inner Palace and Sivalai Gardens; a city wall 1,900 m (2,078 yds) long that surrounds the 'city within the city' housing Wat Phra Kaeo, Thailand's most sacred temple

Phitsanulok Road and the government buildings.

Worth seeing in the town centre are the old foreigns' quarter with the Assumption Cathedral (1910), the Oriental Hotel, and the Jim Thomson House, a traditional Thai living quarter with museum.

Thon Buri has a number of other attractions as well – Wat Arun with its chedi covered in thousands of porcelain fragments, and the old Khlongs with their floating markets and traditional buildings.

Route 16

Detour

Batu Caves

The Batu Caves are among the most visited attractions in the Kuala Lumpur area. They are located 15 km (9 miles) north of the city on Highway 68 to Kuntan.

These giant limestone caves are part of a huge labyrinth of rock openings and tunnels. Because of a shrine inaugurated in the main cave in 1892, this is one of the most important pilgrimage destinations for Malay Hindus.

Top: Hindu shrine in the central cave at Batu.
Bottom: A Hindu pilgrim.

Every year in January and February thousands of Hindu faithful come to the Batu Caves during the festival of Thaipusam, celebrated here for two days. Its highlight is a procession of penitents with metal hooks poked into their backs and chests.

13 Krabi Most visitors come here because of the dream beaches and limestone cliffs in the area to the south and west of town. These are the 'beach images' that most people have come to associate with Thailand nowadays and some are truly spectacular.

Krabi, which is surrounded by karst cliff formations, has 21,000 inhabitants and is a good jumping-off point for boat trips into Phang Nga Bay; the famous Phi Phi Islands 40 km (25 miles) south with their magnificent beaches, steep karst rock faces and good diving; and a host of other white sand beaches and islands.

The temple compound of Wat Tham Sua with its beautiful view of the bay and the surrounding countryside is located on a rock outcrop 8 km (5 miles) north of Krabi.

From here we carry on across the southern Thai plains, which are among the most fertile in the country.

14 Hat Yai For many Thais this city is a shopping paradise because there are a lot of goods smuggled from Malaysia in the shops and markets.

West of the town centre at Wat Hat Yai Nai is the world's third-largest reclining Buddha at 35 m (115 ft) long and 15 m (50 ft) tall. From Hat Yai you can do a little detour to Songkhla

about 25 km (16 miles) and the lakes on the east coast north of town.

A short drive south to Sadao takes you to the Malay border where the road turns into Malaysia's Highway 1. As an alternative to the North-South Highway, which is a dual carriageway, you can take the old road, which mostly runs parallel to the new one.

15 Alor Setar The state capital of Kedah is located in the middle of a wide, fertile plain with picturesque rice paddies. The region is known as 'Malaysia's rice bowl'.

The town landmark, the Zahir Mosque (1912), is one of the largest and most beautiful in Malaysia. With its very slender minarets and onion domes it embodies beautifully everyone's mental image of an oriental mosque.

16 Penang Island The tropical island of Penang, which is up to 700 m (2,300 ft) high in places, is located in the Gulf of Bengal and connected to the mainland by a bridge. Visitors from around the globe are attracted to the beaches at its northern end and to Georgetown, its lively capital. With Chinese shopping streets, narrow alleyways, numerous temples, magnificent clan houses (such as Khoo Kongsi) and colonial buildings such as Fort Cornwallis (18th century) it always makes for a pleasant stroll.

17 Kuala Kangsar For more than 150 years Kuala Kangsar, located 110 km (68 miles) further south, has been the residence of the Sultans of Perak. This pleasant town on the wide Perak River has two cultural monuments worth seeing – the former sultan's palace of Istana Kenangan built in 1926, and Masjid Ubudi-

ah, which was built 1913–17 and whose golden domes and minarets make it one of the country's finest mosques.

18 Ipoh The state capital of Perak has 500,000 inhabitants and owes its economic rise to the profitable tin deposits in the area. These were exploited well into the 1980s. Ipoh seems quite provincial for a city its size. The Kinta Valley to the north and south of the town is dominated by steep, partly

1 The temple of Kek Lok Si, also known as the Temple of a Thousand Buddhas, is in Georgetown on the island of Penang. Construction began in 1890.

2 Tea plantations in the Cameron Highlands in Malaysia at 2,000 m (6,500 ft). These highlands are renowned for their pleasant climate.

At 452 m (1,483 ft), the Petronas Towers are among the highest buildings in the world and have certainly become Kuala Lumpur's most recognizable landmark. A 'sky bridge' 58 m (64 yds) long connects the two towers at a height of 170 m (558 ft). The towers were designed by Cesar Pelli and inaugurated in 1998.

Singapore

The city state of Singapore is located on a small island in the Malacca Straits at the southern tip of the Malay Peninsula. It was founded as a trading post in 1819 and in the space of only a few years became South-East Asia's most important traffic hub as well as a major financial centre.

Singapore is Asia's cleanest city and it has the best air quality of any of the world's large urban centres. The city charges high fines for environmental offences such as throwing away cigarette ends, and there are also high road tolls, horrendous car taxes and strict limits on registration quotas for new vehicles. With this draconic set of measures, the local government has long since managed to effectively ban cars from the city. Its outstanding public transport network makes it very easy to get to any point within the city limits quickly.

Singapore's population of roughly 4.5 million people is two-thirds Chinese, while the remainder is a mix of mostly Indian and Malay people. During the colonial period each of these ethnicities had its own neighbourhood, each of which has been meticulously reconstructed in recent years. Their markets, shops and restaurants are particularly full of atmosphere in the evening. The most colourful markets are in Little India.

Present and future coexist peacefully in this city. The commercial centre is home to one skyscraper after another, the airport is one of Asia's busiest and the container terminal is the largest in the world. But quite a number of historic buildings survive to keep Old Singapore alive.

Many of the colonial buildings in this neighbourhood along the Singapore River, where the city was founded in 1819, have also been meticulously restored over the years. They now house government buildings as well as a handful of museums and a small concert hall.

Sentosa Island, located just off the main island, is one of Singapore's most popular tourist destinations. In fact, its countless leisure attractions make it really quite similar to Disneyland.

If you are seeking some peace and quiet in nature, you can retreat to the heartland of Singapore Island. It is hard to believe but even in this modern city there is still a small area of the island's original tropical rainforest. Bukit Timah Nature Reserve protects that last remnant very strictly.

At Sungei Buloh Nature Park there are more than 120 species of birds living in the mangrove swamps. Singapore Botanic Gardens and Singapore Zoological Gardens enjoy good reputations around the world.

Sights in the Colonial Core include Padang with the Supreme Court, the Victoria Theatre (1862), the Old Parliament House (1826–27) and City Hall (1929), the famous Raffles Hotel (1887) and Fort Canning Park.

A Singapore's view of Orchard Road, central street.

Chinatown also has a number of interesting sights to behold – Sri Mariamman Temple with its seventy-two Hindu gods, the Jamae Mosque (1830), Boat Quay with its romantic seaside promenade, and Thian Hock Keng Temple (1839), the oldest of the Chinese temples in Singapore.

Sights in Little India and Kampong Glam include the Sultan Mosque, the city's largest mosque; Istana Kampgong Glam, the former sultan's palace; Arab Street; several temples, including Leong San See Temple (1917), Sakya Muni Buddha Temple (Temple of a Thousand Lights), and Sri Srinivasa Perumal Temple (1855); and Orchard Road, a lively shopping street.

1

Tioman Island

Tioman, the largest in a group of sixty-four volcanic islands, is located just off Pahang's east coast. The archipelago is accessible by boat or small aircraft from Mersing, Kuala Lumpur and Singapore.

Palm-lined white sandy beaches – some of the most beautiful in the world – and numerous wild flowers and waterfalls in its green mountains make this island a worthwhile destination at the end of our long journey. The waters around this island, which is 35 km (22 miles) long

Fishing boats on Tioman Island.

and almost 11 km (7 miles) wide, are clear down to a depth of 30 m (100 ft); its reefs and coral gardens and its abundant marine life make the island ideal for diving and snorkelling. The densely forested Kajang Mountain Range is home to monkeys, bats, reptiles and pythons as well as twenty-five other species of snake. On the island, there are very few fishing villages and holiday resorts. The main town is Tekek on the island's western side.

forested limestone cliffs. There are some caves with Buddhist sanctuaries here.

South of Ipoh the highway runs along the foothills of the Cameron Highlands. These highlands enjoy comparatively moderate temperatures and their gently sloping hills are home to a long tradition of tea cultivation. In some places the plantations extend right up to the highway.

19 Kellie's Castle On a small hill above the Kinta Valley are the ruins of Kellie's Castle. Construction began in 1915 for a Scottish plantation owner who never returned from a trip home to Europe in 1926. It is said that his ghost has haunted the castle ever since. Further south the highway rolls past some seemingly endless plantations of rubber and oil palm.

20 Kuala Lumpur Malaysia's largest city (1.3 million inhabitants) is this South-East Asian country's political and economic centre. Today there is nothing that recalls the 'Muddy River Mouth' (the translation of its name) of the old days.

No other Malaysian city is quite as outspoken about the fact that the country is aiming to distinguish itself as an up-and-coming industrial nation. Its modern hotels and high-rises such as the Petronas Towers, which house the headquarters of many companies, banks and institutions, illustrate this aim impressively. Kuala Lumpur is an attractive city because it balances lively urban elements with a healthy

amount of greenery in the centre and suburbs.

Its chief attraction, however, lies in its multicultural mix of people – Chinese, Malay and Indian peoples with very different cultures, traditions and lifestyles all seem to carry on in peaceful coexistence.

Tucked in below its modern skyline are the city's older sector: the administrative buildings of the former British colonials, the mansions of the tin barons, and traditional Indian and Chinese neighbourhoods.

21 Melaka A visit to historic Malacca is truly a journey into Malaysia's past. Unlike most other places in the country, this town looks back upon a long history. For a long time Melaka was an international port and transportation centre for sea trade with China, and was coveted by

the likes of the Portuguese, Dutch and British.

The former presence of these colonial powers is still demonstrated by the ruins of the mighty Portuguese castle, A Famosa, Dutch buildings around Red Square and many British colonial buildings.

In Chinatown on the other side of the Melaka River you'll find the most original part of town with houses more than 200 years old. Many of them were built in the so-called Chinese baroque style, a mix of Chinese architectural elements and colonial and classical European borrowings. Between Melaka and Johor Bahru the flat landscape, dense plantations and mangrove swamps mostly obstruct any view of the Malacca Straits.

22 Johor Bahru The southernmost town on the Malay Pen-

insula is the capital of the Johor Sultanate. Many locals have become rich here due to its proximity to Singapore. Numerous historic streets have been razed to the ground and replaced with modern blocks.

A causeway takes you across to the island of Singapore, which is located in the Malacca Straits.

23 Singapore For more detailed information on this interesting city, (see pp. 212–213).

1 Life in the centre of Singapore never stops. In the foreground is Boat Quay on the southern banks of the Singapore River.

2 Buildings in the Dutch Quarter, such as the Christ Church Melaka dating from 1753, recall the city's colonial period in the 18th century.

Chiang Rai Rice is the most important staple food in Asia. Whereas mountain rice is cultivated on terraces and does not require irrigation, water rice grows mainly on flood plains and near the mouths of large rivers such as this one near Chiang Rai.

Ayutthaya At its zenith, this former capital of Siam (1350–1767) was one of the most magnificent cities in Asia. To this day the ruins of its numerous palaces, halls, fortifications and temples and its countless stupas and Buddhas continue to recall this era in a most impressive fashion.

Phuket This island used to be an important trading post for European merchants. Its magnificent bays and palm-lined beaches now make it a first-class tourist destination.

Phi Phi Islands This archipelago located about 50 km (31 miles) south of Phuket has some excellent diving and some bizarre rock formations in the Ko Phi Phi Marine National Park.

Penang Its dream beaches have turned this tropical island into Malaysia's best-known tourist destination, but it also has some interesting colonial buildings and temples. The picture shows the Buddhist temple Kek Lok Si located in a southern suburb of Georgetown, the island's capital.

Singapore Founded as recently as 1819 as a trading post, Singapore has quickly become one of the most important traffic hubs and financial and commercial centres in South-East Asia. The picture is of Orchard Road, the city's main artery.

Melaka Under the name of Malacca, this town was an important transportation centre for trade with China. This can still be seen today in its numerous European-style colonial buildings and an extensive Chinatown. The Portuguese built here the fortress A Famosa.

Chiang Mai Thailand's second-largest city has some famous temple compounds built in the Lanna style: Wat Phra Sing, Wat Chedi Luang, Wat Chiang Man, and Wat Phra That Doi Suthep a little further out. It is also a centre for outstanding arts and crafts.

Sukhothai The extensive palaces and temples of the Sukhothai Kingdom (13th–14th centuries) extend over an area of 70 sq km (27 sq mi). In 1991 the compound was declared a UNESCO World Heritage Site. The picture shows a Buddha at Wat Mahathat.

Bangkok This city of twelve million inhabitants is the political, cultural and social heart of Thailand. One of its main sights is the Old King's Palace and Wat Phra Kaeo, the most important temple in Thailand. The traffic here can be horrendous, but the nightlife can still entertain.

Kuala Lumpur A testimony to the dynamic nature of Malaysia's capital are the Petronas Towers, until recently the highest buildings in the world. They were inaugurated in 1998.

Tioman This tropical island, which is accessible by plane or express boat from Singapore, has every ingredient of a dream holiday: white sandy beaches, reefs and coral gardens, and mountains and forests that are home to monkeys and reptiles. Its beaches starred in the movie *South Pacific*.

Kakadu National Park is characterized by broad lowlands and dry sandstone plateaus.

Route 17

Australia

On Stuart Highway through the 'Red Centre'

The Stuart Highway stretches 3,200 km (1,987 miles) from Adelaide on the south coast all the way across the legendary outback, the 'Red Centre' of the continent, to Darwin in the north on the Timor Sea. Along this dream route you pass some of Australia's most impressive natural sights. Indeed, long portions of the journey are devoid of any signs of life, much less human settlements, but it is precisely this emptiness and solitude that make this journey so fascinating.

The starting point for the adventure across the entire Australian continent is Adelaide, known as the 'greenest town' in the country. Today, tree-lined streets in this tidy city have replaced the rugged seaport where, in 1836, about 550 German settlers arrived bearing grape vines and a vision for the future. The heart of Australian wine production is now concentrated in a handful of picturesque regions including the Adelaide Hills, the Barossa Valley and the Clare Valley.

Port Augusta, 317 km (197 miles) further north, is the real starting point of the Stuart Highway. It is named after John McDouall Stuart, an explorer who in 1862 became the first white man to cross the continent from north to south. At one time known for being one of the country's most hazardous roads, the highway, which has been surfaced now since 1987, has become a fully developed traffic route. Parts of the road can become impassable after unusually heavy rainfall.

Aborigine with impressive body paint.

The first stretch of your route, from Port Augusta to Glendambo, is marked by dried-out salt lakes that are visible from the road. The first real town to the north after Port Augusta is Coober Pedy in the Stuart Range, a relatively inhospitable area where dramatic sandstorms are commonplace. It was here, in the 'opal capital of the world', that the first opal was discovered by chance during the gold rush of 1915.

In general, between Port Augusta and Darwin what may look like a town along the highway on the map is often nothing more than a roadhouse where you can buy fuel, spend the night and stock up on basic food supplies. One of these is the Kulgera Roadhouse, just 'across the border' in the Northern Territory. There are only 185,000 people living in this massive state (six times the size of Great Britain),

The Kakadu National Park covers almost the entire catchment area of the South Alligator River, which crashes over the cliffs of Twin Falls and Jim Jim Falls.

The Stuart Highway leads hundreds of kilometres through the desert landscape of the 'Red Centre'.

and half of them live in Darwin. Coarse, rocky terrain and the endless spinifex grass steppe cover the land as far as the eye can see. The land is rusty red for hundreds of kilometres, with termite hills shimmering dark red in the hot sun. It is a unique symphony of shifting shades of red earth in which you will only rarely see anything other than natural landscapes. Roughly 80 km (50 miles) over the border at Erlunda, the Lasseter Highway turns off towards Uluru National Park where two of Australia's most famous landmarks are located – Uluru (Ayers Rock) and Kata Tjuta (The Olgas).

The most important city in the area is Alice Springs in the Macdonnell Ranges, a town that is also the geographical centre of the country and a comfortable starting point for trips to many well-known national parks – Finke Gorge, Watarrka and the West Macdonnell Ranges. The next tourist highlight on the way to 'Top End' are the bizarre spheres of the Devils Marbles. Tennant Creek has been known as 'Gold Town' ever since the short gold rush that took place there in 1932. At Renner Spring one finally leaves the inhospitable arid plains of the 'Red Centre' behind and the coastal savannah comes into view.

From the town of Katherine you can reach the Cutta Cutta Caves Nature Park as well as the Nitmiluk National Park with the spectacular canyons of Katherine Gorge. At Pine Creek, you have a choice between taking the road to Darwin or the drive through Kakadu National Park towards Jabiru.

Either way, after 3,200 km (1,987 miles) of hard going, you have finally reached the 'Top End'.

The giant red kangaroo measures up to 2 m (6.5 ft) when standing on its hind legs.

Giant kangaroos

If you follow the Stuart Highway north towards Darwin you will regularly come across signs warning you of kangaroos crossing the road. These marsupials are the continent's national animal with an estimated population of about twenty-five million. Despite their cuddly popularity with tourists, these vegetarian creatures are viewed by local farmers as pests because they graze uncontrollably on valuable sheep pastures.

In Australia there are fifty-six kangaroo species, divided into two families – the 'real' kangaroos and the 'rat' kangaroos, a newer species. During your trip, you will mostly come across the 'real' kangaroos, the hopping kind with extremely short forearms and powerful legs and tails.

Giant red kangaroo.

Some are as small as large rabbits while others, like the giant red kangaroo, can reach 2 m (6.5 ft) standing on their hind legs. Cape York is home to two species of tree kangaroo.

Kangaroo offspring are actually born during a late phase of embryonic development, the rest of which is completed from within the mother's pouch. Females have only one baby per year, which then feed for seven to ten months in her pouch while she feeds another offspring with milk outside the pouch.

Kangaroos' long and powerful tails are used as counterweights for hopping and jumping, but their soft leathery feet do not damage the ground below them. In the open grasslands of the dry centre, you regularly come across giant red kangaroos which, like all kangaroos, live in herds.

Shortly after starting out from Adelaide, the Stuart Highway leads straight into the outback. Ayers Rock and Alice Springs lie at the halfway point of the route. The landscape turns into savannah in the far northern sections, and numerous national parks give travellers an idea of the Northern Territory's flora and fauna.

❶ Adelaide With more than a million inhabitants, Adelaide lies on the north and south sides of the Torrens River. The city's many parks, gardens, historic arcades and churches give it a very European flair. Yet despite all this, Adelaide is often considered a bit of a backwater by people from other Australian cities, or is even called 'wowserville', but this seems off the mark.

Every two years one of the world's most important cultural festivals takes place here – the Festival of Arts, held in the Adelaide Festival Centre. It is a tolerant and multicultural city with several museums along the 'Cultural Mile', including the Art Gallery of South Australia, the Ayers House Historical Museum (one of the most attractive colonial buildings in Australia), the Migration Museum on the history of immigration, and the South Australia Museum, with a good collection of Aboriginal tools, weapons and everyday items.

For a great view of the city go up to Montefiori Hill. Then take a break in the enchanting Botanic Gardens. If you feel like a swim, take one of the nostalgic trams down to Glenelg or Henley Beach. A worthwhile day trip is the drive into the Adelaide Hills or to the Barossa Valley. The first vineyards were planted here in 1847 by a German immigrant, Johann Cramp. Today in the Barossa Valley, 40 km (25 miles) long and 10 km (6 miles) wide, there are over 400 vineyards producing wines that have slowly but surely gained recognition around the world. One of the year's cultural highlights is the Vintage Festival with music, sauerkraut, brown bread, apple strudel, and of course wine.

Another interesting detour takes you to Kangaroo Island, 113 km (70 miles) south-west of Adelaide, which can be reached via the Fleurieu peninsula with its inviting sandy beaches. Australia's third-largest island is 155 km (96 miles) long and 55 km (34 miles) wide. You will come face to face here with the kangaroos that gave the island its name.

In the Seal Bay Conservation Park, thousands of sea lions bask on rocks in the sun. In Flinders Chase National Park, koalas lounge in the eucalyptus trees.

Travel information

Route profile
Length: approx. 3,200 km (1,987 miles), excluding detours
Time required: 3 weeks
Start: Adelaide
End: Darwin
Route (main locations): Adelaide, Port Augusta, Coober Pedy, Alice Springs, Wauchope, Tennant Creek, Katherine, Pine Creek, Darwin.

Accommodation:
Aside from signposted campsites, it's always possible to spend the night in a highway 'roadhouse'.

Traffic information:
Drive on the left in Australia. The Stuart Highway is completely tarmac from Adelaide to Darwin. In general, the driving conditions on auxil-iary roads east and west of the highway are good. International driving licences are required for some nations. If you want to explore the outback, a four-wheel drive vehicle is recommended. There are service stations and rest areas about every 200–300 km (124–186 miles) along the highway. Speed limits are 50 km/h (30 mph) in town and 100 km/h (62 mph) outside towns. The blood alcohol limit is 0.05 per cent and there are severe penalties if it is exceeded.

Information:
Australian Government
www.dfat.gov.au
General information:
www.australia.com
National Parks:
www.atn.com.au/parks

Detour

Flinders Ranges National Park

From Port Augusta take scenic Highway 47 through Quorn and Hawker to the mighty wall of the Wilpena Pound. Gravel roads then lead to the most important sights of the 950-sq-km (370-sq-mi) Flinders National Park, one of the most beautiful in South Australia. It protects the 400-km-long (240-mile) Flinders Range, which extends like a wedge between the salt lakes of Lake Torrens, Lake Eyre and Lake Frome and continues far into the outback, providing life support to many of the animal and plant species in this arid region.

The often bizarre rock formations come in red and violet hues, especially at sunrise and sunset. Bright,

Flinders National Park is one of the earth's oldest geological formations.

colourful flowers also grow in the valleys and gorges of the mountains in springtime. Giant red kangaroos live here, as do yellow-footed rock wallabies and other smaller species of rock wallabies. Bearded dragons (a type of monitor lizard) sun themselves on the hot rocks while broad-tailed eagles and brown falcons circle in the sky above.

The highlight of a trip into the national park is the Wilpena Pound, one of Australia's greatest natural wonders: a 17-km (10.5-mile) by 7-km (4.3-mile) crater-like 'cauldron' that resembles a natural amphitheatre with its ring of high, pointed rocks. A small passage is the only way into the bowl, which is an Aboriginal sacred place. You will get the best view from the scenic outlook point.

The real trip to the far north begins on Highway 1 from Adelaide. On the northern banks of Spencer Gulf is the industrial harbour town of Port Pirie, 250 km (155 miles) from Adelaide. Enormous grain silos bear witness to the extensive wheat farming in this region. Zinc and silver ore are processed here too, as is lead.

About 65 km (40 miles) further north, on the way to Port Augusta, it is worth taking the scenic detour into Mount Remarkable National Park at the south end of the Flinders Range. From the 959-m-high (3,146-ft) Mount Remarkable you can get a fabulous panoramic view of the entire region.

After another 70 km (43 miles) along Spencer Gulf, the indus-trial port town of Augusta awaits you and marks the actual starting point of Stuart Highway (Highway 87).

2 Port Augusta This town is often called the 'Gateway to the outback'. In preparation for the trip, a visit to the Wadlata Outback Centre is highly recommended. A few historically important buildings including the Town Hall (1887), the Court House (1884) and St Augustine's Church, with lovely stained-glass windows, are worth seeing. The Australian Arid Lands Botanic Gardens north of town familiarize you with the flora and fauna of the outback.

A short detour to the nearby Flinders Ranges National Park is an absolute must.

3 Pimba This little town is right next to the enormous Woomera military base. Interestingly, the 'restricted area' on the base contains the largest uranium source in the world.

Australia's largest natural lakes can also be found outside of Pimba. These salt lakes are only periodically filled with water and are the remnants of what was once a huge inland sea. In the dry season they transform into salt marshes or salt pans.

To the east of Stuart Highway is Lake Torrens, in the national park of the same name, which covers an area of 5,800 sq km (2,240 sq mi). Frome Lake and Eyre Lake are also in the park. Further west is Lake Gairdner, another salt lake that is part of a separate national park.

4 Coober Pedy In 1915, fourteen-year-old Willie Hutchinson and his father discovered Australia's first opal completely by chance, about 270 km (168 miles) north of Pimba. The name Coober Pedy originates from the Aborigine 'kupa pitl' (white man in a hole). Since then it has been overrun with pits up to 30 m (98 ft) deep and giant slag heaps that, due to consistent demand for opals, are constantly being expanded. In fact, 70 per cent of the world's opal mining takes place in the Coober Pedy area. The raging sandstorms and intense heat in the area have compelled nearly half of the 3,000 inhabitants to live in 'dugouts', underground homes built in decommissioned opal mines. The often well-furnished apartments maintain consistent temperatures between 23°C and 25°C (73°F and 77°F) and can be up to 400 sq m (4,305 sq ft) in size. There is even an underground church in Coober, as well as underground bed and breakfast accommodation. Be sure to pay a visit to the lovingly restored Old Timers Mine while you are here.

1 Road signs warn of kangaroos.

2 The night skyline of Adelaide reflected in the Torrens River.

3 At the base of the Stuart Range lies Coober Pedy, the 'Opal capital of the world'.

Thousands of Aboriginal rock paintings dot the spectacular landscape of Kings Canyon in Watarrka National Park. A lush oasis has developed in the Garden of Eden (illustrated here), providing ancient cycad palms and river eucalyptuses with plenty of water.

ally impressive show that will dazzle any visitor.

6 The Olgas Known as Kata Tjuta by the Aborigines, the Olgas (1,066 m/ 3,497 ft above sea level) are a similarly spectacular sight. Kata Tjuta, meaning 'many heads', is 32 km (20 miles) to the north-west of Uluru and comprises a group of thirty geologically similar, mainly dome-shaped monoliths that spread over an area of 35 sq km (13.5 sq mi), the highest point peaking at 546 m (1,791 ft).

It would appear that the Olgas were once a single mountain that eroded over time into individual hills. The Valley of Winds traverses a stark mountain range through which either seasonal icy winds blow or burning hot air turns each step into a torturous affair.

7 Henbury Back on Stuart Highway the journey continues to the north. Approximately 2,000–3,000 years ago a meteor impacted not far from Henbury, leaving twelve distinct craters. The largest has a diameter of 180 m (560 ft) and the smallest just 6 m (20 ft).

At Henbury, the Ernest Giles Highway splits off towards Watarrka National Park. It is a dirt track until it joins the Laritja Road where it becomes tarmac

and eventually leads to the Kings Canyon Resort.

0 Watarrka National Park and Finke Gorge National Park The centrepiece of the Watarrka National Park is Kings Canyon on the west end of the George Gill Range. With walls that rise to 200 m (656 ft), the canyon looks as if it were man-made.

A number of Aboriginal rock paintings and carvings adorn the rugged canyon facades. The Aborigines aptly call the beehive-like eroded sandstone dome the 'Lost City'. Kings Canyon is best visited on foot by taking the Kings Creek Walk.

From the resort, the Meerenie Loop (a dirt road) leads to the Aborigine town of Hermannsburg. On this slightly daunting stretch of road you'll cross low sand dunes that lead up to the base of the Macdonnell Range. East of the old Hermannsburger Mission, Larapinta Drive turns south and for the last 16 km (10 miles) it runs through the dried-out Finke riverbed to Palm Valley. This last section is only really accessible with four-wheel

1 Chambers Pillar rises 56 m (184 ft) over the Simpson Desert.

2 The Finke River eroded the steep ravine in Finke Gorge National Park.

Roadtrains

The infamous Australian roadtrains are lorries that can measure up to 53 m (174 ft), have as many as fifteen axles

'Roadtrains' ensure the supply of provisions to isolated areas.

and sixty-two tyres and supply the outback with basic necessities. Without them, life on an isolated farm or an inland mine would be impossible. These monsters of the road have 400–500 horsepower and barrel down highways, gravel roads and sand tracks brushing aside any possible obstacles. The tractors are fitted with large grilles designed to protect the radiator from collisions with animals.

Roadtrains run mostly across the sparsely populated outback. They can carry up to 80 tonnes of freight and regularly travel 4,000 km (2,484 miles). Overtaking a roadtrain can be dangerous: airborne gravel can destroy a windscreen, and they tend to swerve due to heavy winds and massive loads.

Eventually, the Lasseter Highway makes its way west at Erlunda towards the Yulara Resort and the Visitor Centre of the Uluru and Kata Tjuta National Parks (1,325 sq km/511 sq mi).

If you are looking for outdoor adventure, turn left off the highway onto a track towards Chambers Pillar, a 56-m-high (184-ft) sandstone monolith that early settlers used as a point of reference and in which many explorers have carved their names and dedications.

5 Ayers Rock The Aborigines call this massive rock mountain Uluru (863 m/2,831 ft above sea level) and cherish it as a sacred place. Subsequently, since

the path to the top is one of sacred significance, they 'kindly ask' that people do not climb it – but they do not forbid you to do so. Instead, they ask you to admire it from below as you stroll along the 9.4-km (5.8-mile) 'base walk'.

The rock itself measures 3.5 km (2.2 miles) by 2.4 km (1.5 miles), and extends several kilometres down into the earth. It rises to 348 m (1,142 ft) above the steppe landscape like a whale stranded on a deserted beach. Due to its high iron content it changes colour with the movement of the sun – from crimson, rust, pink, brown and grey to a deep blue. After rainfall it even goes a silvery shade – a perpetu-

drive vehicles. The main attraction of the Finke Gorge National Park is Palm Valley, home to more than 3,000 species of palm trees – all of them unique to this area – that line the picturesque watering holes.

The route then leads via Hermannsburg and Larapinta Drive to the turn-off for Namatjira Drive, which will take you further to the north-west.

⑨ West Macdonnell National Park The Tropic of Capricorn runs straight across these mountains to the east of Alice Springs, which rise to heights of 1,524 m (5,000 ft). The principal attractions of the park are the numerous gorges that lie on a fault line alongside Larapinta Drive and Namatjira Drive. The most spectacular one is near Alice Springs and is called Simpsons Gap. The Standley Chasm, with depths of up to 100 m (328 ft), only gets sunshine for twenty minutes in the middle of the day.

Ellery Creek Big Hole, Serpentine Gorge, Ormiston Gorge (giant blocks in Ormiston Pound) and Glen Helen Gorge are 133 km

(83 miles) further down the road. The small lake there is sacred to the Aborigines because the mythical giant water snake is said to live there. The return route or continuing drive to Alice Springs follows the same road.

⑩ Alice Springs The geographical centre of Australia is about 1,700 km (1,055 miles) north of Adelaide and 1,500 km (931 miles) south of Darwin.

Alice Springs was founded in 1872 and its main attractions are the carefully restored Old Telegraph Station (1872) and the Flying Doctors centre from which medical assistance has been organized to serve the outback since 1939. You can enjoy a magnificent view of the nearby Macdonnell Range from Anzac Hill. The famous Camel Cup takes place in July when up to fifteen dromedaries take part in a hard desert race. At the comical Henley-on-Todd regatta in springtime, 'oarsmen' race each other on foot in bottomless boats along the usually dry Todd River. North-east of the town is the Trephina Gorge National Park in

the East Macdonnell Range. It can be reached via the paved Ross Highway. Eucalyptus trees grow alongside watering holes tucked between the steep walls of the gorge. A dirt track to the N'dhala Gorge Nature Park also branches off the Stuart Highway. Another track leads to Maryvale, the last outpost of civilization in

the Simson Desert. From there it is about 58 km (36 miles) to Chambers Pillar.

On the way to the Devils Marbles near Wauchope, the view to your right overlooks the Davenport Range, another national park. To the north of the West Macdonnell Range there are Aborigine reserves on both sides

of Stuart Highway, for example the Pawu Aboriginal Land west of Borrow Creek. It was not until the end of the 20th century that the lands were returned to the indigenous people.

⑪ Devils Marbles These eroded granite spheres look as if a mightier power had scattered

road takes you to Renner Springs. This small town marks both the climatic and geographical border between the outback of the 'Red Centre' and the savannah of the northern coastal areas.

Newcastle Waters to the north was once an important telegraph station and crossing point for livestock herds.

⑭ Daly Waters Still further north, it is definitely worth making a stop in Daly Waters, where the oldest pub in the Northern Territory has been wetting whistles since 1893. For decades, travellers have left various utensils here – from tickets for the legendary Ghan Express to autographed underwear. These are now all carefully arranged to decorate the walls of the pub. In this hot, dry environment, a cold beer tastes even better than in other roadhouses along the highway.

The next stop is Larrimah with its historic train station. From there it's on to Mataranka where you should not miss out on a refreshing dip in Mataranka Pool in Elsey National Park,

roughly 9 km (5.5 miles) away. Accommodation is also available at the Mataranka Homestead Resort.

The thermal hotsprings are surrounded by paperbark trees, from which hang long strips of bark. The Aborigines used this bark for thousands of years as wrapping for their food. From Mataranka it's now only 110 km (68 miles) to Katherine on the banks of the Katherine River, a river that never dries out.

⑮ Katherine This town offers limited attractions, but there is a nostalgic train station dating from 1926 and the first biplane used by the Flying Doctors is on

1 As if the gods had tossed them – the Devils Marbles.

2 Bizarre rock formations in the West Macdonnell Range.

3 The desert lives, even on this red sand dune in the Northern Territory.

4 The most impressive way to view the cliffs of Katherine Gorge is on a boat trip down the Katherine River.

them across the rocky plateau with mathematical precision. It seems as if the slightest breeze could blow them away. The Aborigines believe the marbles to be rainbow water snake eggs.

⑫ Tennant Creek When the last gold rush began in Australia in 1932, Tennant Creek was

known as 'Gold Town'. Within a few years, however, it became more of a ghost town until it was eventually reawakened by the discovery of nearby silver and copper mines. The Nobles Nob Mine and the Tennant Creek Stamp Battery Museum recall the short-lived bonanza. Some 11 km (7 miles) north-west of here are

the Devils Pebbles, another scattering of granite boulders. A roadside memorial for John Flynn, the founder of the Flying Doctors, lies some 20 km (12 miles) in the same direction.

⑬ Renner Springs Further along the route towards Katherine, north of Helen Springs, the

Aborigines

When the European settlement of Australia began at the end of the 18th century, they saw the country as 'terra nullius' or unknowed land, but at least 350,000 Aborigines (from the Latin 'ab origine', meaning from the origin or the beginning) had lived on the continent for more than 50,000 years. The Aborigines were organised in kinships, clans and tribes and roamed the continent as hunters and gatherers. What they needed to live, they found in the desert or the rainforest.

The Aborigines' totemic and magical beliefs have been around for thousands of years: mountains, rocks, rivers, lakes and trees all have souls.

One of the many X-ray-style rock drawings in the Kakadu National Park.

Their perception of the world is influenced by the 'Dreamtime' in which past, present and future are permanently interlinked.

In the beginning, the world was a flat disk shrouded in darkness until the giants came with light, water, clouds and rain and created all forms of life. The giants then turned into mountains, rivers, lakes, trees and animals. Nature as a whole is therefore divine in Aboriginal 'Dreamtime'.

All of these concepts feature heavily in Aborigine rites, traditions and customs such as body painting, magical songs and rock paintings. The indigenous Australians have been fighting hard for the return of their lands and social recognition from European descendants for more than fifty years.

display here. Nature lovers in particular stop in Katherine because the Cutta Cutta Caves Nature Park is just 24 km (15 miles) away to the south-east. The stalactite and stalagmite formations in the caves are an important refuge for rare bats and tree snakes.

16 Nitmiluk National Park This impressive network of canyons formed over thousands of years by the Katherine River is one of the greatest natural wonders of Australia – Katherine Gorge. Red-brown limestone canyon walls rise up to 100 m (328 ft) above the river. The best way to view them is from a sightseeing boat that embarks in Katherine, or you can explore the river by canoe when it is not the rainy season. During the rainy season the otherwise calm river turns

into a raging torrent and is not really navigable.

Biologists often marvel at Katherine Gorge for its unbelievable variety of wildlife – freshwater crocodiles live here, along with more than 160 species of birds and numerous butterfly species. All in all, nine of the thirteen gorges in the park are open to visitors.

Edith Falls is a particularly spectacular natural phenomenon. You can reach the falls by either taking the rough 75-km (48-mile) track, or the more comfortabe Stuart Highway. Smaller pools and waterfalls invite sun-weary visitors to take a refreshing swim.

17 Pine Creek This town, 90 km (56 miles) north-west of Katherine, was once a hot spot for gold diggers. Today it's a supply station for those on their way

to Darwin, or the starting point for excursions to the Kakadu National Park to the east.

If you would like to visit that world-famous national park, leave the Stuart Highway at Pine Creek and take the Kakadu Highway towards Jabiru. You will find the park visitor centre there and can plan your trip.

18 Kakadu National Park Covering an area of 20,000 sq km (7,800 sq mi), this national park in Arnhem Land is one of the largest and most attractive in Australia. The scenery shifts from the tidal zone at Van Diemen Gulf and the flood plains of the lowlands to the escarpment and the arid plateaus of Arnhem Land. The most impressive attraction is the escarpment, a craggy 500-km-long (310-mile) outcrop with

spectacular waterfalls such as the Jim Jim Falls, Tain Falls and Twin Falls, which are at their best towards the end of the rainy season. The name of the park comes from 'Gagudju', which is the name of an Aboriginal language originating in this flood-plain region.

Biologists have counted 1,300 plant, 10,000 insect, 240 bird and seventy reptile species, including the feared saltwater crocodile. The rare mountain kangaroos, wallabies and one-third of the country's bird species are also native to this area. Due to its diversity, this impressive park has been made into a UNESCO World Heritage Site.

There are over 5,000 Aborigine rock paintings here, the most famous of which are on Nourlinge Rock, Ubirr Rock and in Nangaluwur. The paintings,

The wildlife of Kakadu National Park

This national park is renowned for its animal diversity. The park is made up of a tidal zone, flood plains, a steppe and the Arnhem Land Plateau. Alone 240 bird species have been counted by ornithologists here, including the Jaribu. The crocodile is the best-known among seventy reptile species here. Daily almost fifty mammal species meet at the watering hole.

The Arnhem Highway leads back through Cooinda and Jabiru to the Stuart Highway. From Noonaman the road leads south before heading west through Batchelor into Litchfield National Park.

19 Litchfield National Park The main attractions of this park are immediately visible – the open eucalyptus forests, the thick rainforest around the escarpment, and the massive, skilfully crafted gravestone-like mounds of the magnetic termites can reach heights of 2 m (6.5 ft). Due to the extreme midday heat the termites have cleverly aligned the long side of their mounds with the north-south axis in order to warm their homes in the morning and evening sun while protecting them from the midday sun.

The Tabletop Range escarpment is a spectacular sight where waterfalls like Sandy Creek Falls, Florence Falls, Tower Falls and Wangi Falls cascade down the ridge even in the dry season. The unique environment around the falls has developed its own unique spectrum of monsoon rainforest wildlife.

20 Darwin Due to its proximity to the South-East Asian countries to the north of Australia, Darwin has developed into a culturally very diverse city, which is reflected in its numerous markets and restaurants. One of the specialities here is the daily, slightly odd Aquascene Fish Feeding at Doctor's Gulley. At high tide various fish swim onto land to be fed by hand from humans. Wonderful white sand beaches can be found on both sides of the scenic harbour town of Beagle Gulf.

Since the destruction caused by Tornado Tracy during Christmas of 1974, the city of Darwin has changed dramatically. After the storm, almost nothing was left of the historic 19th-century buildings apart from the Old Navy Headquarters, Fanny Bay Jail, the Court House, Brown's Mart and the Government House with its seven gables. Your journey across the mighty outback ends here, on the coast at the doorstep to Asia.

1 The Arnhem Land Plateau escarpment in Kakadu National Park.

2 Magnetic termite mounds, bizarre yet clever constructions in Litchfield National Park.

3 The Wangi Falls are one of many waterfalls on the edge of the Tabletop Range plateau.

4 Kakadu National Park: The falls cascade into the depths along the 500-km (310-mile) edge of the escarpment.

some of which date back as many as 18,000–23,000 years, not only demonstrate the area's climate change, but are also a striking portrayal of the culture of the Aborigines, who have allegedly lived on the continent here for 50,000 years. The best time of year to visit the park is in the dry season from May to November, as the roads are otherwise impassable.

Top: The goanna, member of the monitor lizard family, is common in northern Australia.
Middle: Woe betides he who falls into the teeth of the attacking saltwater crocodile.
Bottom: The jaribu is Australia's only indigenous stork.

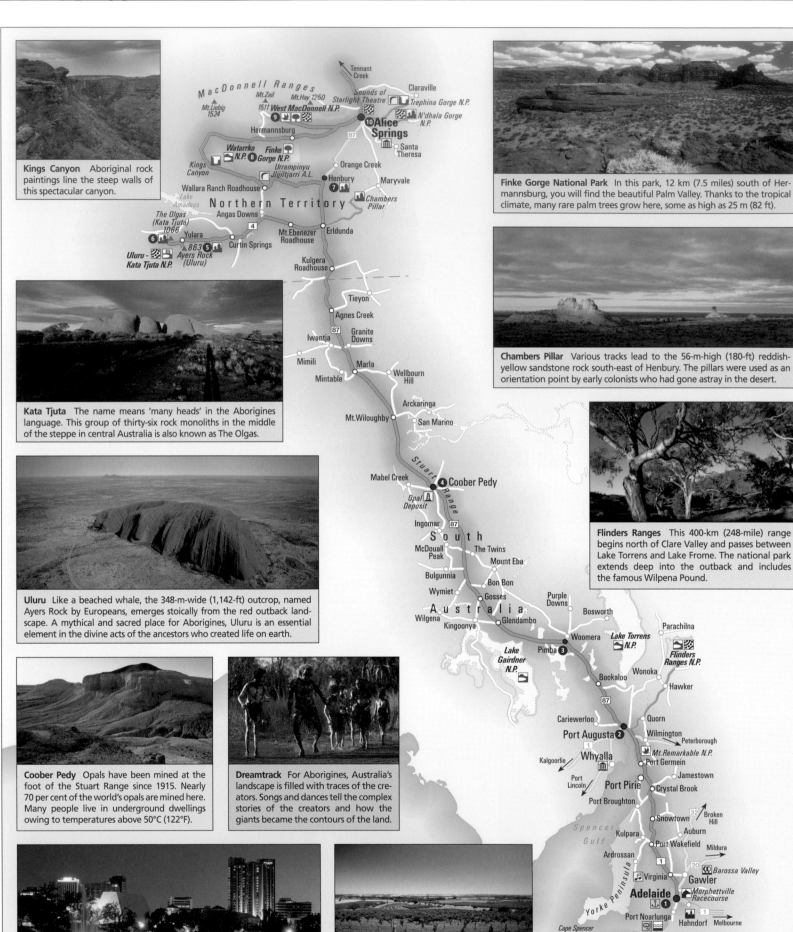

Kings Canyon Aboriginal rock paintings line the steep walls of this spectacular canyon.

Kata Tjuta The name means 'many heads' in the Aborigines language. This group of thirty-six rock monoliths in the middle of the steppe in central Australia is also known as The Olgas.

Uluru Like a beached whale, the 348-m-wide (1,142-ft) outcrop, named Ayers Rock by Europeans, emerges stoically from the red outback landscape. A mythical and sacred place for Aborigines, Uluru is an essential element in the divine acts of the ancestors who created life on earth.

Coober Pedy Opals have been mined at the foot of the Stuart Range since 1915. Nearly 70 per cent of the world's opals are mined here. Many people live in underground dwellings owing to temperatures above 50°C (122°F).

Dreamtrack For Aborigines, Australia's landscape is filled with traces of the creators. Songs and dances tell the complex stories of the creators and how the giants became the contours of the land.

Adelaide The capital of South Australia was founded in 1836 between the beaches of Gulf St Vincent and the Mount Lofty Range. It was named after Queen Adelaide.

Barossa This is the collective name for Barossa Valley and Eden Valley, the best wine-growing region in Australia, originally settled by Germans in the mid 19th century.

Finke Gorge National Park In this park, 12 km (7.5 miles) south of Hermannsburg, you will find the beautiful Palm Valley. Thanks to the tropical climate, many rare palm trees grow here, some as high as 25 m (82 ft).

Chambers Pillar Various tracks lead to the 56-m-high (180-ft) reddish-yellow sandstone rock south-east of Henbury. The pillars were used as an orientation point by early colonists who had gone astray in the desert.

Flinders Ranges This 400-km (248-mile) range begins north of Clare Valley and passes between Lake Torrens and Lake Frome. The national park extends deep into the outback and includes the famous Wilpena Pound.

Fleurieu Peninsula This headland to the south of Adelaide boasts a series of beautiful beaches, bays and harbours. Divers and snorkellers enjoy Port Noarlunga on the north-east side, and surfers head for the high breakers on Waitpinga Beach on the southern side.

Darwin The port on the northern edge of the 'Top End' benefits from a subtropical climate. The few historic buildings include the Old Navy Headquarters, Fannie Bay and Brown's Mart.

Aboriginal rock art Rock carvings, rock and cave paintings, drawings of animals, sand designs, totem poles, carvings that feature and wickerwork are all part of Aborigine culture. The designs in their stone paintings were applied using ochre, charcoal and limestone and symbolize the relationship between humans and their environment, which are believed to mythically coexist in 'Dreamtime'.

Nourlangie Rock The Aborigine rock paintings at Nourlangie Rock in the Kakadu National Park are examples of the so-called 'X-ray style'.

Wangi Falls The waterfalls in Litchfield National Park crash spectacularly into the depths. It is safe to bathe in the bay.

Kakadu National Park Stone plateaus, waterfalls, flood plains and the South Alligator River characterize this park's landscape, one of Australia's best-known attractions in the 'Top End'.

Cutta Cutta Caves Nature Park Rare bat species live alongside equally rare snakes in limestone caves 25 km (15 miles) south-east of Katherine, a jumping off point for the park.

John Flynn Memorial This memorial, located 20 km (12 miles) north of Tennant Creek, is dedicated to John Flynn (1880–1951), founder of the Flying Doctors back in 1939. The service was the most effective way to provide medical assistance to people in the outback.

Litchfield National Park This park is known for its magnetic termite mounds, which are cleverly designed to take advantage of the sunshine.

Nitmiluk National Park Some of the highlights of this park are the rivers and ravines of Katherine Gorge, which go down to depths of 100 m (328 ft).

Tennant Creek The second-largest town on the Stuart Highway was once a telegraph post on the Overland Telegraph Line. Gold was found here in 1932.

Devils Marbles The 170-million-year-old red granite blocks near Wauchope were formed by the constant temperature changes from glowing heat to icy cold.

Davenport Range National Park Waterfoul and giant red kangaroos have found refuge in the mountains and steppes of this park.

Pawu Aboriginal Land The 2,500 sq km (975 sq mi) around Mount Barkly, west of Barrow Creek and south of Willowra, was returned to the Aborigines in 1981, sixty-one years after they were driven off the land by European settlers.

West Macdonnell Ranges The highest peak in this craggy mountain range to the east and west of Alice Springs is Mount Liebig, at 1,524 m (5,000 ft).

Alice Springs At the heart of the 'Red Centre': 1,700 km (1,055 miles) from Adelaide and 1,500 km (931 miles) from Darwin.

Trephina Gorge National Park This park in the East Macdonnell Range is famous for its quartz cliffs and the eucalyptus stands that box in the Trephina Gorge watering holes.

Colourful kilims draw tourists to the small market town of Taddent in the Atlas Mountains.

Morocco

Royal cities, kasbahs and oases

The magic of Oriental medinas and palaces, the austere beauty of the Atlas Mountains, the bright white of the harbour cities, the green of the Saharan palm oases, and the colours and aromas of 'a thousand and one nights' in the souks of the royal cities make this tour an experience for the senses.

Tangiers is the starting point on the Strait of Gibraltar. Strolling through the maze-like medina (old Arab quarters with tiny streets), you get a sense of the special Arabic-Spanish atmosphere that made Tangiers a jet-setters' haunt in the 1960s. East of the city, the rugged mountains of the Rif slope gently back towards the Mediterranean coast. Tétouan, with its well-preserved medina, and the small, picturesque mountain town of Chefchaouen are two fascinating stops on your way south. To the south of the Rif mountains, the columns and gates of the

ruined Roman city of Volubilis soar above golden cornfields. Not far away, the holy city of Moulay Idriss clings to the hillside as if painted on with watercolours. Moulay Idriss I brought Islam to Morocco in the 8th century and founded the first dynasty here. His mausoleum in the city's holy quarter is the most important pilgrimage site in the country. Nearby is the royal city of Meknès with its sturdy walls, storehouses and palaces.

Fez was the first royal city under Moulay Idriss II and his Idriss Dynasty. Above the labyrinth of alleys, squares, markets

Olive sellers in Meknès.

and palaces, the minarets of countless mosques rise up towards the heavens. The architectural treasure of Fez, its colourful, aromatic souks (marketplaces) around the mausoleum of Idriss II, the palace area of the Dar el-Makhzen, and the dignified Kairaouine Mosque make this city of trade and science over a thousand years old, an Oriental gem.

Heading south through the densely forested areas of the Middle Atlas, you pass Ifrane and Azrou and the Col du Zad. Vegetation in this area now becomes more scarce and the nearby desert begins to expand. From Ar-Rachidia onwards, the route follows the palm-filled valley of Oued Ziz on its way to Erfoud, a garrison city that is the jumping-off point for tours into the majestic Erg Chebbi Desert, a dream landscape of extraordinary golden sand dunes.

Tinerhir is one of the largest oases on the Route of the Kasbahs. Many 19th-century clay tiqhremt (family castles) and kasbahs (forts) are found in the lush palm gardens.

The Sultan's love nest – Menara Pavilion, in the garden of the same name, on the outskirts of Marrakech.

From Erfoud, you now follow the famous Route of the Kasbahs where mud fortresses tower above the palm tree oases of Tinerhir and Boumalne Dadès. Both towns lie at the mouth of wildly romantic gorges that lead deep into the mountainous realm of the High Atlas. A day trip south through the Drâa Valley passes Ouarzazate to the old oases of Agdz, Zagora and Tamegroute.

Ksar Aït Ben Haddou is probably the most frequently photographed movie set in Morocco. The mud city was abandoned by its inhabitants and is to be restored under the UNESCO protectorate. Over the Tizi-n' Tichka pass, the route continues north through the 3,000-m (9,843-ft) High Atlas to the royal city of Marrakech. Here, the minaret of the Koutoubia Mosque soars high above this ancient city, and goods from every land fill the souk.

From Marrakech, our dream route heads towards the Atlantic, but before reaching Agadir it briefly breaks south into a landscape where erosion has created some amazing formations. Tafraoute and the Valley of Ammeln in the Anti-Atlas display the ancient world of the Berbers.

The route now passes through the silver city of Tiznit and the resort of Agadir, and follows the Atlantic coast towards Essaouira. The harbour town protected by many forts has a beautiful medina. Further north, the modern metropolis of Casablanca is home to the largest, most magnificent mosque in the Maghreb, while the foundation and base of the Hassan Tower minaret tell of a similarly ambitious mosque project in nearby Rabat that was started in 1150 and never completed. Passing through Larache and Asilah you arrive back in Tangiers.

Horsemen and guards passionately show their might in an historical re-enactment.

Volubilis

Volubilis, near Meknès, is one of the most beautiful ruins in North Africa. In its day, the city had over 15,000 residents, many living in luxurious villas with artistic mosaic floors.

These have been wonderfully preserved, for example in the 'House of the Nymphs', the 'House of the Twelve Labours of Hercules' or the 'House of Venus', where a beauty emerging from the bath adorns the floor mosaic.

The triumphal arch of Caracalla towers imposingly over the Decumanus Maximus. The main axis crosses the ancient city from the south-west to the north-east. In the southern part of the ruins, the basilica, with its elegant porticos, was the place where markets were held and the law administered. Just alongside is the Capitol Temple of Jupiter, Juno and Minerva.

Top: Many of the buildings in Volubilis are well preserved, such as these arcades of the former forum.
Middle: The triumphal arch of Caracalla was constructed in AD 217.
Bottom: Open colonnades border the long side of the basilica.

When Rome's shining star began to fade in North Africa, Volubilis was surrendered. Today, Roman history is vividly presented at these UNESCO World Heritage ruins and in the associated museum.

Our tour through Morocco uniquely combines culture with nature. In addition to royal cities, the journey includes old-style earthen fortresses against the backdrop of the Atlas Mountains as well as resorts on the stunning Atlantic coast.

❶ Tangiers Founded in Roman times, the first impression made by this harbour city on the Strait of Gibraltar is one of a hectic Oriental marketplace. High over the city, the former royal palace is enthroned in the kasbah, which also houses the Archaeological Museum with exhibits from Volubilis. From Tangiers, the N2 winds its way south-east through the foothills of the Rif mountains.

❷ Tétouan The largest city in the Rif is a UNESCO World Heritage Site for its architecture, which is heavily influenced by Andalusian styles and indeed was part of Spain until Moroccan independence in 1956. Within the walled medina you will see numerous vaulted arch alleyways, and many houses with windows covered in wrought-iron bars.

Tétouan's souk is the fourth largest in Morocco. On market days, countrywomen from the Rif bring their products into the city.

The fully restored N2 heads south through the cedar- and holm-oak-covered Rif mountains.

❸ Chefchaouen The white houses of the medina here clutter the mountainside like building blocks, with the high peaks of the central Rif mountains in the background. In 1492, many Jews and Muslims settled here following their expulsion from Spain during the Reconquista. Even today you cannot help but notice the Spanish influence in the architecture of the picturesque labyrinthine alleys in the medina.

After crossing the Rif you reach Ouezzane and follow Highway 417 to the N3 intersection, then head first north-west travelling from Sidi-Kacem, and then south to Volubilis (180 km/ 112 miles).

❹ Volubilis The ruins of this former Roman settlement lie at the foot of the Djebel Zerhoun. Founded in the first century BC, Volubilis was the capital of the Roman province Mauretania Tingitana until AD 285. The city became prosperous through the olive oil trade as well as by selling wild animals for Roman arena events. A mere 2.5 km (1.5 miles) away from Volubis is the pilgrimage site of Moulay Idriss.

❺ Moulay Idriss Your first stop here should be the 'Terrace', a vista point with fantastic views over the maze of the medina with its mosques surrounding the central sanctuary mausoleum of Idriss I. A direct descendant of the prophet Mohammed, Idriss I founded this town around AD 788, succeeded in converting the Berber people to Islam and subsequently formed the first Moroccan

1 The lavishly decorated Bab el-Mansour, completed in 1732, leads to the palace city of Meknès.

2 In the centre of Moulay Idriss is the green-brick mausoleum.

Travel information

Route profile
Length: approx. 3,100 km (1,926 miles), excluding detours
Time required: 21–25 days
Start and end: Tangiers
Route (main locations): Tangiers, Tétouan, Volubilis, Meknès, Fez, Erfoud, Route of the Kasbahs, Ouarzazate, Drâa Valley, Marrakech, Tafraoute, Agadir, Essaouira, Casablanca, Rabat, Tangiers

Traffic information:
Drive on the right in Morocco. It is advisable to avoid travelling after dark as there are often unlit carts, cyclists or pedestrians on the road at night. It is imperative to pay attention to signs, which are unfortunately not always very clear. Between the big cities in the north, the roads are usually asphalt and also relatively wide.
The speed limit for rural roads is 100 km/h (62 mph), and 40–60 km/h (25–37 mph) in built-up areas.
Drivers are strictly forbidden from drinking alcohol.

When to go:
The weather is mild all year in the north, a bit cool in winter. Southern beaches can be foggy in summer. October to April is good for the lowlands with temps of 30°C.

Information:
General and travel:
www.morocco.com
wikitravel.org/en/Morocco
www.arab.net/morocco/
www.visitmorocco.org

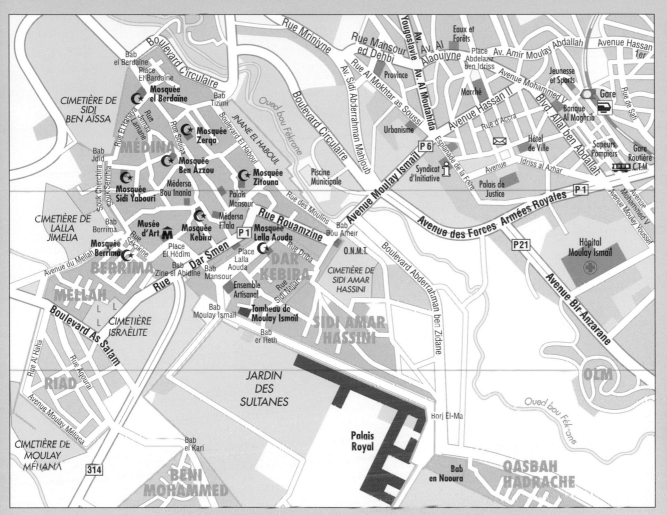

Meknès

Moulay Ismail, who chose Meknès as his royal city at the end of the 17th century, was a megalomaniac ruler and his monumental buildings are testimony to this.

The Ville Impériale, surrounded by mighty walls, the magnificent city gate Bab el-Mansour, the Heri es-Souani storehouse used as a stable and granary, and finally the lavishly decorated mausoleum of the ruler are all part of the city's UNESCO World Heritage offering. The medina, with its colourful souks, is labyrinthine and intimate in comparison. Among the Old City's maze of alleys, the Medersa Bou Inania conceals a special gem of neo-Moorish architecture.

Water sellers in traditional red colours.

Fez

Fez el-Bali, the old Fez, sprawls like a labyrinth in the basin beneath the Marinid fortress. In AD 809, Idriss II deemed the town a royal city. Since then, Fez has become a modern metropolis.

On the other side of the city walls, the tanners leave goat hides out to dry.

Madrasahs and palaces, the mausoleum of the city's founder and the venerated Kairaouine Mosque are adorned with a real fusion of Arabic-Berber decorative art, with carvings, mosaics and gypsum stucco work. In the souks, spice merchants, cobblers, carpet sellers and goldsmiths vie for customers' business while sheep and goat skins are made into leather in the tanners' quarter.

A penetrating smell hovers around the leather tanneries of Fez el-Bali, where skins are first freed from hairs, then smoothed and softened in a variety of different liquids, and finally dyed. Visitors to the tanning yards often hold a bunch of mint leaves in front of their noses.

dynasty. Passing now through an idyllic hill landscape, you will come to the royal city of Meknès just 28 km (17 miles) away.

6 Meknès (see p. 231). Just 70 km (43 miles) down the N6 is Fez.

7 Fez (see p. 231). From Fez, the N13 continues south into the foothills of the Middle Atlas.

8 Ifrane After roughly 60 km (37 miles) you will be pleasantly surprised by picturesque mountain scenery that many say is quaintly reminiscent of Switzerland. The health resort of Ifrane could just as easily be in the European Alps. Gabled houses, cool, fresh mountain air, a few nearby ski lifts – this is what Morocco's alpine holiday destinations look like.

Morocco's most prestigious university is in Ifrane, and the royal family also owns a magnificent palace here. Enjoy a typically Moroccan pastry, the Cornes de Gazelle, before the upcoming 300-km-long (186-mile) stretch through the Middle and High Atlas.

The N8 and, from Azrou onwards, the N13 wind lazily through the impressive cedar forests. With a bit of luck, you will encounter some Barbary Apes. Once you've passed the 2,178-m (7,146-ft) Col du Zad, the landscape becomes more sparse and after the mining city of Midelt, the route winds its way through the enchanting eastern foothills of the High Atlas. North of Ar-Rachidia, the road continues up along the spectacular Gorges du Ziz.

9 Ar-Rachidia This town at 1,060 m (3,477 ft) is an important traffic and trade junction in southern Morocco. Surrounded by oasis gardens, it is the epitome of a typical oasis, but with the added backdrop of the majestic High Atlas. The town itself is rather modern and functional, with very few traces of traditional architecture. This is where the Tafilalt oases begin, fed by the Oued Ziz originating in the Atlas, and where the current royal family resides, the Alouites. The N13 follows the river past oasis gardens and small settlements until it reaches Erfoud 74 km (46 miles) away.

10 Erfoud Founded by the French only in 1917, Erfoud still looks like a desert garrison city with barracks, modern headquarters and wide, dusty streets. It is the centre of the Tafilalt, the largest valley oasis in Morocco. Many souvenir dealers have specialized in selling fossils from the Sahara.

From here you travel another 22 km (13.5 miles) south through the fascinating desert landscape.

11 Rissani Some 3,000 inhabitants populate the narrow, often vaulted-arch alleyways of the medina beyond the town gate. If a market is held on a Sunday, oasis farmers and cattle breeders from the surrounding villages fill the main town square.

It is interesting to do a day trip to the oasis of Rissani, the mausoleum of Moulay Ali Cherif, the founder of the Alouite dynasty, and to Ksar Abbar, whose mud walls are decorated with Islamic geometric patterns. In contrast, the ruins of the once most important trading

1 The sand dunes of Erg Chebbi in the south of Morocco tower up to 100 m (328 ft) high.

2 Only a few sand-blown ruins remain from the once legendary Sijilmassa.

3 Tourists can take camel rides from Merzouga into the dune landscape of the Erg Chebbi.

Detour

Erg Chebbi – in Morocco's 'Sea of Sand'

The adventurous trip to Erg Chebbi can also be done with a suitable off-road vehicle and goes from

The sand dunes of Erg Chebbi near Merzouga.

Rissani (41 km/25 miles, a few sandy sections) or Erfoud (46 km/ 28.5 miles, uneven road) on the marked track to the hamlet of Merzouga and further on into Morocco's largest sand dune region, the Erg Chebbi. This sand sea is part of the eastern foothills of the Great Western Erg.

There are several simple restaurants at the base of the dunes and camel herders offer rides. At dawn and dusk, the sand dunes are bathed in a fire-red light. About 26 km (16 miles) further south, near Taouz, you'll find desert rock drawings (only with police authorization and a guide). From here, the same road leads back to Erfoud.

Detour

Gorges du Dadès and Gorges du Todra

Turning off the N10 for about 1 km (0.6 miles) before Tinerhir brings you approximately 15 km (9 miles) up the winding S6902 to the narrowest point of the Gorges du Todra. Numerous villages and campsites line the road, and there are always amazing panoramic views of the Todra River valley, which originates in the High Atlas. After 15 km (9 miles) you can only continue by foot. The Todra must be repeatedly crossed on artificial fords. The nearly vertical rock faces stretch to the sky on your left and right.

Top: Gorges du Todra.
Bottom: Gorges du Dadès.

Not quite so dramatic is the Gorges du Dadès, which you approach from Boumalne Dadès (S6901 turn-off from the N10 approximately 1 km/0.6 miles after Boumalne Dadès). The access road passes eroded granite sculptures and wide open rock formations. After approximately 10 km (6 miles), the route passes the two impressive kasbahs of Aït Yul and Aït Arbi. Passing by other Kasbahs and villages, it continues on to Aït Oudimar (28 km). This is where the narrowest part of the gorge with steep rock faces starts. The asphalt road ends here after 30 km (18 miles), and you can explore the gorge on foot, returning on the same road.

city in southern Morocco, the legendary Sijilmassa, are disappointing. 100,000 people lived and traded goods here from the 11th to 15th centuries, acquiring caravans from the sub-Saharan African kingdoms of the south. Only a few mud walls have been preserved underneath the desert sand.
From Rissani, you can also make a detour to the sand dunes of Erg Chebbi near Merzouga. Otherwise, return to Ar-Rachidia on the same route through Erfoud and travel west on the N10.

⓬ Tinerhir The majestic range of the High Atlas accompanies the route in the north, while a grey-brown plain sprawls out to the south. You will then see what looks like an oversized molehill. These are the entry craters of the ancient 'foggaras' underground irrigation system. In the canals, water from the High Atlas is channelled into the arid foreland to irrigate the fields. The system must be serviced regularly and cleared of stones and refuse – a dangerous task that is usually carried out by the unlucky descendants of former slaves.
At the mouth of the Gorges du Todra, at 1,342 m (4,403 ft), Tinerhir, the 19th-century kasbah, keeps watch over the town with its old mud houses around

the rosé-coloured minaret of the mosque. The deep-green oasis gardens sprawl around the town, pomegranates, tomatoes, carrots and clover growing in the shade of the palm trees to feed the livestock.
Following the southern edge of the High Atlas, the route continues west to Boumalne Dadès, 53 km (33 miles) away. In the south, the Djebel Sarhro mountain range now draws near. You'll begin to see more and

more mud kasbahs, constructed for the safety of the trade routes and to guard the oases. At the turn of the 20th century, the infamous Pasha of Marrakech, El-Glaoui, built these kasbahs to safeguard his domain and station his loyal troops.

⓭ Boumalne Dadès This oasis at 1,586 m (5,203 ft) is also tucked into the opening of a deep mountain gorge formed by the Dadès. It accompanies the

road from Boumalne to Ouarzazate. The Dadès Valley is also called the Route of the Kasbahs because of its many mud castles. The small market town is made up of several tighremt, Berber family castles built from mud and guarded by four towers, over which the well-fortified kasbah kept watch from high on the plateau. Some tighremt are still inhabited.
Fruit and olive trees as well as vegetables grow in the oasis

15 Ouarzazate Shortly before reaching Ouarzazate, 'The Door of the Desert' (1,160 m/3,800 ft), the waters of the Barrage El Mansour Eddahbi glimmer like a mirage in the otherwise bleak landscape. The golf course, with its deep-green lawn alongside the dam, is an equally unusual sight.

You then reach the Taourirt kasbah, one of Morocco's largest mud settlements and a small city in itself. The mud walls conceal numerous dwellings as well as the palace of Pasha El-Glaoui, where two rooms are open to the public.

Ouarzazate itself is a modern city without any charm as such, but it is an important stopping point thanks to its excellent offering of hotels and restaurants. It owes its nickname of the

The Valley of the Roses

Damascene roses are the most important industry for oasis farmers in El Kelaa M'Gouna. They are the source of extremely valuable rose oil, which is used to make perfume and exported predominantly to Paris. A separate process extracts rose water, which plays a vital role in Moroccan cuisine and cosmetics. Following the annual

Dog roses are also used to border beds in the oasis gardens.

rose harvest in May, a big party is held in El Kelaa M'Gouna.

From El Kelaa M'Gouna, an easily navigated track follows the Assif M'Goun river valley into the mountains. Passing a fascinating series of abandoned kasbahs, you eventually arrive at Tourbist after 18 km (11 miles), an oasis consisting of several abandoned tighremt situated picturesquely on a bend in the river.

---

gardens but palm trees are rarely seen at these heights. Boumalne Dadès is the starting point for day trips to the Gorges du Dadès and the Djebel Sarhro. This high desert mountain range is home to Bedouin folk who roam between the mountains and river oases of the Dadès and the Drâa with goats and camels. Kasbahs and ksars (villages) line the road west to El Kelaa M'Gouna just 24 km (15 miles) away.

14 El Kelaa M'Gouna Just 10,000 people live in this settlement at an altitude of 1,467 m (4,813 ft). They farm the oasis gardens whose most valuable asset is the Damascene Rose (see sidebar at right). El Kelaa M'Gouna is also under the watchful eye of an old kasbah originally built by El-Glaoui to control trade routes. Like other towns along this route, there is also a river here, the Assif M'Goun, that comes down from

the High Atlas Mountains and flows into the Dadès River.

On the 94-km (58-mile) stretch heading toward Ouarzazate, the road is bordered by the High Atlas in the north and the Djebel Sarhro in the south. A series of kasbahs, sometimes in the midst of green palms and other times on stark mountain ledges, once again provides photo opportunities. Of particular interest is the oasis of Skoura with its reddish-brown mud castles.

1 Mud kasbahs and ksars side by side in the Dadès Valley.

2 Markets are held every Wednesday at the large square n Boumalne Dadès.

3 The Route of the Kasbahs, an important caravan route on the western edge of the Sahara.

4 The Drâa River's narrow gorge in the Djebel Sarhro at the southern edge of the High Atlas.

Detour

Drâa Valley

At Ouarzazate, the well-built N9 turns towards the south-east, first crossing a stark pre-desert landscape and finally meandering up the slopes of the Djebel Sarhro to the Tizi-n-Tinififft pass at 1,680 m (5,512 ft). Here you can catch your first glimpse of the verdant Drâa Valley. The road then winds its way back down through the wild craggy highlands.

About 70 km (43 miles) further on, you reach Agdz at the foot of the 1,531-m-high (5,023-ft) Djebel Kissane. This lively market town is the beginning of the river oasis along the Oued Drâa before you reach Mhamid 200 km (124 miles) away. Fields, palm groves, and fruit and olive tree plantations line the river. Even here, the well-fortified kasbahs oversee the villages.

Roughly 4 km (2.5 miles) further on from Agdz, a detour takes you over the river to the Tamnougalt kasbah and the village below it with its mud castles. Back on the N9, you follow the river until reaching Agdz Zagora 96 km (60 miles) away.

Top: A kasbah in the Drâa Valley.
Bottom: Oasis in the Drâa Valley.

Surrounded by the desert mountains of the Djebel Zagora, Zagora is a historically significant stop – It takes fifty-two days for a caravan to reach Timbuktu from here, as a road sign proudly points out. Zagora was an important trading and caravan town for goods from that once legendary city. About 18 km (11 miles) south-east on the N9 takes you to Zaouya Tamegroute, the religious centre of an Islamic brotherhood founded in the 16th century.

'Hollywood of Morocco' to the local film studios that have produced numerous international films in the south of this picturesque country.

The N9 leaves the city to the north-west towards Marrakech. Some 26 km (16 miles) out of Ouarzazate a sign points you to the ksar Aït Ben Haddou.

16 Aït Ben Haddou The 9-km (5.5-mile) access road here ends at one of Morocco's most beautiful vista points looking out over a rocky plateau – the silvery gleaming Asif Mellah River snakes through the valley below while mud castles and storehouses of the ksar on the other side of the valley are piled on top of each other like honeycomb on the hillside. Above it all are the ruins of the kasbah. Cinema-goers will recognize the landscape here. In addition to David Lean's *Lawrence of Arabia* and Orson Welles' *Sodom and Gomorra*, a good many other movies have been filmed here. At high tide, mule herders guide tourists over the river, while at low tide it is possible to cross on foot.

Strolling through the narrow alleys of the ksar, in parts lined with palm trunks, you'll see facades decorated with delightful geometric patterns and artis-

tic palaces at the entrance towers, but also clear traces of decay. Restoration of the castles and granaries is progressing only very slowly due to complicated land tenures.

From Aït Ben Haddou, a rugged track that is only navigable with off-road vehicles leads through spectacular scenery to Telouèt, parts of the road following the Asif Mellah River and traversing dramatic mountain passes along the way. You reach the town

more easily by going back down the N9 and following it into the mountainous region of the High Atlas. The slopes are stony and stark, but in the valleys green terraced fields line the mountain streams and dark-brown mud houses cling to the hillside. In contrast to the tighremt in the Dadès Valley, the houses here are basic and almost bare.

After 65 km (40 miles) of sometimes narrow serpentine roads, you climb 2,280 m (7,480 ft) to

the Tizi-n'Tichka pass. Just 2 km (1 mile) further on, the route branches off towards Telouèt.

17 Telouèt The journey now leads to one of Morocco's most unique kasbahs 20 km (12 miles) down the road. Telouèt was the headquarters of the Glaoua, a powerful subgroup of the Atlas Berbers that controlled much of the southern part of Morocco. Their most famous patriarch, El-Glaoui, also the

Souks

Most Europeans associate the Persian word 'bazaar' with the market area of an Arabian city. In Morocco, this area is called a souk, the Arabic word for market. Morocco's largest souk is found in the royal city of Marrakech. The alleyways are protected from the sun by straw mats or brick arches. In some of the souks, or sellers' alleys, dealers and artisans offer their goods separately according to their trade. Here you find the realm of the goldsmiths and the alleyways of the ceramic sellers gleaming in all the colours of the rainbow. The tailors' souk is filled with the sound of sewing machines.

The Rahba Khedima souk whisks you into the magical world of herbs and esoteric remedies, and carpets are auctioned in the area known as Criée

Morocco. The fields have abundant crops, and early vegetables are grown in the many greenhouses. It becomes clear now that Marrakech is approaching as greater signs of settlement appear and traffic becomes increasingly chaotic.

The clay walls of the 'Red City' can be seen from afar. The N9 opens out into the multi-lane Route des Remparts, which forms a ring road that almost completely encircles Marrakech.

19 Marrakech (see p. 238) The N10 heads south through Asni over a pass in the High Atlas that initially leads through green promontory landscape before finally entering an increasingly sparse mountain region.

20 Tizi-n'Test After approximately 100 km (62 miles) it is

Top: Two women examine the vast range of carpets on offer.
Middle: Market hustle and bustle is also apparent at the Djemma el Fna.
Bottom: Sheltered market alleys invite you to wander around.

Berbère. It is virtually impossible to navigate your way with any purpose through the labyrinth of busy alleys. It is better just to let yourself be led by them.

Pasha of Marrakech, had the former family home converted into a magnificent mud castle but it has been falling to ruin since his death in 1956. Inside, valuable wooden inlays on doors and ceilings, as well as stucco ornaments on the walls, are exposed to the elements without any form of protection. Storks nest in the spires. El-Glaoui was opposed to King Mohammed V and had made an agreement with the French. As

a result, his property was abandoned by the state.
Back on the main route N9 it's another 20 km (12 miles) to the market town of Taddert.

18 Taddert You must drive very carefully here, as children selling minerals and fossils often jump out into the road suddenly to stop passing cars. Taddert is famous for its grill restaurants and takeaway food stores, where you can take a break and

still enjoy the panoramic views of the High Atlas.
Around this striking valley, the peaks of the High Atlas reach 4,000 m (13,124 ft) and even in summer the weather is pleasant and cool. The N9 then winds its way down again, passing pine plantations that are an attempt by the state to reforest the eroded hillsides.
After just 40 km (25 miles) you will arrive at the Haouz plain, one of the most fertile areas of

1 The peaks of the High Atlas are covered with snow until spring.

2 Seemingly calm dealers haggle over the most valuable objects at the carpet bazaar auctions in Marrakech.

3 At the end of the 16th century, artisans displayed their fantastic artistic skills at the Saadier graves in Marrakech.

Marrakech

Some 750,000 people live in Marrakech, 'Pearl of the South'. This vibrant city is surrounded by palm groves and gardens and bordered by the often snow-capped peaks of the High Atlas mountains. With its colourful souks, time-honoured mosques, ornate mausoleums, magnificent palaces and lively night-time bustle on the Djemma el Fna, the almost 1,000-year-old city attracts tourists and locals alike.

Marrakech was founded in 1062 by the Almoravids, a strictly orthodox dynasty with a strong connection to the origins of Islam. In 1126–27, it became the capital of the Almoravid Kingdom.

In the centuries that followed, Marrakech was constantly competing with Fez for the seat of the Sultan. Ultimately, trans-Saharan trade restored Marrakech to its former prosperity and French colonization in the 20th century further shaped the city.

Architectural highlights include the 12th-century Koutoubia Mosque and the magnificent 16th-century mausoleum of the Saadier, with its marble floors and numerous gravestones decorated with calligraphy. Similar in opulence is the 14th-century Medersa Ben Youssef in the medina. The city wall, built of clay bricks, is another

unique monument interspersed with lavishly decorated gates.

You can take a worthwhile and relaxing excursion around the 'Remparts' and a detour to the Jardins Majorelle by calèche, or carriage. The villa and garden of the artist Majorelle form a perfect scene of varying blue and green hues.

Apart from wandering your way through Morocco's largest souks, the undisputed highlight of Marrakech is a visit to the Djemma el Fna, the city's main square and one that is used by both tourists and locals alike.

Amid the bustling food and drinks stalls, the square transforms into a street performers' stage when the sun sets. The nightly shows include acrobats, story-tellers, Chleuh dancing boys, magicians, snake charmers and even traditional medicine peddlers.

The 77-m-high (252-ft) square minaret of the 12th-century Koutoubia mosque is one of the landmarks of Marrakech.

One of the city gates worth seeing in Marrakech is the Bab Aguenaou with its opulent stone relief decoration.

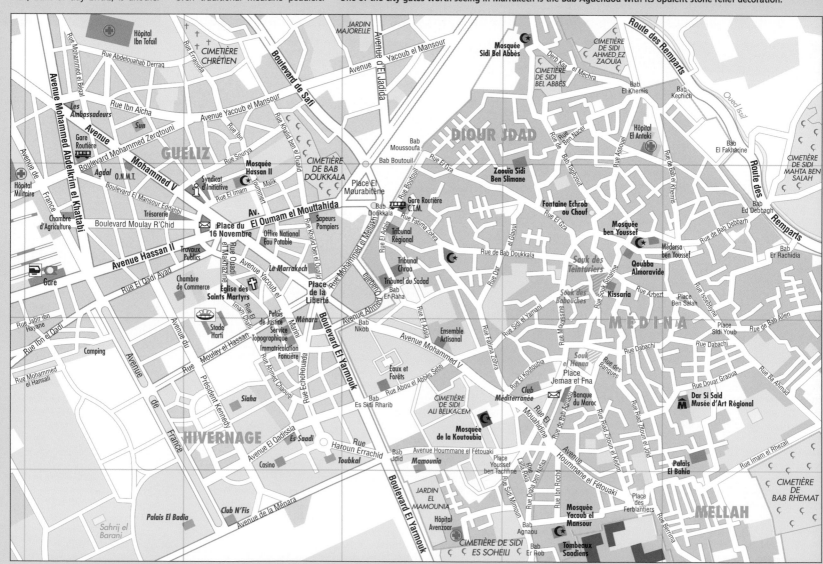

worth stopping at the 12th-century Almohada mosque, Tin Mal. The almost square building, with four corner towers and a crenellation, is more reminiscent of a fortress than a place of worship. Shortly after that begins the steepest and most winding part of the route to the 2,093-m (6,867-ft) Tizi-n'Test Pass, which you have completed after 35 km (22 miles) before arching back towards the valley. The views of the mountains are amazing. You reach Taroudannt after a total of 230 km (143 miles).

㉑ Taroudannt 'Marrakech's younger sister' is completely surrounded by a mud wall with storks nesting on the pinnacles. In the medina it is worth visiting the Place Assarag where Berbers from the surrounding region hold a market on Thursdays and Sundays. This is the start of the maze of souks, which all still have a very original feel. In Taroudannt you'll have the opportunity to stay in one of the most beautiful hotels in Morocco, the 'Salam'.
Leaving the city heading west on the N10, the route now crosses Morocco's most important agri-

cultural region, the Souss plain. In Aït Melloui, just before reaching the spa resort of Agadir, you turn off onto the P509 and head south-east towards Biougra.
In a steady climb, the route crosses the quilt-like mountain landscape of the Anti-Atlas where prickly pears and argania spinosa are the main vegetation, along with the odd almond tree. Storage chambers of the Chleuh Berbers, so-called Agadire, sit on top of table plateaus above the villages.
After 160 km (99 miles), the pinkish houses of Tafraoute come into view, sprawled out in a gorgeous mountain valley.

㉒ Tafraoute Some 1,000 m (3,300 ft) up, and surrounded by a palm oasis, Tafraoute is the main hub of the Ammeln, a subgroup of the Chleuh. From here, it is possible to make detours on foot or by car to villages such as Oumesnat (get back on the P509 heading north, then turn left after 6 km/4 miles), where one of the region's traditional stone houses is open to interested visitors as a museum. Approximately 3 km (2 miles) south

on the S7146 gravel road you then come to a valley full of strangely eroded granite with an array of rock drawings. From Tafraoute the asphalt S7074 heads up and over the 1,200-m-high (3,936-ft) Col du Kerdous into another valley to Tiznit about 114 km (72 miles) away.

㉓ Tiznit This city of silversmiths initially disappoints with its modern outskirts, but a lively souk atmosphere reigns around the Place Mechouar. The Tiznit silversmiths are famous for the quality of their work. They make jewellery as well as traditional dagger accessories.

Your route now heads north, and another 90 km (56 miles) on the N1 takes you through flat, stark terrain until you reach the town of Agadir.

㉔ Agadir This spa resort was rebuilt after a devastating earthquake in 1960. The modern city, located on a wide sandy beach lined with hotels, is a pleasant place to stop before taking the

1 Aday, one of the Ammeln villages in the vicinity of Tafraoute.

2 Agadir Tasguent, a storage chamber in the Anti-Atlas.

Detour

A camel ride through the desert

Tour operators in southern Morocco offer an extraordinary adventure – camel treks with the Tuareg. The 'Blue Men', as they are also known because of their indigo-blue robes, lead their guests through the amazing landscape of the north-western Sahara on their classic mode of desert transport.
They explain the flora and fauna and the old customs and practices of the Tuareg people. In the evening, tents are pitched and food cooked over a bonfire.

The Tuareg, legendary caravan leaders, now use their skills to serve tourists.

Hassan II Mosque

In 1993, King Hassan II dedicated the country's largest mosque in Casablanca to himself. It was built on an artificial platform over the sea and appears to float on the water. More than 3,000 builders from all over the country decorated the mosque in traditional style

'And Allah's throne rests on the water' (Sure 11.7) – Hassan II Mosque in Casablanca.

with majolica mosaics, stucco, the finest inlays and dark cedar-wood carvings.
The prayer room holds 25,000 worshippers, and another 80,000 can pray on the forecourt in the shadow of the 200-m-high (656-ft) minaret. A laser beam from the top of this minaret points to Mecca day and night for correct worship. The Hassan II Mosque is the only place of worship in Morocco where non-Muslims are allowed to visit (daily except Fridays).

N1 coastal road and heading north to Essaouira.
It winds its way along a dramatic, steeply sloping coastline and is bordered with argania groves with a particular attraction – goats climbing to the tops of the trees to nibble at the leaves.

25 Essaouira This harbour city, with its stout walls and the Scala Fortress, has a slightly Portuguese flavour to it, but it was founded in 1760 by the Sultan Mohammed Ben Abdallah and is a UNESCO World Heritage Site. Fishmongers at the harbour, the souk where beautiful thuja-wood furniture is sold, and the many art galleries with their dreamy images of the Gnaoua make the city an extremely popular destination for individual travellers.
The N8 heads inland for a while through argania groves before branching off on the N1 to the intersection with Highway 204, which then continues west and ends in Safi (148 km/92 miles).

26 Safi This harbour city is famous for pottery. North-east of the old city, factories and shops are grouped opposite the Bab Chaaba on 'potters' hill'. Safi's blue-glazed ceramics are in high demand. Heading further north on the narrow but spec-

tacular P121 coastal road you will pass Oualidia, where the Atlantic forms a peaceful lagoon behind a sand bar that is ideal for bathing. About 144 km (89 miles) on, the brilliant white walls of El-Jadida come into view.

27 El-Jadida Behind the fully preserved city wall with numerous bastions lies a lovely medina, whose main attraction is the Portuguese cistern, a water reservoir covered by groined vaults. Only 16 km (10 miles) north is another harbour town of particular charm, Azemmour. Here it's worth visiting the Tuesday market. From there it's another 100 m (62 miles) along the coastal road to Casablanca.

28 Casablanca This metropolis of 3 million people is particularly

worth a stop to take a look at the Hassan II Mosque and the neo-Moorish centre, which originates from the French colonial era. It is not advisable to visit the ruins of the medina.
The route continues for 95 km (59 miles) along a lovely coastline through the popular resorts of Mohammedia and Skhirat Plage, ending at the nation's capital, Rabat.

29 Rabat (see sidebar right). From Rabat, the N1 heads north through Ksar-el-Kebir on its way to Larache.

30 Larache The French poet, Jean Genet, is buried in the cemetery of this small, picturesque harbour town.
The excavation site of the Roman Lixus with an amphitheatre and the ruins of the

ancient fish-processing factory lies 4 km (2.5 miles) further north. Tangiers is another 87 km (54 miles) on the N1 along the Atlantic coast, beyond the small town of Asilah founded in the 15th century. After 84 km (52 miles), it's worth taking a detour of about 9 km (5.5 miles) to Cap Spartel, where the Atlantic meets the Mediterranean Sea, and to the Hercules Grottoes where you get an exceptional view of the sea from a natural crevice shaped like the African continent.

1 The metropolis of Casablanca has numerous colonial buildings that are worth seeing.

2 Essaouira, the 'White City' on the sea, was previously an artist colony and is today a popular tourist destination on the Atlantic coast.

Océan
Atlantique

MÉDINA
DE SALÉ

Bab
Sebta

Bab
Malka

MELLAH

Bab
Bou Haja

Hôtel de Ville

Bab
El Mellah

Bab
Er Rih

Avenue de Plage

Qasbah
des Oudaias

CIMETIÈRE

MUSULMAN

Prison

M Musée

Oued Bou Regreg

Pont
Hassan II

Place
Sidi
Makhlout

Boulevard la Alou

Rue Tariq al Marsa

MEDINA
DE RABAT

Place
Ach
Chouada

Bab
La Alou

Grande
Mosquée

Hassan II

Farah Sofitel

Boulevard Arrahah

OCÉAN

Mosquée
Moulay Sliman

Bab
El Mellah

Douanes

Tour
Hassan

Boulevard du Bou Regreg

Église
St. Joseph

Place
d'Angleterre

Gare
Routière

Bab
Chellah

Boulevard

Mausolée de
Mohammed V

Mosquée
de l'Océan

Bab
al Had

JARDIN
TRIANGLE DE VUE

Place
Melilya

Boulevard Soomat Hassan

Place
de Russia

Avenue Hassan II

Hôtel
des Postes

Théâtre Nat.
Mohammed V

Syndicat
d'Initiative

DIOUR
JAMAA

Rue Jean Jaurès

Université

Parlement

Place de
Ville

Perception
Oudaias

Place de la
Cathédrale

Place
de l'Unité
Africaine

Rue
Al Jazaïr

Place
Abraham
Lincoln

LES
ORANGERS

Gare Centrale D'Orsay
Terminus

Cathédrale
St. Pierre

Place
Moulay
Al Hassan

O.N.M.T.

QUARTIER
DES
AMBASSADES

Mosquée
Diour Jamaâ

Hassan II

Hassan d'Annaba

Chellah

Musée
Archéologique

M

Boulevard Tariq Ibn Ziyad

Place
Bab Tamesna

Avenue Moulay

Bab
er Rouah

Place
An Nasr

Mosquée
As Souna

Irésorerie

QUARTIER
DES
MINISTÈRES

JARDIN

Avenue An Nasr

Faculté
des Lettres

Palais
de Justice

Min. des Eaux
et Forêts

Place
Zerqtouni

D'ESSAIS

Stade

Bibliothèque

TOUARGA

Ministère du
Tourisme

Gare
Routière

Avenue Yacoub el Mansour

Faculté
des Sciences

Institut
Scientifique

MÉCHOUAR

Mosquée
Ahli-Fès

Chellah

Institut
d'Hygiène

Salle
Olympique

Place
Ibn Zohr

Palais
Royal

Bab
Zaers

CIMETIÈRE
MUSULMAN

École
Mahammedia

Faculté
de Droit

de l'U.N.E.S.C.O.

AGDAL

Cité
Universitaire

Avenue John Kennedy

Blvd. Moussa Ibn Noussaïr

CITÉ
KHALIFA

CITÉ
MILITAIRE

Rabat

Along with the twin city of Salé, Morocco's capital has more than 1.5 million inhabitants, yet it is a pleasant experience thanks to the elegant villa neighbourhoods.

In the 12th century, Rabat became the Ribat el Ftah Fortress under the Almohada rule. Buccaneers later settled there and the pirate 'republic' of Rabat-Salé spread terror on the high seas between the 17th and 19th centuries.

In 1956, Rabat became the capital of independent Morocco. The historic heart of the city is the Oudaïa, a kasbah on a bank above the Bou Regreg River. The 12th-century Bab des Oudaï, decorated with magnificent stone masonry, leads to a maze of partly vaulted alleys ending at the 'platform', with a view over neighbouring Salé. East of the kasbah are the 200 pillar bases and the minaret of the Hassan Mosque designed by Yacoub el-Mansour, which was ultimately left incomplete after the death of the sultan in 1199. The charming minaret is often compared to the Giralda in Seville. Opposite this is the neo-Moorish mausoleum of Kings Mohammed V and Hassan II built, in 1967. The royal quarter around the Dar el Makhzen palace is not accessible to tourists.

Top: The Kings Mausoleum in Rabat.
Bottom: The pillars of the incomplete 12th-century Hassan Mosque.

The archaeological museum with the most beautiful finds from the Moroccan excavation sites is well worth a visit. The Marinid necropolis of Chellah south-east of Rabat also makes for an interesting detour. The ruins of a Zaouya (Koran school) and several sultans' graves are a picturesque sight indeed.

El-Jadida The white city walls of this Atlantic coast town were only built in the 19th century. The medina houses a Portuguese cistern with tapering Gothic arches where Orson Welles once filmed scenes from his epic film version of *Othello*.

Rabat The Moroccan capital, with 1.7 million inhabitants, has a picturesque location at the mouth of the Bou Regreg River. The Oudaï kasbah forms the foundation of the royal city.

Tangier This harbour city on the Strait of Gibraltar was once the meeting place for Bohemians. The atmosphere of that time can be somewhat relived over a glass of mint tea at one of the many cafés.

Safi At the edge of the medina, potters manufacture ceramics typical of the region in their traditional workshops. The old harbour city of Safi, guarded by a formidable kasbah, has so far barely been touched by tourists.

Essaouira Although this fishing town appears more Portuguese than Moroccan, it was in fact founded by Arab peoples. Its special atmosphere is adored by alternative lifestyle enthusiasts and artists. The traditional hypnosis rituals of the local Gnaoua, the descendants of black African slaves, are famous here.

Casablanca This metropolis of over 3 million people is home to an awe-inspiring place of worship in honour of Allah and the kings. With capacity for 12,000 people, the Hassan II Mosque is the largest in the Maghreb.

Marrakech The 'red' royal city is surrounded by lush oasis gardens. In the labyrinthine medina, souks entice would-be buyers with their Oriental scents and colours. Every evening in the Djemma el Fna, the street performers' square, people gather to watch acrobats and snake charmers.

Agadir After a devastating earthquake in 1960 destroyed this Atlantic Berber settlement, only the kasbah on the hill remained unscathed. After this, the city was rebuilt. Today, Agadir is primarily known as a spa and holiday resort. Countless hotels, restaurants and a kilometre-long (0.6-mile) sandy beach provide ideal conditions for days of rest and relaxation.

Ouarzazate This kasbah in Taourirt, on the outskirts of the garrison city, once belonged to the mighty Pasha El-Glaoui.

Aït Ben Haddou This UNESCO-protected ksar is at risk of falling into ruin. The former inhabitants abandoned the old mud castle and live in a modern village opposite. The walled city has been a set for films.

Tafraoute Many houses in this oasis city are pink like the granite rock of the Ammeln Valley. Morocco's best almonds thrive in this valley.

Drâa Valley A sea of palms, ordered fields, oasis villages and kasbahs line the Drâa on its way through the arid south. In earlier times, the mud city of Zagora was the starting point for caravans making the 52-day trans-Sahara trade journeys to the legendary city of Timbuktu. The Drâa originally flowed out into the Atlantic, but today it barely makes it to Mhamid in the Sahara.

High Atlas These mountains between the Middle Atlas and the Anti-Atlas form the border between fertile Morocco and the desert. The highest peak is the Toubkal at 4,167 m (13,672 ft).

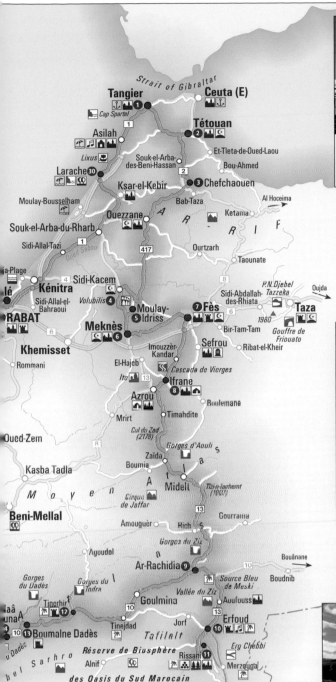

Tétouan Morocco's Spanish legacy becomes evident in the Ville Nouvelle of this Rif mountain town. This is the Place Hassan II. The Moorish tradition is reflected in the medina with its vaulted alleyways.

Chefchaouen This picturesque Rif town, surrounded by mountains reaching 2,000 m (6,562 ft) in height, is a popular summer resort. Rif countrywomen in colourful dress come to the market on Mondays and Thursdays.

Volubilis Between AD 42 and 285, Volubilis was the capital of the Roman province of Mauretania Tingitana. The ruins of the basilica, Capitol Temple, the triumphal arch and the villas with their filigree mosaic floors tower over the fertile landscape of northern Morocco.

Moulay Idriss The founder of the Idriss dynasty is entombed in the holy city named after him. Fleeing the 'fhousand and one nights' sultan, Harun al-Rashid, he sought refuge in Morocco where he was made leader by the Berbers. His son founded the royal city of Fez.

Rissani Water and date palms in the Tafilalt oasis near Rissani ensure survival in the desert.

Meknès The builder of Meknès, Sultan Moulay Ismail, had a fondness for monuments that is reflected in the mighty gates and palaces as well as in the ruler's luxurious tomb complex.

Fez The royal city's medina is a unique work of art, with plenty of Moorish architecture and lively souks. The finest leather is dyed by hand in the tannery pools shown here.

Merzouga The Great Western Erg near Merzouga is a unique sand dune landscape.

Gorges du Ziz At first glance, the southern edge of the High Atlas appears arid and desolate, but in the mud-walled villages along the Ziz Gorge, farmers grow myriad crops near the river.

Vallée du Todra The Todra weaves its way through steep rock faces from the High Atlas down into the Dadès Valley where thousands of palm trees line its banks. The cool gorge is a popular destination for rock climbers and hikers.

Skoura A whole row of well-fortified, ancient-looking kasbahs with decorative brick patterns on their corner towers create a striking contrast to Skoura's other spectacle, its sea of lush palm trees.

Gorges du Dadès In the deep gorges not far from the 'Route of the Kasbahs', farmers make use of every square metre of fertile land. Tomatoes, alfalfa and sorghum are grown on plots of all sizes.

Tinerhir Numerous kasbahs watch over the oasis gardens of Tinerhir at the mouth of the Gorges du Todra in the Dadès Valley. The old trade route passing through here was host not only to caravans, but also to war tribes, against whom the oasis farmers had to defend themselves.

Route 19

Egypt
A journey through the Kingdom of the Pharaohs

The pyramids of Giza are the only ancient wonder of the world still standing today.

The pyramids of Giza are the most powerful emblem of ancient Egypt. The pharaohs who built them instilled the fabulous structures with dreams of immortality. Egypt's cultural legacy was also influenced by Christianity and Islam. In the desert, time-honoured monasteries are evidence of the religious zeal of the Copts, who are still very much alive today. The various Muslim dynasties gave Cairo its numerous mosques.

Egypt gives visitors an insight into an exotic realm situated at the crossroads of African, Asian and European civilizations, and which is indeed an intersection of myriad cultures. Obviously the monumental tombs and temples are still a subject of fascination today, but their mysterious hieroglyphics and ancients scripts also captivate our curiosities.

The ancient societies of Egypt and the pharaohs began over 5,000 years ago. Most of the monuments from the time of

the pharaohs run along the Nile. Along with the pulsating metropolis of Cairo, the 300-km (186-mile) stretch between Luxor and Aswan offers history buffs a multitude of impressive sights. Luxor's attractions include the Valley of the Kings, the tremendous temple complex of Karnak and the funerary temple of the female pharaoh Hatshepsut.

Further south, the temples of Edfu and Kôm Ombo are evidence of the fact that even the Greek and Roman conquerors of

The golden mask of young King Tutankhamun.

Egypt succumbed to a fascination with the Pharaonic culture. Near Aswan, history and the modern world collide. The construction of the Aswan Dam meant the old temples were at risk of being submerged. It was only at great expense that they were relocated in the 1960s. The most famous example of this act of international preservation is the two rock temples of Abu Simbel.

Over 95 per cent of Egypt's total surface area is desert that covers more than one million sq km (386,000 sq mi). Only very few of the 75 million inhabitants earn their living in the oases of the western deserts, on the shores of the Red Sea or on Mount Sinai. The vast majority of the population live close together in the Nile valley. As early as the 5th century BC the Greek historian Herodotus wrote that 'Egypt is a gift of the Nile'.

The four colossal figures of Pharaoh Ramses II tower 20 m (65.5 ft) before the facade of the rock temple of Abu Simbel.

The long avenue of ram's-headed sphinxes in front of the temple of the god Amun in Luxor is particularly impressive at dusk.

The hot climate and the Nile's summer floods, which are nowadays controlled by the Aswan Dam, mean that farmers harvest two to four times a year depending on the crop being cultivated. This enables production of the country's basic food supply despite a rapidly increasing population.

In ancient times the Nile delta in the north of Egypt consisted of five branches bringing fertile alluvial soil with the ever plentiful waters. However, over the course of thousands of years the landscape has changed drastically. Today there are only two remaining branches that stretch from the north of Cairo through Lower Egypt to the Mediterranean Sea and water traffic on the river is now divided up with the help of an extensive canal network.

The Nile delta, which covers an area of 24,000 sq km (9,264 sq mi), is Egypt's most important agricultural region producing everything from corn, vegetables and fruit to the famous Egyptian long-fibre cotton. In the 19th century, Alexandria benefited enormously from this 'white gold' and developed into a modern, Mediterranean port city.

Cairo is located at the southern tip of the delta and connects Upper and Lower Egypt. The nation's capital dazzles visitors with the most diverse of sights. The pyramids in Giza in the west tower above the modern city. In the city centre minarets, church towers and high-rise buildings vie for the attention of worshippers as Christians and Muslims make their way to prayers. Meanwhile, people of all backgrounds and nationalities stroll along the Nile in this, the 'Mother of the World' as locals have come to call their rich city.

The minarets of Cairo silhouetted in a glowing red-gold sunset.

The Copts

Egypt's Christians have been known as Copts since the 7th century. This term originally applied to all people living in Egypt. Following Islamic expansion, it was restricted to just the Christians living in the Nile Valley.

Christianity gained ground in Alexandria as early as the 1st century, from where it quickly spread throughout the country over the following decades. Heavy persecution by the Roman Emperor in the 3rd century led to thousands of people being tortured and killed because of their belief. The calendar of the Coptic Church reflects the particularly cruel persecution of Christians under Diocletian – his accession to power in AD 284 corresponds to the year 0, the Anno Martyrii.

Top: The Coptic monastery in the Wadi el-Natrun.
Bottom: Coptic monks celebrate Christmas.

Not more than 200 years later there were conflicts between Christians that led to the persecution of Egyptian Christians and finally, in AD 451, the separation of the Coptic Church. Even today, Copts do not recognize Rome's pope as their figurehead, but rather follow their own patriarch, who is the successor of the apostle, Mark.

The Copts make up 8 to 14 per cent of Egypt's population, which is itself a hotly disputed number – because of this percentage figure, Copts are entitled to jobs in the public sector, up to and including ministerial positions.

From the Mediterranean to the 'Nubian Sea', Egypt is home to a plethora of sites that are loaded with history. You'll experience both ancient and modern worlds throughout the approximately 1,400-km (870-mile) journey and the route follows large stretches of the country's oldest traffic route, the Nile. The trip only branches off into the desert between Alexandria and Cairo.

1 Alexandria Alexander the Great, after whom this town was named, founded Alexandria in 332 BC. Home to the Ptolemaic Dynasty (323–330 BC), it became the capital of Egypt and gained a great reputation as a centre of scholarship and the sciences. The Temple of Serapi, the famous library and the lighthouse were the icons of the city.

However, after being conquered by the Romans its monuments fell into decay and Alexandria only prospered again under the leadership of Mohammed Ali (1805–49). Fundamental city sanitation measures were introduced at the end of the 20th century and have restored the attractiveness of this important port city. Discoveries dating back to the time of Egypt's last ruler, Cleopatra, were recovered from the eastern port basin and made worldwide headlines.

With a population of close to five million, Alexandria is the country's second-largest city. Its beaches are very popular. Alexandria's eastern sprawl almost reaches the city of Rashid (Rosetta), where French esearchers discov-

ered the famous trilingual Rosetta Stone (now in the British Museum in London) at the end of the 19th century. This stone helped to decipher hieroglyphic scripts that had proved impossible to understand.

South-west of Alexandria you turn off coastal road 55 towards one of the most important early Christian pilgrim sites on the Mediterranean.

2 Abu Mena The martyr Mena was murdered in AD 296 under orders from the Roman emperor, Diocletian, and was buried here, some 50 km (31 miles) from Alexandria. Soon after that the well near his grave was said to possess healing powers. In the 5th century a large public bath was built that attracted tens of thousands of the faithful to its magical waters. The ruins of churches, monastery complexes and pilgrim quarters that were rediscovered in 1905 are now UNESCO World Heritage Sites, though they are severely threatened by rising ground-water levels. In 1959, the new monastery of Abu Mena was

Travel information

Route profile
Length: approx. 1,400 km (870 miles), excluding detours
Time required: 14–20 days
Start: Alexandria
End: Abu Simbel
Route (main locations): Alexandria, Cairo, El-Minia, Assiût, Luxor/Thebes West, Edfu, Aswan, Abu Simbel

Specifics: Special safety regulations apply for off-road journeys, and some stretches can only be driven with an accompanying convoy. Night journeys are to be strictly avoided.

Traffic information:
The speed limit for cars in built-up areas is 50 km/h (31 mph), and 100 km/h

(62 mph) on highways and rural roads. In the cities, Egyptian drivers take up the whole road but in rural areas be careful of forms of traffic such as donkeys, water buffalo or camels. Normally only parking lights are used at night. Oncoming cars briefly turn their headlights up to high beam. Always drive defensively!
Those entering and leaving in their own vehicle must be prepared for customs checks.

When to go:
October to May

General information:
www.egypt.com
www.ancientegypt.co.uk

Detour

The Suez Canal

It was a long-time dream of the Egyptians to connect the Mediterranean Sea with the Red Sea. The dream finally became a reality in the mid 19th century after attempts had already been made as far back as ancient times to integrate the Nile Valley into the trade route.

The first measurements made by Austrian engineer Alois von Negrelli confirmed that a direct waterway without locks between Port Said in the north and Suez in the south would be possible. It was Ferdinand de Lesseps who finally convinced Pasha Ismail to build the canal,

A cargo ship on the sluice-less Suez Canal.

which would shorten the trade routes between Europe and Asia by up to 85 per cent. The Compagnie Universelle du Canal de Suez was then founded in 1858.

Egypt wanted to secure the funds for the construction by selling shares. But due to a lack of interest in Europe, Egypt kept most of its shares and thus fell into enormous national debt. Nevertheless, after eleven years of construction Khedive Ismail held a lavish party to celebrate the opening of the canal in 1869 and state guests from all over the world were invited to Cairo.

Several years later Great Britain took over Egypt's shares. By 1878 it controlled the canal together with France who was still the principal owner of the canal project.

In 1956 President Nasser nationalized the Canal and paid a catastrophic price in the resulting Suez Crisis. Only in 1975 did the canal start bringing profit to Egypt. Every day several convoys with cargo ships carrying 150,000 tonnes (165,000 tons) travel in both directions along the 191 km (118.5 mile) waterway. Passage fees are one of the most important supports for the national budget.

ent looks, the city centre having shifted from the Nile to the citadel in the foothills of the Moqattam mountains and then back to the Nile.

Nowadays, the glass facades of hotels, government offices and shopping malls distinguish the modern heart of Cairo. Residential and office buildings twenty to thirty floors high loom large along the river where the property is most expensive.

Further on from the centre are the old quarters such as Heliopolis or Maadi, filled with elegent villas and green parks. Then there are the concrete jungles of closely packed residential areas for the rest of Cairo's locals. And at the base of the citadel sprawls the Islamic Old Town with its hundreds of mosques.

built. The highway-like desert road 11 takes you further south.

3 Wadi el-Natrun About 110 km (68 miles) south of Alexandria you'll come to a valley that is 22 m (72 ft) below sea level in the desert area west of the delta. Nitrate (sodium bicarbonate) extracted during the time of the pharaohs gave the valley its name, which means Nitrate Valley.

Surrounded by olive and date palm groves, four of the once more than fifty monasteries are still standing. In the 4th century,

hermits would gather around spiritual leaders like the holy Makarios forming what would be the first monasterial communities. The oldest of these monasteries, built in the 4th century, is the Deir el-Baramus in the north of the valley. The monks of the Deir Amba Bschoi and the Dei res-Suryan also accept non-Coptic guests.

Back on the desert road you'll pass Medînet es-Sadat, one of the planned cities built under the rule of President Anwar Sadat (1970–81). These satellite cities were built in circles in the

desert around Cairo. Industrial plants created jobs and kindergartens, schools, parks and leisure activities topped off the activities.

Taking the northern section of the ring road that circumvents most of Cairo's traffic will bring you to the Nile relatively quickly.

4 Cairo (see pp. 248–249). In Arabic, Egypt's capital is called Al-Qahira, 'The Victorious One'. It is home to some 20 million people and counting. Throughout its long history, the Egyptian metropolis has had many differ-

1 Alexandria stretches for miles along the Mediterranean coast.

2 In the year 1356, Emir Sarghatmish, Commander of the Mamluck army, erected his mosque next to the older courtyard mosque of Ibn Tulun in Cairo.

3 The Sultan Hassan Mosque in Cairo is a place of worship, mausoleum and educational site.

4 Some of Egypt's oldest monasteries are found in the Wadi el-Natrun – Nitrate Valley.

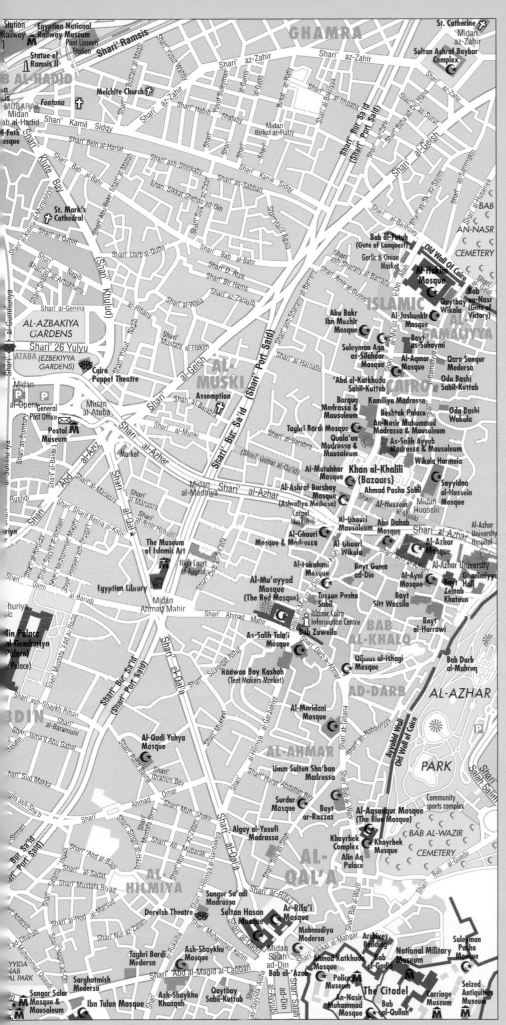

Cairo

The view from the citadel sweeps west over the minarets and the Nile to the silhouettes of the pyramids of Giza – if you're lucky. The Nile city is often hidden from view by the heavy, opaque cloud that floats above it. Humidity from the river, sandstorms from the encroaching desert and pollution from the congested traffic in the inner city are all part of the problem.

A Nilometer at the southern tip of Roda Island is testimony to the Egyptian capital's dignified age. Long before it was given the name of Cairo in the 10th century BC, priests serving ancient Egyptian gods set up wells all over the country to measure the level of the yearly Nile flood and then calculated taxes.

Opposite the island on the eastern bank was one of the country's most important inland ports, Per Hapi en Junu. When the Romans fortified the harbour, the early Christians made use of the well-protected area to build their first churches here. In the 'Candles Quarter' directly next to the Mari Girgis metro station, the Moallka Church, dedicated to the Virgin Mary,

of the most important institutions in the Islamic world. Bejewelled Islamic architecture was created between the city gates Bab el-Futuh and Bab en-Nasr in the north and Bab es-Suweila in the south.

Over a period of 600 years, Fatimids, Ajjubids, Mamlucks and Osmans had elegant mosques, palaces, commercial establishments, wells and schools built in Cairo. Salah ed-Din, who came to power in AD 1171, had his residence moved to the citadel, but Al-Qahira remained the lively centre of the city. Even today, visitors are still fascinated by the bustling bazaars of the Khan el-Khalili. City planners were again kept busy under Mohammed Ali's reign, who used Paris as a model to transform

Top: The skyline at dawn.
Middle: Cairo with the Nile.
Bottom: The muezzin calls the faithful to prayer at the Bussra Mosque.

rises high upon the foundations of the Roman fortress.

In the next neighbourhood is the Ben-Ezra Synagogue where the famous scholar Moses Maimonides presided in the 12th century. It is famed as the location where the pharaoh's daughter rescued the baby Moses from the Nile. Just a few hundred metres north of the synagogue, Africa's oldest mosque gleams after extensive renovations. Amr Ibn el-As had it built in the centre of the new capital, Fustat, in AD 642.

Almost 235 years later, Governor Ibn Tulun, appointed by the Abbasids, created an independent entity here on the Nile. His residence must have been magnificent. The enormous courtyard mosque (AD 876–879) is the only structure to have been preserved from this time and is still one of the largest mosques in the world, covering 2.5 ha (6.2 acres). New rulers arrived in Egypt ninety years later – the Fatimid shi'ites, who also needed their own new residence, of course. Surrounded by well-fortified walls they ensconced themselves in the palaces of Al-Qahira. Their Friday Mosque, el-Azhar, was built in AD 969 and is to this day one

Cairo into a modern metropolis in the 19th century. Art-nouveau facades between the Midan el-Opera and the Midan Talaat Harb are evocative of these times.

From here, it's just a stone's throw into modernity at the Midan et-Tahrir, where the first metro station was built, the Arab League has its headquarters and, at the northern end of the square, the treasures of the national museum take you back to the times of the pharaohs.

1

⑤ Giza The provincial capital of Giza is a close relative of Cairo located on the western bank of the Nile. The three great pyramids of the pharaohs Cheops, Chephren and Mykerinos stand regally on a limestone plateau over the city. The rulers had them constructed in the 3rd millennium BC as tombs to withstand the ages. The blocks piled on top of each other to create the tremendous mountain that is Cheops' pyramid weigh an average of 2 tonnes (2.2 tons) a piece. Even without the finely sanded coating they originally had, the pyramids are a majestic and awe-inspiring sight. They used to stand almost 147 m (482 ft) high, but they have shrunk over time by 10 m (33 ft).

In the Middle Ages, Cairo's master builders helped themselves to the almost endless quarry. Part of the coating has been preserved on the neighbouring pyramid of Chephren. Significantly smaller in size at just 65.5 m (215 ft) is the tomb of Mykerinos, which appears to have missed out on this detail and is humbled by the presence of its formidable neighbours.

The Sphinx lies to the east of these three monuments. Carved out of existing rocks at its loca-

tion, the Sphinx embodies the divine rising sun. A shrine built of blocks of rock soars before its paws. Directly next to it, Chephren had his valley temple constructed out of pink granite and alabaster.

⑥ Memphis The first capital of Egypt, its administrative headquarters, the largest garrison city, and the sacred place of the god Ptah – Memphis covered a lot of bases throughout the course of its long history. Today not much is left of this former cosmopolitan city.

Its palaces and residences of clay bricks have long been reclaimed by the earth and transformed into fertile farmland. The monumental figure of Ramses II and the alabaster sphinx are the only legacy of the city's former glory. They are housed in the open-air museum among palm groves near the small village of Mitrahina on the south-western edge of Giza.

⑦ Sakkara One of Egypt's largest cemeteries sprawls in the desert approximately 20 km (12 miles) south of Giza. Great tombs of kings were already being constructed here in the early civilizations of the

pharaohs. But this cemetery only gained in significance when the first pyramid was built under Djoser's reign (around 2750 BC). Its architect, Imhotep, invented the idea of using stone as a building material and laid the foundations for a tradition that now goes back three thousand years. The step pyramid subsequently attracted many other rulers and dignitaries who had their tombs

erected here. The tomb of Ti, with its illustration of the entombed man hunting in the papyrus coppice, is one of the largest and most beautiful private tombs from the Ancient Kingdom (2750–2195 BC).

Almost a thousand years later, General Haremhab had his 'Eternal House' constructed here before becoming pharaoh in 1320 BC and acquiring an even

more magnificent tomb in the Valley of the Kings.

Another 10 km (6 miles) further south the lane turns off toward the next field of pyramids.

⑧ Dahshûr Snofru was the father of the pharaoh Cheops who set up the 'Pyramid Experimentation Field'. In fact, two of these mighty constructions originate from his reign. The Red

Pyramid gets its name from its red-coloured limestone. Compared to Cheops' majestic edifice, it crouches much lower in the desert landscape.

Snofru's master builders had become cautious following serious problems at the preceding building some 2 km (1 mile) further south – fissures had formed inside the so-called bent pyramid, meaning it had to be com-

pleted with a softened, sloping angle. Further to the south-east are the 'Black Pyramids'. Amenemhet III had them built around 1800 BC using a completely different method. The frame was a cross-shaped limestone shell on top of which a mighty mountain of mud bricks was piled.

After 45 km (28 miles), road 2 runs parallel to the Nile to the turn-off for Meidum.

9 **Meidum** Snofru also carried out work here at the edge of the fertile valley of Faijûm. The ruins of the shell-design pyramids look like gigantic sand cakes. There are some famous murals from the graves of the neighbouring royal suite – the Meidum Geese can be admired in Cairo's National Museum.

Back on road 2 the route heads further south through smaller

settlements before reaching the provincial capital of Beni Suêf after 42 km (26 miles). Here we recommend you drive over the bridge to the eastern bank of the Nile where a quicker desert road makes the rest of the journey to El-Minia a lot easier.

10 **El-Minia** With some 250,000 inhabitants, El-Minia is one of the busiest cities in Middle Egypt. As an administrative headquarters, a university town and an industrial centre it provides employment for people from the surrounding areas while also acting as a popular starting point for interesting sightseeing tours. The large number of churches is a noticeable feature of the city's skyline. Minia is home to a great many Copts.

11 **Beni Hassan** From the western bank of the Nile approximately 25 km (15.5 miles) south of El-Minia you can take a boat to the graves of the princes of Beni Hassan. These structures were hewn into the precipice during the 11th and 12th dynasties between 2000 and 1755 BC. The murals on the walls depict interesting scenes: children dancing and playing with balls, craftsmen, mythical creatures in the

desert and the famous wrestling scenes of Egyptian soldiers practising martial arts. The choice of themes is an indication of the independence and creativity of the provincial rulers.

12 **Ashmunein/Hermopolis** On the western bank 8 km (5 miles) north of Mallawî are the ruins of Ashmunein. This is where Thot was worshipped, the god of wisdom. Statues of baboons are still testimony to his cult where they were one of the sacred animals. In Christian times a St Mary's basilica was built over the ruins of a Ptolemaic temple.

13 **Tuna el-Gebel** This graveyard of Ashmunein is located in the adjacent desert area west of town. The large, underground burial complex for the sacred animals of Thot is rather unusual and includes a wide array of mummified animals in addition

1 A desert camel ride in front of the pyramids of Giza.

2 Colourfully bridled camels wait in Sakkara.

3 Waterwheels are a very rare sight on the Nile.

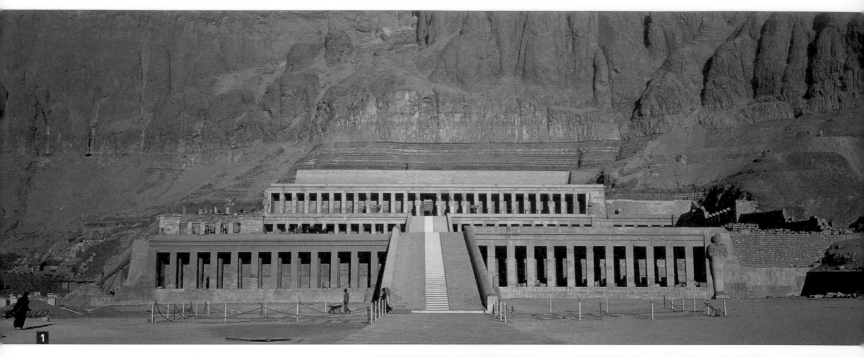

to ibises and baboons. Even crocodiles and fish were found in the maze of crypts.

Priests at the temple of Thot were also laid to rest here. The tomb of the high priest Petosiris from early Ptolemaic times displays ancient Egyptian and Greek art side by side.

The journey continues south through Mallawî and over a narrow lane near the village of Deir Mawas towards the banks of the Nile. A boat can take you to the other side of the river where off-road vehicles are ready to take visitors to the very widely scattered tourist sites.

14 Tell el-Amârna In around 1350 BC, Akhenaten founded the new capital of Akhetaten, meaning the 'Horizon of Aten', in an expansive valley. Palace complexes and residences for the new elite were built along with new temples for the only god, Aten. Luckily for archaeologists, the city was abandoned after the heretic king's death and despite heavy destruction the excavations at the start of the 20th century revealed that many of the unique artworks from this time were still intact. The famous bust of Queen Nerfertiti (today in the Egyptian Museum in Berlin) was discovered on 6 December 1912.

15 Assiût After travelling approximately 75 km (46.5 miles) through the many villages and towns along the Nile you will eventually reach the next provincial capital on the trip, Assiût. Here, the long desert road turns off towards the oases of Kharga and Dakhla where a 19th-century dam regulates the Nile floods.

We recommend you go back over the bridge to the less developed eastern bank before continuing on.

16 Sohâg/Akhmîm These two sister cities 120 km (74.5 miles) south of Assiût are connected by one of the few Nile bridges. Outside Sohâg on the western bank are the ruins of Deir el-Abjad, the 'White Monastery', evidence of Egypt's early Christian history. Many of the blocks used to build the Deir el-Abjad and the accompanying church originate from pharaoh-era constructions.

The monastery, which housed up to 4,000 monks in its heyday, became famous under its abbot Schenute (AD 348–466), the father of Coptic literature, who fought fiercely against the still existing ancient Egyptian cults and traditions.

On the western bank it's another 50 km (31 miles) on the main road until a sign at Balyana points to the turn-off to Abydos.

17 Abydos In ancient Egypt's early days, Abydos was already of paramount significance as a burial site for kings and princes. It was the main cult town for the god of life, death and fertility, Osiris, and one of the country's most important pilgrimage destinations. The belief in life after death is illustrated in tomb complexes, funerary temples and memorial stones.

Greatly worshiped as the rightful judge and ruler of the afterlife, Osiris also symbolized the hope for resurrection. The funerary temple of Sethos I (1290–79 BC) is an impressive sight with a series of very elegant reliefs.

After Nag Hammâdi, another 35 km (22 miles) south, the main road 2 continues along the eastern bank. The stretch on the western bank leads through rural areas and a number of villages. Following a bend in the Nile that sweeps around to the east, you will reach the turn-off to the temple of the ancient goddess Hathor in Dendera after approximately 60 km (37 miles).

18 Dendera Hathor was celestial goddess of a great many things including love, music and debauchery. She was very popular among the Egyptians. Her temple, which was fitted with proper public baths, was visited by pilgrims in their droves even

until Roman times. The 'caring mother' aspect of the great goddess was embodied through her sacred animal, the cow – the reason Hathor was often depicted as a woman with cow ears.

The astronomical images on the ceilings of the entrance hall and the so-called animal circle in an oratory on the roof are some of the interesting details of this Ptolemaic-Roman temple. Crypts embedded in the masonry were used as secret storage places for valuable cult devices.

From Dendera the journey continues over the bridge to the eastern bank towards Qena, one of the country's best-tended provincial capitals. A 160-km (99-mile) route through the east-

ern desert to Safâga on the Red Sea begins here. Luxor is just 60 km (37 miles) away to the south.

19 Luxor The city of Luxor is one of the main destinations for tourists visiting Egypt. It has had its own international airport for many years with commercial as well as chartered traffic. There is a wide selection of hotels to suit all budgets here. Tourism is the region's main source of income and employment.

Right in the centre of the city the columns of the Temple of Amun loom large. Built during the Amenhotep III (1390–53 BC) and Ramses II (1279–13 BC) eras, this extremely important temple in

the history of Egyptian priest-king worship is particularly spectacular at dusk when its reliefs are accentuated. It is connected to the second temple for Amun by a 3-km (1.8-mile) avenue lined with sphinxes. This impressive complex, Al-Karnak, spreads over an area of approximately 30 ha (74 acres) and is the largest ancient religious site in the world, second only to Giza in terms of visitors.

The Al-Karnak complex includes the secondary temples of the lion-headed Mut, the mother goddess, Montu the god of war and Maat the goddess of truth as well as a holy forum. The temple complex was under construction for nearly 2,000 years.

The great columned hall is an impressive site with a total of 134 gigantic papyrus columns towering over a vast area of 5,000 sq m (5,980 sq yds). Numerous discoveries from both temples and other surrounding sites are displayed in the interesting Luxor Museum and include the blocks from a Temple of Aten dating back to the reign of the later ostracized pharaoh Amenhotep IV. The museum's treasures include statues from the time of Amenhotep III and Haremhab discovered in 1989 in the Luxor Temple.

A small mummification museum below the road along the Nile gives an overview of the preservation process.

20 Thebes West The area on the opposite side of the river is home to one of the most famous cemeteries in the world. In a remote basin of crumbling limestone mountains, pharaohs of the New Kingdom (1540–1075 BC) had their tombs built in what became known as the Valley of the Kings.

The world public got its first glimpse of this in 1922 when Howard Carter discovered the still unlooted tomb of the young King Tutankhamun. The small tomb's opulent adornments are today exhibited in the National Museum of Cairo. In the valley itself, people continue to marvel at the incredible murals whose bright colours are still preserved in some areas. Painted on the walls of the long passages and in the coffin chambers, these murals describe Ra the Sun god's journey through the night to the sunrise. The pharaohs hoped to take part in this journey and the daily rejuvenation that went with it.

The funerary temples built at the edges of the fertile land here were used for the cultish care of the pharaohs in the afterlife. The most unique of these was constructed for the female pharaoh Hatshepsut (1479–58 BC). Divided into three monumental terraces, the perfectly symmetrical modern-looking building is nestled in the valley of Deir el-Bahri. Officers, priests and other dignitaries built their own magnificent tombs on the path leading to the Temple of the Pharaohs as well as on the northern and southern mountainsides. The reliefs and murals in these cave tombs, ranging from very small to imposingly large depending on their wealth, often depict scenes from everyday life.

Believing in eternal life, the tomb owners are shown having frivolous parties with their family and friends. Important stages of their careers are also illustrated. The artisan colony of Deir el-Medina is quite famous for its colourful tombs, where religious themes are shown on the walls. The Valley of the Queens is home to the tombs not only of the great pharaohs' wives, but also of the young princes of the kingdoms. The tomb of Nefertari, the royal wife of Ramses II (also known as Ramses the Great), was restored at great expense here. Only very few parts of this funerary temple have been preserved, mainly because his successor, Ramses III, used blocks from the older construction to build his temple in Medînet Habu.

21 Esna Just 60 km (37 miles) south of Luxor down the main road on the eastern bank is Esna. Cross the bridge to the western bank. Keep in mind that the bridge is closed twice a day to let the cruise ships pass.

Deep under the bustling bazaar are the remains of a Roman temple to the god of creation, Khnum. You can only see the atrium with its columns of plants. Other parts of the temple are possibly still underneath the modern buildings above.

22 El Kab The journey continues back over to the eastern bank, where rock tombs on the eastern side of the mountains draw you to a halt after some 35 km (22 miles). El Kab was a significant place early on, being the cult site of the goddess of Upper

1 Restoration work renewed the grandeur of the terrace temple of Hatshepsut.

2 These monumental figures of Amenhotep III in Luxor are as famous as the Colossi of Memnon.

3 In the second courtyard of the funerary temple of Ramses III in Thebes, reliefs depict a procession of Min, the god of fertility.

4 Luxor: In some parts of the Temple of Ramses III in Medînet Habu, the colours still retain their original brilliance.

Egypt, Nechbet. Two of these tombs are of historic interest – that of Ahmose Son of Ibana who was a naval commander during the reign of Ahmose I (roughly 1550–25 BC) and helped expel the Hyksos who had occupied Lower and Middle Egypt for more than 100 years. He even documented the event in an inscription due to its far-reaching effects for the whole of Egypt.

His grandson, Paheri, earned the respect of the royals by educating the prince under the reign of Thutmosis III. On his tomb he is depicted with the king's son on his lap. South of the graves the Wadi Hilal opens up and its entrance is marked with small temple buildings.

23 Edfu It is just another 30 km (18.5 miles) to the country's best-preserved ancient Egyptian temple. On the outskirts of the vibrant city of Edfu on the west bank of the Nile is a massive Ptolemaic temple that is still surrounded by a mighty clay brick wall. Horus, with his human body and falcon head and one of the longest surviving cult gods in Egypt, was worshipped here. As the son of Osiris, who was murdered by his brother Set, it was his job to get revenge on his father's death. Horus thus came to represent new beginnings and was the guarantor for law and justice. The pictures in the temple's tower gallery make reference to the mystery theatre performances that took place every year depicting the battle between Horus and his father's murderer. The temple's inscriptions contain very precise instructions for the priests in their important task of reconstructing the ancient Egyptian cults.

24 Gebel el-Silsila A good 40 km (25 miles) south of Edfu are the sandstone formations of Gebel el-Silsila close to the banks of the Nile. In the time of the pharaohs, sandstone was quarried on both the banks for their many construction projects. Today the mountains further south give way to fertile land where sugar cane is the predominant crop processed in local refineries. After the Aswan Dam was built, this region became the home for resettled Nubians.

25 Kôm Ombo The picturesque remains of the mighty double temple of Kôm Ombo rise up next to the banks of the river. Built in Ptolemaic-Roman times for the falcon-headed Horus and the crocodile-shaped Sobek, the extraordinary details on this temple include the depiction of the Roman Emperor Trajan who dedicated medical devices to the deity, Imhotep.

Crocodiles, kept by the priests as the sacred animals of Sobek, were carefully mummified after their deaths and buried near the temple. A few examples of these can be seen today in a small chapel dating back to the time of Hadrian.

26 Aswan Aswan is considered one of the most beautiful cities in Egypt because of its location at the first Nile cataract. Numerous small islands made from granite blocks worn smooth by the water rise up out of the river. A sailing trip in a traditional felucca should be part of a visit to the Nubian capital.

Elephantine Island, the actual birthplace of the city, lies in the centre of Aswan. Taking a walk

through the excavations around its southern tip transport you back to the early times of the ancient Egyptian settlement of Abu, which means 'ivory'. German and Swiss archaeologists discovered Egypt's earliest cult site here – one of the recesses between the granite blocks dedicated to the goddess Satet. Over the centuries these humble beginnings were developed into an impressive temple. From the end of the Old Kingdom, rulers

to Lake Nasser, which is 500 km (311 miles) long. Its construction (1960–71) had economic, developmental and political consequences. After the US and Britain backed out of the financing of the project, President Nasser decided to nationalize the Suez Canal to pay for the dam. This led to the Suez Crisis and tensions between Egypt and the West. Egypt subsequently accepted an offer from the Soviets to finance the dam.

As part of the construction of the Aswan High Dam, the flood-threatened area of Nubia was explored and a number of monuments moved to other locations. New areas of settlement were developed for Nubia's population in Egypt and Sudan. The Nubian Museum was opened in 1997 and has a memorial to their history.

27 Philae The temple complex of the goddess Isis is sitated on an island between the two dams that is only accessible by boat. This was one of the monuments moved to higher ground before the dam was built. Isis' followers continued to render homage to

their goddess in the Ptolemaic temple until the 6th century AD. The first hall of columns was transformed into a church of St Stephen under the reign of Emperor Justinian to replace old Egyptian beliefs.

28 Kalabsha Directly south of the High Dam on the western bank is the new location of four ancient temples. A boat ride takes you to the Temple of Kalabsha.

During its relocation by German archaeologists, blocks from an older temple were discovered inside the walls. These blocks have been put back together and are today displayed as the Kalabsha Gate in the Egyptian Museum in Berlin. The temple,

1 A natural granite threshold cuts through the river valley and shapes the landscape near Aswan.

2 The Temple of Horus in Edfu has gigantic columns.

3 The Temple of Isis in Philae was relocated to higher ground on a neighbouring island.

of this border town had their tombs constructed in the mountainside on the western bank. Steep slopes lead to the burial sites. The ruins of the Simeon Monastery, home to a great many monks between the 7th

and 13th centuries, are also located on the western bank. Looming large on a nearby hill is the Fatimid mosque-style mausoleum of the 48th imam of the Shia Ismaili Muslims, Aga Khan III (1877–1957).

South of the city two dams seal off the Nile Valley. The older dam was built as a water-regulating mechanism between 1898 and 1902, while the second is known as the High Dam (Sadd Ali). It holds back the waters of the Nile

Lake Nasser

Roughly two-thirds of Lake Nasser's 5,000 sq km (1,930 sq mi) belong to Egypt while one-third is in Sudan. The lake is of utmost importance to Egypt as a water reservoir to control the fluctuations of the Nile flood. It has helped to increase agricultural

The rock temples of Ramses II.

revenues and provide Upper Egypt with electricity. The hydroelectric power station can generate up to 10 billion kWh a year.
Loss of agriculturally viable territory on the Mediterranean coast, soil salinity and the usage of artificial fertilizers are the negative aspects of the project.

which was built in Roman times, was built for the god Mandulis, a Nubian version of the falcon god, Horus. At its southern edge are blocks containing prehistoric petroglyphs depicting giraffes and elephants, thus providing information on the essentially humid climate of the times 5,000 years before Christ. The columns and statues of the temple of Gerf Hussein are a stout reminder of the time of Ramses II. Reliefs in the rock temple of Beit el-Wali, which were relocated just 100 m (328 yds) west of the Kalabsha Temple and created in the same era, are much more elegant in comparison. The graceful kiosk with Hathor column capitals was originally located at the Kertassi quarry and promised divine protection for the men working there.

29 Neu-Sebua The asphalt road now stretches through the desert west of Lake Nasser. Abu Simbel is about 300 km (186 miles) from Aswan. Halfway down, an access road leads to the shores of the lake near New Sebua, where you can see three temples at their new locations.
The largest of the three was named for the sphinx figures in front of it – Wadi es-Sebua means

'Valley of the Lions'. Ramses II appears arrogantly on the temple walls; inside, he sits on an equal level with the gods.
The Temple of Ad Dakkah was dedicated to Thot, the god of wisdom. Thot had travelled to Nubia as a messenger from the gods to entice Tefnut to Egypt, the daughter of the Sun god Ra. The scene of an ape dancing in front of a lioness plays on this divine myth.
The Chapel of el-Maharraka is still small and incomplete. In Roman times its location marked the border between the Roman Empire and the Kingdom of Meroë whose capital was unearthed north of Khartoum. Finally, it's back on the main road for another 40 km (25 miles) to the south until the next road turns east.

30 New Amada When Thutmosis III (1479–26 BC) was pharaoh, Egypt had expanded its empire to the south. The temple for Amun-Ra and Ra-Harakhte symbolizes the power of the Egyptian gods. In the 20th century archaeologists put the temple on a track and pulled it to this higher, drier bank.
The neighbouring temple of ed-Derr was also built by Ramses II. The scenes in the hall of columns are stunning. The third monument in New Amada is the small rock tomb of Pennut, a reputable administrator in the conquered province.

31 Toshka Canal This canal goes straight through the desert for 50 km (31 miles) to Abu Simbel. It is the most recent land reclamation project. The hope is to cre-

ate a new Nile Valley. Green open spaces seem to indicate success.

32 Abu Simbel The relocation of this rock temple in the 1960s made worldwide headlines. Four colossal figures of Ramses II were cut out of the rock and rebuilt at a site 64 m (210 ft) higher. Inside, the walls display images of historic battles and ritual scenes. Ramses dedicated this smaller temple to his wife Nefertari and the goddess Hathor.

1 The Temple of Wadi es-Sebua is one of many buildings constructed under Ramses II in Nubia.

2 The southernmost destination for many travellers in Egypt is the famous rock temples of Ramses II in Abu Simbel.

Alexandria This city was founded by Alexander the Great in 332 BC and was once home to one of the most important libraries in the world, which was replaced in 2002 with a worthy successor.

Cairo In just a few decades the population of Egypt's capital grew from 3 million to over 20 million people – a real melting pot. In 1979, UNESCO declared the Islamic Old City a World Heritage Site.

Valley of the Kings Starting with the 11th dynasty, the pharaohs built their tombs on the western bank of the Nile near Thebes. It is still an enormous necropolis.

Temple of Queen Hatshepsut This temple near Deir el-Bahri is a spectacular sight below the 300-m (984 ft) rock face. Perfect symmetry well pre-dates the Parthenon.

Edfu The Temple of Horus is an example of Ptolemaic architecture located at the site of an older temple. Horus and Set, who killed his father Osiris, were important Egyptian deities worshipped here.

Esna Far below today's ground level is the Temple of Esna, a significant monument from Ptolemaic times (332–30 BC). The Nile Perch was worshipped here.

Abu Simbel The four mighty statues of Pharaoh Ramses II (c. 1200 BC) were relocated with the support of UNESCO when Egypt's President Gamal Abdel Nasser built the Aswan High Dam and Lake Nasser in the 1950s that would have flooded the ancient ruins.

Philae The main temple in the complex on this island in the Nile near Aswan is dedicated to the goddess Isis and her son Horus.

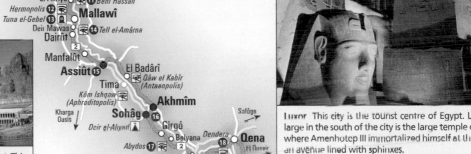

The pyramids of Giza Built over 4,500 years ago (around 2700–500 BC), Egypt's largest and most famous pyramids are found in the Cairo suburb of Giza. The mighty Sphinx next to the pyramids has the body of a lion and a human face. Nobody knows who destroyed its nose.

Dendera This temple complex was the most important cult site of the goddess Hathor. Her divine husband Thoh was also worshipped here.

Sakkara The step pyramid of the pharaoh Djoser lies in the middle of a large temple area west of Memphis.

Luxor This city is the tourist centre of Egypt. Looming large in the south of the city is the large temple complex where Amenhotep III immortalized himself at the end of an avenue lined with sphinxes.

Al-Karnak This vast temple city near Luxor was built over 2,000 years ago and is one of the ancient wonders of the world.

Kôm Ombo This double temple is dedicated to the deities Sobek and Horus. Its magical location is captivating.

Aswan Egypt is dominated by the desert, but the Nile enabled civilization to prosper. A highlight of any Egypt trip is a cruise on the Nile to Aswan in a stylish felucca, a traditional Arab sailing boat.

Route 20

South Africa

Taking the Garden Route through the Garden of Eden

Our drive along the African continent's evergreen southern tip offers a series of enchanting natural spectacles. Animal lovers and amateur botanists will get their money's worth, as will wine-lovers, water-sports enthusiasts and fans of Cape Dutch architecture. Cape Town, a truly cosmopolitan city below the famous Table Mountain, is an experience of itself, while the drive back through the colourful Little Karoo Valley makes a fascinating contrast to urban life.

In many respects, the southern tip of Africa is really a world of its own. Well-groomed parklands, orchards, vineyards and forest jungles are all set against a backdrop of striking mountain ranges and breathtaking coastline. Beautiful beaches vie for attention with rugged rock promontories, seaside resorts and fishing villages on the oceanside. What's more, the region is blessed with a mild climate throughout the year and it rains regularly, so that the vegetation is abundant and colourful. It is no coincidence that the area is often called an 'earthly paradise' or that the English explorer Sir Francis Drake called it the 'earth's finest cape' when he first came here in the late 16th century.

The drive along the N2 coastal road (the Garden Route) from Cape Town to Port Elizabeth and returning through the stunning backcountry is one of the main

Greater double-collared sunbird.

highlights of any trip to South Africa. If at any time you want to leave your car behind, you can take a ride on the luxurious Blue Train, a rail line that runs parallel to the coastal road here as part of its route from Pretoria to Cape Town.

Without doubt, however, the chief attraction of this 'Garden of Eden' is its nature, which is at its most spectacular on the Garden Route between Mossel Bay and the mouth of the Storm River. Nature-lovers can make good use of a well-organized and expansive network of hiking trails that run along the coast and through the forests.

The area also offers plenty of opportunities to watch elephants, whales and a host of other exotic animals in their natural habitats. The Addo Elephant National Park is a good example of a wildlife experience. And for those who want

Table Mountain near Cape Town at sunrise – a classic scene taken from Blouberg Beach.

The Little Karoo's hot and arid climate makes it ideal for ostrich breeding. Most farms are located in the Oudtshoorn area.

nothing more than to sit on the beach and enjoy the consistently sunny weather, the entire south coast is a virtual paradise. Water sports are also fantastic in the dynamic surf of the Indian Ocean.

Up country from Cape Town, in the hills around Paarl, Franschhoek and Stellenbosch to the east, there are some magnificent vineyards where wine-lovers can taste some of the classier local wines. Culture and history buffs will enjoy the beautifully maintained villages from the pioneer days of European settlement, where Cape Dutch-style buildings and a few interesting museums recount a not-so-distant past when the Dutch East India Company established its first stations here, and both Amsterdam and London vied for this profitable new colony.

In the far west, against the commanding backdrop of Table Mountain, the lively metropolis of Cape Town provides a charming contrast to the pristine natural landscapes. Every year millions of visitors from around the globe are attracted by its lively markets, noble Wilhelminian architecture, elegant mansions set away from the coast, sandy bays and hip quarters like the 'Waterfront' with its trendy cafés, restaurants and boutiques.

To get away from it all, you can take a spin along the scenic Chapman's Peak Drive towards the Cape of Good Hope on Africa's southern tip. The heather-clad countryside and colourful fishing villages in the area evoke scenes of Scandinavia. The beauty of South Africa is unrelenting as you move away from the coast to the starkly contrasting desert interior, where the arid steppe of Little Karoo is world-famous for its ostrich farms and stalactite caves.

Colourful beach huts like these in Muizenberg create a Scandinavian atmosphere.

Cape fauna

On the Garden Route you usually have to visit game reserves if you want to see some of the stars of the safari world up close: giraffes, lions, cheetahs, hippos, rhinos and elephants. Yet the wildlife specific to the southern cape is also incredibly varied. In many places along the coast you can see mongoose, baboons, chivet cats and even porcupines. Some species of antelope are also common, among them springbok gazelles, the national animals of South Africa. The most famous animals of the Little Karoo, however, are its ostriches.

Top: A cape gannet just off the Cape coast.
Middle: Cape fur seals.
Bottom: Springbok gazelles, the South African national animal.

Marine life is even more varied. Antarctic plankton, which washes up on the beaches, is the base of a long food chain comprising rich stocks of fish, seal colonies and sea birds including penguins, cape gannets and cormorants. Even the 'kings of the sea', blue whales and sperm whales, breach off the Cape coast.

A drive from Cape Town to Port Elizabeth is definitely the crown jewel of a trip to South Africa. Starting in the metropolis at the foot of Table Mountain, this round trip takes you across the Cape Peninsula on the famous Garden Route along the south coast to Port Elizabeth, and from there back to Cape Town via the Little Karoo and the vineyards around Stellenbosch.

1 **Cape Town** (see pp. 262–263). Before heading out immediately from Cape Town on the N2, you should definitely take a day trip out to the famous Cape of Good Hope.

2 **Cape Peninsula** 'The fairest cape in the whole circumference of the earth.' These enthusiastic words about Africa's rocky southern tip were uttered by none other than Sir Francis Drake, the second captain to circumnavigate the globe. Later generations of seafarers surely felt the words were nothing but mockery, as the Cape came to be feared for its storms and high waves, and dozens of ships have run aground on its reefs. Shipwrecks testify to the perils of the passage. In fact, you should check the weather before setting off in a rental car, and remember to take a windcheater.
There are two ways to get out to the Cape – the route west of Table Mountain and the Twelve Apostles along the idyllic beach-

es past decadent mansions such as Sea Point, Clifton, Camps Bay and Llandudno, or the route further south-east via Kirstenbosch and Groot Constantia. They both reconnect at Hout Bay, a charming fishing town mainly famous for its langoustines.
Now take Chapman's Peak Drive to Noordhoek and carry on to Kommetjie and Scarborough, a pair of idyllic fishing villages on the small road to Smitswinkelbay. On the last 13 km (8 miles) you cross the southern part of the 'Cape of Good Hope Nature Reserve'. The low scrub and heathers of this reserve are distinctly reminiscent of Scotland. You're likely to see antelope, ostrich, wildebeest and zebras and almost certainly some baboons.
The last few hundred yards are covered by shuttle bus. Then it's 133 steps to Cape Point 200 m (650 ft) above the waves where you get an absolutely magnificent view over the peninsula and False Bay – you'll know what

Travel information

Route profile
Length: approx. 1,800 km (1,120 miles), excluding detours
Time required:
at least 7–10 days
Start and end: Cape Town
Route (main locations):
Cape Town, Cape Peninsula, Hermanus, Swellendam, Mossel Bay, Knysna, Port Elizabeth, Oudtshoorn, Robertson, Paarl, Stellenbosch, Cape Town

When to go:
The best months for visiting are February, March and April when the long school holidays are over and the air and water are still pleasantly warm.

Traffic information:
Drive on the left in South Africa. Car rentals require a valid international driving licence. Petrol is always paid for in cash.

Blue Train:
A luxury alternative to the car is a ride on the legendary Blue Train from Cape Town to Port Elizabeth:
www.bluetrain.co.za

Information:
General:
www.gov.za
www.southafrica.net
Garden Route:
www.gardenroute.co.za
Cape Province:
www.tourismcapetown.co.za

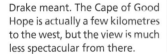

Cape flora

Botanists have divided the earth's plants into seven floral kingdoms. The smallest but by far the most varied of these is the Cape floristic region. On roughly 70,000 sq km (27,000 sq mi) of space there are approximately 8,600 species of flowering plants. A third of these are native to just the Cape Peninsula, an area measuring only 518 sq km (200 sq mi).

The most characteristic element of the local flora is the so-called fynbos vegetation, which primarily consists of heather and protea plants. The coastal regions receive high levels of rain during the colder months. By contrast, the

Drake meant. The Cape of Good Hope is actually a few kilometres to the west, but the view is much less spectacular from there.

Chapman's Peak Drive

It may only be a drive of 10 km (6 miles), but you will never forget this scenic road cut directly into the steep coastal rock faces south of Hout Bay by Italian prisoners-of-war during World War II. Starting in an idyllic fishing port, the road winds its way around the colourful cliffs up to Noordhoek. From its highest point at 600 m (1,970 ft) above Chapman's Bay there is a breathtaking view across to Hout Bay, a rocky outcrop called 'The Sentinel' and the hills around Constantia.

Your return journey goes along a wild, rocky coastline via Simon's Town with its pretty Victorian centre and the fishing ports of

Fish Hoek and Kalk Bay. In the surfers' paradise of Muizenberg beach, the colourful huts recall times gone by.

After 20 km (12 miles) or so eastbound on Baden Powell Drive, which runs in a large arc along the flat beaches of False Bay, you get back to the N2. But at Somerset West you leave it behind again. For 60 km (40 miles) you then drive along the so-called Whale Route at the base of the Koeeberg mountains where lovely coastal scenery, and possibly some majestic marine mammals, will accompany you via Kleinmond to Hermanus.

❸ Hermanus This picturesque town, founded by fishermen in 1855, is located on the northern shore of Walker Bay between Kleinrivierberge and the sea. It is famous not only for its many wild flowers, magnificent beaches and outstanding water-sports

options, but also for its deep-sea fishing.

Many people from Cape Town come to spend their weekends in this holiday village where fishing boats, dreamy cottages and the old harbour give it the feel of an open-air museum.

During the winter, from July to November, Hermanus is a hot spot for whale-watchers from all around the world. They even have a bellman employed at the beach to ring when humpbacks, right whales or even orcas are

1 Fishing ports like Kalk Bay dot the rocky western shore of False Bay.

2 Rocky coastline in the Cape Province.

3 The Cape of Good Hope – every globetrotter's dream.

4 Penguin colonies swimming in the ocean near Table Mountain.

Top: There are more than 100 species of heather (Ericaceae) on the Cape Peninsula.
Middle: The King Protea is South Africa's national flower.
Bottom: Blood flowers bloom from December to April.

inland Karoo steppe is semi-arid with vegetation mostly made up of succulents – herbs and shrubs with fleshy leaves and magnificent flowers. Large forests like the ones near George are relatively rare in South Africa.

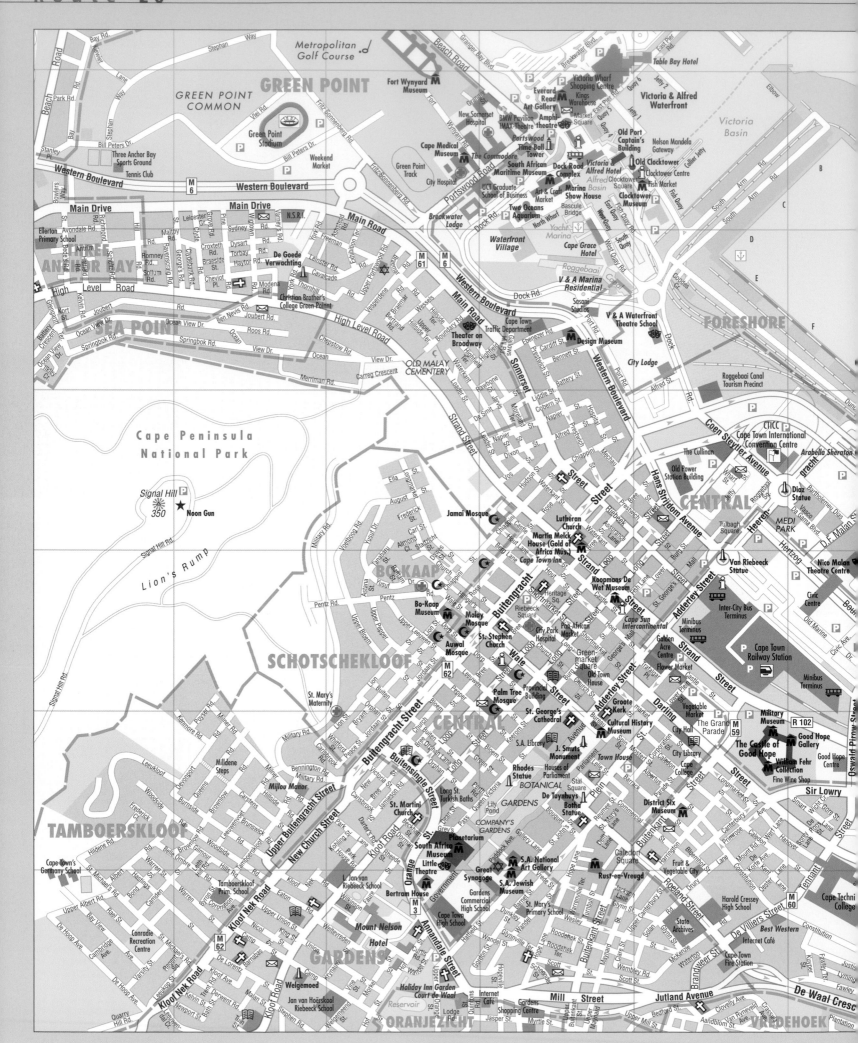

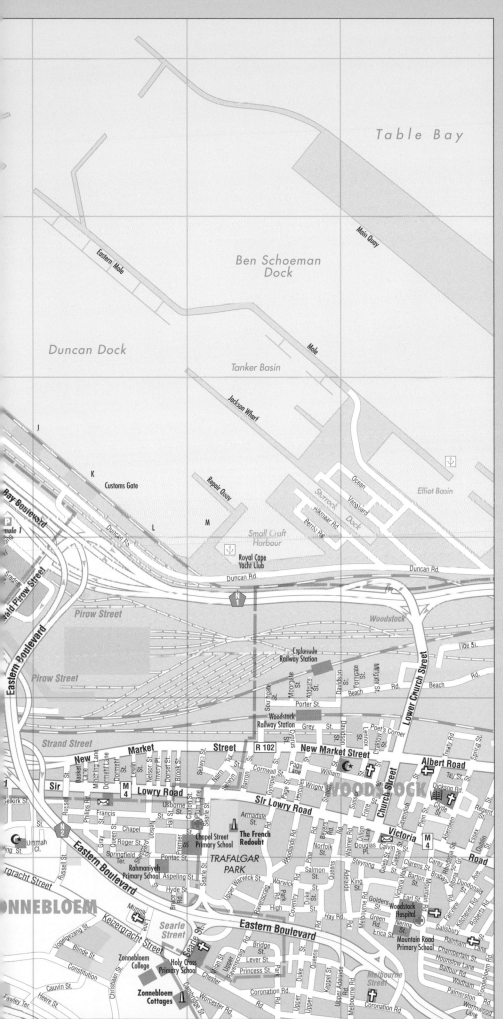

Cape Town

To many globetrotters, the 'Mother City', as South Africans fondly call the oldest city in their country, is the world's most beautiful port city. It is mainly Cape Town's unique location against the imposing backdrop of Table Mountain that makes it special – on the cape where the Atlantic and Indian Oceans meet.

'Cape Town is different.' As any new-comer to this city will immediately notice, this simplistic and superficial advertising slogan really is justified, and in more ways than one. When the Dutchman Jan van Riebeeck moored in Table Bay for the Dutch East India Company on 7 April 1652, he and his handful of pioneers were the first

Blacks, whites, Cape Coloureds, Chinese, Malays, Indians, Jews and countless immigrants from around the globe all contribute to the fascinating mix of colours, cultures and cuisine.

A handful of must-sees while you are there are the Castle of Good Hope, which is more than 300 years old, the Bo Kaap Malay Quarter, the Houses of

Top: Dream mansions in Clifton, Cape Town.
Top right: Cape Town and Table Mountain at dusk.
Middle right: Victoria & Alfred Waterfront – the stylish entertainment mile at the East Pier of Cape Town port.
Bottom right: Bright residential houses are typical of Cape Town's famous Malay Quarter.

white people ever to land here. They were met by Khoikhoi ('Men of men' in their language) and San ('Bushmen'). 'Hottentots' is a term given to the Khoikhoi by the Dutch to mean 'stutterer'. San in turn is Khoikhoi for 'outsider'. 'Bushmen' is more acceptable, but sometimes pejorative.

The fortifications on the cape quickly became a kind of 'tavern of the seas', a refuge and supply station for seafarers on the way between Europe and Asia. Many lives were saved here.

The city's backdrop is second to none. The entire 3 km (2 miles) of the mountain plateau are often draped in clouds and the city is sprawled out at its feet. Outside, in the port of Table Bay, cargo ships and sailing vessels ply the busy waters.

The climate here is Mediterranean, with none of the drastic temperature changes that are so typical of the inland areas. A constant sea breeze seems even to blow away most germs and smog, inspiring the locals to gratefully call it the 'cape doctor'. Beyond its natural setting, the city's population is also far more cosmopolitan than any other in sub-Saharan Africa.

Parliament, Kirstenbosch Gardens, the South African Museum, the National Gallery, Signal Hill, a view from Table Mountain by cable car, and the busy waterfront by the port with its choice of stylish restaurants, boutiques and galleries.

And last but by no means least, do not forget Robben Island, home to the prison where Nelson Mandela was forced to wait half his life for Apartheid finally to come to an end.

Detour

Cape Agulhas

The bearing is 34° 52' south of the equator – Africa's southernmost point! This headland is located 160 km (100 miles) south-east of Cape Town and was christened Agulhas ('needle cape') by Portuguese sailors, supposedly because of the sharp-edged reefs just off the coast. To get there, take the R316 from Hermanus via Napier and Bredasdorp. The local countryside is full of sheep pastures and corn fields and is not very spectacular by South African standards. The more sensational aspect is the sea just off the rocky shore.

Why? It is where the Atlantic meets the Indian Ocean. Two powerful ocean currents meet here – the

The Cape Agulhas Lighthouse.

Agulhas current and the Benguelas current. The former carries water at temperatures of around 20°C (68°F) from equatorial regions, which evaporates easily and thus provides the Eastern Cape with plenty of rainfall and luscious vegetation. The latter carries nutrient-rich but colder water from the Antarctic in the south-west, creating next to no clouds but only fog. This ocean current is the reason that the coastline in South Africa's western regions and Namibia is so bare. The constant temperature differences at the Cape cause pretty severe weather conditions including winds and high waves.

It turns out the South Africans were well-advised when they built the second-oldest lighthouse in the country on this dynamic promontory back in 1848.

sighted. Harold Porter National Botanic Gardens in the Kogelberg Nature Reserve west of the town have a good exhibition of Cape flora.

Before returning to the N2 take the scenic detour via Cape Agulhas. Passing through Bredasdorp, the R3l8 will take you back to the N2 and on to Swellendam.

4 Swellendam The country's third-oldest town was founded by the Dutch East India Company in 1745. It is located against the impressive backdrop of the Langeberg Mountain Range, whose ridge is called the '12 O'Clock Rock' by locals because at noon the sun is vertically above it. Long alleyways of ancient oak trees are the town's landmark and in many places you can still feel a bit of atmosphere from the pioneer days.

The town's biggest attraction is 'The Drostdy', the erstwhile residence of the bailiff (landdrost), which was built in 1747. This thatched mansion, which was renovated and enlarged between 1812 and 1825, now houses a stylish museum with furniture and common household objects dating from the 18th and 19th centuries. An old post office and a vivid documentation of old arts and crafts complete the museum compound.

About 6 km (4 miles) south of Swellendam is Bontebok National Park, home to numerous very rare species of bird and various antelopes. The park is 18 sq km (7 sq mi). One of these birds is the pied buck (Bontebok), which gave the park its name. It is nearly extinct in the wild. If the weather is good, take a swim in the wonderful Breede River.

Just after the bridge across Kafferkuils River, exit the N2 once again and take a detour (about 20 km/13 miles) to Stilbaai at the coast.

5 Stilbaai Even prehistoric fishermen who settled in this

area valued 'Still Bay' as a plentiful fishing ground. Its remarkably long beaches have turned it into a classic holiday resort. For nine months of the year the holiday cottages along its flat sandy shores remain closed up. Many of them are built on stilts. At the end of the school year, however, they come back to life almost overnight.

6 Mossel Bay Mossel Bay marks the beginning of the real Garden Route, where the N2 drops right down to the coast. It is also the location where explorers Bartholomeu Diaz and Vasco da Gama landed before 1500.

Offshore oil and gas discoveries have added an industrial feel to this much-visited holiday village, but around the turn of the last century it was briefly famous for the export of ostrich plumes. During the holiday season local beaches, which are separated by rocky outcrops, are crowded. Sun worshippers and swimmers go to Munro's Bay, Santos Beach and Diaz Beach, whereas surfers prefer The Point and De Bakke. In the historic town centre, the Bartholomeu Diaz Museum Complex is well worth a visit. It houses a reconstruction of the vessel used by Diaz in 1488 when he was the first European to

Long before the young Steven Spielberg directed his classic film in 1974, these sharks were infamous throughout the world. They were and still are considered bloodthirsty beasts and they can grow to more than 7 m (23 ft) in length.

In reality, however, sharks are in great need of protection from human predators, not the other way round. Their

White sharks are a constant presence in the coastal waters around the South African cape.

navigate the Cape. This reconstructed caravel is only 23 m (75 ft) long.

The neighbouring Shell Museum displays a large collection of seashells. A local curiosity is a 500-year-old milkwood tree that seafarers used as a 'post office'. They deposited their letters in a boot hung in the branches of the tree, where they would then be picked up by vessels bound for home.

7 George The Garden Route's 'unofficial' capital is about 50 km (31 miles) further on, just away from the coast at the base of the Outeniqua Mountain Range.

The range peaks at just under 1,600 m (5,250 ft). The name means something like 'they who bear honey'.

Moist sea air causes plenty of rainfall here, ensuring an abundance of verdant green vegetation. George is surrounded by forests and towards the sea there are some park-like landscapes. In the town centre Cape Dutch and classical-style buildings stand alongside the oldest Catholic church in the country, 'Moederkerk', which is adorned with beautiful wood carvings. Next to it stands an almost 200-year-old oak. Slaves were once chained to it before being sold.

A ride on the Outeniqua Choo-Tjoe Train across to Knysna goes through some striking coastal scenery and is a unique experience. The train crosses a long bridge (2 km/1.5 miles) over the Knysna Lagoon before entering the town of Knysna.

8 Wilderness National Park These days the resort town of Wilderness on the N2 does not really do justice to its name. About 12 m (7.5 miles) east of the Kaaiman River's deep gorge you are confronted with an excessive number of holiday cottages and hotels. But the town's fine sandy beach and the

luscious forests in the surrounding countryside do make it a sight to behold.

The neighbouring Wilderness National Park is a stretch of coast around 20 km (13 miles) long interspersed with a number of lagoons and lakes surrounded by dense forests. It's a picture-book natural paradise that is most famous for its seabirds, but you can also go fishing, surfing, canoeing and boating. A hike on Kingfisher Trail along the mouth of the Touw river is perfect for a day trip.

Just outside Knysna you pass the Goukamma Nature Reserve, a strip of rocky coastline that stretches 14 km (9 miles) and can only be explored on foot.

9 Knysna A hundred years ago this holiday resort located at the northern shore of a huge lagoon was the centrepoint of a tempestuous gold rush. These days it is mainly known for its oysters and the substantial

1 Outeniqua Choo-Tjoe Train – bay to bay on steam power.

2 Mossel Bay is where the real Garden Route starts.

3 Coastline and wilderness – dream beaches for lazy strolls.

huge jaws and long rows of razor-sharp teeth may instill fear in many a water-sports enthusiast, and attacks do happen. But attacks on humans are actually much rarer than myths would lead us to believe, and they are usually caused by curiosity, not sheer lust to kill. 'Carcharodon carcharias', as this predator is also known, habitually tests out unknown objects simply by taking a bite. White sharks live all around the globe, which makes it surprising that so little conclusive research has been carried out on them. But their mysterious patterns and elusive behaviour make this difficult.

What we do know is that their numbers are declining dramatically. The reason is that collectors on the black market pay up to 50,000 dollars for a set of shark teeth, and in Asia their fins are considered a delicacy for soup. There are probably no more than 10,000 of these sharks left in the world's oceans. The World Conservation Union placed them on its 'red list' of endangered species, and in some countries, like South Africa, they are strictly protected.

Detour

Addo Elephant National Park

The addo elephants that live here are only a small relic of the giant herds that once roamed freely across the Eastern Cape. However, an encounter with one of them is still a very impressive experience. About 200 of these reddish and slightly smaller variants of the true African elephants live in this national park, which is located just 70 km (43 miles) north of Port Elizabeth. When the first settlers arrived in the area near the Sunday River in the 1820s, a peaceful coexistence of humans and elephants proved to be impossible. The giant animals continuously devastated local harvests. In 1919, the farmers hired a game hunter to put an end to the problem. The man did a very

As well as elephants, the Addo Elephant National Park is home to mountain zebras (top) and warthogs (bottom).

thorough job. Only around a dozen addo elephants survived.
In 1931, in order to protect the remaining specimens, some farmers established a reserve measuring 86 sq km (33 sq mi) and providing the herbivorous animals with ideal conditions for their survival. Today, a total of 45 km (28 miles) of roads and tracks criss-cross the national park.
Artificial watering holes make popular observation points where along with the elephants you can see lions, leopards, antelopes, buffalo and perhaps even a specimen of the extremely rare black rhino.

forests nearby that have provided generations of local people with the economic base for a thriving timber industry. The forests are also home to a small herd of free-roaming elephants. A regional speciality is hand-crafted hardwood furniture made from yellow wood, iron wood and stink wood.
The town's landmarks are two giant sandstone cliffs called 'The Heads', which tower above the small canal connecting the lagoon to the open ocean. West of Knysna is the Featherbed Nature Reserve, home to the rare blue duikers and a host of other rare bird species.
The most magnificent beaches in the area are called Brenton and Noetzie. The Elephant Nature Walk in Diepwalle State Forest offers some truly outstanding hiking. You get to it along the N9, which branches off inland a few miles after Knysna heading towards Prince Alfred's Pass and Avontour.

⓾ Plettenberg Bay There are some ideal opportunities for hiking in the forests of Kranshoek and Harkerville, approximately 30 km (18 miles) east of Knysna. A few minutes after that in the car take a look to your right off the N2 to see some truly fantastic scenery.
Plettenberg Bay, with its almost 10 km (6 miles) of immaculate sandy beaches and crystal blue waters, really is the essence of the 'South African Riviera'. From July to September there are whales calving within sight of numerous exclusive hotels.

⓫ Tsitsikamma National Park This national park, covering 5,000 ha (12,350 acres) of land, has everything that nature-lovers may desire – bizarre cliffs, lonely beaches, steep gorges and luscious vegetation if you make it further up country. Founded in 1962, the area also includes the rich coastal waters.
The Otter Trail, which starts in Nature's Valley and runs along the rocky shore for 42 km (26 miles) right up to the mouth of the Storms River, is one of the country's most attractive long-distance hiking trails. To do it you first have to acquire a permit – only the first 3 km (2 miles) from the eastern entrance are open to those without one. However, even within that distance you are fortunate enough to be able to visit the huge waterfalls and a spectacular hanging bridge that stretches 190 m (623 ft) over the chasm at

a height of 130 m (427 ft). If you are into snorkelling, there is an underwater nature trail where you can go exploring the large variety of marine plants and animals.

⓬ Cape St Francis Near Humansdorp a road turns off to Cape St Francis on your right. This jaunt towards the coast is about 60 km (40 miles) and is well worth doing for a few reasons. First is that the village at the end of the cape really does have a charm of its own with its whitewashed houses and black rooftops. Second is that the long beaches towards Oyster Bay and Jeffrey's Bay to the east are among the most beautiful in South Africa. The third reason has to do with the waves that break here.
In the 1960s Jeffrey's Bay was made legend in the movie *The Endless Summer*, and the waves

still break perfectly here, sometimes for hundreds of yards from the point into the bay. Watching the surfers on this world-famous wave is an enjoyable way to spend a day at the lovely beach. Back on the N2 it is only 70 km (43 miles) to Port Elizabeth.

⓭ Port Elizabeth P. E., as the locals call this important port city, has the gold and diamond trade to thank for its rise. These days the heart of the South African car industry beats a little upriver in Port Elizabeth's 'twin city' of Uitenhage on the banks of the sizeable Swartkops River.

1 An especially spectacular stretch of coastline in Tsitsikamma National Park.

2 Subtropical climate and vegetation – the rain-forests in Tsitsikamma National Park.

Scene at a watering hole in Addo Elephant National Park. 100 years ago these elephants were almost extinct. Today nearly 200 of the giants live on 9,000 ha (22,000 acres) of reserve land. The elephant population density at this park is four times that of Kruger National Park.

1

Although 'Cape Detroit' is definitely not known for its scenic beauty, this port metropolis with its one million inhabitants still exudes its own personal brand of Victorian charm.

Its lively centre and the starting point for guided tours is called Market Square, where the town hall is magnificent and the 'campanile' tower (52 m/170 ft) even has a viewing platform. From Park Donkin Reserve, you have a magnificent view over Algoa Bay and there are some beautifully restored houses from the Victorian era as well as an old lighthouse.

The Museum Complex includes a snake park, dolphin shows in the Oceanium and a regional museum that promise a good variety of entertainment. Close by there are some exquisite beaches such as Kings Beach and Humewood Beach.

Instead of taking the same coastal route back towards Cape Town, we recommend driving the N62/60, which takes you further into the heartland of South

Africa. This inland route branches off about 20 km (13 miles) west of Humansdorp, winding its way westwards past Joubertina, Avontour, Uniondale and De Rust – all of which are smart and tidy but otherwise unremarkable agricultural towns.

The landscape of the Little Karoo, as this interior plateau is called, extends over 250 km (155 miles) over a swathe of land about 60 km (40 miles) wide and is strikingly different to the coastal areas. This area, sandwiched between the Kouga and Swart Ranges to the north and the Outeniqua and Langeberg Ranges to the south, gets very little rain. There are colourful rock formations on either side of the road and large areas of the abundant fertile soil are irrigated. Over the years, ostrich farms have developed into a hugely important impetus for the local economy.

⑭ Oudtshoorn This provincial town with 50,000 inhabitants is the 'urban centre' of the Little

Karoo. You can hardly imagine it these days, but in the late 19th century it was even a fashion hub and, at one point, a group of inventive farmers decided on a new tack for the fashion scene. They started large-scale ostrich breeding operations in this dry valley and subsequently managed to convince the haute cou-

ture of Vienna, Paris and New York that feather boas, capes or fans made from ostrich plumes were indispensable accessories for the fashionably up-to-date. At the height of the resulting boom around 750,000 birds were delivering 500 tonnes of feathers a year. Having become rich overnight, these ostrich

'barons', as they now called themselves, erected decadent mansions of stone and cast iron, the so-called 'feather palaces'. After a downturn lasting several decades, the ostrich business has recently regained some momentum in the wake of the low-cholesterol craze. Ostrich meat is now exported on a large scale,

as is their leather. On some farms, you can try out specialities such as ostrich steaks and omelettes made from the birds' giant eggs, watch ostrich races or even risk a ride on one.

Located 30 km (18 miles) north of the town is an absolute five-star attraction – the Cango Caves. These are some of the world's most terrific stalactite caves and you get to see all their beauty during the course of a two-hour guided tour.

Ostrich farms and other plantations, neat towns with names such as Calitzdorp, Ladismith or Barrydale, and an imposing backdrop of mountain ranges accompany you through this charming region. After passing Montagu, a charming centre for growing fruit and wine at the western end of Little Karoo Valley with numerous historic buildings, the road winds its way up more than 6 km (4 miles) to Cogmanskloof Pass. It then goes through a tunnel under a jagged barrier called 'Turkey Rock' and carries on down into the wide and fertile Bree Valley.

15 Robertson This small town is blessed with a wonderfully mild climate and extremely fertile soil. High-quality apples, apricots and above all grapes grow here in luscious abundance. Wild roses, old oak trees and jacaranda trees grow by the roadside. A long sandy beach along the riverbank is reminiscent of the French Riviera.

The area also has a plethora of accommodation in the form of holiday apartments or campsites. Sheilam Cactus Garden is a must for hobby botanists. It is located 8 km (5 miles) outside the town and has one of the most comprehensive cactus collections anywhere in the world. The next main town on the N60 is Worcester, which has few attractions apart from its botanic gardens and Kleinplasie Farm Museum, which invites you to take a touching journey back in time to the daily routine of an 18th-century farm.

There is a worthwhile detour here via Wolseley to the small town of Tulbagh, which is 70 km (43 miles) north of our route.

16 Tulbagh Also surrounded by extensive orchards and vineyards, Tulbagh was devastated by an earthquake in 1969 but has since been fully restored. The town centre around Church Street is considered to be the most complete collection of Cape Dutch architecture in the country. The town's oldest building is Oude Kerk (Old Church), which was built in 1743.

17 Paarl To reach this small town on the Berg River from

1 Scenic Karoo landscape.

2 Ostrich plumes, meat and leather are sought-after export goods.

3 In many places, irrigation turns the Little Karoo into a Garden of Eden.

Cape vineyards

Even if you aren't a huge wine fan, you should not miss the opportunity to try and perhaps buy some of the Cape's more precious offerings.

Cape Dutch-style winery, surrounded by endless vineyards.

Wine has been grown in the Cape region for nearly 300 years now. The conditions are ideal for red wines, with plenty of sunshine and no frosts. Numerous signposted wine routes make exploration easy. The oldest of these runs around Stellenbosch. The smallest and most exclusive is the 'Constantia' wine route connecting three wineries built in Cape Dutch style.

The wine-growing town of Franschhoek, founded in the late 17th century by French Huguenots, is also worth a visit, as is a tour of the vintner's co-operative KWV in Paarl, whose cellars contain what are supposedly the world's largest casks.

Tulbagh follow the narrow, winding R44 via the jagged Bain's Pass. It is the industrial centre of the wine-growing region and the seat of the wine-growers' co-operative KWV, which was founded in 1918 and now looks after more than 5,000 individual vintners.

It stores more than 300 million litres (66 million gal) of wine, and more than three times this amount is processed here every year. There are guided tours that take you to five wine barrels alleged to be the largest in the world. Each of them holds more than 200,000 litres (909,000 gal), was made without nails and weighs 25 tonnes (27.5 tons). The town was named after 'The Pears' ('De Paarl'), giant granite summits that sparkle in the sunlight after it rains. On one slope of Paarl Mountain, 600 m (1,970 ft) high, the Tall Monument, an imposing granite needle, commemorates the development and spread of Afrikaans, the Boer language. Local vineyards such as Nederburg, Rhebokshof, Fairview, Backsberg or Kanonkop are considered the very best by wine enthusiasts.

18 Franschhoek This wine-growing town has some extensive vineyards with their typically large mansions. Huguenots fleeing from religious persecution in Europe at the end of the 17th century came to South Africa

and settled in this picturesque valley. Farm names such as Dieu Donné, La Provence or Mont Rochelle testify to the pioneers' provenance.

A large monument at the exit of the village commemorates their achievements. The unusually large number of first-class restaurants, bistros and small inns also hints strongly at the town's French heritage.

19 Stellenbosch Nicknamed 'Boer Oxford' because of its venerable elite university, this town is the cultural heart of the winelands. In 1679 the governor Van der Stel established a border settlement on Eerste River. A stroll across the De Braak central square and along Dorp Straat, with its long rows of bright white, partly thatched buildings in classic Cape Dutch style, testify to its rank as South Africa's second-oldest town.

The Burgerhuis with its small town museum is worth a visit, as are the old stagecoach house, the Rhineland missionary church and the beautifully restored mansion of Libertas Parva, which houses an interesting wine museum as well as an art gallery. Well-manicured lawns, shaded oak lanes and the botanical gardens right next to the university campus are definitely worth a leisurely stroll.

The hiking and bicycle trails through the surrounding vineyards are very well-signposted

and nothing if not idyllic. They are certainly a safer option than driving if you have enjoyed some of the local wine!

There are two routes back into Cape Town: either take the N1 back directly, or follow the road south to Somerset West and turn onto the N2 at the starting point of this journey.

1 The Stellenbosch vineyards grow some renowned high-quality wines.

2 It does not get more picturesque than this – the winery at Boschendal is attractive not only because of its excellent wines, but also because of its excellent cuisine and meticulously maintained Cape Dutch architecture.

The Twelve Apostles The coastal road between Cape Town and Llandudno is also called Cape Riviera. The Twelve Apostles make a charming backdrop to any beach holiday on Camps Bay.

Paarl The largest town away from the coast is said to be the cradle of Afrikaans, the Boer language. Alongside its museum and many historical buildings, the cellars of the KWV vintner's co-operative and the magnificent wineries in the surrounding area are well worth a visit.

Addo Elephant National Park This protected area houses 200 addo elephants, which were nearly wiped out 100 years ago. It is also home to the last Cape buffalo herd.

Cango Caves The stalactite caves in the Swart Mountains are among the world's most impressive. The 'Big Hall' is 107 m (351 ft) long and 16 m (52 ft) high.

Cape Town Globetrotters say that this city, founded in the 17th century, is one of the world's most beautiful. Its port, its hillside houses and Table Mountain itself make a stunning sight.

Franschhoek This wine-growing town located in a picturesque valley was founded by Huguenots some 300 years ago. The French heritage is visible not only in an interesting museum and monument, but also in a large number of excellent restaurants and wineries.

Port Elizabeth This port city with its Victorian charm has gold and diamonds to thank for its rise. The museum compound includes a snake park and the regional museum is well worth visiting.

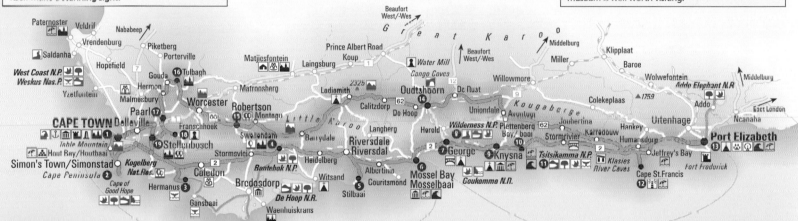

Chapman's Peak Drive The coastal road between Noordhoek and Hout Bay is one of the most spectacular in the world, with breathtaking views, such as this one looking east.

Kogelberg Nature Reserve This protected area west of Hermanus is the heart of the Cape floral kingdom.

Wilderness National Park East of George there is an extensive area of freshwater and saltwater lakes that are home to innumerable birds. Some of the lakes are connected via the Serpentine.

Outeniqua Choo-Tjoe Train A ride on this nostalgic steam train from George to Knysna across the Knysna lagoon is one of the highlights of the magnificent Garden Route.

Cape of Good Hope A visit to the southern tip of the Cape Peninsula is a must for any visitor to South Africa. Once seafarers had passed the 'Cape of Storms', they were safely on their way home.

Swellendam This small town was founded in 1745 and still exudes the pioneer spirit with its Cape Dutch buildings.

Bontebok National Park These days there are around 300 of the once-endangered pied buck roaming the park.

Tsitsikamma National Park This park of 5,000 ha (12,350 acres) has some bizarre cliffs, lonely beaches and a heartland rich in abundant vegetation.

Route 21

Alaska

Far North on the Alaska Highway

Icebergs floating on Lynn Canal (145 km/90 miles) between Skagway and Juneau.

Americans like to call their 49th state 'The Last Frontier'. In Alaska, seashores, rivers, forests, mountains and glaciers remain almost untouched, brown bears fish for salmon, sea lions fight for territory, and herds of caribou trek across the tundra. But even this far north the cities are expanding, oil production is becoming a hazard for the wilderness and civilization is encroaching slowly but steadily on the pristine landscape. Fortunately, several national parks have been established, and this route takes you there.

When William Seward, the US Secretary of State, bought Alaska from the Russians for two cents per acre in 1867, this vast empty expanse of land was quickly derided as 'Seward's folly'. But the billions of barrels of oil that have since flown through the Alaskan Pipeline have more than earned the initial purchase price he paid.

In Alaska, there are eight national parks protecting the state's valuable natural

resources. By area, the Alaskan peninsula in the north-west of the American continent is the largest state in the US. It measures 1.5 million sq km (1.3 sq mi), easily big enough to fit Western Europe into it. From the Canadian border, which is 2,500 km (1,550 miles) long, the peninsula stretches nearly 4,000 km (2,480 miles) to the furthest of the Aleutian Islands on the western tip of the state. To the north of Alaska is the Beaufort Sea, to the west

A walrus herd on the Alaskan coast.

the Bering Straits, and to the south the Pacific Ocean.

The Pacific coast is broken up into innumerable islands, peninsulas and deep fjords that reach far into the interior. Mount McKinley is North America's highest mountain at 6,194 m (20,323 ft), and Juneau is the only state capital that is accessible only by boat, via the Alaska Marine Highway, or by plane. Of its highland plains, 40,000 sq km (15,000 sq mi) are covered by glaciers. North of the Arctic Circle, the permafrost soil only thaws to a maximum depth of half a metre, but agriculture is still possible in the Matanuska Valley.

Until 1942, there was no way to get to Alaska by land, and only when the Japanese threatened to close in on Alaska did the US government decide to build a road connection through Canada. On 9 March

Mount Wrangell (4,317 m/14,164 ft) is an extinct volcano clearly visible from Glenn Highway, which connects Tok Junction with Anchorage.

Carved out by glaciers, Wonder Lake provides an Impressive reflection of Mount McKinley, North America's highest mountain.

1942, a total of 11,000 people began construction on this road, about 2,300 km (1,430 miles) long, between Dawson Creek in Canada to the south and Delta Junction to the north. Despite the huge difficulties encountered, this pioneer route was in use by 20 November 1942 after an impressively short construction period of only eight months.

After the war it was handed over to the civil authorities and gradually improved. Today it is open year-round and in all weather conditions. It remains the only land connection between the USA and Alaska, and despite a tarmac surface along its entire length, the highway is indeed still a challenge. Be prepared for summer snowstorms, mud-slides and washed-out bridges.

The challenge has its rewards, however. Unforgettable scenery awaits you, often right by the roadside, where you occasionally see bears with their cubs, or elks with giant antlers.

Fairbanks and Anchorage are modern cities, but even here the wilderness comes right to your doorstep. A trip into Denali National Park with the mighty Mount McKinley (6,194 m/20,323 ft) is a challenging and unique experience for any visitor. If you want to get even closer to the 'real' Alaska, you can fly from Anchorage to King Salmon in the west and then take a hydroplane to Katmai National Park and Preserve. In July you can watch bears catching salmon from incredibly close range, a world-class sight. Or pay a visit to Kodiak Island with its massive Kodiak bears that weigh up to 500 kg (1,100 lbs) and reach heights of up to 3 m (10 ft). Wilderness in its purest form.

The Arctic tundra is home to small herds of shaggy musk oxen.

Alaska's Whales

'Whale ahead!' That cry means it is time to pay attention. Whale-watching is a truly impressive spectacle. The fountains of water that they blast from their blowholes and the grace of their dorsal fins sliding through the surface of the water as they prepare to dive is something to behold.

Off the Alaskan coast, whale-watching is possible from early summer through to September. During this time, humpback whales come here from their winter quarters off the Mexican coast or from Hawaii, 4,500 km (3,000 miles) away. They come to feed on the large shoals of herring and other fish that abound in these cold waters.

Only rarely do humpback whales make their own rainbow.

These dark grey whales can grow to 16 m (52 ft) in length and weigh up to 40 tons. Their flukes are their individual 'fingerprints'. Each whale has its own unique pattern that does not recur anywhere else in the entire population. These patterns are used by scientists to help identify and study individuals.

Studies have shown that male whales are quite 'musical'. Swimming at 30–50 m (100–150 ft) below the surface, they perform bizarre 'solos' composed of intricate, recurring patterns of sound in hopes of attracting females. Whales give birth to their young in their winter quarters just off the Californian and Mexican coasts. At birth, baby whales already weigh as much as 1.65 tonnes (1.5 tons).

Many places in the south-east of Alaska are good for whale-watching. Some can be reached by boat from Juneau or Haines, including the Inside Passage (Alaska Marine Highway) with its abundance of fish, Sitka, Chatham Straits, Glacier Bay and Frederick Sound.

Our Alaskan dream route begins in Juneau, the capital. After a boat trip across to Haines we take the Haines Highway to the Alaska Highway as far as Border City Lodge where the route actually goes through Canada. Back in Alaska via Fairbanks and Anchorage, the route takes us to Homer on the Kenai Peninsula.

1 Juneau Alaska's capital is located on a narrow stretch of coastal plain between Gastineau Channel and the steep slopes of Mount Juneau (1,091 m/3,580 ft). Right outside town are the towering Coast Mountains with spectacular glaciers.

In 1880, gold diggers Joe Juneau and Dick Harris first found gold in what is now the town's river. By World War II more than 150 million dollars' worth of the precious metal had been discovered in the area.

As early as 1906 the Alaskan state government was moved to this northern El Dorado. The mines have long been shut down now, and Juneau has become a quiet governmental town. More than half the town's population is involved in running the state.

Both of the town's most important sights are located on

Travel information

Route profile

Length: approx. 3,000 km (1,850 miles), excluding detours

Time required: 3 weeks

Start: Juneau

End: Homer

Route (main locations):
Juneau, Glacier Bay National Park, Skagway, Haines, Haines Junction, Whitehorse, Kluane National Park, Tok Junction, Delta Junction, Fairbanks, Denali National Park, Eklutna, Anchorage, Portage, Seward, Kenai, Homer

Traffic information:
Drive on the right in the USA. Speed limits in towns are 25–30 mph (40–48 km/h), and outside towns 65 mph (105 km/h). You must stop when you see a school bus with the indicators on.
In Canada, distances are indicated in kilometres, in Alaska in miles. Side roads are commonly unsurfaced – watch out for airborne gravel.

When to go:
The best time to go is from mid-May to late September.

The road into Denali National Park is only open from mid-June.

Information:
Alaska general:
www.alaska.com
www.travelalaska.com
Ferries in Alaska:
Alaska Marine Highway
www.dot.state.ak.us/amhs
Alaska Ferry
www.akferry.org
National Parks:
www.us-national-parks.net

The north-west coastal Indians were real masters of the art of wood carving. From Vancouver to Prince Rupert to Ketchikan you can find their characteristic totem poles depicting Indian myths and legends.

The Tlingit Indians on Alaska's southern coast were particularly expressive,

On Canada's west coast and in Alaska, there are many Indian totem poles and long houses with fascinating patterns.

carving important images from their spiritual universe right into the cedar trees. The depictions cover events such as the births, marriages and deaths of local chieftains, or they illustrate entire mythologies.

The most prevalent images are human faces and indigenous animals such as eagles, bears, salmon, whales and frogs. Ravens are a very common theme. To the Indians, these birds were the ancestors of all humankind. Indian totem poles often represent a clan's mythical family tree.

The animals serve to recall the stories of achievements and character traits of important clan members, as well as record legendary events such as storms or battles. They also indicate the privileges and social standing of individual families.

The largest number of these elaborate totem poles can be found in Ketchikan in Alaska's southern regions. At the Totem Heritage Center, a total of thirty-three poles have been resurrected. A further thirteen poles have been put up in a totem park near a beautifully carved and painted Potlatch house, a place where ceremonies were held.

Haines or Skagway you can also take scenic flights over Glacier Bay. The first leg on our route to the north is completed by boat.

3 Haines This town at the northern end of Lynn Canal used to be a Chilkat settlement. The Chilkats are a sub-tribe of the Tlingit Indians. Worth seeing are the old military outpost 'Fort William H. Seward', the Chilkat Center and a reconstructed Tlingit tribal house.
Before carrying on, you should take the ferry across to Skagway (1 hour) at the end of Taiya Inlet and visit the former gold-diggers' settlement there.

4 Skagway When gold was discovered on the Klondike River in October 1897, the population of Skagway grew to more than 20,000 almost overnight as

Franklin Street, the town's main road. One of them is the Red Dog Saloon, which was already infamous during the gold rush. The other is the Russian Orthodox Church of St Nicholas, which keeps a close watch over the moral fibre of the townsfolk. The church was erected by Russian fur traders in 1894, making it the oldest Russian church in the south-eastern part of Alaska. Another must-see is the Alaska State Museum on Whittier Street, with an exhibition of indigenous Indian culture and a bit of history of the white settlements in the area.
The terrace on the State Office Building offers the best view of Juneau, the straits and Douglas

Island just off the coast. An excursion to Mendenhall Glacier, about 20 km (13 miles) north of town, is a must. This glacier calves out of the 10,000-sq km (3,650-sq-mi) Juneau Icefield, with a face 2.5 km (1.6 miles) long where it breaks off into the lake.
The visitor centre offers comprehensive documentation on the glacier, and you can go hiking along its edges.

2 Glacier Bay National Park
You should not leave Juneau without taking a boat or plane trip to this national park 85 km (53 miles) away. Giant glaciers detach themselves directly into the sea here, and giant ice flows

descend from mountains that tower above 4,000 m (13,000 ft). No fewer than sixteen glaciers terminate in this large bay, which was completely covered in pack ice as recently as 100 years ago. Since then, the ice has receded by more than 100 km (62 miles), faster than anywhere else on earth.
These days, seals lounge on the ice floes of Glacier Bay, and humpback whales and orcas ply the chilly waters, breaching, hunting and carrying on.
From mid-May to mid-September you can take day trips and longer excursions both by boat and by air from Juneau to Gustavus, a small settlement at the entrance to this huge bay. From

1 Mendenhall Glacier feeds off the massive Juneau Icefield (10,000 sq km/ 3,860 sq mi). Its glacial tongue is 2.5 km (1.6 miles) wide.

2 Haines is located at the end of Inside Passage, where the Chilkat River flows into Lynn Canal, a fjord that stretches 145 km (90 miles).

3 In Glacier Bay National Park, glaciers have carved out some inviting beaches that are now popular with walruses.

The fauna of the Alaskan mountains

In addition to the state's fabulous natural scenery, the animals of Alaska are among the chief attractions of 'The Last Frontier'. Of all the Alaskan animals, bears and moose are the most impressive, but caribou, elk, mountain sheep and mountain goats can be just as fascinating, as can the various wolves and foxes.

You will certainly never forget seeing the gleaming eyes and pointed ears of a lynx next to your camper at dusk, or watching a moose cow with her young cross the highway right in front of you. But it is easy to forget that there are so many other kinds of furry creatures here, like martens, minks, ermines, beavers, wolverines and foxes.

Dall sheep (top) and Rocky Mountain goats (bottom) live in Alaska's mountainous regions.

Dall sheep and Rocky Mountain goats are natural rock-climbers, living at altitudes of up to 3,000 m (10,000 ft). If you are lucky, you'll see small herds of females with their young scouring the slopes for food.

The variety of bird species here is difficult to appreciate initially, but Alaska's extensive wetlands are home to countless waterfowl. Among them are a number of species of wild geese and ducks, as well as the endangered whooping crane.

most gold seekers landed here before hiking along the Chilkoot Trail to the Yukon River. Between 1897 and 1898, a Wild-West-style town developed that has remained almost intact to this day. The town's Broadway Street is now an historical park. You can't miss the impressive Arctic Brotherhood building, with more than 20,000 wooden sticks decorating its facade, or the Red Onion Saloon, where the floor is still covered in sawdust. Every evening a play is performed in Eagles Hall, bringing the time of the gold diggers to life.

Although the gold rush was past its peak by then, the year 1900 saw the construction of a narrow-gauge railway across White Pass, between Skagway and Whitehorse. The most scenic stretch up to White Pass at 889 m (2,917 ft) is now maintained as a heritage railway and will give you some unforgettable views of this wild and romantic landscape. The different climate zones produce myriad vegetation, from wet coastal forests right up to alpine tundras at the top of the pass.

5 Haines Highway/Haines Junction From Haines, the Haines Highway winds its way across the foothills of the Alsek Range. At Porcupine it crosses

the border into Canadian British Columbia, and just after that you get to Chilkat Pass at an altitude of 1,065 m (3,494 ft).

West of the road, the Tatshenshini-Alsek Preserve connects Glacier Bay National Park to the south and Kluane National Park in the north.

Heading north, the nature reserve joins Wrangell-St Elias National Park back in Alaska. People on both sides of the border have worked together to

create this park, the largest protected area on the North American continent. As the crow flies, it stretches more than 700 km (435 miles) from Gustavus at the southern tip of Glacier Bay National Park to Richardson Highway in the north. There are no roads anywhere in the park, but mountains up to 6,000 m (19,500 ft), massive glaciers and pristine forests.

The town of Haines Junction has 500 inhabitants and originally

developed from what was once a soldiers' camp during the construction of the Alaska Highway. Here, the Haines Highway meets the Alaska Highway coming from Whitehorse, which itself is also worth an extra detour (111 km/69 miles).

6 Whitehorse This is where the exhausted gold diggers would arrive after crossing White Pass. Downriver from the large rapids they were able to

Logan is Canada's highest mountain. Down at more 'moderate' altitudes there are large populations of black bears, brown bears, wolves, mountain sheep, caribou and elk. Further to the west are the inaccessible Icefield Ranges. From the air these look something like a giant lunar landscape made of ice and snow. Given its extraordinary dimensions, it is hardly surprising that Kluane National Park was declared a UNESCO World Heritage Site as early as 1980, alongside Wrangell-St Elias Park, which borders it to the west.

There are very few places on the Alaska Highway to access Kluane National Park on foot, and you can never go any further than to the foot of the icy giants. As an alternative, it is well worth taking a scenic flight across this breathtaking mountain landscape. Small aircraft take off from the town of Burwash at the northern end of Lake Kluane.

Or maybe you are into old ghost towns? At the eastern end of Lake Kluane, a short access road takes you down to Silver City on the lakeshore. This old trading post, long since abandoned, really does give you that 'ghost-town' feel.

From Burwash Landing, the Alaska Highway winds its lonely way through a largely pristine landscape of mountains, forests and tundra all in seemingly endless repetition. Towards the west there are some impressive views of the mighty St Elias Mountains, Canada's highest mountain range. The road first crosses Donjek River, then White River and finally, just before you get to the Alaskan border, there is Beaver Creek, Canada's westernmost settlement with roughly 100 inhabitants.

In October 1942 the last section of the Alaska Highway was completed here.

8 Tok Junction Our first stop back in Alaska is Tetlin Junction, and after another 19 km (12 miles) you get to the small town of Tok.

Founded in 1942 as a soldier's camp when the Alaska Highway was being built, Tok is considered to be the gateway to Alaska. From here, Fairbanks

1 The icy world of Wrangell-St Elias National Park is only visible from a helicopter or glacier plane.

2 A reflection of Mount Huxley (3,828 m/12,560 ft) in a temporarily ice-free pond in Wrangell-St Elias National Park.

3 Ice on lakes such as Kathleen Lake in Kluane National Park does not melt until late in the spring.

take a paddle steamer further north along the Yukon River. When the Alaska Highway was being built, Whitehorse developed into the largest settlement in the territory.

Today, at the McBride Museum, you can see old gold-digging and mining equipment as well as Indian arts and crafts. Old Log Church, built in 1900, houses an exhibition on the Yukon Territory's missionary history. The paddle steamer permanently moored at the southern end of Second Avenue is called the 'SS Klondike'. During the gold rush, it regularly plied the Yukon between Whitehorse and Dawson City.

Back at Haines Junction you take the Alaska Highway to Kluane Lake at the eastern end of Kluane National Park.

7 Kluane National Park North of Haines Junction the road rises up to Bear Creek Summit at 997 m (3,271 ft) shortly before coming to Boutillier Summit at 1,000 m (3,281 ft). Just beneath the pass is Kluane Lake, the largest lake in the Yukon Territory at 400 sq km (155 sq m). The highway runs along its western shore.

The national park covers an area of 22,000 sq km (8,492 sq mi) and has plenty of untouched nature including high peaks, huge glaciers and sub-Arctic vegetation. At 5,959 m (19,551 ft), Mount

Alaska's bears

In addition to numerous black bears, there are between 30,000 and 40,000 brown bears in Alaska. They populate the entire state, from coastal forests up to the northern tundra.

Depending on food supplies, these adaptable creatures can vary greatly both in fur colour and in size. Let's face it – if all you get to eat is berries and gophers, you're just not going to grow as tall as your coastal cousin who can gorge on salmon.

The largest brown bears are usually found in Katmai National Park and on Kodiak Island where they grow to 3 m (10 ft) tall and weigh up to 500 kg

Top: In Alaska, polar bears can only be seen on the Arctic Ocean coast.
Middle: Grizzlies are Alaska's largest beasts of prey.
Bottom: Black bears are all over Alaska.

(1,100 lbs). Kodiaks and grizzlies are the largest terrestrial predators on the planet. If you think you can outrun one, be warned – bears can run at top speeds of 60 km/h (40 mph) and they really are outstanding climbers!

and Anchorage are the same distance away.

The visitor centre at the crossroads has an interesting exhibition of stuffed animals from Alaska, and Tok is also a centre for husky breeding. Dogs-led races start here in winter and in the summer you can see teams practising on a 20-km (12-mile) track that runs parallel to the Alaska Highway.

From Tok Junction, the remaining 111 m (69 miles) of the Alaska Highway follow the mighty Tanana River. The broad flood plains on either side of the road remind us that the glaciers of the Alaska Range once extended all the way down to here.

⑨ Delta Junction We have now reached the northern end of the 2,300-km (1,430-mile) Alaska Highway. The terminus is located at the junction with Richardson Highway, where a visitors centre offers all kinds of information about the construction of the highway and the Trans-Alaska Pipeline.

At Delta Junction the pipeline crosses the Tanana River in a wide arc and it is quite a sight in its own right. Its construction became a necessity when, in

1968, the USA's largest oil fields were discovered north of the Brooks Range in Prudhoe Bay. Starting in March 1975 about 22,000 workers were involved in the two-year construction of the line, which now extends 1,280 km (795 miles) straight through the heart of the peninsula and down to the port city of Valdez.

Half the pipeline was installed underground and the rest, nearly 700 km (435 miles) of it, is supported by a system of 78,000 stilts. The pipeline has to be continuously cooled in order to keep the 60°C (140°F) oil from destroying it. Another 153 km (95 miles) down Alaska's oldest highway, the Richardson Highway, you come to Fairbanks.

⑩ Fairbanks This city on the Tanana River owes its existence to the 1903 gold rush. Within seven years 11,000 people had set up shop on its primitive campsite. In World War II, large military settlements and the construction of the Alaska Highway fostered an economic boom in the town. After 1974 the construction headquarters of the

At the park headquarters you can visit the dog pens where the park rangers breed huskies. During the summer they train them as sled dogs for winter when that is the only mode of transport allowed in the park.

The George Parks Highway now takes us towards Anchorage. Roughly halfway along it you get to the picture-book town of Talkeetna. You get yet another view of Denali from here. It is also the take-off point for scenic flights around the national park.

12 Eklutna About 33 km (20 miles) outside Anchorage you pass the Indian village of Eklutna. The St Nicholas Russian Orthodox Church is oddly located right in the middle of an Indian Cemetery. There is also a Siberian chapel.

Bright wooden houses are set on the graves here, their eaves

1 Denali (Mount McKinley), has a higher rise than Everest: 5,500 m (18,000 ft). The peak is at 6,194 m (20,323 ft) above sea level.

2 A solitary grizzly bear roaming the autumnal tundra in search of food.

Fairbanks: Pioneer Park Open-Air Museum

Pioneer Park (18 ha/45 acres) provides a good introduction to the 100 years of

Timber houses from the 19th century.

Fairbanks' history. In total, twenty-nine houses have been rebuilt to create 'Gold Rush Town', an historic gold-digger settlement. The First Presbyterian Church and the Pioneer Museum are also worth visiting here.

Crookes Creek & Whiskey Island Railroad is a reconstructed miniature train engine that used to transport food to Fairbanks and now takes visitors through the park. HMS *Nenana* is Alaska's only stern-wheeler and is made entirely out of wood.

Trans-Alaska Pipeline were relocated here. Today, Fairbanks is a modern city. The Otto William Geist Museum tells you everything about the history and culture of Alaska's indigenous people.

Before carrying on, take the opportunity to relax and enjoy Chena Hot Springs about 100 km (62 miles) east of the city.

11 Denali National Park Our next destination is the highlight of the entire trip – Denali National Park. To get there take the George Parks Highway from Riley Creek. If you want to see the 24,000 sq km (9,265 sq mi) of the park and the highest mountain in North America (Mount McKinley), you have to take one of the shuttle buses operated by

the park authority. These regularly run the 140 km (87 miles) into the park to Kantishna at Wonder Lake. The trip takes eleven hours, and if you picked a sunny day, you will even get a glimpse of Denali, the High One, at a glorious 6,194 m (20,323 ft). The road runs through some hilly tundra with mountains in the 2,000 m (6,560 ft) range.

Detour

In the land of the bears – Katmai National Park and Preserve and Kodiak National Wildlife Refuge

Few national parks in Alaska are accessible by car. Most can only be reached by plane or boat. In the south-west of the state, Katmai National Park and Preserve and Lake Clark form the Alaskan section of the Pacific Ring of Fire, where active volcanoes are as much a part of the scenery as brown bears and salmon.

In the south-east, whales, sea lions and giant flocks of seabirds liven up the coastal areas around Glacier Bay. Weather conditions in Wrangell-St Elias National Park are so hostile that some of its summits and glaciers remain nameless to this day.

Katmai National Park and Preserve

Located in the northern part of the Aleutian Range, this park measures 16,500 sq km (6,370 sq mi). It is home to approximately 1,000 brown bears, innumerable moose, caribou, wolves and foxes. The rivers are famous for their salmon, hence the name on the park gate – King Salmon. The entrance to the park is 465 km (289 miles) from

Anchorage and only accessible by scheduled flight. From early June to mid-September, there are daily seaplane connections to the park's visitor centre at Brooks Camp, another 53 km (33 miles) down the road.

Alternatively, from King Salmon you can take a taxi to Lake Camp 15 km (9 miles) away. From here, a motorboat takes visitors across to Brooks Camp, to the Bay of Islands and to other destinations on Naknek Lake. The hub for all activities in the park is Brooks Camp. Everything meets up here – humans, bears, boats, fish and aircraft. In theory, the park is accessible year-round, but you'll need dogs-leds and skis from mid September to late May. At higher altitudes, the snow may hang around well into July. The best time for those spectacular bear snapshots is July, when the red salmon come up the rivers to spawn and the bears go fishing in the rapids.

Volcanoes and bears are the two defining features of the national park.

Fifteen of the former are still active since the tremendous 1912 eruption. The results of this monstrous outburst can still be seen in the Valley of Ten Thousand Smokes where a number of hissing, steaming and smoking fumaroles remind us that the earth's crust is really quite fragile.

Throughout the summer the valley can be reached by bus from Brooks Camp. If you want to go hiking in the valley, you can stay overnight at the Baked Mountain Cabin and (provided you have the necessary equipment) climb some of the mountains in the area.

If you have only come to see the bears, things are much easier. From Brooks Camp there is a trail just under 1 km

(0.6 miles) long that leads to Brooks Falls and a viewing platform right above the rapids. When the salmon come upriver, the fishing bears just stand in the river and lazily yet skilfully build up their winter layers. Dumpling Mountain is also quite easy to get to. It takes less than two hours to climb the 744 m (2,441 ft) to its summit. From there you have some terrific views over the tundra, Naknek Lake and the surrounding mountains.

The absolute highlight of a visit to Katmai National Park, however, is a scenic flight above those areas that are not accessible on foot. The standard flight takes you via the Valley of Ten Thousand Smokes, through Katmai Pass,

along the shore of Katmai Bay up to Swikshak Bay, and then via Kaguyak Crater and Savonoski River back to Brooks Camp.

Kodiak National Wildlife Refuge

Kodiak Island is located in the south of Katmai National Park. The indigenous people of the Aleutian Islands inhabited this area as early as 6,000 years ago. In 1784, Russian trappers and fur traders made Kodiak the first capital of Russian America. To this day, several Russian Orthodox churches bear witness to this period.

Kodiak is the largest island in Alaska and the second-largest in the United

3

4

States at 6,000 sq km (2,315 sq mi). It is characterized by deep fjords, forests and alpine tundra. The climate is moist and cold throughout the year. Today

the south-western part of the island is a protected wildlife refuge that is home to numerous brown bear populations as well as 250 bird species. The

bald eagles are abundant here, as are the millions of seabirds who spend the winters on Kodiak. They find plenty of food in the shallow coastal waters.

Visitors to the reserve can find valuable information at the visitor centre, which is just about 8 km (5 miles) south of the small town of Kodiak. The island can be reached by plane from Anchorage or by ferry via the Alaska Marine Highway. As there are no roads in the reserve, you will need a boat or seaplane. If you want to go fishing for a day, keep your ear to the ground in Kodiak. It is relatively affordable to get yourself taken to the fishing grounds by plane in the morning and be picked up again in the evening.

If, however, you would like to explore the reserve on foot, you are largely left to your own devices. Overnight stays are possible in designated spots, but only in your own tent. For your own safety, you'll need more than just respect for the ubiquitous bears. Never set off without a 'bear bell' attached to your trousers or backpack. As bears are better at hearing than at seeing, these bells serve to forestall any nasty surprises. If you get too close to a bear by mistake, it can easily feel threatened and you will not be able to run away. At 60 km/h (40 mph) bears are always going to be faster!

It is essential to wrap your food in airtight containers. Do not take anything

smelly into the tent. Neither cook nor eat in your tent as bears can detect the smell of food for days afterwards. A bar of chocolate in your coat pocket is enough to attract an unwanted visit. There are 'bear gallows' in the designated campsites, gates 4 m (13 ft) high with posts wrapped in sheet metal. You hang your food here overnight, securely fastening the pack high up in the air. If you keep these basic rules in mind and keep a healthy distance between yourself and the bears, you can move around their Kodiak Island in relative safety, and enjoy wilderness in its purest form.

1 Salmon-fishing brown bears at Katmai National Park.

2 The 1912 eruption of the Novarupta volcano gave Katmai National Park its current shape.

3 Karluk Bay on Kodiak Island.

4 In 1784 the Russians founded the first permanent settlement on Kodiak Island.

Bald Eagles

In 1782, the bald eagle was chosen as the national animal of the United States. These huge birds of prey can have wingspans of more than 2 m (6.5 ft), helping them glide majestically through the air. Their dark-brown, airfoil-like wings have hundreds of individual feathers that aerodynamically increase wingspan. Their stout heads with pronounced beaks are white, as are their broad tail feathers. Bald eagles are monogamous and use the same nesting tree throughout their lives. Every year they redo the nest for the new brood. Old nests can weigh up to a tonne!

Bald eagles have wingspans of more than 2 m (6.5 ft).

In Katmai National Park alone there are more than 600 breeding pairs of these regal birds. Eagle-watching is particularly good on the Chilkat River near Haines and on the Ninilchik River on the Kenai Peninsula. At the peak of the salmon season, it is not uncommon to see several hundred eagles gathering in both these places to catch fish.

lavishly decorated with wood-carvings. The Indians believe they house the spirits of the dead.

Just south of Eagle River, it is worth taking a 20-km (13-mile) detour to visit Chugach State Park. From here you can do day hikes to the glaciers further up country.

13 Anchorage This city owes its existence to the construction of the railway line between Fairbanks and the ice-free port of Seward on the Kenai Peninsula. Originally a builders' settlement established in 1914, Anchorage eventually developed into a modern aviation hub. It is now home to half of Alaska's entire population. As you enter the city via Glenn Highway you'll see thousands of small- and medium-size aircraft parked at Merill Field. Lake Hood is one of the largest hydroplane airports in the world.

14 Portage After 60 km (37 miles) on Seward Highway, you come to this town at the end of Turnagain Bay. At Girdwood,

just before you get to Portage, is Alaska's northernmost alpine ski resort at Mount Alyeska (1,201 m/3,940 ft). Take a chairlift up to 610 m (2,000 ft) and enjoy a view of the Chugach Mountain Range glaciers.

At the end of the bay is Portage Lake. There are usually some oddly shaped ice floes bobbing on its deep-blue waters. On the far side, Portage Glacier drops into the lake like a giant wall.

15 Seward The natural deep-water port here is the economic engine of this town. The most important annual event is the Silver Salmon Derby in August, a salmon-fishing competition. You'll most likely want to check the Kenai Fjords National Park Visitor Center for information on the 780-sq-km (300-sq-mi) Harding Icefield.

Leaving Kenai you first take Seward Highway back towards Anchorage before turning onto Sterling Highway at Moose Pass.

16 Kenai In 1791 the Russians built their second Alaskan settlement here. After 1846 it became

the centre of the Russian Orthodox Church in Alaska. The Holy Assumption Church and its three onion-domed spires are icons of the period, along with an old bible. The bible, like the other equipment in the church, was brought to Alaska from Siberia.

17 Homer Down on the southwest side of the Kenai Peninsula is the 'Halibut Capital', Homer. In this town at the end of Sterling Highway, it's all about fish. A giant fleet of vessels is always ready to set off for the next

catch. If you are into fishing, rent a boat here or book one of the numerous deep-sea fishing tours.

1 Portage Glacier calving into the lake of the same name.

2 The snowy mountains behind the Anchorage Skyline. The wilderness starts right outside the city.

3 Lakes are typical of the Kenai Peninsula, most beautiful during the Indian summer.

Kodiak Island This island is home to the famous Kodiak brown bears, the largest carnivorous land animal in the world. They can weigh up to 500 kg (1,100 lbs).

Kenai Peninsula There are some large lakes on this mountainous peninsula that extends 200 km (135 miles) into the Gulf of Alaska.

Homer This port town on the Kenai Peninsula at the end of Highway 1 is a mecca for deep-sea fishermen.

Denali National Park The centre of this park (24,000 sq km/9,265 sq mi), is Denali (Mount McKinley) at 6,194 m (20,323 ft). There are about 430 species of wild flowers here along with grizzlies, moose and caribou.

Anchorage The skyline of this boom town looks a lot like other American cities. Half of Alaska's population lives here and its airport is the eighth largest in the USA. Planes are an indispensable mode of transport in the remote regions here. Many people even have their own.

Chena Hot Springs This oasis of relaxation is located 100 km (62 miles) east of Fairbanks on Steese Highway amid the dense forests of the Chena Valley. A small access road takes you to the sulphur springs where you can enjoy the healing waters. But be careful of any black bears that might be in the car park.

Portage Glacier This glacier south of Anchorage has a giant wall calving right into Portage Lake. Below the green mountains, bizarrely shaped ice floes with a bluish hue float aimlessly on the lake.

Wrangell-St Elias National Park Two mountain ranges are protected by this park – the volcanic Wrangell Mountains and the St Elias Mountains with the striking Mount St Elias (5,489 m/18,009 ft).

Kluane National Park Huge glaciers, sub-Arctic vegetation, bears, wolves, caribou and moose are all integral elements of this park in the Yukon Territory around Mount Logan (5,959 m/19,551 ft).

Glacier Bay National Park In Alaska's southernmost national park there are no fewer than sixteen glaciers terminating in Glacier Bay. The bay is over 100 km (62 miles) long and has only been free of ice for the last 100 years.

Mendenhall Glacier This glacier, which is 20 km (13 miles) north of Juneau, Alaska's capital, is part of the gigantic Juneau Icefield, which measures almost 10,000 sq km (3,860 sq mi). The glacier tongue calves at a width of 2.5 km (1.6 miles) into Mendenhall Lake.

Haines This town at the mouth of the Chilkat River is an area where the Indians are famous for their totem poles.

Route 22

USA

From Bass Harbor Lighthouse in Maine to Cape Lookout Lighthouse in Maryland

Typical for Maine and the whole of New

A fairly narrow coastal plain stretches between the Atlantic Ocean in the East and the Appalachians in the West. Here on the East Coast the cities line up like pearls on a chain forming a massive conurbation that is also referred to as 'Boswash' (Boston to Washington). However, despite the high population densities there are still a number of remote natural landscapes to be found.

In 1620, when they disembarked from the *Mayflower* at Plymouth Rock in present-day Massachusetts, the Pilgrim Fathers could not have dreamt that they were playing 'midwife' to what is now the most powerful nation on earth, the United States of America. What they encountered was a largely untouched natural environment only sparsely populated by a number of Native North American tribes. Today the fascination of the US Atlantic coast derives not only from

the bustling cities and the centres of political and economic power, but also from the peace and solitude of its idyllic natural setting. The mountain scenery of the Appalachians, which stretch from New England along the East Coast states to the south, can be demanding for hikers on parts of the famous Appalachian Trail. On the coast, beaches close to the metropolitan areas may be crowded, but further afield they are relatively untouched for miles and are a fantastic

George Washington crossing the Delaware, painting by Emanuel G. Leutze, 1851.

People all over the world recognize the New York skyline, the 'city that never sleeps'. The city has provided a better life for many an immigrant, but is also the scene of many a broken dream.

England – rocky headlands with a picturesque lighthouse.

invitation to simply relax and unwind. Here you can also begin to imagine the courage the first settlers must have needed to set sail across the expansive ocean in their none-too-seaworthy sailing ships. The rich history can be seen at a number of places along the Atlantic Coast – from Plymouth Rock, where the Pilgrim Fathers landed, to Salem, where the witch hunts took place (described so exactingly by the writers Nathaniel Hawthorne in *The Scarlet Letter*, and Arthur Miller in *The Crucible*), on through to Boston, the starting point of the rebellion against England.

The Declaration of Independence was proclaimed in Philadelphia, Pennsylvania, while Williamsburg presents itself as an historical picture book when actors in traditional costumes take to the streets to relive days of yore.

The eastern USA is also the political nerve centre of the USA as a superpower: Washington, with the White House, Capitol Hill and the Pentagon, has formed the backdrop for the making and implementing of decisions with far-reaching historical impact. And then of course there is the city that, for many people, is the very embodiment of the 'American dream'. It's 'the city that never sleeps the 'Big Apple'. It's New York.

Nestled between the Hudson and East rivers, New York is a melting pot of folks with an incredible diversity of languages, skin colours and religions, a shopping paradise with the most exclusive shops for the appropriate wallets, and a cultural centre with theatres and museums of international standing. In short, it's a truly cosmopolitan city that captivates nearly every one of its millions of visitors.

The White House in Washington, seat of the US President and the nerve centre of power.

Lobster

Colourfully painted lobster pots decorate many of the fishermen's houses. For many gourmets, lobster, which loves cold, clear water, is one of the main reasons for visiting Maine. Lobster stocks have dropped dramatically in recent decades and strict fishing

A magnificent lobster in the hands of a breeder.

conditions are now in force. Having now become a rarity, *Homarus americanus* is now considered a particular delicacy. Yes, it's expensive, but in Maine it's still relatively affordable.

The dream route travels through the forests of New England via Boston and New York to Washington. It returns to the coast via Virginia. All twelve of the East Coast states have one thing in common – a view of the endless ocean.

❶ Portland The route begins in the largest city in the state of Maine. Henry W Longfellow, a writer born here in 1807, often extolled Portland's attractive location on Casco Bay. Many parts of the city have been rebuilt after a series of disastrous fires. One of the few historical buildings left is the Wadsworth-Longfellow House, the oldest brick building in the city (1786). The Old Port, with its warehouses, new office buildings, and a variety of numerous shops and restaurants, is ideal for a relaxing stroll.

The route initially heads north via Rockland towards the Acadia National Park. Interstate 95 and

Travel information

Route profile
Length: approx. 1,700 km (1,056 miles), excluding detours
Time required: at least 2 weeks
Start: Portland, Maine
End: Washington, DC
Route (main locations): Portland, Bar Harbor, Boston, Newport, New York, Philadelphia, Baltimore, Williamsburg, Cape Hatteras, Ocean City

Traffic information:
Drive on the right in the USA. There are numerous

interstates, highways or freeways running parallel to one another along the North American coast and orientating yourself through them is not always easy. The typical speed limit (55–65 mph/ 90–105 km/h) can vary from state to state and breaches receive harsh penalties. Drink-driving is strictly prohibited.

Indian Summer:
A number of Internet sites in the New England states provide updates on the chang-

ing autumn colours during the so-called Indian Summer, which often occurs between early/mid September and the end of October:
www.gonewengland. about.com
www.foliagenetwork.com
www.state.me.us/doc/foliage

Information:
General
www.usa.gov
www.usembassy.gov
National parks
www.us-national-parks.net

3

Indian Summer

Autumn stages a very spectacular display in the forests of New England – sometimes referred to as 'fall colours' or 'foliage' by Americans. Europeans tend to refer to it as Indian Summer.

The Native North Americans had a very poetic explanation for the magnificent colouring of their forests in the autumn. They believed it was the blood of the big bear that gave the leaves their wonderful red, and its fat the yellow tones.

The botanists have a more prosaic explanation. There are significant differences in temperature during the autumn in New England, between the sunny, warm days and the very cold nights. During this time the trees produce a cork-like substance that blocks the exchange of liquid between

During the so-called Indian Summers, trees put on a symphony of yellow, orange and red tones.

the leaves and the branches. The level of chlorophyll in the trees drops while sugar and a variety of pigments remain. The red pigment anthocyan, which is especially prevalent in the American maple and oak species, is produced in greater quantities.

'Leaf-peepers' wanting to make their way to the autumn spectacle are best advised to consult the internet site www.foliagenetwork.com, which contains regular reports on where the autumn foliage is currently displaying the best of its red, orange, gold and yellow tones, sometimes even with a touch of violet.

Highway 1 run parallel to the coast and always offer wonderful views of the rocky cliffs and islands, scenic bays, and small harbour villages such as Bath, the 'City of Ships'.

2 Rockland This city at the south-west end of Penobscot Bay calls itself the 'Lobster Capital of the World' and attracts visitors en masse at the beginning of August every year for its Maine Seafood Festival. Two lighthouses ensure a safe approach to Penobscot Bay: Rockland Lighthouse and Owls Head Lighthouse. Information about the lighthouses can be

found at the Shore Village Museum. Highway 1 continues via the harbour town of Camden, especially popular with sailors and windsurfers, before passing through Belfast and Bucksport on the way to Ellsworth. Highway 3 takes you over a bridge to Mount Desert Island.

3 Acadia National Park Still outside of the National Park is the fishing village of Bar Harbor, once a popular summer resort among American millionaires. Today, stately mansions reminiscent of this era still line the coast. The National Park, set up in 1916, encompasses half of

Mount Desert Island and also includes the smaller islands of Isle au Haut, Baker and Little Cranberry. When timber companies began felling timber on the islands at the end of the 19th century, Bar Harbor's 'high society' bought the endangered land and donated it to the nation on condition that it be declared a national park.

The 500-m-high (1,640-ft) Cadillac Mountain is located within the park and attracts large numbers of visitors, especially during elusive Indian Summer days. The stark cliffs of Acadia National Park are constantly pounded by Atlantic surf. The park coinci-

dentally lies on a migratory bird route and can be explored on foot, by boat or by bicycle.

Back on the mainland, the return journey to Portland provides the opportunity to stop off at any of the quaint harbour towns on the coast road, stroll along one of the piers, or take a sailing trip on a windjammer. It is difficult to resist the fascination of the boats anchored so majestically in the harbours, or a graceful cruise along the coast at full sail. From Portsmouth, the only harbour in New Hampshire, it is only 29 km (18 miles) to the next state, Massachusetts.

1 At the southern end of Mount Desert Island in the Acadia National Park is the Bass Harbor Lighthouse.

2 Today it is mainly yachts that are anchored in the Camden harbour in Maine. In centuries gone by the whalers made it a lively place.

3 The Atlantic breakers pound the weather-beaten coast of the Acadia National Park.

Boston

The capital of Massachusetts resembles a giant open-air museum, a European enclave with historic buildings and winding streets amid a modern inner city with glazed office towers, world-renowned universities and leading research establishments.

It was in 1776 that the Declaration of Independence was first read out from the balcony of the Old State House in Boston, a red-brown brick building erected in 1712 as the seat of the English colonial government. Today there is a modern subway station below the historic building, but there is still no avoiding history in Boston. There has been a settlement on the hills around Massachusetts Bay from as far back as the 1720s. The settlement grew into an important harbour and, with its strategic position, became the economic and intellectual focus of the colony. The conflict with the colonial power exploded onto the public scene in 1770 when a number of citizens rebelled against the harsh tax policies of the British Crown and staged a boycott of all European goods. On 16 December 1773 the

they boarded three British ships and threw the tea bales into the sea. Paul Revere was to become a hero in the war of independence that followed when on the evening of 18 April 1775 he rode from Boston to Lexington to warn citizens that 'the British are coming!'. The Paul Revere House, the oldest building in the city, has been converted into a museum and is located in North End, a few blocks away from the Old North Church, which housed the two lanterns that gave Paul Revere warning of the approach of the British forces.

The Freedom Trail begins at Boston Common, the first public park in the USA, which in 1634 was originally set aside as pasture for livestock. Today it is the city's green belt and a popular leisure area for people working downtown. North of the park shines

the golden dome of the new State House. The King's Chapel, built in 1754, was the first Anglican church in Boston. The Old Corner Bookstore, one of the best bookshops in the city, was already the literary centre of Boston in the 19th century. Other key points on the Freedom Trail are the Benjamin Franklin Statue, erected in honour of the scholars and signatories of the Declaration of Independence; the Old South Meeting House, a former church in which the 'Boston Tea Party' was plotted; the Faneuil Hall, another of the colonists' meeting places; and Bunker Hill, scene of an important battle in the American War of Independence.

Apart from the Freedom Trail, the historic area of Beacon Hill is reminiscent of the city's history and its rich tradition. Little has changed here since the 17th century. Romantic patrician houses still stand on both sides of the cobblestone streets.

The country's academic elite are gathered at Harvard University on the other side of the Charles River. The centre of Cambridge offers a diverse combination of bookshops, bars and nightclubs and has become a popular meeting place for foreigners and tourists.

Top: Numerous skyscrapers characterize the Boston skyline.
Centre: One of the covered markets dating back to 1826 at the lively Quincy Market.
Bottom: The narrow Acorn Street in the romantic Beacon Hill area.

colonists met in the Faneuil Hall, moved on to the Old South Meeting House – both significant points on the present-day Freedom Trail – and gathered in the harbour where, dressed as Native North Americans,

1

John F. Kennedy

In 1960 the American people elected the 42-year-old Democratic Senator from Massachusetts, John F. Kennedy, as the 35th President of the United States by a narrow majority over his opponent, Richard Nixon. He proclaimed his political vision and goals in his famous inaugural speech on 20 January 1961.

With his charm and charisma he inspired countless, especially young, people throughout the world to confront the political and social problems in their countries. He rose to global

John F. Kennedy.

political challenges such as the Cuban Missile Crisis with political skill and fortune.

His Berlin speech of 1963, when he proclaimed 'Ich bin ein Berliner' (I am a Berliner) will always be remembered by millions of Germans. Only seldom are the darker sides of his policies mentioned today, such as increasing the military involvement in Vietnam. His death on 22 November 1963 in Dallas from an assassin's bullet ensured that the dynamic President's legend lives on.

Martha's Vineyard and Nantucket

These two islands off the coast of Cape Cod are among the most popular holiday destinations on the Atlantic coast. Martha's Vineyard is closer to the mainland, while the ferry crossing to Nantucket takes a good three hours.

Martha's Vineyard

The 32-km-long (20-mile) and 16-km-wide (10-mile) island was named by Bartholomew Gosnold after the grapes growing there and after his daughter, Martha. With its four harbours, Martha's Vineyard became a wealthy town in the heyday of the whaling industry. Today, expensive yachts are moored where the schooners used to anchor.

The island is a popular location for the holiday homes of New York and Boston 'high society' types who, despite usually keeping to themselves, have unfortunately rendered large areas on the east of the island inaccessible to 'mere mortals'. Today the main harbour of Tisbury is usually referred to as Vineyard Haven, but when it comes to romantic flair it cannot compete with the other two larger locations on the island, Oak Bluffs and Edgartown. Oak Bluffs was originally founded by the Methodists of Edgartown as a religious gathering place. Colourfully painted, picturesque wooden houses thus replaced the original tented camp and have now become popular as holiday homes.

In Edgartown, numerous 'captains' cabins' are reminiscent of the town's heyday as a whaling harbour. The houses often have a roof terrace of sorts, the balustrades of which are

known as the Widow Walk – it was from here that the wives used to keep a lookout for their seafaring husbands, often in vain. Bicycles are available for hire in many places and you can take off on your own to explore the island and its numerous beaches. Martha's Vineyard lies off Chappaquiddick, ideal for a lazy day on the beach or a walk through one of the nature reserves.

Nantucket Island

Nantucket Island, which was inhabited by the Native North Americans until the middle of the 17th century, experienced its heyday in the 18th century as an important whaling harbour. Today it is a popular holiday destination. Much of the main town and ferry harbour, Nantucket Town – one of the best maintained towns in New Eng-

land – is reminiscent of days gone by. Main Street – paved with cobblestones like many of the streets in town – has an historic flair and attracts visitors with its inviting shops and good restaurants. The Whaling Museum is housed in a former candle factory where the raw materials – spermaceti and blubber from the giants of the ocean – were processed. The museum provides graphic displays of the history and methods of whale hunting. The numerous 'captains' cabins' in town are easily recognized by their Widow Walks. Sicasconset was discovered by artists at the end of the 19th century and continues to attract countless bohemian types today. Many of the clapboard houses are framed by an attractive display of roses.

Plants and nature in general are rated highly on Nantucket. About one third

of the island is nature reserve, like the Nantucket Moors near Nantucket Town or the Nantucket State Forest. There are also countless gardens, lovingly tended, which bloom and blossom all summer long. The Daffodil Festival takes place in April when the daffodils bloom everywhere. In October, cranberries are the main attraction. Like Martha's Vineyard, bicycles are also an important means of transport and can be hired everywhere.

1 Since Nantucket was founded, the ocean has determined the way of life in fishing towns. Many houses have direct access to the sea.

2 The popular holiday island of Martha's Vineyard is home to pristine nature, for example on the western tip at Gay Head Lighthouse.

2

Newport and the coast of the wealthy

The Gilded Age, Newport's hey-day, began towards the end of the 19th century. Anybody who was any-body in New York built a 'summer house' in this harbour town with its picturesque alleyways, colonial-style houses and fantastic views of the bay and the ocean. These man-sions often bore a striking resemblance to the European castles their owners had seen on trips in Europe. Some of these dream mansions are

④ Salem This harbour town, founded in 1626 about 25 km (16 miles) north of Boston, achieved its tragic claim to fame when the devout Puritans of Salem staged a crazed witch hunt in 1692 where twenty people were brought to 'trial' and executed. The town has sev-eral museums dedicated to these woeful events – Salem Witch Museum, Salem Witch Village, Witch Dungeon Museum and the Witch House. The mansions, among the most attractive in the country, bear witness to the for-mer wealth of this trading town. They also include the birthplace of author Nathaniel Hawthorne (1804–64), and the House of the Seven Gables.

⑤ Boston (see pp. 288–289). Via Interstate 3 it is 65 km (40 miles) to Plymouth which, due to its long coastline and more than 300 lakes and sprawling forests, is a populated commuter area.

⑥ Plymouth The harbour town is itself a milestone in American history – it was here that the *Mayflower* landed on 21 December 1620 after a per-ilous crossing, and it was here that the Pilgrim Fathers first set

foot on American soil. A replica of the ship, the *Mayflower II*, is anchored in the harbour. The museum village Plimoth Planta-tion provides an interesting insight into the world of the first settlers. Not only does it have 17th-century houses and tools on display, but actors also re-enact everyday life at the begin-ning of that century. The Pilgrim Hall Museum has artefacts from the Pilgrim Fathers on display, and Cole's Hill is the site of the graves of those who died in the first winter. From Cape Cod Bay the journey continues towards Hyannis on Cape Cod.

⑦ Hyannis The Steamship Authority ferries set off from Hyannis to Nantucket and Martha's Vineyard all year round.

⑧ Provincetown This little town at the northernmost end of the Cape Cod headland was founded by artists around 1900. Numerous writers and painters such as Edward Hopper and Jackson Pollock lived there for a time. Today the town still retains its artistic flair. Spec-tacular Whale-watching trips by boat are also on offer in Provincetown.

Cape Cod's elbow shape dates back to the ice age. The retreat-ing glaciers left behind some 365 lakes that are ideal for swimming, fishing and boating. The beautiful Atlantic beaches are extremely popular today, particularly thanks to their warm waters. If you have time you really ought to take a detour to the nearby islands of Martha's Vineyard and Nantucket.
From Falmouth to the south of the peninsula the route initially takes you along Buzzards Bay to Wareham. After crossing the Fall River, it then continues to Newport in Rhode Island (High-way 24).

⑨ Newport Founded in 1639, this town, which has 27,000 residents, is among the most beautiful places on the East Coast. Further along there are lovely views of the islands in the bay, with Providence lying at the northern end.

⑩ Providence The capital and economic centre of Rhode Island was founded in 1636 by Roger Williams, whom the Puritans had driven out of Salem because of his reputedly heretical, i.e. cosmopolitan, views. The most

impressive building in the town is the State House, built entirely of white marble and with the second-largest self-supporting dome in the world.
Coastal Road 1 leads through a series of quaint villages and along the lovely beaches to Mystic Seaport.

⑪ Mystic Seaport This recon-struction of a harbour village from the 19th century in the south-east of Connecticut has now become an open-air muse-um. Since the end of the 1920s around sixty historic buildings have been reconstructed as replicas of the originals. There are up to 430 historic ships anchored in the large museum harbour. One of the yards spe-cializes in the repair of historical ships. The modern neighbour-ing town of Mystic is a small coastal resort with an aquarium

1 The centre of Providence straddles the Seekonk River.

2 Provincetown became known for its artists' colony from 1900.

3 Newport is home to magnificent mansions built at the close of the 19th century.

The Breakers, Cornelius Vanderbilt's house, has 72 rooms.

open to the public today, such as The Breakers, the property belonging to Cornelius Vanderbilt and built in the style of the Italian Renaissance; or Marble House, built by William K. Vanderbilt in the French style. The 5-km-long (3-mile) Cliff Walk from Easton's Beach to Bailey's Beach takes you past some of these grand man-sions.

New York

New York City comprises Manhattan, Brooklyn, Queens, the Bronx and Staten Island. New York means the Statue of Liberty, the Empire State Building, the Chrysler Building, the Brooklyn Bridge, Broadway, Fifth Avenue, but also the ghettos of the now up-and-coming Bronx.

New York is sort of the 'capital of the Western world', a melting pot where immigrants from around the globe have gathered to become an intrinsic part of America's cultural fabric. Of course, many ethnic groups have retained their cultural identity by developing neighbourhoods such as Little Italy or Chinatown, just as they would in Palermo or Beijing. Indeed, New York gladly retreats into its 'villages', creating its own worlds in neighbourhoods such as Tribeca, Soho, Chelsea and Greenwich Village. Yet the chaos continues in Midtown and on the wide avenues: the wailing of police sirens, the honking horns of taxis and the pounding of jackhammers. The office towers rise up into the clouds. Be sure to check out Broadway, from the Battery in southern Manhattan as far as Yonkers and Albany in

Top: The magnificent bronze 'Atlas with the globe' in the Rockefeller Center.
Middle top: View over Manhattan from the north.
Middle bottom: The famous sea of lights on Times Square.
Bottom: For a few months in 1930 the Chrysler Building was the highest building in the world. Parts of its facade resemble the radiator grilles of the Chrysler cars of the period.

Upstate New York. It is the city's lifeline – in the financial district in the south and especially in the theatre neighbourhood around Times Square.
One of the most famous buildings in the world, the Empire State Building (1929–31), was built in art deco style and is 381 m (1,257 ft) high – with the aerial mast, 448 m (1,588 ft.).
Central Park, the green oasis in the mega metropolis, stretches from 59th to 110th Street over an area of 340 ha (840 acres). People of all kinds, ball-playing teenagers, picnicking families and disabled variety artists make for interesting encounters.
The Rockefeller Center (1930–40) is a giant complex with offices, television studios, restaurants and shops. Concerts and other events take place in the Radio City Music Hall (1930). The neo-Gothic St Patrick's Cathedral (1858–87) is a replica of the cathedral

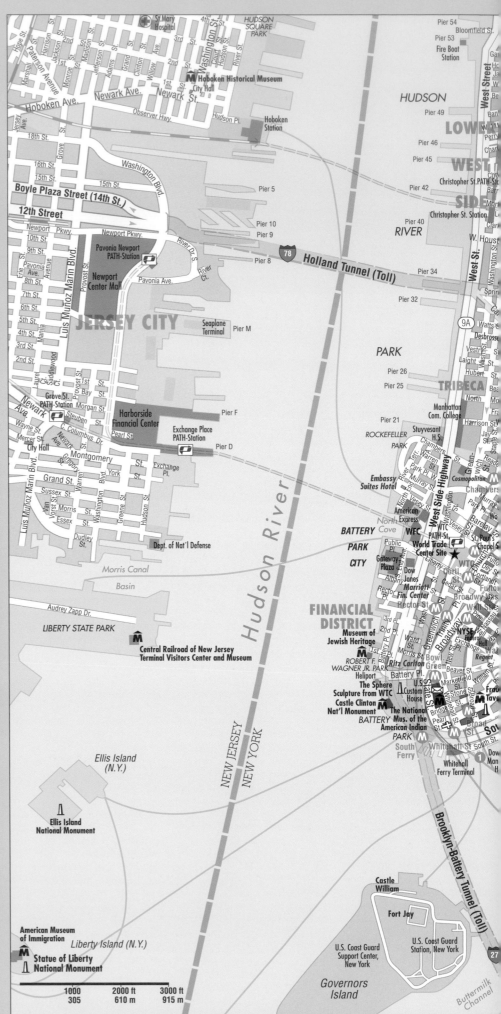

in Cologne. The main train station, opened in 1913 as Grand Central Station after several years under construction, was built in the beaux arts style and decorated with baroque and Renaissance elements. An artificial sky sprinkled with 2,500 stars stretches over the somewhat ostentatious main hall.

Once completed, the Chrysler Building (1930) was the highest building in the world for just one year. Specific aspects resemble the radiator grilles of the Chrysler cars of that period. The United Nations building (1949–53) looks over the East River. A number of works of art are on display in the entrance hall.

The financial district, Wall Street, takes its name from a solid protective wall intended to protect the Dutch Nieuw Amsterdam from enemies such as the English and the Native North Americans.

The Brooklyn Bridge is the most recognizable bridge in the Big Apple. Opened in May 1883 after sixteen years under construction, it is 1,052 m long (1,180 yds), excluding the access roads.

of Modern Art (MoMa) complex was designed by the Japanese architect, Yoshio Taniguchi, and takes up an entire city block. Its galleries house the world's largest collection of valuable paintings from the late 19th century to the present.

The Statue of Liberty stands out on Liber-ty Island (formerly Bedloe's Island), a small rock between Manhattan and Staten Island. In her right hand she holds a torch, in the left the Declaration of Independence. The statue became a symbol of freedom for immigrants on the approaching ships.

The 'path to freedom' used to lead through Ellis Island where every immigrant was registered between 1892 and 1917. In the museum you trace the process from the luggage room to the Great Hall where checks were carried out.

With its winding, tree-lined streets, the famous artists' neighbourhood of Greenwich Village between 12th St, Houston St, Lafayette St and the Hudson River is reminiscent of the 'Old Europe' that early immigrants left behind.

The Metropolitan Opera, or the 'Met', one of the most well-known opera houses in the world, is part of the Lincoln Center, a giant complex of theatres and concert halls. The Guggenheim Museum, built by architect Frank Lloyd Wright, was disparagingly referred to as the 'snail building' but there is no dispute over its art treasures. The new Museum

Top: The Statue of Liberty, donated by France, has been a New York landmark since 1886.
Middle top: Brooklyn Bridge, linking Brooklyn and Manhattan since 1883.
Middle bottom: Soho is known for its lofts.
Bottom: Historic ships have found their last mooring at the South Street Seaport.

Detour

Atlantic City

Atlantic City, in the state of New Jersey, enjoyed its first heyday as a popular seaside resort in 1880. Some fourty years later its reputation for lively nightlife extended way beyond the city limits. Beauty contests and trial runs for Broadway Shows took place here before their New Yorker premiers want live. Alas, the demise of many a popular seaside resort began in earnest in the 1950s with the advent of long-haul travel. Atlantic City was no exception.

Today, modern architecture dominates the boardwalk in Atlantic City.

However, in 1976 the citizens of New Jersey voted to have gambling legalized in Atlantic City, and with that law the East Coast counterpart to Las Vegas and Reno was born. Today, Atlantic City has an international draw with its attractions and theme hotels that take guests back in time to ancient Rome, or to the world of the Maharajas. A relaxing walk along the once-famous 5-km-long (3-mile) wooden boardwalk on the Atlantic is recommended as an alternative to the glitz, glamour and gambling.

worth seeing. A few kilometres west of Mystic is the harbour of New London, where the ferries to Long Island set out.

Via Highway 25 along the coast of the Long Island Sound you can reach New York in around two hours.

12 New York (see pp. 292–295). If you want to discover the rural charm of the state of New York, then you are best advised to go for an outing to the Hudson River Valley, which stretches north from New York City to Albany.

13 Hudson Valley Pine forests sprinkled with lakes, farms and small villages are what characterize the landscape along the Hudson River. Given the wonderful views, it is not surprising that many of the well-to-do from New York have built themselves stately homes here with well-tended parks. 100 km (62 miles) north of Yonkers is New Paltz, founded by the Huguenots in 1692.

The next section of the river is lined with historically signifi-

cant properties. Springwood (Franklin D. Roosevelt Historic Site), the property where the later US President was born and grew up, is located there. Even more stately is the Vanderbilt National Historic Site, the palace built by the industrialist Frederick W. Vanderbilt in 1890 in the style of the Italian Renaissance. The trip along the Hudson Valley ends in Kingston, the gateway to the Catskills, an important recreational area for New Yorkers.

14 Philadelphia From the outskirts of New York the route continues towards Philadelphia, Pennsylvania. Up until the completion of the various government buildings in Washington, Congress was housed in the Congress Hall of this, the most historically significant city in the USA. The centre of the city is the Independence National Historical Park, with Independence Hall where the representatives of the thirteen colonies signed the Declaration of Independence on 4 July 1776. The Liberty Bell, which was rung

to mark the occasion, is housed in the Liberty Bell Pavilion. Numerous significant museums line the Benjamin Franklin Parkway, including the Philadelphia Museum of Art, the Rodin Museum and the Franklin Institute Science Museum.

From here it is around 100 km (62 miles) along Highway 30 to Atlantic City, the 'Las Vegas of the East'. Back on Interstate 95, Baltimore in the state of Maryland is the next stop.

15 Baltimore This small city only has a few historic buildings left to show for itself after a large majority of them were destroyed by fire in 1904. Little Italy still gives some impression of how the city must have looked in the past. The renovated harbour area (Harbor Place) has become an attractive area again since the 1970s. Not to be missed are the National Aquarium, 19th-century Fort Henry and the *Constellation* in the docks, a triple-mast sailing ship built in 1854. The outskirts of Washington extend far into surrounding Maryland and Virginia, and it is

therefore not long before you encounter the first suburbs of the capital city 50 km (31 miles) away.

16 Washington (see p. 297). In Washington you leave the coast for a short while and travel along the Manassas (Highway 29) and Warrenton (Highway 211) towards Washington, Virginia. Shortly before you enter town, Highway 522 branches off to Front Royal. The broad cave complex, Skyline Caverns, near Front Royal lies at the edge of the Shenandoah National Park.

17 Shenandoah National Park You should plan five hours for the 170-km-long (106-mile) Skyline Drive through the national park because it is worth making multiple stops at the

1 The Philadelphia skyline along the Delaware River at twilight.

2 The Capitol, built by Pierre Charles L'Enfant, has been the seat of the Senate since 1800.

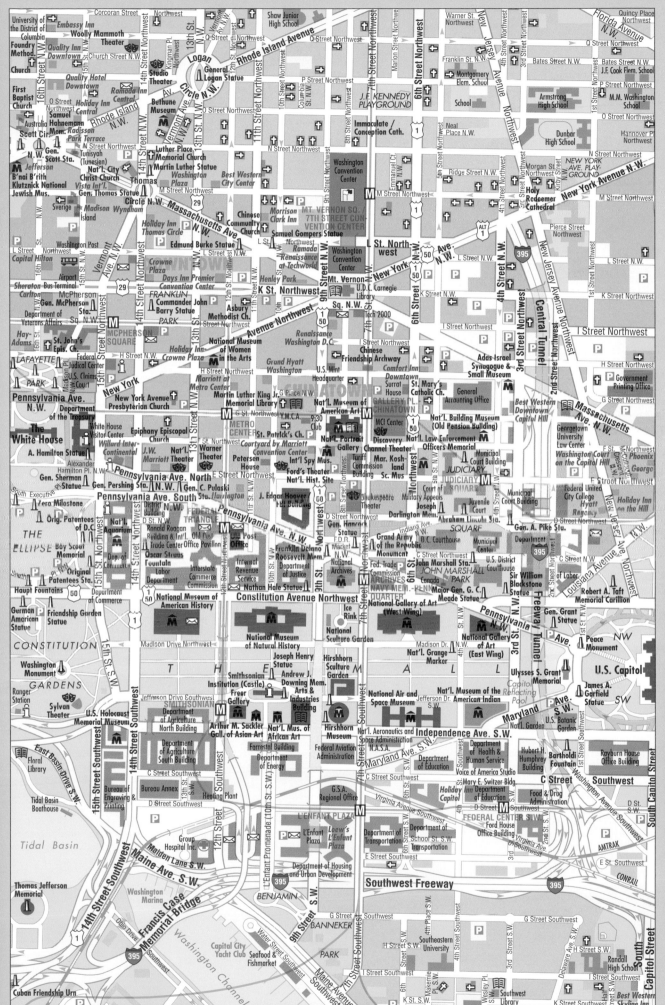

Washington

Washington, DC is the centre of Western democracy and the seat of the US President, a focal point of political power.

The capital of the United States derives its importance from its central geographic location between the northern and southern regions of the original Thirteen Colonies – and also its proximity to Mount Vernon, home of first US President George Washington. Many of the city's buildings, including the Capitol Building, were set on fire during the war of 1812, and the city's present-day appearance is the result of a 'beautification plan' implemented at the end of the 19th century. Today DC is one of the most attractive travel destinations in the USA.

The Capitol sits on top of Capitol Hill opposite the Supreme Court and the Library of Congress. This neoclassical building represents the centre point of the city and is one of America's most important political icons. The National Mall, a mile-long boulevard between the Capitol and the Washington Monument, is renowned for its cultural institutions. Numerous first-class museums such as the National Museum of Natural History and the National Air & Space Museum attract visitors all year round. The White House has been the office and residence of the US President since 1800. The Washington Monument, a 170-m-high (560-ft) obelisk made of granite and marble, commemorates the first president of the USA. The extermination of the Jews in

The majestic Capitol dominates the cityscape of Washington, DC.

World War II is documented in the United States Holocaust Memorial Museum. The Jefferson Memorial is a circular colonnade structure erected in 1943 in honour of Thomas Jefferson. The names of the Americans who fell in the Vietnam War are listed on the black granite walls of the Vietnam Veterans Memorial.

1

Williamsburg

Many of the countless colonial-era houses in Williamsburg were built in the 18th century, but when Rich-

The most attractive building in Williamsburg is the Governor's Palace.

mond was declared the capital of the state of Virginia in 1780, the city gradually faded into insignificance. Today Williamsburg resembles an open-air museum. Employees in shops and restaurants often wear 18th-century costumes and on the Fourth of July a parade is staged in historic uniforms. The most impressive buildings are the State House and the British Governor's official residence.

viewing points to take a look at the Shenandoah Valley. The park covers a particularly scenic part of the Appalachians with the panoramic route ending in Waynesboro. From there it is another 60 km (37 miles) to Monticello.

18 Monticello This property, which once belonged to Thomas Jefferson (1743–1826), is located to the east of Charlottesville. Jefferson designed the building for the Monticello plantation in Palladian style. Construction began in 1770. After 100 km (62 miles) on Interstate 64 you reach Richmond, the capital of Virginia.

19 Richmond The State Capitol on Capitol Square, designed by Thomas Jefferson, is considered to be the first neoclassical building in the USA. Here you will find the only statue for which George Washington modelled in person. The Canal Walk on the northern bank of the James River is ideal for a leisurely stroll. With its Victorian houses the city has retained the flair of the Old South.

20 Williamsburg During the 18th century the town was the capital of Virginia. 'Colonial Williamsburg', as the town calls itself, is home to eighty-eight buildings restored as facsimiles of the originals. Parks in the style

of the 18th century complete the scene. Highway 158 leads you to Point Harbor via Hampton, Norfolk and Chesapeake (Highway 64). The harbour town of Albermarle Sound is the gateway to the Cape Hatteras National Seashore. The nearby Wright Brothers National Monument commemorates the Wright Brothers' attempted flights in 1903.

21 Cape Hatteras National Seashore The 210-km-long (130-mile) group of islands off the east coast of North Carolina

is known as the Outer Banks. The only road that goes there is the 150-km-long (93-mile) Highway 12, which connects the islands of Hatteras and Roanoke with each other.

The Outer Banks were once frequently targeted by pirates, and countless ships have been wrecked along the rocky coast. These days the often empty beaches, picturesque lighthouses and other monuments attract nature lovers, recreational sports enthusiasts and even the odd surfer. The majority of the islands are protected areas within the

Cape Hatteras and Cape Lookout National Seashores.

On the return journey to Washington, DC take Highway 13 after leaving Chesapeake. At Salisbury turn off towards Ocean City (Highway 50) via Highway 611 and the bridge over Sinepuxent Bay. There you come to Assateague Island.

22 Assateague Island National Seashore Due to its exposure to wind and waves, this island is constantly changing shape. A diverse animal and plant world braves the raw climate here. From the only small road on the island you can even see herds of wild horses roaming this narrow spit of windswept dunes and grass.

The return to Washington takes you via Highway 50. A bridge links the eastern side of Chesapeake Bay with quaint Annapolis, Maryland. Picturesque fishing villages, quaint historic towns and scenic bathing spots line the shores of the bay. The founding of Annapolis, the capital of the state of Maryland, dates back to 1649. From Annapolis you are just a few kilometres away from Washington DC.

1 Not far from the busy American capital there are idyllic spots to be found on Chesapeake Bay.

2 The lighthouse at Cape Hatteras is popular with photographers.

Nantucket Island Prosperity here came in the 18th and 19th centuries from whale hunting, as documented in the Whaling Museum.

Boston The colonial revolt against the English hegemony began with the 'Boston Tea Party'. You still encounter traces of history in many of Boston's neighbourhoods. It is also home to important research institutions and universities such as Harvard University and MIT.

Acadia National Park Mount Desert Island, with its impressive craggy coast, is home to majestic Cadillac Mountain, also part of this striking national park.

New York The heart of this megacity beats loudly in places like Times Square. Every year thousands of people gather here on New Year's Eve to ring in the new year together. Here, in the middle of downtown Manhattan, the impressive skyscrapers rise up into the clouds.

Bath Both the town and its shipyards are rich in tradition. The Maine Maritime Museum and the Bath Iron Works document the history of shipping and shipbuilding in the area.

Philadelphia This is where the Declaration of Independence was signed and the constitution drawn up. Today the metropolis is an important commercial centre.

Martha's Vineyard The 'Vineyard' is a popular getaway among East Coast urbanites and plays host to the summer homes of the elite.

Washington The main American political nerve centres are in DC: the White House, the Capitol and the Pentagon, seat of the Dept of Defense.

Atlantic City This East Coast counterpart to Las Vegas attracts visitors with the promise of big winnings and glamorous shows. The boardwalk along the Atlantic is especially scenic.

Shenandoah National Park This beautiful park contains part of the Appalachian Trail, which stretches from Maine to Georgia.

Cape Hatteras Lighthouse The highest lighthouse in the USA has been warning ships of the shallows off Cape Hatteras for more than 100 years.

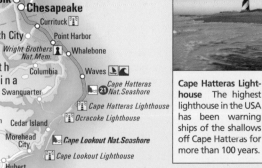

Monticello This classic Palladian mansion was once the home of Thomas Jefferson, the third President of the United States.

Richmond This defiant granite building was constructed in 1894 and was for a long time the city hall in Virginia's capital.

Cape Lookout The 51-m-high (168-ft) lighthouse at Cape Lookout, built in 1859, rises above the shallows of Core Sound. It is characterized by its unusual decoration – black stripes on a white background.

Williamsburg The many old buildings in Williamsburg, such as the Governor's Palace (1706–22), bring the colonial history of this coastal town back to life.

Map labels (Maine): Woodstock, Bangor, St. John, Bucksport, Ellsworth, Bar Harbor, Waterville, Belfast, Camden, Mt. Desert I., Acadia N.P., Augusta, Rockland, Penobscot Bay, Wiscasset, Brunswick, Bath, Portland, Cape Elizabeth, Biddeford, New Hampshire, North Windham, Sanford, Rochester, Sherbrooke, Concord, Portsmouth, Lebanon, Newburyport, Manchester, Gloucester, Lowell, Salem, Leominster, BOSTON, Provincetown, Worcester, Cape Cod Nat. Seashore, Massachusetts, Plymouth, Providence, Hyannis, Albany, Fall River, Nantucket, New York, Hartford, Connecticut, Martha's Vineyard, Kingston, New Haven, Newport, Rhode Island, Catskill Park, New Paltz, New London, Mystic Seaport, Binghamton, Newburgh, Orient Point, Scranton, Hudson Valley, Long Island, Yonkers, Fire Island Nat. Seashore, Akron, Jersey City, Newark, NEW YORK, Statue of Liberty, Allentown, New Brunswick, Long Branch, Pennsylvania, Trenton, Lakewood, PHILADELPHIA, Island Beach S.P., Lancaster, New Jersey, Harrisburg, York, Elkton, Hammonton, Gettysburg, Wilmington, Atlantic City, Hagerstown, Dover, Ocean City, BALTIMORE, Delaware Bay, Cape May, Frederick, Annapolis, Winchester, Arlington, Delaware, Front Royal, Manassas, WASHINGTON, Ocean City, Skyline Caverns, Salisbury, Elkins, Washington, G. Washington Birthplace Nat. Mon., Assateague I. Nat. Seashore, Shenandoah N.P., Fredericksburg, Harrisonburg, Ruckersville, Modest Town, Waynesboro, Monticello, Exmore, Charlottesville, Dixie, Richmond, Williamsburg, Lewisburg, Pocahontas S.P., Cape Charles Lighthouse, Roanoke, Virginia, Petersburg, Norfolk, Virginia Beach, Lynchburg, Greensboro, Chesapeake, Chesapeake Bay, Currituck, Point Harbor, Elizabeth City, Wright Brothers Nat. Mem., Whalebone, North Carolina, Columbia, Waves, Swanquarter, Cape Hatteras Nat. Seashore, Cape Hatteras Lighthouse, Ocracoke Lighthouse, Kinston, Cedar Island, Cape Lookout Nat. Seashore, Kinston, Morehead City, Cape Lookout Lighthouse, Jacksonville, Folkstone, Hubert

Route 23

Canada and the USA

Old farmhouse in Grand Teton National Park in the north-west of the state of Wyoming.

On the Pan-American Highway from British Columbia to New Mexico

A journey through the North American West is a journey of contrasts. The route passes through mountain landscapes and open plains, pine forests and vast deserts, mining villages and megacities, and illustrates the impressive diversity of this enormous continent.

The full diversity of North America reveals itself in its entirety along the wide open stretches of the Pan-American Highway. From its begining on the Canadian Pacific coast to its end near the border between the USA and Mexico, this route initially travels in a south-easterly and then southerly direction. The roads on this long route are in exceptionally good condition but some of the side roads can be closed during the colder times of the year, especially in the north.

The northern section takes you through the Canadian provinces of British Columbia and Alberta as well as the US state of

Montana. Larger towns are the exception here and the individual towns are often separated by large distances. Newer settlements originally developed from either trading posts or supply centres for the white fur hunters. There are also a number of old gold-digging locations along the Pan-American Highway, where visitors are taken back in time to the gold rush of the 19th century. In some places there are also remnants of Native American Indian cultures, such as the impressive totem poles, longhouses and pueblos.

The Canadian part of the route is loaded with absolutely breathtaking natural

Mount Assiniboine after the first snow.

landscapes. Majestic, snowy mountains reflect in the shimmering turquoise hues of Rocky Mountain lakes. To the east of the highway Mount Robson rises to 3,954 m (12,973 ft) above sea level, the highest peak in the Canadian Rocky Mountains. Glaciers and waterfalls drop powerfully to great depths from high cliffs. The Pan-American Highway is also lined with vast expanses of forest. In a number of areas such as Banff National Park, the oldest National Park in Canada, the natural environment is protected from development.

Further south the scenery changes. In the distance you see the skyscrapers of Calgary, a modern metropolis built on wealth generated by oil and natural resources, and given a makeover for the 1988 Winter Olympics. Some three hours from Calgary are the spectacular lakes

Sunset over Jackson Lake and the granite mountains of the Teton Range.

Banff National Park will show you everything that makes the Canadian Rocky Mountains such an attraction – rugged peaks, dense forests, vast open spaces and scenic lakes like Moraine Lake, shown here.

and mountains of Waterton-Glacier International Peace Park, a union of Glacier and Waterton National Parks.

The route continues through Idaho, Wyoming, Utah and Arizona. There are a number of remarkable contrasts here as well. Remnants of Native American cultures and the Spanish colonial era mix with modern cities and skyscrapers, and extensive forest areas stand in contrast to desert landscapes.

A major highlight of this particular section of North America is Yellowstone National Park in Wyoming. Salt Lake City, the capital of Utah and the centre of Mormonism, is also an Olympic city, having hosted the 2002 winter games. In the vast desert expanses of Utah and Arizona the light and landscape change dramatically with the movement of the sun, producing impressive interplays of colours and shad-

ows, and the rocky landscape of the Colorado Plateau is also impressive in places like Bryce Canyon National Park. The Grand Canyon, stretching over 350 km (217 miles) of magnificent desert, is one of the most visited sightseeing attractions in the USA – some 4 million people come here every year.

Sunset Crater, the youngest of Arizona's volcanoes, can be seen near Flagstaff and is today a training area for astronauts. In the adjoining 'Valley of the Sun' to the south the towns appear like oases in the desert. The exclusive golf courses and fields exist only due to artificial irrigation. Phoenix, the capital of Arizona, still has a slight touch of the Wild West to it, but as a centre for the aircraft construction and high-tech industries, the city is part of the modern world. Tucson, the 'City of Sunshine', has 350 days of sunshine a year.

Spirit Island in Maligne Lake in Jasper National Park – postcard views par excellence.

1

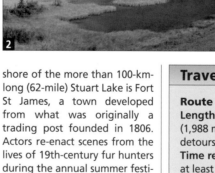

2

Whale-Watching

There are only a few other places on earth where they are better observed, these majestic giants of the ocean. Along the Canadian Pacific coast, in places like Prince Rupert Sound you can go on spectacular whale-watching excursions that last several hours.

A whale-watcher's dream – a breaching killer whale in Prince Rupert Sound.

Between March and July, grey whales are spotted frequently along the North American west coast, migrating to rich feeding grounds in the waters off British Columbia and Alaska. Killer whales and minke whales are also a regular sight in these frigid coastal waters.

The North American section of the Pan-American Highway leads from the Pacific coast via the Rocky Mountains to the arid regions of the American south-west. The route is lined with natural beauty that is protected in a series of spectacular national parks.

❶ Prince Rupert The Pan-American Highway comes up with important cultural and historic sights right from the start. The creative carved totem poles of a variety of Indian tribes can be found all over the harbour town, and the pristine wilderness in the province of British Columbia awaits you just outside the city limits.
Highway 16 initially takes you through the Skeena Valley. At Hazelton it is worth taking a detour to the Gitksan Indian villages. The Ksan Native Village is an open-air museum with several longhouses. In Kitwancool you can see what is alleged to be the largest standing totem pole. After 242 km (150 miles) a small road branches off at Vanderhoof towards Fort St James to the north (66 km/41 miles)

❷ Fort St James National Historic Site On the eastern shore of the more than 100-km-long (62-mile) Stuart Lake is Fort St James, a town developed from what was originally a trading post founded in 1806. Actors re-enact scenes from the lives of 19th-century fur hunters during the annual summer festival in the reconstructed fort. For fishing enthusiasts there are a number of isolated lakes nearby to drop a line.

❸ Prince George The Pan-American Highway crosses the Cariboo Highway (Highway 97) here. Once a satellite of Fort St James, Prince George grew into a lively town in the 19th century with the construction of a railway that brought new settlers and adventurers. The Railway Museum has an historic steam train on display.

❹ Bowron Lake Provincial Park A little detour leads you

Travel Information

Route profile
Length: approx. 3,200 km (1,988 miles), excluding detours
Time required: at least 3 weeks
Start : Prince Rupert, BC
End: Tucson, Arizona
Route (main locations): Prince Rupert, Jasper National Park, Calgary, Yellowstone National Park, Salt Lake City, Grand Canyon National Park, Phoenix, Tucson

Traffic information:
Drive on the right in US and Canada. Highways are also called Interstates or freeways. Speed limits vary in the individual provinces and states. Violations are met with stringent penalties. Air conditioning is essential in the southern US. The network of petrol stations and other supply facilities is good. This portion of the Pan-American Highway is in very good condition. In Canada some smaller roads are closed in winter. Closures are shorter the further south you go.

When to go:
The best time to go is summer when it is mild in the north and roads are open. Extreme heat in the southern US can be uncomfortable.

Information:
Canada:
www.trailcanada.com
USA:
www.travel-america.co.uk
National parks:
www.nps.gov/

400 glaciers give the Glacier National Park its name.

formed and teaches you about the flora and fauna. The low-lying areas are covered with rainforest as a result of the high rainfall and trees species include the hemlock fir and red cedar. Grizzlies are also at home in the Glacier National Park as are caribou and Rocky Mountain goats.

There are about 140 km (87 miles) of hiking trails to enjoy here, including the fantastic Avalanche Crest Trail and Great Glacier Trail. Glacier National Park boasts a number of attractions from under the earth's surface as well – go spelunking in Nakimu Cave, one of the largest in Canada.

The avalanche lanes are especially awe-inspiring and are the result of extreme winter weather conditions. It is recommended that you obtain up-to-date information at the visitor centre on Rogers Pass before setting off on a hike. The climate in the national park is as raw as the scenery is attractive. It rains or snows two out of three days and the weather changes constantly. In the west, Highway 1 also provides access to the Mount Revelstoke National Park.

majestically over what is the largest national park in the Canadian Rockies. It covers an area totalling 10,878 sq km (6,760 sq mi). You get closest to the natural beauty of the park either on foot or in a canoe, the latter of which is perfectly suited to the 22-km-long (14-mile) Maligne Lake.

The Icefields Parkway (Highway 93) is the next portion of the route and is a highlight of the Pan-American Highway. It runs 230 km (143 miles) along the gorgeous panoramic route at the foot of the glacial ridge of the Rocky Mountains and past the Columbia Ice Field, the largest ice field in North America. The Athabasca Falls and the Sunwapta Falls are also worth seeing.

⑦ Banff National Park The road then takes you past the smaller Yoho National Park and

1 A mountain lake in Jasper National Park.

2 Icefields Parkway travels 230 km (143 miles) through the Canadian Rockies.

3 Boating on Maligne Lake in Jasper National Park.

4 The Calgary skyline – an up-and-coming metroplis.

through Quesnel and Barkerville (the centre of a gold rush here in the 19th century) on your way to the wilderness around Bowron Lake. The drive over a gravel road at the end can be somewhat tedious but the effort is rewarded with fantastic landscape. The eleven lakes in the area are a major attraction for fans of canoeing. You can paddle through the entire lake landscape in the course of eight

days. Back on the Pan-American Highway, after driving 270 km (168 miles) through Fraser Valley, you reach Tête Jaune Cache, the gateway to the lovely Mount Robson Provincial Park.

⑤ Mount Robson Provincial Park The highest mountain in the Canadian Rocky Mountains is Mount Robson at an impressive (3,954 m/12,973 ft). It is the king of this unique protected

area (2,200 sq km/1,367 sq mi) and is beloved among hikers and mountaineers. High altitude glaciers, crystal-clear mountain lakes, tumbling waterfalls and exhilarating pine forests characterize this jewel of the Rockies. After 100 km (62 miles) on Yellowhead Pass you reach Jasper in the Jasper National Park.

⑥ Jasper National Park The huge mountains here tower

Head-Smashed-In Buffalo Jump

The Pan-American Highway takes you from Calgary south towards Fort Macleod. At the end of the 19th century the town made a name for itself as a trading centre for both legal and illegal goods. Indians from the Blackfoot tribe traded bison skins for cheap whisky from white settlers. The Fort Macleod Museum has exhibitions covering the history of the Blackfoot Indians.

At Head-Smashed-In Buffalo Jump, around 18 km (11 miles) north-west of Fort Macleod, you can see an example, and now a protected one, of one of the Blackfoot traditions and customs. For thousands of years these Indians used a spectacular cliff formation approximately 300 m (984 ft) long as a tool to hunt bison, an essential element of their livelihood.

The strategy was very simple. Bison herds were rounded up by hundreds of hunters on foot and sent running in a panic towards the cliff edge. Their frenzy to escape combined with the blind herd instinct sent throngs of them falling to their deaths. Honourable or not, the tactic was usually successful.

A UNESCO World Heritage Site – Head-Smashed-In Buffalo Jump.

On a 'good day', a large number of bison lay piled on top of each other at the foot of the cliff and were dissected on the spot. This form of hunting was used until the Indians began acquiring guns and horses from white settlers in the 18th century, mostly in exchange for bison skins and meat. In 1981 UNESCO declared the Head-Smashed-In Buffalo Jump cliff a World Heritage Site as testimony to the way of life of the local Indians.

An interpretive centre was opened in 1987 which, in addition to insights into the traditional techniques of bison hunting, also has a number of archaeological finds on display. The end of bison hunting is symbolic of the change in the Blackfoot Indian's culture.

on to the shimmering turquoise waters of Lake Louise. Nearby Moraine Lake is somewhat quieter. There are more than twenty-four 3,000-m (10,000-ft) peaks in this national park.

Highway 1 turns off westwards near Lake Louise and heads over the Rogers Pass towards Glacier National Park.

8 Calgary The largest city in the area is Calgary on the western edge of the vast prairie. The approach from the west is especially impressive on days when the Chinooks, warm, dry autumn winds, are blowing down from the Rocky Mountains. They ensure grand views of the peaks towering behind the city and create the bizarre illusion that you could reach out and touch the mountains.

The largest city in the province of Alberta can be seen from far away. The downtown high-rises, largely housing the offices of oil companies, banks and insurance companies, rise grandiosely against the backdrop of the mighty Rockies. The city has developed from an agricultural centre to a modern metropolis that attracts a great deal of foreign capital. A milestone in this development was the hosting of the 1988 Winter Olympics. Isolated though it may be in the middle of Alberta, Calgary is

well on its way to becoming a million-strong metropolis and is an important inter-regional traffic hub.

Landmark, symbol and the most important orientation point in the city is the Calgary Tower, standing at a proud 191 m (627 ft). The Olympic Saddledome ice sport arena provides an architectural link between tradition and modernity, and is one of the most advanced of its kind in the world. The design

of the arena in the shape of a saddle also reflects the spirit of the Wild West, which is really brought back to life in July every year during the hugely popular ten-day Stampede, when the ten-gallon cowboy hats, cowboy boots and blue jeans dictate the dress code throughout the city. Rodeos and covered wagon races bring back the 'good old days'.

Heading south again, after 170 km (106 miles) you reach

Fort Macleod. About 18 km (11 miles) north-west of the Fort is the World Heritage Site of Head-Smashed-In Buffalo Jump (see sidebar left). From here, take Highways 6 (via Pincher) or 5 (via Cardston) to reach Waterton, the entrance to another breathtaking Canadian national park.

9 Waterton Lakes National Park There are two national parks near the border between

Little Bighorn

From Livingston, Highway 90 heads east to Billings, Montana, 110 km (68 miles) down the road, the starting point for a visit to the Little Bighorn National Battlefield. The battlefield is the most significant historic location in the state. It is where, on 25 June 1876, a regiment of the US army under the command of Colonel George Custer clashed with Indians from the Cheyenne and Sioux tribes on the Little Bighorn River.

The details of the battle are patchy at best, but US government troops were outnumbered by the Indian forces. Custer had apparently made a fatal error in estimating the number of warriors under the command of the legendary Sioux chief, Crazy Horse. The US troops were soon surrounded by the Indians and killed to the last man in heavy but short-lived fighting.

The victory at Little Bighorn against the government troops achieved almost mythical status among the Indians. Yet the tables quickly turned in their fight to maintain independence and remain on what was rightfully their land. With more efficient weapons, the white man carried out further attacks against

Colonel Custer was defeated and killed at Little Bighorn.

the descendants of the territory's original inhabitants. The Indian resistance, however, was largely suppressed within just a year of the famed battle at Little Bighorn, and most of the Cheyenne and Sioux tribesmen eventually surrendered to increasing numbers of government forces.

The Indians' battles against the white man finally came to an end in December 1890 with another massacre, this time of Indians, at Wounded Knee in South Dakota. It was here that government troops slaughtered several hundred Sioux Indians, including many women and children. The battlefield at Little Bighorn River was declared the 'Little Bighorn National Battlefield' memorial site in 1886.

same name in Canada), slowly comes into view after crossing the border. Dense pine forests in the low-lying areas are home to elks, grizzly bears, pumas and lynxes.

Shortly before reaching St Mary, the road, which is closed in winter, branches off to Many Glaciers. The scenic landscape here, with a total of fifty glaciers, is criss-crossed by hiking routes, of which the Swiftcurrent Lake Nature Trail is especially impressive.

An 80-km-long (50-mile) road takes you from St Mary over the Logan Pass at 2,026 m (6,647 ft) to West Glacier. The route, which is only passable between June and mid-September, is considered one of the most beautiful mountain routes in the whole of North America.

Canada and the USA – Waterton Lakes National Park in the Canadian province of Alberta, and Glacier National Park in the US state of Montana. In 1932 the two were combined as the Waterton-Glacier International Peace Park. For local Indians the entire area has always been known as the 'Land of the Shining Mountains'.

Just after entering the park from the north-east (Highway 5 and 6) you reach Bison Paddocks. A few kilometres further down, a narrow road branches off to the west towards Red Rock Canyon, named as such due to the red sedimentary rock in the area. The route continues to the 2,940-m-high (9,646-ft) Mount Blakiston, the highest peak in the Waterton Lakes National Park. The Prince of Wales Hotel is one of the most striking buildings in the reserve, with stunning views of two lakes, Middle and Upper Waterton.

Access to Glacier National Park is via the Chief Mountain International Highway which travels along the eastern side of the park. The road was built in 1935 and is in good condition but is only passable between mid-May and mid-September.

10 Glacier National Park Mount Cleveland, at 3,185 m (10,450 ft) the highest mountain in the national park (not to be confused with the park of the

1 An ideal location – the historic Prince of Wales Hotel in Waterton Lakes National Park.

2 Sinopah Mountain in Glacier National Park is an almost perfect pyramid.

3 St Mary Lake in Glacier National Park, Montana.

4 Fascinating Glacier National Park is reached via Logan Pass.

Geysers in Yellowstone National Park

The earth displays its powerful forces in a fascinating array of ways in Yellowstone National Park – not with destructive earthquakes or violent volcanic eruptions, but with natural water fountains called geysers that visitors can observe from close up.

The geysers erupt when water boils below the earth's surface, blasting steam and water from their deep shafts. Some of them are incredibly consistent, others erupt at irregular intervals. The forces involved sometimes push the fountains to heights as tall as trees or even buildings. The highest geyser, which only erupts from time to time, is Steamboat. Its blasts sometimes reach 120 m (394 ft), each eruption releasing several thousands

Castle Geyser in Yellowstone National Park.

of litres of water. But its full force is only released every ten years or so.

Geysers are only found in areas with volcanic activity and are subject to specific conditions. What is important is a network of caves in the rock that works its way to the earth's surface. The groundwater collects in this tunnel system and is warmed by the heat of the earth. When the pressure is released the water is forced out. There are only a few places on earth where this natural spectacle occurs as impressively as it does in the Yellowstone National Park. Old Faithful Geyser is the first one in the park to receive a name.

The journey then continues via Browning to Shelby. From here it is a further 82 km (51 miles) on Highway 15 to Great Falls.

11 Great Falls The city's sightseeing attractions include the Giant Springs, one of the largest freshwater springs in North America, and the Lewis and Clark National Forest, named after the explorers who traversed much of western North America at the start of the 19th century.

About 44 km (27 miles) northeast of the city is Fort Benton, founded in 1846 as a trading post on the upper reaches of the Missouri River. Continuing south you pass more springs, including White Sulphur Springs. Continuing to Yellowstone National Park it is worth taking a detour near Livingston to the battlefield of Little Bighorn 110 km (68 miles) away.

12 Yellowstone National Park From Montana you continue

along the Pan-American Highway to the state of Wyoming, which boasts one of the continent's main attractions. Yellowstone National Park is indeed in a league of its own, not least because it is the oldest and largest in the USA. It receives around 3 million visitors a year, and it is easily accessible by car, although some roads are closed between November and April. The Grand Loop Road meanders 230 km (143 miles) through the park.

If you are approaching from the north it is worth making a short stop at Mammoth Hot Springs where information material and updates on the passability of the side roads are available from the park office.

The significance of the reserve (8,983 sq km/5,582 sq mi) in the midst of the Rocky Mountains and the Grand Tetons was recognized early on as a natural treasure and was declared a national park in 1872. Mother Nature shows her most spectacular side

Animals of Yellowstone National Park

For European visitors, bison in the wild are a special experience and sometimes even cause real traffic jams on the Grand Loop Road. Other animals

Bison fighting for territory.

on this high plateau, which ranges from 2,100 to 2,400 m (6,890 to 7,874 ft). The forces of the earth's core come to the surface in the Yellowstone National Park where the world's most impressive and powerful geysers can be seen. The highest of the roughly 300 geysers is Steamboat.
Approaching from the north you first reach the Norris Geyser Basin where, in addition to the Steamboat, the Echinus Geyser also puts on a show from time to

time. A short distance further on to the south-west you reach the Fountain Paint Pot, a basin of bubbling red-brown mud. Upper Geyser Basin has the most geysers in the whole of the national park. It is therefore no surprise that this is where the highest number of visitors will be found. You can even set your watch by some of the geysers and can plan your arrival accordingly.
Old Faithful is one of the most 'punctual', displaying its skills almost every 80 minutes for a

few minutes at a time, sending huge quantities of water about 50 m (164 ft) into the air. Other well-known geysers are Giant Geyser and Castle Geyser. And it's not just a visual experience. The accompanying noises as you approach are also fascinating. Make sure you stick to the marked pathways at all times as the unstable ground bubbles and hisses at many places in the park. Steam clouds sometimes even reach as far as the Grand Loop Road.

1 Yellowstone River near the 94-m-high (308-ft) Lower Falls.

2 The tranquil river landscape is ideal bison territory.

3 In summer bison graze on the wide open spaces of the park.

4 Old Faithful Geyser in Yellowstone National Park.

5 A 34-km (21-mile) shoreline road provides access to Yellowstone Lake in the south-west of the park.

such as elks and mountain goats as well as pumas, coyotes and lynx are also at home here. Wolves have also been successfully reintegrated in recent years. Parts of the pine forests in Yellowstone are subject to recurring forest fires.

Detour

Great Salt Lake

About half an hour north-west of Salt Lake City is the Great Salt Lake at an altitude of almost 1,300 m (4,265 ft). Approximately 120 km (75 miles) long, and about 60 km (37 miles) at its widest point, it is the largest inland lake west of the Mississippi.

For its size, however, the lake is relatively shallow and only during the rainy season does it reach a depth of more than 10 m (33 ft). The lake is all that's left of a much larger body of water, Lake Bonneville, which had a surface area of 50,000 sq km (31,070 sq mi) in the last ice age more than 10,000 years ago. Since then both the surface area and the volume have constantly decreased as a result of rising temperatures and evaporation.

Salt in the water has also crystallized. Today the lake's salt content is several times higher than that of the ocean. With no outflow, there is nowhere for the saline water to escape. Nevertheless, some animals are still able to survive here. Saltwater prawns in particular have adapted to the prevailing conditions.

For many, however, the southern shore of Great Salt Lake State Park is simply good for its beaches.

All of this is evidence of volcanic activity within the park. Violent volcanic eruptions are not to be feared, however, as the last major eruption took place around 600,000 years ago.

The waterfalls along the Yellowstone River in the south of the park are another striking attraction. At Upper Falls the river drops 33 m (108 ft) over the cliffs. At Lower Falls – only a few 100 m away – the drop is as much as 94 m (308 ft). The viewing points in the Lookout Point and Grandview Point parking areas offer especially dramatic views.

⑬ Grand Teton National Park
From Yellowstone National Park, John D. Rockefeller Jr. Memorial Parkway takes you to a much smaller park, Grand Teton National Park (1,257 sq km/ 781 sq mi), which is often over-shadowed by its famous neighbour. This is unjustified to say the least, however, as it also has a number of attractions on offer and is a more relaxed experience altogether.

The jagged peaks of the Teton Range, dominated by Grand Teton at 4,197 m (13,770 ft), are accompanied by glaciers that extend far into the steep valleys. The park's main axis is Jackson Hole, an 80-km (50-mile)

valley through which the idyllic Snake River passes on part of its 1,670-km (1,038-mile) journey to the Columbia River, which eventually flows through Idaho, Oregon and Washington into the Pacific. There are also a number of lakes in the valley.

Teton Park Road takes you from Jackson Lake to the south-east, the panoramic road offering continuously lovely views of the mountain landscape.

Jackson Hole boasts one superlative in particular. In 1933 the lowest temperature ever recorded in Wyoming, -54°C, was measured here. Even though it can be very cold in winter, such temperatures are obviously not typical. This park is open all year and the best time to go is between June and September. Most of the tourist facilities are closed in the winter but winter sports are popular here.

14 Jackson Situated on the southern rim of Jackson Hole, this is the ideal starting point for hikes in Grand Teton National Park as well as for white-water rafting on the Snake River. And, with its Wild-West-style saloons and bars, Jackson is more than just a tourist staging post. The place retains an authentic Wild West atmosphere and can be a lot of fun.

The Wildlife of the American West Art Museum has a worthwhile collection of paintings featuring the wild animals of the region. The cultural history of the local Indians is illustrated in the Teton County Historical Center. A few kilometres south of Jackson a turn-off near Alpine heads west towards Idaho. Idaho Falls are a good distance beyond the state line. In addition to a Mormon temple that is worth seeing, the city is home to the Intermountain Science Experience Center, a first-class natural history museum.

Back on Highway 89 you continue south from Montpellier through the Wasatch Mountains, which emerge abruptly from the plains. The area, at more than 3,500 m (11,484 ft), is covered in snow all year and is a popular winter sport area for residents of Salt Lake City. One of the main attractions here is the large salt lake to the west of the road, which you can reach by making a detour on Highway 80.

15 Salt Lake City The capital of Utah is one of the largest cities along the Pan-American Highway. Initially it seems an intimidating location for a city, with the Great Salt Lake to the west, the Wasatch Mountains forming a natural border to the east, and

the Great Salt Lake Desert stretching west to the horizon. However, in the middle of the 19th century the Mormons were in search of just this type of environment, remote and inhospitable.

Yet the gold rush and the completion of the transcontinental railroad brought more and more people to the town, which had developed into a lively city by the start of the 20th century. A century later the city received further impetus from the Winter Olympics in 2002.

The classical Capitol building (1915) is visible from afar and is the city's primary landmark, but Temple Square is really where things happen here. The 4-ha (10-acre) square is considered to be the Mormons' 'holy square' and the temple is accessible only to members of the Mormon church.

The city's highest building at 128 m (420 ft) is the Church Office Building, also a Mormon building, which houses the central administration of this religious community. The view from the platform on the 26th floor is especially popular with visitors to the city.

16 Timpanogos Cave National Monument On the northern slope of the 3,581-m (11,749-ft)

Mount Timpanogo are three caves that have been formed over a long period of time due to the porosity of the limestone that is characteristic of the area. The bizarre stalactites are a real sight to behold. The three caves are connected by a man-made tunnel and can be viewed as part of a guided tour.

Due to its extraordinary nature the entire area has been declared a National Monument.

17 Capitol Reef National Park The Pan-American Highway is well-maintained in Utah. After having covered more than half of this state you will reach some of the absolute highlights along this dream route. Leave Highway 15 at Scipio and turn off onto Highway 50 for around 30 km (19 miles). Highway 12 turns off at Salina to the next national park.

1 The Snake River flows through Grand Teton National Park.

2 The Teton Range reaches more than 4,000 m (13,124 ft) and gave the national park its name.

3 Salt Lake City, the capital of Utah founded in 1915, lit up at night against the background of the surrounding mountains.

The wonders of erosion

Bizarre rock formations display a wide array of colours depending on the angle of the sun and characterize the image of the south-western United States. Nature presents a very mixed palette of colours here, but it is not only the colours, ranging from violet and all imaginable shades of red and orange to yellow and brown, that fascinate visitors but also the bizarre shapes. They are the work of erosion caused by water and wind that has modelled a magical rock landscape over millions of years.

Rivers like the Colorado have cut deep into the rock layers. The region also rose at the same time, but the cutting strength of the rivers was able to keep up with the rising earth. Over the

Bizarre rock landscapes in Bryce Canyon National Park.

course of time deep canyons were formed. The most spectacular of these is of course the Grand Canyon, but Bryce Canyon, Escalante Canyon or Glen Canyon are certainly not to be missed.

A further force has also played a key role in shaping the landscape – the wind. Smaller rocks are often exposed to the winds, particularly in drier areas with little vegetation. Through the ages the wind has carved these compact stone blocks into shapes that often look like they have been sculpted. Eye-catching needles, archways and mushrooms have been shaped from the rock in this way.

It therefore comes as no surprise that these fascinating canyons and plateaus have frequently served as film sets. Indeed, nowhere else is the vast expanse of this country more impressive.

The Capitol Reef National Park is characterized by a colourful cliff face towering above the Fremont River. The Fremont River has cut its way deep into a geological shift known as the Waterpocket Fold. Parallel ridges rise out of the desert sands here in a wave formation over a distance of 160 km (99 miles). Water and wind have fashioned the unique shapes, which invite comparisons with chimneys, roofs and even fortresses. There are also rock paintings from the Fremont Indians, which frequently depict animals.

Continuing along scenic Highway 12 you will reach Escalante where the road turns off to the south towards the Grand Staircase Escalante National Monument.

18 Grand Staircase Escalante National Monument Those in search of pristine nature will not be disappointed by this reserve between Bryce Canyon National Park to the south and west, the Capitol Reef National Park in the north, and the Glen Canyon National Recreation Area to the east. The National Monument was named after four towering layers of rock. The beauty of the landscape is characterized by gorges, rows of cliffs and plateaus and is best experienced from the dirt roads off the main highway.

The drive along the 200-km (124-mile) Burr Trail Loop weaves its way through the entire area. Initially a tarred road, it takes you along Deer Creek and then through the rocky labyrinth of Long Canyon. It later becomes a bit more challenging but is easily done with an off-road vehicle.

Back on Highway 12 head towards Bryce Canyon Airport. Shortly thereafter, Highway 63 turns off right to the Bryce Canyon Visitors Center.

19 Bryce Canyon National Park Unlike the rest of the landscape in the region, Bryce Canyon is not a canyon in the strict sense of the word. Rather, it is a series of crevices and smaller gullies. Some of the eroded gullies are more than 300 m (984 ft) deep. A lovely panoramic route takes you 30 km (19 miles) through the park,

which was founded in 1928, and leads to the southernmost point, Rainbow Point. The drive and its many vista points constantly provide splendid views over the dense pine forests.

Many of the orange, salmon-pink or red rock formations have characteristic names, such as Sunrise Point, Inspiration Point, Thor's Hammer or Chinese Wall. The landscape is other-worldly and is especially impressive at sunset or sunrise.

After Bryce Canyon it is worth making a detour some 100 km (62 miles) to the west to the Cedar Breaks National Monument. The turn-off to Cedar City is a few kilometres after the junction of Highway 12 and Highway 89.

20 Cedar Breaks National Monument Founded by the Mormons in 1851, Cedar City's Iron Mission State Park and

Museum, with more than 300 old vehicles, documents the pioneering spirit of the Mormons. The Shakespeare Festival also takes place here every summer in the Globe Theater. The National Monument's dimensions may be somewhat smaller than those of Bryce Canyon but the colours are just as enticing. The next stop is Zion National Park, reached from the turn-off at Mount Carmel Junction (Highway 9).

21 Zion National Park This area was declared a national park in 1919 and has several entrances. The most important attractions are found in the southern part, and the Zion-Mount Carmel Highway (9) takes you via the plateau at the East Entrance 600 m (1,969 ft) downhill to the more deserty South Entrance. The Canyon Overlook provides one of the best views of the

beauty. The canyon is traversed by the Colorado River and is spanned by a road bridge. Turn onto Highway 89 where it joins the A89 and drive a short distance north towards Page. From here you can either continue to Glen Canyon Dam or make a detour to Antelope Canyon.

23 Lake Powell Since 1963 the Glen Canyon Dam has held back the Colorado River to create the 653-sq-km (405-sq-mi) Lake Powell, built to generate hydro-electric power.

The lake is now a haven for water-sports enthusiasts. There are also marvellous views of the sandstone formations whose perfectly flat plateaus look like they were measured with a ruler. On the southern shore is the nearly 90-m-high (295-ft) Rainbow Bridge, considered the largest natural bridge in North America. The area around the

Detour

Antelope Canyon

The two canyons of Antelope Creek are only a few metres wide, but the water has cut all the deeper into the rock here. During dry weather you

Midday sunshine in Antelope Canyon.

can hike through the Lower Antelope Canyon, but after it has rained there is too much water in the river. It is particularly fascinating to visit the canyon at midday when the sun's rays shine directly into the depths of the canyon.

heart of the national park, Zion Canyon, created by the Virgin River, a tributary of the Colorado River.

A tunnel built 255 m (837 ft) above the valley floor makes the drive to the Zion Canyon Visitor Center all the more dramatic. From here the Zion Canyon Scenic Drive follows numerous serpentine bends of the winding Virgin River for 12 km (7.5 miles). The most well-known hike in the

park, the 2-km (1.2-mile) River Walk, starts at the end of the road and leads to the 600-m (1,969-ft) canyon walls. The waterfalls on the Emerald Pools Trail are also worth seeing, as are the Hanging Gardens, a cliff overgrown with vegetation.

If you have time, take the park's southern exit and return via the Pipe Spring National Monument and the Pan-American Highway where the A89 turns off from

Highway 89 at Kanab heading south. At Jacob Lake a side road leads to the northern entrance of the Grand Canyon (North Rim), or you can continue along the A89 to the next stop, Marble Canyon.

22 Marble Canyon Close to the town of the same name in the far north of Arizona is Marble Canyon, a prime example of the state's diverse natural

1 Walls of rock in Capitol Reef National Park.

2 View over the countless needles of Bryce Canyon at twilight.

3 The Colorado River cuts through the horizontal layers of fascinating Marble Canyon.

4 A bold bridge over Marble Canyon.

Phoenix

A metropolis in the midst of a dry desert landscape, Phoenix, Arizona attracts visitors with more than 300 days of sunshine a year. In the summer in particular, Phoenix and the surrounding area are characterized by the massive irrigation units that make decadent golf courses and the cultivation of vegetables possible.

Old and modern architecture in Downtown Phoenix.

There is also a bit of culture here. Heritage Square is lined with Victorian houses that are worth a look. The Heard Museum houses an extensive collection of Indian art with sculptures, weaving and paintings. The Arizona Science Center documents the world of science in all its many facets.

lake was declared the Glen Canyon National Recreation Area in 1972.

24 Grand Canyon National Park This world-famous national park can be reached from the north via the turn-off at Jacob Lake and from the south via Cameron (Highway 64) or Flagstaff (Highway 180), both of which lead to the South Rim. The northern side of the canyon, which is 30 km at its widest point, is about 360 m (1,181 ft) higher than the southern side and the canyon walls drop nearly 1,800 m (5,906 ft) down to the Colorado River here.

As the northern Kaibab Plateau is significantly higher than the southern Coconino Plateau, the North Rim provides a completely different perspective of the canyon landscape than the South Rim. Bright Angel Point provides a marvellous backdrop near the Grand Canyon Lodge. Shortly before this viewing point there is a 35-km-long (22-mile) road that branches off to the north to Point Imperial which, at 2,683 m (8,803 ft), is the highest point in the national park.

The southern part receives considerably more visitors. Grand Canyon Village is recommended as the starting point. From here a panoramic route provides access to West Rim Drive and East Rim Drive.

25 Flagstaff The drive from Cameron to Flagstaff passes the Wupatki National Monument with more than 2,000 historical sites once inhabited by Hopi Indians. Just outside Flagstaff is the 120-m-deep (394-ft) crater created in 1064 by a volcanic eruption. The volcanic cone is called Sunset Crater Volcano because of its colour.

The centre of Flagstaff is characterized by red-brick buildings.

It is worth paying a visit to the Lowell Observatory from which scientists discovered Pluto in 1930. The cultural highlight is the Museum of Northern Arizona with archaeological and ethnological displays.

26 Walnut Canyon South of town close to Interstate 40/ Route 66, head west to Walnut Canyon with its famous Sinagua Indian dwellings. More than

twenty of the dwellings open to visitors were built into the cliffs in the 12th and 13th centuries, and some of them are in especially adventurous locations.

27 Montezuma Castle National Monument This Indian site close to the town of Cottonwood was declared a National Monument in 1906 and comprises the remnants of a Sinagua Indian dwelling that was fitted

into the recess of a rock face 30 m (98 ft) high. The Sinagua built twenty rooms in the dwelling more than 600 years ago and used ladders for access. An exhibition in the visitor centre beneath the cliffs documents the Sinagua culture. The trailhead along Beaver Creek is also here.

From Cottonwood it is around 80 km (50 miles) to the junction of Highway 89 and Highway 60, which takes you to Phoenix.

28 Phoenix (see sidebar left). In Phoenix you join Interstate 10 going towards Tucson. The last stop before Tucson is an American Indian memorial.

29 Casa Grande Ruins National Monument Agriculture has been practised in the Gila River Valley south of Phoenix for thousands of years. Local Hohokam Indian culture was already cultivating the land in this area in 200 BC using sophisticated canal systems.

The most important remnants of this culture include the Casa Grande, or 'Big House', a four-storey clay building constructed at the start of the 14th century, the last period of the Hohokam. With walls 1.20 m (4 ft) thick it is more like a fortress, but was abandoned in the 14th century. The building can only be viewed from the outside.

30 Tucson After about three hours on the road you reach Tucson, the 'City of Sunshine'. The approach is an experience in itself. Once you have crossed the last chain of mountains outside the city, gleaming skyscrapers appear, towering out of the Santa Cruz River valley. The colonial era neighbourhood lies in the shadows of these massive buildings and gives Tucson much of its charm.

Due to its climate and mountainous surroundings, the city is a popular winter sports destination, especially during the 'cold' season when the temperature is a consistent 20 to 25°C (68 to 77°F).

Tucson is situated in the Sonoran Desert where the Saguaro cacti reach heights of 10 m (33 ft). The contrast between the end of the North American portion of the Pan-American Highway in the desert and its start in the cold coastal forests of Canada's Prince Rupert could hardly be greater.

1 Grand Canyon – view of the canyon from Toroweap Point.

2 The Wupatki National Monument is about 96 km (60 miles) south-east of Grand Canyon National Park and is a testimony to the American Indian way of life.

3 Montezuma Castle Valley and the ruins of an Indian pueblo.

Mission San Xavier del Bac

Some 15 km (9 miles) south of Tucson is the oldest and best-preserved mission church in south-western USA. It is an exceptional example of Spanish colonial architecture.

The Jesuit priest Eusebio Kino founded the first mission here in 1700. The complex as it is today was completed by the Franciscans in 1790. The masonry work around the entrance and the painted ceilings

Mission San Xavier del Bac – the church is also known as the 'White Dove of Peace'.

inside the church are of exceptional artistic quality. The main altar is adorned with richly decorated pillars and gold-plated wood carvings. Regular church services are still held in the mission church today.

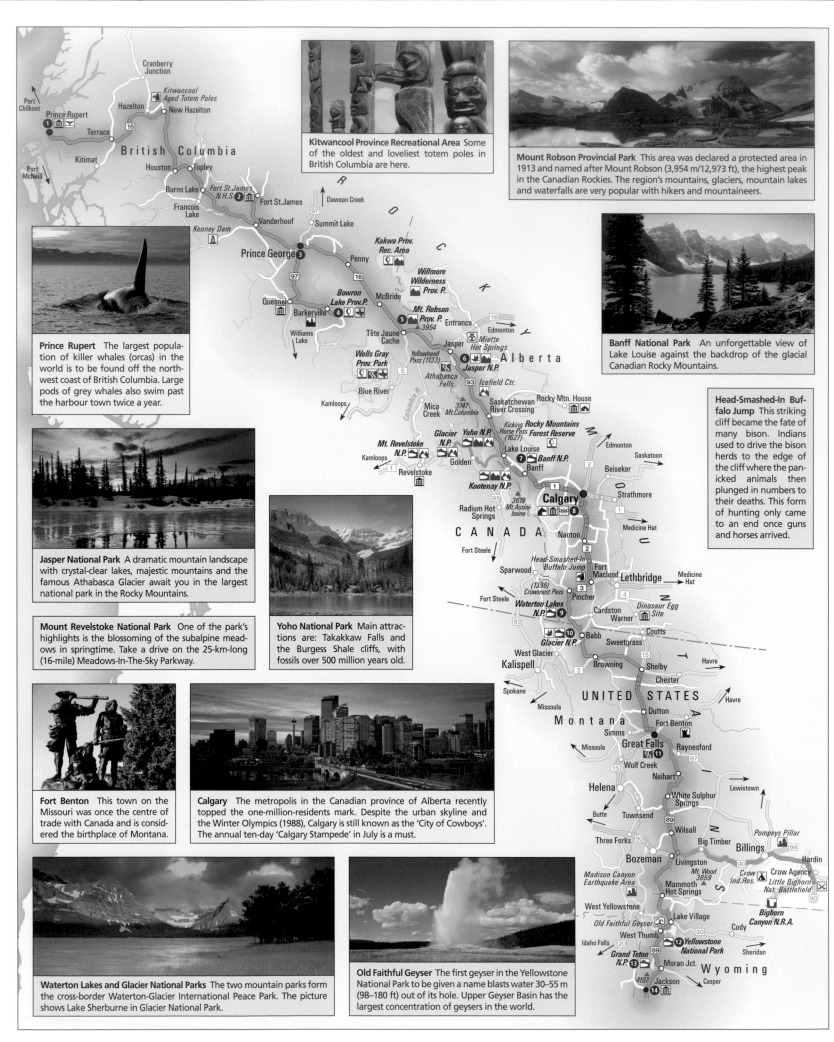

Kitwancool Province Recreational Area Some of the oldest and loveliest totem poles in British Columbia are here.

Mount Robson Provincial Park This area was declared a protected area in 1913 and named after Mount Robson (3,954 m/12,973 ft), the highest peak in the Canadian Rockies. The region's mountains, glaciers, mountain lakes and waterfalls are very popular with hikers and mountaineers.

Prince Rupert The largest population of killer whales (orcas) in the world is to be found off the northwest coast of British Columbia. Large pods of grey whales also swim past the harbour town twice a year.

Banff National Park An unforgettable view of Lake Louise against the backdrop of the glacial Canadian Rocky Mountains.

Head-Smashed-In Buffalo Jump This striking cliff became the fate of many bison. Indians used to drive the bison herds to the edge of the cliff where the panicked animals then plunged in numbers to their deaths. This form of hunting only came to an end once guns and horses arrived.

Jasper National Park A dramatic mountain landscape with crystal-clear lakes, majestic mountains and the famous Athabasca Glacier await you in the largest national park in the Rocky Mountains.

Mount Revelstoke National Park One of the park's highlights is the blossoming of the subalpine meadows in springtime. Take a drive on the 25-km-long (16-mile) Meadows-In-The-Sky Parkway.

Yoho National Park Main attractions are: Takakkaw Falls and the Burgess Shale cliffs, with fossils over 500 million years old.

Fort Benton This town on the Missouri was once the centre of trade with Canada and is considered the birthplace of Montana.

Calgary The metropolis in the Canadian province of Alberta recently topped the one-million-residents mark. Despite the urban skyline and the Winter Olympics (1988), Calgary is still known as the 'City of Cowboys'. The annual ten-day 'Calgary Stampede' in July is a must.

Waterton Lakes and Glacier National Parks The two mountain parks form the cross-border Waterton-Glacier International Peace Park. The picture shows Lake Sherburne in Glacier National Park.

Old Faithful Geyser The first geyser in the Yellowstone National Park to be given a name blasts water 30–55 m (98–180 ft) out of its hole. Upper Geyser Basin has the largest concentration of geysers in the world.

Grand Teton National Park Elk roam the low-lying areas of the Teton Range, one of the most impressive mountain chains in the USA. The highest peak, Grand Teton, is 4,197 m (13,770 ft). Some of the mountains are covered with glaciers while former glaciers have formed deep lakes in the basins.

Salt Lake City The skyline of the Utah capital is dominated by the Capitol building (1915). Salt Lake City, venue for the 2002 Winter Olympics, is the centre of the growing global Mormon community.

Grand Canyon The canyon in north-west Arizona was formed by the Colorado River cutting into the Colorado Plateau. The 350-km-long (217-mile) and up to 1.8-km-deep (1-mile) canyon is one of the most impressive natural wonders in the USA.

Phoenix Once an Indian settlement, Phoenix is today an important high-tech centre. It boasts buildings from all eras, like this colonial-era mission church. The palms that grow throughout the city are characteristic of Phoenix.

Mission San Xavier del Bac This bright white mission church was completed in 1790 by Franciscans. It is an impressive example of Spanish mission architecture and one of the best-preserved churches in the whole of the United States.

Pima Air and Space Museum There are over 200 planes on display here at the south-eastern edge of Tucson. The collection ranges from Wright Brothers-era models to the most modern of supersonic jets.

Yellowstone National Park Geysers and hot springs – in this case Morning Glory Prismatic Spring – are the most spectacular attractions in the largest and oldest national park in the USA, situated in the Rocky Mountains at an altitude of 2,400 m (7,874 ft).

Bryce Canyon National Park The forces of erosion make an impressive display here, especially in the Bryce Amphitheater.

Capitol Reef National Park Rock needles tower over a sandstone cliff 150 km (93 miles) long.

Wupatki National Monument The largest and best-preserved pueblo ruins, built by prehistoric Indians, are to be found north of Sunset Crater in the midst of a desert landscape. In total there are around 2,000 Sinagua and Anasazi dwellings.

Meteor Crater Some 50,000 years ago a meteorite landed in northern Arizona. It left behind a crater with a circumference of 1.3 km (0.81 miles) and a depth of 170 m (558 ft). Because of its geological similarity to the craters on the moon it is used as a NASA training ground for astronauts.

Montezuma Castle National Monument 600 years ago the Sinagua Indians built a twentyroom dwelling in a 30-m-high (98-ft) sandstone cliff face, extending over five storeys.

Tucson The centre of the second-largest city in Arizona, after Phoenix, is dominated by skyscrapers. A colonial-era neighbourhood with a number of adobe houses has been preserved in the shadows of the skyscrapers and makes a significant contribution to Tucson's charm.

Route 24

USA

The awe-inspiring sequoias in Redwood National Park can reach heights of up to 112 m (367 ft).

'The American Way of Life' between the Pacific coast and the Sierra Nevada

Sun, sea and tanned surfers. It's a popular cliché image that many people have of California and, as with many such clichés, it has an element of truth to it. But the Golden State on the west coast of the USA has myriad other facets as well – majestic mountains, ancient forests with giant redwood trees, superb alpine lakes, breathtaking deserts and one of the most beautiful coastal roads in the country, Highway 1. On top of that there are lively cities such as Los Angeles, San Francisco and San Diego.

'Go West, young man, and grow up with the country!' Since the middle of the 19th century this call has inspired countless people to seek their fortunes in the promised lands of California. Today, millions of tourists from all over the world are also drawn by the magic of this region on the West Coast. Highway 1, with its magnificent views of the mighty Pacific Ocean, could easily be considered one of the most beautiful roads in the world. Yet the

'hinterland' offers equally spectacular natural wonders, from the rock walls and waterfalls of Yosemite National Park and the bizarre limestone formations of Mono Lake to the glorious giant sequoias (redwood trees) scattered throughout the numerous parks around the state. They flourish wonderfully along the misty Pacific coast as well as in the cool Sierra

Nevada mountains. Then there are arid regions such as the Mojave Desert which, at first glance, seem devoid of almost any life. After the brief, irregular showers of rain, however, the desert produces a magical variety of plant life. Death Valley, somewhat off this tour's path, is surrounded by mountains rising to more than 3,000 m (9,843 ft) and evokes lunar landscapes of spectacular proportions. It also boasts such superlatives as the lowest point in the Western Hemisphere and the highest temperature ever recorded. European travellers are continually overwhelmed by the diversity and beauty of these magnificent natural landscapes.

Indeed, Mother Nature has been generous to this Pacific region. Gold discoveries in 1849 brought about the first major wave of settlement. Hollywood, synonymous with the glamorous world of film,

In the late 1980s the famous Santa Monica Pier was restored to its former glory.

Population growth in Los Angeles in the mid-1900s depleted water levels in Mono Lake to such an extent that evaporation became faster than inflow. These exposed tufa towers are a result of these developments. Successful efforts are now being made to restore the lake's former state.

San Francisco by moonlight. The 2.7-km (1.7-mile) Golden Gate Bridge, at the entrance to San Francisco Bay, was completed in 1937 and links the city with Marin County to the north.

has the sunny Southern California climate to thank for its existence. Yet the same sun that draws tourists to the beaches also makes the hugely important agricultural business here a major challenge, one that is really only possible with the help of sophisticated and far-reaching irrigation systems. The Californians have artfully mastered their often tough natural environment and do not even seem too distracted by the San Andreas Fault, repeatedly the cause of disastrous earthquakes here.

A tour through California brings to life the many places linked to the region's Spanish and Mexican legacy, like Santa Barbara, San Luis Obispo or Carmel, all of which play host to mission churches founded by Spanish monks along 'El Camino Real', the Royal Road. San Francisco, often considered the most 'European' city in the USA and a dream destination for people around the world, originally boomed after the discovery of gold in the foothills of the Sierra Nevada. It was only in the 20th century that its rival to the south, Los Angeles, grew to its current sprawling size – life without a car is inconceivable here.

California's open-mindedness has often promoted important subculture movements that have even had global influence – the Beat Generation, the Hippies, the Gay Movement, rural communes, ecological movements and other milieus experimenting with alternative lifestyles. Not to be forgotten is of course Silicon Valley, the pioneer site of the digital revolution in the 20th century.

As a whole, a trip through California reflects a sort of microcosm of what the 'American Dream' is all about.

El Capitan and the Merced River in a wintry Yosemite National Park.

Detour

San Diego

This city, very close to the Mexican border, has a lively downtown. Today Old Town, the Spanish-style heart of the city, has been made into a pedestrian zone. For people interested in the city's history and the origins of San Diego in the 18th century, we recommend a visit to the Old Town State Historic Park. Some of the restored adobe houses are open to visitors and provide insight into life in Southern California in the 18th and 19th centuries. The Serra Museum provides further information on this former Spanish settlement on the Pacific west coast. Downtown San Diego is a combination of both historic and

View over the harbour and the San Diego skyline.

modern streets. The heart of the city centre is the Gaslamp Quarter where the architecture brings the turn of the 20th century back to life. Once a dubious area of brothels and gambling houses, the quarter has been the focus of a preservation order since 1980 and has become a popular residential and nightlife area. Many of the old Victorian houses have been renovated, and the cobblestones and gas lamps give it a romantic air, particularly in the evening. The nearby Horton Plaza and the Gaslamp Quarter combine to create a sort of post-modern shopping experience in the heart of a carefully renovated downtown area.

Plan at least a day for Balboa Park, where a number of the pavilions are still reminiscent of the Panama Pacific Exposition of 1915. The zoo in the northern part of the expansive grounds is world-renowned and a must-see. The famous museums in the park include the San Diego Museum of Art, with works by North American and European artists, the San Diego Museum of Man in the California Building (1915), the Timkin Museum of Art, and the Mingei International Museum, with folk art from all over the world. The Aerospace Museum gives good insight into aerospace technology.

In addition to numerous cultural highlights, our tour through California offers a look at some breathtaking natural landscapes. The drive up Highway 1 from Los Angeles to San Francisco is one of the best parts, running high above the spectacular Pacific coast for most of the way.

1 Los Angeles (see pp. 320–321). Our route begins in Los Angeles on Highway 101 (the Ventura Highway). From there, the most famous stretch of Highway 1 branches off at Las Cruces (called Cabrillo Highway here), a few miles beyond Santa Barbara. It covers an often breathtaking route over bridges or directly along the steep Pacific coastline, providing continuously spectacular views.

2 Santa Barbara Founded in 1782 as a Spanish garrison, the city's architecture fascinates visitors. After being reduced to rubble in 1925 by a heavy earthquake, the city took the opportunity to rebuild the entire downtown in Spanish colonial style, an example of which is the County Courthouse built in 1929. From the bell tower you can enjoy a wonderful view of the city. Mission Santa Barbara, officially nicknamed the 'Queen of the Missions', also suffered severe damage in the 1925 earthquake and was initially restored before further rebuilding took place in the 1950s. The mission's charac-

Travel Information

Route profile

Length: approx. 2,500 km (1,554 miles), excluding detours

Time required: 3–4 weeks

Start and end: Los Angeles

Route (main locations): Los Angeles, Monterey, San Francisco, Eureka, Redwood National Park, Mount Shasta, Lassen Volcanic National Park, Lake Tahoe, Yosemite National Park, Sequoia and Kings Canyon National Park, Mono Lake, Mojave, Los Angeles

Traffic information:

Drive on the right in the USA. In autumn and spring you should enquire as to the condition of the roads in the national parks of the Cascade Range (Mount Shasta, Mount Lassen) and the Sierra Nevada (Yosemite, Sequoia and Kings Canyon) as the roads close in winter. Toll roads along the route: the 17-Mile Drive on the Monterey Peninsula and the Golden Gate Bridge (travelling into San Francisco).

Information:

Detailed information on national parks in California: *www.nps.gov*
Information and departure times for ferries to Santa Cruz Island from Ventura: *www.islandpackers.com* and from Santa Barbara: *www.truthaquatics.com* Napa Valley information: *www.napavalley.com*

taking in the many Bohemians who left the destroyed city. The town retains this character even today. The most original house in the town is the Tor House, carved out of stone blocks and built by the poet Robinson Jeffers. During the heyday of the missions, the Mission San Carlos Borromeodel Rio Carmelo (Mission Carmel) was established in 1770 and served as a centre of religious activities due to its proximity to the then capital of 'Alta California', Monterey. The old mission kitchen, garden and housing have been reconstructed according to the originals.

⑦ **Monterey** During the colonial era this city, with its historically significant centre, was the capital of 'Alta California' and

Craggy coast on Santa Cruz Island.

teristic combination of Roman, Moorish and Spanish elements became the archetype of the California mission style. The mission church is the only one of the original California missions that is still being used as a church.

③ **San Luis Obispo** The heart of this tranquil little town at the base of the Santa Lucia Mountains is the San Luis Obispo de Tolosa Mission, founded in 1772 as the fifth of more than twenty Californian missions. One of the mission buildings adjoining the church has a museum with interesting art works by the Chumash Indians, once present in the area.

④ **Hearst Castle, San Simeon** Hearst Castle, completed in 1947, is without doubt one of the classic tourist attractions along Highway 1. This bizarre 'castle', situated above the town of San Simeon, was built by one of America's legendary newspaper magnates, William Randolph Hearst. Gothic and Renaissance features are combined with Moorish ornaments, while the Neptune Pool bears traces of Ancient Rome. But the 155 rooms of this kitschy, decadent setting also host valuable art treasures, from Ancient Egyptian, Greek and Roman artefacts, and paintings from the Flemish, Gothic and Italian Renaissance eras, to baroque pieces and priceless books.

⑤ **Big Sur** The name refers to a 160-km (99-mile) stretch of coast-line between San Simeon and Carmel. Sections of this frequently untouched landscape are indeed easy to reach thanks to Highway 1, but there are still remote, deserted bays, a magnificently rocky coast and backcountry that is easily accessible via the state park. North America's largest kelp forest (a type of seaweed) lies off the coast, as does the Monterey Canyon, which is similar in size to the actual Grand Canyon in Arizona. The unique attraction of this stretch of the highway is the Central Coast Range's sharp descent into the sea.

Architectural attractions include the 80-m (262-ft) Bixby Creek Bridge, an arch bridge dating from 1932.

⑥ **Carmel** This settlement at the southern end of the Monterey Peninsula was established as an artists' colony after the San Francisco earthquake of 1906,

① Highway 1 joins the 160-km (99-mile) Big Sur Coast between San Simeon and Carmel.

② Church services have been held here since the foundation stone was laid at the Santa Barbara Mission in 1786.

③ The pounding Pacific surf continues to erode the steep cliffs along the coast in Big Sur.

④ Once home to a millionaire eccentric, Hearst Castle, San Simeon is now an impressive museum.

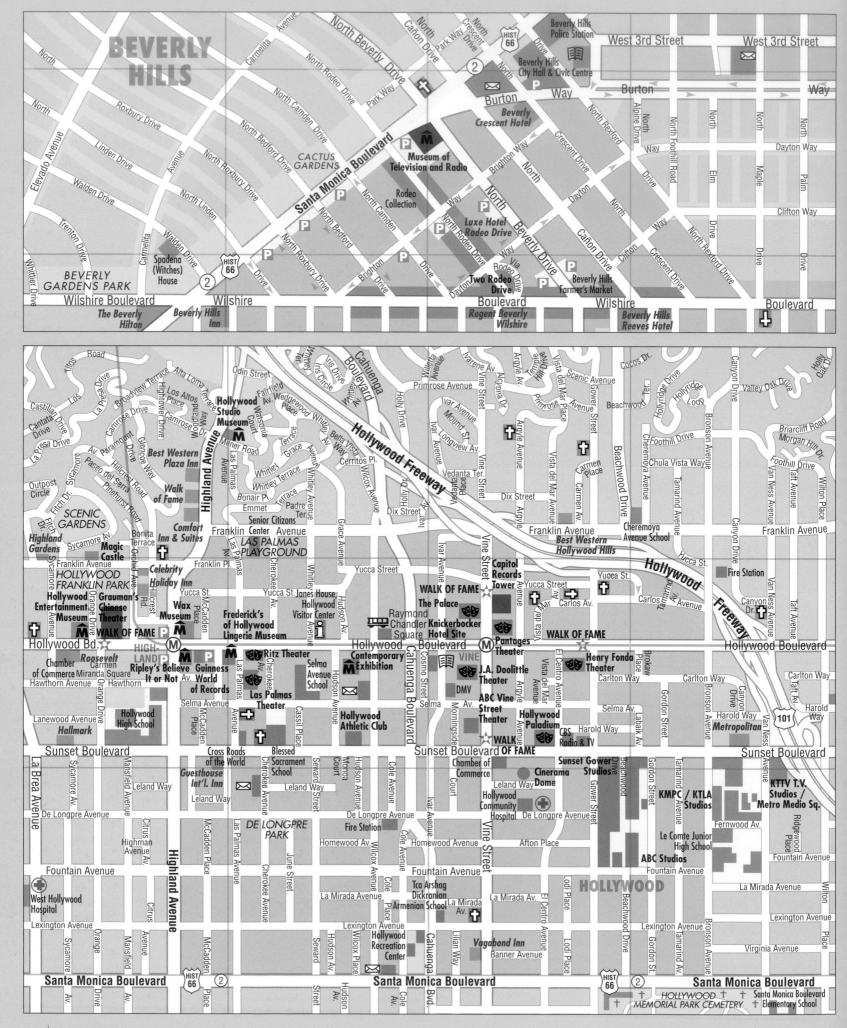

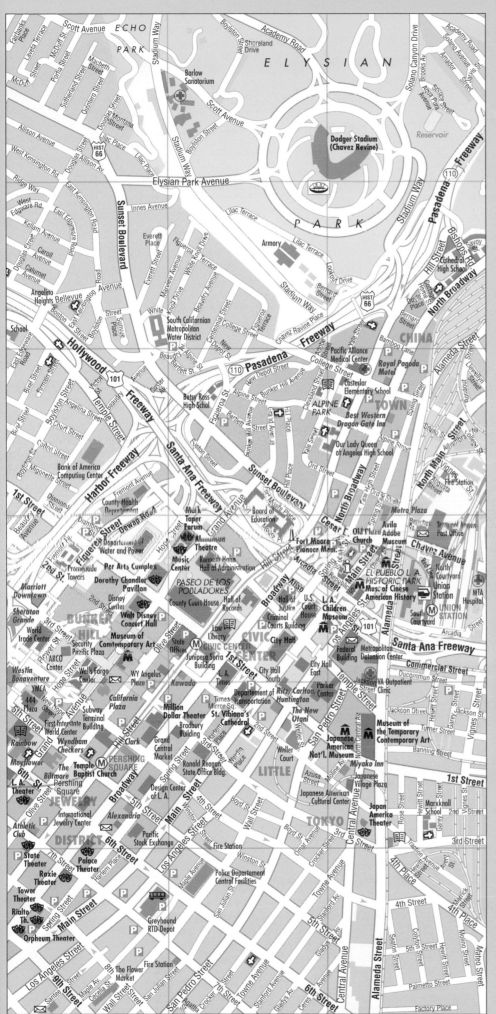

Los Angeles

The 'City of Angels' actually comprises several independent neighbourhoods and a multitude of massive freeways. Some traces of the Spanish past can still be seen today in the old town, while Hollywood has become a modern legend. On the periphery are the beaches – Santa Monica, Malibu and Venice.

Mann's Chinese Theater, a luxurious cinema in the style of a Chinese temple, was built in 1927 by Sid Grauman and was the scene of elaborate premieres during Hollywood's golden years. Legendary stars such as Elizabeth Taylor, Humphrey Bogart and John Wayne have been immortalized with their hand- and footprints in the cement in front of the entrance.

The best view of Los Angeles is from the Griffith Observatory on Mount Hollywood. There are also still numerous adobe buildings from the 19th century in the old town. In this 'El Pueblo de Los Angeles', Olvera Street is the scene of an annual carnival with street artists and colourful stalls.

Union Station is the name of the magnificent railway station built in 1939 in the style of a Spanish mission. It was once a stop for legendary trains such as the *Daylight Special* or the *City of Los Angeles*. In the 1960s Venice Beach was the in-beach for spaced-out Beat-

arts, furniture and other exhibitions of note.

The broad, palm-lined Sunset Boulevard takes you through Bel Air and Beverly Hills. Even the smog seems to have disappeared from this artificial luxury oasis with its waving palm trees, blossoming gardens and magnificent villas. There is hardly a single house without its own pool and tennis court. The rich and famous live behind these walls, and they don't seem to want company.

The Beverly Hills Hotel (1912) on Sunset Boulevard was thoroughly renovated in 2005. Marilyn Monroe was a frequent guest of the famous Polo Lounge. Italian and French designer names dominate the expensive fashion shops on nearby Rodeo Drive.

The famous pier in Santa Monica was built in 1909 and renovated in the 1980s to its former glory. Even the wooden carousel still operates. Three streets away, on the Third Street

Top: Numerous impressive skyscrapers dominate the skyline of downtown Los Angeles.
Middle: The Boulevard of Broken Dreams – an evening street scene in Hollywood.
Bottom: Rodeo Drive in Beverly Hills, one of the most elegant shopping miles in the world.

niks and Hippies. Today it is frequented by countless street performers, skaters, rappers and bodybuilders. Front Walk is full of stalls selling T-shirts and sunglasses.

The J. Paul Getty Museum at the Getty Center is more than just an architectural sensation. The millionaire's legacy includes valuable paintings, graphic

Promenade between Broadway and Wilshire Boulevard, is a pedestrian zone with the usual chain stores as well as exclusive boutiques.

Malibu 30 km (17 miles) north of Santa Monica, once a private ranch, has been home to famous film stars and singers since the 1940s. The numerous beaches are especially popular with surfers.

Detour

Napa Valley

Highway 29 (the Great Wine Way) extends from San Francisco to the nearby 50-km-long (31-mile) Napa Valley. The centre of this wine growing area is the town of Napa, about an hour from San Francisco. Vines have been grown on the fertile volcanic soils of the Napa Valley since the middle of the 19th century. Both red and white wines have often outdone the European competition at blind tastings.

Numerous vineyards, including some of the largest such as Beringer Vineyards, Robert Mondavi Winery or Charles Krug Winery (the oldest vineyard in the Napa Valley), are

Top and middle: Vines are grown over large areas of the long valley between Napa and Calisto.
Bottom: At Clos Pegase the wine barrels are stored in a stone cellar.

open to visitors for tastings. In addition to wine, Le Clos Pegase also houses an art collection of note in its architecturally unique buildings.

An unusual way to explore the valley is with the Napa Valley Wine Train, a restored Pullman dining car from 1917, in which exquisite food is served with fine wines.

also the site of another famous mission. The Monterey State Historic Park includes over thirty historic sites including the oldest government building in California, the Customs House, built in 1840. The signposted 'Path of History' takes you to all the important historic buildings. The Monterey Bay Aquarium presents the flora and fauna of the four large habitats of Monterey Bay – the kelp forest, the reef, the rocky coast and the outer bay. Our journey then continues to San Francisco via the delightful seaside town of Santa Cruz.

8 San Francisco (see pp. 324–325). You depart San Francisco via its most famous landmark, the Golden Gate Bridge, towards the north, passing through Sausalito with its original houseboats and Victorian houses perched on the slopes above the North Bay. After a short distance on Highway 101 along the waterfront, Highway 1

turns off towards the Pacific at the town of Belvedere. From there it continues through the fabulous Point Reyes National Seashore to Fort Ross, 19 km (12 miles) north of Jenner.

9 Fort Ross State Historic Park This fortified complex was founded in 1812 by Russian traders sent by the Tsars to supply their fellow fur hunters living in Alaska. The fort was abandoned in 1839 and part of the original complex still remains. The Russian Orthodox chapel (1824) is especially attractive and the cemetery with its Russian crosses is also worth visiting.

10 Mendocino Fishermen from New England first settled here in 1852. Later adopted by artists as a place of residence, the town has a spectacular location high above the sea and still retains some of its East Coast character. It has often served as a set for Hollywood films.

Highway 1, still offering magnificent views of the Pacific, leaves the coast just north of Westport and joins up with Highway 101 again at Leggett.

11 Humboldt Redwoods State Park The 53-km-long (33-mile) Avenue of Giants was originally built as a stagecoach road and runs through the park for about 1 km (0.6 miles) parallel to Highway 101. As the park's name indicates, redwood trees are the main attraction here, and you'll see them in all their colossal glory as they dwarf the humans that marvel at them. Loads of trails lead deep into the realm of the coastal giants. The trees are often more than 500 years old and they flourish in the mild, misty climate on the coast. Despite extensive deforestation in the past there are still dense clusters in places. One oddity is the almost 100-m (328-ft) Chandelier Tree – it has a passage cut into it that is large enough for cars.

12 Eureka Today the most important industrial centre on the northern Californian coast, this town was founded by gold diggers in 1850. The examples of Victorian architecture include the unusual William Carson Mansion, which resembles a haunted castle with numerous towers and gables. Local timber businessman Carson built it in the 1880s. Another must-see is the Clarke Museum with its Victorian age exhibits and its fine collection of Indian artworks.

13 Redwood National Park This national park (a UNESCO World Heritage Site), founded in 1968, protects some of the largest redwood forests in the world. It extends over a total of 125 km (78 miles) from Arcata (north of Eureka) to Crescent City (centre of the national park). Historic Crescent City was largely destroyed on 28 March 1964 by a tsunami with 6-m-high (20-ft) waves, caused by an earthquake in Alaska.

Reno

Reno, Nevada, was founded in the 1860s as a station along the Central Pacific Railroad. With the discovery of gold and silver in the region the town soon enjoyed its first boom. Its second heyday began in 1931 when gambling was legalized in the state (Las Vegas is also in Nevada). The initiators hoped that this would bring an upsurge in tourism during the Depression. In 1956 a further attraction was added to the flourishing casinos – the first Wedding Chapel. Today Reno is a paradise for gamblers and newlyweds. In contrast to other states in the USA and to other countries in the world, weddings and divorces are carried out with a strikingly minimal degree of bureaucracy.

Night-time in the gambling town of Reno.

In Crescent City you turn onto Highway 99, travelling for about 110 km (68 miles) via Grant's Pass into Oregon where Highway 199 joins Interstate Highway 5. Cave fans can visit the Oregon Caves on the way. The mighty Cascade Range begins with the climb up to the 1,361-m (4,465-ft) Siskiyou Pass beyond Medford.

14 Mount Shasta This 4,317-m (14,165-ft) volcano towers majestically over the much lower peaks around it. A mountain road with fantastic views climbs up to an altitude of 2,400 m (7,874 ft), but an ascent on foot to the peak of the stratovolcano should only be attempted by experienced mountaineers. On the south-western side of the mountain is the little village of Mount Shasta City with a ranger station.
Highway 89 turns off to the south-east directly after Mount Shasta before making its way through the mountains of the Mount Shasta National Forest past the 40-m (131-ft) Burney

Falls in Lassen National Forest. At Subway Cave, a 396-m (1,299-ft) lava pipe, a well-signposted road turns off to the south west in the direction of Lassen Volcanic National Park, the entrance to which is near Manzanita Lake.

15 Lassen Volcanic National Park This national park takes its name from the volcano in the Cascade Range. The last dramatic eruption of the 3,187-m (10,457-ft) Mount Lassen took place in 1915 and destroyed some 40,500 ha (100,076 acres) of land. The Bumpass Hell trail is especially impressive, with hot springs, mud pools and smoke columns highlighting the undisturbed tectonic activity in the area.
As Lassen Park Road, Highway 89 leads through the national park to Mineral where you then turn east onto Highway 36 to Susanville. From there you continue on Highway 395 between the Diamond Mountains in the west and Honey Lake

in the east towards the south and over the border to Reno in Nevada. Here, Highway 80 turns off westwards to San Francisco, but you exit the highway after 30 km (19 miles) at Truckee and continue south to Lake Tahoe.

16 Lake Tahoe At an elevation of 1,920 m (6,300 ft), this alpine lake is 35 km (22 miles) long and 13 km (8 miles) wide. It reaches a depth of more than 500 m (1,641 ft) in parts and is one of the deepest inland lakes in the world. The majesty of this place is especially apparent from out on the lake itself. The border between California and Nevada actually runs through the middle of it. The 72-Mile Drive circles the lake, includes sightseeing attractions along the shore and is the access road to the state park there. On the southern shore is South Lake Tahoe, which attracts many visitors with its casinos. North of the city the replica of a 10th-century Viking fortress stands in Emerald Bay

State Park. The backcountry offers perfect conditions for skiers. The 1960 Winter Olympics were held at Squaw Valley on the north-western side of the lake.

1 When it opened in 1937, the almost 3-km (1.9-mile) Golden Gate was the world's longest bridge.

2 A storm on the Pacific coast close to Fort Bragg in Mendocino.

3 Deer tongue and sword ferns flourish in the moist climate of Redwood National Park.

4 The 4,317-m (14,164-ft) Mount Shasta is snow-capped most of the year.

5 Mount Lassen reflected off Manzanita Lake. The volcano erupted often between 1914 and 1921.

6 Emerald Bay, 15 km (9 miles) north of the town of South Lake Tahoe, is in the state park of the same name.

Ultimately, however, the majority of visitors come in hopes of making their fortune at the gambling tables or slot machines, the infamous 'one-armed bandits'. Accommodation and food in the hotels are usually relatively good value because their profits are actually generated by the gambling activities of their guests. Many of the hotels stage shows with international stars, and anyone interested in culture will not be disappointed either. The Nevada Museum of Art is dedicated to art from 1900 to the present. The modern building, designed by Will Bruder and first opened in spring 2003, is representative of contemporary art.

San Francisco

A unique location overlooking an expansive bay on the Pacific Ocean, historic cable cars, unique neighbourhoods like Chinatown and North Beach, bustling Market Street, Fisherman's Wharf and the Golden Gate Bridge have all made San Francisco, the 'Paris of the American West', into a revered travel destination.

The city was founded by the Spanish in 1776 and named Yerba Buena. Only in 1847 was the name changed to San Francisco after the San Francisco de Asís Mission was founded by Father Junípero Serra.

The city's most turbulent period began in January 1848 when gold was discovered in northern California. San Francisco became a base for many gold diggers heading north. More than 40,000 adventurers and profiteers settled in the city in 1849 alone. It soon grew to become an important trading centre, and has remained so even after the massive earthquake destroyed entire neighbourhoods throughout the city in 1906.

Alcatraz lies in San Francisco Bay. The rocky island was discovered by the Spanish and named after the pelicans that used to inhabit the

The famous cable cars were developed by Andrew S. Hallidie in 1869, the first of them rolling through town in 1873. By 1880 there were already eight lines and since 1964 they have been protected as part of the city's heritage.

One of the USA's most well-known landmarks, the Golden Gate Bridge, opened for traffic in 1937 following four years of construction. Including its access roads, the bridge is 11 km (9 miles) long, and the pylons extend 228 m (748 ft) out of the water. Following the California gold rush of 1849, Fisherman's Wharf was the primary mooring for commercial boats. Today it is geared toward shopping and tourism.

San Francisco's distinct neighbourhoods are a joy to explore. Chinatown, for example, between Broadway, Bush, Kearny and Stockton Street is the

Top: The characteristic triangular shape of the Transamerica Pyramid is clearly recognizable among the skyscrapers.
Middle: With their pastel colours and stylish detail, the so-called Painted Ladies are excellent examples of Victorian architecture.
Bottom: A football game in the university town of Berkeley, across the San Francisco Bay to the east.

island. In the 19th century the US Army built a fort there, which was converted to a military prison in 1909. The first civil prisoners were brought in 1934 to 'The Rock', at the time considered the most secure prison in the world.

second largest Chinese community in the USA (after New York). The official entrance is marked by a large red-green gate at the junction of Grant and Bush streets. The first Star-Spangled Banner was raised in California in 1846 at Portsmouth Square.

Free climbing at Half Dome

Free climbing is an extreme form of rock climbing. Climbers secure themselves to the rock face (it is only with free solo climbing that no protection is used), but on the most famous of the routes there are no fixed hooks or rope protection.

The 2,695-m (8,842-ft) Half Dome in Yosemite National Park is one of the

Top: View of Half Dome from Olmstead Point.
Bottom: The dream of many a climber – to ascend the vertical face of Half Dome.

most revered climbing locations in the world. The route on the north-west flank is the fiercest challenge for even the best climbers. The record for this route is 9.5 hours, but most climbers need more than a day for it. There are other routes on El Capitan at the western end of Yosemite Valley, where The Nose is especially well-known.

Highway 395 continues through the sparsely populated mountains to the eastern entrance of Yosemite National Park at Lee Vining. Highway 120 takes you over the Tioga Pass at an elevation of 3,031 m (9,945 ft) and heads west towards Tuolumne Grove 56 km (35 miles) away at the north-west entrance of the park.

17 Yosemite National Park Not only one of the most renowned parks in the USA, but also one of the oldest – the initial areas were first declared a national park in the 1860s. This protected area was extended in around 1890, and in 1905 it was enlarged to its present size.

Many of the main attractions here are in the 10-km-long (6-mile) Yosemite Valley, at the epicentre of the park – majestic peaks such as El Capitan or Half Dome, and the glorious Yosemite Falls, over 739 m (2,425 ft) high. Around 500 giant redwoods, some of them over 75 m (246 ft) high, can be found in Mariposa Grove on the park's southern border. The early summer blossoms of subalpine plants in the Tuolumne Meadows are a special treat. Glacier Point, at 2,138 m (7,015 ft), towers almost 1,000 m (3,281 ft) over the valley and offers spectacular panoramic views over large areas of the

park. Get there via Glacier Point Road. The visitor centre provides background details on the park and the Yosemite Museum gives you an idea of the history of the Miwok and Paiute Indians. The Pioneer Center is another museum made up of blockhouses from various parts of the park and documents the life of the early Wild West settlers.

The approach to the adjoining Sequoia and Kings Canyon National Park is difficult as this is

accessible only from the southern side. To reach it you need to leave Yosemite via Highway 41 in the south and head to Fresno. From there Highway 180 leads to the Big Stump Entrance in the west of the park.

18 Sequoia and Kings Canyon National Park These two national parks, which are administered as one entity, are perhaps less famous than their northern neighbour but they offer breath-

taking scenery nonetheless: mountain forests, granite domes and giant canyons, including Kings Canyon, one of the deepest in America. The Sequoia National Park protects an impressive number of giant redwoods in various sections – Cedar Grove, Grant Grove and Giant Forest. The 'General Sherman' tree in the Giant Forest, standing at 85 m (279 ft), is said to be the largest tree in the world by volume, and five of the world's ten

Redwood trees

The name 'redwood' includes two tree species that are known worldwide by the botanical name *Sequoia sempervirens* (coastal redwoods) and *Sequoiadendron giganteum* (giant sequoia). They include the oldest and highest trees in the world. They occur only in North America, especially in the Sierra Nevada (giant sequoia) and along the Pacific coast between Los Angeles and Seattle (coastal redwoods). The evergreen conifers reproduce by means of seeds within their cones. The record-holders among

Giant redwoods are often several hundred years old.

The road then continues south through the scenic Owens Valley between the White Mountains and the Sierra Nevada. To the west is Sequoia and Kings Canyon National Park. On the south-eastern edge of the park stands mighty Mount Whitney, at 4,418 m (14,495 ft) the tallest mountain in the continental United States, towering over the spaghetti-western backdrop town of Lone Pine. Those heading for the desert can take Highway 190 from here to Death Valley National Park (80 km/50 miles). Death Valley hosts the lowest point in North America, Badwater, and is 193 km (120 miles) long. If you follow Highway 395 further south, the foothills of the

these two species boast incredible dimensions – at 112 m (367 ft), 'Tall Tree' in Redwood National Park is the highest tree in the world, while 'General Sherman' in Sequoia National Park has a circumference of 33 m (108 ft) and is said to be approximately 2,200-years-old.

The 'Grizzly Giant' in Yosemite National Park is allegedly 2,700 years old, but this figure is disputed. What is certain, however, is that some of the trees have definitely broken the 2,000-year mark.

4

1 Yosemite National Park. Even in winter, El Capitan and the 190-m-high (623-ft) Bridal Veil Falls make an impressive picture.

2 The bizarre tufa stone formations in Mono Lake were formed by underwater chemical reactions.

3 Large parts of Kings Canyon National Park are more than 3,000 m (9,834 ft) above sea level.

4 The Sequoia and Kings Canyon National Park covers the southern end of the Sierra Nevada Range.

largest trees are in this park. The viewing point at Moro Rock provides a fantastic panorama of the area and is reached via more than one hundred stone steps. If the 150-km (93-mile) detour is too far for you, then leave Yosemite Park via the same route, return to Highway 395, and then continue to the 'most beautiful lake in California'.

19 Mono Lake Due to Southern California's need for water since

the early 1940s, the tributaries that once fed Mono Lake have been drastically depleted. Until 1994, when the lake was afforded official protection, evaporation had exceeded inflow rates and the salt content of the lake rose to a level three times greater than that of the Pacific. This cycle turned the lake's islands into peninsulas and exposed the breeding grounds of a number of already endangered waterfowl to predators

and threatened their existence. This problem has been reversed and the lake is recovering.
For visitors, however, the lower water level makes the landscape on and around the lake even more attractive because the bizarre tufa pillars that formed under the water over centuries now rise out of the water. On the southern shores there are a number of hiking trails leading to these extraordinary formations.

1

The living desert

Walt Disney's 1955 film of the same name made it clear to many people that a desert is in no way a landscape devoid of life.

Many plants and animals have adapted well to an existence in arid regions and know how to survive on the scarce food and water resources. When the infrequent rain does fall, the plants are able to germinate and grow quickly. Cacti, yuccas and Joshua trees burst into blossom when the rains come. Many plants have deep roots, making it possible for them to reach underground water tables. Some plants use less 'clean' methods: the creosote bush, for example, sprays a poisonous substance in order to keep other plants and animals out of its space.

2

The rattlesnake, sometimes 2.4-m (7.9-ft) long, is only found in the south-western United States.

Most desert animals, such as the rattlesnake, need only very little liquid, and many are nocturnal, when temperatures are lower. Some bird species get their moisture requirements from the juice of cacti, while other animals are able to store large quantities of water after the infrequent rain showers.

Sierra Nevada are visible to the west, while to the east it becomes increasingly flat and dry. Parts of the Mojave Desert are used for military purposes, including the US Naval Weapons Center, for example, which occupies a huge tract of land between the now dry Owens Lake and Ridgecrest.

20 Red Rock Canyon State Park This park is located in the Paso Mountains at the far southern foothills of the Sierra Nevada and is a source of fascination with its canyons, bizarrely eroded rock formations and impressive display of colours – red, white and brown sandstone alternate with the white clay layers and dark lava tones. While the western side of the mountains rise gently, the eastern side dazzles with its steep cliffs. This landscape has been used as the set for so many Hollywood westerns that it evokes a feeling of déjà vu in some visitors. South of the small town of Mojave you pass

Edwards Air Force Base, internationally known as the space shuttle landing site. The NASA Dryden Flight Research Center is open to visitors but only by prior appointment. It was from here that Chuck Yeager took off in the aircraft that broke the sound barrier for the first time. The journey then continues via Highway 14 back towards Los Angeles. The San Gabriel Mountains, with peaks rising to nearly 2,000 m (6,562 ft), begin 100 km (62 miles) beyond the town of Mojave and border the greater metropolitan area on its northeast side.

North-west of San Fernando, Highway 14 joins Interstate Highway 5, which you will take back into Los Angeles before exiting at the Hollywood Freeway (170).

21 Hollywood The view from Sunset Boulevard of the 'Hollywood' sign on the slopes of this Los Angeles district is world famous. The letters originally read 'Hollywoodland' and were

erected in 1923 as an advertisement for a property scheme. However, they have now long been the symbol of a place synonymous the world over with the film industry, and of course all of its glamour and glitter. Made out to be the main streets of the city in many a film, Sunset Boulevard and Hollywood Boulevard are in fact relatively unspectacular, but there are a few places to get a feel for the stars of Hollywood's more appealing heyday.

The famous Walk of Fame is part of Hollywood Boulevard. In 1960 golden stars bearing the names of legendary film actors were engraved and set in the pavement. There are now more than 2,000 of them.

Mann's Chinese Theater, where countless noteworthy Hollywood films celebrated their premiers, is also on Hollywood Boulevard (address 6925). The concrete hand- and footprints of many stars, as well as their signatures, can be seen in front of the Chinese-style building.

Today, the majority of the studios have moved to other parts of Los Angeles such as Burbank or San Fernando Valley. You can visit the final resting places of many stars such as Cecil B. de Mille, Rudolph Valentino, Peter Finch or Jayne Mansfield in Hollywood Memorial Park.

From Hollywood the route continues via Beverly Hills for a few kilometres to the beaches in Santa Monica or Venice. In nearby Anaheim, Disneyland attracts visitors with its numerous fairground rides and classic comic figures such as Mickey Mouse and Donald Duck.

1 Since many desert tracks and roads, such as this one at Little Lake, run through remote areas, you should make sure the tank is full and you have sufficient water in the car.

2 A thunderstorm approaches over the Mojave Desert.

Redwood National Park Humans are dwarfed by the redwoods (sequoias) that can grow to 112 m (367 ft) – the tallest trees in the world.

San Francisco The imposing Golden Gate Bridge is the landmark of this, the 'most European city in the USA'. San Francisco is a magnet for many subcultures with the motto 'live and let live'.

Big Sur Since the 1930s, Highway 1 has run directly along the steep coast, with fantastic views over the mighty Pacific.

Monterey This little town owes its fame to writer John Steinbeck, born in 1902 in neighbouring Salinas, who immortalized it in novels such as *Tortilla Flat* or *Cannery Row*.

Hearst Castle Newspaper tycoon William Randolph Hearst built himself a more than ample residence to house his collection of art treasures.

Los Angeles The 'city in search of a centre' displays its Mediterranean charm in many of its neighbourhoods, be it Malibu or Venice Beach on the coast, the celebrity neighbourhood of Beverly Hills or the slightly more bohemian Westwood.

Oregon Caves National Monument Visit a fascinating underground labyrinth of marble caves with bizarre shapes, created by water over thousands of years. in the Siskiyou Mountains in southern Oregon. The Oregon pine (also called the Douglasie) is one of the tallest trees in the world and grows in this region.

Hollywood The reality of this town on the north side of Los Angeles is not as glamorous as the name might imply, but the Walk of Fame or Mann's Chinese Theater still evoke the golden age of American film.

Lassen Volcanic National Park Lassen Peak is within this national park. It is 3,187 m (10,457 ft) high and the only active volcano left in California. Sulphur leaks out of the ground in fizzing, stinking plumes at the Sulphur Works Thermal Area.

Yosemite National Park One of the first national parks in the USA boasts many attractions – rock faces like El Capitan with its extreme vertical face, or impressive waterfalls like Yosemite Falls (739 m/2,425 ft).

Kings Canyon Majestic redwoods that reach heights of over 80 m (262 ft) are the main attraction in this wonderful park. Some of the trees have been here for more than 2,000 years.

Mount Whitney California is the state of superlatives – Mount Whitney, at 4,418 m (14,495 ft), is the highest mountain in the USA, excluding Alaska.

Disneyland Mickey Mouse's Empire has been drawing innumerable visitors since 1955 with its various theme parks.

San Diego A metropolis has arisen around the Old Town, and it radiates a holiday atmosphere thanks to a sunny climate. Balboa Park is certainly worth a visit, with museums and one of the world's most diverse zoos.

Map labels:

Coos Bay, Grants Pass, Eugene, Cave Junction, 199, Medford, Klamath Falls, Oregon, Crescent City, Oregon Caves Nat. Mon., Siskiyou Pass (1361), Klamath, Klamath Mountains, Yreka, Klamath Falls, Redwood N.P., 13, 4317 Mt. Shasta, Eureka, 12, Mount Shasta, 14, 89, Burney Falls, 299, Shasta Lake, Humboldt Redwoods S.P., 11, Redding, Subway Cave, Lassen Volcanic N.P., 15, Leggett, 101, Red Bluff, Mineral, Susanville, Fort Bragg, 395, Alturas, Honey Lake, Mendocino, 10, Ukiah, Doyle, Point Arena, 1, Clear Lake, Yuba City, Truckee, Reno, Salt Lake City, Fort Ross S.H.P., 9, Jenner, Squaw Valley, Carson City, Lake Tahoe, 16, Sacramento, 80, South Lake Tahoe, Point Reyes Nat. Seashore, Napa, 5, Topaz, Golden Gate Bridge, 8, Berkeley, 395, Nevada, SAN FRANCISCO, Oakland, Stockton, San Mateo, San Jose, Yosemite N.P., 17, Mono Lake, 19, Lee Vining, Ano Nuevo, Santa Cruz, 4000, Tonopah, Monterey, Los Banos, Devils Postpile, Monterey Peninsula, 7, Carmel, 6, 4263 Boundary Peak, Bishop, Pfeiffer Big Sur S.P., Pinnacles Nat. Mon., Kings Canyon N.P., Big Sur, 5, Fresno, Julia Pfeiffer S.P., 101, Mt. Whitney 4418, Lone Pine, Hearst San Simeon S.H.M., 4, 18, Sequoia N.P., Owens Lake, Death Valley N.P., Paso Robles, Abalones Beach, Morro Bay, San Luis Obispo, 5, Little Lake, Pismo Beach, 3, 14, Santa Maria, Bakersfield, Ridgecrest, Jalama, Mt. Pinos 2092, Mojave, 20 Red Rock Canyon S.P., Lompoc, Mission Santa Barbara, 58, Edwards Air Force Base, Gaviota Beach, Santa Barbara, 2, Ventura, Palmdale, Getty Center, Hollywood, Barstow, Channel Islands N.P., Santa Cruz I., Oxnard, 21, Pasadena, Phoenix, Santa Monica, LOS ANGELES, 1, Anaheim, Long Beach, Disneyland, Huntington Beach, Mission San Juan Capistrano, 5, 15, Oceanside, Escondido, SAN DIEGO, Yuma, TIJUANA, Ensenada, MÉXICO

The Big Red Lighthouse was erected by the Dutch in 1847 on southern Lake Michigan when they founded the little town of Holland.

Route 25

USA

Route 66: The American Myth

The first continuous road link between Chicago and Los Angeles still evokes nostalgia today. It is synonymous with freedom and wide open country, cruisers and 'Easy Rider', neon signs and diners – in short, the symbol of a nation whose identity is characterized by being on the road. The West was all about promises and aspirations, a paradise on earth. 'Go California' was the motto – Route 66 was the way there.

The first link between the Great Lakes and the Pacific Ocean has been a continuing legend and the symbol of the American dream ever since Bobby Troup's 'Get your kicks on Route 66'. It was Horace Greely who popularized the phrase 'Go West, young man, and grow up with the country' in the New York Herald Tribune, and with it created the creed of an entire nation. What came of this creed and the people who later followed it through the Depression and droughts of the 1930s has

nowhere been described as tellingly as in John Steinbeck's *The Grapes of Wrath* in which the Joad family heads out on what later became known as the 'Mother Road' to the West.

The clash between dreams and reality remains part of the Route 66 legend today. What has since become a long forgotten chapter in the history of fast-moving America began less than 100 years ago as cars began to make a show of competition for the railways. The 'National

Route 66 in Arizona.

Old Trails Highway' developed from the first 'highways' in the individual states and thus became the predecessor of Route 66. But the nice name still did not stand for much more than sand, gravel and strip roads. It was only on 11 November 1926 that the eight Federal states of Illinois, Missouri, Kansas, Oklahoma, Texas, New Mexico, Arizona and California completed the uniform 4,000-km (2,486-mile) route between Chicago and Los Angeles, and the highway was officially opened as Route 66.

The start of Route 66 is marked by a signpost at the Michigan Avenue/Jackson Drive intersection in Chicago. The idyllic countryside of Illinois begins directly after the suburban neighbourhoods to the west of town. Remote farms and tranquil villages characterize Abraham Lincoln's home country. The Amish people's rejec-

View of the Chicago skyline by night from Sears Tower. Left in the background is the tapered 344-m-high (1,129-ft) John Hancock Center adorned with two antennae.

In the state of New Mexico Route 66 passes through a stark landscape of bizarre rock formations.

tion of the technological age takes the traveller back into a bygone era. You finally reach the 'Gateway to the West' in St Louis where the road crosses the expanse of the Mississippi and through the 192-m-high (630-ft) steel archway designed by Eero Saarinen.

The gentle hills of the Ozark Mountains and the 'glitter world' of the Meramec Caverns are hard to resist. Upon reaching Oklahoma, the 'Native American State', you are finally in the land of cowboys and Indians with its seemingly never-ending plains. The cowboys are still in charge on the giant cattle ranches in the area, and this applies to the 290 km (180 miles) where Route 66 crosses the narrow panhandle in northern Texas.

In New Mexico there is a whole new world waiting to greet the visitor. The special light in the valleys and canyons glows mysteriously on the red and brown cliffs and gentle mountains. Between Santa Fe and Taos you will experience an enchanted landscape with a harmonious combination of Spanish charm and Indian culture.

Next comes Arizona, which is not only the state with the largest Indian reservations, but also an area of spectacular rock formations in Red Rock Country, Oak Creek Canyon and of course the Grand Canyon. Intoxicated by the beauty of the landscape, you enter California, crossing the daunting Mojave Desert with its cacti as the last obstacle before heading down towards the Pacific.

San Bernardino marks the start of the fertile 'Orange Empire' as Route 66 is slowly swallowed up by Los Angeles' endless sea of buildings. It all finally comes to an end in Palisades Park near Santa Monica.

Mexican children pose in traditional costume in Santa Fe, New Mexico.

Detour

The Big Red Lighthouse

When the Dutch founded the small town of Holland on the southern shore of Lake Macatawa (Lake Michigan) in 1847, they immediately recognized its potential as a harbour. However, the ships had to pass through a narrow passage – only

The Big Red Lighthouse on the eastern shore of Lake Michigan.

70 m (230 ft) in width – between extensive sand dunes.
In order to ensure their safe passage, a bonfire was lit from 1870 at the end of a long wooden pier. With its increasing importance for shipping, this grew to become a building that took on its current shape by 1956. Its nickname 'Big Red' is due to its red colour.

The first continuous East-West connection in the USA from Chicago to Los Angeles remains something of a legend today. Even though during the course of the 20th century large parts of the original Route 66 gave way to more modern Interstate highways, there are still many original stretches where the legend lives on.

1 Chicago (see pp. 334–335). Before starting off towards the south it is worth taking a detour to the town of Holland 110 km (68 miles) away. This reconstructed village is a memorial to the region's Dutch immigrants.
The journey along the legendary Route 66 begins at the Michigan Avenue/Jackson Drive intersection in Chicago and from there Interstate Highway 55 takes you to Springfield. North of Springfield is the Chautauqua National Wildlife Reserve.

2 Springfield The capital of Illinois still has the aura of an idyllic country town today. A little further north, New Salem was the home of the famous president (Lincoln) who lived here in humble circumstances from 1831–37. The village has now been reconstructed as an open-air museum with staff in period costume who demonstrate how hard life was here 200 years ago.
In Springfield itself the focus is also on President Lincoln and

his carefully restored house on Jackson Street is open to visitors, as is his law office on Adams Street where he practised as a lawyer from 1843–53. He found his final resting place in Oak Ridge Cemetery.
Lincoln was a parliamentarian in the Old State Capitol in the Downtown Mall but since 1877 state business has been conducted in the opulent new Illinois State Capitol. Shea's Gas Station Museum imparts true Route 66 feeling.
The journey continues southwards via Interstate Highway 55 toward St Louis.

3 St Louis The largest city in the state of Missouri lies on the western bank of the Mississippi just before the confluence with the Missouri River. The Mark Twain National Wildlife Reserve was established on the river north of the city. The city was founded in 1764 by a French fur trader, Pierre Liguest, and it was fur traders who first brought wealth to the new settlement.

Travel information

Route profile
Length: approx. 4,000 km (2,486 miles), excluding detours
Time required: 3 weeks
Start: Chicago
End: Santa Monica
Route (main locations): Chicago, St Louis, Tulsa, Oklahoma City, Santa Fe, Albuquerque, Flagstaff, Barstow, Santa Monica

Traffic information:
Drive on the right in the USA. Maximum speed limits in built-up areas are 25 to 30 mph (40–48 km/h); on the highways 55–70 mph

(88–115 km/h). Speed checks (with tough penalties) are also conducted from the air. Drink-driving is strictly prohibited in all of the states here, with heavy fines. It is prohibited to carry open or even empty bottles or cans of alcoholic beverages in the car (not even in the boot).

Information:
Detailed information on the historical Route 66 as well as the most important sight-seeing attractions can be found at:
www.historic66.com or
www.theroadwanderer.net

Sears Tower

Chicago's skyline is dominated by one of the tallest buildings in the world, the 443-m (1,453-ft) Sears Tower. Its 108 floors were completed in 1973 following thirty years of construction, making it the tallest building in the world until 1998 when the Petronas Towers were built in Kuala Lumpur, Malaysia. However, there is controversy regarding what 'tallest' means. With its antennae the Sears Tower is still the highest point on any building worldwide (520 m/1,706 ft).

The tower's simple design is based on narrow, quadratic pillars, with nine on the lowest level supporting four, then three and then two right at the top. The facade is made from black aluminium sheets and more than

The Sears Tower in Chicago is adorned by two giant antennae.

16,000 bronze-coloured windows. In the lobby visitors are greeted by 'The Universe', a famous hanging mobile by Alexander Calder.

Of course the giant tower also has record-breaking elevators – as double deckers they are always travelling to the 33rd/34th or the 66th/67th floors simultaneously – at a speed of 8.5 m/sec (29 ft/sec).

The most interesting part for visitors is the Skydeck on the 103rd floor at a height of 412 m (1,352 ft). It has its own entrance on Jackson Boulevard and draws some two million visitors every year.

'America's Biggest Little Town' and the new Mecca of American country music. As such, it has outdone legendary Nashville, Tennessee.

Traditional handicrafts and nostalgic events are staged in 'Silver Dollar City'. Highway 13 takes you to the Talking Rock Caverns, considered the most scenic of the 5,000 caves in Missouri. Those interested in history can make a detour to the Pea Ridge National Monument.

Back in Springfield continue along Interstate 44 westwards.

⑥ Joplin A part of the original Route 66 turns right from Highway 44 shortly before the small town of Joplin, Missouri. Continue through Joplin and shortly thereafter you reach the little town of Galena where time appears to have stood still. The whole town is like an open-air museum.

The next little village is Riverton where the old Marsh Arch Bridge, an arched concrete suspension bridge, was built in 1923

Large parts of the American west were then settled from here. It was from here that the endless wagon trains began their journey across the prairies and it was to here that the riches of the grasslands and the Rocky Mountains were brought back and traded.

The 192-m-high (630-ft) Gateway Arch designed by the Finn, Eero Saarinen, is St Louis' primary landmark and is purposely visible from great distances. As a symbolic 'Gateway to the West', the arch is a reminder that this is where the great tide of settlers heading for the coast began the often perilous expedition.

A short distance south of the Gateway Arch is the Old Cathedral dating from 1834 with its attractive mosaics and a museum of the city's history in the basement. Market Street begins on the Gateway Arch axis and its notable attractions include the dome of the Old Court House from 1864, the magnificent round building that is the Busch Memorial Stadium and the City Hall, which is based on its counterpart in Paris.

On Lindell Boulevard is the splendid St Louis Cathedral built in 1907 in Byzantine style. It has a spectacular mosaic dome. You leave St Louis via Interstate Highway 44 and make your way towards Stanton.

④ Meramec Caverns A visit to the Meramec Caverns about 5 km (3 miles) south of Stanton is not to be missed. They are among the largest stalactite caves in the USA and include some fascinating formations. Some doubt that the famous bandit Jesse James and his gang used the caves as a hideout, but legends certainly tell of their presence here.

For the onward journey you continue down Interstate 44 to Springfield, Missouri.

⑤ Branson South of Springfield, the third-largest city in Missouri, are the Ozark Mountains, which attract a great number of visitors, particularly in autumn.

The small town of Branson is your specific destination reached via Highway 65. It is known as

1 The harbour and skyline of Chicago. The Sears Tower (second from the left) was the tallest building in the world until 1998.

2 At the height of summer, the St Louis sun sets in the middle of the Gateway Arc.

Chicago

Including its outer suburbs, Chicago sprawls over 100 km (62 miles) along the southern shores of Lake Michigan. The city is a fantastic destination for anyone interested in architecture – Downtown Chicago has been highlighted by the works of renowned architects. The city also attracts throngs of visitors with its lively music, museum and multicultural scenes.

Chicago was already an important transport hub and trading centre in the 19th century. Cattle and pigs were unloaded here at the largest livestock station in the country and driven to urban slaughterhouses, of which there are only a few remaining.

In the 'Roaring Twenties', the 'Windy City' gained the dubious reputation of being a gangster metropolis, but Al Capone is all but legend now. The skyline of the new Chicago rose up out of the ruins of the old city and is the best proof of the determination and initiative of its residents.

The 'Great Chicago Fire' of 9 October 1871 almost completely destroyed the city. Over 200 people died and more than 90,000 lost everything they had. Today all that remains of the old Chicago is the water tower.

Picasso; 'Flamingo', the bright red giant spider by Alexander Calder in front of the Chicago Federal Center; 'Universe', a gigantic mobile by the same artist in the lobby of the Sears Tower; or 'The Fours Seasons', a 20-m-long (66-ft) mosaic by Marc Chagall in front of the First National Bank.

Then there is also a series of museums worth visiting – the Museum of Science and Industry houses an underground coal mine and a 5-m-high (16-ft) model of a human heart. A reproduction of the largest saurian (dinosaur lizard) in the world awaits you in the Museum of Natural History. The Art Institute of Chicago is renowned for its collection of modern art. The Adler Planetarium, a star-shaped granite building with a copper dome, has a number of surprising special effects. The attractions

Chicago shows off its impressive skyline on both sides of the Chicago River (top). The city established itself as a centre of modern architecture at the start of the 20th century. Whether by day (middle) or by night (bottom), the numerous unique skyscrapers are there to be admired on a walk through the streets of Chicago.

State Street is considered the largest pedestrian zone in the world and attracts crowds with its department stores, boutiques, restaurants, cinemas and theatres. Passers-by encounter a number of remarkable artworks on the pavements – a 16-m (52-ft) statue left to the citizens of Chicago by Pablo

in the John G. Shedd Aquarium include a huge coral reef and a shark habitat. There are numerous restaurants and bars to choose from at the Navy Pier. Chicago continues to be a city of jazz and blues and a live concert in one of the very diverse clubs or bars should not be missed.

The Plains Indians

The vast North American plains are the true heart of the country. The land of grass, wind and sunshine extends from Saskatchewan, Canada, in the north more than 3,000 km (1,864 miles) to the south as far as the Rio Grande in Mexico. In total, the plains cover an area of some 2.5 million sq km (1.6 million sq mi). Some of the tribes that dominated this area were the Sioux, the Blackfoot, the Crow and the Cheyenne Indians.

Vast herds of bison grazed on the seemingly endless grasslands and formed the basis of the Indians' livelihood. Before the Europeans came and horses were introduced in the late 600s, Indians hunted bison on foot by driving entire herds to a cliff edge, over which the animals then fell to their deaths. The most famous of these cliff edges in North America is the UNESCO-protected

Top: Shawnee Indians at the Red Earth Festival in Oklahoma. Below: Anadarko – the 'Indian Capital of the Nation'.

Head-Smashed-In Buffalo Jump south of Calgary, Canada.

Some of the Indians lived from hunting and others as resident farmers, with a healthy exchange of goods taking place between the various groups. The beginning of the end of the Plains Indians came in the middle of the 19th century with the white man's massive slaughter of bison. The massacre robbed these hunter Indians of their livelihood, and the inexorable advance of the white man from the east did the rest. The end came in December 1890 with the massacre at Wounded Knee. South-west of Oklahoma City, in Anadarko, an open-air museum with seven Indian villages, the 'Indian Capital of the Nation' commemorates the culture of the Plains Indians.

to span Brush Creek. Route 66 passed over this bridge until 1960. The next stop is Baxter Springs where under no circumstances should you miss a visit to Murphey's Restaurant in the Baxter National Bank, which was closed in 1952. Part of the decor comprises former bank furniture, and old cheques from the 1920s lie on the tables under glass.

❼ Miami Here too, little appears to have changed on the outside. Miami developed from a trading station set up in 1890. In 1905 lead and zinc brought a boom to the town. The main attraction is the Coleman Theatre, built in 1929, a cinema with magnificently crafted balconies

and a ceiling lined with gold leaf. On the first floor there is a small exhibition about Route 66 and its history.

❽ Tulsa The former 'Oil Capital of the World', Tulsa has long been stripped of this title, but some of the oil barons' art deco villas are still a sign of the city's former wealth.

Waite Phillips' mansion still houses works of art from the Italian Renaissance. The original Route 66 follows Eleventh Street through downtown. Between Tulsa and Oklahoma City you can also travel along lengthy stretches of the historic Route 66, which maintain their rustic charm.

❾ Oklahoma City Founded in 1889 – after Indian territories were opened to whites – the capital of Oklahoma owes its wealth to oil. There are still a good 2,000 wells within the city limits today, one of which is directly in front of the Capitol. The spirit of the Wild West is still

alive and well in the National Cowboy Hall of Fame on Persimmon Hill, which includes the replica of an old western town called 'Prosperity Junction'. 'The American Cowboy Gallery' documents the life of the cowboys, and the 'American Rodeo Gallery' is dedicated to that

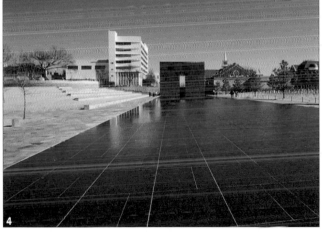

long-standing western tradition. South-west of the city centre is the historic neighbourhood Stockyards City, where you can get a feeling for the way things might have been in the heyday of the cattle business here. South of the city are the Wichita Mountains, a hiking area, and to the north-west is the Washita Battlefield where Custer staged an attack on the Cheyenne Indians in the ongoing and tragic clash of cultures that took place in the area. The journey continues via Interstate 40 westwards to Clinton.

🔟 **Clinton** The most interesting Route 66 museums on the whole trip are to be found here. Films,

photos and original exhibition pieces document the route's heyday. Beyond Clinton you stay on Interstate 40. Once you get to Amarillo, a detour on Interstate 27 leads to one of the most interesting canyons in the area.

⓫ **Palo Duro Canyon State Park** This canyon is surrounded by cliffs some 350 m (1,148 ft) high where remote Indian trails lead deep into the canyon to the most spectacular cliff formations. Also called the 'Grand Canyon of Texas', Palo Duro is the second-largest canyon in the USA: 195 km (121 miles) long, 32 km (20 miles) wide and 243 m (797 ft) deep – a good warm-up for the real thing.

⓬ **Amarillo** Route 66 used to pass along Sixth Avenue in this Texas town, a street lined with some restored buildings from the route's heyday. The American Quarter Horse Heritage Center documents the history of the breeding of the American Quarter Horse.
Cadillac Ranch 15 km (9 miles) to the west is, a bizarre desert exhibition of old Cadillacs. There is a flint quarry further north, Alibates Flint Quarries National Monument. The route continues on Interstate 40 over the border into New Mexico towards Albuquerque.

⓭ **Fort Sumner** Before reaching the little town of Santa Rosa, it is worth taking a brief detour to the south on Highway 84 to Fort Sumner where 8,000 Navajo and Apache Indians were rounded up in 1864 and forcefully relocated to the fort to survive on their own. Many of them died. The visitor centre and adjacent museum tell the story of this gruesome incident.
The town went down in American history a second time as well, as it was here on 16 July 1881 that Pat Garrett shot the famous Billy the Kid. A small museum has been erected in his memory. Back in Santa Rosa, continue to follow Interstate 40. To reach

Santa Fe you need to leave the actual Route 66 at Clines Corners, the intersection of Interstate 40 and Highway 285, then head north toward Santa Fe.

⓮ **Santa Fe** The second oldest city in the USA and the capital of New Mexico is characterized by both Indian and Spanish culture. There are eight large museums and a multitude of art galleries, jewellery shops and handicraft stores here. When the Spanish arrived in 1542, there was already a large Pueblo Indian settlement here, which later revolted against the colonials and sent them packing. In the meantime, however, the Spanish made Santa Fe the capital of

1 They're back: nostalgic diners and the cars to match.

2 Some of the buildings in the Old Town of Muskogee, south-east of Tulsa, are reminiscent of the city's early days.

3 Stark cliffs rise 350 m (1,148 ft) in the Palo Duro Canyon.

4 The Oklahoma City National Memorial was erected to commemorate the victims of the attack on the Alfred P. Murrah Federal Building in 1995.

Cadillac Ranch

The Texas town of Amarillo boasts two superlatives. On the one hand, it draws the crowds with the Big Texan Steak Ranch where you can have a 2-kg (4-lbs) steak for free if you can eat it, including side dishes and dessert, in one hour. On the other hand, 15 km (9 miles) west of the city is the Cadillac Ranch where ten old Cadillacs from

Cadillac Ranch: a bizarre reminder of the golden age of the Cadillac.

between 1948 and 1963 are buried halfway in the ground.
This bizarre exhibit is a homage to the American sense of mobility and style. The ten Cadillacs are painted in all the colours of the rainbow and covered in graffiti of all kinds. The front ends are buried in the ground while the rear ends, with the characteristic tail fins, stick up in the air.

Pueblo culture

The Indian tribes of the south-west were mostly resident farmers. By around 1000 BC they had already built their first pithouses, which were covered with branches and furs. These then became the first buildings, erected around 700 BC and later called 'pueblos' (villages) by the Spanish.

Taos Pueblo north of Santa Fe.

The Anasazi Indians located their villages under dramatic overhanging cliffs or on safe, flat-topped mountains. The best example of this is Pueblo Bonito in Chaco Canyon. The main building consisted of 650 rooms and some forty 'kivas' (religious rooms). Up to five storeys, these complexes were built from air-dried adobe. The pueblo designs were based on a closed maze of living quarters and inaccessibility to outsiders. Originally, there were no doors and the only access was via ladder.

their new colony. Today the architectural mix of Indian, Spanish, European American and Mexican influences is the special attraction of Santa Fe's old town.

The famous Santa Fe Trail, an historic trading route running from Independence in the west of Missouri to Santa Fe, ends at the Plaza built in 1610 in the historic heart of the city. This is also the site of the Palace of the Governors (1614), the governor's residence dating from the 17th century. The oldest buildings are situated south of the Santa Fe River in the Indian settlement of Barrio de Analco, established in the early 17th century by the Tlaxcala Indians.

The Museum of Fine Arts shows the work of regional artists. Those especially interested in Indian culture ought not to miss the museums on Camino Lejo. The Museum of Indian Arts and Culture displays artworks from the Indian tribes of New Mexico. The Museum of International Folk Art is one of the largest ethnographic museums in the USA, while the Wheelwright Museum of the American Indian is dedicated to all the Indian cultures of North America.

The numerous interesting Indian pueblos in the area are worth visiting. The Interstate High-

way 25 takes you directly to Albuquerque and back to the original Route 66.

⑮ Albuquerque The largest city in New Mexico is situated on the Rio Grande at an altitude of 1,600 m (5,250 ft) and is overshadowed by Sandia Peak. There is a 4-km-long (2.5-mile) cable car ride that takes you up to 3,163 m (10,378 ft) above sea level.

Founded by the Anasazi Indians, who had already been living here between 1100 and 1300, the town was then settled by the Spanish at the beginning of the

18th century and they built what is today known as Old Town. About 170 years later the town was linked to the rail network. There is a series of museums worth visiting here – the Albuquerque Museum has a collection of exhibits from the Spanish colonial era; nature fans will want to see the New Mexico Museum of National History, with exhibits on the natural history of the south-west (such as dinosaurs); and the largest collection of rock paintings is to be found in the Petroglyph National Monument north of the city.

The Indian Pueblo Cultural Center north of Interstate 40 is an absolute must-see.

⑯ Laguna Pueblo About 10 km (6 miles) west of Albuquerque, north of Interstate 40, is a Keresan pueblo made up of six villages – Encinal, Laguna, Mesita, Paguate, Paraje and Seama. The site has been in existence since the middle of the 15th century. Colourful local pottery is on sale in every village. The St Joseph Mission on the lake in Old Laguna is also worth a visit.

17 **Acoma Pueblo** Roughly 48 km (30 miles) south-east of the small town of Grant is Acoma, considered the most attractive pueblo far and wide. The village, which is also known as 'Sky City' because of its spectacular location, sits on top of a mesa (table mountain) 10 m (361 ft) above the plain.

The pueblo has been a settlement for over 1,200 years and is considered to be the oldest continually inhabited settlement in the USA. Today, however, there are only about fifty residents, most of the tribe's members hav-

ing moved to the villages on the plain. As the village is sometimes closed for religious ceremonies, it is best to enquire beforehand whether it is open to visitors. There is a fantastic view of the hinterland from the pueblo. West of Acoma is the El Malpais National Monument, famous for its bizarre rock formations and the more than 150 local bird species.

In the state of Arizona, Interstate 40 continues on more or less the old Route 66. At Thoreau, Highway 371 branches off towards Crownpoint to the

Chaco Culture National History Park. Continuing westwards, south of the road is the El Morro National Monument on Highway 53. Both the Indian tribes and the Spanish have left their mark on the 60-m (197-ft) sandstone cliffs.

Sanders, in the 'Grand Canyon State' Arizona, is the starting point for a detour to the north.

18 **Hubbel Trading Post** West of Sanders you should not miss the 50-km (31-mile) detour via Highway 191 to the Hubbel Trading Post. The trading post

was founded in 1890 by John Lorenzo Hubbel in the middle of Navajo territory. The buildings date back to the turn of the last century and the Navajo have quality handicrafts on sale here. Back on Interstate 40, the next highlight is only 30 km (19 miles) away to the west.

19 **Petrified Forest National Park** This park, spread out over 379 sq km (236 sq mi), offers insight into a geological world that is 200 million years old. Around 100 species of fossilized plants and animals have been identified to date. The most impressive examples are the petrified tree trunks that were infused with quartz

1 Indian and Spanish cultures characterize the Old Town of Santa Fe. The picture features Canyon Road.

2 Old Town Albuquerque shares Spanish and Indian origins.

3 The El Morro National Monument is a 60-m-high (197-ft) sandstone cliff. The numerous inscriptions have led to the cliff's nickname 'Inscription Rock'.

4 Acoma Pueblo sits on top of a majestic cliff plateau.

Detour

Chaco Culture National Historical Park

Between 900 and 1200 the Anasazi Indians in north-eastern New Mexico developed their culture to a high level of sophistication. The intellectual and cultural centre was in the Chaco Canyon, a 15-km by 3-km (9-mile by 1.8-mile) basin where numerous buildings still remain today. The oldest evidence dates

The Chaco Canyon was a regional cultural centre between 850 and 1250.

as far back as the 9th century BC. The first pithouses were built 2,500 years ago and the first adobe buildings in the 7th century. The huge pueblos were built in the 9th century. There were twelve large settlements in Chaco Canyon alone and about 400 separate villages.

Flagstaff Indian Day

A powwow – a colourful Indian gathering – takes place every July in the Coconino County Fairground in Flagstaff where Indian traditions are observed with dancing and singing. The Indians have struggled to retain

Participants at the Flagstaff Indian Day.

their culture, but the songs and dances help keep some of their traditions alive.

Part of the powwow therefore always comprises the large counsel fire where tribal politics are discussed, successes celebrated and losses lamented. The traditional 'giveaway' provides the opportunity to present valuable gifts and to gather money for charity. The dancers are motivated with substantial money prizes and there are also awards for costumes and jewellery. It is a point of honour for everyone to take part – the tribe benefits from a successful powwow the whole year long until the next one.

around 200 million years ago. Today their fractures glimmer with all the colours of the rainbow. The park, which extends both north and south of Interstate 40, is accessed via the 43-km (27-mile) park road and has two information centres, one of which is located at the north entrance, directly accessible from Interstate 40.

Pintado Point, right at the start of the park road, offers the best overview of the Painted Desert. All the colours of the glowing badlands are seen at their best from here.

Blue Mesa Point, reached by the 4.8-km (3-mile) access road, offers a second spectacular overview. Agate House is an 800-year-old Anasazi pueblo, the walls of which are made of petrified wood that glitters in a myriad of colours. The most beautiful of the petrified trees can be found in the southern part of the park. The Giant Logs Trail leads to Old Faithful, a conifer tree that has a diameter of 2.9 m (9.5 ft).

A visit to the Rainbow Forest Museum ought not to be missed either. The exhibition includes a variety of pre-Columbian Indian artefacts fashioned from petrified wood. At the southern end of the park you will reach Highway 180, which will take you directly back to Holbrook and Interstate 40.

20 Winslow About 20,000 years ago a space 'bomb' landed a little further south of the village. The meteorite created a 180-m-deep (591-ft) crater with a circumference of around 1,300 m (4,265 ft). The visitor centre has all the details about the meteorite and has pieces of the celestial body on display. It is now a further 70 km (43 miles) on Interstate 40 to Flagstaff.

21 Sunset Crater Before visiting Flagstaff, it is worth making a detour to the north on Highway 89. On the eastern side of the highway is a bizarre volcanic landscape surrounding the Sunset Crater National Monument. The focal point of the volcanic

area is the over 300-m-wide (984-ft) cinder cone of the Sunset Crater. It is the youngest volcano in Arizona and has been active for some 200 years. It first erupted in 1064 and the layer of ash covered an area of over 2,000 sq km (1,243 sq mi). In 1250 the volcano discharged the red and yellow oxidized lava that today still causes the edge of the crater to glow with the colours of a permanent sunset. The area is accessed via Scenic Drive, with spectacular views of the spooky volcanic landscape.

If you take the Sunset Crater National Monument park road a little further north, you soon reach another noteworthy Indian site.

22 Wupatki National Monument There used to be more than 2,000 settlements here that were part of the ancient Indian Sinagua culture. The Indians settled in this region between 500 and 1400. The Wupatki Pueblo, dating back to the 12th and 13th centuries, is relatively well-preserved. The three-storey pueblo had more than 100 rooms, all ventilated by means of a sophisticated system of wall and floor openings. It could also be heated if necessary.

You can learn anything and everything you want to know about the culture of the Sinagua Indians (Sinagua = sine, aqua = without water) in the visitor centre.

Detour

Grand Canyon

The canyon landscape created by the Colorado River in north-western Arizona is one of the world's greatest natural wonders. It is here that the Colorado River has carved a 450-km-long (280-mile) path leaving a spectacular gorge landscape in its wake. In places it is up to 1,800 m (5,906 ft) deep.

The canyon walls are sheer rock faces which, at the upper rim of the canyon, are up to 30 km (19 miles) apart. Much of the massive canyon is located within the 4,933-sq-km (3,065-sq-mi) confines of Grand Canyon National Park.

View of the Grand Canyon from Toroweap Point.

The Grand Canyon can be reached from both the north and the south but the southern side offers the most spectacular views (South Rim). This is where most of the tourist facilities are. Due to the volume of visitors, the entire southern rim has now been closed to private cars. A shuttle service brings visitors to the main viewing points.

㉓ Flagstaff This city on the southern edge of the San Francisco Mountains was founded in about 1870 when gold diggers followed farmers and ranchers. The railway followed as soon as 1882 and with the completion of Route 66 the transit traffic continued to increase. Flagstaff's sightseeing attractions include the Museum of Northern Arizona with a range of exhibits from the various cultural strata of the Pueblo Indians. Flagstaff's real attraction, however, is its surrounding natural landscape. North of town are the fantastic San Francisco Mountains with the highest point in Arizona. Take a chair lift up the 3,854-m (12,645-ft) Humphrey's Peak.

South-east of Flagstaff is Walnut Canyon, 36 km (22 miles) long and 12 m (39 ft) deep, definitely worth exploring on foot. The canyon conceals around 300 Zinagua Indian cliff dwellings; they lived here from the 10th century and built their dwellings solely under overhanging cliffs. From Flagstaff you can directly to the Grand Canyon on Highways 89 and 64 or 180 and 64. On Interstate 40 follow the highway as far as Seligman and then take the Highway 66 turn-off. The most scenic stretch of old Route 66, which is still largely in its original condition, takes you to the next stop, Kingman. Access roads lead to the Grand Canyon Caverns and to the

Havasupai Indian Reservation. You then end up in central Kingman after crossing the Interstate Highway 40.

㉔ Kingman Between the Cerbat Mountains in the north and the over 2,500-m (8,203-ft) Hualapai Mountains in the south is a traffic interchange in the middle of a desert landscape. Nowhere else on the entire Route 66 has there been a greater investment in nostalgia than here. Old petrol stations and snack bars have been brought back to life, and road signs and signposts have been saved from obsolescence. The entire town is full of unadulterated Route 66 nostalgia. In the

Mohave Museum of History and Arts, with its extensive collection of turquoise jewellery, you learn that the area had already been settled by the Hohokam Indians

1 Sinagua Indian dwellings used to cover the area that is now the Wupatki National Monument.

2 The Wigwam Hotel in Holbrook. An affordable Indian tradition for modern nomads.

3 The 300-m (984-ft) cinder cone of the Sunset Crater is the product of Arizona's youngest volcano.

4 The historic railway station in Flagstaff dates from the 19th century.

Joshua Tree National Park

Joshua Tree National Park covers 3,213 sq km (1,997 sq mi) in California and is part of two different deserts – the cooler, slightly more humid and higher Mojave Desert in the north, and the drier Colorado Desert in the south-east. The park, which is ninety per cent wilderness, shows very vividly how plants can thrive even in arid regions. In addition to the distinctive Joshua trees, the Colorado Desert is also home to palm groves and cactus gardens as well as the thorny juniper bush.

The 'Joshua tree' (*Yucca brevifolia*) is the largest of the yucca trees and grows only in the Mojave Desert, in the northern part of the park. It can reach heights of 18 m (59 ft) and its trunks measure up to 1.2 m (3.9 ft) in circumference. The oldest trees are said to be 900 years old.

The name Joshua tree comes from a group of Mormons who passed through the desert in the middle of the 19th century. The trees reminded them of a story of the prophet Joshua. The rest is history.

The Oasis Visitor Center in Twenty-nine Palms, where two roads begin, is the jumping-off point for excur-

Bizarre rock landscape in Joshua Tree National Park.

sions into the park. One road leads to the north-western part of the park, crosses the Queen and Lost Horse Valleys and provides access to the Jumbo Rocks and the Wonderland of the Rocks. The second road leads to the south-eastern section and provides access to the Cholla Cactus Garden where you will also find the best of the Joshua trees. The best time to go is between March and May when both the Joshua trees and other cacti are in blossom.

If you are planning a visit to the park, make sure that you have a full tank of petrol and sufficient water supplies. In contrast to other national parks, there are neither petrol stations nor hotels or restaurants here. Only two of the basic campsite, Black Rock Canyon and Cottonwood Campgrounds, have water available.

some 1,300 years ago. The museum gives you a history of their work with the precious stones. After Kingman you need to leave Route 66 and Interstate 40 (which goes towards Barstow), to pay homage to the spectacular Hoover Dam and legendary Las Vegas. Both are easy to reach via Highway 93. If you stay on Route 66 you can also visit Lake Havasu south of Kingman.

25 Hoover Dam This dam near Boulder City was once the largest embankment dam in the world. The 221-m-high (725-ft) and 379-m-wide (1,242-ft) construction, which is an amazing 201 m (659 ft) thick at its base, was completed in 1935. The awe-inspiring structure holds back the waters of Lake Mead, a 170-km-long (106-mile) and 150-m-deep (492-ft) body of water. There is a large visitor centre on the dam wall where you learn about the dam's fascinating technical details. You can then take a cruise on Lake Mead with the paddle steamer *Desert Princess*.

After 56 km (35 miles) on Highway 93 you then reach Las Vegas.

26 Las Vegas The world's gambling capital is located in the middle of the desert and really only consists of hotels and casinos. No less than fourteen of the

twenty largest hotels in the world are located here. More than 40 million visitors come to Las Vegas each year to seek their fortune and, more often than not, lose their money to the one-armed bandits and casinos. The big casino hotels stage elaborate shows, revues and circuses in order to provide entertainment for the non-gamblers, or perhaps to raise the spirits of those who do try their hands. The individual casinos each have their own theme and these range from 'Stratosphere Tower' to the 'Venetian', complete with Doge

Palace and Campanile, and the 'Luxor', evoking associations with Ancient Egypt with pyramids and pharaohs.

From Las Vegas, Interstate 15 rejoins the old Route 66 at Barstow. But before you reach Barstow, it is worth paying a brief visit to Calico, a ghost town that was once a very successful mining operation at the end of the 19th century due to the discovery of substantial reserves of silver and borax. The minerals here were extracted from more than 500 mines throughout the area. In 1907 Calico was instant-

ly rendered obsolete, a ghost town, when silver and borax prices dropped sharply.

27 Barstow This town to the east of the Edwards Air Force Base is situated in the middle of the desert and serves as a supply centre for a huge yet sparsely populated hinterland. The California Desert Information Center is very interesting, providing a plethora of details on the Mojave Desert and its difficult living conditions.

Following Interstate 15 you gradually leave the desert

Detour

San Diego

California's southernmost metropolis is directly on the Mexican border. Due to its two protected bays, San Diego has become one of the most important harbour cities on the west coast.

San Diego was founded in the year 1769 when the Franciscan priest Junipero Serra began construction of a mission. The English first arrived in the village in 1803. Today the small Spanish village has grown into a pulsing metropolis.

The historic centre of San Diego is located on Presidio Hill in the north of the town. In Old Town, the San Diego State Historic Park brings Spanish, Mexican and US history to life. Well-restored adobe houses compete with colonial buildings

View over the harbour of the San Diego skyline.

for attention. The Bazaar del Mundo is full of life.

In downtown San Diego the Gaslamp Quarter is a particular attraction with theatres, bars, restaurants and shops. This area still boasts lovely Victorian buildings from between 1880 and 1910. On the shores of the San Diego Bay, Seaport Village attracts visitors looking for a maritime stroll, while to the north-west is the adjoining San Diego Maritime Museum.

The city's real museum centre, however, is the 565-ha (1,396-acre) Balboa Park. Whether you are interested in tropical plants, the Spanish colonial era, the cultural history of the Pueblo Indians, space travel or natural or art history, you will find it all here. The main highlight as far as museums go is the Aerospace Museum and the International Aerospace Hall of Fame. In addition, the San Diego Zoo is an absolute must as it is one of the best zoos in the world. Its counterpart is the Sea World leisure park near Mission Bay.

previously made a living from citrus farming.

If you have plenty of time, it is worth continuing from Anaheim along Interstate 5 to San Diego, 150 km (93 miles) south along the coast.

30 Santa Monica In 1935, Route 66 was extended from Los Angeles to Santa Monica and since then has followed Santa Monica Boulevard, terminating at Ocean Boulevard in Palisades Park, where a modest signpost indicates the end of the legendary route, the 'Mother Road' or 'Main Street USA'.

behind and reach the centre of the Californian citrus-growing region, San Bernardino County.

28 San Bernardino This city, almost 100 km (62 miles) east of Los Angeles, developed from a Franciscan mission founded in 1810. From here you really must do the 'Rim of the World Drive', a panoramic drive through a spectacular high desert and mountain landscape. It passes scenic lakes, reaches an altitude of 2,200 m (7,218 ft) and offers splendid views of the San Bernardino Mountains.

The Joshua Tree National Park is a worthwhile detour from here, if you haven't done it already, and the entrance at Twenty-nine Palms can be reached via Interstate 10 and Highway 62.

The historic Route 66 takes you westwards from San Bernardino, just north of Interstate 10, past Pasadena (Pasadena Freeway) and on towards Los Angeles. Via West Hollywood and Beverly Hills you continue along Santa Monica Boulevard to the famous beach town of Santa Monica. Beforehand, if you want to visit the oldest of Disney's parks, Dis-

neyland, take Interstate 15 and Highway 91 over to Anaheim.

29 Anaheim The ending 'heim' is indicative of the German origins of this settlement near the Santa 'Ana' River, where German immigrants settled in about 1857. Anaheim is in Orange County, around 60 km (37 miles) south-east of Los Angeles. The largest attraction is Disneyland, the leisure park founded by Walt Disney in 1955 and which brought an end to the country tranquillity of this once rustic town. Anaheim had

1 South of Kingman are the Hualapai Mountains, over 2,500-m-high (8,203-ft).

2 In 1885 some 1,200 people lived in Calico and sought their fortunes in one of the 500 silver mines. Calico became a ghost town after 1907 and some of the old buildings, here the old school, have been restored.

3 Downtown Los Angeles is characterized by skyscrapers.

4 Despite high temperatures and irregular rainfall, a great diversity of plant and animal species thrives in the Mojave Desert.

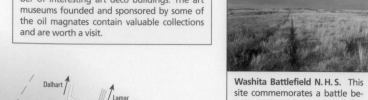

Tulsa Downtown Tulsa has an impressive number of interesting art deco buildings. The art museums founded and sponsored by some of the oil magnates contain valuable collections and are worth a visit.

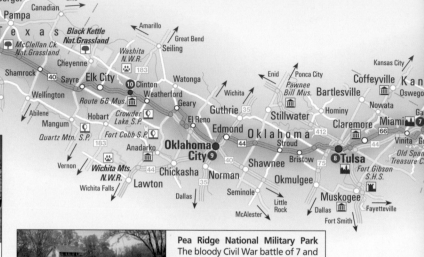

Washita Battlefield N.H.S. This site commemorates a battle between the US cavalry under Custer and the Cheyenne Indians.

Muskogee There are numerous historic buildings to be seen in the Old Town at the railway bridge over the Arkansas River.

Clinton, Oklahoma In addition to other exhibits, the Route 66 Museum displays a farming family's original loaded truck.

Wichita Mountains The mountain range south-west of Oklahoma City is a popular recreational area rich in flora and fauna.

Oklahoma City In front of the Capitol, an oil well and the sculpture of an Indian woman evoke the history and identity of the city.

Anadarko The Southern Plains Museum in the 'Indian Capital of the Nation' brings the culture of the Plains Indians and the Wild West back to life.

Pea Ridge National Military Park The bloody Civil War battle of 7 and 8 March 1862 in which 26,000 soldiers faced each other is commemorated near Rogers.

Los Angeles Palms between the skyscrapers remind passers-by that they are in the 'Golden State' and that Malibu and Venice Beach are not far away.

Calico Ghost Town This town, abandoned following the 'Silver Rush' in 1900, has been restored.

Grand Canyon The largest canyon in the world is about 1,800 m (5,906 ft) deep, up to 30 km (19 miles) wide and some 450 km (280 miles) long. The view of the giant canyon, with its colourful ridges, turrets and free-standing outcrops is overwhelming. At the bottom the Colorado River looks like a tiny little stream.

San Bernardino This is where the 'Orange Empire' begins, where oranges are grown as far as the eye can see. The California Theater evokes the golden age of Hollywood.

Joshua Tree National Park This park near Palm Springs is dedicated to the cactus-like yucca trees. They were given their name by a group of passing Mormons who were reminded of a biblical story about Joshua pointing to the sky.

Hualapai Mountain Park This park near Peach Springs is located in a side valley of the Grand Canyon.

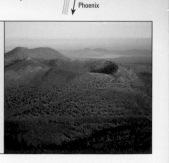

Sunset Crater This crater is part of a huge lava field in the San Francisco Peaks range and is 300 m (984 ft) deep. The best lava cones, flows and pipes are accessed from the panoramic drive.

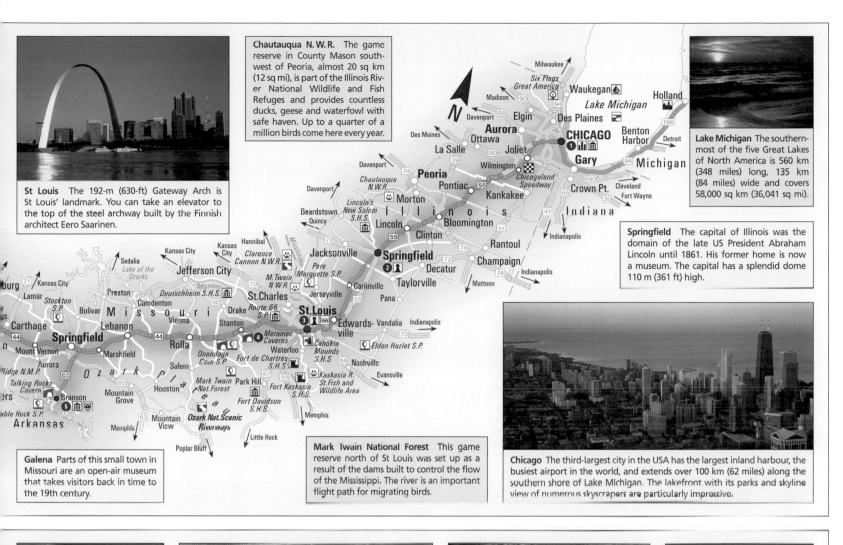

St Louis The 192-m (630-ft) Gateway Arch is St Louis' landmark. You can take an elevator to the top of the steel archway built by the Finnish architect Eero Saarinen.

Chautauqua N.W.R. The game reserve in County Mason southwest of Peoria, almost 20 sq km (12 sq mi), is part of the Illinois River National Wildlife and Fish Refuges and provides countless ducks, geese and waterfowl with safe haven. Up to a quarter of a million birds come here every year.

Lake Michigan The southernmost of the five Great Lakes of North America is 560 km (348 miles) long, 135 km (84 miles) wide and covers 58,000 sq km (36,041 sq mi).

Springfield The capital of Illinois was the domain of the late US President Abraham Lincoln until 1861. His former home is now a museum. The capital has a splendid dome 110 m (361 ft) high.

Galena Parts of this small town in Missouri are an open-air museum that takes visitors back in time to the 19th century.

Mark Twain National Forest This game reserve north of St Louis was set up as a result of the dams built to control the flow of the Mississippi. The river is an important flight path for migrating birds.

Chicago The third-largest city in the USA has the largest inland harbour, the busiest airport in the world, and extends over 100 km (62 miles) along the southern shore of Lake Michigan. The lakefront with its parks and skyline view of numerous skyscrapers are particularly impressive.

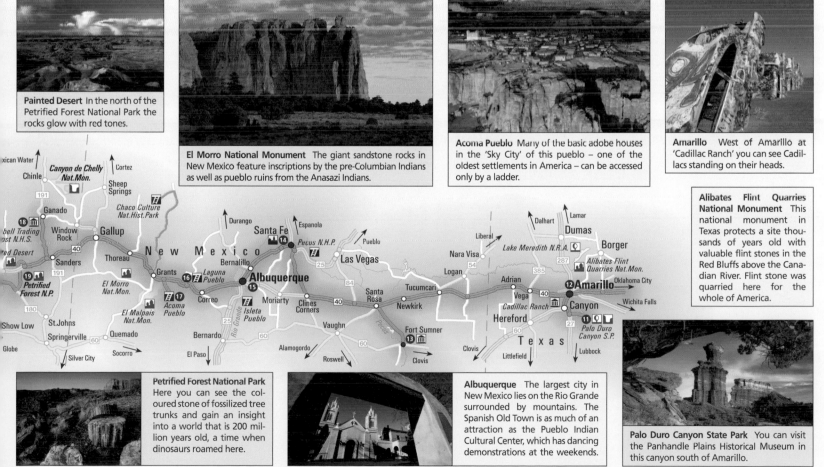

Painted Desert In the north of the Petrified Forest National Park the rocks glow with red tones.

El Morro National Monument The giant sandstone rocks in New Mexico feature inscriptions by the pre-Columbian Indians as well as pueblo ruins from the Anasazi Indians.

Acoma Pueblo Many of the basic adobe houses in the 'Sky City' of this pueblo – one of the oldest settlements in America – can be accessed only by a ladder.

Amarillo West of Amarillo at 'Cadillac Ranch' you can see Cadillacs standing on their heads.

Alibates Flint Quarries National Monument This national monument in Texas protects a site thousands of years old with valuable flint stones in the Red Bluffs above the Canadian River. Flint stone was quarried here for the whole of America.

Petrified Forest National Park Here you can see the coloured stone of fossilized tree trunks and gain an insight into a world that is 200 million years old, a time when dinosaurs roamed here.

Albuquerque The largest city in New Mexico lies on the Rio Grande surrounded by mountains. The Spanish Old Town is as much of an attraction as the Pueblo Indian Cultural Center, which has dancing demonstrations at the weekends.

Palo Duro Canyon State Park You can visit the Panhandle Plains Historical Museum in this canyon south of Amarillo.

Route 26

Mexico, Guatemala and Belize

Through the Kingdom of the Maya

Culture and beaches all in one – a journey through the Yucatán Peninsula. In the heartland of the Mayan region you can marvel at both ancient pyramids and Spanish-colonial-style baroque towns, while the white sand beaches of the Caribbean offer idyllic relaxation after your adventures.

The name of the peninsula separating the Caribbean Sea from the Gulf of Mexico originally arose from a misunderstanding. When the Spanish conquistadors first set foot on the peninsula at the start of the 16th century they addressed the indigenous people in Spanish. The Maya answered in their language: 'Ma c'ubab than', meaning 'We do not understand your words'. This later became Yucatán. Three countries lay claim to the Yucatán Peninsula: the north and west belong to Mexico, the south-east coast and Barrier Reef to Belize, and the mountainous south-east to Guatemala. Detours from

the route also take you to the most significant ruins in Honduras – Copán. When the conquistadors arrived in Mexico they discovered a uniquely advanced civilization. The Maya had both a precise calendar and their own alphabet. Their massive constructions – pyramids, palaces, places of worship – are all the more astounding given that the Maya had neither the wheel as a means of transport nor iron, metal implements, winches, pulleys, ploughs, or pack or draught animals. Mayan ruins are often located in the midst of tropical rainforests, are often overgrown and have only been partly

Mexico: a well-earned siesta in the afternoon.

uncovered. Sites that are easily accessible for tourists along the route we suggest here are Chichén Itzá, Tulum, Tikal, Edzná and Uxmal. The city of San Cristóbal de las Casas and the surrounding Indian villages in the south-west of the peninsula, Chiapas (Mexico), provide wonderful insight into the present-day life of the descendants of the Maya.

The Indian population of Mexico and Belize makes up around one-tenth of the overall population of each country. In Guatemala, however, half of all citizens are of Indian origin. In Mexico and Guatemala numerous Mayan languages are also still spoken. The Spanish who first landed on the Yucatán Peninsula in 1517 greatly underestimated the scale of Mayan civilization and unfortunately destroyed a large part of their physical culture and records. In their place rose

High above the Caribbean Sea sits Tulum, meaning 'fortress', a mighty wall that once encircled the Mayan town. The original Mayan name was Zama, meaning 'City of Dawn'.

San Miguel is the largest town on the holiday island of Cozumel off the coast of Cancún.

a series of colonial cities from the ruins of older Mayan settlements. The Spanish legacy includes baroque monasteries, cathedrals, palaces and large town plazas. The oldest cathedral in the Americas is in Mérida (1560), Campeche was once the most important harbour on the Yucatán Peninsula for goods headed to Europe, and there are important monasteries dating back to the 17th and 18th centuries in Antigua, Guatemala.

The route we recommend includes some of the most scenic nature reserves in Central America. On the north-east coast is the Sian Ka'an biosphere reserve (a UNESCO World Heritage Site) covering 4,500 ha (11,120 acres) of jungle and swamp as well as a 100-km-long (62-mile) coral reef. Belize is home to the Blue Hole National Park and the 300-km-long (186-mile) Belize Barrier Reef (also a UNESCO World Heritage Site). Guatemala is home to the Sierra de Las Minas biosphere reserve. Wild cocoa trees can still be found in the north-east of the peninsula and also in the mountainous regions of the south. Today the east coast, known as the 'Mayan Riviera', is a popular holiday destination – white sand beaches and the splendid reef between Cancún in the north and Tulum Playa in the south provide ideal conditions for both snorkelling and diving.

Yet swimming, diving, snorkelling and relaxing on the 'Mayan Riviera' are just some of the many options for an active holiday on the Yucatán Peninsula. If you go for a hike through the often still pristine tropical rainforests of the national parks and nature reserves in the interior of the peninsula, you will discover an unparalleled wealth of flora and fauna.

'The Old Man from Copán' sculpture in the ruined Mayan town of Copán in the Honduran forest.

Cancún

The modern coastal resort of Cancún lies on the very north-east corner of the Yucatán Peninsula, in the small federal state of Quintana Roo. With its international airport, it is a handy gateway to the rest of the Yucatán Peninsula. Conditions in Cancún are ideal for modern tourism – it has clean, warm, turquoise water all year round, superb white-sand beaches, mild swimming weather and excellent diving along the various coral reefs. Archeologically significant Mayan sites – primarily Chichén Itzá, Uxmal and Tulum – are easy to reach within two or three hours.

Most holidaymakers spend their time on Isla Cancún with its 23-km-long (14-mile) 'zona hotelera'. Near the southern end of Cancún Island is the Mayan site of El Rey with two small pyramids. Two bridges connect the island with Cancún on the mainland with the Laguna Nichupté in between. The resort island of Isla Mujeres off the coast to the north of Cancún was

View of the holiday complexes of Isla Cancún.

once an idyllic Caribbean island with a romantic atmosphere. In recent years it has succumbed to the pressures of increased travel, but it is still a splendid alternative. Ferries dock in Playa Linda in Cancún or in Puerto Juárez and Punta Sam north of the town. There are also ferry connections between Cancún and the island of Cozumel in the south where simpler, traditional accommodation can also be found. European explorers first landed on Cozumel in 1518. Within a few decades the island had been almost completely depopulated.

The Yucatán tour goes through Mexico, Guatemala and Belize, with a detour to the ruins of Copán in Honduras. From the idyllic Caribbean beaches you head to the mountainous regions of Guatemala before visiting the Petén rainforest and the magnificent coast of Belize then heading back to the start.

❶ Cancún The journey across the Yucatán Peninsula begins in Cancún on the north-east coast. The town's name derives from the name of the former Mayan settlement 'Can-Cune' ('End of the Rainbow'). Until the beginning of the 1960s Cancún was a tiny fishing village with barely 100 residents. The Mexican government then decided to create an international seaside resort, a project that met with massive success. Today more than 2.5 million tourists visit this town of 300,000 residents. South of the town the MEX 180 highway

turns towards Mérida. The turn-off to the most architecturally significant Mayan site on the peninsula, Chichén Itzá, is well signposted, 40 km (25 miles) beyond Valladolid.

❷ Chichén Itzá The largest and best preserved pre-Columbian ruins on the Yucatán Peninsula represented an important economic, political and religious centre between the years 400 and 1260, with a population of about 35,000 people. The best-known building at the site is El Castillo, a 24-m-high (79-ft) pyramid. Other buildings worth seeing are the Templo de

Travel information

Route profile
Length: approx. 2,800 km (1,740 miles), excluding detours
Time required: min. 4 weeks
Start and end: Cancún
Route (main locations): Mérida, Campeche, San Cristóbal de las Casas, Antigua, Ciudad de Guatemala, Quiriguá, Tikal, Belmopan, Belize City, Chetumal, Tulum

Traffic information:
Drive on the right on this trip. Most of the roads in Mexico

are decent. In Guatemala expect bad roads, apart from the Pan-American Highway and the main roads – best to travel by day. The roads in Belize are in relatively good condition. Caution during flooding in the rainy season!

Information:
Mexico:
www.mexicotravel101.com
Guatemala:
www.enjoyguatemala.com
Belize:
www.travelbelize.org

Mérida and Campeche

Mérida was built in 1542 on the site of the former Maya settlement, Tihó. The town was built in the early 16th century by Franciscan monks and has the appearance of a town designed at a drafting table. A series of preserved buildings from the Spanish colonial era are worth seeing – the Casa de Montejo (governors' residence), the cathedral San Ildefonso (the oldest in the Americas – construction began in 1560), the Jesuit church Templo de la Tercera Orden (17th century) and the Iglesia de Santa Lucia. The Palacio de Gobierno (1892), the city hall buildings on the Paseo de Montejo and the Museo de Antropologia e Historia date from the 19th century.

Catedral San Ildefonso in Mérida.

Campeche, formerly a Mayan trading centre, also played an important role in the conquest of Yucatán. From the 1550s the Franciscans tried to resettle the Mayan population in 'congregaciones' or 'reducciones' in the region around Campeche.

Two gates within the mighty city walls lead to the historic old city which, with its numerous renovated buildings, is a gem of colonial history. Among the loveliest 17th-century buildings is the Casa del Rey, the military commander's residence. The cathedral is located in the Parque Principal. Historically, two fortresses at each end of the town ensured additional safety. Construction of the Fuerte San Miguel in 1772 finally put an end to the pirate attacks. Today the fort houses the Museo de Cultura Maya. To the north-east lies the fortress Fuerte de San José with a weapon and ship museum.

los Guerreros, the observatory (Caracol) and the Cenote de los Sacrificios, as well as the 168-m-long (180-yd) playing field, the largest of its kind in the whole of Mesoamerica. Four 45° angle steps lead up to the El Castillo platform from where you will have a breathtaking view of the entire site.

❸ Mérida At the turn of the 19th century, the capital of the Federal state of Yucatán was a centre for the cultivation and production of sisal, a type of hemp. Magnificent town villas, spacious plazas and lovely parks are reminiscent of the town's heyday. Today it is an important industrial and commercial centre. At Uman, 20 km (12 miles) south of the town, a road branches off from the MEX 180 to the Parque Natural Rio Celestún.

❹ Parque Natural Rio Celestún Nature Park It is about 70 km (43 miles) to the small fishing village of Celestún on the Bahia de Campeche coast. In addition to the white, sandy beaches, the waterfowl living here are the

main attraction. Fishermen offer boat trips through the mangroves and to a petrified forest on the Isla de Pájaros. The same route takes you back towards the MEX 180. In Uman the MEX 261 branches off towards Muna and Uxmal (60 km/37 miles).

❺ Uxmal Archaeologists presume that the first stages of construction took place in the year AD 1. The majority of the buildings, however, date back to between the 7th and 10th centuries when parts of the peninsula were ruled from Uxmal. Uxmal is the best-known example of the Puuc civilization, represented by elongated buildings with

1 Uxmal: The Palacio del Gobernador from the 9th–10th century is considered a highlight of Puuc architecture.

2 Chichén Itzá: The Warriors' Temple is lined on two sides by '1,000 pillars' that originally supported a roof.

3 Chichén Itzá: The Warriors' Temple with Chac Mool in the foreground.

Mayan writing

One of the features of an advanced civilization is a distinct system of writing, created once a people have reached a specific level of development. It entails the use of graphic symbols to record and communicate important information.

The Mayans did not invent their writing system themselves. Instead they took it from the original writing of the Olmeken (c. 30 BC). Within 1,000 years they had developed this further and become the only civilization in pre-Columbian America to have a complete writing system comprising of logograms and syllables.

Mayan lettering on a wall panel in Palenque.

The writing, which was very similar to other regional languages, was widespread throughout the entire Mayan lowlands. The oldest complete text was found on pillar 29 in Tikal (AD 292).

The written texts, which are mainly preserved on wall panels, door frames, pillars, ceramic pieces and bark, tell of the lives of rulers – births, coronations, marriages, wars and burials. With only a few exceptions, the block-shape hieroglyphics are read in double columns from left to right and from top to bottom.

The Spanish Franciscan monk Diego de Landa was the first to document Mayan writing in his 'Report on Yucatán' in the 16th century. Their writing remained 'encrypted' to outsiders for centuries until the first images were deciphered in 1820. The majority of the works, however, were decoded only after 1950.

attractive courtyards, facades decorated with stone mosaics and the conspicuous lack of cenotes (natural limestone pools) typical of this style. Indeed, it was the ability to build artificial cisterns that enabled the Mayans to settle in this arid region.

Opposite the entrance to Uxmal stands the 35-m (115-ft) 'Fortune Teller's Pyramid', with its oval foundation, dating from the 6th–10th centuries. The steep, 60° staircase up the pyramid has a safety chain for visitors to hold when climbing.

From Muna it is then around 40 km (25 miles) to the MEX 180.

6 Campeche During the colonial era Campeche became an important harbour from which the Spanish shipped wood and other valuable raw materials back to Europe. The mighty city wall was reinforced with eight bastions (baluartes) to protect it from constant pirate attacks. From this significant harbour town on the peninsula we then follow the MEX 180S to Champotón, where we turn onto the MEX 261 towards Francisco Escárcega.

7 Calakmul The detour to Calakmul in the Reserva de la Biósfera Calakmul is around 150 km (93 miles). The reserve protects the largest continuous tropical rainforest area in Mexico and is also host to a number of important Mayan sites – Balamkú, Becán, Xpujil and Calakmul. After around 110 km (68 miles), at Conhuas, a road turns off the two-lane MEX 186 south towards Calakmul. During the rainy season the 60-km (37-mile) surfaced road, first built in 1993, is often passable only with four-wheel-drive vehicles. Although it has not been extensively researched to date, this sprawling settlement, which was continuously inhabited from 500 to 1521, is one of the most important examples of a classic Mayan town and was declared a UNESCO World Heritage Site in 2002. Until the year 1000 Calakmul was the capital of a former kingdom. Thereafter it served merely as a ceremonial centre. The 50-m (164-ft) pyramid is the highest in Mexico and from the top is a breathtaking view of these overgrown rainforest ruins. There are around 100 pillars spread around the site, but more valuable archaeological treasures such as the priceless jade masks have been moved to the museum in Campeche.

Back in Francisco Escárcega take the MEX 186 to Palenque.

8 Palenque These ruins, covering an area of 6 sq km (4 sq mi), are about 12 km (7.5 miles) out-

side of town and surrounded by the last sicable area of rainforest on the peninsula. The town, which must have been an important trading centre in the region, experienced its heyday between 600 and 800.

One important Mayan ruler is still known by name – Pacal the Great, whose reign coincided

Founded in 1528, San Cristóbal has fortunately been able to retain much of its originality. The heart of the town is the Zócalo, a grand plaza surrounded by old mansions. The western side of the square is dominated by the Palacio de Municipio while the north

The oldest church in San Cristóbal de las Casas: Santo Domingo.

with one of the most splendid eras in Mayan history. Today only part of the site is accessible to visitors. Try to plan a whole day for it. Inside the most famous temple, the 20-m (66-ft) Templo de las Inscripciones (Temple of the Inscriptions), sixty steps lead 25 m (83 ft) down into the crypt. Similar to the Egyptian pyramids, the step pyramids of Palenque were also the tombs of rulers. The most valuable possessions are now on display in the Museo Nacional de Antropologica in Ciudad de Mexico. Opposite the Temple of the Inscriptions is the El Palacio, where the royal family lived, while other accessible temples are located on the other side of the Otulum River.

One of the most important discoverers of ancient Mexican cul-

ture was the American John Lloyd Stephens, who visited the Yucatán between 1839 and 1841. According to his report, when Stephens first visited Palenque, 'a single Indian footpath' led to the archaeological site. He travelled all over the Yucatán with English draughtsman and architect Frederick Catherwood. Stephens recorded his impressions in travel journals while Catherwood captured his in drawings.

On the way from Palenque to San Cristóbal de las Casas it is worth making a stop at the Agua Azul National Park. The more than 500 waterfalls are especially worthy of their name, 'blue water', during the dry period between April and May. They vary in height from 3 m (10 ft) to an impressive 50 m (164 ft).

Beyond Palenque the road climbs gradually into the mountainous area of Montañas del Norte de Chiapas.

⑨ San Cristóbal de las Casas
This lovely little town at an altitude of 2,100 m (6,890 ft) carries the name of the Spanish Bishop of Chiapas, who was especially committed to the interests of the indigenous peoples. Particularly noticeable are the low-slung buildings in the town, a result of constant fear of earthquakes.

San Cristóbal is the centre of one of Mexico's important cocoa-growing areas. The Mayans were already growing the wild plant as a monocrop before the arrival of the Europeans, and even used slave labour to work on their plantations. The striking

terrace-like fields on these steep slopes (sometimes at an angle of 45°) date all the way back to the Mayans who built rows of stones running diagonally over the slope in order to fashion fields of up to 50 by 70 m (164 by 230 ft). The fields were enclosed by walls measuring over 1.5 m (5 ft) high.

Many visitors take trips from San Cristóbal into the outlying villages of the Chamula Indians,

1 Cleared ruins in the north of the Palenque archaeological site.

2 In Palenque, nine terraces lead up to the Temple of the Inscriptions.

3 One of the many waterfalls in the Agua Azul National Park.

side hosts the 16th-century Catedral Nuestra Señora de la Asunción with its baroque facade. The terraces of the Templo de Guadalupe and the Templo de San Cristóbal provide impressive views over the town. Santo Domingo is one of the finest examples of Mexican baroque architecture and an arts and crafts market is held on its terrace. The San Jalobil monastery is involved in preserving the Indian weaving traditions of the surrounding villages.

Guatemala's volcanoes

The Central American land bridge, between North and South America, has only existed for a few million years. The North American plate meets the Caribbean plate in Guatemala, where the tectonic fault line runs from west to east right across the country through Montaguatal. Guatemala also lies directly over a subduction zone where the coconut plate is descending into the earth's mantle below Central America (the North American and the Caribbean plate) at a speed of around 6 cm per year. This causes molten magma to rise to the surface. When its gases reach a certain pressure they are discharged in the form of volcanic eruptions,

Top: The Atitlan volcano (3,535 m/ 11,598 ft).
Below: Eruption of the Pakaja volcano in 1994.

which are often accompanied by earthquakes.

In this tectonically active region, thirty-seven volcanoes can be found in Guatemala alone , most of them in the Sierra Madre, which run parallel to the Pacific coast. The country's highest volcano (and the highest in Central America) is the extinct Tajumulco (4,220 m/13,546 ft) south-west of Huehuetenango. In addition to Acatenango, which last erupted in 1972, there are currently three other active volcanoes. The 3,763-m-high (12,346-ft) Fuego volcano (next to Acatenango) is not far from Antigua Guatemala and last erupted in December 2000. Pacaya, a stratovolcano, has been active since 1965 and last erupted in 1994 when its ash rain fell as far as 30 km (19 miles) away in Ciudad de Guatemala. The stratovolcano Santa Maria (3,772 m/12,378 ft) is located behind Quezaltenango. The youngest and perhaps most dangerous volcano, Santiaguito, last spewed lava and ash from its slopes in February 2003.

for example to San Júan Chamula (11 km/7 miles), or to Zinacantán, where the Tzotzil Indians live (8 km/5 miles).

Another worthwhile excursion from San Cristóbal is to Cañon El Sumidero, with fantastic views of gloriously coloured craggy cliffs that tower to heights of 1,000 m (3,281 ft). With a bit of luck you might even see crocodiles during a boat trip on the river.

From San Cristóbal to Ciudad de Guatemala the route follows the Pan-American Highway, known as the CA1 after the border. Around 85 km (53 miles) southeast of San Cristóbal is Comitán de Dominguez. From there you can take an excursion to the Mayan site of Chinkultic. You will reach the border at Paso Hondo after another 80 km (50 miles). On the Guatemalan side a mountain road leads via La Mesilla through the Sierra de los Cuchumatanes to Huehuetenango. The

roads in the rugged mountainous regions of Guatemala are generally in bad condition and are often full of potholes. Turning off at Los Encuentros, Lago de Atitlan is one of the featured sights in these highlands.

⑩ Lago de Atitlan Three volcanoes – San Pedro (3,029 m/ 9,938 ft), Atitlan (3,535 m/11,598) and Toliman (3,158 m/10,361 ft) – are reflected in the water of this alpine lake, which lies at 1,560 m (5,118 ft). Alexander von Humboldt wrote of the beauty of this 130-sq-km (81-sq-mi) azure blue lake, describing it as 'the most beautiful lake in the world'. There are fourteen Indian villages located around the lake, some of which already existed prior to the arrival of the Spanish conquistadors.

Today the residents are farmers or make a living from selling traditional handicrafts. The famous Friday market in Sololá, high

above the lake on the northern shore, is even frequented by hordes of Indians from the surrounding areas. The largest settlement is Santiago Atitlan at the southern end of the lake. In 1955 the government declared the lake and surrounding mountains a national park.

At Los Encuentros a narrow road turns off towards Chichicastenango, 20 km (12 miles) further north.

⑪ Chichicastenango This town, lying at an altitude of 1,965 m (6,447 ft) is characterized by its classic white colonial architecture. In the pre-colonial era the town was an important Mayan trading centre. Markets are the main attraction and draw residents from the surrounding areas in their colourful traditional costumes, who come to sell their textiles and carvings. In 1540 a Spaniard erected the oldest building in the town on the

ruins of a Mayan temple, the Santo-Tomás church. Each of the eighteen roads leading to it represents a month in the Mayan calendar, which comprised 18 months each with 20 days.

⑫ Antigua This village in Panchoytal is situated in a tectonically active region at the foot of three live volcanoes – Agua (3,766 m/12,356 ft), Fuego (3,763 m/12,346 ft) and Acatenango (3,975 m/13,042 ft). In 1541, mud-slides from Agua destroyed the town of Ciudad de Santiago de los Caballeros founded by the Spanish in 1527, but it was rebuilt further north in 1543. Numerous religious orders settled in this Central American capital where monasteries, schools and churches were erected. However, only parts of the Catedral de Santiago (1545) with its five naves have survived the earthquakes of the subsequent centuries. Nuestra

Copán, the southernmost of the Mayan towns close to the Honduran settlement of Copán Ruinas, lies on a promontory at 620 m (2,034 ft). Densely forested mountains surround the ruins on the Copán River, discovered by the Spaniard Diego Garcia de Palacio in the late 16th century. In 1576 he sent a report of his findings to

Señora la Merced is one of the most attractive examples of the Churrigueresque style. Together with the Palacio de los Capitanes Generales and the Palacio del Ayuntamiento, the Capuchin monastery Las Capuchinas is an impressive example of Spanish colonial architecture.

The town was destroyed by strong earthquakes in 1717 and 1773, but the Spanish rebuilt it as La Nueva Guatemala and it later became present day Ciudad de Guatemala. The previous capital was then simply called Antigua. In 1979 the old city, which in the 18th century was one of the most beautiful baroque ensembles of the Spanish colonial era, and which still retains a great deal of flair today, was declared a UNESCO World Heritage Site.

⑬ **Ciudad de Guatemala** The rebuilding of the residential town for the Spanish governor took place at a safer distance of 45 km (30 miles). Today, La Nueva Guatemala de la Asunción is still the economic and political centre of Guatemala. It lies at 1,480 m (4,856 ft) and is the seat of several universities. The main sightseeing attractions include the cathedral (1782–1809), the National Palace (1939–43) and the Archaeological Museum. Another important Mayan site is located in Tazumal, not far from Santa Ana in El Salvador, roughly 200 km (124 miles) away.

From the capital it is about 150 km (93 miles) on the CA9 to Rio Hondo where the asphalt

CA10 takes you via Zacapa, Chiguimula and Vado Hondo to the border post at El Florido. About 12 km (7.5 miles) beyond the Guatemala-Honduras border is Copán. On the return journey along the same road, about 70 km (43 miles) beyond Rio Hondo, you reach another UNESCO World Heritage Site – the ruins of Quiriguá.

⑭ **Quiriguá** This Mayan town on the lower Rio Motagua saw its heyday between 500 and 800. Its layout is very similar to that of Copá, only 50 km (31 miles) away. Explorer John Lloyd Stephens discovered Quiriguá in 1840.

Today the archaeological site at the edge of the Sierra del Espiritu Santo is still surrounded by thick jungle, and this is a major part of its attraction. The large mythical creatures carved in stone and the pillars measuring over 10 m (33 ft) in height, which constitute a high point of Mayan sculpture, are among the special attractions here. The highest pillar, E, is 10.5 m (34 ft) high and weighs 65 tonnes (71.5 tons).

Approximately 45 km (28 miles) beyond Quiriguá you leave the CA9 and turn to the north-west towards Lago de Izabal. The lake, 590 sq km (367 sq mi) in size, is surrounded by dense rainforest. Between the largest lake in Guatemala and the Rio Dulce, lined by rainforest, is the Spanish Fort Castillo de San Felipe. The fortress was originally constructed in 1595 to defend the arsenals on the eastern shore

of the lake from the repeated attacks of determined pirates plying the broad river.

The national road CA13 now crosses the foothills of the Sierra de Santa Cruz and continues via Semox into the lowlands of Petén. The small town of Flores on an island in Lago Petén Itzá is a good starting point for a visit to Tikal.

1 The Toliman and San Pedro volcanoes form an impressive backdrop to Lago de Atitlan in the Guatemalan highlands.

2 Universidad de San Carlos (1763) in Antigua.

3 Relief of a high priest in the Quiriguá Archaeological Park, also home to the tallest Mayan pillars.

Tombstone in Copán.

the Spanish king, Philip II. By the time John Lloyd Stephens wanted to visit the Mayan town of Copán in 1839, none of the residents in surrounding villages was able to answer his questions about the ruins.

Copán appears to have been one of the oldest and most important Mayan religious sites. According to archaeologist estimates, the town had as many as 40,000 inhabitants. Copán's 'Acropolis', said to have been 600-m-long (1,969-ft) and 300-m-wide (1,086-ft) included pyramids, temples and plazas. The pillars, some of which were as high as 3 m (11 ft), are among the most impressive examples of Mayan sculpture. Copán had already been abandoned 500–600 years prior to the Spanish, but the reasons are unclear. Skeletons found in Copán indicate malnutrition and chronic illness.

15 Tikal National Park This 576-sq-km (358-sq-mi) national park is surrounded by dense forest and includes one of the most important Mayan sites on the peninsula. Together, the park and rainforest, one of the largest continuous forests in Central America with over 2,000 plant varieties, has been declared a UNESCO World Heritage Site. Between 600 BC and AD 900 as many as 55,000 people lived in Tikal. Today, many of the 4,000 temples, palaces, houses and playing fields are buried under the encroaching forest.

A climb up one of the pyramids, the most important of which are on the Gran Plaza, gives visitors an impressive view of the 16-sq-km (10-sq-mi) Tikal National Park. The Jaguar Temple, some 45 m (148 ft) high, houses a burial chamber where the ruler Ah Cacao lies at rest. From Flores it is about 100 km (62 miles) to the border with Belize, and from there it is another 50 km (31 miles) to Belmopan, which has been the capital of Belize since 1970.

16 Guanacaste National Park 3 km (2 miles) north of Belmopan

is the 20-ha (49-acre) national park named after the large Guanacaste tree (Tubroos). It grows in the south of the park and is one of the largest tree types in Central America. The many tree species in the park also include mahogany, the national tree of Belize. South of Belmopan is the Blue Hole National Park, on the road to Dangriga.

17 Blue Hole National Park This 2.3-ha (5.7-acre) national park is a popular leisure area for the residents of Belmopan. Large areas of the park contain cave formations and are covered by dense rainforest. Sightseeing attractions include the 33-m (108-ft) collapsed crater that feeds a tributary of the Sibun River. It flows briefly above ground before disappearing into an extensive underground cave system. The 7.5-m (25-ft) 'blue hole' takes its name from its sapphire blue colour. Also within the park is St Herman's Cave, also used by the Mayans as evidenced by the ceramics, spears and torches that have been found inside.

18 Belize City Until 1970, Belize City was the capital of the for-

mer British Honduras. Today it is still the largest city in the country as well as an important seaport. St John Cathedral, the oldest Anglican cathedral in Central America, was built in 1812 from bricks that sailing ships from Europe had used as ballast.

The British Governor lived at Government House starting in

1814 (today it is the House of Culture museum). The city is an ideal base for excursions to the Belize Barrier Reef, a renowned diving paradise.

19 Belize Barrier Reef System The 300-km (186-mile) Barrier Reef is one of the longest in the northern hemisphere. The many islands and cays off the coast are

1 Guanacaste National Park: The jaguar is the most well-known wild cat on the Yucatán Peninsula.

2 Tikal: Temple 1 is one of the most attractive pyramid tombs of the late classic Mayan period. It rises about 45 m (148 ft) above the central square. Around 55,000 people lived here in the town's heyday. It was abandoned in the 10th or 11th century.

Spectacular diving territory: the Blue Hole in Belize's Barrier Reef is 80 km (50 miles) east of Belize City. Charles Darwin had already provided a description of the reefs back in 1842. About 10,000 years ago a cave collapsed here as land sank into the sea. The hole has a diameter of 300 m (984 ft) and is 125 m (410 ft) deep.

1

2

Reserva de la Biósfera Sian Ka'an

This biosphere reserve on the east coast of the Yucatán Peninsula close to Tulum (declared a UNESCO World Heritage Site in 1987) covers

At home in the biosphere reserve – the bottlenose dolphin.

around 100 km (62 miles) of beach as well as coral reefs, bays and lagoons. In the Mayan language the name Sian Ka'an means 'the origin of the heavens'. Tropical rainforest, mangroves and swamps are all close together here and there is a large reef off the coast. Beyond the underwater world, there are numerous bird and reptile species to be observed as well.

covered with mangroves and palms. The cays that are within reach include Ambergris Cay some 58 km (36 miles) north of Belize City as well as the Turneffe Islands. The reef's main attraction is its underwater world, with visibility of up to 30 m (98 ft), the bird reserve, Half Moon Cay and the Blue Hole, a massive collapsed cave.

20 Altun Ha The ruins of Altun Ha are close to the village of Rockstone Pond. It is postulated that this Mayan ceremonial centre was originally settled over 2,000 years ago. The Mayans built up much of their trading around Altun Ha. The most valuable finds from Altun Ha include a jade head of the Mayan Sun god that weighs 4.5 kg (9.9 lbs). Via Orange Walk the road continues through the lowlands of Belize to the Mexican harbour town of Chetumal and along the second largest lake in Mexico,

Laguna de Bacalar (MEX 307), to Felipe Carrillo Puerto. Here an access road branches off to the Sian Ka'an biosphere reserve.

21 Tulum This ancient Mayan town is a popular destination on the peninsula, primarily due to its spectacular location on a cliff overlooking the sea. The conquistadors were impressed by its imposing and protective walls. Five narrow gates opened the way into town. Outside the walls there were two ancient Mayan temple sites north of town.
Tulum has always had a safe harbour from which pilgrims in the pre-Columbian era once travelled to the island of Cozumel to honour the Moon god Ixchel with sacrifices.
After 1540 Tulum was engulfed by tropical vegetation and forgotten until 1840. From Tulum there is a road leading to the small fishing village of Punta Allen in the Reserva de la Biós-

fera Sian Ka´an. In the forest 48 km (30 miles) north-west of Tulum you can visit another ruins complex – Cobá.

22 Cobá You can reach the site of the ruins on the well-made road in half an hour. US archaeologists began the first excavations of the complex (210 sq km/130 sq mi) in the 1920s, and further excavation projects that are still going on today began in the 1970s. Cobá also has a pyramid. From the top you can see smaller pyramids, temples, a series of procession streets, a playing field, pillars with life-size images of kings and queens, and of course dense forest. In Cobá you can see peccaris (wild pigs), iguanas, tortoises and the colourful toucan.
The 130-km (81-mile) stretch of coast between Tulum and Cancún is also known as the 'Mayan Riviera'. Small villages

and bays such as Puerto Morelos provide swimming and diving opportunities for water enthusiasts. The seaside resort of Playa del Carmen is only a few kilometres south of the more upmarket Cancún, which is the start and end point of this round trip through the Yucatán Peninsulua.

1 Belize's main attraction is the Barrier Reef. At just less than 300 km (186 miles) in length, it is the longest barrier reef in the western hemisphere. Divers will find unique coral, good visibility and more than 350 types of fish. Hundreds of small islands (cays) are scattered along the length of the reef.

2 Never-ending white Caribbean beaches with crystal-clear water characterize the north-east coast of the Yucatán Peninsula, also known as the 'Mayan Riviera'.

Mérida The 'white town' was founded in the 16th century. At its centre are the Montejo Palast and the cathedral, one of the first sacral buildings in Mexico.

Chichén Itzá The highlights of the complex in the northern part of the Yucatán Peninsula are the Kukulcán and El Castillo pyramids, probably constructed by the Mayas and the Tolteken. Close by is a deep cenote, an underground limestone well from which water rises and forms a pool.

Cancún With its magnificent beaches and tropical climate the former fishing village in the north-east of the Yucatán has become Mexico's most popular holiday destination. With 20,000 beds and all-night entertainment options, more than 2.5 million tourists visit the giant hotel town each year.

Uxmal The 'Fortune Teller's Pyramid' is a highlight of Mayan architecture. The name dates back to the Spanish era but does not have anything to do with the actual purpose of the construction.

Tulum Situated on a cliff over the Caribbean Sea south of Cancún, the ruins of this Mayan town are easily accessible for even the laziest of beachcombers.

Palenque This archaeological site in the middle of the rainforest is among the most attractive in Mexico. Many of the buildings date from the reign of King Pacal and his son, Chan Balum.

Altun Ha The largest archaeological site in Belize is made up of two plazas with temple and residential complexes. Important jade artefacts have been found here, including a magnificent axe.

Lago de Atitlan This lake in the highlands of Guatemala (1,560 m/5,118 ft) is tucked between the San Pedro, Atitlan and Toliman volcanoes.

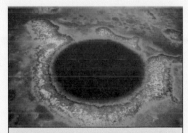

The Blue Hole In the Lighthouse Reef Atoll off the coast of Belize is one of the most beautiful coral reefs in the world. The Blue Hole has a diameter of 300 m (984 ft) and a depth of 125 m (410 ft).

Map labels

Parque Natural Río Lagartos · Ecab · Río Lagartos · Parque Natural San Felipe · 295 · Culuba · Yucatán · Cancún ① · Progreso · Tizimín · 176 · ❸ MÉRIDA · Ek Balam · Valladolid · Playa del Carmen · Celestún · Uman · ② · Cobá ㉒ · 307 · Cozumel · Parque Natural Río Celestún ④ · 281 · Muna · Chichén Itzá · Parque Natural de Quintana Roo · Tulum ㉑ · Jaina · ❺ Uxmal · Kabah · Yucatán · Chamax · 180 · 261 · 184 · Felipe Carrillo Puerto · Punta Allen · Campeche ⑥ · M É X I C O · 295 · Champotón · Edzná · Polyuc · Reserva de la Biósfera Sian Ka'an · Pustunich · Tixmul · 307 · Sabancuy · 261 · P e n í n s u l a · 293 · Cafotal · Majahual · R. de la Biósfera Calakmul · Ciudad del Carmen · Laguna de Términos · Francisco Escárcega · Balamkú · Becán · Dzibanché · Chetumal · Reserva de la Biósfera Pantanos de Centla · Palizada · 186 · Xpujil · Chicanná · Kohunlich · Cerros · Colha · 186 · Villahermosa · Coatzacoalcos · Catazajá · San Marco · Calakmul · Orange Walk · Altun Ha ⑳ · Belize City ⑱ · Turneffe Islands · 203 · Nuevo Coahuila · 106 · Palenque ⑧ · Ténosique · Reserva de la Biósfera Maya · El Tintal · B E L I Z E · Guanacaste N.P. · ⑯ · Blue Hole · Cascadas Agua Azul · P.N. Cañón del Sumidero · Toniná · El Cayo · P.N. Sierra del Lacandón · P.N. Tikal · Tikal · Belmopán · ⑰ · Blue Hole N.P. · Dangriga · ⑲ · Belize Barrier Reef System · San Cristóbal de las Casas ⑨ · Ocosingo · Planchón · Flores · Chiquibul N.P. · Mango Creek · Juchitán de Zaragoza · Tuxtla Gutiérrez · Comitán de Domínguez · Chinkultic · R. de la Biósfera Montes Azules · El Ceibal · Naj Tunich · Punta Gorda · Tenam Puente · Chinkultic · G U A T E M A L A · 13 · Sarstoon N.P. · Mesa de la Angostura · 190 · P.N. Los Cuchumatanes · Semox · Puerto Barrins · Paso Hondo · Lago de Izabal · Castillo de San Felipe · La Rúidosa · Tapachula · Cobán · R. de la Biósfera de Sierra de Las Minas · Quiriguá ⑭ · Vol. Tacana 4093 · Huehuetenango · 9 · Río Hondo · Los Encuentros · Chichicastenango · El Progreso · Copán · H O N D U R A S · Quezaltenango · 1 · ⑪ · Chimaltenango · Esquipulas · Tapachula · ⑩ · Lago de Atitlan · Antigua ⑫ · ⑬ CIUDAD DE GUATEMALA · 1 · Abaj Takalik · Santa Ana · 2 · Ahuachapán · Joya de Cerén · Puerto Quetzal · Tazumal · 1 · SAN SALVADOR · 2 · San Miguel · La Libertad · EL SALVADOR

Antigua The Spanish Governor used to rule Central America from this Guatemalan town. A number of baroque churches and palaces from the Spanish colonial era survived the earthquakes of 1717 and 1773, and are definitely worth seeing.

Tazumal Close to Santa Ana in El Salvador is the country's oldest Mayan settlement. The ruins of the 10-sq-km (6-sq-mi) complex with five temples were first cleared only 40 years ago.

Quiriguá The tallest and most artistic Mayan pillars can be found here. Their multitude of shapes evokes associations with the surrounding rainforest.

Tikal These ruins, buried in the jungle in the heart of the Mayan lowlands in present-day Guatemala, have inspired awe in many a visitor. Gustav Bernoulli discovered the ruins in 1877.

Stone pillars at the sun gate of the ruined city of Tiahuanaca, south of Lake Titicaca.

Peru and Bolivia

The Inca Trail

The Inca Trail connects the capitals of Peru and Bolivia and passes through culturally and historically significant sites in the highlands of the Andes Mountains. Travellers will be amazed by magnificent monuments dating back to early Inca civilization and Spanish colonial times.

The Inca Trail begins in the Peruvian capital of Lima, extends through the western cordilleras (range) of the Andes and runs right across Peru to Lake Titicaca. From there, one of the most spectacular routes in the whole of South America travels over Bolivian territory through the basin scenery of the Altiplano to the south-east and finally terminates in the eastern cordilleras of the Andes, in Sucre, the country's constitutional capital.

A fascinating natural environment, protected in a number of national parks such as the Parque Nacional Manú, provides

a stunning backdrop for the region's cultural treasures.

At the beginning of the 16th century, before the arrival of the Spanish, the Inca Empire covered almost the entire Andes region, including parts of the Andean foreland. A large number of the architectural treasures of this advanced civilization have been preserved along the Inca Trail. The architectural highlights include spectacular temples and palaces as well as a series of fortresses built at impressively shrewd locations. Most of these huge buildings, such as the large sun temple at

Highland Indians with their llamas.

Cuzco, were also built without significant technological assistance. A prime example of the strategic locations selected for Inca settlements is Machu Picchu, an extraordinary terraced site and one of the Inca's last places of refuge from advancing colonial troops.

Ironically, the Spanish never actually discovered this well-hidden settlement, which lies at around 2,800 m (9,187 ft). It was an American explorer who first discovered it in 1911. However, the discovery brought with it more riddles than answers regarding Inca culture.

Lake Titicaca, which still has a healthy fish population, straddles the Peru-Bolivia border. It lies 3,812 m (12,507 ft) above sea level and is not only the largest lake in South America, it is also the highest navigable lake in the world. Close to its southern shores is the town of Tiahuanaco (also

A view of the ruins of Machu Picchu, a glorious terraced Inca city in the high Andes.

In Sillustani, a peninsula on Laky Umayo, the Colla cultures buried their important citizens under chullpas, or burial mounds, measuring over 10 m (6 ft) in height and dating back to the 13th century.

known as Tiwanaku) which, up until the 10th century, was the religious and administrative centre of an important pre-Columbian civilization. The natural environment in the region around Lake Titicaca is also spectacular. Some of the highest mountains in the Andes are here, including the 6,880-m (22,573-ft) Nevado del Illimani south-east of Bolivia's largest city and administrative capital, La Paz.

Numerous remnants of the Spanish colonial era can also be seen here, in particular in the area around Lago de Poopó. The Europeans were especially interested in the mineral wealth of the 'New World', and many Indians were forced to work as slaves in Spanish mines, many of them losing their lives in the process. At the beginning of the 17th century Potosí was the world's most important centre for silver mining. As a result of its historical

significance the town has been declared a World Heritage Site, together with Cuzco, Machu Picchu and the Old Town in Lima. The distinction is intended for both the time-honoured Inca sites and for some of the architectural achievements of the Spanish colonial rulers.

In addition to these cultural and historical features, the diverse natural environment in this South American region has also been given its share of attention – the Manú National Park, in the transition zone between the Amazon lowlands and the middle Andes, has also been declared a UNESCO World Heritage Site.

With its dramatic differences in altitude, the Inca Trail provides a wonderful cross-section not only of Peru and the northern reaches of Bolivia, but also of the history and natural environment of an entire continent.

Women with traditional headwear offer their produce at the market in Cuzco.

Pachacámac

Pachacámac was a popular pilgrimage destination as far back as the 9th century – long before the advance of the Inca. The sites are around 30 km

Remains of a pyramid in Pachacámac.

(19 miles) south-east of Lima and are still shrouded in legend. Pilgrims covered great distances on difficult routes to come and consult the oracle. Interestingly, Pachacámac lost none of its mystery following the Inca invasion in the 15th century. On the contrary, not only did the new rulers take over the existing temples, they also extended the site to include the 80-m-high (262-ft) sun pyramid. Pachacámac subsequently became one of the most important administrative centres in the Inca Empire. The excellent condition of the ruins is particularly remarkable.

The Inca Trail runs from Lima on the Peruvian Pacific coast through countless Andean passes, majestic mountains and high plateaus on its way to Sucre in Bolivia. The route features both desert landscapes and tropical rainforests as well as high mountain lakes. The well-preserved Inca ruins make the journey an unforgettable experience.

❶ Lima Our journey begins in the largest city on the Inca Trail, where traffic is characterized by the expected noise and chaos of a large urban centre. Lima was founded by the Spanish in 1535 and they quickly established it as the focal point of their colonial empire in South America. In 1826 Lima replaced Cuzco as the capital and grew into a wealthy metropolis.

Some of the most magnificent buildings from this era – both palaces and churches – have since been beautifully restored to their original glory. The main cathedral (1535–1625) is located on Plaza San Martín in the historic Old Town, which itself has been declared a World Heritage Site in its entirety. The tomb of the conqueror Francisco Pizarro, the founder of Lima, is also said to be somewhere in the city.

Lima is a junction for important transcontinental routes such as the Pan-American Highway. When you leave Lima heading east you will unfortunately encounter few inviting locations. Due to significant migration from the countryside, sprawling slums have developed on the outskirts of the city. Road conditions in the outer areas can be very bad at times. The multi-lane Pan-American Highway runs past these outskirts before heading south towards Pachacámac.

You will soon leave the coastal flats as the road climbs quickly into the Andean foothills toward the market town of La Oroya. There are some steep, winding sections here. From there a detour (64 km/40 miles) heads north to Junín. Several memorials here commemorate the battle of Junín in 1824 between Simon Bolívar's troops and Spanish soldiers, one of many South American battles for independence. The journey then continues through the narrow Mantaro valley towards Huáncayo.

❷ Huáncayo The Mantaro Valley is renowned for its numerous

Travel information

Route profile
Length: approx. 2,000 km (1,243 miles), excluding detours
Time required: 3 weeks
Start: Lima, Peru
End: Sucre, Bolivia
Route (main locations): Lima, Ayacucho, Cuzco, Machu Picchu, Lake Titicaca, La Paz, Cochabamba, Oruro, Potosí, Sucre

Traffic information:
Drive on the right side. Road conditions vary considerably. Heavy rainfall and the resulting landslides can make some mountain routes impassable.

When to go:
The best time for travelling to the Andes is during the southern hemisphere winter (May to September), as the southern summer (December to March) is the rainy season. The temperature range between night and day is considerable.

Information:
Peru travel info:
www.peru.info/perueng.asp
Bolivian travel info:
www.boliviaweb.com
Peruvian and Bolivian embassies around the world:
www.embassyworld.com

Inca architecture

Where they came from is uncertain, but it is beyond dispute that the Inca's architectural legacy is the most magnificent on the South American continent. Their monumental buildings are considered the most important cultural achievements of the Inca, despite the fact that the craftsmen of this advanced Indian civilization had no significant technological aids at their disposal.

Today it still seems barely conceivable that huge blocks of stone could be worked so smoothly without the use of metal tools, much less assembled without the use of joints. And yet it was not just individual houses, temples, palaces and tombs that were built. Whole cities were constructed without even the use of the wheel.

Top: Stone circle in the Inca fortress Sacsayhuamán.
Bottom: The almost seamless stone walls at Sacsayhuamán.

Furthermore, the materials often had to be transported to remote, nearly inaccessible locations at high altitudes, such as Machu Picchu. The remains of Inca architecture can also be found in the beautiful city of Cuzco and a number of other places.

All the sites have in common a high degree of functionality (even the religious buildings) and a simplicity of decoration. One essential function of the monumental buildings was to intimidate enemies. To this end, the Inca secured their settlements with mighty walls. Despite, or perhaps because of the aura of magic that still pervades their architecture today, Inca architecture is among the best researched architecture of the pre-Columbian era.

most important of their kind in South America, drawing visitors from all parts of the country.

4 Huari Approximately 22 km (14 miles) north-east of Ayacucho is Huari, once the centre of the culture of the same name (6th–12th centuries). Nearly 100,000 people lived here during the heyday of the Huari Empire in the 9th century. The city was carefully planned and the grid-like layout of the streets can still be seen today. The well-organized Huari armies had a history of subordinating enemy peoples, but the city was ultimately abandoned in the 10th century. Back on the main route we now head east past more Andean peaks towards Cuzco, the red

1 Rooftop view of the Renaissance-style cathedral in Cuzco (17th century).

2 Plaza San Martín, the lively centre of the Peruvian capital, Lima.

3 Near Cuzco, a high-altitude basin framed by snow-capped Andean peaks.

4 The Corpus Christi procession is one of the most important religious ceremonies in Cuzco.

pre-Columbian ruins. It ends in Huáncayo, the largest town in the region. Maize, potatoes and vegetables are grown outside the town using irrigation and in some places the allotments seem to stretch beyond the horizon. Huáncayo, at an altitude of roughly 3,350 m (10,991 ft), is an important regional trading centre. Today there is little left as a reminder that the town was once a centre of the Inca Empire.

It is now characterized by Spanish colonial architecture.
The route now heads along a valley towards the south and the climate becomes milder with the decreasing altitude. Prickly pears grow right up to the roadside, their fruit highly prized by the Peruvians.

3 Ayacucho This city, at an elevation of 2,760 m (9,056 ft), is an interesting combination of

past and present. Ayacucho was at one time the capital of the Huari Empire, one of the first advanced civilizations in the Andes and, as such, a predecessor to the Incas.
The city was discovered and refounded in 1539 by Francisco Pizarro. It is known as the 'City of 33 churches' and religious ceremonies play an important role here. The Holy Week processions (Semana Santa) are among the

Valle Sagrado de los Incas

One of the most revered destinations on a journey through Peru is the Sacred Valley of the Incas, best reached via Pisac. The Spanish name for the central section of the Urubamba Valley, Valle Sagrado de los Incas, refers to its fertile soils – and it's no surprise. The mild climate and the protected location made it possible for the Inca to make incredibly productive use of the land.

It was here, between Pisac and Ollanta, that the foundation for this advanced Indian civilization was formed. It was here that the staple crops were cultivated and the seeds sold for distribution throughout the country. And it is here that evidence still indicates the sophisticated methods used by the Incas to work the land.

Farming (top) and salt mining (bottom) have been carried out in the Sacred Valley of the Incas for centuries.

The steep slopes here were laboriously terraced in order to grow staple crops like potatoes, maize and quinoa, among other things. Land in this region was thus made available for agriculture up to an astounding altitude of about 4,000 m (13,120 ft). The terraces built in hollows are even reminiscent of amphitheatres. These fields are still worked by family groups to this day.

The villages, which seem to have remained untouched by the passing of time, are further testimony to the Sacred Valley's cultural legacy – dusty roads between simple adobe houses, wobbly wooden stands at the markets and people in traditional costumes retain the valley's authenticity. But it was not always so tranquil here. This valley was the scene of bloody battles between the Inca and Spanish invaders, who even managed to take the fortress of Ollantaytambo.

tiled roofs of which can be seen from miles away.

5 Cuzco For many travellers, Cuzco is one of the most important destinations in Peru. With its scenic location in the Andes, relaxed atmosphere, easy access to its attractions, and especially as a base for tours to the Urubamba Valley and Machu Picchu, the city is indeed a highlight along the Inca Trail.

For the Incas, Cuzco was the focal point of their empire and therefore the centre of the world as they knew it. They established the city as a political, religious and cultural hub. Upon their arrival the Spanish knew of the city's importance but were dazzled by its wealth and grandeur. Unlike other Inca strongholds, the Spanish destroyed only a few of the buildings when they invaded Cuzco, and only the most significant structures with political or religious functions were razed. On those foundations the colonial rulers then erected a series of their own buildings, some stately in scale, others of religious importance. The Plaza de Armas, for example, was constructed on the site of the former main square, Huacaypata, at the time 600 m (1,969 ft) long. Santo Domingo monastery was built from the ruins of the Coricancha sun temple. The Jesuit church La Compañia (1571) was constructed on the foundations of the grand Inca palace, Huayna Capac.

In 1950, parts of the city were destroyed by a strong earthquake. Fortuitously, however, the quake actually unearthed a number of Inca remains that had been previously hidden from view.

Cuzco's importance remains unchanged for the descendants of the Inca. The Quechua-speaking Indians hold colourful ceremonies in the city, in which the customs and traditions of their forebearers are relived, and yet Christian festivals are also celebrated with enthusiasm. The annual Corpus Christi processions in particular attract much attention. In 1983 the Old Town was declared a UNESCO World Heritage Site.

6 Sacsayhuamán Situated above Cuzco – about 3 km (2 miles) north of the city – are the remains of a mighty fortress. Between 1440 and 1532 the Inca built an imposing citadel here encircled by three concentric walls.

Sacsayhuamán can be reached on foot from Cuzco in just under half an hour. The path leads from the Plaza de Armas via the Calle Suecia, past San Cristobal church and via the old Inca path up to the fortress.

In their time the stone blocks, which are up to 5 m (16 ft) high and weigh 200 tonnes (220 tons), intimidated many a would-be attacker and thus fulfilled their purpose as a demonstration of the power of their owners. The fortress is a main attraction in the Cuzco area. Today it is assumed that the fortress was built to control the most vulnerable entrance to the city. The complex includes a number of store rooms for food and an armory for weapons.

Manú National Park

Some 100 km (62 miles) north of Cuzco is the Manú National Park (15,300 sq km/9,507 sq mi) in the area between the Amazon lowlands and the Andes. Due to the changes in altitude here, from 400–4,000 m (1,312–13,124 ft), the range of habitats extends from tropical lowland rainforest to mountain and cloud forest to highland steppe. The fauna is equally diverse. In addition to some 800 bird, 200 mammal and 120 fish

Top: A colourful scarlet parrot in flight.
Middle: The Manú meanders through the lowlands.
Bottom: The Black Caiman is one of the most striking reptiles in the park.

During the Spanish invasion, hundreds of Inca warriors barricaded themselves within the walls of Sacsayhuamán, right up until the bitter end. In addition to the heavy fighting, strong earthquakes have also caused significant damage to the structure. Today only about one-third of the fortress remains.

❼ Pisac On a 32-km-long (20-mile) detour to the north you are led along a scenic road via the cult site Kenko, the 'Red Fortress' (Puca Pucara), and the sacred spring of Tambo Machay in the idyllic village of Pisac, which can be reached by a metal bridge. Inca influences clash here with colonial era flair.
Market days in Pisac are full of activity. Souvenirs such as flutes, jewellery, and clothing made

from llama wool are traded on the central plaza. Just as attractive, however, are the ruins of an Inca ceremonial site located 600 m (1,969 ft) above the village.

❽ Ollantaytambo At the end of the Sacred Valley, 19 km (12 miles) beyond the main town of Urubamba, is the village of Ollanta (2,800 m/9,187 ft), named after Ollantay, an Inca military leader. The fortress, with its spectacular stone terraces, stands on a bluff above the village. The Inca began construction on the well-fortified complex in 1460, but the project took much longer than planned. Ollantaytambo was not yet complete when the Spanish attacked in 1523.
Despite that, residents of Ollanta are still enjoying the benefits

of the irrigation system developed back then by the Inca. Even during the dry season there was, and is, enough water available for agriculture.
Costumes worn by local residents are especially eye-catching and have hardly changed from those worn by their forefathers 500 years ago. The last few metres to the fortress have to be covered on foot.
While the landscape in the Cuzco hinterland is characterized by sparse vegetation, the scenery changes drastically as you head towards Machu Picchu. It becomes more tropical and the monotone flora of the highlands gives way to dense rainforest. The road starts to wind pretty heavily now, with tight curves and an occasionally hair-raising climb up to the 'City of Clouds'.

❾ Machu Picchu The 'City of Clouds', as Machu Picchu is also known, is about 80 km (50 miles) north-west of Cuzco. Surrounded by imposing mountains and set in the midst of a dense forest is the most significant and fascinating archaeological site in South America. It is spectacularly located on a high

mountain ridge nearly 600 m (1,969 ft) above the Urubamba River. There is hardly any other site where the technical and mechanical skills of the Inca are demonstrated more tangibly than Machu Picchu, and it is therefore no surprise that the site was declared a UNESCO World Heritage Site in 1983. It is also no surprise that myths and legends still surround this magical place today. In fact, its very origins remain unknown.
It is assumed that Machu Picchu was built in the 15th century. One theory holds that Machu Picchu served as a place of refuge during the Spanish invasion.

1 The walls of the Inca fortress Sacsayhuamán were intended to command the respect of attackers.

2 Ruins at the Inca ceremonial centre of Pisac with the typical trapezoid doors.

3 The sun temple and stone terraces of the Ollantaytambo fortress.

4 View from the strategically situated village of Pisac down into the Sacred Valley of the Incas.

species, there are also countless insect species. As a result, the area was declared a National Park in 1973 and a UNESCO World Heritage Site in 1987.
To protect its flora and fauna, the national park has only minimal road infrastructure, but it is not empty of people. There are about thirty villages here. Approach the park via Paucartambo and the Acjanacu Pass to the mountain village of Atalaya on the Río Alto Madre de Dios. From here, boats bring visitors to Boca Manú, at the edge of the area open to tourists.

The condor

A lonely figure circling high above the peaks of the Andes – zologically one of the New World vultures, in the old world the condor was considered the symbol of South America. It is one of the largest volant birds in the world

Condor – King of the Sky.

and its wing-span can reach more than 3 m (10 ft). Its black plumage and fluffy white ruff are especially striking. Condors do not build an eyrie. Instead they lay their only egg in a rock crevice. The carcasses of larger mammals are their main source of food.

Another theory supposes that the Inca relocated their political centre to this barely visible and even more inaccessible site. One thing remains certain, however – the colonial Spanish were fully unaware of the existence of this city. The site was first discovered in 1911.

The city's structure is still easily recognizable. Stone houses comprise one room only and are arranged around small courtyards. What might appear simple at first is in fact the result of considerable technical and mechanical skill on the part of the builders. The structures are grouped around a central, more or less quadratic formation. The most striking buildings include the temple tower, or Torreon, and the Sintihuatana sun temple, with seventy-eight stone steps leading up to it.

From Machu Picchu you first need to return to Pisac via the same road, where another road then branches off toward Huambutiyo. On a narrow, gravel road you will come to Paucartambo and Atalaya, jumping-off point for a visit to the Manú National Park.

From Pisac back on the Inca Trail you soon branch off onto a signposted side road heading north to Tipón. The gravel road here is typically in good condition. After

about 4 km (2.5 miles) you will reach the ruins of the old city of Tipón at an altitude of about 3,500 m (11,454 ft).

🔟 **Tipón** Especially noteworthy here are the well-preserved terraces, where a sophisticated system of irrigation still enables productive cultivation of the land. It is now surmised that the Inca used the site as an experimental area for acclimatizing plants that otherwise only grew in lower-lying areas. On the onward journey from Tipón towards the south-east you pass

the little village of Andahuaylillas where the 17th-century baroque church is worth a brief visit. The peak of Nudo Ausandate towers 6,400 m (20,998 ft) above you on the left.

⓫ **Raqchi** Located at the base of the Quinsachata volcano, this town hosts an important traditional festival every year on the 3rd Sunday of June. From a distance, the temple, which is dedicated to Viracocha, the most important Inca god, resembles a viaduct because of its 15-m-high (49-ft) walls. It provides

an impressive backdrop for the festivities.

1 The ruins of Machu Picchu are even impressive when shrouded in mist. Yet they lay hidden for several centuries without the help of this natural veil. Situated as it is 600 m (1,969 ft) above the Urubamba River on a high mountain bluff, this surprisingly well-preserved Inca ruin is reached only with difficulty.

2 On the Inca Trail, the Nudo Ausandate (6,400 m/20,998 ft) rises out of the high Andean plateau.

It is hard to imagine how the Inca could have transported the stone blocks that were used to build the magnificent structures to Machu Picchu. Both the buildings and the site itself are testimony to their advanced skills and craftsmanship. Sophisticated irrigation systems were constructed for agricultural purposes.

Inti Raymi

The Spanish invaders may have destroyed the Inca Empire but the descendents of this advanced Indian civilization maintain many of the customs and traditions of their forebearers. The result of this is that many of the festivities and rituals have survived to this day.

The most well-known event is the solstice festival, Inti Raymi, which the Indian residents of Peru celebrate in Cuzco every year on 24 June. This date marks the winter solstice in the southern hemisphere. On this, the shortest day of the year, people traditionally brought the sun back to earth with symbolic bonfires. They also celebrated the harvest and the start of the new solar year. Wearing colourful costumes and headdresses, they made sacrifices to the Sun god, Inti.

A dancer with a colourful feathered headdress.

The present-day ceremony is still reminiscent of the sun worship of the early Inca Empire. Celebrations begin at the sun temple and then continue on the main square. The main ceremony takes place in the Sacsayhuamán fortress near Cuzco.

Admittedly, sacrifices are now less spectacular than in the days of the Incas. Today only one white and one black llama are sacrificed. During colonial rule the festival was forbidden. Spanish rulers suppressed the Inca's cultural traditions for fear of an outbreak of resistance.

Times have changed, however, and the festival has become a modern event. The once religious ceremony is now a grand spectacle where music groups come from all over to play the old folk songs. Yet despite the commercialization, Inti Raymi reflects the great importance of sun worship among the Inca.

The ceremonies are also all held in Quechua, the Inca language, a fact that reinforces the immense importance of these traditions for the identity of Peru's Indian residents.

12 Sillustani The well-built road from Raqchi now leads southeast towards Lake Titicaca. Near the northern shore of the lake a road branches off to the right towards one of the architectural attractions on this section of the route – the burial mounds of Sillustani, a peninsula on Lake Umayo.

The mounds, known as chullpas, were constructed out of clay in the pre-Inca era and are up to 12 m (39 ft) high. They served as the burial sites of regional rulers. Some chullpas seem to defy gravity, with base diameters smaller than those of their tops. It is known that the material for the burial mounds comes from quarries near the lake. Particularly noticeable here, too, is the precise working of the stone blocks, which were put together without the use of joints.

It is possible to drive around Lake Titicaca to the north and the south, and both roads run close to the shores almost all the way. You will reach Puno after about 32 km (20 miles) on the southern route of the Inca Trail.

13 Puno The location of this town, directly on Lake Titicaca, is striking enough in itself, giving you the impression that you are

at the coast. Puno is considered to be a cradle of Inca civilization. One legend has it that the first Inca rose from the lake here to create the empire. The surrounding area used to be ruled from Tiahuanaco.

Puno, at an elevation of 3,830 m (12,566 ft), was founded by the Spanish in 1668 and quickly equipped with a number of Christian churches intended to evangelize the Indians living here. Part of this religious centre remains today.

Many Peruvians associate Puno with colourful folklore. Every year in February, residents stage one of the most well-known festivals in the country, named after the Virgen de la Candelaria.

Lively markets are held on the Plaza Mayor, which is flanked by the cathedral completed in 1757. Boats depart from Puno's harbour to some of the islands on the lake.

The region around the city is used intensively for agriculture, and pastures for the llama and alpaca herds extend almost to the edge of the road. After a short drive you will reach Chucuito, a village with two colonial churches and an Inca fertility temple.

14 Lake Titicaca This is a lake in a class of its own. With a surface area of 8,300 sq km (5,158 sq mi), Lake Titicaca is the largest lake in South America and the border

of Peru and Bolivia runs right through it. The water level lies at 3,812 m (12,507 ft).

But it is not only these record features that characterize this unique body of water. The scenery and the remains of Inca civilization in the area around the crystal-clear 'Andean Sea' constitute the real attraction of the lake, which belongs to both Peru and Bolivia.

Ruins and ritual sites exist on the Isla del Sol (Island of the Sun) as well, which rises nearly 200 m (656 ft) out of the lake. The Incas created a variety of myths that proclaimed the island as their place of origin. The Templo del Sol (sun temple) in particular, situated on the highest point

Reed construction on Lake Titicaca

In addition to the 'stationary' islands in Lake Titicaca there are also a number of 'floating' islands. They were constructed by the Uros people, fishermen who lived on them out on the lake. The Uros built these islands, which are named after them, out of reeds, a raw material that is readily available on the shores of the lake.

Initially they simply built the foundations of their houses on land using rushes mixed with soil. With the lake's rising water level, however, they had to keep raising the level of the foundations until some houses began

Top: Reed boats – an important means of transport for the Indians on Titicaca.
Middle: 'Floating' islands on Lake Titicaca.
Bottom: Reed boat with an artistic figurehead.

mountains, is the fishing village of Copacabana, on the peninsula of the same name extending far out into Lake Titicaca.

Excursion boats to the islands of the sun and moon depart from here. The climate is rough and the water temperature is usually quite cool.

Copacabana is an important pilgrimage destination for Bolivians. On 4 August every year a large procession of pilgrims arrives for the Fiesta de la Virgen de Copacabana. The Virgin is also sanctified in the Moorish-style basilica (1820).

From Copacabana you can either return to the southern route via Yunguyo (crossing the border for

1 Many of the massive stone tombs in Sillustani, which are visible from great distances, have been partially destroyed by grave robbers or lightning.

2 Lake Titicaca on the Altiplano has a total of seven large islands.

3 A colonial church in Puno, at an altitude of 3,830 m (12,566 ft), on the western shore of Lake Titicaca.

4 Market day on the main square in front of the cathedral in Copacabana.

to float on the lake during times of flooding.

Since this had advantages for fishing, the Uros decided to make a virtue out of necessity since this way of life also provided protection against attacks by the Inca. When invasion threatened, the Uros retreated to their floating islands on Lake Titicaca. However, the reeds served the Uros not only as 'foundations', they also used them to make their boats. The descendants of the Uros now live on the lake shores and the floating islands have become popular tourist destinations.

of the island, is still shrouded in mystery.

Isla de la Luna (Island of the Moon) is also worth a brief visit. In addition to the 'stationary' islands there is also a series of 'floating' islands, designed by the Uros people in the pre-Inca era and still surviving today (see sidebar on the right).

15 **Copacabana** Turn off the southern coastal road to the border town of Yunguyo. On the Bolivian side, between the Cerro Calvarío and Cerro Sancollani

Detour

Cordillera Real

A lofty name that certainly delivers on its promises as these mountains are indeed majestic. In Bolivia the Cordillera Real (the King's Range) extends east of Lake Titicaca and on sunny days the glittering high-altitude glaciers are visible from miles away.

In addition to the highest peak in the group, the 6,880-m (22,573-ft) Nevado del Illimani, there are quite a few other 'six-thousand-footers' rising up into the cobalt blue skies of the Andes. They are so spectacular that many passionate European climbers and hikers travel to South

Top: The majestic Cordillera Real forms a dramatic background to Lake Titicaca.
Bottom: View of Nevado del Illimani from Achacachi on the eastern shores of Lake Titicaca.

America exclusively for trekking tours in the Cordillera Real.

From La Paz it is a fairly short journey here. The capital city lies just below 4,000 m (13,124 ft) above sea level so it does not take long to acclimatize. Yet the altitude is not without its problems. The air becomes very thin and climbers therefore should proceed slowly, their luggage being carried by llamas. When they finally reach the peak, however, the view over the Andes, Altiplano and Lake Titicaca is simply spectacular.

the second time), or continue your journey without the border crossing by taking the northern route around the lake towards La Paz.

16 Tiahuanaco The ruins of this city (also called Tiwanaku) lie about 20 km (12 miles) from the southern end of Lake Titicaca. The site used to be directly on the lake shore but the lake has become smaller over the centuries. Very close to the former ceremonial site is present-day Tiahuanaco, just a short drive from the ruins.

The first traces of settlement here have been dated back to approximately 1500 BC. Tiahuanaco was probably founded in around AD 300. It subsequently developed into the centre of an empire that covered most of the region and whose cultural and religious influences extended far beyond Peru, even as far as northern Chile and Argentina. The civilization experienced its heyday between 300 and 900. It is meant to have been the most advanced civilization in the central Andes. Around 20,000 residents lived together on only a few square kilometres. Agriculture was the most important economic activity in Tiahuanaco, with nearby Lake Titicaca providing water for effective cultivation. Using an advanced system of canals, farmers here

channelled lake water to their fields, which extended over an area of about 80 sq km (50 sq mi). Most of the temples, pillars and monoliths were built between 700 and 1200. An important place of worship, in this case a step pyramid about 15 m (49 ft) high, is situated in the middle of the city. The most famous construction, however, was the sun gate, sculpted out of one stone that weighs almost 44 t (48 tons). Many buildings were removed by the Spanish who needed ready-made stone blocks for the construction of their own showcase buildings. Blocks from Tiahuanaco were used to build a number of churches in La Paz, for example.

Only a few remains of the site survived the centuries of destruction and overall disregard for their cultural significance. It was only at the beginning of the 20th century that extensive excavations began. The site was reconstructed as precisely as possible to the original once archaeologists were able to clear sufficient remains of the buildings.

Ultimately, the site was declared a UNESCO World Heritage Site in the year 2000. However, there are still many unanswered questions. Why was the city abandoned? Was it due to climate change, or had the population become too large? Without any doubt, the stonemasonry in

Tiahuanaco is among the most skilled in South America. Shortly before La Paz the road following the eastern shore of Lake Titicaca joins National Road 1.

17 La Paz The largest city in Bolivia, and the highest city in the world, is nestled impressively among the slopes of a steep valley. The metropolis is not the constitutional capital but it is the seat of the Bolivian government – and the heartbeat of the country.

The city's neighbourhoods seem to cling to the mountain slopes and are striking even from afar. La Paz is situated at an elevation of between 3,650 and 4,000 m (11,976 and 13,124 ft). Those who can afford it choose to live in the low-lying suburbs as the

climate is somewhat milder in the 'lower city' and the residents are more protected from the Altiplano winds.

If you arrive from the west, the road passes the international airport of El Alto. Temperatures in this now independent suburb are often up to 10°C (50°F) cooler than in the city centre. From El Alto the road crosses a basin where many stop to enjoy the view of the city.

On the onward journey the colourful markets of the famous 'Indio neighbourhood' pop up on the right. Behind that is the Old Town, which has been able to retain its colonial era character. A wide boulevard passes straight through the entire inner city and while the various sections of it have different names,

3

Altiplano and Sajama National Park

The whole of western Bolivia is covered by high mountains. The landscape is characterized by high ranges with extensive basins between them. These contrasts are especially typical of the area near the border with Chile.

The Altiplano Basin extends between the Cordillera Occidental (western Cordillera) and the Cordillera Oriental (eastern Cordillera) of the Andes at an

A clay brick church in front of the Mount Sajama volcano in the national park of the same name.

altitude of between 3,600 and 4,200 m (11,812 and 13,780 ft).

The region is relatively arid as the mountains keep rain clouds away, and vegetation is largely limited to grassland and dwarf shrubs, with minimal tree growth. Agriculture in the raw Altiplano climate is laborious, but a number of local grain types yield satisfactory harvests. Livestock farming also plays an important role for residents.

To the west of the Altiplano the road diverging to Patacamaya passes the village of Curahuara, site of a thatched-roof church dating from the 16th century, which is the main sightseeing attraction here. The scenery left and right of the road is impressively dramatic.

The next highlight is the Cañon de Sajama with its fantastic cliff formations. As you make your way down the road, Mount Sajama (6,520-m/ 21,392-ft) and its neighbours, the Parinacota (6,342 m/20,808 ft) and Pomerape volcanoes (6,282 m/ 20,611 ft), will continue to draw your attention.

At an elevation of more than 5,300 m (17,389 ft), this extinct volcano is permanently covered in snow. Mount Sajama itself is inactive but the tectonic activity in the entire region is so substantial that volcanic eruptions and earthquakes are frequent occurrences.

4

the locals simply call the road the 'Prado'.

From here it is not far to the sightseeing attractions such as the cathedral, which was completed in 1933 and has capacity for 12,000 people. The Bolivian metropolis is a good base for tours to the Nevado del Illimani, the highest mountain in the country, to the east of the city.

18 Nevado del Illimani The journey to this 6,880-m-high (22,573-ft) mountain in the Cordillera Real can be tedious as the road leading directly to the base of Illimani is occasionally closed. The road to the small Indian village of Comunidad Uno is recommended as an alternate route. Climbers can start the ascent of the mountain from

here too, and base camp is reached in about five hours of hiking.

For locals the mountain is not only a symbol, it also represents an image of their country. With a little imagination you can recognize the outline of an Indian with wife, child and llama in the three peaks of the Nevado del Illimani. The southernmost of the three peaks is the highest and easily the most accessible, but it takes several days to complete the challenging hike.

Another awe-inspiring peak, the Mount Sajama volcano, lies to the west of the Inca Trail. From La Paz travel south-east to Patacamaya. From there a well-paved road branches off to the south-west. After 150 km (93 miles) on this road you reach the Sajama

National Park in the centre of which is the majestic 6,520-m (21,392-ft) volcano of the same name.

Back in Patacamaya, follow National Road 1, which has oil and gas pipelines running parallel to it. After 90 km (56 miles) turn off to the south-east at Caracollo, taking National Road 4 towards Cochabamba. The road passes a vast expanse of fertile farmland where grain, fruit and vegetables are grown.

19 Cochabamba In contrast to the raw climate of the highlands, the weather is much milder in Cochabamba, which is situated at 'only' 2,570 m (1,597 ft) above sea level. This city on the eastern slopes of the Andes has appropriately earned the name 'The city of eternal springtime'. The name Cochabamba, however, actually derives from the Quechua language and basically means 'swampy flatland'. It is home to a renowned university and, with about 600,000 residents, is one of the largest cities in Bolivia.

Unlike most of the cities along the Inca Trail it has no pre-colonial history, having been first founded by the Spanish in 1574. Many Spanish immigrants settled here due to the comfortable climate. In the centre of the city there are a number of houses and churches dating back to the city's early history.

A poor-quality road leads from Cochabamba to the Tunari National Park, which extends to the mountain of the same name.

20 Oruro Back in Caracollo, continue for a few kilometres through some pretty bleak scenery until you reach the city of Oruro, elevation 3,710 m (12,173 ft). At the height of the tin-mining era, from the early 19th century to the middle of the 20th century, Oruro was one of the most important economic locations in Bolivia. That has changed since the mines were closed.

The locals' zest for life, however, remains the same and Oruro continues to be the centre of the Bolivian carnival, which is celebrated here with sophisticated revelry. The dancers adorn them-

1 Tiahuanaco, the sacred site and capital of an Andean culture of the same name that experienced its heyday between the 3rd and 9th centuries.

2 Cacti on the Altiplano, testimony to this arid high Andean region.

3 View over La Paz with snow-capped volcano.

4 Salar de Uyuni and Salar de Coipas, the two largest saltwater lakes in the Bolivian Altiplano.

The Quechua

The term Quechua refers both to a group of Indian peoples and to their language. The Quechua live in the Andes, mainly in Peru but also in parts of neighbouring Bolivia and Ecuador. Most of them have retreated to the high-altitude regions above 4,000 m (13,124 ft).

Agriculture is hardly possible at these altitudes and most Quechua make a living from raising llama and alpaca. Lamas serve principally as pack animals and sources of meat while the closely related alpacas are kept for their high-quality wool.

The Quechua Indian culture had already achieved a high degree of sophistication before the arrival of European colonialists, especially in the areas of social organization and architecture.

Two Quechua women from the highlands of Peru.

Even during the colonial era the Quechua language remained the predominant language in the middle Andes region. The European missionaries first achieved greater success when they addressed the Indians, as would-be converts, in the Quechua language.

The language is still maintained today, and in Peru and Bolivia Quechua is even an official language, along with Spanish. It is one of the few Indian languages to have been granted this status.

According to estimates the language is spoken by approximately 8 million people and is therefore more widespread than any other Indian language in South America.

selves with colourful, ornately carved devil and ghost masks.

㉑ Lago de Poopó Only a short distance beyond Oruro is Lake Poopó. With a surface area of 2,800 sq km (1,740 sq mi), it is the second-largest lake in Bolivia after Lake Titicaca. Lake Poopó receives some of its water from the outflow of Lake Titicaca from the Río Desaguadero. The lake is very shallow in comparison to the up to 280-m-deep (919-ft) Lake Titicaca, with a depth of just a few meters. High levels of evaporation over the decades have caused a slow but consistent drop in the water level and surface area of the lake. Its swampy shores are only sparsely populated.

㉒ Laguna Tarapaya The road now heads south-east to another scenic highlight of the region, an almost perfectly circular lake with a diameter of some 100 m (328 ft) in the crater of an extinct volcano, Laguna Tarapaya. This thermal pool has a temperature of about 35°C (95°F). The Balneario de Tarapaya, at 3,400 m (11,155 ft), is a perfect place to relax, especially after long hikes at this altitude.

The onward journey is a steep climb towards Potosí, about 25 km (15 miles) away.

㉓ Potosí At just below 4,000 m (13,124 ft), Potosí was one of the wealthiest cities in all of South America between the 16th and 18th centuries. The wealth came from a mountain with relatively unspectacular looks, but of spectacular intrinsic value – the conical, 4,830-m-high (815,847-ft) Cerro Rico ('Rich Mountain').

The Spanish colonial rulers were fortunate enough to discover extensive silver reserves within this mountain, which they then proceeded to mine mercilessly. Tens of thousands of tonnes of silver were extracted but the lucrative mining activities had another side to them, namely Indian slave labour that led to countless deaths.

The silver mines have since been abandoned but tin-mining has become increasingly important in recent decades. Unfortunately for the people of Potosí, tin mining is not nearly as lucrative as silver.

Traces of the former wealth can be found in the city centre – stately homes and churches from the Spanish colonial era, some of which have striking facades. The city and the neighbouring silver mines were declared a UNESCO World Heritage Site in 1987 and a bumpy road leads to the visitors' mine, located at an altitude of 4,300 m (14,108 ft).

Beyond Potosí the road (No 5) winds its way north. En route to the much lower-lying city of Sucre you descend some 1,400 m (4,593 ft) in altitude over a relatively short distance, with very steep gradients in places.

㉔ Sucre On the approach to the capital, at an altitude of about 2,600 m (8,531 ft), the glittering buildings of the 'White City' are visible even from a distance. Ivory-coloured baroque churches and religious buildings, whitewashed houses and regal palaces define Sucre, which was founded in 1538.

There are only a few Spanish colonial cities that are as well-preserved as this one. Buildings with stylish balconies and lovely arcades characterize the Old Town, which was declared a UNESCO World Heritage Site in

1990. Even though Sucre has been the capital of Bolivia since 1828, there are only a few civil authorities here. The government and its ministries are based in La Paz.

The university here, founded in 1624, is one of the oldest in South America. Celebrated as the jewel of Bolivian colonial architecture, Sucre makes a fitting conclusion to the Inca Trail, running through two countries and two worlds.

1 A view over Potosí, the 'Silver City', towards the snow-capped peak of Cerro Rico.

2 The Universidad de San Francisco Xavier in Sucre has an impressive courtyard. Founded in 1624, it is one of the oldest universities in South America.

Lima With its two towers, the 16th-century cathedral here is one of the Peruvian capital's featured architectural treasures.

Pachacámac Located directly outside Lima are the remains of the temple complex of Pachacámac. One of the most important buildings in the complex was the 80-m-high (262-ft) sun pyramid, the ruins of which sit on top of an artificially constructed hill.

Machu Picchu These ruins represent the zenith of Inca architecture. Built in the 15th century, the city was situated on sophisticated terraces and its construction is profound evidence of highly accomplished technical skill and know-how. This unique complex is a UNESCO World Heritage Site.

Huari In its heyday (6th–10th century), the Huari Empire extended over almost the whole of Peru. Theories postulate that up to 100,000 people lived in this centre of Huari power. The giant stone sculptures are testimony to their high degree of artistic ability.

Tipón Inca settlements such as Tipón arose around Cuzco. The remains of the now uncovered village are open to visitors.

Manú National Park This national park extends from the central Andes to the rainforest in the Amazon lowlands.

Sacsayhuamán Built at the end of the 15th century, this fortress is one of many outstanding examples of Inca architecture. It was impregnable for centuries.

Cuzco This city, at 3,500 m (11,484 ft), is characterized not only by buildings from the Inca era but also by those from the Spanish colonial period. The Renaissance-style cathedral (17th century) is an example.

Lake Titicaca The 8,300-sq-km (5,158-sq-mi) lake at 3,812 m (12,507 ft) belongs to both Peru and Bolivia. Descendants of the Uros people living on the lake are renowned for their 'floating' islands built from reeds.

Tiahuanaco So-called 'nail heads' portray priests on a temple wall of the former centre of an Andean culture, Tiahuanaco. The town was founded in around AD 300.

La Paz The highest city in the world (4,000 m/13,124 ft) sprawls in a basin at the foot of the Andes. There are only a few old buildings, one of which is a prominent cathedral with capacity for 12,000 people.

Potosí Following the discovery of a silver mine in Cerro Rico in 1545, this town became one of the largest cities in the world. It then went into decline once the silver reserves were depleted around 1800.

Sucre Bolivia's official capital (La Paz is the seat of government) is home to one of the oldest universities in South America (1624).

Argentina and Chile
Through the Pampas and Patagonia

The common rhea or nandu, a flightless bird, lives on the Pampas and in Argentinian Patagonia.

Argentina is characterized by three major geographical regions that could scarcely be more different from one another – the endless Pampas, the high peaks of the Andes, and the plains of Patagonia with their steep isolated mountains and glaciers. Part of the Andes and some of the southern foothills of Patagonia near the Tierra del Fuego belong to Chile.

Covering an area of more than 2.8 million sq km (1 million sq mi), Argentina is the second-largest country in South America after its signficantly larger neighbour Brazil. The Pampas, which make up the heartland of Argentina, are a vast green expanse on which isolated mountain ranges emerge like islands in an ocean, from Buenos Aires all the way to the western border with Chile.

One such 'island' is the Sierra de Córdoba, a range that rises west of Córdoba in the Cerro Champaqui to a height of 2,884 m (9,614 ft), indeed a considerable height, but that is nothing compared to the peaks west of Mendoza. There, the Cerro Aconcagua, or 'Stone Sentinel', towers to 6,963 m (23,000 ft) and is both the highest peak in the Andes and the highest mountain in the Americas.

The Andes Mountains mark the natural border between Argentina and neighbouring Chile. National parks have been established on both sides of the border in magnificent mountain landscapes containing virgin forests interspersed with

An Argentinian gaucho herding his cattle on the Pampas.

Like an impregnable fortress, the granite towers of the Torres del Paine in Chile rise from the plains of southern Patagonia. They are a favourite destination for adventurous trekkers from all over the world.

The tongue of the Perito Morena Glacier in Los Glaciares National Park is some 70 m (233 ft) high.

shimmering blue and green lakes and rivers of cloudy glacier water. The areas are a paradise for hikers and include the Lanín National Park, where dense forests of araucaria and Antarctic beech engulf the mighty Lanín volcano. At the base of this 3,747-m (12,290-ft) volcano is a deep blue lake, Lago Huechulafquén.

While northern Patagonia occasionally offers gentle landscapes such as that of the Nahuel Huapi National Park, in the south the landscape becomes progressively more windswept and barren. The constant Westerlies bring humidity from the Pacific, falling as rain on the Chilean side of the Andes. They then sweep over the icy inland regions, glaciers and ice fields of Patagonia, which chill them before they whip over the eastern plains. The Andes open up here and there, revealing gaps between the peaks like the ones at Lago Buenos Aires – known as the Lago General Carrera on the Chilean side – and at the Los Glaciares National Park. Also typical of southern Patagonia are the isolated granite peaks that dominate the plains: the FitzRoy Massif and the Torres del Paine, for example.

It was not until the last ice age that the Strait of Magellan, once just a cleft in the Andes, split off from the mainland and created the island of Tierra del Fuego. This main island in the archipelago is 47,000 sq km (20,000 sq mi) with a landscape that clearly resembles that of Patagonia. In the north is a broad plateau while in the south the last foothills of the Cordilleras reach heights of 2,500 m (9,000 ft), finally sinking spectacularly into the sea at the notorious Cape Horn, whose perpetually stormy seas have been the bane of so many a brave sailor.

An impressive landscape of gorges and ravines east of San Carlos de Bariloche.

Aconcagua

The 'Stone Sentinel' – translated from the Quechua term *Ackon-Cauak*, from which the name Aconcagua is derived – is not only the highest mountain in Argentina at 6,963 m (23,000 ft), but also the highest in the Andes, the Americas, and in the entire southern hemisphere.

Aconcagua, in the centre of the Provincial Park Aconcagua, is a favourite destination for thousands of mountaineers from all over the world, for it is considered a relatively easy climb. First, mountaineers need to acclimatize themselves by scaling the Puente del Inca,

Top: Aconcagua, the highest peak in the Americas.
Bottom: Puente del Inca.

a mere 2,720 m (9,000 ft) above sea level, then move to the base camp at about 4,000 m (13,333 ft). From there, the ascent begins on the glacial northern route.

The Swiss climber Matthias Zurbriggen was the first in modern times to get to the top, on 18 January 1897, but the peak was almost certainly conquered much earlier by the native inhabitants. After all, in 1982 a 500-year-old Inca mummy was found at an elevation of 5,200 m (17,333 ft). It was the body of a boy aged about seven who had been given a ritual burial.

From the Pampas through the mountains, past the granite massifs and glaciers of Patagonia, through the Strait of Magellan to Ushuaia, this dream route leads you all the way down through Argentina along the Pan-American Highway to the southern tip of Tierra del Fuego on Lapataia Bay.

❶ Córdoba Argentina's second-largest city, with 1.5 million inhabitants, is known as 'La Docta', 'the Erudite', and it bears the nickname with pride. For it was here in 1614 that the country's first university was founded, and Córdoba still possesses excellent university faculties.

The city, founded in 1573, is surprisingly tranquil in its centre. The plaza contains the arcaded Cabildo, the colonial-style government building, and the cathedral, built in 1574 in a mixed baroque and neoclassical style. A few steps further, through the pedestrian zone, you come to the so-called Manzana Jesuítica, the Jesuit quarter, with a Jesuit church and the first university buildings.

Passing through some dull suburbs, we leave Córdoba on Ruta 20 in the direction of Carlos Paz and reach the Sierra de Córdoba, which rises impressively from the Pampas to a height of 2,884 m (9,614 ft) in the Cerro Champaqui. At Villa Dolores, some 170 km (105 miles) south-

west of Córdoba, you will leave the mountains behind and enter a flatter landscape that remains as such for the next 500 km (310 miles) until Mendoza.

❷ Mendoza The green countryside around Mendoza is deceptive, as this city of 600,000 is located in a desert known as the Cuyo, meaning 'sandy earth'. Plentiful water from the nearby mountains has allowed the desert to bloom, and it is here that the finest Argentinian wines are produced.

Although Mendoza was founded as early as 1561, the city centre is mostly modern because older portions have been repeatedly razed by earthquakes, most severely in 1861. All that remains is the Church of San Francisco, dating from 1638. The pedestrian area of the Calle Sarmiento, with its cafés and restaurants, and the suburb of Maipú, with bodegas that offer wine tastings, are worth a visit.

From Mendoza, take a detour to the stunning Puente del Inca.

Travel information

Route profile
Length: approx. 5,300 km (3,315 miles), excluding detours
Time required: 4 weeks
Start: Córdoba
End: Ushuaia
Route (main locations): Córdoba, Mendoza, Puente del Inca, San Carlos de Bariloche, Parque Nacional Los Glaciares, Parque Nacional Torres del Paine, Punta Arenas, Parque Nacional Tierra del Fuego,

Traffic information:
The trip mostly follows the Argentinian Ruta 40, which runs north-south along the eastern edge of the Andes. The highway is mostly sur-

faced, although a few of the side-roads in southern Patagonia are gravel. You will need to watch for oncoming traffic and pass close to it, otherwise loose stones flying up from the road could damage the windshield. It is generally not advisable to drive at night outside the cities.

Strait of Magellan:
There is a good ferry connection from the mainland to Tierra del Fuego; in summer, the ferries operate hourly.

More information:
www.ontheroadtravel.com
www.parquesnacionales.gov.ar
www.travelsur.net

The Pampas

The word 'pampa' is taken from the language of the Quechua Indians. It means 'treeless plain', which aptly describes this vast region. The Pampas extend from the Atlantic to the Andes, and are bordered to the north by the Chaco, to the north-east by the Río Paraná and to the south by Patagonia.

This grassy plain is the classic landscape of Patagonia. Herds of cattle here look like little brown or black dots on an endless field of varying shades of glowing green and brown.

The Pampas make up the heartland of Argentina. Two-thirds of the country's cattle breeding and about ninety per cent of its agriculture are based here. It is a natural grassland as the

Top: Skulls of horses in the Pampas.
Bottom: Gauchos at work.

❸ Puente del Inca The 'Inca Bridge', at a height of 2,720 m (9,000 ft), is a natural arch over the Río Mendoza that was formed by mineral deposits. Following the road westwards, you soon come to the best view of Aconcagua (see sidebar left). A dirt road then leads up to the old border zone on the Bermejo Pass at 3,750 m (12,500 ft). From there your climb will be rewarded by a wonderful view over the High Andes.

From Mendoza, Ruta 40 leads south. After about 300 km (190 miles) through the Cuyo, a road branches at El Sosneada to the west towards Las Leñas, Argentina's greatest skiing area. You will then head another 490 km (310 miles) south, parallel to the Andes, to Zapala.

This city has a museum displaying beautiful local minerals and

fossils. The distances are great in Argentina, but after another 156 km (100 miles) on Ruta 40 there is a road turning off to the west, leading to San Martín de los Andes, a little mountain town with the best approach to Lanín National Park.

❹ Lanín National Park This park surrounds the extinct volcano for which the park is named. The 3,747-m (12,490-ft) volcano, which has a perfectly formed cone peak, is mirrored in glorious Lago Huechulafquén. It is the ideal backdrop for extended hikes. Back on Ruta 40, San Carlos de Bariloche is not far away.

❺ San Carlos de Bariloche Bariloche was founded by Swiss immigrants, and is the 'Swiss side' of Argentina. The Centro

Cívico, the community centre, is built to resemble a Swiss chalet. Best of all, the main shopping street features one chocolate factory after another, and all the restaurants have cheese fondue on the menu.

The first settlers sought and found a rural idyll here. Bariloche lies on one of Argentina's most beautiful lakes, Lago Nahuel Huapi, at the heart of the national park of the same name. The road leads further south through a magnificent mountain landscape until you reach Los Alerces National Park near the town of Esquel.

❻ Los Alerces National Park This national park covers an area of 260,000 ha (650,000 acres) and is dedicated to the preservation of the alerces, gigantic evergreen trees that can reach

heights of 70 m (235 ft) and have diameters of 4 m (14 ft). Some of them are estimated to be 3,500 years old. In the centre of the park is the 78-sq-km (30-sq-mi) Lake Futalaufquén. From the national park, Ruta 40 continues

1 Steppe as far as the eye can see – beginning just east of San Carlos de Bariloche, the vast Patagonian plains extend all the way out to the Atlantic Ocean.

2 A peak in the southern Pampas – the 3,680-m (12,266-ft) Cerro Payún south-east of Bardas Blancas.

3 Autumnal mood on Lake Nahuel Huapi in the national park of the same name.

4 The 3,500-year-old trees in Los Alerces National Park can reach 70 m (235 ft) in height.

compact and firm soil encourages the growth of grasses, but it is so hostile to trees that they are unable to take root here of their own accord.

Yet despite all its natural appearance, the Pampas are the landscape in Argentina where flora and fauna have undergone the greatest changes as the result of human intervention. Many new grasses were introduced, and the Pampas became a cultivated steppe. In addition, cattle-breeders planted trees to give their cattle shelter from the temperature extremes on the vast open plains.

In some places, grassland and cattle-breeding have been abandoned in favor of more lucrative soybean cultivation. The Pampas were once a haven of local wildlife, and even today the common rhea or nandu, the smaller cousin of the South African ostrich, as well as armadillos and skunks still roam the steppes. The Pampas deer, however, is on the verge of extinction.

José Ormachea Petrified Forest

If you turn west at the Río Mayo, after about 100 km (62 miles) you will come to the town of Sarmiento on Lake Muster. South of Sarmiento, in the José Ormachea Petrified Forest, one of several petrified forests in Patagonia, it becomes clear that this region was not always an empty, stark plain, overgrown with short, coarse grass. Approximately 150 million years ago, dense forests grew here, with giant trees (including araucaria) that were up to 100 m (330 ft) in height and more than 1,000 years old.

Movements in the earth's crust then created the Andes, which resulted in numerous volcanic eruptions. A formidable layer of ash covered Patagonia up to 20 m (65 ft) deep.

Above and below: Remains of the primeval forest in the Bosque Petrificado José Ormachea.

Plants and animals suffocated, died and were buried under the thick layer of ash, but because these ashen graves were airtight, they did not decompose.

Over the course of hundreds of thousands of years, water permeated through the ash layers. As it did so, it dissolved some of the minerals and silicates in the ash. The water then flowed into the dead tree trunks and, as it dried out, minerals gradually replaced the cell walls of the organic matter, turning them into stone. The tree trunks thus remained exactly the way they fell some sixty-five million years ago, gradually being exposed to air, erosion and the various movements of the earth's crust.

on to the south. It is 381 km (237 miles) from Esquel to Río Mayo, but shortly before this, Ruta 26 branches off to the east towards Sarmiento via the petrified forests (see sidebar left).

To the west, Ruta 26 winds through the Andes to the Chilean city of Coyhaique. From this crossroads it is another 129 km (80 miles) south to Perito Moreno.

7 Perito Moreno This small town does not offer anything special, but it is the starting point for excursions to the milky, teal-coloured Lake Buenos Aires, the second-largest lake in South America after Lake Titicaca. The Argentinean side of the lake lies in the middle of the Patagonian plains; the Chilean side is surrounded by snow-covered peaks. You can cross the Chilean border at Los Antiguos, on the southern edge of the lake.

Some 56 km (35 miles) south of Perito Moreno, the road forks, one branch leading to Cueva de las Manos (see sidebar right). It is another 239 km (148 miles) from Perito Moreno through the desolate Patagonian plains to the next settlement, Hotel las Horquetas, just a handful of houses in the Río Chico Valley. At an intersection here, a gravel road branches off to the west in the direction of Estancia la Oriental and Lake Belgrano. This is the route to the Perito Moreno National Park.

8 Perito Moreno National Park This is one of Argentina's most isolated and spectacular national parks. There are glaciers and shimmering mountain lakes with floating blocks of ice, and the park is teeming with wildlife such as pumas, foxes, wildcats, guanacos and waterfowl.

The second-highest mountain in Patagonia, Monte San Lorenzo (3,706 m/12,159 ft), is the home of the condor. The park can only be explored on foot or on horseback. There are hardly any roads or facilities – only campsites.

Tres Lagos is the name of the next crossroads on Ruta 40, about 235 km (146 miles) further on. At this point, Ruta 288 goes east towards the Atlantic. After another 45 km (28 miles) heading

park, near El Calafate, than in the northern part. This is due to the spectacular glaciers that can be much more easily accessed from here than from anywhere else. Large slabs of ice break off from the 70-m (230-ft) glacial walls, landing in the lake with an immense crash.

The biggest of these giants is the Upsala Glacier, with a surface area of 595 sq km (230 sq mi). The most popular spot, however, is the Perito Moreno Glacier about 80 km (50 miles) from El Calafate, whose glacial tongue pushes out into Lake

1 The drastic edge of the Perito Moreno Glacier in Los Glaciares is up to 70 m (230 ft) high. With a great roar, ice chunks the size of houses continually break off from its walls.

2 The icy blue-green waters of Lake del Grano in the Perito Moreno National Park.

3 Colourful sandstone cliffs near Sarmiento between Lake Musters and Lake Colhué Huapí.

4 The expansive green steppe in the Los Glaciares National Park with the Andes in the background.

5 The jagged peaks of the FitzRoy Massif tower over the rugged Patagonian plains.

Cuevas de las Manos

The cave paintings discovered in the Río Pinturas Canyon are among the oldest human artifacts in South America. The local inhabitants, who lived here between 9500 BC and 1000 BC, left behind depictions of animals,

Handprints in the Cueva de las Manos.

often hunting scenes, as well as palm prints in various colours.

The drawings date mainly from between 5000 BC and 1500 BC. The cave has been designated a UNESCO World Heritage Site.

south is Lake Viedma. The road on this lake's northern bank leads westward and, on clear days, there is a fantastic view of the FitzRoy Massif.

9 El Chaltén This small town is the northern access point for Los Glaciares National Park,

a dream destination for mountaineers from all over the world as it is home to the 3,375-m (11,072-ft) Mount FitzRoy. But it is not just for climbers. Hikers will also find a plethora of activities. You can organize one-day or multi-day excursions from El Chaltén.

Back on Ruta 40, you pass through the Leona Valley and along the eastern bank of Lake Argentino to the junction to El Calafate.

10 Los Glaciares National Park There is considerably more activity at the southern end of this

Patagonia's animals

Most visitors to Patagonia will first encounter guanacos and rheas. The guanaco, a dark-brown type of camel and a relative of the llama, live in herds of five to twenty-five animals in the national parks of the south. The steppes of Argentina are also home to

Top: The Pampas hare covers long distances in search of food.
Bottom: The Pampas fox is mostly active at night.

the ostrich-like common rhea or nandu. At the beginning of incubation, the males of the species carve out their territories while the females gad about in groups. Rarer sights are the Pampas hare (maras), the pudu, and the Patagonian huemul, a species of deer about 1.5 m (5 ft) in height. The red fox and the puma are the only predators in this part of the world.

Argentino to such an extent that every few years it completely seals off the Brazo Rico, one of the lake's offshoots.

11 Puerto Natales The town, situated on the Ultima Esperanza Estuary, was the last hope of sailors who had got lost in the countless channels of southern Patagonia in their search for an east-west passage. Puerto Natales is the best starting point for a visit to nearby Torres del Paine National Park, and also a worthwhile stop for arranging various excursions.

For example, you could take a boat ride on Seno de la Ultima Esperanza (Last Hope Sound) up to the border of the Bernardo O'Higgins National Park to Cerro Balmaceda (2,035 m/6,676 ft) with its impressive glaciers. Bird lovers should visit the town's old pier in the late afternoon. It's a meeting place for hundreds of cormorants.

12 Cueva del Milodón En route to the Torres del Paine National Park, it is well worth taking time to pay a short visit to Cueva del Milodón. To get there, go 8 km (5 miles) north out of Puerto Natales and head west. After 5 km (3 miles) you reach the cave where German immigrant Hermann Eberhard found remains of a huge dinosaur, a 4-m (13-ft) megatherium, in 1896. A replica of the creature by the entrance to the cave shows how it may have looked.

13 Torres del Paine National Park The peaks of the Torres del

Paine Massif rise dramatically from the windswept plain. These steep, seemingly impregnable mountains have granite peaks, the highest of which is Cerro Torre Grande at 3,050 m (10,007 ft), surrounded by the peaks of Paine Chico, Torres del Paine and Cuernos del Paine.

This is Chile's adventure paradise. Visitors can choose between embarking on long hiking trails in the park, daylong tours, or a hiking trail around the entire massif. All these trails pass by bluish-white, opaque, glacial lakes with floating icebergs. They include Grey Glacier and the amazing Río Paine, which plummets into Lake Pehoe as a cascading waterfall.

The stunted trees brace themselves against the wind here, but in early summer the plains form a sea of flowers. In addition to guanacos, you will likely spot condors and sundry waterfowl. Remember to take warm clothing.

To the south of Puerto Natales, the route continues straight through the plains. Stubby grass grows on both sides of the road. You'll often see guanacos, rheas and sheep. This is Ruta 9 to Punta Arenas.

Some 34 km (21 miles) before the city, a road branches westwards. After 23 km (14 miles) you reach Otway Sound, home to a large penguin colony.

14 Monumento Natural Los Pingüinos There is another

large penguin colony to the north-east of Punta Arenas, right on the Strait of Magellan. In the summer months, some 2,500 Magellan penguins, the smallest of the species, live in this colony. They only grow to between 50 and 70 cm (20 and 28 in) and weigh a mere 5 kg (11 lbs). They can be easily recognized by their black-and-white heads and the black stripe running across the upper part of their torsos.

1 Guanacos, relatives of the llama, in a flowery meadow in the Torres del Paine National Park.

2 Rider on the Patagonian plains north of Punta Arenas.

One of the wonders of nature – a cluster of flowers, mainly lupins, in the Torres del Paine National Park, with snowy peaks in the background. This magnificent sight can be seen only in late spring and early summer.

The Patagonia coast and its marine life

The Patagonian coastal areas are rich in species variety, but the true animal paradise is located far to the east of the route on the Váldes Peninsula, where every year from July through to mid December you can see black-and-white killer whales (orcas) and

Above: Macaroni penguins, recognizable by the feathers over their eyes. Below: The sea lion can weigh up to 320 kg (700 lbs).

loads of southern right whales. In many coastal waters, you can catch sight of sea lions – especially in Tierra del Fuego's Beagle Channel – as well as dolphins, which are crossing the Strait of Magellan. The largest colony of the 70-cm-tall (28-in) Magellan penguins along your route lives at Seno Otway near Punta Arenas.

15 Punta Arenas This city, founded in the mid 19th century as a penal colony, grew quickly and was an important port for ships plying the west coast of America until the construction of the Panama Canal in 1914. Patagonia's profitable sheep-farming also made its contribution to the city's success, allowing wealthy inhabitants to build large sheep estancias (ranches) around the city centre.

The Palacio Braun-Menéndez, today a museum, shows how the upper class lived in those days: walls covered in fabric imported from France, billiard tables from England, gold-plated fireguards from Flanders and Carrara marble decorations from Italy. Burials were no less regal here. The Punta Arenas cemetery contains the enormous mausoleums of the city's wealthier families. The Museo Regional Mayorino Borgatallo is also worth a visit.

From Punta Arenas you can drive 50 km (31 miles) back to the intersection of Ruta 9 and Ruta 255. Then follow Ruta 255 in a northeast direction until you reach Punta Delgada. From there, Ruta 3, which starts in Argentina, leads south and soon reaches the Strait, where a ferry transports travellers to Puerto Espora in Tierra del Fuego.

16 Strait of Magellan/Tierra del Fuego In 1520, Fernando de Magellan was the first to sail through the Strait later named after him. As he skirted the mainland and the islands, he saw fire and smoke, hence the archipelago's name. The island group covers an area of 73,500 sq km (28,378 sq mi). Its main island, the

western part of which belongs to Chile, covers an area of about 47,000 sq km (18,147 sq mi).

It is some 280 km (174 miles) from Puerto Espora to the Río Grande through vast, open countryside. At San Sebastián Bay, you can cross the border into Argentina. South of the Río Grande, the landscape changes – the valleys become narrower, the hills higher, and dense forests come into view. After about 250 km (155 miles), you reach Ushuaia and the adjacent Tierra del Fuego National Park.

17 Tierra del Fuego National Park Hikers will enjoy Tierra del Fuego National Park, which begins 18 km (11 miles) west

of Ushuaia. It is easily accessible in its southern part but inaccessible in the north, and stretches along the Chilean border offering marshes, rocky cliffs and temperate rainforests.

Ruta 3, the Argentinean part of the southern Pan-American Highway, leads directly into the park and ends picturesquely at the Bahía Lapataía.

18 Ushuaia The southernmost city in the world is set between the icy waters of the deep Beagle Channel and the peaks of the Cordillera which, despite being only 1,500 m (4,921 feet) high, are always covered in snow. Originally founded as a penal colony, the city lives most-

ly from tourism these days. The Museo Fin del Mundo has a collection depicting the early and colonial history of the region. If the weather is good, take a boat trip to the glorious 'End of the World', Cape Horn.

1 The Tierra del Fuego National Park entices adventuresome travellers with its expansive steppe, mountainous landscape and impenetrable jungles and rainforests.

2 Punta Arenas harbour in the Strait of Magellan.

3 View of Ushuaia harbour, the southernmost city in the world. The foothills of the Darwin Cordillera rise up in the background.

Aconcagua The highest mountain in the Americas at 6,963 m (23,000 ft), Aconcagua is near Mendoza on the Chilean border. It was first 'officially' climbed in 1897. Today, 2,000 to 4,000 mountaineers enjoy it every year.

Mendoza This modern city of 600,000 also has a colonial past, though it has largely been destroyed by earth-quakes. Mendoza has now become the hub of Argentina's flourishing grape grow-ing and wine industry. It has many wineries and bodegas where visitors can get a taste of the local wine amid some stunning landscape.

Los Alerces National Park Massive alerces trees, some are believed to be over 3,500 years old, grow to a massive height and girth.

Villa el Chocón Jurassic Park in Argentina: dinosaur fossils and models are on show at Neuquén.

Los Glaciares National Park This park consists mainly of two formations, the high mountain landscape in the north, with the FitzRoy Massif, and the inland glaciers in the south, with the Upsala and Perito-Moreno Glaciers.

The Torres del Paine National Park The highest peak in the park is the 3,050-m-high (10,007-ft) Cerro Torre Grande, surrounded by Paine Chico, Torres del Paine and Cuernas del Paine.

Ushuaia This city, the southernmost in Argentina, lies on the Beagle Channel. The Museo del Fin del Mundo (End of the World Museum) dis-plays exhibits from the prehistoric and colonial history of Tierra del Fuego.

Córdoba Argentina's second-largest city (1.5 million inhabi-tants) is home to the country's oldest university. The picture shows the cathedral and Cabildo in the central plaza of town.

Cueva de las Manos In a sizeable cave in the Río Pinturas Canyon, the original inhabitants of this area left behind the oldest indi-cations of human settlement in South America.

Nahuel Huapi National Park This park near Bariloche has several different landscape zones includ-ing the High Andes, rainforest, transitional forest and steppe.

Perito Moreno National Park The national park surrounding Lake Belgra-no (the picture shows the broad Belgrano Peninsula) showcases wild and pristine Patagonian nature. Numerous indigenous animals live here, including pumas, guanacos, nandus, flamingos and condors.

Tierra del Fuego National Park This national park, close to Ushuaia in Terra del Fuego, runs to the Chilean border with its lakes, glaciers and rainforests.

Punta Arenas Until the Panama Canal was built in 1914, this port town was of great importance at the tip of South America. Some of the typical houses from that period still remain.

The Los Pingüinos and Seno Otway Penguin Colonies Thousands of Magellan penguins live here near Punta Arenas in the summer. They are the smallest species of penguin in South America.

Map labels:
Cerro Colorado, Laguna Mar Chiquita, Cruz del Eje, Villa del Totoral, Miramar, La Rioja, Cosquín, CÓRDOBA ❶, La Rioja, Difunta Correa, P.N.Uda. del Condorito, Villa Dolores, Alta Gracia, Santa Fé, San Juan, Encón, P.N.Sierra de las Quijadas, Quines, Villa General Belgrano, Villa María, Termas de Villavicencio, Mendoza ❷, Gruta de Intihuasi, Río Cuarto, Co.Aconcagua 6963, Santiago, San Luis, La Loma, Rosario, Puente del Inca ❸, San Martín, La Paz, Beazley, Villa Mercedes, Tunuyán, Pareditas, Monte Comán, Santa Rosa, San Rafael, Molina, Pozo de las Ánimas, Fuerte San Rafael, General Alvear, El Sosneado, Fortín Malal-Hué, R.N.Gil de Vilches, Bardas Blancas, Cueva de las Brujas, Cerro Payún 3600, Ranquil del Norte, Volcán Tromen 3978, P.N.Laguna del Laja, Chos Malal, Copahue, CHILE, ARGENTINA, Curacautín, Las Lajas, Añelo, Bahía Blanca, Zapala, Cutral-Có, Neuquén, P.N.Conguillio, P.N.Laguna Blanca, Villa El Chocón, P.N.Huerquehue, La Ofelia, Catán Lil, San Martín de los Andes, Piedra del Aguila, Osorno, P.N.Lanín ❹, P.N.Nahuel Huapi, Paso Flores, P.N.Puyehue, Valle Encantado, Pilcaniyeu, San Carlos de Bariloche ❺, P.N.Lago Puelo, El Maitén, P.N.Los Alerces, Esquel, Futaleufú, Tecka, Pampa de Agnia, R.N.Lago Rosselot, Lago Vintter, P.N.Queulat, Nueva Lubecka, Buen Pasto, Villa Amengual, Alto Río Senguer, Sarmiento, Bosque Petrificado J.Urmacheá, Coihaique, Río Mayo, Bosque Petrificado Victor Szlapelis, L.Buenos Aires, Perito Moreno ❼, Las Heras, Chile Chico, Cueva de las Manos, Monte San Lorenzo o Cochrane 3706, Bajo Caracoles, Lago Belgrano, P.N.Perito Moreno ❽, Gobernador Gregores, Monte Fitz Roy 3375, El Chaltén ❾, La Julia, Tres Lagos, P.N.Los Glaciares, Lago Viedma, El Calafate, El Cerrito, P.N.Torres del Paine, Ea.Cerro Guido ⓭, Esperanza, Cueva del Milodón ⓬, Tapi Aike, Güer Aike, Pasada Conaf, P.N.Pali-Aike, Río Gallegos, Puerto Natales ⓫, Punta Delgada, Morro Chico, Puerto Espora, Strait of Magellan, M.N. Los Pingüinos ⓮, Cullén, Punta Arenas ⓯, San Sebastián, Porvenir, Tierra del Fuego, Río Grande, Fuerte Bulnes, Puerto Arturo, P.N.Tierra del Fuego ⓱, Estancia San Pablo, P.N.Alberto de Agostini, Ushuaia ⓲, Puerto Toro, Puerto Williams, P.N.Cabo de Hornos, Cape Horn

L_Specht; ifa_Aberham; ifa_Thouvenin; ifa_Diaf; 493 map (from t.l. to b.r.): C_Bennett; C_Lisle; Mau_Thamm; P_Vidler; ifa_Welsh; C_Holmes; P_Hummel; C_Tidman; P_Prisma; P_ImageState; ifa_Aberham; C_Lisle.

Route 19: 244 big picture: Hub; 244 c.+b.: P_Janek; 245 c.: P_StockImage/S.Harris, 245 b.: ifa_Harris; 246 sidebar t.: C_O.Lang; 246 sidebar b.: C_H.G.Roth; 246.1: ifa_W.Grubb; 246.2: P_Buss; 247.3: P; 247.4: C_D.Bartruff; 247 sidebar: ifa_PictureFinders; 249 t.: ifa_Panstock; 249 c.: DFA_Riedmiller; 249 b.: laif_Krause; 250.1: ifa_Shashin Koubou; 250.2: ifa_J.ArnoldImages; 251.3: N.N.; 252.1: P_T.Smith; 252.2: P_NawrockiStock/ S.Vidler; 253.3: ifa_Panstock; 253.4: ifa_J.ArnoldImages; 254.1: Hub_Zoom; 254.2: laif_Krause; 255.3: stone_Press, 256 sidebar: P_Boyer; 256.1: ifa; 256.2: P_s.Bunka; 257 map (from l. to r., from t. to b.): C_P.Nilson; G_Armand; ifa_JAI; C_W.Kaehler; ifa_Harris; laif_Emmler; ifa_TPC; G_Westmorland; C_S.Vannini; C_N. Wheeler; ifa_Alexandre; C_W.Forman; Hub_Damm; stone_Press; DFA_A.Buck.

Route 20: 258 big picture: ifa_Aberham; 258 b.: ifa_Sohns; 259 c.: ifa_Sohns; 259 b.: ifa_Index Stock; 260.1: ifa_J. ArnoldImages; 260.2: ifa_FischerB.; 260 sidebar t.: P_ImageState; 260 sidebar c.: ifa_Becker; 260 sidebar b.: P_Digital Vision; 261 picture in box: P_Kiefner; 261.3: Ifa_Aberham; 261.4: C_Reuters; 261 sidebar t.: ifa_Sohns; 261 sidebar c.: ifa_Picture Finders; 261 sidebar b.: P_Prisma; 263 t.: ifa_J.ArnoldImages; 263 c.t.: ifa_LDW; 263 sidebar c.: ifa_J.ArnoldImages; 263 sidebar b.: P_Raga; 264 sidebar: ifa_J.ArnoldImages; 264.1 DFA/Tack; 264.2: C_Krist; 265.3: ifa_Aberham; 265 sidebar: P_Watt, 266 sidebar t.: C; 266 sidebar b.: ifa_Aberham; 266.1: C_O'Rear; 266.2: ifa_Aberham; 267: P_Lanting/Minden; 268.1: ifa_J.ArnoldImages; 268.2: ifa_Sohns; 269.3: L; 270 sidebar: P_AnkaAgency/N.Austen; 270.1 Alamy/D.Sanger; 270.2: ifa_J.ArnoldImages; 271 map (from l. to r., from t. to b.): P_Herzog; C_Souders; C_Krist; ifa_LDW; ifa_PictureFinders; P_Hilger; ifa_Aberham; C_Harvey; ifa_Aberham; ifa_PictureFinders; P_Image State; C_Gallo Images/Hosten; C_Harvey; C_Alamany&Vlcen

Route 39/21: 272 big picture: ifa_Warter; 272 M: P; 272 b.: P_Wisniewski; 273 c.: P_Prier; 273 b.: C_Widstrand; 274 sidebar: ifa_Int.Stock; 274.1: P_Schott; 274.2: P_Minden; 275.3: Mau_Rosing; 275 sidebar: C_Peebles; 276 sidebar t.: P; 276 sidebar b.: P; 276.1: C_Sohm; 276.2: P_Clifton; 277.3: C_Keaton; 278 sidebar t.: P; 278 sidebar c.: P; 278 sidebar b.: P; 278.1: C_Sohm; 278.2: P; 279 sidebar: C_Thompson; 280.1: ifa_Panstock; 280.2: ifa_Warter; 281.3: C_Cooke; 281.4: C_Cooke, 282 sidebar: C_Allofs; 282.1: C_Sohm; 282.2: C; 282.3: ifa_BCI; 283 map (from l. to r., from t. to b.): P_Wothe; ifa_BCI; C_Streano; ifa_Kokta; ifa_Peebles; C_Krist; C_Sohm; C_Keaton; C_Johnson; C_Hymans; C_Peebles.

Route 22: 284 big picture: TheStockMarket/ Berenholtz; 284 c.: C_R.Ono; 284 b.: AKG; 285 b.: ifa_PictureFinders; 286.1+2: C_Sohm; 286 sidebar: C_Owaki-Kulla; 287.3: C_R.Ono; 287 sidebar t.+b.: ifa_Panstock; 288 t.: P_Image State/C.Waite; 288 c.: C_B.Krist; 288 b.: C_R. Nowitz; 290.1: C_C.Karnow; 290.2: C_R.Berenholtz; 290 sidebar: C_Bettmann; 291.1: C_Sohm; 291.2: C_R.Howard; 291.3+sidebar: C_B.Krist; 292 t.: P_FirstLight/F.Hudec; 292 c.t.+c.b.: P; 292 b.: P_Hicks; 295 t.: ifa_IT/tpl; 295 c.t.: C_R.Berenholtz; 295 c.b.: C_J.Hicks; 295 b.: C_A.Schein; 296.1: Hub_Giovanni; 296.2: Stone/C; 297: P_Pan.Images; 296 sidebar: C; 297: Stone/Armand; 298.1: C_J.Amos; 298.2: C_Kulla; 298 sidebar: ifa_J.ArnoldImages; 299 map (clockwise from t.l.): C_C.Karnow; C_J.Sohm; C_R.Berenholtz; C_R.Cummins; ifa_J.ArnoldImages; C_Owaki-Kulla; C_RoyaltyFree; Mau_GFP; C_D.Muench; stone_Armand; P_Schwabel; P_V.Palmisant.

Route 23: 300 big picture: P_Stock Image; 300 c.: ifa_Harris; 300 b.: P_Wiggett; 301 c.: C_Ono;

301 b.: ifa_Lahall; 302 sidebar: P_FirstLight; 302.1: P_Watts; 302.2: ifa_Panstock; 303.3 P_S.Bunka; 303.4: ifa_Panstock; 304 sidebar: P_FirstLight; 304.1: P_Sisk; 304.2: C_Muench; 305.3: ifa_Panstock; 305.4: ifa_J.Arnold Images; 305 sidebar: ifa_J.ArnoldImages; 306 sidebar: ifa_BCI; 306.1: ifa_Harris; 306.2: Pix/Minden/Mangesen; 306.3: ifa_BCI; 307.4: ifa_Panstock; 307.5: Pix/Minden/Fitzharris; 307 sidebar: P; 308.1: P; 308.2: P_Larson; 308.3: C_Sohm; 310 sidebar: ifa_J.ArnoldImages; 310.1: ifa_Panstock; 310.2: ifa_Panstock; 311.3: P_Sisk; 311.4: P_Milbradt; 311 sidebar: P_Wittek; 312 sidebar: C_Lovell; 312.1: P_Sisk; 312.2: ifa_Siebig; 313.3: ifa_Siebig; 313 sidebar: C_Mays; 314 map (from t.l. to b.r.): C_Marx; C; P_Image State; ifa_Panstock; C_FirstLight; P_FirstLight/Wiggett; C_Ricca; ifa J. ArnoldImages; C_Rowell; ifa_Panstock; 315 map (from t.l. r. page) C_Sohm; C_Sohm; C_sidebarklev; C_Lovell; C_Mays: (right page) NOK; ifa_NHPA; C_Sedam; C_Huey; P_NGS/ Blair; C_Cummins.

Route 24: 316 big picture: G_Layda; 316 c.: P_Gilchrist; 316 b.: P_Hympendahl; 317 c.: P_Watts; 317 b.: C_Rowell; 318 sidebar: C_Ross; 318.1: P; 318.2: C_Muench; 318.3 C_Muench; 319.4: C_Krist; 319 sidebar: C_Muench; 321 t.: Mau_Visalmage; 321 c.: C_Saloutos; 321 b.: C_Sinibaldi; 322 sidebar t.: C_O'Rear; 322 sidebar c.: C_Tharp; 322 sidebar b.: C_Streano; 322.1: P_Stimpson; 322.2: P_PanoramicImages; 322.3: P_Watts; 323.4: P_PanoramicImages; 323.5: C; 323.6: C_Sohm; 323 sidebar.: C_Sedam; 324 t.: P_Wheelan; 324 c.: P_StockImage; 324 b.: P_Sanford; 326 sidebar t.: Mediacolor's; 326 sidebar c.: C_Rowell; 326.1: P; 326.2: P_Sisk; 326.3: P_PanoramicImages; 327.4: P_C.Cliffton; 327 sidebar: P; 328 sidebar: König; 328.1: P_Winz; 328.2: P_Foott; 329 map (clockwise from t.l.): C_Gulin; C_Bean; C_Sohm; C_Watts; C_Sinibaldi; N.N.; C_Saloutos; P_AGF; C_Schermeister; ifa_Hicks; P_Hicks; P_Winz.

Route 25: 330 big picture: P; 330 c.: P_Palmisano: 330 b.: ifa_Index Stock; 331 c.: P_Schwabel; 331 b.: ifa_indexstock; 332 sidebar: P; 332.1: ifa_Panstock; 332.2: P_Bunka; 333 sidebar: G_Wells; 335 t.: ifa_Panstock; 335 c.: P_Schramm; 335 b.: ifa_Panstock; 336 sidebar t.: C_Turnley; 336 sidebar b.: C_Hebbert; 336.1: P; 336.2: C_Lehman; 336.3: C_Muench; 337.4: C_Vadnai; 337 sidebar: ifa_TPC; 338 sidebar: ifa_Koubou; 338.1: P_Frilet; 338.2: C_Cummins; 339.3: C_Huey; 339.4: C_Fleming; 339 sidebar: P; 340 sidebar: C_Bean; 340.1: ifa_Siebig; 340.2: ifa_Siebig; 341.3: ifa_Gottschalk; 341.4: C_French; 341 sidebar: P_Sisk; 342 sidebar: ifa_Visions OfAmerica; 342.1: C_Muench; 342.2: C_Zaska; 343.3: P_ImageState; 343.4: P_StockImage; 343 sidebar: ifa_J.Arnold Images; 344/345 map top (clockwise from t.l.): C_Faris; C_Bean; C_Lehman; P_Vidler; C; P_Raga; C_Ergenbright; C_Hebbert; C_Lehman; C_Bake; 344/345 map bottom (clockwise from t.l.): C_Saloutos; C_Corwin; P_PanoramicImages; ifa_Siebig; C_Huey; C_Fleming; ifa_TPD; C_Muench; C_Cummins; C_Huey; C_Bean; C_Muench; C_Krist.

Route 26: 346 big picture: P, 346 b.: P_StockImage/ C.Sarramon; 347 c.: ifa_LDW; 347 b.: C_Arthus-Bertrand; 348.1: ifa_Panstock; 348.2: Kohlhas; 348 sidebar: ifa_J.ArnoldImages; 349.3: P_Nawrocki Stock/S.Vidler; 349 sidebar: ifa_Held; 350.1: ifa_Panstock; 350.2: P_StockImage/J.Brunton; 350 sidebar: laif_Eid; 351.3: ifa_AP&F; 351 sidebar: ifa_PictureFinders; 352.1: ifa_IndexStock; 352.2: P_Pan.Images; 352 sidebar t.: ifa_Int.Stock; 352 b.: ifa_AP&F; 353.3: C_Lenars; 353 sidebar: C_R.A.Cooke; 354.1: P; 354.2: P_ImageState/T.Booth; 355 Hub_Giovanni; 356.1: ifa_BCI; 356.2: ifa_Panstock; 356 sidebar: P_Pacificstock/D.Perrine; 357 map (clockwise from t.l.): C_M.Everton; ifa_Marr; ifa_J.Arnold Images; P_Buss; C_B.Mays; C_R.Watts; stone_Hiser; C_C.& J.Lenars; C_J.Poblete; 2 x ifa_K.Welsh; ifa_Panstock; ifa_Koub.

Route 27: 358 big picture: P_PanoramicImages; 358 c.: C_Stadler; 358 b.: C_Horner; 359 c.: C_Stadler; 359 b.: P_Raga; 360 sidebar: C_Donoso; 360.1: C_Vega; 360.2: P_Roda; 361.3: P_Roda; 361.4: C_Vega; 361 sidebar t.: C_Vega; 361 sidebar b.: laif_Gonzalez; 362 sidebar t.: C_Stadler; 362 sidebar b.: C_Stadler; 362.1: P_Pecha; 362.2: C_Rowell; 362.3: C_Lovell; 363.4: C_Stadler; 363 sidebar t.: C_Allofs; 363 sidebar c.;363 sidebar b.;; 364 sidebar: C_Mays; 364.1: C_Vikander; 364.2: C_Lovell; 365 t.l.: laif_Gonzalez; 365 t.r.: laif_Gonzalez; 365 b.l.: laif_Gonzalez; 365 b.r.: laif_Gonzalez; 366 sidebar: C_Horner; 366.1: C_Stadler; 366.2: Woodhouse; 367.3: Woodhouse; 367.4 C_Baldizzone; 367 sidebar t.: ifa_J.ArnoldImages; 367 sidebar c.: C_Houck; 367 sidebar b.: P_Japack; 368 sidebar t.: C_Vega; 368 sidebar b.: C_Vega; 368.1: C_Houck; 368.2: C_Wright; 369.3: C_Horner; 369.4: C_Wright; 369 sidebar: C_Vega; 369 sidebar: P; 370.1: C_Spashatt; 370.2: C_Pepita; 371 map (from l. to r., from t. to b.): L_Gonzalez; C_Donoso; P_Roda; C_Horner; G_Lanting; L_Gonzalez; C_Johnson; Mau_Vidler; C_Kaehler; Stone_Allison; C_Sparshatt; C_Pepita.

Route 28: 372 big picture: P_PanoramicImages; 372 c.: P; 372 b.: C; 373 c.: G_Stone_Klevansky; 373 b.: C_Stadler; 374 sidebar t.: C; 374 sidebar b.: C_Stadler; 374.1: C_Johnson; 374.2: C_Y.Arthus-Bertrand; 375.3 C_Y.Arthus-Bertrand; 375.4 C_Picimpact; 375 sidebar t.: C_Picimpact; 375 sidebar b.: C_Houghton; 376 sidebar t.: C_Stadler; 376 sidebar b.: C_Stadler; 376.1: P_Maywald; 376.2: C_Picimpact; 376.3: C_Modic; 377.4: C_Lovell; 377.5: C_Stadler; 377.6: C_Stadler; 378 sidebar t.: P; 378 sidebar b.: P; 378.1 C_Rowell; 378.2: C_Stadler; 379: C_Rowell; 380 sidebar t.: P; 380 sidebar b.: P; 380.1: C_Picimpact; 380.2: C_Everton; 380.3: C_Schafer; 381 map (from l. to r., from t. to b.): C_Keaton; ifa_Koubou; C_Rowell; C_Vo TrungDung; C_Stadler; C_Ergenbright; C_Neden; C_West; C_Rowell; C_Pikamitz; C_Ergenbright; 2 x C_Lovell.

IMPRINT

This edition is published on behalf of APA Publications GmbH & Co. Verlag KG, Singapore Branch, Singapore
by Verlag Wolfgang GmbH & Co. KG, Munich, Germany

© 2007 Verlag Wolfgang Kunth GmbH & Co. KG, Munich, Germany
Königinstr. 11
80539 Munich
Tel. +49.89.45 80 20-0
Fax +49.89.45 80 20-21
www.kunth-verlag.de

Cartography: © GeoGraphic Publishers GmbH & Co. KG, Munich, Germany
Topographical Imaging MHM ® Copyright © Digital Wisdom, Inc.
Translation: Silva Editions Ltd., Coordination: bookwise GmbH, Munich

Distribution of this edition:
GeoCenter International Ltd
Meridian House, Churchill Way West
Basingstoke, Hampshire RG21 6YR
Great Britain
Tel. (44) 1256 817 987
Fax (44) 1256 817 988
sales@geocenter.co.uk
www.insightguides.com

Printed in Slovakia

The information and facts presented in this book have been extensively researched and edited for accuracy.
The publishers, authors, and editors, cannot, however, guarantee that all of the information in the book is entirely
accurate or up to date at the time of publication. The publishers are grateful for any suggestions or corrections that
would improve the content of this book.